PLACES TO VISIT
in Southern Africa

PLACES TO VISIT
in Southern Africa

AA The Motorist Publications (Pty) Limited, Cape Town

ACKNOWLEDGEMENTS

First edition ©1995 AA The Motorist Publications (Pty) Limited, 130 Strand Street, Cape Town 8001

All rights reserved. No part of this book may be reproduced, translated, stored in a retrieval system, or transmitted in any form or by any means, electronic, electrostatic, magnetic tape, mechanical, photocopying, recording or otherwise, without permission in writing from the publishers.

ISBN 1-874912-38-6

Places to Visit in Southern Africa was edited and designed by AA The Motorist Publications (Pty) Limited, Cape Town

Editor: Tim O'Hagan
Designers: Valerie Phipps-Smith, Stuart Nix
Research editor: Judy Beyer
Project co-ordinator: Carol Adams
Picture researchers: Rose-Ann Myers, Vivian Baard, Nazreen Garder
Cartography: Linda Stevenson
Indexer: Sandie Vahl

Title page: From the air the Lowveld town of Pilgrim's Rest appears as a scattering of red-roofed houses in an emerald countryside.

Writers: Vivian Baard, Brian Johnson Barker, Judy Beyer, Jose Burman, Ellen Fitz-Patrick, Jill Gowans, Jane-Anne Hobbs, Peter Joyce, Paul Tingay

The publishers would like to thank the following individuals and organizations for their valuable assistance in helping to produce this book:
Albany Museum; Algoa Regional Services Council; Aventura Limited; Bartolomeu Dias Museum; Beaufort West Publicity Association; Val Bell; Bloemfontein Publicity Association; Marita Blom; Bulawayo Publicity Association; Eric Canterbury; Cape Nature Conservation; Captour; Chiping Rural Council; Clanwilliam Tourism Association; Department of Agriculture and Forestry, Umtata; Department of Culture and Recreation, Pretoria; Department of Nature Conservation, Pietermaritzburg; Department of Tourism, Gaborone; Department of Wildlife and National Parks, Gaborone; Lungile de Vletter; Directorate of Forestry, Southern Cape; Dundee Publicity Association; Durban Unlimited; Eastern Cape Tourism Board; East London Metropolitan Tourism Association; Sheldon Erasmus; Eshowe Publicity Association; Mary (Fred) Forrest; Franschhoek Vallée Tourisme; Gaborone National Museum and Art Gallery; George Tourism Association; Cynthia Giddy; Gordon's Bay Municipality; Graaff-Reinet Publicity Association; Grahamstown Publicity Association; Groot Marico Information Centre; Harare Publicity Bureau; Jenny Hawke; Hermanus Publicity Association; Highland Tourism Association; Jeffreys Bay Publicity Association; Johannesburg Municipality; Johannesburg Publicity Association; Kariba Publicity Association; Kimberley Tourist Information Office; Klein Karoo Marketing Association; Knysna Publicity Association; Kuruman Municipality; KwaZulu Monuments Council; Lesotho Tourist Board; Local History Museum, Durban; Luderitz Foundation and Tourist Information; Malolotja Nature Reserve; Manicaland Publicity Association; Masvingo Publicity Association; McGregor Museum; Ministry of Broadcasting, Information and Tourism, Swaziland; Ministry of Wildlife, Conservation and Tourism, Windhoek; Mlilwane Wildlife Sanctuary; Montagu Tourism Information Bureau; Municipal Information Office, Walvis Bay; MuseumAfrica; Namaqualand Regional Tourism Information Office; Namib Publicity and Tourism Association; Natal Parks Board; National Botanical Institute; National Cultural History Museum; National Parks and Wildlife Management, Harare; National Parks Board; Paarl Publicity Association; Paarl Wine Route Publicity Association; Pietermaritzburg Publicity Association; Pilgrim's Rest Information Centre; Port Alfred Publicity Association; Port Elizabeth Publicity Association; Ted Reilly; SAFCOL; SA Museums Association; Sasolburg Town Council; SA Tourism Board; Simon's Town Publicity Association; Somerset West Information Bureau; Sondela Tourist Information; Southern African Regional Tourism Council; Stellenbosch Tourist Information Bureau; Stellenbosch Village Museum; Stellenbosch Wine Route Office; Suidpunt Publicity Association; Sun International; Swellendam Publicity Association; Talana Museum; Tourist Rendezvous Travel Centre, Pretoria; Tourist Rendezvous, Windhoek; Tsumeb Tourism Centre; Tulbagh Valley Publicity Association; Tzaneen Municipal Tourist Office; Felix Unite; Upington Tourist Bureau; Valley Trust; Victoria and Alfred Waterfront Information Centre; Victoria Falls Publicity Association; Vignerons de Franschhoek; Wellington Publicity Association; Wild Coast Hotels; Wilderness Information Centre; Worcester Publicity Association; Zimbabwe Tourist Development Corporation

INTRODUCTION

Southern Africa has an extraordinary array of wonderful places to visit, from the teeming game parks of the Lowveld and northern KwaZulu-Natal, to the sweeping beaches of the Cape Peninsula and southern Cape. In between there are beautiful country towns, glittering casino resorts, bird sanctuaries and nature reserves, and an endless procession of mountains, lakes, dams, rivers, waterfalls and other scenic splendours.

On the cultural side there are fascinating monuments, memorials, museums, and a host of scenic drives – through historic battlefields, gracious wine estates and goldrush towns, built on the promise of instant wealth.

Places to Visit in Southern Africa features the very best of these destinations, taking you through 25 touring regions, from the western Cape to Namibia, Botswana and Zimbabwe. On this journey, more than 500 fascinating places are carefully and colourfully described, illustrated and mapped. Each entry is accompanied by a panel bristling with information on how to get there, opening times, where you can stay, how you can book, and what restrictions, if any, apply.

The really great places within each region are treated as special features, most of them illustrated with detailed maps or aerial photographs, and give you a comprehensive insight into what to do, where to go and what to see.

HOW TO USE THIS BOOK

Places to Visit in Southern Africa covers 25 touring regions (see map opposite) spanning the entire subcontinent, from the Zambezi River to Cape Agulhas.

The entries within each region run in alphabetical sequence, and each one is accompanied by a text panel giving such vital details as directions, opening and closing times throughout the year, where to stay and booking information.

Each entry also features a map reference, directing you to a page on which the entry is mapped. There are two kinds of map in this book: those appearing at the start of each region (regional maps), and those which appear as part of a special feature within the region (special feature maps). By consulting one or the other of these maps you will be able to plot your movements within the region, and see at a glance all the other special places you can visit. Note that the maps are intended only to help you locate the place you want to visit, and should be used in conjunction with a good road atlas, such as the *New Southern African Book of the Road*.

CONTENTS

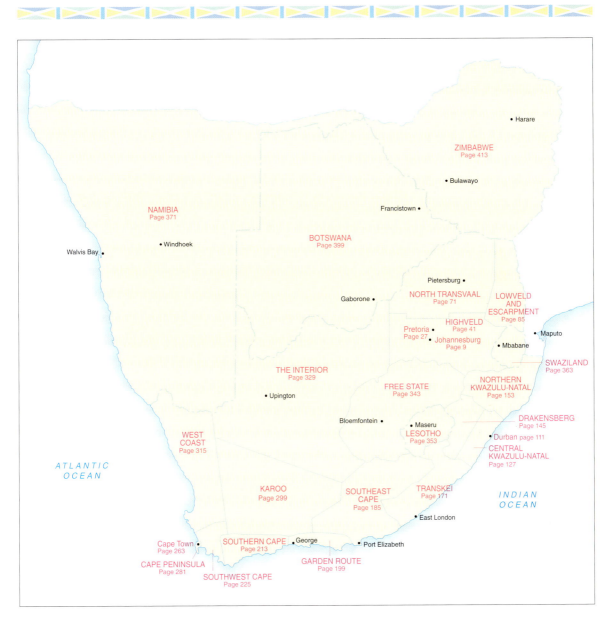

Johannesburg 9
Pretoria 27
Highveld 41
North Transvaal 71
Lowveld and Escarpment 85
Durban 111
Central KwaZulu-Natal 127
Drakensberg 145
Northern KwaZulu-Natal 153

Transkei 171
Southeast Cape 185
Garden Route 199
Southern Cape 213
Southwest Cape 225
Cape Town 263
Cape Peninsula 281
Karoo 299
West Coast 315

The Interior 329
Free State 343
Lesotho 353
Swaziland 363
Namibia 371
Botswana 399
Zimbabwe 413
Index 447

The blazing lights of high-rise buildings in downtown Johannesburg dominate the skyline as night falls on the City of Gold.

JOHANNESBURG

1. Adler Museum of the History of Medicine
2. Bensusan Museum of Photography
3. Braamfontein Spruit Trail
4. Carlton Centre Panorama
5. Civic Theatre
6. Fleamarket World
7. Florence Bloom Bird Sanctuary
8. Geological Museum
9. Gold Reef City
10. James Hall Museum of Transport
11. Johannesburg Art Gallery
12. Johannesburg Botanic Garden
13. Johannesburg Stock Exchange
14. Market Theatre
15. Multiflora (Flower Market)
16. MuseumAfrica
17. National Exhibition Centre
18. National Museum of Military History
19. Organic Market
20. Oriental Plaza
21. Planetarium
22. SABC Broadcasting Centre
23. Sandton City
24. Santarama Miniland
25. Soweto Tours
26. Transnet Museum
27. Zoo Lake Park

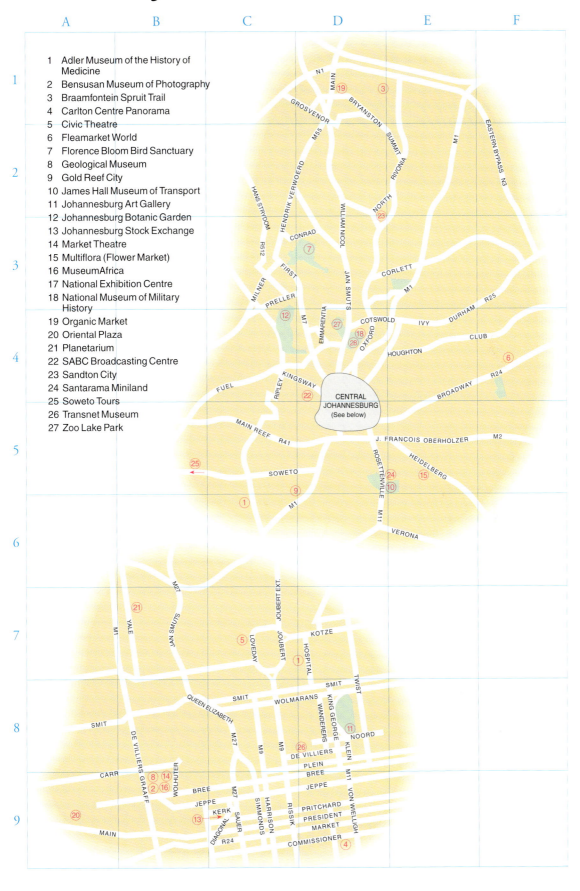

JOHANNESBURG

ADLER MUSEUM OF THE HISTORY OF MEDICINE
Hillbrow

Map: page 9, 7D
The museum is situated in the grounds of the South African Institute for Medical Research, corner De Korte and Hospital streets, Hillbrow. The entrance is in Hospital Street; the museum is the double-storey house situated to right of the gate.
Details: Open Monday to Friday 09h00-16h00; closed public holidays, on 21 March, 16 June and from 24 December to 1 January. Guided tours by appointment. Admission free. Accessible to the handicapped. Parking available in Hospital and De Korte streets. Refreshments from canteen on premises.
Further information: The Curator, Adler Museum of the History of Medicine, P O Box 1038, Johannesburg 2000, tel (011) 725-1704/725-1793.

A device for reshaping your nose, a ceramic jar for storing blood-sucking leeches and traditional healers' throwing-bones are some of the fascinating artefacts on display at the Adler Museum.

Housed in a building designed by Sir Herbert Baker, this impressive collection of old instruments and machines chronicles the triumphs and failures in the history of medicine. It's certainly Johannesburg's most unusual museum, and the guided tours are recommended for anyone who has ever paid a visit to the doctor or dentist.

Several reconstructed rooms recapture Johannesburg's medical past – such as the Edwardian pharmacy, with its handsome mahogany fittings, which once stood in Beit Street, Doornfontein. There are also a doctor's and a dentist's surgery, the latter equipped with some alarmingly primitive instruments. An African herbalist's shop, crammed with powders, potions, roots and bones, offers visitors a glimpse into the powers of the traditional healer.

An interesting variety of old instruments is on display, several of them grisly enough to send a shiver down the spine: look out for the old surgical instruments – which include a formidable-looking saw, a ship surgeon's kit dating back to the 18th century, an iron lung and early anaesthetic apparatus.

And if you want to know even more, the museum presents an interesting selection of video documentaries.

An early 20th-century pharmacy attracts visitors to the Adler Museum of the History of Medicine.

BENSUSAN MUSEUM OF PHOTOGRAPHY
Newtown

Map: page 9, 9B
Level Four of the new MuseumAfrica, 121 Bree Street, Newtown, Johannesburg (between Goch and Wolhuter streets).
Details: Open Tuesday to Sunday 09h00-17h00 (closed Mondays). Admission fee charged. Secure parking in Mary Fitzgerald Square, Bree Street. Refreshments available.
Further information: The Custodian, Bensusan Museum, P O Box 517, Newtown 2113, tel (011) 833-5624.

Much more than a collection of old cameras, this interesting museum documents the extraordinary strides made in photographic technology during this century. Laser beams, holographs, videos, computers and sophisticated cameras are used in imaginative interactive displays, offering a unique glimpse into the production of photographs, film and other visual images.

There are displays of cameras and photographic equipment, both antique and new, as well as many fine photographic prints, together with hints on how to take and develop your own photographs. History enthusiasts will really enjoy the 3-D display which portrays images of early Johannesburg, while children of all ages will be intrigued by the 'Alhazen's Light House', a darkened room that uses some dramatic special effects to demonstrate the intriguing properties of light, colour and shadow.

The Bensusan Museum's penny-farthing bicycle evokes a more leisurely era, complementing the displays of antique cameras and other photographic equipment. Exhibits date from 1839 right up to today's hi-tech wizardry. Of special interest are items relating to the Anglo-Boer War.

BRAAMFONTEIN SPRUIT TRAIL
Northern suburbs

Crisscrossing the metropolitan area like a great green web, the Braamfontein Spruit Trail follows rocky ridges and willow-fringed rivers, passing dams, waterfalls and golf courses, and going through bird sanctuaries, botanical gardens and nature reserves. This is where the people of Johannesburg come to relax, to ramble along the river banks, ride bicycles, jog, walk their dogs, watch birds, to worship, play sport and enjoy picnics and braais.

At least 14 streams rise in the ridges of the Witwatersrand, but over the decades many of these waterways have become choked by the detritus of urban sprawl. In recent years, however, the rivers have been upgraded and renewed by local authorities, providing the citizens of Johannesburg, Sandton, Randburg and Alexandra with much-needed recreational space. The Braamfontein Spruit, a 25-km-long river course with several tributaries, rises in Hillbrow and meanders north, flowing into the Jukskei River and eventually joining the mighty Limpopo.

A wide variety of indigenous fauna and flora is to be seen along the trail – there are more than 200 species of bird, as well as frogs, snakes, lizards, tortoises, and mammals such as water mongooses and meerkats. Among the other attractions of the walks are the interesting archaeological and historical features, including some iron-smelting works in Melville, farmhouse ruins, historical mansions and stone weirs.

Melville Koppies Nature Reserve, an unspoilt sanctuary that's open only a few days of the year, is well worth a visit if you are keen on indigenous flora and archaeology. Other wide-open spaces along the way include Emmarentia Dam, the Johannesburg Botanic Gardens and the Florence Bloom Bird Sanctuary, home to over 180 species of bird.

The Sandton section of the trail meanders along wide, shady banks, past pools and boulders, finally meeting up with the Sandspruit, a tributary which has its own 12-km trail starting in The Wilds in Houghton, and passing through the Melrose Bird Sanctuary.

Map: page 9, 1D
The trail starts at Westdene and Houghton, and stretches to the boundaries of Sandton and Randburg in the north. You can join the trail at any point.
Details: Parking, fresh water and picnic spots at many places along the trail.
Further information: Consult one of the several maps and brochures available from the Sandton Town Council, Parks Division, P O Box 78001, Sandton 2146, tel (011) 803-9132/3; Johannesburg Publicity Association, P O Box 4580, Johannesburg 2000, tel (011) 337-6650 or the Braamfontein Spruit Trail, P O Box 44538, Linden 2104, tel (011) 782-5169/ 882-7337.

The waters of Braamfontein Spruit meander through northern Johannesburg, marking the course of South Africa's oldest urban trail.

The Parktown/Westcliff Urban Walk

Forming part of the larger Braamfontein Spruit Trail, these five circular walks introduce visitors to the beautiful old suburbs of Parktown and Westcliff, which were once the exclusive enclaves of Johannesburg's early mining magnates. Using the millions they made on the goldfields of the Reef, these 'randlords' built their splendid mansions on the lonely rocky ridges north of town, preferring the sound of birdsong and spectacular views to the dust and noise of the little mining town. Thomas Cullinan, Sir Percy Fitzpatrick and the Oppenheimers were among the famous personalities who lived here; another resident was the architect Sir Herbert Baker, whose handsome houses, many built from locally quarried quartzite, have come to characterize the suburbs. The hour-long Baker Walk, between Oxford Road and Jan Smuts Avenue, is of great architectural appeal; equally interesting is the Jubilee Walk through the oldest part of Parktown, which takes many visitors past some of Johannesburg's grandest mansions, such as *Dolobran* and *Emoyeni*.

A guide to the walk is available from the Westcliff Heritage Trust, 39 Barkly Road, Parktown 2193, tel (011) 482-3349 (open weekdays 09h00-13h00).

JOHANNESBURG

Map: page 9, 9D
Central Johannesburg on Commissioner Street, between Kruis and Von Wielligh streets. The entrance to the observation deck is on the top level of the Carlton Shopping Centre.
Details: Open daily 09h00-23h00. Admission fee charged. Parking in the Carlton Centre car park (entrance in Kruis Street).
Further information: The Carlton Centre, P O Box 99019, Johannesburg 2000, tel (011) 331-1010.

CARLTON CENTRE PANORAMA
City centre

Anyone unfamiliar with Johannesburg can enjoy a splendid bird's-eye view of the entire metropolitan area by visiting the Carlton Centre, in the heart of the city. Lifts ferry visitors up 50 floors (202 m) to an observation deck at the top of South Africa's most famous skyscraper.

The views are spectacular. Far, far below are the tiny streets of the city centre, with their scurrying pedestrians and matchbox cars; to the south are the mine dumps; to the north the leafy suburbs of Sandton and other satellite towns. On a clear day it's possible to see as far as the Magaliesberg mountains, some 75 km to the north, and by night the views are equally breathtaking, as the city stretches out in a glittering carpet of light to distant horizons.

Coin-operated telescopes placed at intervals along the perimeter wall provide close-up views.

The interior of Johannesburg's Carlton Centre in downtown Johannesburg is a busy concourse for retailers, shoppers and sightseers heading for the observation deck.

CIVIC THEATRE
Braamfontein

Map: page 9, 7C
Loveday Street, Braamfontein, opposite the Civic Centre.
Details: Tours Tuesdays and Thursdays at 11h00 and 14h00. Small fee charged. Free, secure night-time parking available under the theatre building and diagonally opposite the main entrance. Refreshments from theatre cafe, open Monday to Saturday for light meals.
Further information: The Civic Theatre, P O Box 31900, Braamfontein 2017, tel (011) 403-3408.

If you've ever wondered what goes on behind the scenes during a major theatrical production, take one of the guided tours of the Civic Theatre – which boasts some of the most modern technical facilities in the country.

The theatre has existed 30 years, but recently underwent a drastic refurbishment and upgrading programme that stirred much controversy because of its staggeringly high cost. It's easy to see where the money went when you tour the four theatres, with their lavish fittings and state-of-the-art computerized equipment.

As a result, the Civic is no longer the cheerless mausoleum it once was, and its critics have been subdued by a bold and creative management programme that effectively has converted it into a vibrant cultural platform for many new and untried artistes.

The one-and-a-half-hour tour starts in the foyer, takes visitors backstage and into the dressing rooms, and then finishes with tea in the centre's canteen.

Futuristic statuary draws the eye as you enter Johannesburg's Civic Theatre. The recently refashioned theatre complex embraces four fine auditoria and a superb array of equipment.

FLEAMARKET WORLD
Bruma

Anything from an antique cupboard to a cucumber, a T-shirt to a bag of tomatoes, can be bought at the very popular Fleamarket World, a thriving and sophisticated shoppers' complex established to accommodate the many entrepreneurs who used to ply their wares at the old fleamarket at nearby Bruma Lake.

Many thousands of local and foreign visitors come to Fleamarket World, especially over weekends, to browse through the 550-odd stalls, hunt for hidden bargains and to soak in the carnival-like atmosphere created by strolling buskers and live bands.

This is a good place to shop for inexpensive new clothing, leatherwork, crafts and African curios.

There are also several stalls selling a startling variety of vegetables and fruit, brought in direct from the farm at competitive prices.

Other attractions at Fleamarket World include continuous, live entertainment (including excellent live theatre and an array of symphony orchestras), plenty of secure parking on the premises, foreign exchange facilities and a 'News and Views' stall, which presents alternative ideas and environmental information to the general public.

At the European Food Market, a variety of fast-food restaurants, kiosks and coffee shops provides sustenance for hungry shoppers.

South Africa's thriving 'informal economy' can be seen at its most colourful at the Bruma Lake and other open-air markets in the Johannesburg metropolitan area. Shoppers and browsers have a huge range of items from which to choose.

Map: page 9, 4F
Corner of Ernest Oppenheimer Avenue and Marcia Street, Bruma. Turn off the R24 over the N3, turn right at the first set of traffic lights into Marcia Street, then first right into Ernest Oppenheimer Avenue.
Details: Open Tuesday to Thursday 10h00-19h00; Fridays 10h00-21h00; Saturdays 08h30-21h00; and Sundays 09h00-19h00. Small admission fee charged. Free, secure parking. Refreshments.
Further information: Fleamarket World, P O Box 39620, Bramley 2018, tel (011) 786-0776.

FLORENCE BLOOM BIRD SANCTUARY
Victory Park

You can spot up to 40 species in just a few hours' viewing at the Florence Bloom Bird Sanctuary, a secluded, leafy reserve which is tucked away in Delta Municipal Park, a 100-ha piece of open parkland northwest of the city.

Although the reserve is not open to walkers, the birds may be viewed and photographed from hides overlooking the two dams.

The sanctuary covers only 10 ha, but encompasses several different habitats. These include reedbeds, grasses and a small, forested area – which attract a great diversity of birds. More than 120 species have been recorded in the greater Delta Park area, including African black ducks, tawny-flanked prinias, Egyptian geese, blacksmith plovers, hamerkops, sacred ibises, as well as a variety of owls, woodpeckers and kingfishers.

Delta Park and the Florence Bloom Bird Sanctuary form part of the Braamfontein Spruit Trail *(see separate entry)*.

Map: page 9, 3D
Situated in Delta Municipal Park, Road No. 3, Victory Park. From the city, travel north along Barry Hertzog Avenue, which becomes Rustenburg Road, and turn right into Road No. 3.
Details: Open daily, sunrise to sunset. Parking available. Admission free.
Further information: The Witwatersrand Bird Club, P O Box 72091, Parkview 2122, tel (011) 782-7134.

GEOLOGICAL MUSEUM
Newtown

The romance and hardship of Johannesburg's early prospecting days are evoked under the lofty ceilings of the Geological Museum, where sturdy display cases are crammed with thousands of rocks, minerals, fossils and gems.

The more than 25 000 specimens are mainly from South Africa, although there are also many rare and beautiful specimens which have been imported from other parts of the world. Gold and its history feature prominently – look out for the display of the world's most fabulous solid-gold nuggets.

Other highlights found here include a wide range of fluorescent minerals that glow eerily in their darkened case, a fine display of cut and uncut gems, models of the world's most famous diamonds, and a fascinating chronological display of South Africa's geological formations covering 3,2 billion years.

Map: page 9, 9B
Situated in the new MuseumAfrica complex, 121 Bree Street, Newtown (between Goch and Wolhuter streets).
Details: Contact the museum for hours of opening. Admission fee charged. Secure parking at Mary Fitzgerald Square, Bree Street.
Further information: The Curator, Geological Museum, P O Box 517, Newtown 2113, tel (011) 833-5624.

PLACES TO VISIT

GOLD REEF CITY

Map: page 9, 5/6C
Eight kilometres south of the city centre. Take the M1 South (Ben Schoeman Highway) and turn off at the Xavier Street off-ramp. Turn right at the traffic lights and follow the signposts.

Details: Open daily, including all public holidays, 09h30-17h00. Closed on Mondays and Christmas Day. Restaurants and bars stay open after hours; gates close at 23h00. Admission charged – all rides and shows included. Free parking available. Refreshments.

Further information: Gold Reef City, Private Bag 1890, Gold Reef City 2159, tel (011) 496-1600.

This vast, historical theme park is a reconstruction of pioneer Johannesburg during the heady days of the gold rush. Since it opened in 1987 it has become one of the city's main tourist attractions, drawing many thousands of visitors.

Designed to appeal to all ages and tastes, Gold Reef City provides value-for-money enjoyment for the whole family. Another attraction is the happy festival-like atmosphere created by the many dancers, singers and musicians who entertain the crowds.

Gold Reef City is situated eight kilometres outside central Johannesburg, on the site of Crown Mines which, until it ceased production in 1975, was the world's richest gold mine. The reconstructed town, with its charming tin-roofed houses and shops, gives visitors a good idea of what Johannesburg must have looked like after the discovery of gold a century ago, when prospectors from all over the world poured into the Reef in their thousands, transforming a dusty, tented camp into a thriving boom town in a matter of months. Thankfully, none of the dirt, vice and squalor that characterized the pioneer town is to be found at Gold Reef City, which imaginatively combines an old-world setting with every modern convenience.

There is a bewildering choice of things to see and do at Gold Reef City. Sixteen museums are to be found in the park, many of them portraying the history of gold – a highlight is the Underground Mine Tour.

A wide selection of speciality shops, many of them quaint reconstructions of Victorian originals, sells everything from diamonds to doughnuts, while there are over 12 comfortable restaurants, saloons and snack bars providing refreshment for hungry revellers.

One of the most appealing aspects of Gold Reef City is the excellent entertainment, which continues nonstop throughout the day: a company of 20 energetic dancers performs indigenous African dances and the mineworkers' traditional gumboot dance. A marimba band and a roving penny-whistler keep visitors' feet tapping during the day, and by night the pubs and saloons host cabarets and other live performances.

Horse-drawn carriage rides are popular with children, who also enjoy taking a trip in the vintage steam train that puffs all the way round the park on a narrow-gauge railway track. The delightful Victorian-style Funfair provides sedate rides, but those in search of thrills and spills should head for the amusement park, which offers some hair-raising adventures.

Try to set aside a whole day to explore Gold Reef City, preferably over a weekend or during school holidays, when extra shows and activities are staged.

The Old Crown Mines headgear is just one of the fascinating showpieces at Gold Reef City.

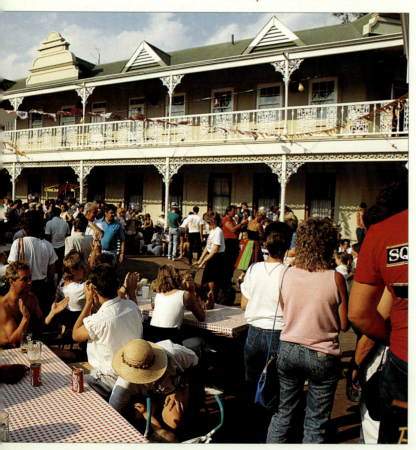

A regiment of restaurants, bistros, takeaways and taverns caters for thousands at Gold Reef City. Attractions range from gumboot dances to steam-train trips.

GOLD REEF CITY

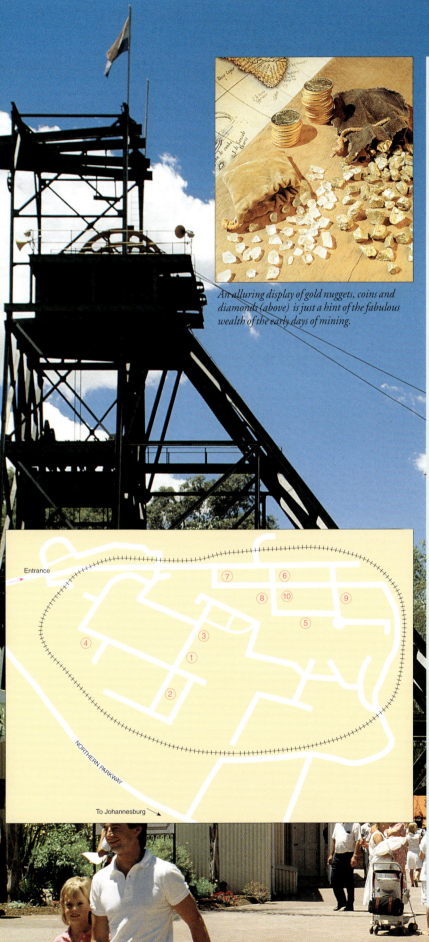

An alluring display of gold nuggets, coins and diamonds (above) is just a hint of the fabulous wealth of the early days of mining.

KEY TO THE MAP

1 Underground Mine Tour Experience first-hand what it's like to labour at a rock face in the dark and steamy tunnels of a gold mine during the 30-minute Underground Mine Tour. A two-tier lift carries visitors down to the 5th level, some 220 m below the surface.

2 Gold Pour Watch a gold bar being smelted in an 'arc' furnace, heated to 110°C. The molten gold is then cast into a bullion bar.

3 The Mint The most impressive exhibit is a huge coin press, nicknamed 'Oom Paul', after President Paul Kruger, who imported it from Germany in 1892 for minting coins for the South African Republic. It's the oldest working coin press in the world.

4 The Olthaver House This fully furnished house-museum is characteristic of the type of dwelling built by early mining companies for their officials and engineers. These houses were constructed of sun-dried bricks, and covered with corrugated iron to prevent the bricks from disintegrating during Highveld rainstorms.

5 *The Star* Newspaper A replica of the old newspaper offices that once stood on the corner of Sauer and President streets. The 80-year-old press housed in the building is still in use, printing personalized copies of the newspaper.

6 First National Bank Museum With its chequered marble floor and handsome Burmese teak counters, the interior is typical of banks at the turn of the century. The counter comes from an old bank in Springfontein in the Free State.

7 Rosie O'Grady's Action Bar The nightclub is housed in a replica of a prefabricated wood-and-iron theatre brought to the Reef, together with a complete operatic company, by an imaginative impresario named Luscombe Searelle in 1888.

8 Barney's The only brewery tavern in Gauteng. Look out for the bullet hole in the wooden counter, which comes from the old Sacks Hotel in Fordsburg, scene of bitter fighting during the 1922 miners' strike.

9 Gold Reef City Hotel A luxury hotel built and furnished in the style of a grand Victorian hotel with updated accommodation.

10 Gold Reef City Chemist Re-creation of a Victorian chemist shop with original fittings rescued from an old pharmacy in Wynberg, Cape Town.

JOHANNESBURG

JAMES HALL MUSEUM OF TRANSPORT
La Rochelle

Map: page 9, 5E
Situated in Pioneers' Park, Rosettenville Road, La Rochelle. From the city centre, drive south along Von Wielligh Street (which becomes Rosettenville Road) for 2km or until you see the entrance to the museum on the left-hand side.
Details: Open Tuesday to Sunday 09h00-17h00. Closed Christmas Day, Day of Goodwill and Good Friday. Tours for school groups and special-interest groups may be arranged. Parking available. Refreshments.
Further information: The Curator, James Hall Museum of Transport, Rosettenville Road, La Rochelle 2197, tel (011) 435-9718.

Ever fancied to take a closer look at a velocipede? This early bicycle, which was known to outdoor enthusiasts as a 'bone-shaker' because of its iron-rimmed wooden wheels, is one of the many fascinating items on show at the James Hall Museum of Transport – together with wagons, carts, trams, locomotives, vintage cars and motorbikes.

The south hall is where you'll find the velocipede, which is displayed alongside an interesting collection of other early bicycles and vintage motorcycles. Also in this area are many animal-drawn vehicles, including Voortrekker wagons and that unique South African invention, the Cape cart.

In the museum's courtyard area is a world-renowned collection of steam-powered vehicles, including steam rollers, tractors and locomotives.

Nearby is an old pont, which was once used to ferry transport riders, their wagons and oxen across the crocodile-infested Komati River. This pont lay buried on the banks of the river for over 70 years before it was unearthed and brought to the museum.

A stunning contrast of art forms on display in the Johannesburg Art Gallery.

JOHANNESBURG ART GALLERY
Joubert Park

Map: page 9, 8D
Southern end of Joubert Park, between King George and Twist streets. Entrance on the north side of the building, accessible from King George Street.
Details: Open Tuesday to Sunday 10h00-17h00; closed Mondays. Guided tours on Wednesdays at 13h00, Saturdays at 15h00, and the first Sunday of every month at 11h00. Admission free. Parking in the gallery grounds. Light meals and refreshments at the gallery's coffee shop.
Further information: The Director, Johannesburg Art Gallery, P O Box 23561, Joubert Park 2044, tel (011) 725-3130/725-3180/1.

A restful and tranquil haven amid the hurly-burly goings-on of the city centre, the Johannesburg Art Gallery provides hours of free stimulation for visitors who choose to wander at leisure through its airy interleading halls, soaking up an inspiring collection of modern and traditional art.

The gallery is also well worth a visit for anyone who is interested in architecture, with its grand façade designed by Sir Edwin Lutyens.

The gallery's original collection, started in 1909 by benefactor Lady Florence Phillips, comprised 19th-century and contemporary art (including works by Monet, Sisley and Rodin) and was later expanded to include South African and 17th-century Dutch art.

Among the many treasures of the gallery's Print Collection are various works by artists as Dürer, Rembrandt, Whistler and Toulouse-Lautrec. Also included are Japanese woodblock prints and contemporary international works. If you happen to take a keen interest in African and traditional art, you will find that artists from all over the subcontinent are well represented.

The coffee shop, a popular meeting place, overlooks a sculpture garden where large works are displayed, and there's a small shop selling good-quality arts and crafts, posters and souvenirs.

JOHANNESBURG BOTANIC GARDEN
Emmarentia

With its interesting collection of rare plants, trees, lawns and ponds, the Botanic Garden has a quiet magic all of its own. Gardeners and plant-lovers come here for inspiration, others simply to relax in the fresh air. It's also a lovely unspoiled place for a picnic.

Established in 1968, this stretch of undulating garden and veld is set on the western shores of Emmarentia Dam, close to the ancient quartzite ridges of Melville. Over 30 000 trees have been planted, among them numerous exotic varieties, such as the many silver birches and cork oaks that provide shade and greenery throughout the garden. The ponds, islands and reedbeds attract many species of breeding waterfowl, including moorhens, crested grebes, dabchicks and Egyptian geese.

The large, formal rose garden, containing over 4 500 varieties, is laid out on a series of terraces, making a spectacular sight in the spring and ensuing summer months, with pretty displays of flowering cherries, thousands of fragrant blooms, secluded bowers and waterfalls.

In the herb garden the air is filled with the pungent fragrance of hundreds of indigenous and exotic herbs; included in the collection are many ancient medicinal herbs that were widely used by early Voortrekkers and *sangomas* (traditional healers) alike.

Anyone interested in gleaning valuable gardening ideas might like to visit the Hedge Demonstration section and, close by, the Ground Cover Demonstration Garden. The succulent collection (viewed by appointment only) is famous throughout the world, containing over 2 500 rare and beautiful species.

Map: page 9, 4C
The main entrance is in Olifants Road, Emmarentia. There are several other entrances on the garden's perimeter.
Details: Open daily, sunrise to sunset. Guided tours take place in summer on the first Tuesday of every month at 09h00. Admission free. Parking on premises. Refreshments at weekends and public holidays only.
Further information: The Information Officer, Johannesburg Botanic Garden, P O Box 85481, Emmarentia 2029, tel (011) 782-0517.

Emmarentia Dam provides a tranquil weekend venue for keen city yachtsmen, canoeists and windsurfers.

Brick-paved pathways wind their way through the Botanic Garden's splendours. Fountains, pools and secluded corners invite quiet contemplation.

JOHANNESBURG

JOHANNESBURG STOCK EXCHANGE
Johannesburg

Map: page 9, 9C
17 Diagonal Street, Johannesburg (between Kerk and Pritchard streets).
Details: Audiovisual presentations in the auditorium on the lower plaza level, Monday to Friday at 11h00. Admission free. Parking at West Street Parkade, corner West and Jeppe streets.
Further information: The Public Relations Department, P O Box 1174, Johannesburg 2000, tel (011) 833-6580.

A constant hum of activity welcomes you to South Africa's only stock exchange. The atmosphere crackles with excitement; this is where hundreds of thousands of shares are traded every day, a place where fortunes are made and lost in the twinkling of an eye.

Trading takes place on one large market floor, which visitors can view through a glass wall from the public gallery. The 'open outcry' method is still used, with brokers and their authorized clerks shouting out orders to buy or sell; in many other stock exchanges in the world this method has been virtually replaced by screen trading.

The Johannesburg Stock Exchange was founded by Benjamin Woollan in 1887 in order to provide a marketplace for investors to buy and sell the shares of the many mining and finance companies that were established after the discovery of gold on the Witwatersrand (Gauteng) the previous year. It has occupied five buildings since then, moving to its current Diagonal Street premises – right in the heart of the country's financial market – in 1978.

The Johannesburg Stock Exchange, located on, and popularly known as, Diagonal Street, towers above Johannesburg's financial district. The exchange was established in 1887, and since then has served hundreds of thousands of traders in the world of South African business.

MARKET THEATRE
Newtown

If Johannesburg has a heart, then the Market Theatre must surely be it. More than any other place, this arts complex reflects the spirit of the city; it's a cultural melting pot, a showcase for talent, the place where everything seems to be happening. Patrons come to the Market to enjoy some of the best theatre, dance and music that South Africa has to offer; they come to savour the good food, prowl the various art galleries and browse at the city's most colourful fleamarket. Most of all, they come here to enjoy the warm, vibrant atmosphere.

The Market Theatre's metamorphosis from run-down Edwardian market hall to a cultural arena of international renown has made it an important symbol of urban renewal. In 1975 a small group of dedicated actors scraped together the funds to save this grand old building, devoting their own physical labour to the conversion. Over the years, the Market has played a pivotal role in the development of indigenous theatre, at the same time providing a platform for many of South Africa's best-known actors and playwrights.

The biggest of the complex's three theatres is situated in the old Indian Produce Market; be sure to look out for the vendors' signs that still hang from the gallery. Also situated within the complex are two art galleries that hold regular exhibitions of contemporary South African art.

For those wanting to socialize, the small bar in the main theatre has a congenial atmosphere, while the ever-popular Kippies, named after legendary saxophonist Kippie Moeketsi, is a wonderfully atmospheric venue that offers live jazz late into the night. There are several eateries from which to choose, including a restaurant specializing in traditional South African fare.

The Saturday fleamarket is a colourful and offbeat affair with a unique African atmosphere; hundreds of stallholders sell every conceivable item, including crafts, clothing, antiques and a wide selection of sculptures, masks, beads and other artefacts from all over Africa.

There is no better place to go to soak up the soul of Johannesburg.

Map: page 9, 9B
Corner of Bree and Wolhuter streets, Newtown, to the west of the central business district.
Details: Tours of the Market Theatre are offered daily; please phone to book. Fleamarket on Saturdays 08h00-17h00. Admission free. Secure parking available in Mary Fitzgerald Square, opposite the complex in Bree Street. Refreshments.
Further information: The Market Theatre, P O Box 8656, Johannesburg 2000, tel (011) 832-1641.

Colourful canopies shade a wide variety of stalls that offer visitors to the Saturday fleamarket everything from finely crafted curios and printed fabrics to genuine antiques.

The roof that came by sea

The vast hall that accommodates both the Market Theatre complex and the new MuseumAfrica may look undistinguished to the casual observer, but this immense structure is considered by architects in the city to be one of Johannesburg's major buildings because of its very unusual roof construction.

Two hundred metres in length, the roof of this complex spans 36 metres. Its graceful metal trusses and other components were manufactured in Glasgow in about 1911, and the parts were shipped to South Africa, where they were eventually assembled.

The building was completed in 1913 and it served as a produce market for the people of Johannesburg for more than 60 years. The handsome Edwardian façade in Wolhuter Street, which has three grand arched windows, flanked by twin domed towers, serves as the main entrance to the Market Theatre complex. The old Indian Produce Market, to the east of the main hall, houses the main theatre.

JOHANNESBURG

MULTIFLORA (FLOWER MARKET)
City Deep

Map: page 9, 5E
Southeast of Johannesburg in Marjorie Street, City Deep. Leave the M2 on the Benrose off-ramp. Turn south and drive for 4 km or until you see the market on the left-hand side.
Details: Open Monday to Friday 07h30-17h00; Saturdays 07h30-15h30. Admission free. Parking and cafeteria on the premises.
Further information: Multiflora, P O Box 86060, City Deep 2049, tel (011) 613-4011.

Whether you're looking for a rare orchid or a subtropical flower, a protea or a perfect rose; whether you'd like to buy just one or a whole truckload, Multiflora is the place to go. This huge market is the nerve centre of South Africa's cut-flower industry. Every day buyers bid from seven in the morning for farm-fresh blooms, which are then systematically distributed all over the country.

The market is open to the public too, who come here to admire the rather extraordinary array of flowers and to buy from the numerous wholesalers situated within the complex.

It's fascinating to wander among the many stalls, with their banks of brilliantly coloured blooms filling the huge warehouses with fragrance. And if you're shopping for a special occasion, such as a wedding or large function, you'll find every conceivable accessory for entertaining and floral art at Grandiflora next door, which also sells gardening products.

MUSEUMAFRICA
Newtown

Map: page 9, 9B
The museum is situated in Bree Street, between Wolhuter and Goch streets (in the same building complex as the Market Theatre).
Details: Open Tuesday to Sunday 09h00-17h00. Admission fee charged. Secure parking available in Bree Street.
Further information: The Curator, MuseumAfrica, P O Box 517, Newtown 2113, tel (011) 833-5624.

An essential stop for anyone who has an interest in South African history, MuseumAfrica is the custodian of one of the most important collections of historical documents and artefacts on the subcontinent.

The museum, in its modern, new building, reflects the changing focus of southern Africa. Exhibits are centred around the interests of the population, for example, a temporary exhibit entitled 'Johannesburg Transformations' reflects a period of change in both the country and the museum.

Also on display is an exhibition of South African Rock Art, with its fascinating collection of Bushman paintings depicting the interests of the San, and their understanding of the world and wildlife around them.

Satirical images of the apartheid era (left) feature in MuseumAfrica's showcase of recent politics. Other exhibits include aspects of township life, and key events in the struggle against white domination. Below: Much of the emphasis is on the often tragically violent years just before and after Nelson Mandela's release from prison in 1990.

NATIONAL EXHIBITION CENTRE
Nasrec

A railway station, a lake and parking for some 20 000 vehicles make the National Exhibition Centre, 12 km southwest of Johannesburg, one of the biggest and most sophisticated complexes of its kind in the world.

This is where Johannesburg's famous Rand Easter Show takes place every year, a massive and spectacular consumer exhibition that draws some 700 000 visitors and over 1 200 exhibitors, many of them coming from overseas to show off their various products.

An annual visit to the Rand Easter Show has become a time-honoured tradition among many of Johannesburg's citizens, who come along to watch the pageantry, and sample the attractions. Among these are a thrill-a-minute fairground, helicopter rides, parades, heart-stopping bungee jumping, displays, showjumping, agricultural shows, open-air music concerts, competitions and, of course, the many huge halls exhibiting a seemingly endless range of products and services.

Map: page 9, 6C
Situated in Nasrec, southwest of Johannesburg. Travel along the M1 South and take the Nasrec Road/M5 off-ramp; the centre is well signposted.
Details: The Rand Easter Show takes place at Easter every year. Admission charged. Ample parking available on premises. Refreshments.
Further information: The National Exhibition Centre, Private Bag X07, Bertsham 2013, tel (011) 494-9111.

MuseumAfrica has exquisite examples of San (Bushman) rock art. The culture and lifestyle of these hunter-gatherers are introduced to visitors by an expert guide.

Pickhandle Mary

Across the road from the MuseumAfrica is a parking lot where a fleamarket is held every Saturday. This was once a dusty, open square known as 'the Outspan' where wagons from surrounding farms came to unload their variety of produce and make use of the weighbridge facilities.

Now it's called Mary Fitzgerald Square, in memory of 'Pickhandle Mary', a feisty and fearless activist whose passionate involvement in labour issues made her very popular among Johannesburg's workers. Irish-born Mary earned her nickname during the 1911 tramwaymen's strike, when she and other workers collected the pickhandles that mounted police had used to break up a meeting in Market Square. When she addressed public meetings after that, she always carried her famous pickhandle. A committed socialist, Mary became deputy mayor of Johannesburg during the 1920s.

NATIONAL MUSEUM OF MILITARY HISTORY
Saxonwold

Map: page 9, 4D
20 Erlswold Way, Saxonwold, at the northeastern end of the Johannesburg Zoological Gardens.
Details: Open daily 09h00-16h30; closed Good Friday and Christmas Day. Admission charged. Parking available on premises. Refreshments. Book and souvenir shop. Conference and function facilities available.
Further information: The Public Relations Officer, South African National Museum of Military History, P O Box 52090, Saxonwold 2132, tel (011) 646-5256.

Anyone with a boyhood dream to fly fighter aircraft will spend many blissful hours at the Museum of Military History; so too will history enthusiasts, collectors and anybody with a passion for things military. The museum's function is to collect, preserve and study items concerned with South Africa's military history, focusing on the period of the First and Second World Wars. It's famous for its fine collection of First and Second World War aircraft, and it also houses a vast collection of military equipment and memorabilia.

There are about 30 000 main exhibits, including some tanks, armoured vehicles, uniforms, flags, rifles, helmets, daggers, knives, swords and bayonets, and some 19 000 smaller items, including badges, medals and insignia. The museum's displays change constantly as the artefacts are rotated.

One of the museum's treasures is the world's only surviving German Messerschmitt Me-262 two-seater, a radar-equipped night fighter. Another prized exhibit is a very rare German Molch (Salamander) midget submarine.

The museum's very large artillery collection is laid out on rolling green lawns in a peaceful garden setting. Nearby is a special area where children may spend happy hours climbing on and exploring a variety of military vehicles.

The museum is the custodian of South Africa's official military art collection, and many superb portraits and battle scenes hang in the gallery.

Other attractions are a huge reference library, extensive archives and a world-famous photograph collection, including the National Collection of Second World War photographs, all of which visitors may see on weekdays.

With so much to see and do, it's not surprising that this museum attracts more visitors annually than any other museum in the city.

Beautiful memorial to the 'khakis'

One of Johannesburg's most outstanding memorials, the Rand Regiments Memorial, stands adjacent to the grounds of the Museum of Military History.

This grand, triumphal archway, which was built in sandstone, was completed in 1913, and commemorates the men of the Rand Regiments who fell in action during the South African War.

Originally, the archway was conceived as a peace memorial that would honour lives which were lost on both sides, but sadly this was not to be the case; at one time it was scathingly referred to as 'die kakie-monument' (the khaki monument) by descendants of Boer soldiers, a reference to the impression that it commemorated British soldiers only.

The monument is square in plan, with a flattened dome supporting a vast, bronze 'Angel of Peace'. It was designed by Sir Edwin Lutyens (who also designed the Johannesburg Art Gallery) after Sir Herbert Baker had declined the task due to having accepted the commission for Pretoria's Union Buildings. Famous French sculptor Auguste Rodin was approached to sculpt the bronze figure but, for reasons unknown, he was unwilling to do so, and eventually the Russian sculptor Naoum Aronson, who had studied under Rodin, accepted the commission.

The memorial was erected in the beautiful Sachsenwald forest, now the suburb of Saxonwold, where it still stands, largely invisible to the wider audience it deserves.

ORGANIC MARKET
Bryanston

Map: page 9, 1D
The Michael Mount Waldorf School, corner Culross and Main roads, Bryanston, Sandton (entrance in Culross Road).
Details: Open Thursdays and Saturdays 09h00-13h00. Moonlight markets take place on Tuesdays closest to full moon 17h00-21h00. Admission free. Free parking available on premises. Refreshments.
Further information: The Organic Market, P O Box 4406, Rivonia 2128, tel (011) 706-3671.

Open-air markets have mushroomed all over Johannesburg and other parts of South Africa in recent years, and this craft and produce market is without a doubt the cream of the crop.

A gentle, relaxing ambience and a rural atmosphere are part of the attraction; another drawcard is the exceptionally high quality of the goods on sale.

More than a hundred covered stalls are clustered around a shady tea garden where shoppers can enjoy home-baked treats, and listen to live classical or folk music. Part of the market's general philosophy is to emphasize organically grown products, so this is undoubtedly the place to buy farm-fresh vegetables, fruit, herbs, flowers and a range of excellent cheeses.

The pride that the craftspeople take in their work is reflected in the superior quality of their wares, which include attractive handmade clothing, prints, sculptures, a fascinating range of jewellery (featuring anything from tiny, inexpensive trinkets to more expensive gold and silver pendants), linen, old and new furniture, dried flowers and pottery.

ORIENTAL PLAZA
Fordsburg

Affectionately known as 'the Plaza', this enormous complex of some 300 shops is a paradise for bargain-hunters. With its numerous traders plying their wares, its exotic scents of incense and fresh spices, its cave-like shops festooned with all sorts of colourful fabrics, the Plaza has the vibrant, chaotic atmosphere of a busy Eastern bazaar, and hums with activity from morning till late in the afternoon.

The shops in the Plaza are mostly family businesses, because it was to this complex that the Indian traders of the colourful old suburb of Pageview (or Fietas) were forcibly relocated by apartheid 20 years ago. The centre is perhaps best known for its many small fabric and curtaining shops, but you can buy virtually anything, and at very reasonable prices too: good-quality clothing, shoes, gifts, household linen, crockery, brassware, baskets, toys, rare spices and fresh fruit and vegetables, as well as Indian clothing and freshly cooked delicacies. Feel free to haggle, as most prices are negotiable.

Map: page 9, 9A
Between Bree Street and Main Road in Fordsburg. From the Carlton Centre, travel west along Commissioner Street (which becomes Main Road) for approximately 20 blocks or until you see the Plaza on your right-hand side.
Details: Open Monday to Saturday during regular business hours. Ample free parking on secured premises.
Further information: The Manager, Oriental Plaza, P O Box 42096, Fordsburg 2033, tel (011) 838-6752.

PLANETARIUM
Braamfontein

A fascinating armchair adventure to the 'final frontiers of space' awaits you at the fascinating Johannesburg Planetarium, where visitors are dazzled by the mystery and grandeur of the cosmos without leaving the air-conditioned comfort of their seats. A variety of interesting and topical shows, ranging from multivisual extravaganzas to live lectures, is offered throughout the year at less than the price of a movie ticket.

You can travel the glittering length of the Milky Way, or enjoy close-up views of the planets and their moons within our solar system, as observed through the beady 'eyes' of the Mariner, Viking, Voyager, Magellan and Galileo space probes, or travel back across the centuries to puzzle over the grand and ancient enigmas of the pyramids, Stonehenge or the Star of Bethlehem.

Opened in 1960, the Planetarium auditorium – four storeys high – has a dome measuring 22 m in diameter. It was the first to be built in Africa and the second in the southern hemisphere.

Map: page 9, 7B
Yale Road, Milner Park, Braamfontein, on the campus of the University of the Witwatersrand.
Details: Evening shows: Fridays and Saturdays 20h00. Matinées: Saturdays 15h00; and Sundays 16h00. Tickets for the hour-long shows are available at the door 30 minutes before starting time. Parking in Yale Road or on the university campus.
Further information: The Liaison Officer, Planetarium, P O Box 31149, Braamfontein 2017, tel (011) 716-3199.

Attractively garlanded grounds embrace Johannesburg's domed Planetarium, where visitors explore the mysteries of the universe.

JOHANNESBURG

Map: page 9, 4D
Corner of Kingsway and Henley roads, Auckland Park; entrance in Henley Road.
Details: Organized tours take place Monday to Friday at 09h00 and 10h30. Children under 12 not permitted. Booking essential. Parking in Symons Road.
Further information: The SABC, Private Bag X1, Auckland Park 2006, tel (011) 714-3744.

SABC BROADCASTING CENTRE
Auckland Park

Put on your most comfortable walking shoes for tours of the SABC's massive Broadcasting Centre – covering three kilometres in just one and a half hours. That's what it takes to explore some of the inner workings of this labyrinth, one of the most advanced of its kind in the world. Straddling a ridge west of the city, Broadcasting Centre covers an area of 15 hectares. It is situated in a suburb all of its own, which was declared a separate municipal area in 1980.

Dominating the complex is a 36-storey head-office building. Nearby is Radio Centre, housing 22 radio stations broadcasting in 11 languages, and reaching over 17 million adult listeners daily. The vast Television Centre has numerous studios boasting state-of-the-art equipment, including one that measures more than a quarter of an acre.

A highlight of the tour is a visit to the complex's broadcasting museum; another is the studio in the reception area, which has glass windows through which visitors can watch radio presenters at work.

Illuminated by floodlights, the imposing Brixton radio and television tower, also known as the SABC Tower, looms high above the suburbs of Johannesburg.

Map: page 9, 3D
Corner of Rivonia Road and Sandton Drive, Sandton. Most major routes in the vicinity have green directional signposts showing the way to the centre.
Details: Open during business hours. Restaurants open until 22h00 weekdays and Sundays, and 24h00 Saturdays.
Further information: The Public Relations Officer, Sandton City, P O Box 78100, Sandton 2146, tel (011) 783-7413.

SANDTON CITY
Sandton

This vast, glittering shopping centre is testimony to the immense spending power of the citizens of Johannesburg's prosperous northern suburbs. Built in 1973, it became the forerunner of giant shopping complexes in South Africa.

Since then it has expanded several times to become one of the biggest and most sophisticated retail centres in the southern hemisphere, offering shoppers every possible convenience and facility.

The centre is well known for its exclusive clothing boutiques and its jewellers. Being adjacent to two luxury hotels, there are also up-market curio, leather and African art shops.

But it's not only the affluent who shop at Sandton City: in many ways, the complex functions as the central business district for Sandton, and there are always shoppers browsing through the centre's six major department and food stores and its 200 speciality shops.

When the shopping's done, there's entertainment galore: the centre has 16 cinemas, including a show scan-theatre, and more than 20 restaurants.

Sandton City's five-star hotel has direct access to an elegant concourse.

JOHANNESBURG

SANTARAMA MINILAND
La Rochelle

This miniature city, situated four kilometres south of the Carlton Centre on Rosettenville Road, offers visitors an entertaining whistle-stop tour of some of South Africa's noteworthy landmarks. Inspired by Holland's famous Madurodam miniature city, this miniaturized world is built on a scale of 1:25.

Among the interesting landmarks which are represented in small scale are Cape Town's Castle, Matjiesfontein Village, Groot Constantia, Knysna's tiny Belvidere Church, and Pietermaritzburg Station. Many of the exhibits are working scale models: there are trains, aircraft and several ships and boats, including various tugs, a container ship, minesweeper, fishing trawler, tanker and dredger.

Not everything is Lilliputian, however. One of the main attractions is a splendid full-sized replica of the *Dromedaris*, the vessel in which Jan van Riebeeck's party sailed to the Cape in 1652. Some other attractions include a riverboat, a train and a paddle steamer – small, but big enough for children to take a ride.

The town is named in honour of the South African National Tuberculosis Association (SANTA), to which all the proceeds go.

Two other worthwhile tourist attractions are to be found in the vicinity of Wemmer Pan: the James Hall Museum of Transport *(see separate entry)* and the famous Musical Fountains, which operate every night except Mondays.

Map: page 9, 5D/E
Northern shores of Wemmer Pan, in Pioneer Park, Rosettenville Road, La Rochelle. From the Carlton Centre, drive south along Von Wielligh Street (which becomes Rosettenville Road) for 2km or until you see Miniland on the left-hand side.
Details: Open daily 10h00-17h00. Admission charged. Parking. Refreshments.
Further information: Santarama Miniland, P O Box 57111, Springfield 2137, tel (011) 435-0543.

Santarama Miniland brings the magical world of miniatures to thousands of visitors every year.

SOWETO TOURS
Soweto

Since the 1976 student revolt, the name 'Soweto' has almost become synonymous internationally with black resistance to oppression, so it's hardly surprising that few tourists visit this sprawling, smoky, poverty-stricken satellite city.

Add to this the fact that there are no important sights to see – no museums, no luxury shopping malls, no leafy parks or nature reserves – and it's clear why this vast ghetto is not one of South Africa's major attractions. Still, a tour through Soweto can be intriguing, and for many turns out to be the highlight of their visit to Johannesburg. It's certainly a must for anybody who would like to experience everyday life in Africa's largest city.

Soweto, which is sometimes referred to as Johannesburg's alter ego, consists largely of row after monotonous row of 'matchbox' houses, accommodating some two million people, mostly workers who commute long distances by train or taxi every day to factories, mines and offices. But for all its poverty, it's a place of poignant contrasts and startling enterprise, an exuberant melting pot that pulsates with energy from early morning to late, late at night.

Several reliable companies offer guided tours into Soweto. These can be individually tailored to take in various places of interest; some even include visits to a shebeen (informal tavern).

Map: page 9, 5B
Details: Tours daily.
Further information: The Johannesburg Publicity Association, P O Box 4580, Johannesburg 2000, tel (011) 337-6650.

TRANSNET MUSEUM
Johannesburg

Railway buffs who mourn the passing of the great locomotives of yesteryear will find more than just a touch of nostalgia at this museum.

Some very fine scale models of locomotives and other rolling stock are displayed, along with miniature replicas of ships and aircraft. The museum also houses many of the trappings of yesterday's trains and stations.

The museum is the custodian of all the remaining steam locomotives in South Africa, and is committed to preserving them. Funds for this purpose are raised through various steam safaris: beautifully restored vintage locomotives and coaches take visitors to many of South Africa's most scenic spots, and also to Zimbabwe, Swaziland and Namibia. Day-trips to the Magaliesberg are also offered.

Map: page 9, 8D
Downstairs in the old concourse of Johannesburg Station, corner Eloff and De Villiers streets, Johannesburg.
Details: Open Monday to Friday 07h30-16h00; closed public holidays. Admission free. Parking on premises (entrance in Wolmarans Street).
Further information: The Transnet Museum, P O Box 3753, Johannesburg 2000, tel (011) 773-9118.

JOHANNESBURG

ZOO LAKE PARK
Parkview

Map: page 9, 4D
Between Jan Smuts Avenue and Lower Park Drive in Parkview, opposite the Zoological Gardens.
Details: Open every day of the year (including all holidays). Admission free. Parking in the grounds. Refreshments at the park's tea garden and at kiosks. Avoid walking through Zoo Lake Park after dark.
Further information: The Department of Culture and Recreation, Municipality of Johannesburg, P O Box 2824, Johannesburg 2000, tel (011) 407-6111.

Zoo Lake is more than just the city's most popular recreation spot – it's virtually an institution. There can be hardly a citizen of Johannesburg who has not at one time or another come to Zoo Lake to throw bread crusts to the ducks, take a leisurely row across the lake, walk the dogs or enjoy a picnic in the shade of the many tall trees.

Forming part of Hermann Eckstein Park (which includes the Zoological Gardens across Jan Smuts Avenue), this 45-ha piece of landscaped parkland, with its attractive artificial lake, is the Johannesburg equivalent – albeit much smaller – of New York's Central Park. It is often used as a venue for recreational events, such as musical concerts, art exhibitions and sporting activities.

A popular pastime is to rent a rowing boat and explore the lake, which has a central island where waterfowl breed, and an ornamental fountain commemorating the coronation of King George VI. Other attractions include a public swimming pool, a pleasant tea garden and the Zoo Lake Restaurant, offering fine cuisine in elegant surroundings.

Zoo Lake provides a peaceful refuge for picnickers and strollers near the heart of the city.

ZOOLOGICAL GARDENS
Parkview

Map: page 9, 4D
Jan Smuts Avenue in Parkview, opposite Zoo Lake. From the M1 South take the Riviera Road off-ramp, or the Jan Smuts Drive off-ramp from the M1 North, and follow the signs.
Details: Open every day of the year (including all holidays) 08h30-17h30. Admission fee charged. Ample parking. Refreshments obtainable at the restaurant and from several kiosks.
Further information: The Director, Johannesburg Zoological Gardens, P O Box 2824, Johannesburg 2000, tel (011) 646-2000.

It's worth setting aside at least half a day to visit Johannesburg's Zoological Gardens, because there's much to see and do in this enormous animal sanctuary – home to 3 500 birds, mammals and reptiles, including many endangered species. With its dynamic education and conservation programme, the zoo is particularly geared towards children, who will find a surprise around every corner. And with its 54 ha planted with rolling lawns, flowerbeds and shady old trees, it's a splendid place for a picnic.

Old-fashioned cages are a thing of the past here, replaced in the early Sixties by barless enclosures surrounded by moats, allowing many of the animals to roam freely in their habitats. Perhaps the most popular animals with children are the tigers, the gorillas, the seals, the polar bears and the rare white lions. There's also a farmyard where children may interact with animals. Nearby, there's a walk-through aviary where the air vibrates with the chirrups of hundreds of birds.

Seals, cheetahs, chimpanzees and wild dogs are fed at various times of the day; enquire at the gate for further details.

One of the zoo's famed white lions. These animals were first seen and documented in the Timbavati area in the Lowveld and Escarpment.

PRETORIA

1. Aquarium and Reptile Park
2. Austin Roberts Bird Sanctuary
3. Church Square
4. Fountains Valley
5. Jacaranda Route (starting point)
6. Kruger House Museum
7. Melrose House
8. Museum of Science and Technology
9. National Zoological Gardens
10. Pierneef Museum
11. Police Museum
12. Pretoria Art Museum
13. Pretoria National Botanical Garden
14. State Theatre
15. Union Buildings
16. Voortrekker Monument, including Museum
17. Wonderboom Nature Reserve

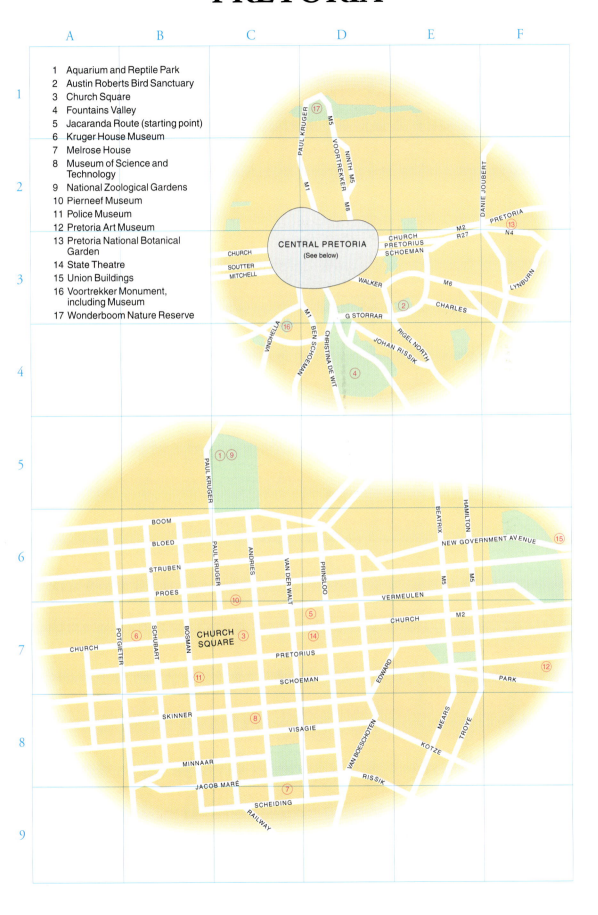

AQUARIUM AND REPTILE PARK
Boom Street

Map: page 27, 5C
Next to the zoo in Boom Street. From Church Square, drive north for 5 blocks along Paul Kruger Street and turn right into Boom Street.
Details: Open daily (including all holidays). Summer 08h00-18h00; winter 08h00-17h30. Admission charged. Parking available diagonally opposite the aquarium in Boom Street. Refreshments.
Further information: National Zoological Gardens, P O Box 754, Pretoria 0001, tel (012) 328-3265/ 328-6020.

Not a single drop of real sea water is to be found in the Pretoria Aquarium, which is remarkable when you consider that this is the largest inland saltwater aquarium in South Africa. One hundred and thirty marine species thrive in its watery, man-made habitats, while the freshwater tanks are home to some 177 species, including several endangered breeds. Rare and exotic creatures of the creepy, crawly, and sometimes clawed, variety are to be found at the Reptile Park nearby, which houses a fascinating, spine-tingling collection of live snakes and reptiles from all over the world.

Both the Aquarium and the Reptile Park pursue active breeding programmes, raising funds by selling surplus animals to zoos and collectors. Among the species that have been successfully bred by the Aquarium are the endangered *Otjikoto* tilapia and the strange *Ancistris* or 'bristle-nosed' catfish from the Amazon River in South America. Other interesting marine animals to be seen at the Aquarium are stonefish – the most venomous fish in the sea – and horseshoe crabs, an ancient species that has not changed since the time of the dinosaurs.

Snakes, crocodiles, lizards, iguanas and tortoises are among the scaly creatures housed in the Reptile Park. Look out for the highly endangered rhinoceros iguana (indigenous to Haiti and the Dominican Republic), which is one of the rarest specimens in the collection, and which was successfully bred in the Aquarium and the Reptile Park in 1993 and 1994.

Among the many fascinating reptiles to be seen at the Pretoria Aquarium and Reptile Park are these rhinoceros iguanas, the first to be bred in the park. The iguanas are a highly endangered species.

AUSTIN ROBERTS BIRD SANCTUARY
New Muckleneuk

Map: page 27, 3E
Boshoff Street, New Muckleneuk. From Church Square, drive south along Paul Kruger Street and turn left into Jacob Maré Street, which becomes Rissik Street, then Walker Street. Turn right into Queen Wilhelmina Avenue, then left into Boshoff Street.
Details: Hide open weekends and public holidays 07h00-17h00. Admission free. Parking available.
Further information: Parks and Recreation Department, P O Box 1454, Pretoria 0001, tel (012) 313-7830.

Great flocks of herons and egrets return at dusk every evening to roost in this leafy nature reserve in the middle of Pretoria's built-up eastern suburbs. Many other birds that forage in and around the city by day find shelter in the sanctuary – about 170 species have been recorded – and it is also home to several small types of antelope.

Although you may not enter the 11-ha sanctuary, the four roads that border the reserve provide an easy two-kilometre, 20-minute walk. Close-up viewing of the birds is possible from the Louis van Bergen hide, a superb vantage point overlooking a willow-fringed dam in the northwestern portion of the reserve. From here a variety of breeding waterfowl may be viewed at close quarters, including herons, egrets, ducks, cormorants and weavers. Look out for blue cranes, South Africa's national bird, and for the rare black swans that also make their home on the dam.

The sanctuary was established by the city council in 1955 on the site of a brick factory, and is named after South Africa's most famous ornithologist, Dr Austin Roberts, author of the bird-watcher's bible, *Roberts' Birds of South Africa*.

CHURCH SQUARE
City centre

Church Square, an open, sunny space in the heart of Pretoria, has been at the centre of the city's social and political life for well over a century. A tour of the square, with its grand old buildings, offers some interesting insights into Pretoria's history. A few private companies offer guided tours, but for those who would prefer a self-guided walk, an informative brochure (with a map) is available from the city's Tourist Rendezvous Travel Centre.

Over the past 130 years Church Square has been used as a market, an auction venue, a sportsfield and tram terminus, its changing face reflecting the turbulent history of Pretoria as it evolved from a sleepy farming centre into the seat of government of a prosperous Boer republic, and finally into a humming commercial centre that is also South Africa's administrative capital.

A simple, mud-walled church once stood at the centre of the square; in the early days, farming families trekked hundreds of kilometres to *nagmaal* (quarterly communion service), outspanning their oxen on the dusty floor of the square.

When Pretoria became the seat of the Transvaal Republican Government in 1860, several imposing buildings were erected around Church Square, among them the Raadsaal (parliamentary building), the Palace of Justice and the old State Bank and Mint. The central focus of the square is Anton van Wouw's massive and imposing statue of President Paul Kruger *(see box)*.

Map: page 27, 7C
Intersection of Church and Paul Kruger streets.

Details: A comprehensive tourist information brochure may be obtained from the Pretoria Information Bureau at the Tourist Rendezvous Travel Centre. Guided tours of the Raadsaal are offered by appointment.

Further information: Tourist Rendezvous Travel Centre, P O Box 440, Pretoria 0001, tel (012) 313-7694/313-7980.

Finally, a place to call home

The famous statue of President Paul Kruger that stands at the centre of Church Square has led a nomadic existence since it was cast in bronze in Rome in 1899. The sculptor, Anton van Wouw, was commissioned by the well-known millionaire industrialist Sammy Marks, a close friend and adviser of President Kruger, who wanted to show his gratitude for having been allowed to build Pretoria's first synagogue. The statue arrived by ship in Delagoa Bay, but for the next 12 years it was to languish in a small store, prevented by the hostilities of the Anglo-Boer War from taking its intended place on a specially built plinth in Church Square. The public-spirited Sammy Marks donated a quite splendid cast-iron fountain to take its place, but this was eventually banished to the Zoological Gardens. In 1913 the statue was dusted off and erected in Prince's Park, and then 12 years later, on the centenary of Paul Kruger's birth, it was moved again, this time to a place in front of the railway station. It was only in 1954 that it finally took up its place in Church Square. The statues of four burghers at the base of the plinth are also well travelled: two were given to Lord Kitchener by Marks at the end of the Anglo-Boer War, and were eventually located at Kitchener's estate in England.

The Raadsaal (parliamentary building) in Pretoria's Church Square dates back to the time of Paul Kruger. This imposing edifice is open to members of the public by prior appointment.

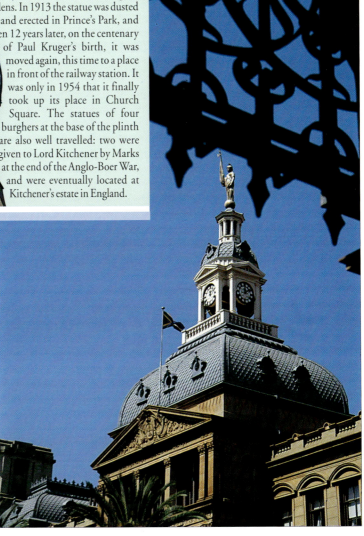

FOUNTAINS VALLEY RECREATION RESORT AND NATURE RESERVE
Verwoerdburg

Map: page 27, 4D
Five kilometres south of Pretoria city centre. About 1 km from Fountains Circle, take the Verwoerdburg/Fountains Valley turn-off. The entrance to the resort is signposted on the left.
Details: Open 24 hours a day, including public holidays, although the office closes at 21h00. Admission charged. Parking. Refreshments.
Further information: Department of Culture and Recreation, P O Box 1454, Pretoria 0001, tel (012) 543-0918.

Fountains Valley is something of an institution in Pretoria. For a great many years this nature reserve and resort have been a favoured destination for the citizens of the city, who come here to enjoy the fresh air and open spaces, the abundant bird life, the indigenous flora and the many excellent recreational facilities.

The nature reserve and resort are situated five kilometres south of the city, at the source of the Apies River. Covering just on 500 ha, the reserve has been in existence for more than a century, making it the country's oldest reserve and the first in Africa.

Although it is situated close to the bustle and grime of the city, the reserve is surprisingly unspoiled, especially in areas where the indigenous vegetation has survived. Many species of bird are to be seen, along with several mammals, including zebras and blesbok.

Most people head for the recreational section of the reserve, which covers an area of about 60 ha, and offers a wide range of facilities, including shaded lawns, picnic spots, a swimming pool, tennis courts, caves, fountains, a restaurant and a caravan park.

For the children there are plenty of attractions, among which are a tidy playground, pens with rabbits and tortoises, and a delightful miniature train with puffing engine.

A dual highway skirts the Fountains Valley Recreation Resort and Nature Reserve, just five kilometres south of Pretoria. The resort is a favourite recreational area, particularly over weekends.

JACARANDA ROUTE
Pretoria

Map: page 27, 7D
Start at the Tourist Rendezvous Travel Centre, corner Vermeulen and Prinsloo streets, Pretoria.
Details: A brochure with a map showing the Jacaranda Route may be obtained from the Pretoria Information Bureau at the Tourist Rendezvous Travel Centre. Parking available in garages in Vermeulen Street and Prinsloo Street.
Further information: Tourist Rendezvous Travel Centre, P O Box 440, Pretoria 0001, tel (012) 313-7694/313-7980.

Every October, Pretoria's 70 000 jacaranda trees explode into billowing clouds of purple blossoms that rain down from the branches to form pools of vivid colour on the streets and sidewalks. The Jacaranda Route, consisting of three separate circular drives, is designed to show off Pretoria's finest jacaranda avenues, at the same time introducing visitors to the city's lovely parks, its historical buildings and various important landmarks. If you are a stranger to Pretoria, these whistle-stop tours are an excellent way to familiarize yourself with the layout of the city, and will help you decide which places to explore further at your leisure.

The starting point for all the routes is the Tourist Rendezvous Travel Centre in the city centre. This is also where to obtain a brochure, which contains a colour map and some useful information about the places of interest on the jacaranda routes.

Varying in distance from 11 km to 26 km, the routes are designed to be driven, although there is no reason why an energetic walker shouldn't explore the various circuits on foot.

Route One, which is coded blue on the map, takes visitors past Sir Herbert Baker's imposing Union Buildings, Venning Park, Arcadia Park and the Pretoria Art Museum.

Jacaranda petals form a carpet of mauve around a park bench along Pretoria's Jacaranda Route, one of the city's more attractive drives.

The second route, coded yellow, winds through the southwestern part of central Pretoria, introducing tourists to the University of Pretoria, the Austin Roberts Bird Sanctuary, Magnolia Dell, Burgers Park and historic Melrose House.

Fort Klapperkop, Unisa, Protea Park and the famous white jacarandas in Herbert Baker Street are the highlights of the third route (coded purple), a scenic drive that meanders through the hilly, southern part of the city.

KRUGER HOUSE MUSEUM
Church Street

This old Church Street house, now a museum, was home to President Paul Kruger for 17 years, and it has not changed much since the days when the irascible leader of the South African Republic (Zuid-Afrikaansche Republiek) dared to challenge the might of the British Empire: the old 'vierkleur' (four-colour) flag still flutters in front of the building, and inside are many original pieces of furniture and smaller personal items that belonged to President Kruger and his wife. Also of great historical interest is the museum's extensive collection of tributes – including documents, medals, ornaments and furniture – which were presented to President Kruger and his countrymen during the Anglo-Boer War by people and countries who were fairly sympathetic to the Boer cause.

For the president of such a prosperous republic, the house is surprisingly modest – a clear reflection of Paul Kruger's unobtrusive lifestyle. The dwelling's exterior design is simple and sober, with a deep stoep, tin roof, pointed gables and wooden posts and railings. The only sign of opulence is a pair of stone lions at the gate – a birthday gift from mining magnate Barney Barnato. An unusual aspect of the house's construction is the fact that the cement was mixed with milk, which was considered to have superior binding qualities to water.

Inside are displayed items of furniture, documents, photographs, mementos and many small, personal possessions, including the president's pipe, saddle, rifle and pocketknife. The house also contains some interesting Victoriana, such as the old brass light switches, harmonium, brass spittoons and wrought-iron heater in the president's official reception room. In the West Hall is a fine old stinkwood trek-wagon and the president's state coach, and at the back of the house stands his private railway coach. A particularly poignant exhibit is a reconstruction of the room in Clarens, Switzerland, where the president died in exile in 1904.

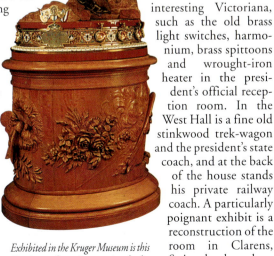

Exhibited in the Kruger Museum is this Bratina, or fraternity cup, given by the Russian community to General Piet Cronje during the Anglo-Boer War.

Map: page 27, 7B
Church Street, between Booth and Potgieter streets. From Church Square, walk west along Church Street for two and a half blocks. The museum is on the right.

Details: Open Monday to Saturday 08h30-16h00; Sundays and public holidays 11h00-16h00. Closed Christmas Day and Good Friday. Admission charged. Refreshments.

Further information: The Curator, Kruger House Museum, P O Box 28088, Sunnyside 0132, tel (012) 326-9172; or National Cultural History Museum, P O Box 28088, Sunnyside 0132, tel (012) 341-1320.

MELROSE HOUSE
Jacob Maré Street

Map: page 27, 9C
From Church Square in central Pretoria, drive south along Paul Kruger Street for 5 blocks. Turn left into Jacob Maré Street; Melrose House is on the right.
Details: Open Tuesday to Saturday 10h00-17h00; Sundays 12h00-17h00; Thursdays 10h00-20h00. Closed Mondays and public holidays. Talks, workshops, temporary exhibitions and antique fairs held regularly. Admission charged. Parking available behind Melrose House (entrance in Scheiding Street). Refreshments from museum's tearoom.
Further information: Melrose House, 275 Jacob Maré Street, Pretoria 0002, tel (012) 322-2805.

History comes alive when you step through the front door of Melrose House and wander through the cool, high-ceilinged rooms, crammed with the treasured possessions of a well-to-do Victorian family. This grand old mansion, now a museum, is one of South Africa's best-preserved examples of Victorian domestic architecture. It's also a place of great historic significance, because it was here that representatives of the British government and the Boer republics came together in 1902 to sign the Treaty of the Peace of Vereeniging, finally bringing to an end the war that had ravaged the land and its people.

Melrose House was the home of millionaire entrepreneur George Heys, whose transport company, Geo. Heys & Co., owned a fleet of horse-drawn coaches that carried passengers and goods to various destinations in the Boer

The lavishly furnished interior of Melrose House reflects the Victorian elegance of its former days. The Treaty of Vereeniging, marking the end of the Anglo-Boer War, was signed here on 31 May 1902.

A hygienic house by Victorian standards

To the modern eye the fittings in Melrose House may seem quaintly outdated, but at the time that the house was built they were considered to be the very last word in fashion.

The discovery of microbes by Pasteur influenced the design of the house, which incorporated many 'hygienic' modern conveniences. Some walls were painted white, the kitchen was tiled, and the entire house was kept warm by means of central steam heating. Most importantly, the house had indoor bathrooms, one fitted with steam-heated towel rails and a luxurious 'closed box' steam bath, the other boasting an elaborate shower-and-bath unit. Ever conscious of the need for fresh air, the owners had ventilators installed in the roof, and to the kitchen added an unusual ventilation shaft.

Air was circulated through the rooms by means of 'Tobin's Tubes' – ventilation ducts operated by levers in the shape of brass hands.

republics. In the 1880s he bought the erven on which the house stands and commissioned London architect W T Vale to design an elegant residence for himself and his family.

The end result was both romantic and extravagant, a sumptuous mansion decorated inside and out with almost every conceivable form of architectural embellishment. Completed in 1886, the house was enlarged substantially during the 1890s when several rooms – including a conservatory and magnificent billiard room – were added.

While the house was being built, George and Emma Heys visited Scotland and were so taken by the haunting beauty of the ruins of Melrose Abbey that they immediately decided to name their new residence after it.

When the time came, no expense was spared to furnish Melrose House; it was on frequent holidays to the East and Europe that George and Emma bought much of the rare and beautiful Victoriana that can be seen in the museum today. The lavish rooms are crammed with ornaments, including silverware, marble statues, paintings and many items of fine porcelain. Of particular interest is the dining-room table, which bears a commemorative silver plaque engraved with facsimiles of all the signatures of the delegates who signed the peace treaty.

A colourful avenue of flowers greets visitors to Melrose House, whose external grandeur is matched by the Victorian treasures within.

MUSEUM OF SCIENCE AND TECHNOLOGY
Skinner Street

Not only for science boffins, technology wizards and other eggheads, a trip to the Museum of Science and Technology is a must; even those who aren't particularly knowledgeable about scientific matters will be surprised at how entertaining a visit to this unusual museum can be. It's the only 'hands-on' museum of its kind in the country, housing dozens of interactive displays and models that visitors are encouraged to handle and manipulate, the ultimate aim being to convey underlying scientific and technological principles in an enjoyable way.

The museum is designed to cater to the tastes of both young and old, with displays covering subjects as diverse as biology, space, nuclear energy, mechanics, water, optics and electricity. Youngsters are particularly attracted to 'Physikon' – an unusual physics playground where the children are encouraged to scramble all over the various models. The Optikon is a similar 'play-as-you-learn' area, containing models that explain light and its properties.

A display that never fails to delight children is the space exhibit, which contains real space artefacts from early American spacecraft; these were recovered in Northern Transvaal after they fell back to earth. Other interesting displays include holograms, a real-time weather satellite receiving station and a plasma ball – in which miniature lightning bolts may be activated by the touch of a hand. Groups may arrange to attend a spectacular chemistry and physics demonstration, or to see the museum's walking, talking robot in action. Group bookings are essential.

Youngsters who are doing research for school projects will appreciate the museum's well-equipped resources centre, which contains books, magazines and audiovisual aids.

Map: page 27, 8C
Didacta Building, 211 Skinner Street, Pretoria Central (between Andries and Paul Kruger streets).
Details: Open Monday to Friday 08h00-16h00; Sundays 14h00-17h00. Closed public holidays. Small admission fee charged. Refreshments.
Further information: Museum of Science and Technology, P O Box 1758, Pretoria 0001, tel (012) 322-6406.

The Museum of Science and Technology enables children to play as they learn.

NATIONAL ZOOLOGICAL GARDENS
Boom Street

Map: page 27, 5C
From Church Square, drive north for 5 blocks along Paul Kruger Street. Turn right into Boom Street; the zoo is on the left.
Details: Open daily (including all holidays). Summer 08h00-18h00; winter 08h00-17h30. Admission charged. Parking available opposite the zoo in Boom Street. Refreshments.
Further information: National Zoological Gardens, P O Box 754, Pretoria 0001, tel (012) 328-3265/ 328-6020.

Flamingoes are just one of 200 different bird species to be found at Pretoria's National Zoological Gardens.

A million visitors a year pass through the gates of the National Zoological Gardens of South Africa, and small wonder: this zoo, comprising 60 ha of beautiful parkland in the heart of Pretoria, has few rivals anywhere in the world. This is where to go to see all the majestic creatures of the African savannah. And if that isn't enough to satisfy you, the zoo's fascinating collection of rare and endangered animals – including a Brazilian maned wolf, Arabian oryx, Indian gaurs, Przewalski horses from Poland and our own bateleur eagle – surely will.

The National Zoological Gardens is considered one of the top 10 zoos in the world and is the largest in South Africa, housing over 120 mammal species and 200 varieties of bird, and boasting its own Aquarium and Reptile Park *(see separate entry)*. It is a dynamic, conservation-orientated place where animals are treated as pampered guests and where the breeding of endangered species takes top priority.

In keeping with its philosophy of playing an educational role, the zoo holds regular exhibitions and offers a variety of courses for young and old. The popular night tour comprises an audiovisual presentation and a moonlight ramble past the enclosures of the zoo's nocturnal creatures. Other interesting initiatives include 'adoption' schemes – where members of the public may sponsor individual animals and indigenous trees – and a Friends of the Zoo Society.

Children will not want to miss a visit to the zoo's farmyard where they can meet all the animals face to face.

Some great aerial views of the zoo and the surrounding city can be enjoyed by members of the public from the overhead cableway. There is a fine restaurant set within the grounds, but visitors are free to take along their own refreshments which may be enjoyed at leisure on the banks of the Apies River, where shady picnic spots and braai facilities are provided.

PIERNEEF MUSEUM
Vermeulen Street

Map: page 27, 7C
218 Vermeulen Street, Pretoria, next to the offices of *The Pretoria News*.
Details: Open Monday to Friday 08h30-16h00. Closed public holidays. Admission free. Parking available in Hallmark Garage (entrance in Vermeulen Street). Refreshments.
Further information: Pierneef Museum, P O Box 28088, Sunnyside 0132, tel (012) 323-1419 (museum), 323-0731 (tearoom).

This art museum offers visitors a unique insight into the life, work and artistic vision of Jacob Hendrik Pierneef, South Africa's best-known landscape painter. The museum, housed in a restored 1920s building, is the custodian of many of the artist's treasured personal possessions, displayed alongside 75 oil paintings, watercolours, pencil sketches, pastels, and pen-and-ink drawings.

The artist experimented with a variety of styles and media during his career, but it is his stylized landscape paintings that are most familiar to South Africans. With their flat colours, linear rhythms and precise geometric forms, they brilliantly evoke the harsh, brooding beauty of the African landscape, which held a great fascination for Pierneef. One of Pierneef's most famous works, *The Study in Blue*, done at the height of his career, can be seen at the museum.

Pierneef was born in Pretoria, but left when his family was deported to Holland

PRETORIA

This entrancing work by the South African artist Pierneef hangs proud among the 75 paintings, drawings and sketches of the museum named after him.

Jan Hendrik Pierneef was born in Pretoria in 1886 to a Dutch father and Afrikaans-speaking mother. Known by his friends as Henk, Pierneef's illustrious career started at an early age. He died in 1957.

for siding with the Boers after Lord Roberts occupied Pretoria in 1900. He studied at the Rotterdam Academy, returning to Pretoria in 1902. Here he worked as a tobacconist, art lecturer and librarian, before finally devoting himself full time to painting in 1923.

The domestic minutiae on display in the museum offer a glimpse into the personal life of Pierneef and his wife Mae: while you're browsing around, look out for the sturdy, wooden camp-stools which were made by the artist, his easel and etching press, and the ceramic ginger jar in which he kept his paintbrushes. A small shop in the museum sells prints of some of Pierneef's works, and various other handcrafted items.

POLICE MUSEUM
Pretorius Street

Crime and punishment, infamy, evil and corruption are the themes of Pretoria's Police Museum, which houses what is surely the most sinister collection of artefacts in the country. The museum is divided into two sections, one of which chronicles the history of the South African Police Force by means of weapons, insignia, uniforms, a reconstruction of an old charge office, and so on. But what really draws visitors to the museum is the other section, which contains representations of South Africa's most shocking crimes: infamous killers and their weapons, pictures of their victims, reconstructions of the crime scenes and other grisly remnants that will send a shudder down the spine of even the most hardened murder-mystery reader.

This criminal hall of horrors introduces visitors to a selection of South Africa's most frightful characters. Meet Daisy de Melker – who poisoned her two husbands and her son – and Pangaman, who terrorized the citizens of Pretoria by attacking couples as they sat in their cars. Then there are the dreaded *muti* (ritual medicine) murderers, whose grisly methods and weapons are displayed alongside chilling photographs of victims. The eeriest display is the 'lake' scene, depicting one of the locations used by murderer Ronald Burch to dispose of the carved-up pieces of his wife.

Several displays are devoted to terrorism and espionage, while the seedy 'gambling and drugs hall' contains some fearsome exhibits designed to warn the public about the dangers of drug and alcohol abuse.

This museum is definitely not for the faint-hearted, but worth a visit for anyone with an interest in crime, mystery and the darker side of human nature.

Map: page 27, 7B
Compol Building, corner Pretorius Street and Volkstem Avenue, Pretoria.
Details: Open Monday to Friday 08h00-15h30; Saturdays 08h30-12h30; Sundays 13h30-16h30. Closed public holidays. Admission free.
Further information: South African Police Museum, P O Box 4866, Pretoria 0001, tel (012) 21-1678/21-2063.

PRETORIA

PRETORIA ART MUSEUM
Arcadia

Map: page 27, 7F
Arcadia Park, corner Schoeman and Wessels streets, Arcadia. From Church Square, drive east along Church Street for about 10 blocks. Turn right into Wessels Street; the museum is 2 blocks further along, on the left.
Details: Open Tuesday to Saturday 10h00-17h00, closing at 20h00 on Wednesdays. Open Sundays 13h00-18h00; closed Mondays and public holidays. Admission charged. Parking available on premises. Refreshments.
Further information: Pretoria Art Museum, P O Box 40925, Arcadia 0007, tel (012) 344-1807/8.

Lovers of fine art should not miss a visit to the Pretoria Art Museum, where they can view a very fine collection of works by some of South Africa's leading artists. Pierneef, Frans Oerder, Pieter Wenning, Anton van Wouw, Walter Battiss, Maud Sumner and Judith Mason are among the famous painters whose works are on display. Sculptures, tapestries, photographs, graphics and ceramics also form an important part of the museum's total collection of 3 000 works of art.

Among the many treasures of the museum is its small but fascinating collection of valuable 17th-century Dutch paintings, some of which are listed in international catalogues.

Having built up a collection of the foremost South African artists of the past, the museum is now acquiring exciting works by contemporary, younger artists. It has also built up a sizable collection of international graphics.

The museum attempts to foster a wider appreciation for its collections by holding regular exhibitions, lectures, guided tours and film shows.

This engaging work by Maud Sumner, entitled 'Flight from Egypt', is among the 3 000 works of art which are exhibited at the Pretoria Art Museum.

PRETORIA NATIONAL BOTANICAL GARDEN
Brummeria

Map: page 27, 2F
Cussonia Road, Brummeria, 10 km east of the city centre. From Church Square, drive east along Church Street for approximately 9 kilometres. Turn right into Cussonia Road; the garden is on the left-hand side.
Details: Open every day 08h00-18h00. Guided tours by arrangement. Admission charged. Parking on premises. Refreshments from tea garden.
Further information: The Curator, Pretoria National Botanical Garden, Private Bag X101, Pretoria 0001, tel (012) 804-3200.

Although it's only 76 ha in extent, this garden contains an astonishing diversity of plant life. Of the 1 700 flowering plants that occur in the Pretoria region, more than half are to be found growing naturally in the garden; it is also home to 500 of South Africa's 1 000 indigenous tree species.

The garden is situated a mere 10 km from the city centre, yet it is remarkably pristine, a tranquil haven where the breeze is scented with the fragrance of indigenous shrubs, and the air reverberates with the ceaseless 'kek-kek-kek!' of flocks of guinea fowl.

Anyone who has a particular interest in indigenous flora will spend many a fascinating hour getting to know the 5 000 species that occur in the garden, and it's also a delightful place for a picnic.

The garden was declared a national monument in 1979 and serves as the headquarters for the National Herbarium. Running from east to west is a rocky outcrop known as the Silverton Ridge; this entire area comprises natural bankenveld. The ridge divides the garden into warmer and cooler sections that accommodate different vegetation types, including bushveld, grassland, succulent karoo, savannah and coastal forest.

Special sections are set aside for aloes, fynbos and some splendid cycad specimens, while the more delicate species are cultivated in hothouses and shade-houses (the nursery can be viewed by appointment only). A good time to visit is in late winter, when the garden is ablaze with the vivid pinks, oranges and yellows of aloes and indigenous daisies.

Perhaps the best way to get a feel for the layout of the garden is to take the Bankenveld Trail, an easy, two-kilometre circular walk that follows the Silverton Ridge. Many small mammals, including dassies, small buck and hares, live among the rocks, and bird-watchers will not be disappointed by the garden's many bushveld birds – all in all over 185 species have been recorded. Plants are labelled, and the annotated map provides details of the various viewpoints.

STATE THEATRE
Church Street

The State Theatre is nothing short of breathtaking in aspect, a mammoth state-owned arts complex that is among the most modern of its kind in the world, and certainly the most sophisticated in Africa. Since it opened in 1981, the complex has attracted its share of controversy – it is regarded in some quarters as an expensive and elitist folly – but there is no denying that it has become Pretoria's most important cultural arena. A guided tour of the complex provides a fascinating glimpse into behind-the-scenes activities, and fascinating specialist tours of the various décor studios and wardrobe department are also offered.

Once described as 'a factory for the performing arts', the complex has five auditoria for opera, ballet, drama and symphony concerts. Each theatre boasts its own dazzling array of state-of-the-art equipment: the 1 300-seat Opera has five sophisticated scenery lifts and a 55-m flytower (used for storing equipment above the stage). The tower is probably the highest of its kind in the world. The splendid costumes and scenery are produced by a small army of technicians in the vast production workshops and wardrobe, and the complex also boasts 88 dressing rooms, nine soundproof rehearsal venues, a restaurant, coffee shop and souvenir shop.

No expense has been spared in fitting out the immense foyers, where marble finishes, thick carpets and a variety of sculptures, paintings and tapestries by well-known artists create a grand, if somewhat overpowering, atmosphere.

In contrast to this rarefied atmosphere is the craft market that takes place in Strijdom Square, adjacent to the theatre complex. It's a colourful, vibrant affair, with stallholders selling a variety of goods, including clothing, curios and fresh produce.

Map: page 27, 7D
Church Street, between Van der Walt and Prinsloo streets. From Church Square, travel 3 blocks east along Church Street; the State Theatre is on the right-hand side.

Details: Tours on Wednesdays at 14h30. Private tours on Thursdays at 09h30 and 14h30; book 1 week in advance. Admission to complex free; small fee charged for guided tour. Secure nighttime parking available under the complex (entrance in Prinsloo Street). Refreshments.

Further information: State Theatre, P O Box 566, Pretoria 0001, tel (012) 322-1665.

One of the outstanding sculptures on display at Pretoria's State Theatre. This is the city's most important cultural centre, where visitors may attend ballet, opera or drama productions in one of five auditoria.

A nightmare for window cleaners

It took 12 million bricks and about 60 000 cubic metres of concrete to build the mammoth State Theatre, and the logistics of maintaining such an enormous building are staggering. Nine kilometres of passage link the offices, workshops, dressing rooms, auditoria and foyers. There are 1 732 doors, 16 passenger lifts, 145 toilet blocks and 3 500 chairs. Pity the poor window cleaners, who have to polish almost 10 000 square metres of glass, while the floor cleaners are not much better off, having to contend with 72 000 square metres of floor covering. When the painters pay a visit, they are faced with a wall and ceiling area of 176 000 square metres: that's over 17 ha, or approximately the area of 40 rugby fields. There are about 12 000 household electric light bulbs to be changed at regular intervals, and some 1 250 wall sockets to keep in perfect working order.

An interesting feature of the building is its paint workshop, which contains the world's largest single paint frame. Measuring 23 m by 17 m, it is set perpendicularly against a wall, eliminating the backbreaking work of painting a stage cloth on the floor.

PRETORIA

The Union Buildings stand in floodlit grandeur above the city of Pretoria, as a full moon rises in the night sky.

UNION BUILDINGS
Arcadia

Map: page 27, 6F
From Church Square in central Pretoria, drive east along Church Street for 7 blocks. Turn left into Zeederberg Street; 1 block further along, on the right, are the gardens of the Union Buildings.
Details: The Union Buildings grounds are open to the public Monday to Friday; the buildings themselves are closed to the public. Admission free.
Further information: Tourist Rendezvous Travel Centre, P O Box 440, Pretoria 0001, tel (012) 313-7694/313-7980.

Grand, majestic and inspiring are adjectives that have all been used to describe the Union Buildings. Symbolizing the unity of the country's former four provinces, the buildings have also served as the seat of government since Pretoria became South Africa's administrative capital in 1910. The formal terraced gardens of the buildings are open to the public: with their manicured lawns and jewel-bright flowerbeds, they are a spectacular sight in springtime and are probably the most photographed location in the whole of Pretoria.

The Union Buildings were designed by Sir Herbert Baker, whose distinctive style was already stamped on hundreds of buildings in the Cape and Highveld. When Baker received the commission, he was offered a site in central Pretoria but, considering it too humdrum for such an important building, rejected it in favour of Meintjeskop, an undeveloped koppie above the city that commanded sweeping views and overlooked a natural amphitheatre. His design, inspired by memories of some Greek and Roman temples, incorporates two graceful, domed towers linked by a curved colonnaded section – the towers are said to represent the English and the Afrikaans people. Locally quarried sandstone was used for the buildings, which incorporated many other indigenous materials, including stinkwood panelling and Vereeniging tiles. Not surprisingly, the Union Buildings are considered to be the crowning achievement of all Baker's work in Africa.

Three statues of former South African prime ministers – Louis Botha, Jan Smuts and J B M Hertzog – are to be found in the grounds, and there are several memorials, including one commemorating the South Africans who lost their lives at the Battle of Delville Wood during the First World War.

VOORTREKKER MONUMENT AND MUSEUM
Pretoria South

To some, it's a cherished symbol of their nationhood and the most important memorial in Afrikanerdom; to others, a threatening monolith representing the bad old days. But whatever way you look at it, the Voortrekker Monument is certainly awe-inspiring in its immensity. Its formidable 41-m-high granite bulk broods over the Pretoria skyline, a lasting memorial to the fortitude and perseverance of the doughty pioneers who avoided British rule in the Cape Colony by trekking into the unknown interior between 1834 and 1840.

Architects from all over the world submitted plans for the monument, but it was the uniquely African design of Gerard Moerdijk that was finally accepted. He envisaged a simple altar of thanksgiving, and turned for inspiration to the medieval stone ruins of North Transvaal and present-day Zimbabwe. The chevron patterns that adorn the massive granite edifice are drawn from traditional African designs, but many of the other decorative elements of the monument are decidedly Art Deco in concept, reflecting the fashion of the time (1937-49).

The rather gloomy lower hall has in its centre an inscribed cenotaph of polished granite, which is dramatically illuminated by a shaft of light falling through the ceiling at noon on 16 December every year (the anniversary of the Battle of Blood River in 1938). The most impressive feature of the monument is the splendid Hall of Heroes, with its ripple-patterned floor and great domed ceiling. Running along its walls is a 92-m-long marble frieze depicting the events of the Great Trek; this is the largest marble frieze in the world. One hundred and sixty-nine steps lead to an observation platform on the roof where visitors can enjoy panoramic views of Pretoria.

Symbolic protection of the monument comes in the form of an encircling wall of 64 covered Voortrekker wagons cast in terrazzo. A very fine bronze statue by Anton van Wouw, depicting a Voortrekker woman and her children, stands at the entrance to the monument.

The Voortrekker Monument Museum nearby contains a fascinating selection of Voortrekker memorabilia. These include an oxwagon, simple kitchen utensils, tools, farming implements, furniture, clothing and guns.

A particularly interesting Voortrekker exhibit is the replica of a typical three-room pioneer house, a simple structure with a floor made of antheap, dung and animal blood.

Pride of the museum is the magnificent set of tapestries depicting the life and times of the Voortrekkers. These were embroidered by nine needlewomen, and took eight years to complete.

Map: page 27, 4C
Six kilometres south of Pretoria. From Fountains Circle, take the Verwoerdburg/Fountains Valley turn-off and turn right at the first traffic lights. The monument is about 2 km further along, on the right-hand side.
Details: Monument and museum open daily 09h00-16h45. Closed Christmas Day and Good Friday. Admission fee is charged at the monument and the museum. Parking on premises. Refreshments.
Further information: Voortrekker Monument, P O Box 1595, Pretoria 0001, tel (012) 326-6770; Voortrekker Monument Museum, P O Box 28088, Sunnyside 0132, tel (012) 323-0682.

The monolithic face of the Voortrekker Monument towers above the surrounding countryside just outside Pretoria.

Visitors are dwarfed by the immensity of the ripple-patterned floors inside the Voortrekker Monument, as seen from the top balcony.

WONDERBOOM NATURE RESERVE
Near Pretoria

Map: page 27, 1D

From Church Square, drive west along Church Street and turn right into D F Malan Drive. Continue north until the road merges with Paul Kruger Street. About 2 km further along, turn right at turning marked Wonderboom/Old Warmbaths Road, and follow the signposts to the reserve.

Details: Open daily, including public holidays, 06h00-18h00. Admission charged. Parking.

Further information: Department of Culture and Recreation, P O Box 1454, Pretoria 0001, tel (012) 543-0918; or Tourist Rendezvous Travel Centre, P O Box 440, Pretoria 0001, tel (012) 313-7694/313-7980.

Around the time of the Crusades, a fig sapling sprang up on the slopes of the Magaliesberg, 10 km north of present-day Pretoria. Today, a thousand years on, it still flourishes, an ancient giant that was christened 'Wonderboom' (wonderful tree) by Voortrekker Hendrik Potgieter when he happened upon it in 1836. Growing on the sheltered approach to the Wonderboom Ridge, near the site of an old fort, the tree has lent its name not only to the Pretoria suburb of Wonderboom but also to the 450-ha nature reserve that surrounds it.

The tree is *Ficus salicifolia*, a species of wild fig with leathery leaves, rough, grey bark and tiny clusters of figs. This particular specimen has spread itself over a huge area by a process of natural layering. Where the drooping branches of the original tree touched the ground, they took root and produced a circle of new trees, which in turn produced another generation. Today there is a central trunk 5,5 m in diameter and 12 distinct auxiliary trunks, although the original 'umbilical cords' linking them to the parent tree have long since vanished. The vast canopy covers 55 square metres, and can easily accommodate 1 000 people in its shade.

With its many birds, buck, dassies and other small mammals, the reserve is a pleasant place for nature rambles and picnics – braai facilities and ablution block are provided. A footpath leads up the Magaliesberg, where you can see the ruins of the old Wonderboom Fort. No shot was ever fired from the fortress, which was built for the defence of Pretoria after the Jameson Raid.

The ruins of the old Wonderboom Fort, originally built to defend Pretoria, attract visitors to the Wonderboom Nature Reserve, an easy drive from central Pretoria.

HIGHVELD

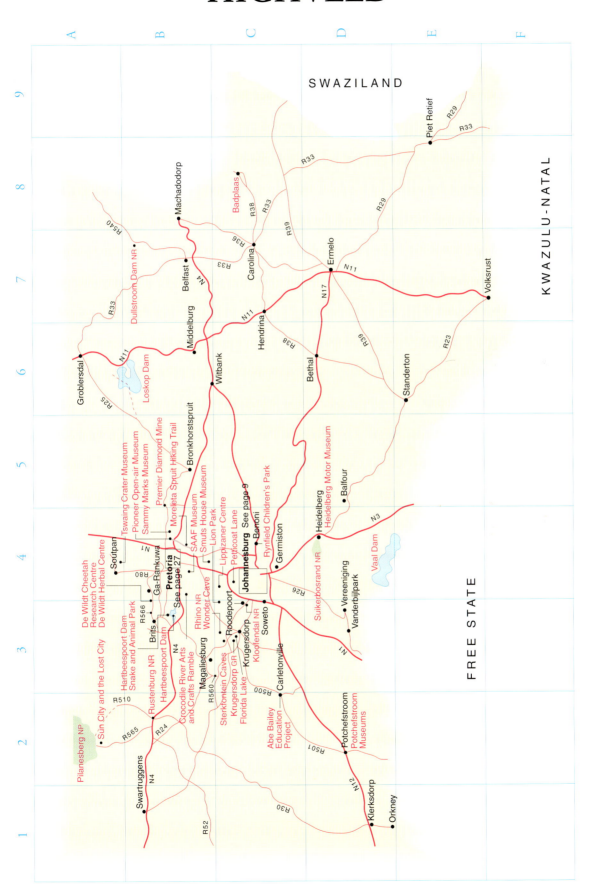

HIGHVELD

ABE BAILEY EDUCATION PROJECT
Carletonville

Map: page 41, 2C
Situated just northwest of Carletonville. Leave Carletonville by the Pretoria road, and after about 5 km turn left at the signpost marked 'Welverdiend/Khutsong'. The reserve is 5 km further along on the right.
Details: Open daily 08h00-16h30. Entrance fee charged.
Accommodation: Four self-catering bungalows (booking essential); caravan/camping facilities. Bush camp available for larger parties.
Further information: The Education Officer, Abe Bailey Education Project, P O Box 6444, Oberholzer 2502, tel (01491) 788-3015.

When you look out over the still waters of the many vleis in this reserve, it's difficult to believe that this vast and lonely wetland was created artificially by pumping water in from nearby mines. Man-made it might be, and rather bleak at first glance, but this valuable reserve teems with wildlife, including many species of waterfowl and grassland bird, as well as buck and smaller mammals. Two interesting day-walks, the Guineafowl Trail and the Avocet Trail, wind through the reserve, and an overnight trail is being developed. Other attractions are a hide on the edge of the vlei, and a dolomitic cave that you can visit by arrangement.

The farm is named in honour of well-known mining magnate Sir Abe Bailey, who once owned a hunting lodge and stud farm here.

The property was enlarged by the then Transvaal branch of the Wildlife Society of Southern Africa as a conservation education centre, and is administered by the Gauteng provincial authorities.

The reserve comprises four ecozones: wetland, grassland, acacia woodland and acacia bushveld, which together support Burchell's zebras, wildebeest, springbok, red hartebeest, duiker and steenbok. Migrating flamingoes are sometimes seen here, along with over 220 resident species of bird, including ducks, geese, cormorants, gallinules, teals, herons, kingfishers, avocets, cranes and storks.

Some tame animals, including a lynx, are used for educational purposes.

Various guided outings, all with an environmental theme, are available to schools and special-interest groups.

Joyous children are propelled into the water by one of Badplaas's colourful switchback slides. The family-style resort offers everything, from spa baths and minigolf, to game-viewing in the next-door reserve.

BADPLAAS
East of Carolina

Map: page 41, 8C
About 48 km east of Carolina. Can be reached by tarred and gravel roads from Carolina, Machadodorp and Barberton.
Details: Aventura Resort and game reserve open every day 07h00-17h00.
Accommodation: Chalets, flatlets, rondavels, camp site and hotel.
Further information: Aventura Badplaas, P O Box 15, Badplaas 1190, tel (01344) 4-1020. Bookings: Aventura Central Reservations, P O Box 720, Groenkloof 0027, tel (012) 346-2277.

The hot mineral waters that filter from a natural spring at Badplaas were first visited by travellers in the mid-1870s, but their extraordinary curative powers had been known to the local tribesmen long before that: they called them *Emanzana*, or 'healing waters'.

Today, people with rheumatic ailments still travel to Badplaas to soak away their aches and pains, but they are largely outnumbered by the many holiday-makers who come to enjoy the superb facilities offered by the large, modern resort and nature reserve here.

The thermal springs are situated in the valley of the Komati River, 48 km east of Carolina, on the Barberton road. Legend has it that the spring was presented as a gift to a Jacob de Clerq by a Swazi chief. The fame of the waters spread rapidly, especially after the discovery of gold in the De Kaap Valley nearby, and by 1893 the spring was proclaimed State property.

The alkaline waters contain sodium bicarbonate, and are a steaming 50°C when they filter from the earth. The water, flowing at a rate of about 32 000 litres per hour, is pumped into a warm mineral pool and into private baths at the Aventura Resort.

The resort caters for action-packed family holidays, and the only worrying moment you're likely to experience here is deciding what to do next! Facilities include minigolf, water slides, a bowling green, tennis, beach volleyball, roller-skating rink, a restaurant and all sorts of indoor activities.

There's a 1 500-ha reserve adjoining the resort, which is set in the foothills of the Hlumuhlumu Mountains. The reserve caters for nature-lovers who prefer to get away from it all. The grassveld vegetation supports a wide variety of bird and animal life, including rhinos, black wildebeest, eland, gemsbok and red hartebeest. A network of roads allows you to drive through the reserve on your own, while the walking trails offer opportunities for close-up encounters with animals. For a quite different game-watching experience, you may ride on horseback through the reserve. Horses may be hired from the resort.

CROCODILE RIVER ARTS AND CRAFTS RAMBLE
Muldersdrift and Broederstroom

The Crocodile River rises near Krugersdorp, and flows lazily northeastwards, cutting a secret, willow-fringed pathway through the grassy hills of Muldersdrift and Broederstroom, and pouring eventually into the Hartbeespoort Dam. All along the river's banks are the homes of a variety of talented artists and craftsmen, who produce everything from fine art to furniture in their studios and workshops.

Some seven years ago these artists joined forces with local restaurants, hotels and farms to create the Crocodile River Ramble, a delightfully different tourist route that has now established itself as the country's foremost arts and crafts route.

The ramble offers tourists the unique opportunity to visit artists and craftsmen in their home studios, to watch them at work, and to browse at leisure through

Map: page 41 2/3B, and below
The route passes through Honeydew and Muldersdrift, one arm extending west towards Krugersdorp and Kromdraai, then proceeds past Lanseria to end near Pelindaba in Broederstroom.
Details: Open Saturday and Sunday of the first weekend of every month 09h00-17h00. Several studios are open by appointment on other days. Admission free. Refreshments. Parking. No dogs.
Accommodation: There are several hotels and guest farms along the route.
Further information: A free map and brochure are available at any of the stops on the route, from tourist information centres in Johannesburg and Pretoria, or from the Secretary, Crocodile River Arts and Crafts Ramble, P O Box 231, Lanseria 1748, tel (011) 659-2486.

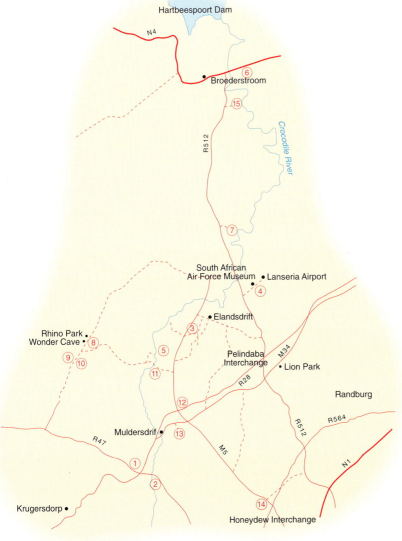

KEY TO THE MAP
1 Chris Patton Studio
2 John Dunn Studio
3 Mickey Korzennik
4 Lindele
5 Riverbend Gallery
6 Preller House Restaurant
7 New Vaalie Farm Stall
8 River Country Estates
9 Rainbow Trout Farm
10 Ibis Ridge Gallery
11 Khanya Craft
12 The Right Track
13 John Curteis Forged Ironwork
14 Gallery Tres Jolie
15 SVR Creations

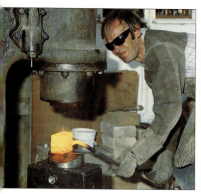

This home-based craftsman is smelting his raw material, first stage in the fashioning of ironwork. The Crocodile River's workshops range through the creative spectrum.

the many galleries. It operates only on the first weekend of every month, and there is no fixed sequence. 'Doing' the route is as simple as hopping into the car, grabbing a map *(see panel)* and heading for the studios and workshops that appeal to you most. A wonderful diversity of arts and crafts is to be found along the route, including ceramics, paintings, furniture, jewellery, antiques, knitware, clothing, lace, dolls, ironwork and stained glass, all of which may be purchased at very reasonable prices. Don't miss the studios of potters Chris Patton and John Dunn. Equally inspiring is the gallery of well-known sculptor and muralist Mickey Korzennik.

At Lindele, near Lanseria Airport, you can buy a range of beautiful angora and woollen jerseys and hand-spun yarns, while the zany Riverbend Gallery specializes in handmade rustic furniture.

Gourmets will enjoy exploring the fine hotels, restaurants and farm stalls along the route. The Preller House Restaurant is set in an old stone farmhouse – once the home of Gustav Preller and Eugene Marais. The Hertford Hotel is famed for its country lunches. Tea and cream scones are a staple at the various tea gardens along the route, some of which also provide picnic hampers crammed with delicious home-made comestibles.

The New Vaalie Farm Stall specializes in a range of wittily named preserves, such as 'Knobkiwi Jam'. If a fresh trout is your idea of heaven, then head for River Country Estates, set on the banks of the Crocodile River, or for the Rainbow Trout Farm in Kromdraai, where you can hire a rod and catch your own.

Guided coach tours of the ramble may be arranged, and for the intrepid adventurer there's the option of hiring a hot-air balloon for an unforgettable aerial view of the river's course.

A pair of cheetahs covers the De Wildt terrain at high speed. These graceful hunters of the open plains are an endangered species.

DE WILDT CHEETAH RESEARCH CENTRE
De Wildt

Map: page 41, 3B
From Johannesburg drive north along the R511. Note your kilometre reading as you cross the N1. Continue along the R511 for 49,6 km, then turn right onto the R513. The entrance to the centre is 5 km further on.

Details: Guided tours by arrangement only: Saturdays and Sundays 09h00 and 14h15; Thursdays 10h00. Book well in advance. No children under six. Admission charged.

Further information: De Wildt Cheetah Research Centre, P O Box 16, De Wildt 0251, tel (012) 504-1921.

A perfect synthesis of strength, agility and grace makes the cheetah the fastest mammal on earth, capable of moving at speeds of up to 110 km/hour. But this phenomenal swiftness has not been enough to ensure the continued survival of the species, and the total number of cheetahs in southern Africa has declined alarmingly over the years.

The De Wildt Cheetah Research Centre, which nestles in the shadow of the Magaliesberg, near Brits, was established with the purpose of breeding cheetahs in captivity. A guided tour of the research centre offers visitors a fascinating insight into the breeding programme, and also the rare opportunity to view cheetahs and their cubs at close quarters.

The centre was established in 1971 for the specific purpose of breeding cheetahs in semicaptive conditions.

Initially the project was greeted with scepticism in some quarters because of the extreme difficulty of breeding these shy cats in captivity, but the results of the

Designed for speed

With the swiftness of a sprinter and the grace and suppleness of a dancer, cheetahs are creatures custom-designed for speed. Their legs are long and supple, their shoulders high and muscular, allowing them to take strides of up to seven metres, with the long tail acting as a stabilizing mechanism.

Although a cheetah can reach speeds of up to 110 km/h, it tends to tire easily – after about 300 m – because it cannot sustain the enormous muscular effort required to keep the elongated spine springing back and forth. The cheetah stalks its prey carefully, sometimes taking hours to come within range. Then it attacks in a terrifying burst of speed, its head held steady, eyes fastened on its quarry. In a blurred flurry of fur it knocks its prey over and clamps its powerful jaws over the throat for up to 10 minutes.

Cheetahs hunt alone, in pairs or in groups, in the mornings and late afternoons, preying on buck, hares, jackals, young warthogs, birds and even young ostriches and porcupines.

Apart from its speed, there are several other characteristics that set the cheetah apart from its other feline cousins. Unlike leopards and lions, an adult cheetah has partially retractable claws and lacks the protective sheaths found in other cat species. It also lacks the ability to roar, communicating instead by deep purrs, growls and hisses. Cheetahs are by nature peace-loving, which is why they are often driven from their kills by lions and hyaenas. Their timid nature makes them easy to tame. In India, cheetahs were once trained to hunt gazelles for their masters.

This young cheetah is one of more than 400 animals reared at the De Wildt centre. Other residents include wild dogs and brown hyaenas.

researchers' efforts are nothing short of spectacular. To date, more than 400 cheetah cubs have been born at the research centre, and attempts have been made to reintroduce them into the wild.

In recent years, the centre has successfully begun breeding a variety of other rare and endangered species, whose very survival hangs on a thread. You would be extremely lucky to spot any one of these elusive creatures in the country's game parks. Here, however, you can encounter them face to face. The centre has raised several litters of Cape hunting dogs, one of Africa's most endangered carnivores. Some of these have been released into the wild. Other animals that are being bred here include brown hyaenas, Cape vultures, sunis, blue duiker and the riverine rabbit. Aviaries have also been erected for two pairs of Egyptian vulture to be used for breeding purposes.

The most prized of all the centre's inhabitants are the king cheetahs – the only specimens ever to have been bred in captivity. These creatures are distinguished from ordinary cheetahs by their extraordinary markings. Their spots are enlarged, flowing into heavy black stripes and blotches. For a while scientists mistakenly believed that this was a separate species, but it is now known to be a genetic variation.

HIGHVELD

An elegantly arched walkway leads through one of herbalist Margaret Roberts's delightful gardens. On show are a myriad different plants.

DE WILDT HERBAL CENTRE
De Wildt

The heady fragrance of thousands of exotic and indigenous herbs fills the air as you drive up a dusty farm road between thorn trees. Up ahead, tucked up against the sun-soaked northern flank of the Magaliesberg lies the popular De Wildt Herbal Centre. This is the home of Margaret Roberts, the herbalist whose many books and appearances on television have created an unprecedented surge of interest in the cultivation and use of herbs in South Africa.

Her extensive gardens, shop, demonstration kitchen and nursery, situated in De Wildt, north of Pretoria, are open to the public on Wednesdays every week, offering visitors an inspiring opportunity to see how the herbs are grown, harvested and used, and to soak up some fascinating herb lore.

Margaret's abiding interest in herbs and her encyclopedic knowledge of plants are evident everywhere. It's worth taking along pen and paper to take notes. Keen gardeners, especially, will delight in exploring the various herb gardens where plants grow in rampant profusion, testimony to the success of the organic gardening principles that are followed with religious zeal. The main formal herb garden contains every conceivable medicinal, culinary and fragrance herb, each one clearly labelled. There are several handsome *parterre* gardens (laid out in patterns to resemble a glowing Persian carpet) and a rock garden, cooking garden, container garden and charming 'fairy garden' that features a diversity of indigenous healing herbs. The 'fairy garden' is unique in that, among the herbs, an enchanting miniature village of 26 buildings has been painstakingly created, with each structure relating to a companion herb plant. The 'fragrant walk' is a colonnaded avenue overgrown with honeysuckle, stephanotis and jasmine that burst into flower in springtime, attracting clouds of bees and butterflies.

Flavoured vinegars and oils, potpourris, pomanders, dried flowers and seeds, syrups, soaps, creams and lotions are some of the fragrant herbal products on sale at the shop. Every single item is grown, made and packaged on the farm. When you're finished shopping, head for the shady tea garden, where you can enjoy herbal teas (coffee is frowned upon!) and geranium-scented scones, with lashings of jam and farm cream. If you're thinking of creating your own herb garden or extending an existing one, stop off at the farm's nursery, where you can buy a huge range of herbs for just a few rands each. Many of them are rare plants, unavailable elsewhere in the country.

The Herbal Centre also offers various lectures and special courses to groups by prior arrangement.

Map: page 41, 3B
About an hour's drive from Johannesburg and Pretoria. From Johannesburg take the R511 to Hartbeespoort Dam. Cross over the N4, and continue until you see the Aquarium on the right-hand side. Turn right immediately afterwards onto the Tunnel Bypass Road at the garage on the corner (still the R511), and continue for about 3 km, to where the road forks. Keep to the left (still following the R511), drive for 2,8 km, and then turn right at the top of the mountain onto the Pretoria North road. At the T-junction turn right again onto the R513. About 4 km further along, on the right-hand side, is the turn-off to the Herbal Centre. Follow this untarred road for 1,5 km up the mountain to the garden.

Details: Open Wednesdays 08h30-16h00. Parking. Teas and light lunches.

Further information: De Wildt Herbal Centre, P O Box 41, De Wildt 0251, tel (012) 504-1729 (mornings only).

DULLSTROOM DAM NATURE RESERVE
Dullstroom

Crystal-clear, fast-running waters and dams that boil with trout have made the Dullstroom area one of the Highveld's premier fly-fishing spots, and the many exclusive lodges, hotels and shops that have sprung up around the town are proof of its popularity among anglers who have money to spend. But there's more to Dullstroom than just trout. Nature-lovers, especially, will find many botanical delights to interest them in this region, renowned for its unique sub-Alpine climate. The Dullstroom Dam Nature Reserve, on the fringes of the village, is an ideal base from which to explore the area.

Dullstroom lies 33 km north of Belfast, and is overlooked by the Steenkampsberg range, of which Die Berg, at 2331 m, is the highest point in the Highveld. The village has the unusual distinction of having the highest railway station in the country, and it is also one of South Africa's coldest towns. Here, the air is as clear and as bracing as icy champagne, with temperatures plummeting as low as –10°C in winter.

Proclaimed in 1893, and named after Wolterus Dull, a merchant from Amsterdam, the town was originally settled in by Dutch immigrants. Several charming, historic buildings are to be seen here, among them the old post office and church. The town is famous for its magnificent deciduous trees, including beeches, elms, lindens and cherry trees, some of which are proclaimed national monuments.

Trout is the area's major industry, and the municipal dam, situated in the nature reserve just outside Dullstroom, is administered by a club known as the Dullstroom Fly-fishers. Nonmembers are allowed day access to the dam for a fee, and for those who wish to stay overnight there's a very pleasant caravan and camping site.

The dam is the starting point for the Steenkampsberg Hiking Trail, which passes through the town for one kilometre, before winding up onto the plateau, where it then passes deep gulleys, streams, dramatic rock formations and a vlei, where rare wattled cranes breed. Between October and February hikers are dazzled by the great diversity of indigenous wildflowers that grow on the high-lying grasslands, among them ericas, purple arum lilies, blue scilla, red-hot pokers and pineapple lilies.

At peace with the world: a fly-fisherman angles for trout in one of Dullstroom's dams. Superb scenery, a bracing climate and two charming hotels are among the area's other attractions.

Map: page 41, 7B
From Johannesburg/Pretoria, drive east along the N4, and turn off at Belfast. Follow the R540 for about 33 km to Dullstroom. Drive through the village, turn left at the garage and follow the signs for about 800 m to the gates of the reserve.

Details: Open daily, including public holidays, 06h00-18h00. Admission charged.

Accommodation: Camping/caravan sites in nature reserve. Alternative accommodation at several hotels, lodges and on private farms. Booking essential for hiking trail.

Further information: The Town Clerk, P O Box 1, Dullstroom 1110, tel (01325) 4-0151/2.

HIGHVELD

Usually seen in pairs or small groups, the wattled crane is easily identified by its striking plumage.

FLORIDA LAKE
Florida

Map: page 41, 3C
Situated in Florida, west of Johannesburg, bounded by Swan Avenue, Fourth Avenue, Kathleen Avenue and Eisteddfod Road.
Details: Open daily. Admission free. Park along Fourth Avenue or at the western end along Westlake Road. Refreshments.
Accommodation: There are sites for caravans at the lake, and a variety of hotels in Florida.
Further information: Parks and Recreation Division, Roodepoort City Council, Private Bag X30, Roodepoort 1725, tel (011) 472-1439.

If your idea of blissful relaxation is lazing on a lawn on the shores of a huge lake, then Florida Lake will appeal to you. This enormous sheet of water and its adjoining park are one of the finest recreational areas on the Witwatersrand, and offer something for everyone. Watersport enthusiasts come to enjoy themselves on windsurfers, yachts and canoes (provided that they are members of the yacht club); walkers come to take pleasant rambles around the perimeter of the lake; and nature enthusiasts come to watch the abundant bird life in the adjoining bird sanctuary. With its rolling lawns and groves of shady trees, it is also a very popular picnic place.

Florida is a suburb forming part of the city of Roodepoort, west of Johannesburg. Many early miners worked the reefs in this area, and as early as 1890 the dam was used as a recreational area for residents. A monument on the shores of the lake commemorates the discovery of gold in the area.

The western shore of the lake is fenced off, and is an important breeding area for egrets, herons, cormorants and other waterfowl.

There are plenty of attractions for landlubbers, including lovely picnic places with braai facilities, a putt-putt course for the kids, a swimming pool and, on Sundays and public holidays, a miniature train. Every two years, in springtime, an international dance and music eisteddfod are held here.

The placid surface and embowered shores of Florida Lake beckon the picnicker, the nature-lover, the rambler and the yachtsman.

HARTBEESPOORT DAM
Broederstroom

The sizzle of meat on the braai, the happy shouts of children wading knee-deep in water, and the arc of glittering spray as a water-skier whizzes past, are some of the familiar sights and sounds of a weekend in the sun at Hartbeespoort Dam. This enormous sheet of water, with its lovely backdrop of blue-grey Magaliesberg Mountains, is one of the Highveld's premier recreation spots. Over weekends, a small flotilla of yachts, speedboats and sailboards is launched onto the dam's 12 square kilometres of water, while the various nature reserves strung out along the shores attract many picnickers, campers and anglers.

The dam has become a favourite destination for city dwellers keen to escape the pressures of urban living; its convenient location, some 35 km west of Pretoria (about 50 minutes' drive from Johannesburg) makes it particularly popular among day-trippers. Areas of the dam tend to become unbearably crowded in peak season, but there are still several remote pockets where nature-lovers can unwind in peace.

Lovely views over the water may be enjoyed by taking a scenic drive around the dam. The road that encircles the dam passes through a short tunnel blasted through the mountain, and then over the 59-m-high dam wall. All along its length are kiosks, farm stalls, curio shops, restaurants, resorts and private holiday homes, as well as tourist attractions, such as the Hartbeespoort Dam Snake and Animal Park *(see separate entry)*, and an aquarium. Perched on sloping mountainside at the northern end of the dam is Cosmos, a holiday village that is every bit as pretty as its name.

An aerial cableway on the eastern side of the dam swoops visitors 400 m up to the craggy, red heights of the Magaliesberg, from where they can enjoy breathtaking vistas and, at certain times, watch hang-gliders taking off from the mountainside and drifting on the thermals like petals in the wind.

The Hartbeespoort Dam Nature Reserve comprises the dam itself and five other conservation areas. On the water's edge are Schoemansville, Oberon, Ifafi and Meerhof. Camping is permitted at the first three, and all are popular among anglers who come to fish for kurper, carp and yellowtail. Kommandosnek, on the Cosmos Road, is a 200-ha reserve with camping facilities and an enclosed game camp where kudu, bushbuck and zebras roam free.

Map: page 41, 3B
About 70 km north of Johannesburg. From Four Ways, take either the R512, which passes through Broederstroom to the western end of the dam, or the R511, which takes you through Hennops River to the eastern shores. From Pretoria travel along Church Street West, and then take the N4 to Hartbeespoort Dam.

Details: Nature reserves open 06h00-18h00.

Accommodation: At camping sites, resorts and the Lake Hotel, P O Box 1, Hartbeespoort 0216, tel (01211) 3-0001/3-0053.

Further information: Tourist Rendezvous Travel Centre, P O Box 440, Pretoria 0001, tel (012) 313-7694/313-7980; Hartbeespoort City Council, P O Box 976, Hartbeespoort 0216, tel (01211) 3-0037/53-0600.

The day's last soft light gilds the waters of Hartbeespoort Dam, a pleasant refuge from the urban jungles of the Witwatersrand.

HIGHVELD

HARTBEESPOORT DAM SNAKE AND ANIMAL PARK
Scott Street, Hartbeespoort

Map: page 41, 3B
North side of Hartbeespoort Dam, east of the dam wall. From Four Ways, follow the R512. After passing beneath the R28, continue until you reach the turn-off to Brits. Turn left, and follow this road until you reach the park on the left-hand side of the lake, before the dam wall. Alternatively, if you're coming from Pretoria, you can take either Church Street to the Pelindaba fourway, or Van der Hoff Street, following the Hartbeespoort sign.
Details: Open daily, including public holidays, 08h00-17h00 (later during summer months). Chimp and seal demonstrations at 12h00 and 15h00 on weekends and public holidays. Regular boat trips on dam. Educational programmes offered. Admission charged. Parking on premises. Curio shop. Refreshments.
Accommodation: Lake Hotel, P O Box 1, Hartbeespoort 0216, tel (01211) 3-0001/3-0053.
Further information: Hartbeespoort Dam Snake and Animal Park, P O Box 109, Hartbeespoort 0216, tel (01211) 3-0162 (administration 53-0195/6).

A fine collection of fanged slitherers and other reptilian relatives is to be found at this small zoo, set on sloping mountainside, and lapped by the waters of Hartbeespoort Dam. But it is not only hissing sounds that you'll hear emanating from cages: there are also the roars and growls of many big cats, including Kalahari lions, tigers, cheetahs, panthers, pumas and leopards, and a large variety of other animal species.

This private zoo is one of the smallest in the country, but its position near the dam wall ensures a steady stream of visitors who come to watch entertaining chimp and seal shows, as well as snake-handling demonstrations in the park's large arena. (These shows take place on weekends and public holidays.)

Many of the animals kept here are movie stars which have appeared in a variety of local as well as overseas films and television advertisements.

Zoos may not be everyone's cup of tea, but the enclosures here conform to international specifications, and the animals are well cared for. The zoo also plays an important educational role: thousands of schoolchildren, including many under-privileged city kids, have had their first close contact here with a creature from the wild.

The zoo serves as a starting point for relaxing and scenic 20-minute cruises on a passenger launch, and also offers tours up the nearby aerial cableway.

One of the park's well-schooled pythons drapes itself around a young visitor. Other drawcards are performing chimpanzees and seals.

HEIDELBERG MOTOR MUSEUM
Heidelberg

Map: page 41, 4D
From Johannesburg drive south along the N3. Take the Nigel off-ramp (exit 66) and turn right towards Heidelberg. After about 3 km, turn left into Voortrekker Street, and follow the signposts to the museum.
Details: Open Tuesday to Saturday 10h00-13h00 and 14h00-17h00. Closed Mondays and religious holidays. Admission charged. Parking. Refreshments.
Accommodation: Heidelberg Guest House, P O Box 62, Heidelberg 2400, tel (0151) 9-5387.
Further information: Heidelberg Motor Museum, P O Box 320, Heidelberg 2400, tel (0151) 6303.

The holiday-makers who whizz past Heidelberg on their annual stampede to the KwaZulu-Natal coast represent but a fraction of the parade of many thousands of vehicles that have passed this way during the last 100 years. Heidelberg's long and romantic association with the history of transport is admirably preserved at its Motor Museum, which traces the history of land transport, from the days of four-footed travel, to the dawn of the mechanized age.

Containing several rare and unusual exhibits, including some splendid vintage cars and motorcycles, the museum is definitely worth a detour, even if it means adding a half-hour or so to your travelling time to the coast.

It was at Heidelberg, set below the ridge of the Suikerbosrand, that the old wagon trails converged, those highways of the veld that linked far-flung settlements. Transport riders, ivory hunters, prospectors, politicians and soldiers all passed this way, on horseback, in ox-wagons, Cape carts, buggies, hansom cabs and stagecoaches. After the last rail of Paul Kruger's Zuid-Oosterlijn to Natal was coupled at Heidelberg in 1895, the whistle of steam locomotives was added to the chorus of clopping hooves and rattling wheels, heralding the age of rail

This 18th-century sedan chair once plied the cobbled streets of Paris. Most of the museum's many exhibits, though, relate to travel in the old Transvaal.

travel in the Highveld. With the railway line came a station, and it is this handsome old sandstone building that now houses the motor museum.

A Velocipede, a Boneshaker and a Penny Farthing are among the delightful early bicycles on display, while the museum's collection of veteran cars and motorcycles includes a 1913 Humberette, and a 1913 Beeston Tricar. Look out for the rare Louis XV sedan chair, a field ambulance from the Boer War, and a fascinating old horse-drawn Merryweather fire engine.

Slumbering in happy retirement alongside the platform is Locomotive 816, a splendid old Type 16C workhorse which, for 55 years, hauled the Corridor Dining Express on the Johannesburg-Durban run. Behind it are passenger coaches and elegant dining saloons that will bring a lump to the throat of anyone who recalls with fondness the romantic early days of rail travel.

Kloofendal's rocky hills and wooded valleys sustain a fascinating variety of plants, and provide the setting for pleasant nature-walks. Other features include the first of the region's mines to produce viable quantities of gold, and an amphitheatre in which open-air events are staged.

KLOOFENDAL NATURE RESERVE
Roodepoort

Roodepoort's Kloofendal Nature Reserve is just a short drive away from the cheerless concrete canyons of central Johannesburg, yet for the most part this 150-ha sanctuary is remarkably pristine. Here, on these protea-covered ridges, the air is sweet and reverberates with the song of over 120 species of bird, while the whistle of the wind in the grass all but drowns out the distant murmur of traffic. The two circular walking trails that pass through the reserve will appeal to hikers and nature-lovers. For the less energetic there's a pleasant picnic place and a stone amphitheatre that is often used as a venue for outdoor music concerts.

This reserve is a fine example of what can be done to conserve nature in a built-up area. The fact that it includes large sections of the rather inaccessible koppies of the Witwatersrand ridge system has undoubtedly helped preserve the indigenous flora. The ancient quartzites and shales of this region are more than 3 000 million years old, forming the basis of fertile soil in which a wonderful diversity of indigenous plant life flourishes. The two trails that wind up over the koppies through the kloofs and past a small dam are well marked, with interesting geological, historical and botanical features highlighted along the way.

This is also gold-mining country. Kloofendal is part of the old farm *Wilgerspruit*, where the first payable deposits of gold on the Witwatersrand were discovered by Fred Struben and his brother Harry. The old Confidence Reef mine shaft, now restored as a national monument, is an interesting reminder of the early days of prospecting, when intrepid fortune-hunters combed these ridges in search of the yellow metal that could bring them riches. Guided tours to Confidence Reef are organized by the Roodepoort Museum.

Map: page 41, 3C
From Johannesburg drive west to Roodepoort along Ontdekkers Road. Turn right into Christiaan de Wet Road, third left into Wilgeroord Road, second left into Topaz Avenue and then immediately right into Galena Road, which leads to the entrance.
Details: Open daily 08h00-18h00. Closed between 1 May and 1 September because of the risk of fire. Admission free. Map available at the Parks, Sport and Recreation Division of the Roodepoort City Council office. Parking. Tours of the Confidence Reef on the first Sunday of every month at 14h00. Book through the Roodepoort Museum, Private Bag X30, Roodepoort 1725, tel (011) 672-2147 or 761-0225.
Further information: Parks, Sport and Recreation Division, Roodepoort City Council, Private Bag X30, Roodepoort 1725, tel (011) 472-1439.

HIGHVELD

Map: page 41, 3C
Drive west out of Krugersdorp on the R24 (Rustenburg Road). The entrance to the reserve is on the right-hand side.
Details: Open daily 08h00-17h00. Visitors may stay in the reserve until 18h00. Game drives by arrangement. Admission charged. Parking. Refreshments at kiosk and restaurant.
Accommodation: Rondavels, chalets, family units, and caravan sites.
Further information: Krugersdorp Game Reserve, P O Box 5237, Krugersdorp West 1742, tel (011) 665-4342.

KRUGERSDORP GAME RESERVE
Krugersdorp

Visitors to Johannesburg who yearn for a wilderness experience but have little time on their hands need no longer contemplate a whistle-stop tour of Lowveld reserves. At the Krugersdorp Game Reserve, just 40 minutes' drive west of central Johannesburg, you can see white rhinos, lions, buffaloes, giraffes and a number of hippos roaming free in a sanctuary comprising 1 400 ha of golden grassland and wooded ravine. The reserve is also home to a great diversity of smaller game – including brown hyaenas, the rare roan and sable antelope, tsessebe, waterbuck, hartebeest, impala, zebras and springbok. The 150 bird species attract bird-watchers from all over Gauteng. A special attraction is the 100-ha lion camp on the western side of the park, where visitors can view the big cats at close quarters. Feeding times (Sundays at 10h00) are especially popular.

Several demarcated game-viewing sites wind through the reserve and, although walking is not permitted, it is possible to arrange day and night game drives in open Land Rovers.

The reserve caters mainly for day-visitors, and has very pleasant picnic places and braai facilities, as well as swimming pools for visitors who would like to cool off after a hot morning in the car. A game lodge situated in a lovely valley offers comfortable overnight accommodation in chalets and rondavels; there is also a restaurant, cocktail bar and conference facilities, and *lapas* can be hired for self-catering functions.

A special section of the reserve is home to this lion and its endearing offspring. Rhinos and buffaloes also have enclosures. Among other residents are giraffes and kudu.

The male sable antelope below is wrinkling his nose in an action known as flehmen – a reaction to the stimulation of sensory receptors in the nasal cavities.

HIGHVELD

LION PARK
Muldersdrift

The roar of a lion is the last sound you'd expect to hear just 10 minutes' drive out of deepest suburbia, but that is one of the familiar sounds that reverberates through the night air in the vicinity of the Lion Park, a 60-ha reserve near Muldersdrift, north of Sandton. More than 60 lions, lionesses and their cubs roam free in an area of grassland scattered with boulders and trees, existing alongside (but fenced off from) a variety of other species of game. A drive around the reserve offers visitors the rare opportunity to view the lions at close quarters from the comfort of their cars.

The 10-km, one-way game drive winds through the park, taking you first past the game area, where you can see buck, zebras, ostriches and black wildebeest, and then into the enormous lion enclosure. Although they are well camouflaged against the grass, the lions exist here in such great numbers that they are easy to spot.

These magnificent big cats tend to appear sluggish and tame, especially in the heat of the day, but don't be fooled into leaving the safety of your car. The Lion Park made headlines in 1993 when two students were tragically mauled to death after they climbed out of their vehicle to take photographs.

The drive ends at the reserve's entertainment area, which has a restaurant, swimming pool, curio shop and reconstructed Ndebele village.

Map: page 41, 3C
From Johannesburg drive north along the William Nicol Drive to Four Ways. Turn left onto Witkoppen Road, drive for 400 m and then turn right at the next traffic light into Cedar Road. Travel for about 8 km, until you reach a stop street. Turn left. The Lion Park is about 2 km further along, on the left-hand side.
Details: Open daily, including all public holidays, 08h00-16h30. Admission charged. Parking. Refreshments.
Further information: Lion Park, P O Box 11346, Johannesburg 2000, tel (011) 460-1814 or 37-6978.

The Lippizaners of Kyalami. The demands of medieval nobility, and centuries of careful breeding and training, have combined to produce equestrian shows of breathtaking precision.

LIPPIZANER CENTRE
Kyalami

Strength, stamina, beauty, docility and intelligence are some of the attributes demanded of a Lippizaner horse before it can be trained in the art of classical riding. The magnificent white Lippizaner stallions of Kyalami, which perform every Sunday morning, have all these qualities, and more. Breathtakingly beautiful and superbly controlled, they move with balletic precision as they prance into the indoor stadium to the strains of a Strauss waltz. Later in the show the stallions perform spectacular leaps known as 'Airs Above Ground', so demanding that they can only be performed by Lippizaners, and then after years of intensive training.

Lippizaners have been selectively bred over centuries to perform the highest art of classical riding, or dressage, in the style of the famous Spanish Riding School in Vienna. The movements of this style of riding are derived from cavalry exercises used during the Middle Ages to terrify and disperse unmounted troops.

South Africa's white Lippizaners have an interesting history. Their forebears actually belonged to a nobleman, Count Jankovich Besan, who fled his native Hungary during the turmoil and uncertainty of post-war Europe. Twelve horses from his stud were transferred to Bavaria, then England, and in 1948 the Count brought them to South Africa where they were used to establish the South African Lippizaner breed.

The team of dancing white horses was formed under the direction of Major George Ivanowski, a former Polish cavalry officer, and they first performed at Kyalami in 1965.

Map: page 41, 4C
Dahlia Road, Kyalami. From Johannesburg travel along the N1 (Ben Schoeman Highway) to Pretoria, take the off-ramp marked Midrand-Allandale Road, and turn left. Continue along this road until you reach the main gates of Kyalami Race Track. Turn right, and continue for about 500 m until you see the Lippizaner Centre signpost. Turn left and follow the signs.
Details: Performances every Sunday at 11h00. No performances between mid-October and mid-November. Book at the door, or through Computicket, tel (011) 331-9991.
Accommodation: In Johannesburg and the surrounding areas.
Further information: Lippizaner Centre, P O Box 1039, Rivonia 2128, tel (011) 702-2103.

HIGHVELD

LOSKOP DAM
Near Middelburg

Map: page 41, 6A/B
From Johannesburg take the N12 to Witbank and Middelburg, and turn off onto the N4 towards Middelburg. The dam is situated about 50 km north of Middelburg. From the east take the Machadodorp/Middelburg trunk road. From the north use the Potgietersrus/Groblersdal/Middelburg road.
Details: Aventura Loskop Dam Resort is open every day of the year.
Accommodation: Log cabins, chalets and camping sites.
Further information: Aventura Resorts, Private Bag X1525, Middelburg 1050, tel (01202) 3075/6. Book through Aventura Central Reservations, P O Box 3046, Pretoria 0001, tel (012) 346-2277.

Any angler will tell you that there are only three reasons to visit Loskop Dam, and those are fishing, fishing and fishing – it is, after all, one of the Highveld's finest angling dams, its waters boiling with kurper, yellowfish, barbel and carp. But this vast stretch of water, pooled like melted sky between rolling bush-covered hills, has many other attractions: a particularly mild climate, peaceful scenery, diverse vegetation and a well-stocked game reserve. The dam is a magnet for boaters and yachtsmen, while holidaymakers who simply want to relax in the sunshine make a beeline for the large and well-appointed resort on the north shore of the dam.

The dam is conveniently situated about two hours' drive northeast of the Witwatersrand, some 50 km north of Middelburg. The vegetation in this part of South Africa is remarkably varied because the dam lies at the interface of two very distinct ecological zones: the Highveld, with its rolling grasslands, and the Lowveld, with its healthy abundance of thorny trees and shrubs.

Most of the area surrounding the dam, including the 14 000-ha game reserve on the northern shores, comprises combretum-dominated woodland, which provides an ideal habitat for a variety of game, including white rhinos, buffaloes, giraffes and sable antelope. The bush pulsates with the song of many bushveld species of bird, such as kingfishers, bee-eaters, francolin, wood hoopoes, hornbills, barbets and fly-catchers. Where bush meets water, you'll hear the cry of the African fish eagle, and see many other types of waterfowl.

The Aventura Resort, situated two kilometres from the dam wall, offers accommodation in the form of log cabins, chalets and pleasantly shaded caravan sites. The emphasis here is on family fun: facilities include a restaurant, swimming pool, trampolines, water slides, tennis court and minigolf. Boating enthusiasts use this as a launching point for their craft, and pleasure cruises also depart from this point. Across the road from the reserve is a short nature-walk which leads to a lookout point high above the dam.

Leafless trees create a symphony of pinks and golds on and around Loskop. The dam and surrounds are a mecca for keen fishermen, bird-watchers and nature-lovers.

MORELETA SPRUIT HIKING TRAIL
Pretoria

Suburbs of even the busiest cities have their secret, shaded pathways, where gurgling water, rustling leaves and softly chirruping birds drown out the incessant rumbles of urban life. The Moreleta Spruit, flowing through eastern Pretoria, is one such green artery, hemmed in on all sides by suburbs, but still pulsing with a vibrant life-force. Along its banks a delightful walking trail has been laid out, taking walkers past willow-fringed pools, reedbeds, open grasslands and areas of dense indigenous bush. For bird-watchers, the trail is particularly worthwhile for its remarkably varied bird life. Pretoria marks the southern limit of the habitat of several bushveld species.

The Moreleta Spruit rises southeast of Pretoria and meanders gently northwards through the suburbs of Garsfontein, Lynwood Glen, Murrayfield, Meyerspark and Silverton.

At present about eight kilometres of the trail are marked out, beginning at Menlyn Drive, where a stone beacon marks the starting point, and ending finally at the Pioneer Open-air Museum in Silverton *(see separate entry)*.

The trail passes through several urban sanctuaries, including the Meyerspark Bird Sanctuary, Struben Dam and the Faerie Glen Nature Reserve, which boasts some of Pretoria's loveliest scenery.

Strenuous efforts have been made to preserve the natural character of the river and its banks: alien invaders have been cleared, and a variety of indigenous trees, such as acacias, bushwillows and karees, planted. There are no water points along the way, but numerous natural pools and old dams are strung like pearls along the river, their willow-shaded banks providing tranquil and pleasant picnic places for weary walkers.

The trail can be joined at any point. Walking at a brisk pace you should be able to complete the entire trail in two hours. Although the trail is well marked with signposts, it's advisable to obtain a map if you are unfamiliar with the terrain. These are available from the Pretoria Tourist Rendezvous Travel Centre.

Map: page 41, 4B
The start of the trail is marked by signposts in Menlyn Drive.
Details: The trail is always open and no permits are required. Take your own water. There are no toilet or braai facilities provided.
Further information: Tourist Rendezvous Travel Centre, P O Box 440, Pretoria 0001, tel (012) 313-7694/ 313-7980.

PETTICOAT LANE
Near Four Ways

You can buy anything from a silk shirt to a silver teaspoon to a samoosa at this delightful open-air country market, situated just beyond Four Ways, on the northern fringes of Sandton. It's one of the finest of the many fleamarkets that have sprung up on the Witwatersrand in recent years, offering budding entrepreneurs and talented craftspeople the chance to ply their wares in pleasant rural surroundings. The emphasis here is on family entertainment, and there's a happy carnival-like atmosphere that makes the market the ideal place to take young children.

Petticoat Lane covers 26 ha, with stalls housed in graceful Victorian-style gazebos, clustered on the banks of two willow-fringed dams. There are some 500 traders selling a bewildering diversity of goods, including clothing, antiques, ironwork, toys, ceramics, jewellery, leather goods and furniture. Fresh farm produce can be purchased directly from farmers, while several stalls specialize in good-quality gourmet fare, including home-made cheeses, salamis, jams, preserves and fresh herbs.

Additional sustenance for hungry shoppers is provided by 20 fast-food stalls that sell food from all over the world. You can enjoy your picnic on the shaded banks of the dam, while listening to a jazz band and strolling buskers. For children there are pony rides, go-carts and four-wheel bicycles, paddle-boat trips and a farmyard. Grown-up visitors with nerves of steel will relish the chance to try bungee-jumping (over water!) for the first time. After their exertions, visitors can relax in the shady beer garden on the banks of the Jukskei River.

Gilding the lily: fresh young faces are brightened with paint applied by one of Petticoat Lane's many sidewalk entrepreneurs.

Map: page 41, 4C
From Sandton, drive north along William Nicol Drive to Four Ways. Cross over the R564, and continue north along the R511, passing the Karos Indaba Hotel on your left. The road crosses over the Jukskei River a little further along. The turn-off to Petticoat Lane is on the right-hand side, and is clearly signposted.
Details: Open Saturdays, Sundays and public holidays 09h00-17h00. Admission free. Parking. Refreshments.
Further information: Petticoat Lane, P O Box 2088, Gallo Manor 2052, tel (011) 464-1780.

PILANESBERG NATIONAL PARK
Mogwase

Map: page 41, 2A

Pilanesberg has three entrances. The southern gate, Bakubung, is situated 175 km from Johannesburg, and is reached via the R565 to Sun City. The Bakgatla gate is reached from the road that approaches from Northam and Thabazimbi. The main entrance is Manyane gate at Mogwase, reached from the main road between Rustenburg and Thabazimbi.

Details: Open daily throughout the year. Reception times 07h30-20h00. Gates open 05h30-19h00 in summer and 06h30-18h30 in winter. Game-viewing is best between April and September. Restaurant and shops at Manyane Camp.

Accommodation: Huts, chalets, safari tents and camp sites. Luxury hotel accommodation at Kwa Maritane Lodge, tel (01465) 2-1820; and Bakubung, tel (01465) 2-1861.

Further information: Central Reservations Office, P O Box 937, Lonehill 2062, tel (011) 465-5423.

It's not easy to believe, looking out over the peaceful, bush-covered ridges of the Pilanesberg National Park, that a thousand million years ago this area was one huge, seething volcano, higher even than present-day Kilimanjaro. A more desirable site for a game reserve is difficult to imagine – not only is the geology of this area unique, but its rugged and varied topography has given rise to a diversity of vegetation types which support a splendid abundance of animal and bird life. With its sound conservation strategies, its well-maintained facilities, good roads and lovely rest camps, this wilderness area has developed, in a matter of 15 years, into one of South Africa's finest game reserves.

The reserve's location adjacent to the pleasure palaces of Sun City and the Lost City has no doubt also contributed to its popularity.

Established in 1979 by the former Government of Bophuthatswana, the Pilanesberg National Park comprises about 500 square kilometres of rugged, hilly terrain and is the fourth-largest national park in South Africa. The highest peak, Pilanesberg, overlooks Mankwe Lake, which fills what was once the main lava vent of the long-extinct volcano. The vegetation is broadly defined as sour bushveld, with grasslands in the valleys and densely wooded areas on the hillsides.

The ambitious game reintroduction programme, known as 'Operation Genesis', has been a resounding success and the reserve now has over 8 000 head of game, including the third-largest white rhino population in the world. Visitors are likely to spot the 'Big Five', as well as many of the 300 bird species here.

There is an extensive network of good gravel roads, but for those who prefer a close-up wilderness experience, there are hiking and bird-watching trails, and also game-watching hides.

The reserve caters for all tastes and pockets when it comes to accommodation. Manyane Camp, with its pleasantly shaded camping sites, safari tents, restaurant, shop and swimming pool, has been rated one of the country's finest caravan parks. It also offers a fine chalet camp and conference centre.

For a tranquil bushveld experience, guests should opt to stay in one of the reserve's three tented camps, with their delightful, 'Out of Africa' safari tents. Kwa Maritane Lodge, Tshukudu Lodge and Bakubung Lodge are luxury hotel and timeshare resorts situated within the boundaries of the park.

Hot-air balloons provide a novel and colourful means of exploring the Pilanesberg. Centrepiece of the park is the volcanic Pilanesberg massif.

The Kwa Maritane complex, huddled among the rocks and trees of the southern Pilanesberg, offers luxury living just a step away from the wild.

PIONEER OPEN-AIR MUSEUM
Silverton

The aromas of freshly baked bread and hot, bitter coffee drift from the old farmhouse, evocative reminders of a simple pioneer way of life that has disappeared for ever. This unusual open-air museum recalls the tenacity and resourcefulness of the earliest white settlers in the Pretoria district. Comprising a humble Voortrekker farmhouse, furnishings, household items, implements, outbuildings and live farm animals, the museum also offers regular demonstrations of many almost-forgotten domestic skills from yesteryear.

The centrepiece of the museum is the original farmhouse, built in about 1840 by Cape farmer David Botha. This low-slung, thatched and whitewashed dwelling was constructed with a mixture of raw earth and anthill, with dung-smeared floors.

The other outbuildings, including a water-driven mill, threshing floor, stables and animal pens, were added later by the Mundts, a family of German immigrants who converted the farm into a halfway station on the busy coaching route to the goldfields at Barberton.

The museum has an orchard with some of the oldest fruit trees in the Highveld, including ancient quinces and pomegranates, and a fine old wild mulberry tree. Farm animals roam free in the yard. Visitors are welcome to try their hand at milking the cow.

Regular demonstrations of bread-baking, butter-churning, thong-dressing and soap-making are given by museum staff in period costume during school-term mornings. However, it is safest to book ahead if the demonstrations are to be the main attraction.

Guided tours are arranged. One popular tour ends with a meal of hot bread, jam and biltong under willows, alongside a pond where ducks paddle. The museum's tranquil setting and its picnic and braai facilities make it a good place for family outings.

Simple hardwood furniture, dung-smeared earthen floors and reed-thatched roofing illuminate the early settler lifestyle. The farmstead now functions as a 'living museum'.

Map: page 41, 4B
From Church Square in Pretoria, drive east along Church Street, which becomes Pretoria Road, to Silverton. The museum is situated at the end of Pretoria Road. From Johannesburg take the N1 (Pietersburg Highway), turn off onto the N4 (Witbank Highway), and from there take the Watermeyer Street off-ramp and follow the signposts to the museum.
Details: Open daily, including public holidays, 08h30-16h00. Admission charged. Parking. Refreshments.
Further information: Pioneer Open-Air Museum, P O Box 28088, Sunnyside 0132, tel (012) 803-6086.

POTCHEFSTROOM MUSEUMS
Potchefstroom

The heroic pioneer spirit lives on in Potchefstroom, a town founded on the banks of the Mooi River by Voortrekker leader Andries Pretorius. At one time Potchefstroom was the capital of the South African Republic (ZAR). Later it became an important trading centre used as a base by thousands of prospectors, hunters and adventurers on their way to the interior. These action-packed days are vividly recalled by many interesting exhibits in the Potchefstroom Museum, comprising the Main Museum, Goetz/Fleischack Museum, President Pretorius Museum and Totius House Museum.

The Goetz/Fleischack Museum is the only remaining example of the early town houses which were erected in Potchefstroom around the New Market Square between 1850 and 1855. Nearby is the Main Museum, which contains changing short-term exhibitions with cultural history and art as themes. The Totius House Museum, erstwhile home of well-known Afrikaans poet and theologian, Totius, exhibits many of the author's personal belongings.

Also worth a visit is the restored homestead of President M W Pretorius, a handsome Cape-style dwelling that recalls an urban Boer culture which has long since disappeared.

Map: page 41, 2D
The Main Museum is situated on the corner of Gouws and Wolmarans streets, Potchefstroom. Entering Potchefstroom from Johannesburg along Potgieter Street, turn left into Gouws Street. The Main Museum is the second building on the left-hand side in the Museum and Library Complex. Ask at the museum for directions to the 3 house museums.
Details: Potchefstroom Main Museum open Monday to Friday 09h00-16h30; Saturdays 09h00-13h00; Sundays 14h30-17h00. House museums open Monday to Friday 10h00-13h00 and 14h00-16h30; Saturdays 09h00-13h00; Sundays 14h30-17h00. Closed religious holidays. Parking. No admission charged.
Accommodation: At several hotels and guesthouses.
Further information: Potchefstroom Museum, P O Box 113, Potchefstroom 2520, tel (0148) 99-5024.

HIGHVELD

PREMIER DIAMOND MINE
Cullinan

Map: page 41, 5B

The Premier Diamond Mine is situated in Cullinan, some 45 km east of Pretoria. From Pretoria, travel east along the Witbank Highway (N4) and take the Cullinan/Rayton turn-off. Follow the R515 for about 15 km to Cullinan; the mine is well signposted.

Details: Tours of the mine last about 2 hours, and are conducted Monday to Friday at 09h30, 10h00 and 13h30; Saturdays and Sundays at 10h00 only. No children under 10 admitted. Booking essential. Admission charged. Parking on premises. Tour includes free tea and coffee.

Accommodation: The Oak House is a guesthouse in Oak Avenue, Cullinan, tel (01213) 3-0215.

Further information: Premier Diamond Tours, P O Box 7, Cullinan 1000, tel (01213) 4-0081.

Until the world's biggest diamond was discovered here in 1905, Cullinan was just another Highveld mining camp, a ragtag settlement set amid thorn trees and sun-burnished grasslands, some 40 km east of Pretoria. But after that great chunk of sparkling carbon – roughly the size of an orange – was scooped out of the diggings by a trembling hand, Cullinan's Premier Diamond Mine became world-famous overnight.

Today, thousands of tourists still come to the mine, where they can enjoy a fascinating guided tour of the works and admire replicas of some of the fabulous gems yielded by the oldest and biggest diamond pipe known to man.

Cullinan was laid out on the farm *Elandsfontein* in 1902 after Sir Thomas Major Cullinan discovered an immense diamond pipe there.

Over the past 90 years, this 1 500-million-year-old pipe has produced most of the world's largest stones, and, even today, the citizens of the town still rely for their livelihood on the Premier Mine's seemingly inexhaustible and rich supply of diamonds.

The diamond pipe covers 32 ha, making it the largest man-made hole in Africa. It cannot be entered but may be viewed from a special lookout point. From here visitors are escorted to the mine's diamond display room, which contains numerous interesting exhibits, including rough diamonds yielded by the mine, replicas of the fabulous stones that were cut from the Cullinan diamond, and an exhibit showing the various stages of diamond-cutting. The next stop is the mine's tourist centre, which sells fine gold jewellery, loose diamonds and souvenirs.

The town of Cullinan has some lovely old wood-and-iron miners' houses and several quaint country-style restaurants and craft shops. The old recreation club is worth a visit, because it contains some very fine murals, recently discovered behind boards, that were painted in 1944 by Italian prisoners of war.

A tour group explores the giant Premier Mine's plant area. Visitors are also shown the fabulously rich kimberlite pipe and the exhibits in the glittering display room.

The pink-and-white charm of an early Cullinan miner's cottage. The town was named after turn-of-the-century builder and mining magnate Sir Thomas Cullinan.

RHINO NATURE RESERVE
Kromdraai

Answering the call of the wild is now as easy as hopping into the car and driving 30 km northwest of Johannesburg to the Rhino Nature Reserve.

This small, private game reserve is so close to the city that from certain vantage points you can see the distant blue-grey smudge of the Johannesburg skyline. It's set on the slopes of the twin-peaked Zwartkop Mountain in Kromdraai, comprising about 100 ha of rippling golden grassland, where about 500 head of game roam freely. The recreational facilities here are good, making the reserve a very pleasant place to take the family for weekend outings.

There are no carnivores in the reserve, but you will be able to spot a variety of other animals, including white rhinos, sable antelope, buffaloes, giraffes, jackals and zebras. These may be viewed from an extensive network of gravel roads, while more inaccessible areas can be reached in an open Land Rover, by arrangement with the management. Organized walking trails are also offered.

When you've had your fill of game-watching, head for the visitors' braai area, where you can enjoy a picnic in the shade of trees or soak your cares away in the swimming pool. Overnight accommodation is offered in the form of comfortable thatched chalets.

Adjacent to the reserve is the spectacular Wonder Cave, where fascinating guided tours are offered every 90 minutes *(see separate entry).*

Map: page 41, 3C
From Randburg, drive north towards Honeydew along D F Malan Drive, which becomes Muldersdrift Road. Continue along this road, cross over the R28, and drive for a further 2,8 km, or until you see the turn-off signposted 'Zwartkop/Tweefontein'. Turn left and continue for 8 km, or until you see the signposted turning for the Rhino Nature Reserve on your right.

Details: Open daily, including public holidays, 08h00-17h00. Game drives and walks by arrangement. Admission charged. Parking. Refreshments.

Accommodation: Chalets.

Further information: Rhino Nature Reserve, P O Box 180, Krugersdorp 1740, tel (011) 957-0109.

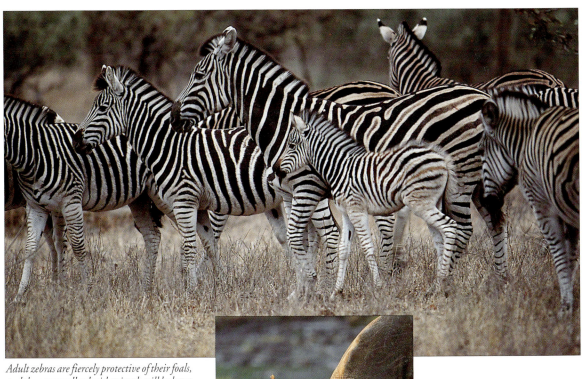

Adult zebras are fiercely protective of their foals, and these normally placid animals will lash out with their hooves at would-be attackers.

The mighty white, or square-lipped, rhinoceros usually grazes on short grasses, which it can trim to a mere centimetre above the ground.

HIGHVELD

RUSTENBURG NATURE RESERVE
Magaliesberg

Map: page 41, 2B
Coming into Rustenburg from Pretoria or Magaliesburg – a set of traffic lights marks the start of the town – you enter on the one-way Van Staden Street. Turn left into Wolmarans Street, cross over Boven Street, and then turn left into Boekenhout Road; 5 km further along are the gates to the reserve.
Details: Open daily, including public holidays, 08h00-16h00 for incoming traffic (campers with reservations 08h00-18h00). Admission charged. Information complex.
Accommodation: Camp sites and picnic spots; overnight huts for hikers. Reservations for overnight stays essential.
Further information: The Officer-in-Charge, Rustenburg Nature Reserve, P O Box 511, Rustenburg 0030, tel (0142) 3-1050.

A rare species of aloe that is endemic to the western Magaliesberg is one of the special features of this lovely reserve, set on the sun-burnished northern slopes of the mountain range near Rustenburg. Other attractions are the rugged scenery and the abundant animal and bird life, both of which are best observed by walking one of the three hiking trails that wind through the 4 200-ha reserve.

The Rustenburg Overnight Trail is a strenuous two-day, 21-km circular trail that passes through a variety of natural landscapes, including a valley basin with reedbeds, open grasslands, shaded kloofs and mountain ridges where clear, cold streams tumble over steep quartzite cliffs. The vegetation in the reserve comprises mainly sour bushveld, with some areas of acacia- and combretum-dominated woodland. Both are good places to spot some of the 210 bird species that have been recorded in the area. On this walk you are also likely to see a wide variety of game, including impala, kudu, red hartebeest, oribi, aardwolfs, brown hyaenas, black-backed jackals and baboons. Look out for the rare sable antelope, which was once found in abundance here and has been recently reintroduced.

The 5-km circular Peglerae Interpretive Trail is a two-hour ramble over the northern crest of the Magaliesberg. A booklet, available at the visitors' centre, points out natural features of the landscape, including geological formations. This is the place to look out for the beautiful *Aloe peglerae*, after which the trail is named. The interesting two-kilometre Vlei Ramble has a game- and bird-watching hut halfway along its length and is ideal for children and for those who tire easily.

Impala, such as this fine specimen, are conspicuous residents of Rustenburg Nature Reserve.

RYNFIELD CHILDREN'S PARK
Benoni

Map: page 41, 4C
From Johannesburg drive east to Benoni along the N12 (Witbank Highway). Turn left at the Morehill/Snake Park off-ramp. Follow this road (Pretoria Road) for approximately 2 kilometres. The Bunny Park is situated on the left.
Details: Open daily, including public holidays, 07h00-17h00. Admission free. Parking. Kiosk open Sundays and during school holidays.
Further information: Parks and Recreation Department, Benoni City Council, Private Bag X014, Benoni 1500, tel (011) 845-1650.

Hundreds of hopping, fluffy rabbits roam free in this 18-ha park, affectionately known as the 'Bunny Park' to generations of city children. For almost 25 years the park has provided hours of hilarious fun for cooped-up children. Shrieks of delight fill the air as children grab a bunny for a quick cuddle. Handling the rabbits is allowed by the administration – but no chasing them! The park is run by the Benoni City Council, and there is no entrance fee. It's safe and well maintained, making it the ideal place for a carefree family outing.

There are many other animals to pet and feed, including donkeys, pigs, sheep, cows, goats, swans, ducks, tortoises and an aviary full of birds. Another huge attraction is the playground, which has separate areas for big and small kids. Remember to take along a bunch of carrots to feed to the rabbits, and a picnic for yourself. A small kiosk sells light refreshments on Sundays, and braai facilities and thatched shelters are provided.

Cuddle-bunnies are the park's major attraction, though plenty of other animals – donkeys, goats and pigs among them – vie for attention.

SAMMY MARKS MUSEUM
Near Pretoria

Close your eyes, and you can almost hear the echoes of a more gracious age: the clink of a spoon on a porcelain teacup, the thwack of a croquet mallet hitting a ball, the silvery laughter of children drifting in from the garden. Like a haunting perfume, the past seems to linger on at Zwartkoppies Hall, the imposing tin-roofed mansion built in the veld not far from Pretoria by Victorian industrialist Sammy Marks. This magnificent period piece was used as a family home by his descendants for a century, and is unique in that it is the only Victorian mansion in South Africa whose interior has been preserved in every detail, as Sammy Marks declared it should be in his will.

Having risen from a penniless Lithuanian pedlar of trinkets to one of the most brilliant entrepreneurs of his day, Sammy Marks made millions, and no expense was spared when the time came to build a home for his wife and eight children. Zwartkoppies Hall has some 20 rooms open to the public (the original house has 48 rooms), and numerous outbuildings, including a coach house and stabling for 14 horses. The rooms are grand in scale and, in the fashion of the day, embellished with all kinds of architectural detail: look out for the delicate frescoes painted by an Italian artist, in the lounge and billiard room.

Each room is crammed with fine furniture, paintings, glassware and porcelain, most of it purchased in England by Bertha Marks after their wedding, and then transported with great care to the house by oxwagon. Because of the value of the house's contents, visitors are admitted to the house only as part of a guided tour.

The mansion stands in beautiful gardens emblazoned with a jewel-bright tapestry of blooms. The pride of the museum is Bertha's formal rose garden, which was recently excavated and then replanted with old-fashioned rose varieties. After the tour, pause a while to browse through the delightful shop housed in the old servants' quarters, or to enjoy tea and scones in the shade of the beefwood trees.

Map: page 41, 4B
From Pretoria, drive east along the N4 (Witbank Highway) and turn off at the Sammy Marks/Hans Strijdom off-ramp (exit 11). Turn left and continue for about 1 km until you reach a T-junction where the road joins the old Bronkhorstspruit Road (R104). Turn right, cross a small bridge and you will see the turn-off to the museum a little further along on your left.
Details: Open Tuesday to Friday 09h00-17h00; Saturdays, Sundays and public holidays 10h00-17h30. Tours every hour, on the hour (on the half-hour on Sundays). The last tour takes place 1 hour before closing time. Admission charged. Parking. Refreshments.
Further information: Sammy Marks Museum, c/o National Cultural History Museum, P O Box 28088, Sunnyside 0132, tel (012) 803-6158.

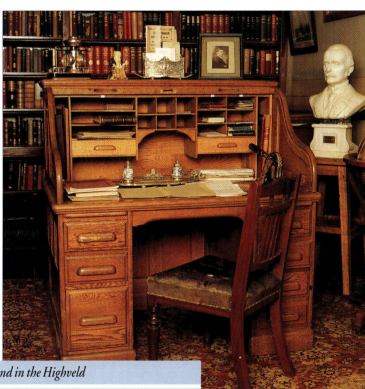

The cosy little study, one of 20 perfectly preserved rooms in Sammy Marks's mansion. Most of them are more grandly proportioned.

A little piece of England in the Highveld

Zwartkoppies Hall may have been built in the middle of the veld in a far-flung corner of Africa, but it was run in much the same manner as any grand English country estate of its time, thanks, no doubt, to the formidable influence of Sammy Marks's English wife Bertha. Croquet, tennis and punting on the farm's canal were favourite pastimes. There were swans on the dam and flocks of guinea fowl – admittedly the indigenous variety – roaming the woods.

The sons of the family were sent for their schooling to Harrow, in England. The eldest, Louis, was nicknamed 'Young Lord', later abbreviated to 'YL', a name that stuck for the rest of his life.

The Markses employed a small army of servants who scrubbed, polished, dusted, cooked, carried water and saw to the grounds and livestock at Zwartkoppies.

There were grooms, coachmen, kitchen-maids, laundry-maids and parlour-maids. Higher up in the hierarchy were Miss Lorimer, the children's governess, and McCracken, the butler, whose duty it was to sound the large brass gong in the hallway half an hour before dinner. The garden and outbuildings were the responsibility of a carpenter and handyman, affectionately known as Daddy Potts. The head gardener was an Austrian, whose hobby was making purses, bags and belts from the skins of snakes he killed on the farm.

HIGHVELD

Map: page 41, 4B
From Johannesburg travel north along the N1, and take the Botha Avenue off-ramp. Follow the signposts to Irene and the museum (about 4,5 km from the highway).
Details: Open daily, including public holidays, 09h00-13h00; 13h30-16h30 (closes at 17h00 on weekends and public holidays). Closed 24 and 25 December and on Good Friday. Admission charged. Parking. Refreshments at tea garden.
Accommodation: Doornkloof Caravan Park, in the museum grounds.
Further information: Smuts House Museum, P O Box 36, Irene 1675, tel (012) 667-1176.

SMUTS HOUSE MUSEUM
Irene

When you walk across the shaded stoep and enter the cool, plainly furnished front room, it's difficult to believe that for 40 years this modest wood-and-iron farmhouse was the cherished family home of one of South Africa's most remarkable leaders. A brilliant, but often misunderstood leader, General Jan Christiaan Smuts was at heart a contemplative man who craved a life of peace and simplicity. Perhaps that is why he selected the farm *Doornkloof*, near the peaceful village of Irene, as a site for his family home (later known as the 'Big House'). Here, he spent many happy hours roaming the veld, indulging his abiding interest in botany. The house has been converted into a museum and holds many interesting mementos, tributes, personal belongings and photographs that tell the story of Jan Smuts's varied career as lawyer, soldier, international statesman, botanist and philosopher. Its setting in wooded parkland makes it the ideal place for a family outing: there is a tea garden, but you are welcome to take along a picnic basket if you wish.

The farmhouse was originally the British officers' mess in Middelburg (Transvaal) during the Anglo-Boer War, but was bought by Jan Smuts in 1909 and rebuilt on his farm at Irene. The house is frugally furnished, much as it was in his day. Smuts's narrow, dim bedroom, with its family photographs, reflects his disregard for ostentation.

Other exhibits include furniture, photographs, his herbarium, which houses his extensive botanical collection, and many small items belonging to his wife Isie. Some of the exhibits have a fascinating story to tell. It's worthwhile arranging one of the excellent guided tours, if you'd like to know more.

Behind the house a footpath leads up to Smuts Koppie, where a granite obelisk marks the spot where the ashes of Smuts and his wife are scattered.

Map: page 41, 4B
The Air Force Museum is situated at Swartkop Air Force Base, near Valhalla, about 13 km south of Pretoria. Take the Ben Schoeman Highway, turn off at the Lyttelton/Voortrekkerhoogte off-ramp, and follow the signposts to the museum.
Details: Open Monday to Sunday 10h00-16h00. Closed Good Friday, 25, 26 December, 1 and 2 January. Aircraft are flown on the third Saturday of the month, February to November. Admission free. Parking. Refreshments from museum shop on air display days only.
Accommodation: The nearest accommodation is in central Pretoria where there are several top-class hotels.
Further information: SAAF Museum, AFB Swartkop, P O Valhalla 0137, tel (012) 351-2911.

SOUTH AFRICAN AIR FORCE MUSEUM
Valhalla

A taste of the romance, the excitement, the thrilling danger of early aviation is what visitors can expect to experience at the South African Air Force Museum. It's the largest military aviation museum in South Africa, its hangars housing an impressive array of splendid historic aircraft, and its display cases bristling with Air Force memorabilia, including uniforms, medals, logbooks, documents and photographs.

Until the museum was established in 1973, no co-ordinated efforts had been made to preserve historic aircraft in this

A De Havilland Hornet Moth, one of the museum's many historic aircraft, takes a spin in company with a more modern Sikorsky S-55 helicopter.

country. Gradually, derelict aircraft were collected from all over the country and brought to the museum where they were restored, some to flying condition.

The historic treasures on display in the museum include a Hornet Moth, a Vampire, a Fieseler Storch, a Shackleton, a Spitfire and a Mustang P-51. More modern aircraft include an Alouette II, Mirage III and Mirage F1. The Vampire T Mk 55 is flown, along with several other aircraft, every third Saturday of the month. Gifts, posters, aircraft models and books are on sale at the museum.

STERKFONTEIN CAVES
Kromdraai

If it's true that Africa is the cradle of all mankind – and most palaeontologists believe this to be so – then Sterkfontein Caves is surely one of the continent's sacred sites.

This rather vast network of caves near Krugersdorp is world-famous because it was here that fossil bones of ancient hominids, including the fossilized skull nicknamed 'Mrs Ples', were discovered by palaeontologist Dr Robert Broom.

These finds supported earlier theories (expounded by Professor Raymond Dart) that a species of ape-like human existed on the African continent millions of years ago.

Palaeontological significance aside, the caves are awe-inspiring, and a tour into their dark, chill, primeval depths leaves a lasting impression on visitors. Discovered by an Italian prospector in 1896, this labyrinth of interconnected caverns was formed over millions of years by underground waters slowly dissolving the dolomitic rock. The largest cavern is the soaring Hall of Elephants, 23 m high and 91 m long. Other imaginatively named chambers include Fairy Chamber, Bridal Arch, Lumbago Alley and the Graveyard. The cave system also has an immense underground lake, whose tranquil, crystal-clear waters extend some distance into unexplored chambers.

Several interesting dripstone formations are to be seen, although, sadly, many of the cave's more spectacular stalactites and stalagmites were removed or damaged by early limestone-mining activities. This quarrying also exposed parts of the caves' ancient consolidated infill, known as breccia, which contains the fossilized bones of extinct hominids, monkeys, antelope, horses, sabre-toothed cats and many other mammals that lived between one and a half and three million years ago. Also found were the earliest stone tools used in South Africa, close to two million years old.

It was from these deposits that, beginning in 1936, Dr Robert Broom of the Transvaal Museum extracted many fossilized bones during the course of his excavations, which culminated in the discovery of an almost perfectly preserved cranium of a female specimen, estimated to be two and a half million years old, which he named *Plesianthropus transvaalensis*. Later, 'Mrs Ples' was reclassified as *Australopithecus africanus* when the skull was positively recognized as belonging to the same species as the 'ape-child' skull discovered by Professor Raymond Dart at Taung in the northern Cape in 1924.

The caves form part of the Isaac Stegmann Nature Reserve and are owned by the University of the Witwatersrand. Guided tours of the cave leave every 30 minutes, and have a taped commentary in three languages. At the mouth of the cave you may browse around a small museum or relax in the restaurant.

The skull of 'Mrs Ples', among the first of the man-ape fossils to be unearthed.

Map: page 41, 3C
North of Krugersdorp. From Johannesburg/Randburg, drive north along D F Malan Drive (which becomes Muldersdrift Road) towards Muldersdrift, and turn left onto the R28 to Krugersdorp. After 5,5 km turn right onto the R47 to Tarlton. Drive for about 10 km, then turn right onto the R563. The turn-off to the caves is some 2 km further along on the right-hand side.
Details: Open Tuesday to Sunday 09h00-16h00; closed Mondays. Conducted tours every 30 minutes. Admission charged. Parking. Refreshments.
Accommodation: Krugersdorp offers hotel, caravan/camping facilities, as well as guesthouses (contact the Krugersdorp Publicity Association, P O Box 1575, Krugersdorp 1740, tel (011) 951-2000.
Further information: Sterkfontein Caves, P O Box 481, Krugersdorp 1740, tel (011) 956-6342.

HIGHVELD

Trailists halt for a moment to take in the rugged beauty of the Suikerbosrand landscape.

SUIKERBOSRAND NATURE RESERVE
Heidelberg

Map: page 41, 4D
From Johannesburg take the N3 towards Heidelberg, and take the R550 turn-off to Nigel and Kliprivier. Turn right towards Kliprivier. About 6 km along, turn left at the turning marked 'Suikerbosrand'. Four kilometres further along is the main entrance to the reserve.
Details: Gates open daily 07h00-18h00. Office open weekdays 07h30-16h00, weekends 07h00-17h00.
Accommodation: Resort at Kareekloof has camp sites, restaurant, swimming pool and kiosk. Admission charged. Permits for day-walks obtained from Diepkloof Visitors' Centre. Overnight trails must be booked in advance.
Further information: Suikerbosrand Nature Reserve, Private Bag H616, Heidelberg 2400, tel (0151) 2181.

It is as if time has stood still on the rocky ridges of the Suikerbosrand: this is what the Witwatersrand, 50 km to the north, must have looked like before the discovery of gold. Here, the air is still sweet and smog-free, and the only sounds are the whistle of the wind and the ceaseless chirrup of birds.

This lovely reserve is certainly one of the Highveld's most precious natural assets, not only because it preserves the fast-disappearing Highveld grassland, but also because of its easy accessibility to both young and old.

The reserve, situated in the range of low hills known as the Suikerbosrand, near Heidelberg, covers some 13 000 ha of ridges, sheltered valleys, kloofs, plateaus and open plains, where the plant communities – including protea veld, acacia bushveld, vlei reedbeds and grasslands – are as diverse as the animal and bird life. For the seasoned hiker, a network of self-guided overnight trails has been laid out in the reserve, covering a representative selection of habitat types and offering unequalled opportunities to view a wide range of Highveld plant, mammal and bird species. The network has a total length of 66 kilometres. Minimal facilities are available, and it is essential to book 10 months in advance.

A meditation hut lies 20 km from the Diepkloof Visitors' Centre.

The animals that roamed these hills for centuries are still found here (although not in abundance as they once were), among them grey duiker, steenbok, mountain reedbuck and baboons. The reserve is also rich in large game that have been introduced more recently, such as zebras, oribi, eland, kudu, brown hyaenas and even cheetahs. Bird-watchers consider the reserve one of the finest birding spots on the Highveld – some 200 species, including several bushveld birds, have been recorded here. Reminders of the human history of the area come in the form of Iron-Age kraal ruins, and a restored 1850 Voortrekker farmhouse.

First-time visitors should head for the excellent visitors' centre at Diepkloof. Here you may obtain an excellent informative map and brochure for two shorter walks, the 4-km Cheetah Trail and the 10- or 17-km Bokmakierie Trail.

PLACES TO VISIT

SUN CITY and THE LOST CITY

A grand, glittering pleasure palace, an outrageous fantasy world, a huge, thrilling playground – love it or loathe it, there's no denying that Sun City is quite extraordinary.

Situated slap-bang in the middle of the African bush, 'the city that never sleeps' is a mammoth resort that offers unparalleled entertainment for the whole family. It's undoubtedly one of the world's most unusual and exciting resorts, not least for its unique African atmosphere – some two million tourists pour through the gates of Sun City every year to throw their money to the four winds and enjoy every action-packed moment.

The driving force behind the creation of the Sun City complex was flamboyant multimillionaire hotelier Sol Kerzner.

When Kerzner first revealed his plans to build a lavish hotel, casino, golf course, man-made lake and entertainment centre in the poverty-stricken backwaters of what was then Bophuthatswana, many wondered if he had gone mad. But his unique vision has paid off: visitors materialized, money in hand, as if by magic, and the complex was expanded with the addition of two further luxury hotels, the Cabanas and the Cascades, in 1980 and 1984, respectively.

All these developments were eclipsed, however, by the opening in December 1992 of the Lost City, a spectacular 'African palace' hotel, complete with soaring domes and columns, aged stonework, crumbling 'ruins', tropical jungle, huge wave-pool and desert-style golf course. The sheer scale of The Palace of the Lost City is breathtaking. There are towers adorned with elephant tusks; palm fronds and sculpted animals rearing upwards, glowing like fiery torches by night; the entrance atrium, with its frescoed six-storey dome and marble floor, almost defies description.

Sun City's attractions are varied enough to appeal to the most divergent of tastes. The chance to win a fortune is a major drawcard for most visitors, who head straight for the Sun City Casino or the R30-million entertainment centre, a huge, kaleidoscopic cavern that hums with feverish excitement as jingling slot-machines disgorge coins and then gobble them up again at a ruthless rate. Lavish extravaganzas, featuring high-kicking, befeathered dancers, take place in the 620-seater Sun City Theatre in the Sun City Hotel. The Superbowl, in the entertainment centre, hosts rock concerts and beauty pageants, world championship boxing events and banquets. Gourmets will delight in exploring the many fine restaurants that offer everything from *haute cuisine* to hamburgers, while those who prefer burning off kilojoules to consuming them can choose from a range of sporting activities. There are two superb golf courses, a driving range, tennis and squash courts, a bowling green, a 10-pin bowling alley, numerous swimming pools and a huge man-made lake where all sorts of watersport can be enjoyed.

Perhaps the most exciting attraction is the Valley of the Waves, where realistic turquoise breakers crash onto an icing-sugar-white beach fringed with palm

Map: page 41, 2A
Sun City is approximately 180 km from central Johannesburg (about two and a half hours by car or bus). Take the R47 west of Johannesburg, bypassing Krugersdorp, then join the R24 at Tarlton. Continue to Rustenburg, then exit onto the R27, from which you turn right onto the R56 past Boshoek, to Sun City. An alternative route passes Hartbeespoort Dam. For directions and advice, contact Sun International Central Reservations.
Details: Open daily throughout the year. Admission charged. Parking. Refreshments.
Further information: Sun International Central Reservations, P O Box 784487, Sandton 2146, tel (011) 780-7800. Various operators run regular bus and plane trips to Sun City.

The minarets, domes, waterways and scattered 'ruins' of the Lost City recapture the grandeur of an ancient and imagined Africa.

SUN CITY/LOST CITY

Seen here, from front to rear, are the lavish Cascades complex, the Sun City Hotel and the family-style Cabanas. In the far background is the highly popular Waterworld.

Cooling off at the Sun City Hotel, part of an extensive entertainment complex.

KEY TO THE AERIAL PHOTOGRAPHS
1 Sun City Hotel Vast, glamorous and glitzy, this stylishly furbished, 340-roomed, six-storey hotel overlooks the lake and the Gary Player Golf Course. It's been overshadowed to some extent by the new Lost City complex, but nevertheless has much to offer the jet-setting clientele that it aims to attract. There are glass lifts, a 620-seat theatre, an enormous pool terrace, several good restaurants and one of the largest casinos outside America.
2 The Cascades Built round the theme of cascading water, this elegant hotel with its newly refurbished rooms commands lovely views over tropical gardens, where 12 waterfalls create a constant, soothing sound of rushing water. There are two fine tree-fringed swimming pools, one of them heated, and also several popular bars and restaurants.

trees. The water is scented with chlorine, and the pool has a concrete floor, but who cares when you're having such fun?

Nature-lovers who tire quickly of the neon caverns and the crowded beach will enjoy exploring the magnificent tropical gardens, where paths meander through 25 ha of full-grown jungle trees and shrubs. Equally lovely is the Pilanesberg National Park next door, an unspoiled bushveld sanctuary set in the crater of a long-extinct volcano *(see separate entry)*. It's worth booking a chalet or camp site at Pilanesberg if you're operating on a tight budget, because the prices of the hotels at Sun City, and particularly of the Lost City (where an ordinary room will set you back a staggering R800 a night), tend to place them beyond the reach of the average family.

SUN CITY/LOST CITY

3 The Cabanas This 284-room hotel is marginally less expensive than the other accommodation at Sun City, and caters largely for families and those with outdoor interests. Attractions include a minigolf course, steakhouse, sundeck, an adventure playground, and direct access to the lake.

4 Entertainment Centre This R30-million pleasure palace offers nonstop, mind-boggling entertainment. The Hall of Treasures, with its domed, star-spangled roof, contains bank after bank of state-of-the-art slot-machines, some of them offering huge progressive jackpots. Other attractions are 'virtual reality' rides, video games, bingo, numerous cinemas, cocktail bars, restaurants and exclusive boutiques. Outside the complex is the amazing Bridge of Time, which is shaken now and then by a realistic fake earthquake.

5 The Valley of the Waves A tropical idyll in the middle of the bushveld has to be worth experiencing. The enormous wave-pool has a sweep of white sand, clear turquoise waters and waving palm trees. The waves are really big, appearing as if by magic from behind a cliff of carved stone. Children will enjoy riding down the Lazy River on tubes, but only the very daring should attempt the 'Temple of Courage', a hair-raising 130-m plunge down a sheer rock face, as well as no fewer than four water slides.

6 Tropical jungle There are half a million exotic and indigenous trees, plants and shrubs in this spectacular 'jungle', which has various subthemes, including swamp area, baobab forest and rainforest. Designed largely for theatrical effect, the gardens were conjured up out of the sun-baked bush by a team of experts in a matter of just two years. There are 5 000 species of forest tree alone, including full-grown baobabs from Venda, and euphorbias from Madagascar.

7 The Palace of the Lost City Unashamedly ostentatious, the Palace of the Lost City is without doubt one of the world's most luxurious hotels, where everything, from the smallest silver teaspoon to the mightiest crystal chandelier, is of the very finest quality, matched by world-class service and cuisine. There's a fantastical air about this huge hotel, with its lofty domes, marble mosaics, atriums, loggias, sweeping staircases and delicate frescoes. No expense has been spared in fitting the 338 rooms with the finest custom-made furnishings. The Crystal Court and the Villa del Palazzo serve exquisite cuisine in truly palatial surroundings. If you can afford to stay here, you'll never forget it.

8 Gary Player Country Club and Lost City Golf Course Fairways and greens unroll like cloths of emerald velvet over the bush-covered Pilanesberg hills. Sun City's original golf course, designed by Gary Player, hosts the annual Sun City Million Dollar Golf Challenge. The new 18-hole desert-style course at the Lost City features a driving range, a halfway house for thirsty golfers and live crocodiles at the 13th hole.

Water is the dominant element of the Lost City's sprawling entertainment area. One of the pools has its own beach, and is swept by artificially created surfing waves.

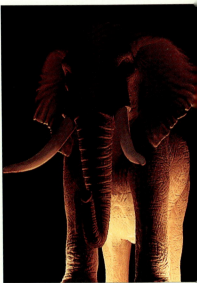

A life-size, illuminated statue of a bull elephant guards the entrance to The Palace of the Lost City, ranked among the world's finest hotels.

HIGHVELD

TSWAING CRATER MUSEUM
Near Pretoria

Map: page 41, 4A
About 40 km northwest of Pretoria. Visitors by arrangement.
Further information: The Curator, Tswaing Crater Museum, National Cultural History Museum, P O Box 28088, Sunnyside 0132, tel (01214) 98-7302.

Two hundred thousand years ago an immense, fiery meteorite came streaking out of the heavens and smashed into the earth's crust, creating a vast circular crater some 40 km northwest of present-day Pretoria. In time, a shallow, saline lake formed, hence its original Tswana name, *Tswaing*, which means 'place of salt'. The huge bowl-shaped depression is of unique interest to scientists. It's one of the best-preserved meteorite craters in the world, and is remarkably rich in animal, bird and plant life. It is also a site of great archaeological significance.

For many years the Pretoria 'Soutpan' has been the exclusive domain of scientists, but now this extraordinary place is being developed into South Africa's first open-air environmental museum.

The National Cultural History Museum is developing the crater in close consultation with local communities. When it is fully functional, the museum will play an important role in environmental education and research. One project is to use it as a base for nucleus herds of Nguni cattle and other indigenous domesticated animals. Another is to establish a nursery for the conservation of numerous valuable wild plants.

The crater comprises acacia- and combretum-dominated bushveld, and has some eight different plant communities. About 300 species of bird have been recorded here, along with many animals, including grey duiker, steenbok, African wild cats and even the nomadic and elusive brown hyaena.

The abundant game in the crater, the salt deposits and the presence of fresh water were the features that attracted the first San hunters to the area some 100 000 years ago. About 1 000 years ago Tswana-Sotho people lived here, tending their herds, growing crops and smelting iron. Numerous Iron-Age potsherds, beads and stone ruins reveal much about their living patterns.

This aerial view of the meteorite crater gives little indication of either its size or the wealth of plants and wildlife it contains. Plans are under way to transform it into an environmental showpiece.

In the 1840s Voortrekkers settled in the area, and after 1858 the crater became an important source of salt for the Highveld. From a geological point of view, the crater provides unique insights into the history of the area over a period which spans thousands of years.

The museum's location on the edges of the Soshunguve and Mabopane Winterveld makes it easily accessible to millions living in the Gauteng area and in the North-West Province. Walking trails, horse trails, bird hides and archaeological digs are planned.

A unique geological treasure house

The blazing meteorite that created the crater at Tswaing struck with a force 60 times greater than the atomic bomb that annihilated Hiroshima. Today the crater is 1,1 km wide and 119 m deep, but at the time the meteorite struck, 200 000 years ago, it was much deeper. Over the centuries, the rim has slowly worn down and the interior has filled with sediment in the form of sand, boulders and debris from the rim. Because the crater floor is slightly below the level of the local water table, a shallow seasonal lake formed. This lake is saline because of the presence of dissolved bicarbonates and carbonates, chiefly of sodium, in the local granitic ground water. The salts deposited on the surface by evaporation have been collected by humans for millennia.

For some years certain geologists believed that the crater was of volcanic origin. Their theories were finally disproved when a 200-m geological borehole was sunk near its centre, its core revealing not volcanic rock, but glass and melt fragments enriched with minerals of meteoric origin. Because these sediments had not been disturbed since the crater was formed, the borehole core could be read like an open book, revealing unique information about the climate and environment over the past 200 000 years.

VAAL DAM
Southern Highveld

For landlocked Highveld residents and Free Staters, the immense Vaal Dam is the next best thing to having the sea virtually on their doorsteps. Crowds of day-trippers and campers flock to the dam at weekends to enjoy themselves along the many kilometres of willow-fringed shore. With its wide, slow-moving, bilharzia-free waters, the Vaal River and its dam, on the border between Gauteng and the Free State, are ideally suited to yachting, swimming, water-skiing, motorboating and angling.

Irregularly shaped like some huge, lazy amoeba, this immense man-made sheet of water extends over a distance of about 104 km, swelling in places to 24 km wide. The dam feeds the Vaal Barrage further downstream, which in turn provides the 1 000 million litres of water a day to the complex of households, mines and industries of Gauteng, the Highveld and Sasolburg, and Deneysville and Heilbron in the northern Free State.

Although the Vaal River itself rises up in the highlands of the Lowveld and Escarpment, much of the water that feeds the dam comes from the KwaZulu-Natal Midlands. This water is pumped over the Drakensberg into the Wilge River, which flows eventually into the Vaal Dam.

Strung out along the serpentine shores of the dam on the Gauteng, as well as the Free State, side are numerous resorts, boat clubs, camping and caravan sites and picnic spots.

The dam is well stocked with barbel, carp and yellowfish, making it very popular among anglers. Deneysville in the Free State is one of the more popular towns, having facilities for all the watersports, and caters for the biggest annual inland yachting regatta in South Africa.

On weekends the busier resorts tend to become overcrowded, but there are still many quiet corners where nature-lovers can relax in peace. One such place is the lovely Vaal Dam Nature Reserve, run by the Gauteng administration, a 350-ha sanctuary situated three kilometres from the dam wall, near Deneysville.

The reserve has three kilometres of water frontage, but rather rudimentary facilities. Another resort is Aloe Fjord, a private venue, catering mainly for boaters and watersport enthusiasts. Oranjeville in the Free State is one of the quieter towns on these shores. Bounded by water on three sides, it is called the Peninsula of the Free State. The only drawback with the dam as a watersport haven is that its level cannot be kept more stable, and millions of rands worth of development lie unused when the water drops.

Map: page 41, 4D/E
From Vereeniging, travel southeast along the R54 and turn right onto the R549. The gates to the reserve are about 14 km further along. From Sasolburg, travel east on the Heilbron road (R26) and turn onto the R716 to Deneysville. Aloe Fjord is situated off the R54 on the northern shore of the dam, and is well signposted.
Details: Nature Reserve open daily 06h00-21h00. Aloe Fjord open daily. Admission charged. Refreshments.
Accommodation: Camping/caravan sites at both resorts; overnight accommodation at Aloe Fjord.
Further information: Vereeniging Public Relations Office, P O Box 135, Vereeniging 1930, tel (016) 50-3009; Sasolburg Town Council, P O Box 60, Sasolburg 9570, tel (016) 76-0029; or Department of Water Affairs, Private Bag X2, Deneysville 1932, tel (01618) 3-1121/2/3.

The waters of the dam are ideal for yachting, and for other water-related sports.

HIGHVELD

WONDER CAVE
Kromdraai

Map: page 41, 3C
From Randburg, drive north towards Honeydew along D F Malan Drive, which becomes Muldersdrift Road. Continue along this road, cross over the R28, and drive for a further 2,8 km, or until you see the turn-off signposted 'Zwartkop/Tweefontein'. Turn left, and continue for 8 km, or until you see the signposted turning for the Rhino Nature Reserve (which adjoins the Wonder Cave) on your right.
Details: Open daily, including public holidays, 08h00-17h00. Guided tours take place every 90 minutes. Admission charged. Parking. Refreshments.
Accommodation: Chalets at the Rhino Nature Reserve adjoining the cave.
Further information: Wonder Cave, P O Box 1859, Krugersdorp 1740, tel (011) 957-0106.

This beautiful subterranean cavern in Kromdraai, north of Johannesburg, was discovered a century ago, but opened to the public for the first time in 1991. For some 2 200 million years this vast, chilly chamber has existed, soaked in darkness, silent except for the slow drip-drip of water on stone.

Nowadays the cave is flooded with lights that allow visitors to marvel at the strange and beautiful rock formations that have been built up, with infinitesimal slowness, over the aeons. There are spectacular stalactites and stalagmites, rimstone dams, cave pearls and even a complete calcified animal skeleton.

The Wonder Cave consists of a single cavern 50 m wide, 125 m long and 40 m deep, its only entrance being an opening in the roof of the chamber. The difficulty in gaining entry to the cave is one of the factors that has helped preserve its formations in a pristine state.

Early speleologists, researchers and miners entered the cave's recesses by means of an iron ladder; nowadays a modern lift offers safe and easy access to the cavern. Remnants of early explorations may be seen scattered about the cave, as well as evidence of early calcite-mining activities.

Fascinating tours of the cave are offered every 90 minutes, and when the tour's over, most visitors head for the Rhino Nature Reserve nearby for a picnic, swim or game drive.

Steep steps lead down into the great cavern. Most visitors descend by lift to view the floodlit fantasia of dripstone formations.

The interior of Wonder Cave is a wonderland of stalactites, stalagmites and small, ancient dams.

NORTH TRANSVAAL

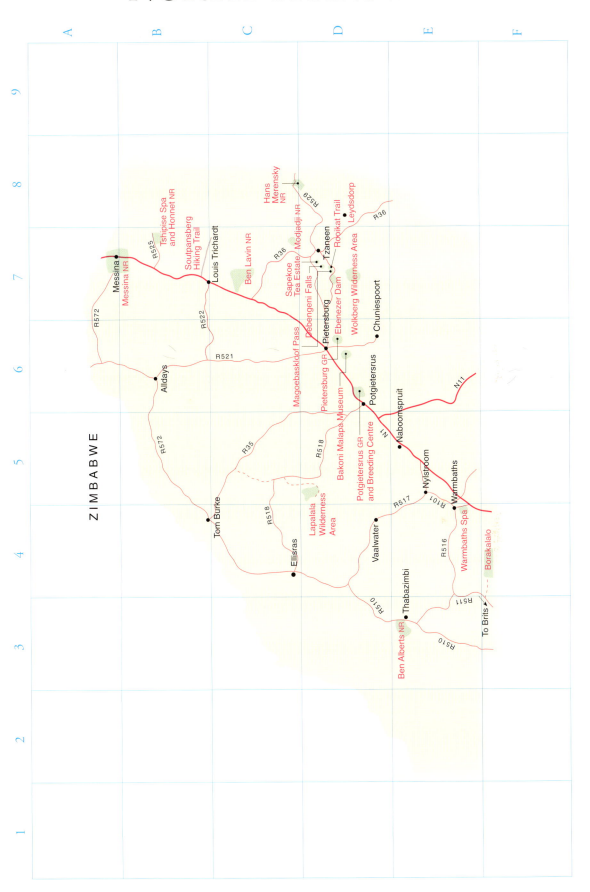

NORTH TRANSVAAL

BAKONI MALAPA MUSEUM
Near Pietersburg

Map: page 71, 6D
The museum is situated 9 km south of Pietersburg, on the Chuenespoort/Burgersfort road (R37).

Details: The museum is open daily 08h30-12h30 and 13h30-15h30. Guided tours offered throughout the day. Braai facilities available. Admission charged.

Accommodation: Self-catering accommodation available at the Union Park Caravan Park, P O Box 111, Pietersburg 0700, tel (0152) 295-2001. Hotel accommodation at the Ranch Hotel, P O Box 77, Pietersburg 0700, tel (0152) 293-7180.

Further information: Bakoni Malapa Museum, P O Box 111, Pietersburg 0700, tel (0152) 295-2011; South African Tourism Board, P O Box 2814, Pietersburg 0700, tel (0152) 295-3025.

Beer-brewing, basket-weaving, maize-grinding and fire-making are some of the age-old traditional techniques that are demonstrated for visitors at the Bakoni Malapa Museum, set at the foot of a large rocky koppie, some nine kilometres south of Pietersburg. This open-air, 'living' museum is one of the most unusual in South Africa, offering visitors a fascinating insight into the everyday life of the Northern Sotho people, of whom the Bakoni of Matlala are a subgroup.

The museum comprises a traditional kraal, with huts made of wood, thatch and anthill clay. Nearby is a modern unit that reflects the influences of Western civilization on the material culture of the Northern Sotho.

At the centre of the traditional kraal is a circular area which is enfenced by thorn trees. This is the *kgr*, the gathering place of the males. Other structures include sleeping huts, initiation hut, cooking huts, witchdoctor's hut, potters' huts and a cattle kraal.

A group of highly skilled craftsmen and women live in and maintain the museum, producing clay pots, baskets, sleeping mats, hides, chairs, spoons, beer strainers, brooms and many other traditional objects. Visitors can purchase a selection of these items at the information centre.

A hiking trail leads over the koppie behind the museum, offering a good bird's-eye view of the kraal layout. The numerous indigenous trees growing here are another attraction.

A woman displays some of the pottery used to prepare meals outside the kraal. Such clay pottery and a variety of local crafts are on sale at the Bakoni Malapa Museum.

The museum features kraals such as this one, enfenced traditionally by the Northern Sotho people to keep out nocturnal predators.

History revealed at Bakoni Malapa

Although the entire Bakoni Malapa Museum is a reconstruction, the site itself is of great archaeological significance. Various groups made their homes at the foot of this koppie over many thousands of years, and the numerous artefacts excavated by the University of the Witwatersrand during 1980 provided fascinating clues about the identity and lifestyle of these people. Stone-Age people lived here between 20 000 and 50 000 years ago, as evidenced by the numerous Middle and Later Stone-Age implements that were discovered on the site.

A rock engraving was found at the southern foot of the koppie, indicating the presence of San (Bushman) hunter-gatherers at some stage. The remains of stone-wall complexes and many pottery shards yielded a wealth of information about groups who occupied the site in later years. It is believed that the Northern Ndebele lived here from around 1600 to 1650, and that they melted both copper and iron on the site. Fifty years later they were succeeded by the Northern Sotho, and from about 1850 the site was occupied by Tsonga-Shangaan people, who finally moved away in about 1900.

The huts that presently form part of the reconstructed kraal were built using traditional methods employed by the Northern Sotho some 250 years ago. No surviving example of this type of hut could be found in the area, so the new huts were constructed with the help and advice of a few elderly men and women of the Matlala people, who could remember having lived in them as children.

BEN ALBERTS NATURE RESERVE
Thabazimbi

The muted colours of the bushveld vegetation – silver and fawn, dun, grey-green and gold – contrast sharply with the rust-red soil of the terrain in this out-of-the-way bushveld sanctuary, lying in rolling hills at the foot of the Ysterberg, near Thabazimbi.

Thabazimbi means 'mountain of iron', and the region's soils and rocks are indeed rich in iron ore, which has been mined here for some centuries, first by Sotho tribes, and now by the Iron and Steel Corporation (Iscor).

Iscor laid out the town of Thabazimbi in 1953, and later established the Ben Alberts Nature Reserve as a recreational facility for its employees.

The reserve covers some 2 000 ha, and is watered by the Crocodile River, which is flanked by steep hillsides. In the background, the Kransberg (highest peak of the Waterberg range) is a magnificent and brooding presence.

A network of good gravel roads criss-crosses the reserve (visitors will find a map printed on the back of their entrance tickets). Some routes take you to lookout points commanding panoramic views of the reserve. Here you can expect to spot an abundance of game, including such mammals as white rhinos, kudu, blue wildebeest, giraffes, eland, zebras and warthogs. There is also a wide variety of bird life for the enthusiast.

Map: page 71, 3E
Drive south out of Thabazimbi on the road to Northam (R510). About 5 km further along, on the right-hand side, is the signposted turn to the reserve.
Details: Open daily throughout the year 07h00-18h00. Admission charged.
Accommodation: Camping and caravan sites at rest camp.
Further information: The Warden, Ben Alberts Nature Reserve, P O Box 50, Thabazimbi 0380, tel (014773) 7-1670.

Cascades and rocky pools such as this one, not far from the Ben Alberts Nature Reserve, bring their own magic to the remoter parts of North Transvaal.

BEN LAVIN NATURE RESERVE
Louis Trichardt

A secluded hutted camp, hidden in singing riverine woodland, is one of the special features of the Ben Lavin Nature Reserve. For a surprisingly low tariff, groups of up to 20 can enjoy the seclusion of a second rustic bush camp, close to several water holes.

But that's only one of the several attractions of this 2 500-ha bushveld sanctuary, situated 12 km southeast of Louis Trichardt, within sight of the rugged Soutpansberg Mountains.

It's one of the few large reserves in the area that allow visitors to explore on foot. Comprising gently undulating terrain cloaked in sweet and mixed bushveld, the reserve has four marked circular trails, ranging from four kilometres to eight kilometres in length. Some wind through thick riverine bush, past dams and water holes where you are likely to spot a wide variety of animals.

More than 50 mammal species are to be found in the reserve, and include such species as giraffes, warthogs, zebras, tsessebe, black-backed jackals, antbears and aardwolfs. There are more than 230 recorded species of bird. For those who prefer to view their game from the comfort of their cars, there is a 40-km network of good gravel roads.

Map: page 71, 7C
Ben Lavin Nature Reserve is situated about 450 km north of Johannesburg. Take the N1 north from Pietersburg, and continue through Bandelierkop. Pass the Adam's Apple Hotel on your right and continue until you reach Fort Edward about 8 km outside Louis Trichardt, on the right-hand side. The gates to the reserve are 5 km further along this road.
Details: Open daily throughout the year. Gates open all hours (additional fee charged for arrivals before 06h00 and after 18h00). Admission charged. Shop selling basic supplies and firewood. Night-drives by arrangement.
Accommodation: Thatched huts and hired tents. Also camp sites for tents.
Further information: The Warden, Ben Lavin Nature Reserve, P O Box 782, Louis Trichardt 0920, tel (01551) 3834.

NORTH TRANSVAAL

BORAKALALO
North of Brits

Map: page 71, 4F
Take the R511 through Brits. Turn right at the last set of traffic lights, onto the R511 for Thabazimbi. After about 10 km turn right at the sign for Lethlabile, then, after a further 4 km, turn left at a second Lethlabile sign. Continue for some 24 km to the T-junction at Jericho. Turn right here and then first left to Leegonyane. The park lies some 26 km from Jericho. The road is tarred all the way, but watch out for animals.
Details: Open daily throughout the year: October to March 05h30-19h00; April to September 06h00-18h30. Admission charged.
Accommodation: Camp sites and, at the more luxurious Phudufudu, in furnished safari tents. Shop selling basic supplies and firewood.
Further information: Central Reservations, Golden Leopard, P O Box 937, Lonehill 2062, tel (011) 465-5423.

There are no fences around the rest camps at this little-known wildlife sanctuary, so you are likely to enjoy startling face-to-face encounters with all manner of game – even elephants and rhinos – as you make the short trip from your safari tent to the reed-walled ablution facilities. The opportunity to experience the quiet magic of the African bush at such close quarters is what draws devoted nature-lovers to Borakalalo, which means 'the place where people relax' in Setswana. Its convenient location (60 km north of Brits, about an hour and a half's drive from Johannesburg) is another plus, while the reasonably priced accommodation makes it the ideal weekend destination for families who'd like to get away from it all.

The reserve covers some 14 000 ha of rolling sandveld, mixed bushveld and grassland. The Moretele River, with its fringes of thick riverine bush, cuts a cool, green swathe across the dry grasslands of the reserve, flowing into the huge, sickle-shaped Klipvoor Dam, where anglers can expect generally good catches of carp, kurper and barbel.

Borakalalo is considered by ornithologists to be one of the Highveld's premier bird-watching locations – some 300 species have been recorded here.

The 60-km network of roads winding through the park offers good viewing of the reserve's abundant game, which includes elephants, giraffes, zebras, white rhinos, sable antelope, leopards and brown hyaenas.

There are lovely camp sites and furnished safari tents scattered in the shade of trees along the banks of the river at Moretele Camp. Anglers generally prefer to camp at the rather more barren Pitjane camp site on the banks of the dam. Ablution facilities are basic, but clean and well maintained.

DEBENGENI FALLS
Magoebaskloof

Map: page 71, 7D
From Tzaneen take the R71 to Pietersburg. After about 18 km, turn right at the turning signposted 'De Hoek Forest'. Follow a gravel road for about 5 km to the entrance to Debengeni Falls.
Details: Open September to March 07h00-18h00; April to August 07h00-17h00. Admission charged. Braai and picnic facilities; toilets. Swimming permitted in specified areas.
Accommodation: Magoebaskloof Hotel, P O Magoebaskloof 0731, tel (015276) 4277; Troutwaters Inn, P O Magoebaskloof 0731, tel (015276) 4245. Self-catering chalets may be rented at the Magoebaskloof Holiday Resort, P O Box 838, Tzaneen 0850, tel (01523) 5-3142; and at The Chalets, P O Box 94, Haenertsburg 0730, tel (015276) 4264.

It's easy to understand why local tribespeople once considered this glorious natural cascade to be inhabited by water spirits: one can almost imagine the wraiths slipping out of the deep green shadows of soaring forest trees to collect the offerings of food and drink that were placed in earlier times alongside the churning waters. Perhaps these are not water spirits, but the ghosts of the several poor souls who lost their lives clambering up the treacherously slippery rocks and trying to ride the waterfall.

Haunted or not, Debengeni is eerily beautiful, an enchanted site hidden in the ancient mist-shrouded forests of Magoebaskloof, some 25 km west of Tzaneen. The sweet mountain waters of the Ramadipa River hiss like liquid smoke as they course down 80 m of sloping rock, cascading at the foot of the falls into a natural basin that has been scoured very smooth and deep over the aeons by countless millions of litres of water. This basin has given the waterfall its name, Debengeni, which means literally 'place of the big pot'.

There's a beautiful picnic place and braai area at the foot of the falls, from where several short walks lead into the De Hoek State Forest.

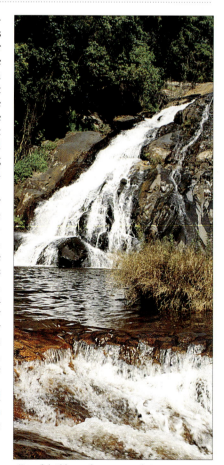

Graceful ribbons of water cascade into Debengeni's 'big pot', set in the deep green woodland magic of the Magoebaskloof. Visitors can relax at a picnic spot laid out close to the pool.

EBENEZER DAM
Haenertsburg

Meandering between pine-scented hills like a glittering stream of melted glass, the Ebenezer Dam near Haenertsburg is one of the loveliest watersport and angling dams in the northeastern Transvaal. The dam is fed by the Letaba River, which flows past pine plantations down into George's Valley, a place of lush, cultivated farmlands where subtropical fruits and nuts thrive in the balmy subtropical air.

In the background, the beautiful, mist-shrouded heights of the Wolkberge ('Cloudy Mountains') soar skywards.

Trout, kurper, eel and barbel are caught here by keen anglers. If you would like to fish, you will need to get a provincial licence in advance (enquire at the Troutwaters Inn, *see panel*).

Watersport enthusiasts come here from many parts of North Transvaal to revel in the large stretches of clean, bilharzia-free water and the wonderful scenery surrounding the dam.

Near the dam wall is a small but very pleasant picnic site. It is difficult to find, so it's best to enquire at a local hotel before you set off.

The road that runs from Haenertsburg to Tzaneen through George's Valley is not really as spectacular as the better-known Magoebaskloof Pass, but nevertheless has a lush beauty all of its own and makes a fine alternative route if you intend making the return journey. The valley is named after the original road builder, who loved these hills and made gratuitous detours along the route simply to afford travellers the best views.

Map: page 71, 7D
The Ebenezer Dam is situated near Haenertsburg, about 35 km west of Tzaneen, and may be reached via either the R71 or the R528. Follow signs from Haenertsburg.
Details: Picnic site open daily. Admission free. No tourist facilities, apart from picnic and braai sites.
Accommodation: Troutwaters Inn, P O Magoebaskloof 0731, tel (015276) 4245. Self-catering chalets may be rented at the Magoebaskloof Holiday Resort, P O Box 838, Tzaneen 0850, tel (01523) 5-3142.
Further information: Tzaneen Municipal Tourist Office, P O Box 24, Tzaneen 0850, tel (0152) 307-1411.

These serene waters lie close to the Ebenezer Dam, venue for boating enthusiasts, anglers and windsurfers. The surrounding pine-mantled countryside is perhaps more reminiscent of the North American wilderness than of Africa.

HANS MERENSKY NATURE RESERVE
Near Letsitele

Hippo footprints the size of dinner plates, squashed into the mud alongside the footpath, are a stern reminder to walkers in the Hans Merensky Nature Reserve that they should keep a sharp lookout for these mighty amphibians. The hippos abandon their wallowing places in the Great Letaba River at dusk to saunter along the banks in search of food. The opportunity to hike through tangled riverine woodland alongside the river, and to explore sun-washed expanses of tranquil bushveld, is one of the main attractions of this 5 200-ha nature sanctuary, situated some 50 km west of the boundaries of the Kruger National Park.

By South African standards the reserve is hardly large, but there's an abundance of game roaming the lovely stretches of grassland and woodland. It's an important breeding area for giraffes and the rare sable antelope, and is also home to spotted hyaenas, zebras, wildebeest, kudu, baboons, warthogs, a few rarely seen leopards, and numerous smaller nocturnal mammals such as antbears, honey badgers and bushbabies. Visitors who follow one or more of the four marked walking trails will be rewarded by sightings of many beautiful bushveld birds: over 300 species have been recorded here.

The trails in the reserve range from the 1,2-km Mopane Interpretive Trail, to the vigorous three-day Giraffe Hiking Trail, which takes visitors into the southern part of the reserve. Walking trips to the ominously named Black Hills, a series of doleritic ridges on the eastern boundary of the reserve, may be organized by arrangement.

The huge, well-maintained Aventura Eiland Resort, which is built over a mineral spring on the banks of the Great Letaba River, is designed for fun-filled family holidays, offering hot and cold mineral baths, sporting facilities, horse-riding, an entertainment hall and a restaurant. For those who'd prefer to get away from it all, it's best to head for a quiet corner of the vast, lawned camping area where graceful bushveld trees offer a shaded place to lie back and enjoy the sounds of the wild.

Map: page 71, 8C/D
From Tzaneen drive east along the R71 for about 27 km, and then turn left onto the R529. The entrance to the reserve is about 38 km further along. The visitors' centre and resort are on the right.
Details: Open daily throughout the year. A course of antimalaria tablets is recommended before setting out.
Accommodation: Comfortable self-catering rondavels; camp sites at the Aventura Eiland Resort. Book through Aventura Central Reservations, P O Box 720, Groenkloof 0027, tel (012) 346-2277.
Further information: The Officer-in-Charge, Hans Merensky Nature Reserve, Private Bag X502, Letsitele 0885, tel (0152) 3-8632/3/4/5.

LAPALALA WILDERNESS
Near Vaalwater

Map: page 71, 5D
Lapalala Wilderness is situated northwest of Nylstroom, a three and a half hour drive from Johannesburg. Drive north on the N1 (Pietersburg road), and turn left towards Nylstroom at the Kranskop Plaza tollgates. Continue for about 60 km to Vaalwater, and then turn right towards Melkrivier. Continue for 40 km until you see the Melkrivier School on your right. Turn left, and drive for 19 km until you reach the left-hand turning to Kolobe Lodge. Turn right, drive for 4,6 km, and then turn left at the signpost marked 'Lapalala Wilderness'. The reception office is 6 km further along this road.
Details: The reserve is open daily throughout the year, closing at 17h30 from April to August and at 18h30 from September to March. There is no shop or filling station in the reserve.
Accommodation: In self-catering camps, and at Kolobe Lodge and Rhino Camp. Booking essential.
Further information: Booking Office, Lapalala Wilderness, P O Box 645, Bedfordview 2008, tel (011) 453-7645.

There are so few areas of true wilderness left in late 20th-century South Africa. Lapalala Wilderness is a notable exception. Up on the rust-coloured krantzes of North Transvaal's Waterberg Mountains the air is sweet and clear, and the shimmering grey-green bushveld stretches into the distance as far as the eye can see, a landscape that has hardly changed since the days when the earliest Stone-Age people roamed the area.

Lapalala is one of the largest singly owned reserves in the country, a pristine 25 000-ha wilderness sanctuary, which has as its prime objectives conservation and the breeding of endangered species.

For lovers of the bushveld, the Lapalala Wilderness has many distinct advantages over the reserves of the Lowveld and Escarpment: it's uncrowded, free of malaria, completely tranquil, and has a mild climate. Its location, three and a half hours from Johannesburg, makes it ideal as a weekend destination.

Comprising mixed and sour bushveld, the reserve is watered by the Palala and Blockland rivers, which wind through magnificent gorges, crashing over rapids into pools of motionless, deep water, where hippos and crocodiles lie half-submerged. Driving is not permitted at Lapalala. Instead, guests are given the freedom to explore the bushveld on foot and to enjoy rare face-to-face encounters with an abundance of game, including a number of white rhinos, black rhinos, giraffes, hippos, sable antelope, roan antelope and over 280 species of bird.

Another special feature of the reserve is its numerous archaeological sites, which include Bushman rock paintings, Stone-Age sites and Iron-Age ruins.

Six self-catering camps are scattered along the Palala and Blockland rivers.

Lapalala Wilderness School

A short stay at the Lapalala Wilderness School can be a thrilling adventure for city kids whose only previous encounter with African wildlife has been on a school trip to the zoo. Since 1985, when the school was founded by conservationist Clive Walker, it has offered a unique wilderness experience to thousands of youngsters, many of them disabled or from underprivileged communities. The school's objective is to create in youngsters an awareness of the environment, and also an understanding of the impact of man on the ecological processes.

By hiking through the bush in the company of experienced education officers, the youngsters gain a rare insight into the intricate natural rhythms of this fragile wilderness. Subjects covered on these hikes include fauna and flora identification, animal behaviour, bushcraft, concepts of ecology, and an appreciation of Stone-Age and Iron-Age cultures. Plenty of action-packed activities are thrown in, including canoeing, climbing, game-viewing, hiking, and swimming in the cool waters of the Palala River.

The courses vary in length from two to five days, and are open to all children between the ages of nine and eighteen.

For further information and details of the school's activities you should contact The Wilderness Trust, P O Box 577, Bedfordview 2008, tel (011) 453-7645/6/7.

LEYDSDORP
Near Gravelotte

Map: page 71, 8D
Leydsdorp is situated 11 km southeast of Gravelotte, which is 53 km southeast of Tzaneen on the R71.
Details: Leydsdorp has no tourist facilities apart from a small hotel that offers meals and limited accommodation. To book, write to Leydsdorp Hotel, P O Box 196, Gravelotte 0895, tel (152312) 7-3111.
Further information: Tzaneen Municipal Tourist Office, P O Box 24, Tzaneen 0850, tel (0152) 307-1411.

Eerily silent and all but deserted, the town of Leydsdorp dozes in the blistering Lowveld heat like some long-abandoned movie set of a Hollywood western. Dust settles in layers on windowsills, painted tin roofs are bleached white, and weeds grow waist-high around sagging wooden verandahs. It's difficult to believe that this forlorn settlement was once a vibrant and bawdy boom town, home to some 600 hard-bitten prospectors who flocked to 'French Bob's camp' after gold was discovered in the Murchison range in 1888.

The town was laid out in 1890 as an administrative centre for the Selati Goldfields, but after the gold deposits proved insubstantial, prospectors began to abandon the town. No doubt they were relieved to be away from the heat and dust of the 'fever flats', where malaria, tsetse fly and yellow fever were the scourge of early pioneers.

For many years there were no tourist facilities in Leydsdorp, but since the town was sold to various private investors some years ago, there have been small stirrings of life. Several historic buildings are now in the process of being restored, but this is still essentially a ghost town, consisting of a dusty main road flanked by deserted Victorian structures. The Leydsdorp Hotel (recently restored) has a charming pub and restaurant, and can accommodate small numbers of guests.

NORTH TRANSVAAL

MAGOEBASKLOOF PASS
Magoebaskloof

Spellbinding, beautiful Magoebaskloof must surely rank as one of South Africa's loveliest corners. Happily for motorists it's also one of the most accessible, because it's traversed by a fine, tarred mountain pass with many gravel detour roads that lead you deep into the silent, green heart of the forest in a matter of just a few minutes.

The 25-km pass links Haenertsburg and Tzaneen, in one section dropping some 600 m in just six kilometres as it swoops over the edge of the Drakensberg escarpment, that great wall of mountains that divides the cool grasslands of the Highveld from the sun-baked thorny savannah of the Lowveld.

The road weaves first through deep indigenous forest, pine plantation and mist-shrouded mountain slopes, emerging eventually into the dazzling sunlight, where you will see the hazy blue-green Lowveld stretching out to the east below you. The great tea plantations of Sapekoe Tea Estate blanket the lower slopes of the escarpment like a rich green quilt. Soon you will pass the lush farmlands that usher in the Lowveld. Here mangoes, litchis, avocados, bananas, citrus fruits and a variety of nuts thrive in the moist, subtropical climate.

The upper area encompasses the Woodbush and De Hoek forest plantations, and it's well worth exploring further by taking one of the numerous gravel roads that disappear like magic between the trees.

The scenically splendid Debengeni Falls and the Ebenezer Dam *(see separate entries)* are lovely places to have a quiet, waterside picnic. Other attractions are guided tours of the Sapekoe Tea Estate, trout-fishing, and the Dokolewa and Grootbosch trails.

Tea-pickers carry large baskets on their backs among the rolling plantations that carpet the slopes of the Magoebaskloof.

Map: page 71, 7D
The Magoebaskloof Pass is situated beyond Haenertsburg on the R71, between Pietersburg and Tzaneen.
Details: The Magoebaskloof area is at its loveliest in September and October, when the azaleas and cherry blossoms are flowering. A cherry festival takes place near Haenertsburg every September.
Accommodation: Magoebaskloof Hotel, P O Magoebaskloof 0731, tel (015276) 4277; Troutwaters Inn, P O Magoebaskloof 0731, tel (015276) 4245. Self-catering chalets may be rented at the Magoebaskloof Holiday Resort, P O Box 838, Tzaneen 0850, tel (01523) 5-3142; and at The Chalets, P O Box 94, Haenertsburg 0730, tel (015276) 4264.
Further information: For details of hiking trails, contact The Regional Director, Eastern Transvaal Region, SAFCOL, Private Bag X503, Sabie 1260, tel (01315) 4-1058/4-1392.
For more information contact the Haenertsburg Town Council, P O Haenertsburg 0730, tel (015276) 1713.

The densely wooded heights of the Magoebaskloof are reached via a good road that rises 600 m in a short six-kilometre stretch. The uplands are covered by pine plantations and lovely patches of natural forest.

MESSINA NATURE RESERVE
Messina

Map: page 71, 7A/B
Drive south out of Messina on the N1; the entrance to the reserve is 6 km further along, on the left-hand side.
Details: Open daily 07h30-16h00. Admission free. Picnic sites and toilets.
Accommodation: The reserve has tented accommodation for 8 people. The municipal camp site in Messina has pleasant grassed sites, laid out in the shade of thorn trees and huge baobabs. Hotel accommodation is available at the Impala Lily Hotel, P O Box 392, Messina 0900, tel (01553) 2197 or 2300.
Further information: The Subsection Head, Messina Nature Reserve, P O Box 78, Messina 0900, tel (01553) 3235/2307; Messina Caravan Park, Private Bag X611, Messina 0900, tel (01553) 4-0211.

The gnarled silhouette of an ancient broad-girthed baobab tree against a blood-red sunset must be one of the most powerful images of the African landscape. For the residents of Messina, this stirring sight is virtually an everyday occurrence. Here, around this small town just south of the Limpopo River, baobabs grow in such astonishing abundance that a special nature reserve has been established for the purpose of protecting these grand monoliths of the bushveld.

The baobab is the elephant of the plant world, an extraordinary botanical curiosity with a gigantic, squat trunk, swollen and twisted lower limbs, and a spreading crown of disproportionately slender branches.

The Messina Nature Reserve covers about 4 900 ha just south of the town, and boasts well over 12 000 baobabs, including some really quite spectacular specimens. This is quintessential, sun-scorched Lowveld country, a place of rippling lion-gold mopane veld dotted with magnificent indigenous trees such as corkwood, shepherd's tree, white seringa and bushwillow. The trees are the reserve's main attraction, but there is also an abundance of animal life, including nyala, kudu, Sharpe's grysbok, sable antelope, giraffes, leopards, and some 187 species of bird. A 23-km circular drive through the reserve passes some of the most impressive trees, and it is also possible to arrange hikes by obtaining permission from the officer-in-charge.

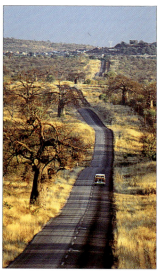

Baobab trees flank the ribbon of tar that stretches towards the town of Messina in far North Transvaal. The Messina Nature Reserve is just south of the town.

Secrets of the ancient baobab

Not only is the baobab tree one of the most imposing and long-lived of African trees – some specimens live as long as 2 000 years – but it is also among the most useful to both animals and humans. An old baobab can create its own distinct ecosystem, swarming with life as it provides shelter and sustenance for thousands of creatures. Elephants browse its leaves and strip its bark, baboons feast on the fruit, birds nest in the branches or in holes in the trunk, fruit bats and bushbabies pollinate the flowers, and a myriad tiny insects scurry about the crevices in its convoluted grey bark.

Humans have also been known to make their homes – at least temporary ones – in the hollowed trunks of giant baobabs, which continue, mysteriously, to thrive even after the pulpy inner flesh of the trunk has burnt away. Over the years, baobabs have been used variously as house, prison, shop, storage barn and bus shelter. One famous tree, outside Leydsdorp in the Lowveld, enjoyed brief fame when it was converted into a pub during the frenzied years of the gold rush; another, in Katima Mulilo, is even equipped with a flushing toilet.

The various parts of the tree have diverse uses: the woody-shelled fruit of the tree contains a whitish powdery pulp which makes a refreshingly tart drink; the pulp is rich in tartaric acid, hence its Afrikaans common name, 'kremetartboom' (cream of tartar tree). The fibrous bark and spongy wood may be used to make rope, matting, baskets, ceiling boards, paper and even cloth; the seeds can be ground and roasted to make a coffee-like beverage, and the pollen to make a type of glue.

The baobab derives its scientific name, *Adansonia digitata*, from Michel Adanson, the naturalist who first saw it while travelling in Senegal in about 1750.

To the African people of southern Africa's rural areas, baobabs are wreathed in legend: some believe that God originally planted them upside down, others that the blossoms are haunted by spirits.

No tree embodies the spirit of wild Africa more than the stately baobab, with its bulbous trunk and gnarled branches. The early San and the animal communities which shared their land drew sustenance and shelter from these trees.

MODJADJI NATURE RESERVE
Near Duiwelskloof

If dinosaurs were alive today, probably one of the last places on earth that these great lumbering reptiles would feel at home would be among the cycads of the Modjadji Nature Reserve, situated in mountainous country 29 km northeast of Duiwelskloof. This is an ancient landscape where thousands of mighty cycads form a dense 305-ha forest.

These cycads are known as 'living fossils' because they are the survivors of a primeval plant group, the Cycadales, that was the dominant vegetation type as long as 300 million years ago.

What is unique about the Modjadji cycad forest is that it represents the largest natural concentration of a single cycad species, *Encephalartos transvenosus*, in the world. Growing to about five metres, sometimes reaching up to a height of 13 m, this species is the biggest and best known of all the cycads.

The position of the cycads against the mountain slopes has undoubtedly helped to preserve them in such large numbers. But another, more compelling, reason for their survival over the last four centuries is the protection they have enjoyed from succeeding generations of the Rain Queen, Modjadji, hereditary ruler of the Lobedu tribe, to whom the plants are sacred. Modjadji is one of the most mysterious of all Africa's tribal rulers, endowed with terrifying powers, including the ability to summon the refreshing rains that soak this lush and lovely corner of North Transvaal.

The original Modjadji is said to have been a princess who fled Zimbabwe in the 16th century to find refuge in the cycad forest. Today's Rain Queen is her direct descendant, a mysterious and shadowy person of enormous influence, who rules her people from her kraal below the cycad forest.

You can see Modjadji's sacred cycad forest by following one of the short walking trails through the nature reserve.

Facilities for visitors include picnic and braai facilities, an information centre, kiosk and curio shop.

Map: page 71, 7C
From Tzaneen drive north on the R36 to Duiwelskloof (about 18 kilometres). Continue north on the R36 towards Mooketsi. After about 6 km, turn right towards Ga-Kgapane, and follow the signposts to the Modjadji Nature Reserve, which is about 23 km further along this road.
Details: Open daily 07h00-17h00. Admission charged. Picnic and braai sites; refreshments from kiosk.
Accommodation: In Duiwelskloof at the Imp Inn, Botha Street, P O Box 17, Duiwelskloof 0835, tel (01523) 9253. Self-catering accommodation at the Duiwelskloof Holiday Resort, P O Box 36, Duiwelskloof 0835, tel (01523) 9651.
Further information: Duiwelskloof Municipality, P O Box 36, Duiwelskloof 0835, tel (01523) 9246.

The realm of Modjadji, mysterious Rain Queen of the Lobedu people and said to be the inspiration for Rider Haggard's 'She'. Thousands of giant cycads, primeval plants that covered parts of the earth 300 million years ago, grow here.

PIETERSBURG GAME RESERVE
Pietersburg

In their haste to reach their holiday destinations in the North Transvaal and Zimbabwe, motorists rarely pause as they speed through Pietersburg on the great north road, but this is a pity, because just south of the town is a fine nature reserve that is well worth the slight detour.

This 3 000-ha wildlife sanctuary is one of the largest municipal reserves in the North Transvaal, comprising rippling golden grassland with scattered patches of dense acacia bush and occasional rocky outcrops. The openness of the terrain means that you can expect good game-viewing throughout the year. The reserve is stocked with a variety of game, including blesbok, springbok, eland, gemsbok, kudu, zebras, sable antelope, white rhinos, giraffes and an abundance of bird life (some 195 species have been identified here).

The reserve is particularly notable for its magnificent aloes, which bloom in winter, lighting up the veld like blazing torches of vivid orange and deep red. Indigenous trees in the reserve are labelled with national tree list numbers.

Perhaps the best way to enjoy the reserve's varied attractions is to follow the Rhino Trail, an 18-km, easy circular walk that can be completed in a day, provided that you walk briskly. For the most part the route leads through an undemanding terrain of acacia-dotted grasslands.

For those who would prefer a more leisurely walk, there is the option of spending a night at the farmhouse at a halfway point on the trail.

There is no other overnight accommodation for visitors, but rondavels and camp sites may be rented at the nearby municipal camp site in Union Park.

Map: page 71, 6D
Drive south out of Pietersburg along the airport road (signposted). The gates to the reserve are about 500 m past the airport turn-off to the right at Union Park.
Details: Open daily throughout the year 07h00-18h00 in summer and 07h00-17h00 in winter. Admission charged. Picnic and braai facilities.
Accommodation: Self-catering accommodation in rondavels at the Union Park Caravan Park (adjacent to the reserve), P O Box 111, Pietersburg 0700, tel (0152) 295-2011; and at Arnotha's, P O Box 1075, Pietersburg 0700, tel (0152) 291-3390. There's also accommodation at the Ranch Hotel, P O Box 77, Pietersburg 0700, tel (0152) 293-7180; and at Holiday Inn Garden Court, P O Box 784, Pietersburg 0700, tel (0152) 291-2030.
Further information: South African Tourism Board, P O Box 111, Pietersburg 0700, tel (0152) 295-3025.

NORTH TRANSVAAL

POTGIETERSRUS GAME RESERVE AND BREEDING CENTRE
Potgietersrus

Map: page 71, 6D
Potgietersrus is about 230 km from Pretoria, on the N1 to Pietersburg. The reserve is on the northern outskirts of Potgietersrus.
Details: The reserve and breeding centre are open Monday to Friday 08h00-16h15; weekends and public holidays 08h00-17h30. Admission charged. Picnic and braai sites.
Accommodation: At the Protea Park Hotel, P O Box 1551, Potgietersrus 0600, tel (0154) 3101; and at Kiepersol Holiday Resort, P O Box 930, Potgietersrus 0600, tel (0154) 5609. There is also a camping and caravan site close to the nature reserve.
Further information: The Town Clerk, P O Box 34, Potgietersrus 0600, tel (0154) 2255.

A Madagascan lemur is the last creature you'd expect to find lurking in the vicinity of a bushveld reserve, but that's exactly what you will see when you visit the Potgietersrus Game Breeding Centre.

This rather unusual wildlife sanctuary is one of two animal-breeding centres established by the National Zoological Gardens of South Africa. The other is near Lichtenburg, in the North-West Province. For many years the Potgietersrus centre concentrated on ensuring the continued survival of a variety of endangered exotic creatures, but in recent years the emphasis has shifted to the breeding of some of Africa's threatened species, such as black rhinos, cheetahs, buffaloes, bushbuck and roan antelope.

The 800-ha bushveld reserve adjoining the breeding centre is crisscrossed by about 30 km of dirt roads which allow for good game-viewing. Visitors can expect to spot giraffes, kudu, impala, nyala, tsessebe, eland and zebras. There's also a 3-km trail that winds through the reserve.

Near the main gates you can view such exotic species as Madagascan lemurs, the pygmy hippo from West Africa and, from the central Amazon, the capybara, which is the world's largest rodent. The reserve has also been home to blackbuck and hog deer from Asia, and moufflon wild sheep.

ROOIKAT TRAIL
Tzaneen

Map: page 71, 7D
The trail starts and ends at the New Agatha Forest. Take the road out of Tzaneen signposted 'Agatha'. Drive for 10 km, turn left at the T-junction, and continue for a further 3 km, or until you see the New Agatha signpost on the right.
Details: Permits for the trail may be obtained for a small fee from the New Agatha Forest Station, open between 07h30 and 16h30 on weekdays. On weekends and public holidays permits are available from the guard on duty.
Accommodation: Close by is the historic Coach House, several times voted South Africa's finest country hotel. The address is: P O Box 544, Tzaneen 0850, tel (0152) 307-3641. You can also stay at the Mountain View Guest House, P O Box 1471, Tzaneen 0850, tel (0152) 307-1802.
Further information: The Plantation Manager, New Agatha Forest, Private Bag X4009, Tzaneen 0850, tel (0152) 307-4310; or The Regional Director, Eastern Transvaal Region, SAFCOL, Private Bag X503, Sabie 1260, tel (01315) 4-1058/4-1392.

This splendid 11-km, five-hour circular trail through montane forest near Tzaneen can be completed in a morning. This makes it ideal for tourists who would like to experience at first hand the hushed green magic of these sylvan corridors, without spending days slogging along with heavy backpacks.

The Rooikat Trail starts and ends at the New Agatha Forest Station, some 18 km southwest of Tzaneen. Part of the trail passes through pine plantation, and the rest through patches of dense indigenous forest similar in character to the fabled forests of Magoebaskloof *(see separate entry)*. Magnificent forest trees form leafy caverns where ferns, mushrooms, mosses and lichens thrive. The only sound is the soft gurgle of the river and the crunch of leaf litter beneath your hiking boots.

The first third of the trail is a steep downhill walk into the valley, where the path meets up with the Bobs River, which it follows closely for about half the total distance of the trail. About six kilometres after the start of the trail you will come to Die Akkers, a beautiful picnic place set in a sunny clearing. Close by is Bobs Glyvalle waterfall. The last third of the trail is a vigorous uphill climb back to the forest station.

A llama shares the bushveld with several other exotic and local species at the Potgietersrus Game Reserve and Breeding Centre. Exotics include Madagascan lemurs and pygmy hippos.

SAPEKOE TEA ESTATE
Tzaneen

First-time visitors to the Tzaneen area are sometimes puzzled by the unfamiliar appearance of the vivid green, waist-high bushes that grow in densely packed swathes on the lower slopes of the Drakensberg escarpment.

These are the well-known Sapekoe tea plantations, Middelkop and Grenshoek, which together cover an area of 900 ha and produce some 2 800 tons of high-grade tea every year.

A guided tour of Middelkop Estate, on the lower slopes of Magoebaskloof, offers visitors some fascinating insights into the tea industry: you will be shown how tea is cultivated, and then taken on a tour of the curing and packing sheds to see how the healthy leaves are processed into the aromatic black dust that fills millions of teapots and teabags each year *(see box)*.

Tea has been cultivated here since 1963, when Douglas Penwill, a tea expert from Kenya, came to South Africa to establish the plantation with finance from the Industrial Development Corporation. The tea grown here is known as Sapekoe, a word derived from 'pekoe', the Chinese word for tea. The best time to visit the estate is during the picking season between October and April.

Map: page 71, 7D
From Tzaneen take the R36 to Duiwelskloof. After some 4 km turn left on to the R71, which is the Magoebaskloof/Pietersburg road. After another 4 km you will see the start of the tea estate. The white-pillared gates to the estate are about 500 m further along on your left, and are signposted 'Middelkop Estate'.

Details: Guided tours take place Tuesday to Friday at 09h00, 10h15, 11h15, 14h00 and 15h00. Saturday tours are available at 10h00 from October to April. Phone in advance for big group tours.

Further information: Middelkop Tea Estate, P O Box 626, Tzaneen 0850, tel (01523) 5-3241/2.

Emerald-hued tea plantations (left) grace the slopes of the beautiful Letaba River Valley.
Below: The tea plant's choicest tip: two leaves and the bud, which are picked on the Sapekoe Tea Estate for processing.

From fresh green leaf to morning cuppa

The Magoebaskloof/Tzaneen region's sub-tropical climate provides the most suitable growing conditions for tea in southern Africa. The two tea estates here produce a significant proportion of the tea needed to brew the 10 000 million cups that are drunk by South Africans each year.

The tea bush *(Camellia sinensis)*, a native of tropical and subtropical Asia, grows to about 15 m in its natural environment, but for the purposes of tea production the trees are pruned to bushes 50 cm high. The plant has large, glossy, green leaves, but most of the tea flavour is concentrated in the smaller, younger leaves at the tips of the branches, known as 'two and a bud'.

After harvesting, the leaves are laid out on 'withering troughs' where air is forced through them to remove 30 percent of the moisture content. The leaves are then broken up, cut and twisted into a mass of small particles, a process that releases the tea juice from the cells. After this, the tea is fed into a 'continuous fermenting unit' where the juice oxidizes, turning the green particles to a coppery brown colour. Hot air is used to dry or 'fire' the tea, a process that takes about 20 minutes. Finally, the tea is sorted to remove particles of stalk and leaf vein or fibre.

The tea is then sorted into different sizes or grades, the most common of which are Flowery Pekoe, Broken Orange Pekoe and Pekoe Dust. The tea is packed in 'breaks' (100 bags of 50 kg each), and samples are sent to the buyers who will eventually purchase the tea for blending and packaging.

NORTH TRANSVAAL

SOUTPANSBERG HIKING TRAIL
Near Louis Trichardt

Map: page 71, 7B/C
The Hanglip section of the trail begins and ends at Hanglip State Forest, about 2 km north of Louis Trichardt. Drive straight through the town on the N1, and take the signposted left-hand turn leading up to the forestry station. The Entabeni Trail begins and ends at Klein Australie Hut in Entabeni State Forest, about 40 km east of Louis Trichardt. Follow the signposts from town.
Details: Permits for the Soutpansberg Hiking Trail must be obtained and bookings made well in advance. There is an information centre and ablution block at the Hanglip Forest Station.
Accommodation: Overnight huts are provided for hikers.
Further information: Department of Forestry, Private Bag X503, Sabie 1260, tel (01315) 4-1058.

The Soutpansberg range is a place of dramatic contrasts: it's possible to pass from hot, thorny savannah to cool, dense, indigenous forest in just a matter of hours. The area's varying topography, its splendid scenery and its great botanical diversity attract many hikers and other nature-lovers, most of whom opt to follow the challenging Soutpansberg Hiking Trail.

The Soutpansberg comprise broken parallel ridges that were formed by extensive faulting of the quartz, shale and sandstone. They extend for about 130 km, from Nylstroom in the west to the Rooirand in the east.

Because of the considerable variations in topography, rainfall and soil, a wide variety of plants is to be found growing here. The hiking trails are specifically designed to take walkers through all the various types of vegetation – grass, bushveld, scrub and high forest. There are many splendid indigenous trees growing sturdily on the mountain slopes, including yellowwood, Transvaal beech, Cape chestnut, lemonwood, white and red stinkwood and cabbage tree (it's well worth taking a tree identification book along with you).

Bird-watchers are kept particularly busy on this trail: a staggering total of 400 species occur in the Soutpansberg area, including loeries, woodpeckers, sunbirds and flycatchers.

Be aware, however, that this is quite a demanding hike that requires a high level of fitness. Entabeni section, near Louis Trichardt, has three circular trails of two to three days, all of which pass through indigenous forest and exotic plantations in the Entabeni State Forest and Ratombo Nature Reserve. The Hanglip section consists of two circular trails that pass through the Hanglip State Forest on the southern slopes of the range.

TSHIPISE SPA AND HONNET NATURE RESERVE
Near Louis Trichardt

Map: page 71, 7B
From Louis Trichardt drive north on the N1 for about 57 km, or until you see the turn-off to Tshipise Spa (R525) on the right-hand side. The resort is 28 km further along this road.
Details: Aventura Resort is open daily throughout the year. Admission charged. Shop and restaurant.
Accommodation: In self-catering rondavels and at camp site. Book through Aventura Central Reservations, P O Box 720, Groenkloof 0027, tel (012) 346-2277.
Further information: Aventura Tshipise, P O Box 4, Tshipise 0901, tel (015539) 624.

The smoky-sweet scent of a leadwood camp fire; mopanes, jackalberries and camelthorn trees etched against glowing copper sunsets; the hushed rustlings of an inky-black bushveld night. These are the sights, sounds and scents of the African savannah. If they evoke in you a yearning nostalgia, then you will cherish a visit to Tshipise Spa.

This little-known resort is situated in the heart of the low, harsh mopane country, 84 km northeast of Louis Trichardt, and it's a place that lovers of the bushveld return to again and again to relax in the healing waters of the spa, soak up the year-round sunshine, and roam the unspoiled expanses of mopane veld in the nearby Honnet Nature Reserve.

The Aventura Tshipise Spa is a large, well-maintained complex that offers every imaginable amenity, including a post office, landing strip, liquor store and supermarket. The resort was developed on the site of two hot mineral springs, whose alkaline waters bubble up out of the earth's crust at a scalding 65°C.

Comfortable, air-conditioned bungalows stand amid lush lawns in the shade of many indigenous trees, together with flamboyants, frangipanis and extravagant tumbles of bougainvillea. There are many swimming pools and therapeutic baths where you can soak your cares away.

Nature-lovers generally eschew the holiday crowds, and head straight for the Honnet Nature Reserve, the 2 200-ha wildlife sanctuary surrounding the spa.

There are plenty of birds and game to be seen, including giraffes, kudu, roan antelope and eland, but the main attraction of the reserve is its splendid indigenous trees, mainly mopanes.

Horseback trails into the reserve may be arranged, but most people opt to follow the Baobab Trail, a 25-km, two-day circular route.

A pleasantly embowered camp site features among Tshipise's drawcards. A major attraction is the surrounding mopane-covered wildlife sanctuary.

WARMBATHS SPA
Warmbaths

To travellers who ventured north of Pretoria late last century, a billowing cloud of steam rising over the bushveld was the first sign that they were getting closer to the hot mineral springs known as Het Bad ('the bath'). In those days early travellers scooped out hollows in the muddy marshland so they could wallow in comfort in the healing waters. Those primitive spa baths have long since faded into memory, however, and today's visitors to the springs – numbering over a million a year – are accommodated in an enormous, internationally renowned resort that has made Warmbaths one of South Africa's busiest and best-known inland holiday destinations.

The springs at Warmbaths bubble out of the earth at a sultry 49°C; they are rich in dissolved salts, chiefly sodium chloride and calcium carbonate.

Their famed therapeutic qualities attract many people with rheumatic complaints, although the vast majority of visitors are families who come to Warmbaths to enjoy an action-packed, affordable holiday at a resort that is designed to cater for their every whim.

The pride of the Aventura Resort is the sophisticated Hidro *(sic)* Spa Centre, an enormous health complex which offers a 21-m-square indoor pool, complete with powerful underwater jets which lead to the warm outdoor pool. Other resort amenities include a cool plunge pool, hot rheumatic pool, fully equipped gymnasium, saunas, professional massage, steam rooms, and a hydrotherapy unit where visitors can enjoy a variety of luxurious water treatments.

The outdoor complex has a series of enormous hot and cold pools set in attractive, landscaped gardens, including an inviting wave-pool, children's pool and 'supertube' water slides.

Visitors to the resort are accommodated in a hotel, in chalets that are spaced well apart in a lovely treed parkland or, for those who prefer total independence, there is the option of the camping and caravan site.

A good way to escape the crowds is to visit the small nature reserve adjoining the spa. Amongst the animals you're likely to see here are Burchell's zebras, ostriches, red hartebeest and impala.

Map: page 71, 4E
Warmbaths is situated about 100 km north of Pretoria. Take the Pietersburg Highway (N1) and follow the signs to Warmbaths.
Details: The Aventura Warmbaths resort is open daily throughout the year 07h00-17h00.
Accommodation: In self-catering chalets and at the hotel or caravan park. Book through Aventura Central Reservations, P O Box 720, Groenkloof 0027, tel (012) 346-2277.
Further information: Aventura Warmbaths, P O Box 75, Warmbaths 0480, tel (014) 736-2200.

Children delight in the monstrous 'supertube' water slide, one of the Spa's many family-orientated attractions.

WOLKBERG WILDERNESS AREA
Magoebaskloof

Map: page 71, 7D

The entry point for the Wolkberg Wilderness Area is Serala Forest Station. From Pietersburg take the R71 east to Tzaneen. After about 35 km turn south at Boyne onto a gravel road. Drive for about 9 km to a four-way intersection, and carry on straight ahead. Continue for a further 7 km until the road forks, and take the left-hand fork. Fourteen kilometres further along, the road forks again. Take the left fork, and continue for a further 6 km to the Serala Forest Station.

Details: Permits are obtainable for a small fee from the Serala Forest Station. However, it's advisable to book well in advance *(see address below)* if you intend to stay overnight.

Accommodation: There are no overnight huts for hikers (it's essential to take your own camping equipment). There is a camp site with showers and toilets at the Serala Forest Station.

Further information: The Officer-in-Charge, Wolkberg Wilderness Area, Private Bag X102, Haenertsburg 0730, tel (015276) 1303.

The silvery veils of mist that swirl over the peaks and buttresses of the Wolkberg range give the 'Cloudy Mountains' an irresistible atmosphere of mystery and danger. This spectacular mountain wonderland, with its deep ravines, dizzying quartzite cliffs and windswept peaks, its crystal-clear rivers, dense rainforests and magnificent waterfalls, was proclaimed a wilderness area in 1977, encompassing about 22 000 ha of terrain.

Because of the ruggedness of the terrain and a lack of visitor facilities, the appeal of the Wolkberg Wilderness Area is largely limited to experienced hikers who are happy to disappear into the mountains for days at a time. But day-visitors are also welcome here.

There are no set routes, and hikers are free to walk along management paths and jeep tracks. You are strongly advised, however, to discuss your proposed route with the officer-in-charge at the entrance to the Serala Forest Station.

The northern part of the reserve comprises montane vegetation where proteas, everlastings, tree ferns and cycads thrive. In the forested ravines there are many splendid indigenous trees, such as wild fig and yellowwood. You may spot such game as reedbuck, klipspringer, samango and vervet monkeys, baboons, caracals, hyaenas and red- and black-backed jackals. About 157 species of bird have been recorded here, including a large variety of raptors.

A waterfall plunges over the rocky heights of the Wolkberg Mountains. This pristine wilderness, favoured by experienced hikers, is a wonderland of indigenous flowers and plants, and also home to a variety of small mammals.

LOWVELD AND ESCARPMENT

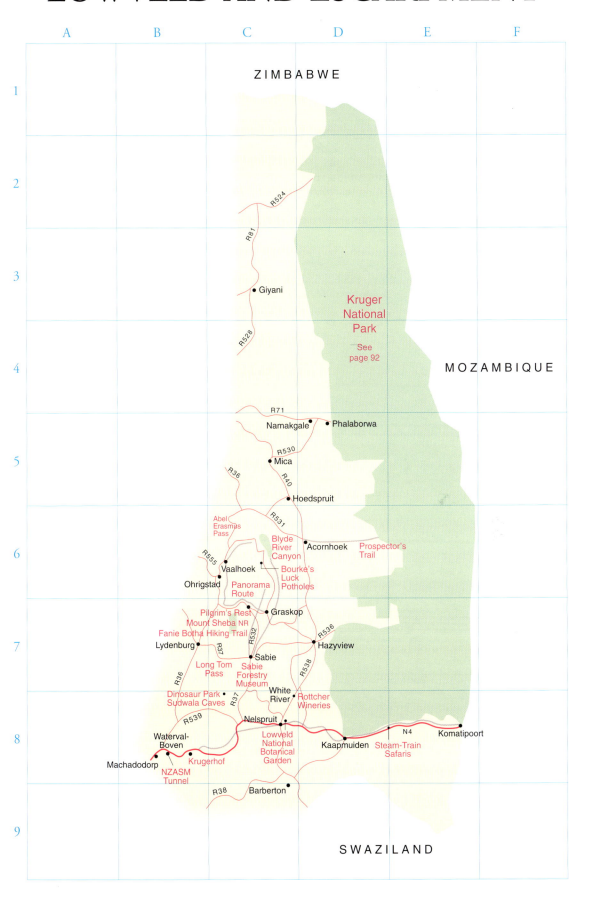

LOWVELD & ESCARPMENT

ABEL ERASMUS PASS
Ohrigstad

Map: page 85, 6C
The Abel Erasmus Pass is situated about 20 km north of Ohrigstad, on the R36 to Tzaneen. The Echo Caves are reached from a signposted turn-off west of the road between Ohrigstad and Strijdom, about 23 km north of Ohrigstad.
Details: Echo Caves open 08h00-17h00 daily; admission fee charged.
Accommodation: Self-catering accommodation and camp sites at the northern end of the pass, at Manoutsa Park, Private Bag X503, Hoedspruit 1380, tel (01528) 3-5125. Hotel accommodation at River Lodge Motel, P O Box 53, Hoedspruit 1380, tel (01528) 3-5134.
Further information: SA Tourism Board, P O Box 5018, Nelspruit 1200, tel (01311) 55-1988/9.

Vivid splotches of yellow and orange lichen, daubed on the sandstone cliffs like the work of some demented artist, are among the really memorable features of the Abel Erasmus Pass, a fine, tarred mountain route that links the scorched plains of the Lowveld to the cooler Drakensberg plateau.

The pass begins on the R36 north of Ohrigstad, and winds up the bush-covered flanks of the Drakensberg. After seven kilometres it reaches the summit, and then the road begins its convoluted descent, dropping some 600 m through dramatic scenery to the valley of the Olifants River.

Opened in 1959, the pass follows the same route as an old wagon trail over the mountains. Some remnants of this old road, signposted 'Old Coach Road', may be seen. Another highlight of the pass is the much-visited viewsite known as the Devil's Pulpit. Soon after the turn-off to the Devil's Pulpit, the road winds through the densely wooded ravines that dominate the northern side of the pass, where lichen-stained krantzes create a striking scenic backdrop.

There are several picnic sites along the pass; another good place to stop is at the southern portal of the 335-m-long J G Strijdom Tunnel, where visitors can enjoy breathtaking views over the valley of the Olifants River and, in the distance, the panorama of sun-burnished Lowveld.

Close to the southern foot of the pass is a turn-off to the Echo Caves, which are well worth a slight detour. These dolomitic caves are famous for the many important archaeological remains they have yielded, and also for their magnificent dripstone formations, which, when tapped, produce the ringing echoes after which the caves are named.

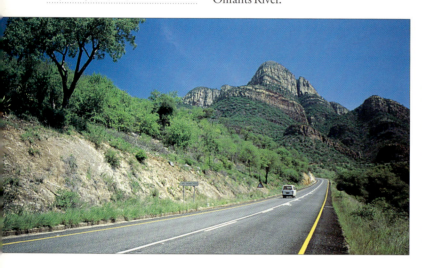

The gentle, northward approach to the Abel Erasmus Pass. After negotiating the summit the road makes a steep 700-m descent to the Olifants River Valley.

BLYDE RIVER CANYON
North of Graskop

Map: page 85, 6C
Blyde River Canyon is about 390 km from Pretoria, via Lydenburg and Ohrigstad. To reach the main scenic route that skirts the western edge of the canyon, continue through Ohrigstad. Just 20 km further north the R532 branches west, and then curves southwards to Graskop and Pilgrim's Rest. The canyon may also be entered from the Hoedspruit or Bosbokrand side (via Nelspruit).
Details: The reserve and its two resorts are open throughout the year.
Accommodation: Self-catering accommodation and camp sites at Aventura Blydepoort Resort, on the edge of the escarpment, and at the Aventura Swadini Resort, just below the Blydepoort Dam: Aventura Blydepoort Resort, Private Bag X368, Ohrigstad 1122, tel (01323) 8-0155; Aventura Swadini Resort, P O Box 281, Hoedspruit 1380, tel (01528) 3-5141.
Further information: The Officer-in-Charge, Information Section, Blyderivierspoort Nature Reserve, Private Bag X431, Graskop 1270, tel (01315) 8-1215.

Rust-coloured sandstone cliffs, bush-covered slopes and craggy buttresses soar above the canyon floor, dimmed to hazy blue-green in the distance. Far, far below, the river snakes its way northwards, a broad, shining ribbon that is sometimes inky blue, sometimes emerald, sometimes a dazzling silver. Few who have visited the Blyde River Canyon will ever forget their first breathtaking glimpse of this spectacular gorge, the third-largest in the world and undoubtedly one of Africa's most splendid scenic wonders.

This 700-m-deep chasm was gouged through the quartzites and shales of the Highveld Drakensberg by the quick-running waters of the Blyde River. It embraces 57 km of the escarpment, that immense, broken wall of mountains that divides the Highveld from the flat, sun-blistered plains of the low country. The canyon forms part of the 27 000-ha Blyderivierspoort Nature Reserve, a vast sanctuary that stretches from Swadini in the north to Graskop in the south.

Natural wonders such as waterfalls, dizzying cliffs and weird rock formations abound, so it is not surprising that this is one of the Lowveld and Escarpment's most popular tourist destinations. There are two different approaches to the canyon, both offering quite distinct touring experiences.

A road leading north from Graskop skirts the western edge of the canyon. From here, several side roads lead to viewsites on the lip of the canyon. These offer awesomely beautiful vistas of the canyon and its dominating features, such as the Three Rondavels, the Blydepoort Dam, Sundial Peak and Mariepskop. Also on this road are Bourke's Luck Potholes, where the reserve's information centre offers visitors a fine introduction to the fauna and flora of the canyon. Sixteen kilometres to the north of Bourke's Luck is the entrance to the popular Aventura Blydepoort Resort.

The other approach to the canyon is from the Lowveld end, where a road enters the reserve southeast of Hoedspruit, and winds past Mariepskop, along the floor of the canyon, to the entrance of the Aventura Swadini Resort, and continues to the visitors' centre in the nature reserve overlooking the dam.

Although the resorts tend to be extremely busy during peak season, the canyon itself is still wild and remote. Numerous footpaths and hiking trails crisscross the canyon walls and floor, the most popular of which is the lovely Blyderivierspoort Hiking Trail, a relatively undemanding five-day route that starts at God's Window near Graskop, and ends at the Swadini Resort, 65 km to the north.

Hikers will be astonished by the great diversity of flora along the trail. Because the canyon lies at the interface of the Highveld and the Lowveld, numerous different vegetation types may be observed here, including sour grasslands, mixed bushveld, montane forest, subtropical forest and even fynbos. Equally impressive is the great diversity of smaller mammals and birds, including several rare and endangered species.

Other attractions in the vicinity of the canyon that are worth a detour are the Abel Erasmus Pass and nearby Echo Caves, the Panorama Route and Bourke's Luck Potholes *(see separate entries)*.

The Blyde River flows swiftly through its majestic gorge before widening into a placid lake created by the dam wall. In places the canyon's cliffs rise more than 700 m above the waters.

BOURKE'S LUCK POTHOLES
Blyde River Canyon

Hundreds of thousands of tourists have peered into the rocky basins known as Bourke's Luck Potholes over the years, and with good reason, because this moonscape of deep hollows and channels is among the Lowveld and Escarpment's most extraordinary landmarks *(see illustrations, page 104)*. Forming part of the Blyderivierspoort Nature Reserve, the potholes are situated at the confluence of the Blyde and Treur rivers, not far from the point where the river makes its spectacular descent into the mighty Blyde River Canyon.

Bourke's Luck Potholes were formed over aeons by the continuous scouring action of sediment, grit and pebbles carried by river waters. Some of these holes are as much as six metres deep. Concrete bridges and walkways span the gorge, offering fine and safe viewing of the potholes. You may be surprised to see a glitter of metal at the bottom of some of the holes: this is not gold, but the 'good luck' coins tossed in by visitors.

This is certainly gold-mining territory, though. Close to the potholes is a disused gold mine that yielded a fortune during the heady days of the gold rush. The name 'Bourke's Luck' refers to the hapless prospector, Thomas Bourke, whose property lay within a stone's throw of the mine but produced no gold at all.

Close to the potholes are the headquarters of the Blyderivierspoort Nature Reserve. The information centre, with its many fascinating displays relating to the fauna, flora and geology of the Blyde River Canyon, is well worth a visit, particularly if you intend touring the canyon. Numerous short and long hikes depart from this point, and picnic places are provided.

Map: page 85, 6C
From Lydenburg travel north on the R36 to Ohrigstad. Continue through the town, and about 20 km later turn east onto the R532 to Graskop. Continue for some 40 km along this road until you see the turning to Bourke's Luck.
Details: Open daily 07h00-17h00. Admission charged. Picnic sites and kiosk.
Accommodation: Self-catering accommodation and camp sites available at Aventura Blydepoort Resort, on the edge of the escarpment, and at Aventura Swadini Resort, just below the Blyderivierspoort Dam: Aventura Blydepoort Resort, Private Bag X368, Ohrigstad 1122, tel (01323) 8-0155; Aventura Swadini Resort, P O Box 281, Hoedspruit 1380, tel (01528) 3-5141.
Further information: The Officer-in-Charge, Information Section, Blyderivierspoort Nature Reserve, Private Bag X431, Graskop 1270, tel (01315) 8-1215.

DINOSAUR PARK
Near Nelspruit

Map: page 85, 8C

The Dinosaur Park is situated next to the Sudwala Caves, 33 km northwest of Nelspruit. A tarred road turns off the N4 about 93 km east of Machadodorp (26 km before Nelspruit). Continue for 8 km along this road until you reach the Sudwala Caves, and then follow signposts to the Dinosaur Park.

Details: Open daily 08h30-16h30. Admission charged. There is a restaurant, a coffee shop and a curio shop adjacent to the park.

Accommodation: At Sudwala Lodge, set below the caves in a wooded valley. Write to Sudwala Lodge, P O Box 30, Schagen 1207, tel (01311) 6-3073/4/5.

Further information: Sudwala Caves, P O Box 48, Schagen 1207, tel (01311) 6-4152.

Small glittering eyes observe you from behind a curtain of shivering leaves. Walk around a corner, and a mighty *Tyrannosaurus rex* looms six metres above you, looking every inch as fearsome as it must have done during its reign of terror some 65 million years ago. This sculpture is one of the highlights of this extraordinary open-air museum, which comprises a collection of terrifyingly realistic life-size models of dinosaurs and various other extinct creatures. The models are scattered among indigenous trees and cycads in a lovely natural park on the Mankelekele Mountain, close to the mouth of the famous Sudwala Caves, northwest of Nelspruit.

The museum was built in 1975 by T C Owen, owner of the farm on which the Dinosaur Park is sited. It's the biggest of its sort in the world, and also the most scientifically accurate.

The reptiles were sculpted from steel, asbestos and cement by Jan Theron van Zijl, in close consultation with palaeontologist Dr Andre Keyser, using available fossil records to ensure that all the models were true to the originals.

A short circular path winds through the park, taking visitors past sculptures of about 100 prehistoric creatures, ranging from the small creeping reptile, *Ichthyostega*, to a mighty *Diplodocus*, which stands knee-deep in a large pond, watching bemusedly as golden carp swirl about its feet. Other models of extinct creatures include those of a Cape quagga and a black-maned Cape lion. Another series of six sculptures depicts the evolution of the horse family, *Equus*. Near the end of the circular walk is a pit where several crocodiles laze in the Lowveld sun – visitors be warned that these reptiles are very much alive.

Many fine trees and plants are to be seen in the Dinosaur Park, including stinkwoods, wild figs, wild pears, cabbage trees, cycads, tree ferns, mlala palms and the magnificent *Aloe aloöides*, which grows only on dolomitic outcrops in the Lowveld and Escarpment.

Life-size and strikingly lifelike replicas of dinosaurs – lords of the earth between 250 and 65 million years ago – graze, browse, hunt and fight in the well-wooded grounds of the park.

FANIE BOTHA HIKING TRAIL
Sabie to God's Window

Map: page 85, 7C

Starting point for the Fanie Botha Hiking Trail and the Loerie Nature Walk is the Ceylon Forest Station, situated 6 km out of Sabie, on the Graskop road. Starting point for the Forest Falls Walk is the Mac-Mac picnic site, near Mac-Mac Forest Station.

Details: You must obtain permits for the 77-km Fanie Botha Trail. Groups are limited to a maximum of 30 people. Permits are not required for the Loerie Nature Walk and the Forest Falls Walk.

Accommodation: There are overnight huts equipped with bunks, mattresses and cooking pots. There are luxury hotels, lodges, self-catering resorts and camp sites in the Sabie region.

Further information: SAFCOL, Private Bag X503, Sabie 1260, tel (01315) 4-1058/4-1392.

The Fanie Botha Hiking Trail is among the best known of all South Africa's nature trails, and deservedly so, because it allows walkers the opportunity to experience at close quarters the Highveld Drakensberg in all of its deep green splendour. The longest section of the trail passes through rugged mountain territory, over expanses of open grassland, through pine plantations and enclaves of ancient indigenous forest, passing many of the region's most spectacular natural beauty spots along the way, including the well-known Mac-Mac Falls, Mac-Mac Pools, the Pinnacle, Lone Creek Falls and God's Window.

The longest section of the Fanie Botha Hiking Trail was first opened in 1973 by its namesake (the Minister of Forestry at the time), and represented the first section of the National Hiking Way System, which today comprises some 300 trails across the country. Since then, many thousands of hikers have tackled this five-day, 77-km trek, which begins at the Ceylon Forest Station, six kilometres west of Sabie.

The trail passes through Tweefontein State Forest, and over the flanks of Mauchsberg Peak, then through Mac-Mac State Forest and Graskop, finally ending at God's Window, northeast of Graskop, where sweeping views over the broken battlements of the escarpment and the distant blue-grey Lowveld provide a breathtaking finale to the walk.

There are several alternative routes, ranging from an easy two-day walk from

Ceylon plantation to the Maritzbos Indigenous Forest and back, as well as other three-, four- and five-day hikes.

Yet another option passes through Pilgrim's Rest to join the Prospector's Trail *(see separate entry)*. This is a demanding trail that requires a reasonable level of fitness; there are many steep climbs and also long stretches between huts. However, the magnificence of the scenery, the wildflowers, and the prolific bird life more than compensate for aching feet and backs, as do the many lovely natural swimming pools along the way.

Also part of the Fanie Botha Hiking Trail is the 12-km, one-day Loerie Nature Walk, which begins at the Ceylon Forest Station, and winds up through pine plantations and some magnificent patches of flower-spangled indigenous forest, passing Bridal Veil Falls and several smaller cascades.

Less energetic walkers, or those with small children, may want to tackle the scenic four-kilometre Forest Falls Walk, a lovely circular route that starts at the Green Heritage Picnic Site, about two kilometres north of the Mac-Mac Falls *(see also Waterfalls feature)*. There is also the very easy Secretary Bird Walk, starting at the Mac-Mac Pools, and winding through the grasslands of Mac-Mac Bluff to the edge of the escarpment and back again, in less than an hour.

A magical moment along the Fanie Botha Trail. The route leads through some of the stateliest of the Highveld Drakensberg's vast pine plantations, past mountain streams, waterfalls and displays of wildflowers.

KRUGERHOF
Waterval-Onder

Singularly sober and lacking in ostentation, this tin-roofed house in the small village of Waterval-Onder aptly reflects the personality of its most famous inhabitant, President Paul Kruger. For two months during the Anglo-Boer War, Krugerhof was home to the 'Old Lion' of the Transvaal. Today, it is a museum housing a photographic exhibition that chronicles events of the war.

When British forces under Lord Roberts approached Pretoria in May 1900, the President of the old South African Republic was forced to move his seat of government to Machadodorp. The climate there disagreed with him, however, and he soon decamped to this house in Waterval-Onder. Every day, members of his executive committee had to travel by train to the village to discuss matters of state. Two months later the seat of government moved yet again, to Nelspruit, where 'Oom Paul' made a temporary home in a railway carriage. In October 1900 he sailed from Delagoa Bay, hoping to enlist support for the Boer cause in Europe. He was never to return – he died in exile in Switzerland in 1904.

The house itself is an annexe of the historic Wayside Inn, which was built in 1879 as a staging post on the road to Delagoa Bay.

Map: page 85, 8B
The entrance to Krugerhof is opposite the Wayside Store, on the road to the Wayside Inn.
Details: Open daily 08h00-16h00. Admission free.
Accommodation: The Wayside Inn, P O Box 425, Waterval-Boven 1195, tel (013262) 128. Self-catering accommodation and camp sites available in Waterval-Boven, at the Elandskrans Holiday Resort, Private Bag X05, Waterval-Boven 1195, tel (013262) 176.
Further information: Village Council of Waterval-Boven, Private Bag X05, Waterval-Boven 1195, tel (013262) 58.

PLACES TO VISIT

KRUGER NATIONAL PARK

Map: page 85, 1-8D/E
Skukuza, the Kruger National Park's largest camp, is approximately 500 km from Johannesburg.

Details: The main entrance gates, and the gates of the rest camps, open 04h30-06h30, and close 17h30-18h30, depending on time of year.

Further information: All enquiries and applications for accommodation should be addressed to the National Parks Board – Pretoria: P O Box 787, Pretoria 0001, tel (012) 343-1991; Cape Town: P O Box 7400, Roggebaai 8012, tel (021) 22-2810. Preference is given to written applications received 13 months in advance.

There is no better place to feel the ancient, steady heartbeat of wild Africa than the Kruger National Park. Here, in this two-million-hectare expanse of shimmering savannah, the sun rises and sets on a landscape that seems not to have changed for thousands of years; its intricate cycles of birth and death seem unaltered, its many living inhabitants as numerous and magnificently diverse as nature originally intended.

Hippos lie motionless in the rivers, their presence betrayed only by the occasional flick of an ear; a leopard slips like a shadow through the dappled branches of a huge old tree; and far, far above the trees, hungry vultures wheel, waiting for a kill, specks of soot against a blazing blue African sky.

It took more than a century to create this precious wildlife sanctuary, and there were long and bitter battles between landowners, politicians, hunters and conservationists. Many decades of intense ecological management have also gone into preserving the park, which today ranks as one of the world's greatest natural wildlife sanctuaries.

The Kruger National Park stretches north to south for about 350 km, a broad band of singing, thorny bushveld that straddles the Tropic of Capricorn, and is bordered by Mozambique to the east and Zimbabwe to the north. Its 19 000 sq km of territory teems with life, like some great, vibrating web, where every living thing, from the humble termite to the majestic bull elephant, is intimately connected to the next.

Dense riverine forests flourish along the courses of the seven rivers that flow east across the park. These leafy green corridors of wild figs, fever trees, mahoganies, apple-leafs and jackalberries create shelter and sustenance for many thousands of mammals, birds, insects, reptiles and amphibians.

The mopane tree dominates the hot, parched country north of the Olifants River. Even further north, the monotonous expanses of mopane are punctuated by increasing numbers of baobab trees.

In the southeast the open savannah is dominated by leadwood, acacia and marula trees. Here, nutritious 'sweet' grasses draw large herds of grazers. Sweet

Moonlight illuminates the Kruger National Park's bushveld spaces, home to a stunning variety of animals, including cheetahs (inset), the fastest land-mammals on earth.

grazing is also found west of the acacia country, between the Olifants and Crocodile rivers, where mixed combretum (bushwillow) dominates the landscape. Even further west, between the Sabie and Crocodile rivers, is a thickly wooded area where many magnificent indigenous trees grow; here the sour grasses are less palatable to grazers.

The types of animal a visitor to the park is likely to see depend to some extent on the type of vegetation in that particular area and, to a lesser degree, on the time of year. Those visitors who wish to see the 'Big Five' will not be disappointed. About 7 600 elephants live permanently in the park, along with 21 000 buffaloes, 2 000 lions, 1 000 leopards, 200 black rhinos and about 1 800 white

The large, terraced and aloe-graced Olifants Rest Camp perches high on a cliff-top; guests enjoy stunning views of the game-filled river valley which stretches out 100m below.

Visiting the Kruger National Park

It's doubtful if there's a single nature sanctuary anywhere that can rival the Kruger National Park's visitor facilities. A 2 300-km network of fine tarred and gravel roads offers easy access to lovely picnic spots, viewsites, water holes, rivers and historical memorials.

Twenty-three lovely rest camps are scattered throughout the park, ranging from rustic outposts where campers can pitch a tent and enjoy a close encounter with the bush, to large, well-maintained complexes that offer every imaginable convenience.

Generally speaking, the southern part of the park tends to be most popular with visitors, because of its abundant game. However, the wild northern extremities of the park have a special beauty of their own and are specially appealing to nature-lovers in search of a quiet bushveld experience.

When to visit
Winter is generally regarded as the best time to visit the park. When the grass is low and the trees leafless, it's easiest to spot game, and large numbers of animals also tend to congregate at water holes and rivers. Days are sunny, mild and clear, but nights can be cold, so remember to take along warm clothing.

The scenery is certainly more beautiful during the summer months, when the grass is lush and green, the rivers full, and the park filled with migrant birds and newborn animals, but visitors must be prepared to endure blisteringly hot days, balmy nights and sudden downpours. The rainy season is from October to March.

Touring in the park
You may leave the camps only during daylight hours, and may only get out of your car at designated viewing spots, monuments and picnic sites. Speed limits are 50km/h on tar and 40 km/h on gravel. Feeding animals is forbidden.

The best times to view game are in the early mornings and late evenings, especially in the scorching heat of summer.

You may also see parts of the park on foot: there's a choice of seven different wilderness trails led by an experienced ranger, during which you sleep in rustic bush camps.

Make sure that you take antimalarial medication before you visit the Kruger National Park.

Accommodation
All the camps of the Kruger National Park are run by a single authority, which means that standards are remarkably consistent. The 23 public rest camps offer guests a very wide choice of accommodation in self-contained huts, cottages, dormitories and even furnished tents. Most huts are placed well apart and set among rolling lawns and tall shady trees where monkeys and birds keep up a ceaseless chatter. All accommodation units are serviced daily, and bedding, towels and soap are provided. Visitors accommodated in units without kitchens must provide their own cooking utensils, crockery and cutlery; communal cooking facilities are available in all camps.

Campers are inevitably impressed by the cleanliness of the camp sites, all of which have well-equipped ablution blocks and communal kitchens. Many sites are situated in shaded areas close to the boundary fences of the rest camps, allowing campers to enjoy the nocturnal sounds of the bush, ranging from the manic cackle of hyaenas to the thoughtful chomping of anonymous browsers.

The larger camps all have shops that sell basic supplies, as well as souvenirs, firewood, wine, beer, spirits, fresh fruit and vegetables. The bigger camps also have a restaurant, petrol garage, electric power, laundromat and telephones, and some of them also offer swimming pools and car repair services.

KRUGER NATIONAL PARK

rhinos. There are 4 600 giraffes, 15 000 wildebeest, 31 000 zebras, 2 600 hippos and over 100 000 impala.

All in all, some 147 species of mammal are to be found in the park, including many lesser-known species such as aardwolfs, civets, genets, caracals, servals, otters, porcupines, pangolins, scrub hares, samango monkeys, bushbabies and many types of antelope.

Birds are another major attraction of the Kruger National Park – 507 of South Africa's 900-odd bird species have been identified here. They include hornbills, masked weavers, woodpeckers, loeries, sunbirds, rollers and bee-eaters.

At the many water holes you'll see such aquatic species as storks, egrets, herons, kingfishers, spoonbills, ducks, geese, cormorants and darters.

There's no shortage of raptors, either: bateleur eagles, martial eagles, lappet-faced vultures and whiteback vultures, to name a few.

Kruger Park is home to some 1 500 lions. The big cats have no natural enemies, but drought, disease and injury take a heavy toll on the prides. This well-drilled female group drinks its fill at one of the park's precious water holes.

See key on opposite page.

KEY TO THE MAP
The rest camps

1 Balule This small camp has six rustic huts and 15 tent sites, and is set on the banks of the Olifants River, 57 km from Phalaborwa Gate. There is no electricity and no shop or restaurant, but visitors can obtain supplies at Olifants Rest Camp, a few kilometres to the north.

2 Berg-en-Dal Situated on the banks of the Matjulu Spruit, some 12 km from Malelane Gate, this fine new camp in the southern part of the park overlooks rolling hills to the east. Visitors are accommodated in modern, face-brick chalets and huts scattered among indigenous trees. Other facilities include a pleasant camp site, conference venue, restaurant, pool, and a walking trail for the blind.

3 Crocodile Bridge This small and pleasant camp is situated in the southeast corner of the park, on the banks of the Crocodile River, and also serves as one of the southerly entrance gates to the reserve. Visitors are accommodated in 2- and 3-bedroomed huts, and there is also a camp site and shop. Zebras, wildebeest, buffaloes, elephants and rhinos are common in the area, and hippos and crocodiles plentiful along the river.

4 Letaba Huge shady trees, mlala palms, green lawns and fine views of the Letaba River make this one of the park's most beautiful camps. Another important attraction of this central region of the park is its abundance of game, which includes several rarer species, such as sable antelope and cheetahs. Letaba is situated on the southern banks of the Letaba River, 50 km from Phalaborwa Gate. Elephants, hippos and crocodiles are common along the river and in the vicinity of the Engelhard and Mingerhout dams. Accommodation: Cottages, huts and furnished tents; there is also a camp site, shop and a fine restaurant overlooking the river.
The tusks of the well-known 'Magnificent Seven' elephants are on display in the recently opened Environmental Centre.

5 Lower Sabie This lovely rest camp, situated on the banks of a dam on the Sabie River, is one of the most popular family destinations in the Kruger National Park. It's a good base from which to explore the southern part of the reserve, which has sweet grazing and numerous water holes that attract an abundance of game and many predators, especially lions. Visitors stay in huts and cottages set among spreading trees and emerald lawns. Facilities include a camp site, shop and restaurant.

6 Maroela This small camping site overlooks the Timbavati River, and is situated about 4 kilometres from Orpen Camp.

7 Mopani Huts and cottages constructed from natural stone, wood and thatch are a feature of this camp (the newest of Kruger's camps), situated 45km north of Letaba, on the east bank of the Pioneer Dam. Facilities include a shop, cafeteria, swimming pool and conference venue.

8 Olifants This modern camp is built on a cliff 100m above the densely wooded Olifants River, providing guests with splendid views of the river and distant sunwashed plains. Other attractions are the beautiful and varied vegetation (including many fine old trees), and a great variety of game, especially on the scenic drives that follow the Olifants and Letaba rivers. There is a good restaurant and shop, and a conference venue. There are no overnight camping facilities, but Balule Camp serves this purpose.

9 Orpen This tranquil little camp, situated at the Orpen Gate, is a good base from which to explore the surrounding countryside. The water hole just outside the camp draws a variety of game; equally rewarding is the Rabelais Dam, 7 kilometres away. A few of the huts have electricity, and there is a small shop and communal kitchen.

10 Pretoriuskop Anyone with an interest in history will enjoy staying at Pretoriuskop, which is situated 9 kilometres from Numbi Gate, on the old wagon trail once used by Voortrekkers and transport riders. There are numerous historic monuments in the vicinity, including Ship Mountain, and the birthplace of Jock of the Bushveld. This large camp, set among rocky granite outcrops, is very picturesque, especially in spring when its coral trees and acacias are in full flower. Game-viewing is excellent – impala, zebras and wildebeest abound, and rhinos and rare sable antelope are often spotted. This camp has a shop, restaurant, pool and camp site.

11 Punda Maria Magnificent fever trees, sycamore figs, mahoganies, jackalberries and baobabs grow in profusion in this northerly part of the Kruger National Park, especially in the hilly country in the vicinity of the Luvuvhu River. Visitors wishing to sample a taste of true Africa will enjoy a stay at this small, rustic camp, which is built on terraces cut into the slopes of a hill.

12 Satara Large concentrations of game, especially lions, hyaenas, zebras and wildebeest, occur in the knobthorn veld of the central Kruger National Park. Although it lacks some of the lush beauty of the other camps, Satara (the second-largest camp in the park) has good, modern facilities, including a fine restaurant. There is a shop and a camp site.

13 Shingwedzi A lovely rustic atmosphere, diverse bird life and excellent game-viewing are the special attractions of this pleasant camp, set in flat mopane country in the northern Kruger National Park, close to the Tropic of Capricorn. A popular scenic drive follows the Shingwedzi River southeast to the Kanniedood Dam. Guests are accommodated in huts and cottages, and there is a restaurant, swimming pool, shop and camp site.

14 Skukuza In the early days of the park, Skukuza was nothing more than a ragtag collection of huts in the middle of the bush; today, it is a large, thriving community that accommodates hundreds of guests and staff members, and also acts as the nerve centre for the administration of the entire park. The camp houses a restaurant, shop, offices, reception area, bank, information centre and post office. The camp has over 600 beds, as well as a very pleasant and well-equipped camp site. Other facilities include a police station, doctor's rooms, open-air cinema and indigenous plant nursery, as well as an *a la carte* restaurant housed in railway coaches of the train that travelled through the park until 1972.

Private camps

There are five private camps in the Kruger National Park *(see map on opposite page)*, namely Malelane (B), Jock of the Bushveld (A), Nwanetsi (C), Roodewal (D) and Boulders (E). All of these may be reserved by groups only; day-visitors are not permitted.

One of the more rewarding sights in the Kruger National Park – a huge tusker lumbering through the bush towards a water hole.

KRUGER NATIONAL PARK

Malaria: The stealthy killer

The delicate *Anopheles* mosquito may seem insignificant when compared to the dangerous wild animals that roam free in the Kruger National Park, but it is in fact a far more sinister presence. This tiny insect is without a doubt the most dangerous creature visitors are likely to encounter in Africa, because it is the carrier of malaria, a disease that kills two million people every year, 85 percent of them in Africa.

The 'malaria belt' in southern Africa is roughly sickle-shaped, encompassing the far North Transvaal, curving south over the Lowveld, down through Swaziland, and finally tapering out just north of Durban.

This threat to public health has been compounded in recent years by the emergence of strains of malaria that are resistant to chloroquine, the drug that is widely used to control malaria in South Africa.

Anyone intending to visit an area where malaria is prevalent must take the appropriate antimalarial medication well in advance of their departure date. It is recommended that you consult your doctor or a knowledgeable pharmacist, who will be able to recommend an appropriate drug or drug combination.

The choice of drug will be determined not only by the area that you intend visiting, but also by the length of your stay, the time of year and your immunity. Babies, children under five years old, the elderly, and pregnant women are all considered to be at high risk of contracting the disease.

Apart from taking antimalarial medication, there are other ways to reduce the risk of disease: wear light-coloured clothing with long sleeves and long trousers, particularly at night; apply insect-repellent ointment or spray to your hands, face and any other exposed areas of skin; avoid wearing perfumes or scented lotions; avoid going out after dark; sleep under mosquito nets, and burn coils. Risk is reduced if you avoid visiting malaria zones during the rainy season, which is from October to March.

By far the largest of the Kruger's camps is Skukuza, close to the western boundary, and 'capital' of the park. More like a self-contained village than the classic African safari venue, it has a supermarket, shop, post office, bank and petrol station.

One of the more old-fashioned and charming of the Kruger's rest camps is Punda Maria, set among the rocks and evergreen trees of the northern section of the park.

LONG TOM PASS
Between Lydenburg and Sabie

Map: page 85, 7C

The Long Tom Pass is situated on the R37 between Lydenburg and Sabie.

Accommodation: There are numerous hotels and self-catering resorts in the Sabie and Lydenburg areas. On the pass itself, self-catering accommodation is available at Misty Mountain Chalets (about 30 km west of Lydenburg), P O Box 115, Sabie 1260, tel (013152) ask for 1403.

Further information: Sondela Tourist Information and Central Reservations, P O Box 494, Sabie 1260, tel (01315) 4-3492.

The spectacular vista from Long Tom Pass. During the Anglo-Boer War the route's twisting course and steep gradients helped Boer leader Louis Botha's retreating troops to fight a successful rearguard action.

Deep ruts carved into solid stone by locked wagon wheels can still be seen close to the Long Tom Pass. These are a stirring reminder of the great hardships endured by early transport riders who laboured over the Drakensberg Mountains on the gruelling 'Hawepad' (Harbour Road) between Lydenburg and Delagoa Bay.

Today, as one sweeps in comfort along the gentle, smoothly tarred curves of this splendidly scenic mountain road, it's almost impossible to imagine how these early travellers managed to hoist their heavy wagons over such rugged terrain.

For many years during the 1900s the Hawepad was a vital trade route to the coast and, in the latter decades of the century, it also served the burgeoning Lowveld and Escarpment goldfields. And although the story of this old transport road is a long and romantic one, the Long Tom Pass is probably more renowned for the bitter battles fought here during the Anglo-Boer War, when the hills echoed with the boom of the famous 'Long Tom' siege cannons, as the Boers bombarded the British forces after the capture of Lydenburg in September 1900.

The present pass, which was opened in 1953, closely follows the route of the original wagon trail, linking Lydenburg in the west with the forestry town of Sabie, 46 km to the east.

Today the pass is the second-highest tarred mountain road in the country, sweeping effortlessly through a landscape of rolling green hills, mist-shrouded mountain peaks and dense pine and eucalyptus plantations.

'The Staircase' is undoubtedly the most scenically attractive part of the pass. Other landmarks which have made a name for themselves over the years are the notorious Devil's Knuckles (a particularly treacherous section once dreaded by transport riders, whose oxen perished from exhaustion here), an old trading post, and the Long Tom Shell Hole, a crater (now overgrown) blasted in the hill by one of the Long Tom guns after which the pass is named.

Four of these Creusot siege cannons were imported from France to defend Boer forts around Pretoria. Two were taken over the pass by General Louis Botha in 1900. A replica of one of the guns may also be seen along the pass.

LOWVELD & ESCARPMENT

LOWVELD NATIONAL BOTANICAL GARDEN
Nelspruit

Map: page 85, 8C
The Lowveld National Botanical Garden is situated about 3 km from the centre of Nelspruit, on the R40 to White River.
Details: Open daily 08h00-18h00 in summer, 08h00-17h15 in winter. Admission charged. Kiosk and tea garden.
Accommodation: Hotel accommodation nearby at the Crocodile Country Inn, P O Box 496, Nelspruit 1200, tel (01311) 6-3040. Camping sites may be rented at Polka Dot Caravan Park, P O Box 837, Nelspruit 1200, tel (01311) 2-5088; and at Montrose Falls Hotel Caravan Park, P O Box 20, Elandshoek 1208, tel (01311) 6-3060.
Further information: The Curator, Lowveld National Botanical Garden, P O Box 1024, Nelspruit 1200, tel (01311) 2-5531; SA Tourism Board, P O Box 5018, Nelspruit 1200, tel (01311) 55-1988/9.

A world-famous collection of rare cycads is one of the star attractions of the Lowveld National Botanical Garden, on the northern outskirts of Nelspruit. These ancient specimens form only a small part of the spectacular variety of summer-rainfall plants and trees to be found in this lush, subtropical Eden, which has few rivals anywhere in South Africa. Because of its outstanding scenic beauty, the garden is a favourite picnic spot for many travellers who stop off *en route* to the Kruger National Park. However, if you are a keen gardener or bird-watcher, you may want to set aside a good few hours to explore the many delights of this secluded paradise.

The garden is located at the junction of the Crocodile and Nels rivers, whose granite cliffs and churning waterfalls provide a magnificent scenic backdrop. Wide, paved paths meander and twist through the garden, allowing visitors to explore the various plant communities. There are dim forest glades where rare, indigenous ferns and orchids thrive, sun-baked, rocky outcrops supporting aloes and figs and other drought-resistant plants, and generous plantings of subtropical species, with their luxuriant foliage and vivid colours.

Quite the most magnificent 'residents' of the garden are the graceful bushveld trees, among them the mighty baobabs, the cabbage trees and the wild figs, whose sinuous roots anchor themselves on rocky cliffsides. About half of South Africa's 1 000 indigenous tree species are represented in the garden.

A great diversity of animals finds shelter and sustenance in the garden, including many beautiful butterflies, some 245 species of bird, baboons, monkeys, buck, snakes, lizards and, occasionally, hippos which stroll up from the river in search of food.

Cycads stand like ancient sentinels above the undulating valleys of the Lowveld and Escarpment.

The Lowveld National Botanical Garden is famous for its cycads, which includes all the South African species, as well as imported specimens. Cycads generally are prized by gardeners because of their great rarity. Some unscrupulous collectors are prepared to pay princely sums for the privilege of displaying such specimens in their gardens, and their survival in the veld has become seriously threatened as a result.

Botanists consider cycads of exceptional importance for another reason: they are the surviving relics of a primeval plant group, the *Cycadales*, which existed some 150 million years ago.

In South Africa the cycads are represented by the *Encephalartos* and *Stangeria* genera, both of which are protected by law.

Ancient survivors of a primeval plant group

Cycads are gymnosperms, and differ from flowering plants in that the seeds are borne on a cone. They are dioecious, which means that male and female cones are produced on separate plants. In order for them to reproduce, cross-pollination is necessary. Pollen is produced by the male cones in autumn and transferred to the swollen seeds on female cones by wind, and also by beetles.

Because gardeners often own only a single specimen of a species, cycads in cultivation seldom reproduce or set fertile seed. In an effort to encourage collectors to hand-pollinate their cycads, the Cycad Society of South Africa has established a pollen bank where quantities of precious cycad pollen are kept frozen. The pollen is made available to the owners of female cycads so that they can hand-pollinate the cones to produce fertile seeds.

For further information about the Cycad Society, write to Professor Hannes Robbertse, 167 Astrid Street, Meyerspark 0184.

MOUNT SHEBA NATURE RESERVE
Near Pilgrim's Rest

A cloud of Knysna loeries rises above the forest canopy in a flurry of brilliant green and purple, a family of rare samango monkeys hurries through the trees, a waterfall sends up a silvery veil of fine mist: these are some of the memorable images of the lovely Mount Sheba Nature Reserve, set in a spectacular amphitheatre of mountains about 25 km by road from the historic mining village of Pilgrim's Rest. Forming part of the reserve is the luxurious Mount Sheba Hotel, a cluster of thatched buildings that clings to a grassed section of mountain slope, surrounded on all sides by dense montane forest where 1 000-year-old yellowwoods and ironwoods thrive in the refreshingly crisp mountain air.

This 1 500-ha private reserve is one of the last surviving stands of indigenous Drakensberg forest in the Highveld, a botanical treasure house featuring some 110 species of forest tree, as well as a variety of ferns, orchids, mosses, forest vines, cycads and tree ferns.

Numerous paths leave from the hotel, leading walkers deep into the silent, leafy forests, past deep, clear pools and many fine waterfalls.

Several old diggings and the remnants of wagon trails are to be seen on these lovely walks, reminders of the hardships endured by the doughty pioneers and prospectors who trekked across this lonely mountain territory.

The hotel itself is among the finest of South Africa's mountain hideaways, offering some excellent accommodation in thatched chalets and suites.

Adjoining the reserve is the wild and lovely Mount Sheba Game Sanctuary. Although this private farm is not yet open to casual visitors, self-catering accommodation is available in an old farmhouse.

Map: page 85, 7C
From Pilgrim's Rest drive west along the R533, up the Mullerseberg Pass. After about 12,5 km take the signposted left-hand turning to Mount Sheba. Follow signs along this road; the hotel is some 8 km further along.
Details: Open daily throughout the year. Meals and refreshments available at hotel restaurant and pub.
Accommodation: In chalets and suites at the Mount Sheba Hotel *(see below)*; farmhouse accommodation at Mount Sheba Game Sanctuary.
Further information: Mount Sheba Hotel, P O Box 100, Pilgrim's Rest 1290, tel (01315) 8-1241.

NZASM TUNNEL
Waterval-Boven

This historic tunnel near Waterval-Boven is an impressive tribute to the ingenuity of early railway engineers, and also a lasting reminder of the sacrifices which were made by the unknown number of men who perished while labouring to construct the famous Eastern Line linking Pretoria to the former Portuguese port of Lourenço Marques.

The Eastern Line was constructed by the Nederlandsch Zuid-Afrikaansche Spoorweg Maatschappij (NZASM) at the behest of President Paul Kruger, who was determined that his South African Republic should have its own corridor to the sea. The most complicated part of the route was the section of line that ascended from the Lowveld, up the Drakensberg escarpment, to the grassy plains of the Highveld plateau. Eventually it was decided to build the line up the slopes of the Elandsberg, between Waterval-Onder and Waterval-Boven. This spectacularly scenic stretch of line climbed 208 m in seven kilometres, with a gradient as steep as 1:20 in places. Special locomotives were needed to hoist the coaches up such a steep incline, and, in order to accommodate them, a four-kilometre section of rack railway was constructed. A portion of the old rack railway may still be seen near the eastern end of the tunnel.

The tunnel is 400 m long and was completed in 1883. It was finally abandoned in 1908 when a new line was constructed. Visitors may walk through the tunnel. At the eastern end of the tunnel there is a lovely picnic spot overlooking the magnificent Elands River Falls.

A short distance away from the tunnel is another national monument, a sturdy five-arch bridge made of dressed stone that once carried the famous Eastern Line right across the precipitous gorge of the Dwaalheuwel Spruit.

The entrance to the tunnel, which stands as a silent monument to Paul Kruger's bid for Boer independence. At the tunnel's eastern end are the splendid 228-m-high Elands River Falls.

Map: page 85, 8B
Travelling east along the N4 towards Nelspruit, pass the right-hand turn-off to Waterval-Boven. About 3 km further along, the road passes through a tunnel. On the other side of the tunnel is a left-hand turning that leads to a car park; the NZASM tunnel is a short walk away.
Details: Open daily. Admission free.
Accommodation: Self-catering accommodation and camp sites available at the Elandskrans Holiday Resort, Private Bag X05, Waterval-Boven 1195, tel (013262) 176; hotel accommodation at the Malanga Hotel, P O Box 136, Waterval-Boven 1195, tel (013262) 431; and at Bergwaters Lodge, P O Box 71, Waterval-Boven 1195, tel (013262) 103.
Further information: Village Council of Waterval-Boven, Private Bag X05, Waterval-Boven 1195, tel (013262) 58.

LOWVELD & ESCARPMENT

PANORAMA ROUTE
Graskop – Pilgrim's Rest – Vaalhoek

Map: page 85, 6/7C
Details: The Panorama Route is a 70-km circular drive on public roads. Admission to waterfalls and viewsites is free.
Accommodation: There are a number of camp sites and self-catering resorts in the vicinity of Graskop and Pilgrim's Rest, including the Panorama Rest Camp, P O Box 29, Graskop 1270, tel (01315) 7-1091; Lisbon Hideaway, P O Box 43, Graskop 1270, tel (01315) 7-1851; Pilgrim's Rest Caravan Park, P O Pilgrim's Rest 1290, tel (01315) 8-1221. Hotel accommodation available at the Kowyn Hotel, P O Box 64, Graskop 1270, and at the Royal Hotel, P O Box 59, Pilgrim's Rest 1290, tel (01315) 8-1100.
Further information: Pilgrim's Rest Information Centre, Private Bag X516, Pilgrim's Rest 1290, tel (01315) 8-1211.

Several scenic routes which track the broken edge of the Lowveld Drakensberg escarpment have been christened the 'Panorama Route' at one time or another, but this 70-km circular drive, arching north of Graskop, is probably the most deserving of the title. There are indeed many spectacular views to be enjoyed as the road winds over mountain and through pine-scented plantation and patches of tangled indigenous forest. Equally impressive are the beautiful waterfalls along the way, which are good places to stop for a leisurely picnic or even an invigorating dip in an ice-cold natural rock pool.

The route begins at Graskop, and may be driven in either a clockwise or an anti-clockwise direction. If you set off in a westerly direction along the R533, you will find yourself twisting and turning through verdant hills and thickly forested slopes as the road snakes over Bonnet Pass and then down to the picturesque village of Pilgrim's Rest *(see separate entry)*.

Just after the village, a gravel road branches northwards and continues along the western side of the Pilgrim's Creek valley to reach Vaalhoek after about 21 kilometres.

From this point the Panorama Route swings southeast along the R532, closely following the edge of the escarpment and passing through the plantations of the London Nature Reserve and the Blyde Forest Reserve.

Highlights of this portion of the route include the magnificent Berlin Falls, and Watervalspruit, where there is a pleasant spot to have a picnic, and a beautiful, fern-fringed natural swimming pool *(see Waterfalls feature)*.

Close by are the lovely Lisbon Falls and also Bourke's Luck Potholes.

Less than a kilometre from the road to Bourke's Luck is the turn-off to a scenic loop road, the R534, which branches off the main road at this point and rejoins it about six kilometres to the south. It will be worth your while to make this slight detour because of the numerous famous viewsites it offers.

Most splendid of all is God's Window, where a deep fissure in the mountain wall affords breathtaking views of the rocky ramparts of the escarpment and of the Lowveld 1 000 m below.

Also along this road is the Pinnacle Nature Reserve, which is named after the much-photographed granite column that rises like a bony finger from the dense indigenous forest that blankets Driekop Gorge. Take your camera along – the sights are worth capturing on film.

The Lisbon Falls are among the delights on the 70-km Panorama Route. Not too far away is the viewing point of God's Window.

PLACES TO VISIT

PILGRIM'S REST

In a country where picturesque historic villages are a rarity, Pilgrim's Rest comes as a delightful surprise to tourists. The little gold-rush village lies snug in the arms of a green valley, its wood-and-iron miners' houses straggling for about two kilometres on either side of the road, their modest façades and shady verandahs resplendent in new coats of paint.

Pilgrim's Rest is the only village in the country to have been declared a national monument in its entirety. The town, and indeed the entire valley, is soaked in the romantic history of the hunt for alluvial gold, a fascinating reminder of the harsh and heady days when the remotest and most inaccessible reaches of the Eastern Transvaal highlands teemed with prospectors who rushed here in their thousands in search of the elusive yellow metal concealed in riverbeds and beneath the mountains' green mantle.

Pilgrim's Rest has become one of the Lowveld and Escarpment's most popular tourist attractions, thanks to a careful restoration project undertaken by the provincial authorities.

Although it presents a picture of tranquillity, the village is anything but sleepy, its six museums, its Victorian hotel, tearooms, restaurants and shops drawing thousands of visitors every year.

But even the busiest peak-season days cannot possibly be compared with the excitement of the gold-rush years, when Pilgrim's Rest was a madhouse, its canteens and inns choked with thirsty, dirt-streaked diggers, its main thoroughfare churned to mud by scores of wagons and coaches, the banks of its creek pockmarked with yawning craters. In the village's heyday, there were 1 400 diggers living here, along with bankers, hoteliers, storekeepers, transport riders, prostitutes and a strange assortment of dreamers, desperadoes and adventurers, all of whom were prepared to put up with bitter weather and chronic shortages of supplies in exchange for a stake in this new El Dorado.

Alluvial gold was first discovered here by the famous Alec 'Wheelbarrow' Patterson, a salty Australian prospector who earned his sobriquet from his habit of transporting his possessions in a wheelbarrow. In 1873 Patterson left behind the goldfields at Mac-Mac and trundled off into the high mountains, where he found alluvial gold in the narrow, quick-running river later christened Pilgrim's Creek.

Hot on his heels followed another prospector, William Trafford, and although they tried to keep their discovery secret, word soon leaked out and treasure hunters from all over the world stampeded to Pilgrim's Rest. Prospectors staked out their claims along the river, each trying to include part of the creek, as well as the banks on either side.

By about 1877 the supply of alluvial gold began to dwindle, and prospectors drifted away, unable to afford the special mining equipment needed to extract the rich deposits of quartz gold that had been discovered in many other places in the valley. Several companies were formed to raise the capital for this equipment, eventually amalgamating in the year 1895 into the Transvaal Gold Mining Estates (TGME), a company which opened a number of new mines. Over the decades the valley yielded in the region of some 20 million pounds worth of gold. The last TGME mine closed in 1972.

There's so much to see in Pilgrim's Rest that it's worth setting aside a good few hours to explore the village on foot.

The best place to start a tour is at the town's information centre, just opposite the Royal Hotel. Here you can obtain a 'rambler's map', buy admission tickets to the museums, and browse through many interesting exhibits, including a pictorial history of Pilgrim's Rest.

Map: page 85, 7C
Pilgrim's Rest is situated 16 km northwest of Graskop, on the R533.
Details: Museums and shops open during regular business hours. A small admission fee is charged at museums; tickets available at the information office (opposite the Royal Hotel).
Accommodation: Luxury hotel accommodation at the Royal Hotel and its annexes: Royal Hotel, P O Box 59, Pilgrim's Rest 1290, tel (01315) 8-1100. Camp sites may be rented at the caravan park on the banks of the Blyde River, just outside town, tel (01315) 8-1367.
Further information: Pilgrim's Rest Information Centre, Private Bag X516, Pilgrim's Rest 1290, tel (01315) 8-1211.

A bird's-eye view of the town of Pilgrim's Rest, once a bustling little mining village and now a 'living museum' of the lively past.

PILGRIM'S REST

The quaint Old Print Shop, which is situated next to the premises of the Pilgrim's and Sabie News, is part museum, part shop.

The village store overflows with wares that sustained the early mining folk. Intrepid transport riders brought most of the goods in over the fever-ridden Lowveld plain.

KEY TO THE MAP

1 The Diggings A tour of this old mining camp (outside town) offers visitors a fascinating insight into the history of the hunt for alluvial gold. Included in the tour are a gold-panning demonstration and a lecture about the history of Pilgrim's Rest. Tours: Monday to Sunday at 10h00, 11h00, 12h00, 14h00 and 15h00.

2 *Pilgrim's and Sabie News* This turn-of-the-century building once housed the *Pilgrim's and Sabie News*. Exhibits include old printing presses, typewriters, linotypes and some early newspapers. The Old Print Shop, next door, sells books and souvenirs.

3 House Museum This museum depicts the domestic scene of a miner between 1910 and 1920. In those early days, miners were forced to improvise: some of the furniture in the house is fashioned from dynamite crates and paraffin boxes.

4 Royal Hotel A modest corrugated-iron façade conceals one of South Africa's most delightful Victorian hotels, carefully furnished in period style. The hotel has only 11 rooms, but seven separate annexes are scattered throughout the village, offering a total of 33 rooms.

5 Cemetery The old cemetery has many interesting old graves, including Robber's Grave, the final resting place of a hapless thief who was banished from Pilgrim's Rest in disgrace. When he tried to sneak back into the village at night, he was shot dead, and was buried where he fell.

6 Dredzen's Store Charmingly reminiscent of the old general dealers' stores that were once found in every country town, Dredzen's Store is crammed from floor to ceiling with every imaginable type of merchandise.

7 Reduction Works For many years the mine reduction works slumbered in a state of sorry repair, but a recent restoration programme has breathed new life into these old wood-and-iron buildings, which include a wheelwright's shop, smithy, carpenter's shop and stables. Tours: Monday to Saturday at 10h30 and 14h00, and Sundays at 10h30.

8 Joubert's Bridge This sturdy old 5-arch bridge spans the Blyde River, marking the northern end of the village. The bridge was built in 1896 and named after the Republic's mining commissioner.

9 Alanglade The neo-Georgian design of this imposing villa, built in 1916 as a home for the mine manager, was inspired by the work of architect Sir Herbert Baker. The house, now a museum, has 35 beautifully restored rooms, furnished in sumptuous colonial style. Tours: Monday to Saturday at 10h30 and 14h00.

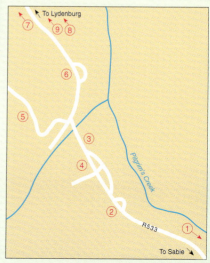

PLACES TO VISIT

PRIVATE GAME RESERVES

For those who yearn for a face-to-face encounter with the hushed majesty of the African bushveld, and don't want to share this experience with hundreds of other car-bound sightseers, the exclusive game sanctuaries of the Lowveld and Escarpment are the perfect solution. Several vast private reserves straddle the western border of the Kruger National Park. Together they comprise the largest privately owned tract of wilderness area in the country.

In size, these reserves cannot compare with the immense area of the Kruger National Park, but they do have the advantage of offering visitors a 'personal touch' that is rarely found in the busy state-run resorts. First-class service, excellent cooking and spacious, air-conditioned accommodation are all part of the package. But what is even more attractive is that these reserves allow visitors the rare opportunity to experience the wild African bush and all its inhabitants at very close quarters.

Experienced rangers and trackers accompany guests on walks and game drives through the reserves, eager to share their intimate knowledge of the rhythms of the African savannah. Because these experts are familiar with the intricate hunting and migratory patterns of the animals, visitors are able to spot a wonderful variety of big game.

Another major advantage of private lodges is that they offer guests the chance to take ranger-escorted night-drives and to view some of the elusive nocturnal inhabitants of the bush as they are frozen in the beam of a powerful spotlight.

There are numerous different lodges situated in the private game reserves of the Lowveld and Escarpment. The ones below are among the best known.

The private game reserves of the Lowveld and Escarpment are situated about 500 km, or six hours' driving time, from Johannesburg and Pretoria. For directions to individual reserves, enquire when booking. All lodges will supply maps. Many of the reserves have private landing strips, and air charters may be arranged. It is also possible to take scheduled flights to Skukuza, where guests are fetched by the staff of the lodges.

Ngala's beautifully thatched buildings grace the mopane woodlands of Timbavati's southern section. The lodge belongs to the Conservation Corporation, a private enterprise that ranks among the leaders in the field of ecotourism.

TIMBAVATI

This 62 000-ha reserve is probably best known for its famous white lions, a trio of which were first recorded here in 1976. Watered by the Timbavati and Nhlaralumi rivers, the reserve borders the central Kruger National Park, west of the Orpen Gate, and is carved into many separate private reserves belonging to some 30 different landowners.

Motswari Private Game Reserve: This private reserve covers just on 14 000 ha of mopane veld in the northern section of Timbavati Private Game Reserve, and has two small but exclusive lodges. Motswari is the more luxurious, its spacious, thatched bungalows set among spreading bushveld trees on the banks of the Sohebele River. Late-afternoon

PRIVATE GAME RESERVES

game-viewing drives extend into the evening and are followed by sumptuous dinners in the boma.

The more adventurous guest may wish to stay at the delightful M'bali Camp, which consists of a cluster of safari-style 'habitents' (tents under thatched roofs) half-hidden among trees overlooking the Nhlaralumi River and offering grand views of the river and the bushveld plains in the distance. The elephant and lion population are excellent in this area.

Tanda Tula Bush Camp: 'Tanda Tula' means 'Love the quiet', a very appropriate name for this lovely oasis in the bushveld. Eight luxury tents, accommodating a maximum of 16 guests, are scattered among bushveld trees overlooking a small water hole.

Each tent has an *en suite* bathroom, and its own patio overlooking the bush and water hole. This private reserve covers about 8 000 ha of open woodland dominated by knobthorn, and is watered by the Nhlaralumi and Machaton rivers. Huge breeding herds of elephants and buffaloes may be seen, but this reserve is perhaps best known for its lions. Long and interesting game drives through the bush are a speciality of Tanda Tula.

Ngala Game Lodge: A deep, shady verandah overlooking a water hole is one of the attractions of this large, sophisticated bushveld lodge, which accommodates guests in 20 thatched rondavels and one luxury safari suite. The reserve covers about 14 000 ha in the southern portion of the Timbavati reserve.

This is big-game country, where white rhinos, elephants, lions and buffaloes often are to be seen in large numbers, along with numerous lesser-known species. One of the special attractions of Ngala is a 'sleep-out' boma where guests are serenaded by the magical sounds of the African night.

Further information: Contact Motswari Private Game Reserve, P O Box 67865, Bryanston 2021, tel (011) 463-1990; Tanda Tula Bush Camp, P O Box 32, Constantia 7848, tel 0800-2200-55 or (021) 794-6500; Ngala Game Reserve, P O Box 1211, Sunninghill Park 2157, tel (011) 803-8421.

MALA MALA

This vast reserve boasts the biggest privately owned tract of big-game country in southern Africa, its 45 000 ha straddling the Sand River for a distance of more than 50 kilometres. There are over 200 species of game to be found in the reserve, including the 'Big Five', many smaller mammals and an abundance of bird life. There are three camps: the Mala Mala Main Camp, Harry's Camp and Kirkman's Kamp.

All three lodges offer luxury accommodation, excellent gourmet cooking with venison specialities, and filtered swimming pools. Game drives are tailor-made to suit guests' requirements and are all accompanied by experienced Shangaan trackers. Walking safaris may also be arranged. Mala Mala Main Camp, one of the world's best-known safari camps, is a favourite stamping ground of celebrities and millionaires, who are accommodated in luxurious ochre-coloured buildings clustered on the banks of the perennial Sand River. Those who wish to get away from it all usually prefer Harry's, the smallest camp, which also overlooks the Sand River. Here, guests stay in Ndebele-style buildings scattered among trees.

Further information: Mala Mala Game Reserve, P O Box 2575, Randburg 2125, tel (011) 789-2677.

Kirkman's Kamp is one of the Mala Mala reserve's several components, each of which has its own and very distinctive character. The main lodge offers the ultimate in safari luxury.

PRIVATE GAME RESERVES

SABI SAND

This vast reserve lies south of the Timbavati Private Game Reserve and is one of the world's most prestigious private game sanctuaries. Its various lodges are famous throughout the world for their unique African atmosphere and superb service, and are priced accordingly, drawing the well-heeled nature-lovers from all over the globe.

Inyati Game Lodge: This small and exclusive camp is situated on the Sand River in a vast area of virgin bush. The word 'Nyati' means buffalo, and guests are certain to see plenty of these, along with numerous species of antelope, wildebeest, giraffes, zebras, lions, crocodiles, hippos, cheetahs and elephants, as well as an abundance of bird life. The camp has a lovely patio overlooking dense riverine vegetation, and accommodates a maximum of 16 people in beautifully furnished thatched chalets.

LONDOLOZI

Londolozi is regarded by many as being the quintessential bushveld game lodge, and enjoys a worldwide reputation for its comfortable accommodation and peaceful African atmosphere. The reserve is situated about 20 km northwest of Skukuza, along a private road. A typical day at Londolozi begins with an early-morning drive in open vehicles and a late breakfast back at camp. Afternoon and evening game drives are followed by superb dinners in the boma under starlit skies. In the main camp, which accommodates 12 couples, guests are accommodated in luxury chalets overlooking lush riverine bush. Even more exclusive is a tree-house that allows a splendid bird's-eye view of the passing parade of bushveld life.

Further information: Contact Inyati Game Lodge, P O Box 38838, Booysens 2091, tel (011) 493-0755; Sabi Sabi Private Game Reserve, P O Box 52665, Saxonwold 2132, tel (011) 483-3939; Londolozi Game Reserve, P O Box 1211, Sunninghill Park 2157, tel (011) 803-8421.

Londolozi landscape at last light. Londolozi is owned and run by leading conservationists Dave and John Varty. John has earned international acclaim for his research on the leopards (left) of the area.

SABI SABI

This world-famous private game reserve lies on the banks of the Sabie River and has three lodges and a tented camp. River Lodge, on the river bank, accommodates guests in 20 luxurious thatched chalets, two suites and the executive Mandleve Suite, while Bush Lodge has 22 chalets and five luxury suites overlooking a water hole. Selati Lodge, on the banks of the Msuthu River, has seven thatched chalets decorated in turn-of-the-century splendour. The Nkombe tented camp uses the wilderness as a classroom for lectures on environmental awareness, and caters for up to seven guests. Guests are taken on safaris in open-air vehicles, and may also enjoy walking safaris. These are always accompanied by qualified rangers and trackers.

Game drives are followed by dinner served in an open-air boma around a roaring log fire.

PROSPECTOR'S TRAIL
Mac-Mac to Bourke's Luck

Map: page 85, 6D
The Prospector's Trail starts at the Green Heritage Picnic Site, 2 km north of Mac-Mac Falls, on the R532 between Sabie and Graskop.
Details: Permits are required. Groups are limited to 30 people.
Accommodation: Hikers are accommodated in huts with bunks, mattresses, firewood and toilets. Hikers must carry their own water. A list of hotels and self-catering resorts may be obtained from Sondela (Sabie's tourist information centre), which is situated on the Lydenburg road, opposite the Old Trading Post, tel (01315) 4-3492.
Further information: SAFCOL, Private Bag X503, Sabie 1260, tel (01315) 4-1058/4-1392.

Derelict mine shafts, abandoned diggings and overgrown wagon trails are among the historic landmarks on the Prospector's Trail, a five-day hike that begins at Mac-Mac Forest Station near Graskop and passes through Pilgrim's Rest and Morgenzon State Forest to end, 69 km to the north, at Bourke's Luck Potholes. The historic theme of this hike makes it unique among South Africa's many walking trails, while the rough terrain over which it passes provides an insight into the hardships suffered by early prospectors who, in a delirium of gold-fever, made the long trek over the mountains to stake their claims along the creek at Pilgrim's Rest.

A good dash of this hardy pioneering spirit is required from hikers who intend to walk this challenging trail, which is noted for its protea veld, cool montane grassland, plantations of pine and eucalyptus, and dwindling pockets of tangled indigenous forest.

The Prospector's Trail was opened in 1983 as part of the National Hiking Way System, connecting the Morgenzon Hiking Trail to the Fanie Botha Hiking Trail and the Blyderivierspoort walks. One of the highlights of the first day of the trail is the tiny village of Pilgrim's Rest *(see separate entry)*, where hikers are accommodated in a historic miner's cottage on the outskirts of the village.

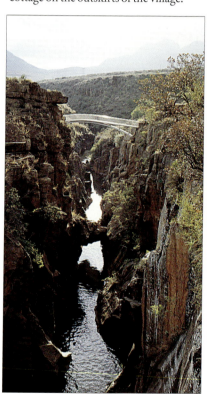

The convoluted Bourke's Luck Potholes (above), product of water erosion at its oddest, mark the finish of the 69-km Prospector's Trail. Attractions en route include old gold diggings, magnificent woodland scenery and the village of Pilgrim's Rest. The potholes are located on a steep-sided section of the Blyde River (right). Blyde means 'joy' in English, and commemorates the happy reunion of a group of 1840s Voortrekker women with their menfolk – pathfinders who had ridden ahead and were presumed lost.

ROTTCHER WINERIES
White River

Map: page 85, 8C
From Nelspruit drive north on the R40 towards White River. Just before entering White River, turn right towards Nutcracker Valley at the turning signposted 'Rottcher Wineries'.
Details: Open Monday to Friday 08h00-17h00; Saturdays 08h00-15h00; Sundays 10h00-15h00. Admission free.
Accommodation: The White River area offers a variety of hotel, resort and self-catering accommodation. There are also camping and caravan sites available.
Further information: Rottcher Wineries, P O Box 487, White River 1240, tel (01311) 3-3884.

Lush, lovely White River, 26 km northeast of Nelspruit, is the fruit basket of the Lowveld and Escarpment, a place of rampant growth and rolling farmlands, where a profusion of fruits, nuts, vegetables and flowers flourishes in the balmy subtropical climate.

Valencia oranges are among the important crops grown here, and at Rottcher Wineries in Nutcracker Valley these are used to make a variety of unusual orange liquors.

This winery is one of only three orange wineries in the country, and is among White River's best-known tourist attractions. Tours are available on a regular basis, and there's also a lovely tea garden where delicious country food is served in the shade of old trees.

Another important crop of Nutcracker Valley is macadamia nuts, which are exported in vast quantities to various countries all over the world.

At Rottcher Wineries you can buy fresh macadamias at reasonable prices, along with a selection of other locally grown nuts, including pecans, almonds and peanuts.

SABIE FORESTRY MUSEUM
Sabie

There could not be a place more fitting for a museum dedicated to wood than Sabie, because this forestry town lies at the heart of the world's biggest man-made forest region, and produces more than half of South Africa's pine timber needs. Part of this unusual museum chronicles the rapid development of forestry in South Africa, but far more interesting from the casual visitor's point of view are the many fascinating exhibits that celebrate the countless uses of wood in the world today, and its properties of insulation, elasticity, resilience, resonance and extreme durability.

The development of Sabie's plantations may be traced to the discovery of gold in the area. Alluvial gold was first discovered at Spitzkop near Sabie in 1871, but by the 1880s the claims were exhausted and large financial mining groups began to extract reef gold. Vast quantities of timber were needed as pit props in the shaft mines, and the few remaining pockets of indigenous forest were plundered for this purpose.

Soon it became clear to the authorities that renewable sources of timber were essential. After extensive research it was established that the Sabie region had similar climatic conditions to parts of Mexico, so the first Mexican pines were planted in 1909. Today various species of Mexican pine cover a total area of some 193 000 hectares.

Interactive displays in the museum include a display demonstrating the musical properties of wood, another showing how the hardness of wood is tested, and a 'talking tree' that tells the story of the evolution of the tree – fascinating stuff for adults and children alike.

Map: page 85, 7C
The Sabie Forestry Museum is situated in Ford Street, Sabie (opposite Sabie Primary School).
Details: Open weekdays 09h00-16h00; Saturdays 09h00-13h00; closed Sundays. Admission charged.
Accommodation: There is a wide choice of accommodation in the Sabie region, ranging from luxury hotels and lodges to self-catering resorts and camp sites.
Further information: The Curator, Sabie Forestry Museum, Sabie Village Council, P O Box 61, Sabie 1260, tel (01315) 4-1241; Sondela Tourist Information and Central Reservations, P O Box 494, Sabie 1260, tel (01315) 4-3492.

STEAM-TRAIN SAFARIS
Pretoria to Maputo

A steam-train safari through the lovely Lowveld and Escarpment will bring a lump to the throat of anyone who recalls the romantic sights and sounds of the golden age of steam travel: the clickety-click of swaying coaches, the distant snorts and hisses of a locomotive toiling up a mountain slope, the wood-panelled dining cars with tables resplendent in white linen and crystal.

If you are a person who enjoys life's little luxuries – and can afford to pay for them – then there is no better way to see the Lowveld and Escarpment than to hop aboard Rovos Rail's exclusive steam train. This stately relic of a fast-receding age regularly chuffs its way from Pretoria to Komatipoort, and on to Maputo in Mozambique and back, its staff pampering guests along the way with first-class service, fine wines and exquisite gourmet cooking.

Rovos Rail's private steam train is South Africa's answer to the Orient Express, an unashamedly exclusive service aimed at the upper end of the tourist market.

Rovos Rail was started by Rohan Vos, who salvaged 12 derelict coaches and three prewar steam engines from various scrapyards and farms around the country. Each coach and locomotive was painstakingly restored, retaining ornate period details but incorporating those modern touches essential to comfortable travel. Pride of Rovos Rail's collection is the 1924-vintage 'Shangani' dining coach, with its elegant wooden pillars and arches, and Art Nouveau light fittings.

The four-day steam-train safaris begin at the restored Victoria Hotel (opposite Pretoria Station), pass through Witbank, and then wind down the slopes of the Drakensberg plateau to Waterval-Boven and Nelspruit.

On you travel to Komatipoort, and there you are taken onto a private game reserve. The train then departs on its last 90-km leg across the border to Maputo, the capital of Mozambique.

You can also travel with Rovos Rail from Pretoria to the Victoria Falls – the widest sheet of falling water in the world. This is an adventure that will stay with you for the rest of your life. Other destinations are Durban, Cape Town and Dar es Salaam in Tanzania.

Map: page 85, 8B/E
Accommodation: Rovos Rail's steam train can accommodate 46 guests in a choice of spacious rooms, ranging from the sumptuous royal suites to the only slightly less plush *de luxe* suites, each sleeping 2 in dignified *en suite* style. Prices include all food and beverages. Safaris take place at set times throughout the year.
Further information: Rovos Rail, P O Box 2837, Pretoria 0001, tel (012) 323-6052.

One of Rovos Rail's grand locomotives. Passengers enjoy old-fashioned comfort and five-star cuisine on their way through the Lowveld to Maputo.

Lights create a ghostly effect in the Sudwala Caves. The caves are thought to penetrate more than 30 km into the dolomite rocks. The air inside remains at a constant 20°C throughout both summer and winter.

SUDWALA CAVES
Near Nelspruit

Map: page 85, 8C
A tarred road signposted 'Sudwala Caves' turns off the N4 about 93 km east of Machadodorp (26 km before Nelspruit). The caves are about 8 km further along this road.
Details: Open daily 08h30-16h30. Guided tours offered throughout the day. Admission charged. There is a restaurant and coffee shop near the cave entrance.
Accommodation: At the Sudwala Lodge, set below the caves in a wooded valley. Contact Sudwala Lodge, P O Box 30, Schagen 1207, tel (01311) 3913.
Further information: Sudwala Caves, P O Box 48, Schagen 1207, tel (01311) 6-4152.

The only doorway to mankind's oldest-known caves, and one of South Africa's most spectacular underground networks, is a fern-fringed opening, half-hidden in a forest on the Mankelekele Mountain. Step into the chill gloom of the caves, and you will find yourself at the start of an immense labyrinth that drives deep into the cold, rocky heart of the mountain. This network of interleading caverns and passages was formed over 300 million years by seeping waters slowly dissolving away the dolomite. Although a large section of the network has been mapped by speleologists, its furthest reaches have never been seen by human eye.

Stone-Age man once made his home in these chilly caverns, but the caves are better known for the bloody battles that were fought here by the Swazis and other groups during the 19th century.

Today the only permanent residents of the caves are three species of bat; their forebears were the source of the rich guano deposits that were once mined here. Fortunately, these mining activities didn't damage the caves' magnificent speleothems, great columns of frozen stone formed over the millennia. These weird dripstone formations include the Screaming Monster, the Rocket Silo and the Weeping Madonna.

The interior of the caves is festooned with a fascinating and bizarre assembly of cream-coloured stalactites, stalagmites and speleothems.

Close by, embedded in the roof of a cave, are collenia. These strange saucer-like depressions are fossilized colonies of a primitive blue-green algae that existed some 2 000 million years ago, around the time that the dolomite was deposited.

These fossils may also be seen in the P R Owen chamber, a vast, ringing cavern that has near-perfect acoustics and which has often been used as a successful venue for concerts.

Tours of the caves last about an hour and a half and cover a distance of 600 metres. If you would like to venture a bit deeper into the cave system, longer tours may be arranged in advance.

The spectacular recesses of the Sudwala Caves reveal a world of grotesque dripstone formations. The maze-like complex of caverns has been hollowed out of a massif known as Mankelekele (which means 'crag-on-crag'), and is rumoured to contain the 'Kruger Millions'. Visitors to Sudwala are restricted to a 600-m section.

Refuge of bats, and fabled home of untold wealth

The whispers of tourists and the rustle of bats' wings are the only sounds to be heard in the Sudwala Caves today, but in earlier times these caverns rang with the clash of spears and the anguished cries of battle.

From about 1815 to 1840, Somcuba, a wily old renegade who was joint regent of the Swazi people after Sobhuza's death, had established a settlement here, and this was where he kept the large numbers of royal cattle he had misappropriated during his reign.

When Mswazi, heir apparent to the throne, came of age, he attempted to recover the stolen cattle. Eventually, Somcuba and several thousand of his supporters were trapped in the caves by Mswazi and his regiments. Later, Somcuba was relieved by a Boer commando from Lydenburg, with whom he had earlier formed an alliance.

Rumour has it that Somcuba stored large numbers of diamonds and other gems in clay pots, and secreted them somewhere in the caves. An equally persistent tale is that the apocryphal 'Kruger Millions' are hidden in their murky depths.

This consignment of gold bullion and sovereigns belonging to the old Republic is said to have disappeared between Waterval-Onder and Nelspruit during the Anglo-Boer War. Boer commandos are known to have hidden ammunition for the heavy 94-pounder Long Tom guns in the caves, but no trace has ever been found of the most fabulous golden hoard in South African legend.

PLACES TO VISIT

Map: page 109

WATERFALLS OF THE LOWVELD AND ESCARPMENT

There is something about the sight of a river plunging over a cliff that is extraordinarily refreshing to the senses: the rainbow haze of spray, the rush of falling water, and the fringes of water-spangled greenery all create an ethereal atmosphere that even the most weary traveller finds irresistible.

The Drakensberg Escarpment, where the Highveld falls away to the hot plains of the low country, has more waterfalls than any other area in southern Africa. Numerous rivers and streams flow over the broken edge of the great plateau, tumbling through precipitous ravines and spectacular forested kloofs as they make their spectacular descent towards the Lowveld floor.

All along their courses, strung like misted diamonds on silver chains, are waterfalls, ranging in size from gentle, tinkling cascades, to dramatic torrents that plunge from dizzying heights. Although some are located in remote forested areas accessible only to hikers, many of the most spectacular waterfalls are to be found a few hundred metres off main roads.

The best time to photograph waterfalls is in the afternoon light.

BERLIN FALLS
Near Graskop

A special observation platform built above these falls allows visitors a fine view of this natural wonder, where the Watervalspruit plunges 80 m over a sheer rocky cliff, falling in a single broad strap of water into a deep green pool. This is one of the many spectacular beauty spots to be seen on the Panorama Route north of Graskop and close to God's Window. The Lisbon Falls, three kilometres to the south, are also well worth visiting *(see below)*. About five kilometres away, on the western side of the R532, is another popular picnic site known as Watervalspruit, where a deep, mirror-smooth pool, set among tree ferns and wildflowers, invites visitors to take a refreshing swim.

The Berlin Falls are 10 km north of Graskop, along a tarred road to the west of the R532 (take the turn-off to the Blyde River Forest Station and State Sawmill).

A graceful sheet of white water plunges from the Berlin Falls near Graskop. The falls are best viewed from the strategically sited observation platform.

WATERFALLS OF THE LOWVELD & ESCARPMENT

ELANDS RIVER FALLS
Waterval-Onder

This stately waterfall has lent its name to not one, but two towns. Waterval-Boven (Dutch for 'above the waterfall') and Waterval-Onder ('below the waterfall') are situated about 10 km apart in the beautiful Elandsberg range, where the Highveld escarpment plunges to meet the Lowveld.

The waters of the Elands River stream in three separate ribbons over a sheer 228-m cliff, splashing onto a tumble of rocky boulders before cascading into a deep, clear pool. The falls have been declared a national monument.

Travelling east on the N4 towards the town of Nelspruit, pass the right-hand turn-off to Waterval-Boven. About three kilometres further along, the road passes through a tunnel.

On the other side of the tunnel is a left-hand turning which leads to the NZASM tunnel and Elands River Falls.

LISBON FALLS
Near Graskop

The Lisbon River gives off a steady roar as it plunges in a double stream down a craggy, semicircular rock face, crashing into a wide, dark pool at the base of the cliff, some 90 m below.

A 100-m footpath leads from the parking area to a vantage point at the base of the falls, from which you get some really panoramic views. Nearby are some very pleasant picnic places.

The Lisbon Falls are situated 2,2 km along a gravel road that leads west from the R532, between Graskop and the Blyde River Canyon. The turn-off to the falls is situated about 800 m south of the junction of the R532 and the R534.

A deep pool, fringed by trees and rocks, receives the plunging waters of the Lisbon Falls. A pleasant picnic site adds to the attractions.

LONE CREEK WATERFALL
Near Sabie

Gauzy veils of spray float outwards as the Sabie River pours in a single, snow-white column over a sheer 68-m cliff draped in trees, ferns and mosses. The waterfall, with its rainforest atmosphere, is a spectacular sight, especially after heavy rains. A tarred road brings visitors to a parking area where there are braai sites and toilets. From here, a short circular walk leads through indigenous forest to the foot of the falls. Lone Creek Waterfall is just one of many waterfalls to be found along the Sabie River; others worth a special detour include Horseshoe Falls, and the beautiful Bridal Veil Falls, not far from Sabie.

Lone Creek Waterfall is situated some 10 km west of Sabie, along the Lone Creek road, and is well signposted.

A cascade of white water plummets over precipitous cliffs at the beautiful Lone Creek Waterfall. The fall's spray nurtures a rainforest.

KEY TO THE MAP
1 Berlin Falls
2 Elands River Falls
3 Lisbon Falls
4 Lone Creek Waterfall
5 Mac-Mac Falls
6 Forest Falls
7 Montrose Falls

WATERFALLS OF THE LOWVELD & ESCARPMENT

MAC-MAC FALLS
Near Sabie

Among the most splendid of all the waterfalls in this region are the Mac-Mac Falls, where the lively Mac-Mac River plummets in twin streams into a dark and densely wooded chasm. The sparkle of the water, the haze of droplets and the shadowy recesses of the ravine create striking contrasts of light and dark, making this one of the most photographed sites in the entire region.

The waterfall is 65 m high, and is named after the nearby village of Mac-Mac, site of a gold rush in 1873. The village is said to have been christened by Rev Thomas Burgers, who, on being handed a list of diggers, remarked that there were so many Scottish men working claims that every second one seemed to be named 'Mac'.

Two kilometres beyond the falls is the lovely Mac-Mac picnic site, which is the starting point for the Forest Falls Nature Walk *(see below)*.

Mac-Mac Pools to the south of the falls consist of a series of rocky basins filled with ice-cold waters; swimming is permitted and change-rooms and ablution facilities are provided.

Among the loveliest but less frequently visited of the escarpment's cascades are the Forest Falls, accessible via a charted four-kilometre nature walk.

FOREST FALLS
Near Sabie

Because it is situated some way off the tourist track, this beautiful waterfall has been spared the ravages of thousands of visitors. The falls may only be viewed by those who are prepared to embark on the four-kilometre Forest Falls Nature Walk, a lovely, undemanding ramble that takes walkers through pine plantation and pockets of indigenous forest.

The Forest Falls Nature Walk begins and ends at the Mac-Mac picnic site, about two kilometres north of Mac-Mac Falls, on the R532 between Sabie and Graskop. Permits are not required. A map is available from SAFCOL, Private Bag X503, Sabie 1260, tel (01315) 4-1058.

MONTROSE FALLS
Near Sudwala Caves

The Montrose Falls are situated at the foot of the Schoemanskloof, west of Nelspruit, where the broad, powerful Crocodile River roars over a 12-m-high rock face into a series of deep pools. There are two other falls, one above, and another below, the main cascade.

The Montrose Falls are reached by means of a 400-m loop road on the south side of the N4, near the junction with the R559 to Schoemanskloof.

Further information: The South African Tourism Board, P O Box 5018, Nelspruit 1200, tel (01311) 55-1988/9; SAFCOL, Private Bag X503, Sabie 1260, tel (01315) 4-1058.

DURBAN

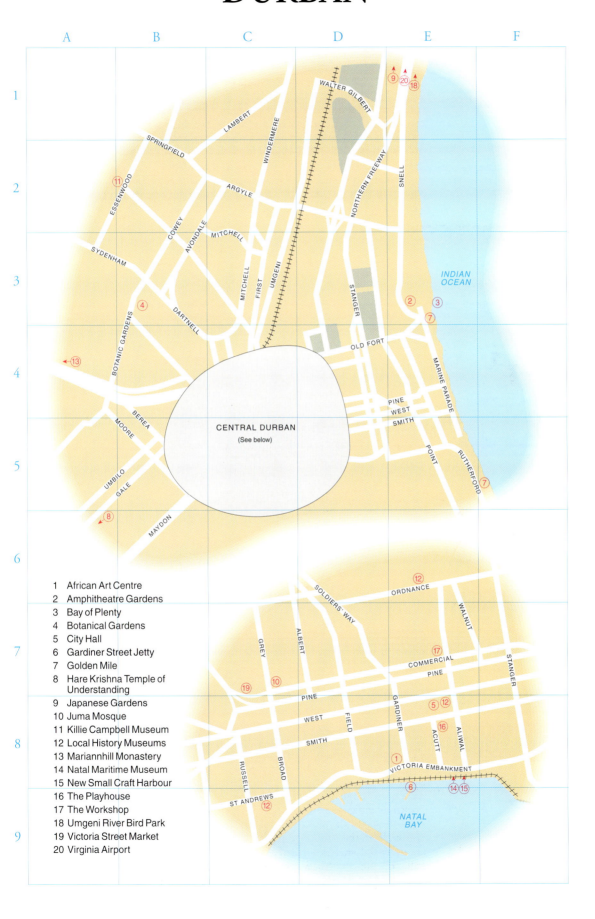

1 African Art Centre
2 Amphitheatre Gardens
3 Bay of Plenty
4 Botanical Gardens
5 City Hall
6 Gardiner Street Jetty
7 Golden Mile
8 Hare Krishna Temple of Understanding
9 Japanese Gardens
10 Juma Mosque
11 Killie Campbell Museum
12 Local History Museums
13 Mariannhill Monastery
14 Natal Maritime Museum
15 New Small Craft Harbour
16 The Playhouse
17 The Workshop
18 Umgeni River Bird Park
19 Victoria Street Market
20 Virginia Airport

AFRICAN ART CENTRE
Gardiner Street

Map: page 111, 8E
The African Art Centre is situated in the Guildhall Arcade at the lower end of Gardiner Street. If you're walking from the Royal Hotel, turn left into Gardiner Street and first right into the Guildhall Arcade.

Details: Open Monday to Friday 08h30-17h00; Saturdays 08h30-12h30. Closed public holidays. Find parking at the Esplanade, towards the Victoria Embankment, or park at The Workshop, and walk across.

Further information: African Art Centre, P O Box 803, Durban 4000, tel (031) 304-7915.

Durban is a city awash with crafts and curios, but for the finest and most original, head straight for the African Art Centre. This art gallery/shop is a non-profit organization committed to promoting African art and artists. The centre provides an important outlet for the work of the individual artist, and also offers a variety of self-help projects. As its role is to nurture and develop new talent, the centre holds exhibitions and arranges workshops in a variety of disciplines, to encourage the exploration of new ideas.

Over the years it has acquired a reputation for quality, originality and authenticity, partly from the individuality and variety of the stock, but also because of its stringent quality controls.

There's a huge range of traditional and contemporary arts and crafts. Apart from various paintings, drawings, linocuts and sculpture, you'll also find pottery, clay beer pots, baskets, carved wooden meat platters and walking sticks.

This is where you will find the Rorke's Drift tapestries and carpets. Heavily

The language of beads

For many people Zulu beadwork, while brightly coloured and cleverly woven, is merely decorative. Certainly, that description fits much of the beadwork that is mass-produced for the tourist trade. Yet, with traditional beadwork, each pattern and colour combination is imbued with a special significance. While woodcarving is the preserve of Zulu men, it is the women who weave the elaborate beaded items, ranging from necklaces to *iincwadi* or love-letters. A complex language of beadlore – which differs from region to region – has evolved over time, and been passed down through the generations.

The life of a traditional Zulu is marked by certain types of dress and beadwork, and it is through the beadwork that a person's status, as well as past and present commitments, can be determined.

As with western culture, courtship is the time of peak adornment. The more beadwork worn by a young man, the more obvious his appeal, and the higher his status, as most of it would have been given to him by girlfriends. In days gone by, young men would flaunt their beadwork in the village (that worn by particularly attractive and eligible young men could weigh as much as 15 kilograms).

A young woman's beadwork would have been given to her by a suitor who had commissioned his sisters or another female relative to make it. So a person's beaded ornamentation has emotional as well as social significance, and is very personal – the sale of particular pieces would mean the same as selling an engagement ring in western society.

The language that has evolved in beadwork is rich in poetry and symbolism, colours and patterns describing a world of meaning. The following guide is rough and superficial.

Pink beads were adopted by the 19th-century king, Mpande, which meant that pink became a symbol of royalty. Conversely, when worn by a commoner, pink means poverty.

The basic colour of most beadwork is white, and in common with other human societies, it means virtue, purity and truth. Conversely, black beads mean evil, but in some contexts can also have a positive connotation, representing marriage.

Different shades of blue mean different things: for example, royal blue stands for loyalty, while pale blue can charge the recipient with spreading gossip. Green symbolizes grass, and therefore home; while red can mean romantic passion or blood and anger.

Before reading and writing became widespread, beadwork served as legal documentation, and pieces were presented as evidence in traditional courts.

A Zulu woman bears a vibrant selection of beadwork. Each item represents a specific message.

The Zulu people are renowned for their fine craftsmanship, exemplified here by the woven rug and the sophisticated clay and straw work.

textured, richly coloured depictions of rural life – beehive huts, thorn trees, people and animals – are beautifully and boldly expressed in rich colours.

The centre is particularly renowned for beadwork, which is among the finest in the country. There is a small selection of antique beadwork, such as traditional Zulu aprons and colourful anklets, from the Tugela Ferry region. Contemporary work from the Valley of a Thousand Hills is original, creative and tightly woven. There are bracelets, belts, love-letters, necklaces, cute *sangoma* dolls, and even a beaded radio, complete with loops representing music.

AMPHITHEATRE GARDENS
North Beach

An oasis of beauty and tranquillity awaits those who have overdosed on the crowds, noise and excitement of Durban's beachfront. Directly in front of the Holiday Inn Garden Court Hotel are the Amphitheatre Gardens, a lovely sunken retreat, with wide lawns, cool fountains and fishponds, subtropical flowers and trees. Here you can sit and relax on a bench shaded by a thatched rondavel, and enjoy the passing parade.

These photogenic surroundings, enhanced by the backdrop of the sea, are a favourite spot for bridal parties to pose for their wedding photographs.

They are also a very popular venue for open-air shows, which can vary from the rich sounds of a Zulu choir, to a laid-back jazz band, or Zulu dancing. Contact the Durban Arts Association *(see right)* for details of what's on.

Every Sunday the gardens are ablaze with colour when vendors set up umbrellas and stalls in preparation for the weekly Amphimarket, Durban's most original fleamarket, where you can buy anything from curries to beads, from a bag of nuts to a warm jersey.

Map: page 111, 3E
You'll find the Amphitheatre Gardens on the Golden Mile, between North Beach and the Snell Parade.
Details: Open all year round. Admission free. Ample parking.
Further information: Durban Arts Association, 316 Avondale Road, Morningside, Durban 4001, tel (031) 23-1236; Durban Unlimited, P O Box 1044, Durban 4000, tel (031) 304-4934.

Tucked between the sea and the ultramodern hotels of Durban, the Amphitheatre Gardens offer a peaceful refuge for city slickers.

DURBAN

BAY OF PLENTY
North Beach

Map: page 111, 3E
The Bay of Plenty is part of North Beach, opposite the Snell Parade.
Details: The main surfing event is the Gunston 500 which takes place in July, although you can surf all year round. Surfboards can be hired from Safari Surf Shop, 28 Somtseu Road, Durban 4001, tel (031) 37-2176, and Surfmaster, tel (031) 37-4038.
Further information: Durban Unlimited, P O Box 1044, Durban 4000, tel (031) 304-4934.

The name Bay of Plenty alone is enough to evoke images of iridescent waves tipped with foam, and no wonder. It is one of the world's prime surfing spots, and the venue for important international and local competitions.

Bay of Plenty is really a misnomer, and actually refers to an attractive stretch of coastline next to North Beach, where the surfing conditions are outstanding and the waves regular.

When the big contests take place in winter, both amateur and professional surfers and their followers arrive from around the globe. The beach takes on the carnival atmosphere that accompanies most major sporting events – there are food, music and an endless parade of bronzed bodies. Surfing is not the only competitive activity: fiercely contested beach volleyball tournaments also attract the crowds.

Although experienced surfers make it look easy, newcomers to the sport are advised to proceed with caution. The sun, sea 'n surf atmosphere at the Bay of Plenty is so seductive that novices tend to get carried away.

The morning sun illuminates Durban's Golden Mile, bristling with pleasure parks, luxury hotels and a variety of holiday accommodation.

BOTANICAL GARDENS
Sydenham Road

Map: page 111, 3B
You'll find the Botanical Gardens adjacent to Greyville Racecourse, with the entrance in Sydenham Road.
Details: Open daily 16 April to 15 September 07h30-17h15; 16 September to 15 April 07h30-17h45. Closed Christmas Day and Good Friday. Refreshments available in the Tea Garden 09h30-16h15. Ample parking.
Further information: Parks Department, Durban Municipality, P O Box 3740, Durban 4000, tel (031) 21-1303.

The longest leaves in the plant kingdom (from the Raffia Palm), the largest seeds in the world (from the Coco de Mer), and the Giant Water Lily are just some of the attractions that lure visitors to Durban's Botanical Gardens.

The impressive cycad collection is internationally known, and includes the Wood's Cycad, which has been around for the past 150 million years, but is now extinct in the wild. These gardens are also famous for the Orchid House, in which the orchids are exhibited in their natural setting, and flower according to the seasons. Displays are changed frequently, so it is always worth a visit.

Appropriately, the Sunken Garden was built during the Great Depression in the 1930s, but year-round it is ablaze with colour, thanks to the thousands of annuals that bloom in abundance. Adjacent to this is the Fragrant Garden for the blind, as well as the Herbarium, which boasts aromatic, medicinal and culinary herbs from all corners of the earth.

Vivid blooms shimmer in the rarefied atmosphere of the exotic Orchid House at the Botanical Gardens.

CITY HALL
Central Durban

The magnificent domes and colonnades of the Durban City Hall have a regal, old-world character about them that contrasts sharply with the brash, multistorey office blocks so typical of the city centre.

One of Durban's most impressive landmarks, the City Hall was completed in 1910, and today forms part of a complex housing an art gallery and natural-science museum.

This art gallery is the second-largest of its kind in the country, and the beautiful interiors of the City Hall are perfectly suited to displaying the large canvasses of artistic luminaries, from Dürer, Degas and Rembrandt, to Kokoschka, Picasso and Rodin.

South African art is also well represented, and includes the works of Pierneef, Gwelo Goodman, Maggie Laubser, Zainib Reddy, Irma Stern, Derek Mumalo, Penny Siopis, Dumile, and many more. The works of these artists comprise the permanent collection, but the quantity of works and lack of hanging space means that they need to be constantly rotated. Displays of Chinese porcelain, Turkish and French ceramics, Eastern ivory carvings and a variety of silver and glassware are also included.

The Natural Science Museum is world-renowned for its ornithological research. The sounds of bird-calls accompany the realistic displays of birds and animals in their natural environment. The museum is renowned for KwaNunu, an insect gallery that includes an impressive collection of cockroaches.

Other exhibits include a life-sized reconstruction of a dinosaur, and an egg of the extinct giant *Aepyornis*, or Elephant Bird. There is also the mummy of an Egyptian priest, whose face has been reconstructed by a forensic expert.

Map: page 111, 8E
The City Hall is hard to miss in the heart of the city and is bounded by West, Smith and Aliwal streets, overlooking Frances Farewell Square.
Details: Art Gallery open daily 09h30-17h00; Wednesdays 09h30-14h00; Sundays 14h30-17h00. Natural Science Museum open Monday to Saturday 08h30-17h00; Sundays 11h00-17h00. The Art Gallery has free programmes for children every Saturday from 09h30. The Natural Science Museum has organized school visits, public film shows and guided tours.
Further information: Durban Art Gallery, P O Box 4085, Durban 4000, tel (031) 302-6231; Natural Science Museum, P O Box 4085, Durban 4000, tel (031) 300-6211.

Durban's bustling harbour, where international vessels berth below the modern skyscrapers of the city.

GARDINER STREET JETTY
Across Victoria Embankment

It's not enough to explore a city like Durban on dry land. For a refreshing perspective, get out on the water. Sarie Marais Pleasure Cruises offers various harbour and deep-sea trips aboard the *Jolly Roger*, the *Sea Isle* and the *Fancy Me*, from the Gardiner Street Jetty.

On the morning cruise you'll get a fascinating glimpse of Africa's busiest port, visiting all the major parts of the harbour, the Small Craft Basin, with tugs bustling back and forth, the T-Jetty, where the big passenger liners dock, and the naval base. You will also probably see coal-loading near the Point, and the awe-inspiring sight of massive containers being shifted at the container terminal near the Bluff.

The deep-sea cruise also explores the harbour before heading out to the open sea. The launch runs parallel to the beach for a sea gull's view of the Golden Mile, and then heads out to deeper waters, before turning back.

Depending on the weather, the seasons and just plain luck, you could see dolphins, whales and even sharks, such as basking sharks or hammerheads, which tend to stay near the surface.

Map: page 111, 8E
The Gardiner Street Jetty is just beyond the statue of Dick King and his horse (it's also known as the Dick King Jetty), at the bottom end of Gardiner Street and across the Victoria Embankment. Simply walk through the subway.
Details: Cruises leave daily (subject to weather conditions) at 11h00 (harbour cruise), and 15h00 (deep-sea cruise). The morning cruise takes an hour, and the afternoon cruise 75 minutes. A commentary is provided on the afternoon cruise only. Take along an anorak.
Further information: Sarie Marais Pleasure Cruises, P O Box 3805, Durban 4000, tel (031) 305-4022.

▶ PLACES TO VISIT ◀

GOLDEN MILE

BEACHES

Map: page 111, 3E

The beaches stretch for kilometres from south to north, the most popular being South Beach, North Beach and the Bay of Plenty. All the beaches are accessible from the city centre, by taxi, bus or a brisk walk.

Details: The beaches are at their busiest over the Christmas, New Year and Easter holidays. Don't leave your valuables unattended, rather lock them in a change room. There's ample parking, if you get there early. Refreshments. Lifeguards are on duty 08h00-17h00 daily.

Further information: Durban Unlimited, P O Box 1044, Durban 4000, tel (031) 304-4934.

From Addington in the south through to Blue Lagoon, there's no doubt that Durban's string of sandy beaches is the city's prime attraction. It is also the most commercialized beachfront in the country, and you are never far from a change room, deck chair or hot dog. The subtropical climate and Agulhas Current ensure year-round swimming in the warm waters of the Indian Ocean. Sea temperatures rarely fall below 17-18°C, even in winter, and summer temperatures can be as high as 25°C.

Although the main beaches are protected by shark nets, and are patrolled by lifeguards, you should not swim before dawn or after dusk. Keep within areas which are clearly marked as safe – the underwater topography is constantly changing, producing unpredictable side- and backwashes.

A number of long jetties extend quite far into the sea, providing a grandstand view of the waves as they pass; you can even study the surfers' techniques without getting wet.

The annual sardine run between June and August is a spectacle worth seeing. Millions of sardines migrate north from the southern and western Cape to breed, followed by shoals of game fish, sea birds and dolphins. During this migration, currents drive the shoals inshore.

The shark nets along parts of the KwaZulu-Natal coast are lifted at this time, so swimming is not recommended. However, if you would like to participate in the churning frenzy of fish that characterizes the sardine run, you are at liberty to join the jostling hordes of people who dash into the shallows, armed with buckets, nets and a variety of vessels to bag a free feast.

At the Umgeni River Mouth there is a spectacular view of Durban's beaches, and all kinds of water-related activities such as pedal-boating, canoeing, water-skiing and speedboat trips.

Early-morning mists shroud Addington Beach, where modern skyscrapers tower above fishermen whose livelihood has been supported by these seas for many generations.

GOLDEN MILE

Exuberantly coloured amusement parks, with their Dodgem cars, swings and roundabouts, provide lavish entertainment for thrill-seeking young visitors to Durban's waterfront esplanades.

Sparkling seas, cloudless skies, entertainment unlimited and luxury hotels combine to make Durban one of the country's most popular holiday cities.

FITZSIMONS SNAKE PARK

Most people relish a good scare, and the Fitzsimons Snake Park offers the incomparable thrill of watching a spitting cobra or deadly black mamba mere centimetres away, a toughened sheet of glass safely between you. Over 300 snakes from all over the world can be viewed at close quarters (the exotic ones housed in thermostatically controlled cages), including fascinating new and rare species. Although snakes are the stars of this show, there's a supporting cast of crocodiles, lizards, iguanas, geckos, tortoises, terrapins, spiders and scorpions.

There are five live venomous snake demonstrations a day, including a 20-minute talk on South Africa's venomous snakes, what to do if you're bitten, and more. Feeding takes place on a Saturday and Sunday after each demonstration, and if you're not squeamish you will enjoy the sight of snakes devouring dead rodents. The crocodiles are fed chickens (also dead) on Saturdays and Sundays.

This park is undoubtedly one of the country's most important snake research centres. Unfortunately, public demonstrations of venom-milking for snake-bite serum no longer take place, as this was found to be 'too stressful' for the snakes. The park offers a snake-catching service for people around Durban who have these unwanted guests in their houses or gardens. The staff's expertise is invaluable to medical practitioners who have to treat snake-bite victims. People who are really keen on snakes can take one of the park's herpetological courses.

Map: page 111, 3E
The Fitzsimons Snake Park is easy to find on the Snell Parade, just above the Bay of Plenty on North Beach.
Details: Open seven days a week: Monday to Friday 09h00-16h30; Saturdays, Sundays and public holidays 09h00-17h00. Snake-handling demonstrations are at 10h00, 11h30, 13h00, 14h30 and 15h30. Children's birthday party packages and concessions for group visits.
Further information: Fitzsimons Snake Park, P O Box 10457, Marine Parade 4056, tel (031) 37-6456.

LITTLE TOP

You don't have to be beautiful or talented to win a contest at the Little Top. Recalling the golden age of beachfront entertainment, it is a well-loved institution which began life as a small circus tent after the Second World War.

The present structure resembles a huge golf ball, and is the venue for contests ranging from beauty pageants to talent shows; Tarzan and Jane to the Biggest Tummy. A holiday favourite is the Lucky Legs contest which, according to compere Dan Bailey, 'is open to all girls over the age of 18 and under the age of 99'.

Prizes range from cooldrinks to free movie tickets and cash, and the winners are chosen by an enthusiastic audience. Off season, the Little Top is popular enough to attract about 1 000 people a day, and, at peak times, five thousand.

Map: page 111, 3E
The Little Top is situated on South Beach. Just look for a huge red-and-white golf ball.
Details: Shows are held daily during the season, and at the busiest times during the rest of the year.
Further information: Durban Unlimited, P O Box 1044, Durban 4000, tel (031) 304-4934.

GOLDEN MILE

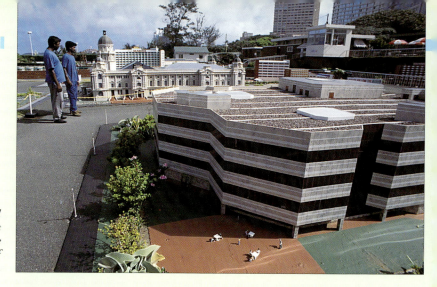

Minitown, built in 1960, was based on the miniature Dutch city at Madurodam, and contains some painstakingly reproduced models of buildings found in Durban.

MINITOWN

Map: page 111, 3E
You'll find Minitown on the Snell Parade, diagonally opposite the Elangeni Hotel.
Details: Open all year round (weather permitting), Tuesday to Saturday 09h00-20h00; Sundays 09h00-17h00. Closed Mondays and all major religious holidays. Ample parking.
Further information: Minitown, P O Box 2354, Durban 4000, tel (031) 37-7892.

For a Gulliver-like experience, visit one of Durban's favourite attractions for both children and adults – Minitown. This miniature city-within-a-city is built on a scale of 1/25 and features many replicas of the city's famous landmarks, like hotels and the City Hall, which you can study in detail without getting dizzy.

Spread out over nearly a hectare are more than 100 different features, including a fully functioning funfair, a highway, game park, factories, churches, hotels, suburban homes, a harbour with more than 200 000 litres of water (complete with ships, cranes and piers), a central railway station, and an impressive airport. All ships, cars, trains and planes are animated.

Like a real city, Minitown is constantly changing and developing, yet still retains many quaint, original features that date from its inception in 1969.

SEA WORLD

Map: page 111, 3E
Sea World is situated right on the beachfront at Marine Parade, roughly halfway between North Beach and South Beach.
Details: Open 365 days of the year 09h00-21h00. Show times vary, depending on the season. There are generally about 4 a day. Fish-feeding daily at 11h00 and 15h00. Shark-feeding on Tuesdays, Thursdays and Sundays at 12h30. Refreshments available.
Further information: Public Relations Department, Sea World, P O Box 10712, Marine Parade 4056, tel (031) 37-4079.

Ragged-tooth sharks – and an incredible array of marine animals – glare balefully at you through viewing ports as they cruise the busy depths of their holding tanks at the Sea World complex on Durban's Golden Mile.

After the beach, Sea World is the next place to visit, if you're at all interested in sea creatures. Year after year thousands of people are drawn to Sea World to visit its dolphinarium and aquarium. The main attractions are the theatricals performed by bottle-nosed and dusky dolphins.

Special shows feature the dolphins streaking through the water, jumping through hoops, 'standing' on their tails, fetching and carrying, and even posing on the slipway. You may even see a baby dolphin make a rare appearance.

The dolphins appear to enjoy their routines immensely, displaying uncannily human traits such as humour and mischief. Jackass penguins and Cape fur seals also perform, much to the delight of the children. It is best to avoid the very front row, as you risk being drenched by the playful dolphins during their momentous leaps from the water. After the show, head downstairs where you can view the huge pool below the surface.

Inside the aquarium an enormous 800 000-litre circular reef tank has spectacular close-up views of a variety of fish and marine life, including stingrays and turtles. Further on is Sea World's pride and joy – the shark tank, which accommodates one of the world's best displays of large sharks, including Zambezi, ragged-tooth and sawfish sharks. Every Tuesday, Thursday and Sunday at 12h30 divers enter the tanks to feed the sharks.

Later, consider retracing your steps to view the individual tanks full of fascinating marine life near the entrance to Sea World. And don't forget the shell room, with its beautiful displays.

Everyone visiting Sea World wittingly or unwittingly contributes to marine research undertaken by the Oceanographic Research Institute, which has a dolphin-, seal- and penguin-breeding programme. The institute also rescues and rehabilitates injured marine animals, and researches our marine resources.

A dolphin performs aerial acrobatics in front of visitors to Sea World.

GOLDEN MILE

WATER WONDERLAND

Kamikaze is the name of a popular ride at Water Wonderland, a tummy-turning plummet few can resist. But those who prefer something less challenging to begin with, can work their way up through other watery adventures, all of which end up in one of several sparkling pools.

The entrance fee entitles you to 'all day fun' and on offer are supertubes, speed slides, a ski jump, a ride on a large blue tube where you pick up enough speed to fly across the water at the bottom, and a long river ride featuring several rapids.

If you'd prefer to watch the action from the sidelines, Water Wonderland sprawls across a park-like tropical paradise with palm trees, shade trees and lawns.

A large tent is permanently erected for extra shade, a restaurant provides fast food and takeaways, and there are also braai facilities, so you can pack a picnic and make a day of it.

Map: page 111, 3E
Water Wonderland forms part of Kings Park, and is situated just off the Snell Parade, opposite Oasis Beach.
Details: Open 7 days a week 09h00-17h00 from late November to the end of April. May, June, July, October and November, weekends only. Water Wonderland closes for maintenance and repairs for 2 months after the July holidays. Parking available.
Further information: Water Wonderland, P O Box 10585, Durban 4056, tel (031) 37-6336/32-9776.

A panoramic view of Water Wonderland, with its turquoise pools, shady terraces and water slides, alive with the wet bodies of youngsters shrieking with delight at the thrill of the ride.

The water chutes at Water Wonderland snake between palm-fringed rocks before dumping their cargo into a pool of cool, sparkling water.

Durban's other marathon: the sardine run

One of those thrilling annual spectacles thoughtfully provided by nature is KwaZulu-Natal's 'sardine run'. It doesn't matter how often you've experienced it, the sight of the shallow waters glittering, heaving and writhing with a dense profusion of silver fish is breathtaking.

Every year in the cool waters off the southern and western Cape, millions of sardines mass in vast shoals, and begin to move northeastwards seeking warmer waters in which to spawn.

The shoals migrate up the coast for hundreds of kilometres, keeping well out to sea until they are driven towards the surf by ocean currents.

Their arrival is heralded by much fanfare. Thousands of sea gulls, cormorants, gannets and other sea birds wheel and circle noisily overhead before plunging into the moving meal.

Beneath the waves each shoal trails in its wake predatory fish such as barracuda, kingfish, queenfish, snoek, skates, rays and, of course, sharks.

The bigger fish have to confine their gorging to the edges of the shoals, as the abundance of small fish could endanger them by clogging up their gills if they ventured too far into the dense mass.

On shore, the appearance of the sardines is greeted with great excitement. Anglers, anxious to make the most of the sport provided by the unusual numbers of big game fish, compete for space; and on the beaches people of all ages are seized with an acquisitive urge, using any available item to gather the fishy harvest.

Millions of sardines are eaten on this migration, but the size of the catches depends on a number of climatic factors: low barometric pressure makes the fish sluggish, and therefore easy prey; but high pressure boosts them with the water's extra oxygen, filling them with energy. Heavy swells will send them into the deep water where they will escape predators, both human and marine.

Each female produces about 100 000 eggs, of which only a few need survive to ensure the survival of the species.

The migration ends just off Durban, when the shoals head out to sea to catch the Mozambique Current which will carry them and their offspring back to the Cape for spring and summer.

HARE KRISHNA TEMPLE OF UNDERSTANDING
Chatsworth

Map: page 111, 6A
The Temple of Understanding is in Chatsworth, south of Durban. To get there, take the N2 south, and the Chatsworth-Mobeni turn-off. Turn inland, and continue on the Higginson Highway until the Chatsworth Centre, where you turn left. The Temple is signposted.
Details: The temple is open daily 07h00-21h00 all year round. Ceremonies are held daily, the main one at 14h00 on Sundays. Guided tours are available. Ample parking. Refreshments.
Further information: Temple of Understanding, P O Box 56003, Chatsworth 4030, tel (031) 43-3384.

The gold-tipped steeples and glittering silver roof of the Temple of Understanding (comprising 35 000 stainless-steel roof tiles), mark it as one of South Africa's unique buildings. Surrounded by a moat and circular walkways which represent the eternal cycle of reincarnation, devotees crossing the water symbolically leave the temporal world and enter the spiritual world of the temple.

Spiritual upliftment is the aim of a visit to this temple and, upon entering its portals, you will be struck by its tranquillity and serenity. After removing your shoes, the sensation of cool marble on bare feet, combined with light streaming through wraparound windows (tinged with gold plating), suffuses visitors with a sense of spiritual wonder. Life-size paintings depicting the pastimes of Lord Krishna adorn the walls and ceilings.

The centuries-old Hare Krishna movement (based on ancient Vedic scriptures) has only existed in South Africa since the mid-Seventies, and this temple was built in the Eighties according to the wishes of

Worshippers at the temple present offerings to the ornate shrine of Lord Krishna daily.

The Temple of Understanding was designed by an Austrian architect, a faithful Krishna devotee.

the spiritual leader of the Hare Krishna movement, His Divine Grace Srila A C Bhaktivedanta Swami Prabhupada. A realistic idol of Srila Prabhupada (who left this world in 1977, shortly after his South African visit) has a significant place and a compelling presence on the left of the entrance, inside the central chamber.

An ornate altar contains the figures of Lord Krishna and his consort Srimati Radharani, who form the focus of the daily rituals. Incense, chanting, dancing and flowers form an important part of the ceremonial format.

Before leaving, end with a meal at the self-service restaurant which has delicious Vedic vegetarian dishes at very cheap prices.

JAPANESE GARDENS
Durban North

Map: page 111, 1E
To get to the Japanese Gardens, take the M4 north from Durban. After crossing the Blue Lagoon bridge, take the Durban North off-ramp. There are signposts to the gardens, which are about 1 km further on.
Details: The gardens are open all year round. Admission free. No refreshments available, but there are toilet facilities.
Further information: Japanese Gardens, P O Box 3740, Durban 4000, tel (031) 84-4606.

A stroll through the Japanese Gardens is like being transported into an animated scene on an oriental porcelain plate. The rolling garden is one of Durban's many green 'lungs', and you would be hard-pressed to find a more tranquil setting.

Winding paths lead through archways, past pagodas and lanterns, and over small wooden bridges. Willows weep into a series of lakes, where giant koi cruise beneath the surface, herons pose photogenically and Egyptian geese bring up their young. To soothe the spirit there are the sounds of cascading water, birdsong and the breeze in the trees.

Of course, such qualities do not go unnoticed, and the Japanese Gardens are well patronized, especially on Sundays. The sweeping Japanese style extends over 89 ha, so there is plenty of space, and the shady expanses have become a favourite place for Durbanites to picnic. There is a large braai area and a children's playground. Children also love the Rotary frog – a large golden frog which stoically accepts money posted into its mouth.

JUMA MOSQUE
Grey Street

In keeping with Islamic philosophy that you pray and worship where you live and work, the beautiful golden-domed Juma Mosque stands proudly amidst the blocks of flats and buildings of the Indian quarter. Built by Moslems who emigrated to Durban in the 19th century, it is the largest mosque in the southern hemisphere – between 4 500 and 5 000 people can worship here – and has recently been extensively refurbished.

The interior matches the outside for beauty, and is enormous, light and airy, with windows facing onto a courtyard. The walls are embellished with exquisite calligraphic texts from the Koran, and the floor is dominated by an oriental carpet that was specially woven for the mosque to mark its refurbishment.

A singular feature from the old days before modern public address systems is a recess – an indentation in the wall – into which the muezzin would call while facing Mecca, and his voice would reverberate back to the masses.

Map: page 111, 7C
The Juma Mosque is centrally situated on the corner of Queen and Grey streets, and is also known as the Grey Street Mosque.
Details: The mosque is open throughout the year. Durban Unlimited arranges Oriental tours, or phone the mosque for a free guide. Remember to remove your shoes before entering. Women should not wear revealing clothes.
Further information: Durban Unlimited, P O Box 1044, Durban 4000, tel (031) 304-4934.

KILLIE CAMPBELL MUSEUM
Berea

An elegant colonial homestead in the leafy suburb of Berea houses one of South Africa's most exciting collections of Africana. *Muckleneuk*, which dates back to 1914, was the dream home of sugar baron Sir Marshall Campbell and his daughter, Dr Killie Campbell, whose insatiable curiosity, energy and enthusiasm led to a wonderfully eclectic collection of art, books, furniture and other treasures.

The house is still furnished as it was when the Campbells lived there, and the magnificent furniture, art and rare oriental rugs, gloriously enhanced by the graceful architecture and grandiose proportions, are a splendid introduction to the museum, which consists of three main sections.

The Mashu Museum of Ethnology is a treasury of weapons, beadwork, ornaments, carvings, utensils and tools, including fascinating items such as the ivory bangle worn by the Zulu chief Shaka, and a stool carved with a small knife from a single block of wood by chief Dinizulu, while incarcerated on St Helena.

This collection is complemented by over 250 Barbara Tyrrell paintings depicting southern Africa's diverse customs, rituals and dress.

The bulk of the William Campbell Furniture Museum (named after Killie's brother) consists of furniture brought to Natal by the early English settlers. There are also superb pieces of 18th- and 19th-century Cape furniture such as *rusbanke* (settees), as well as contemporary and 19th-century African art.

A new wing houses the Killie Campbell Africana Library, Dr Campbell's lifetime collection of rare books, manuscripts, maps and prints which she assembled over many years on her travels all over the world. Notable items include early missionary imprints, photographs, letters and diaries.

Muckleneuk is now maintained by the University of Natal.

Map: page 111, 2A/B
Muckleneuk is situated on the corner of Marriott and Essenwood roads, Berea. From the centre of Durban, take the Berea Road and turn right into Essenwood Road. You will pass the Musgrave Centre on your right, and Marriott Road is further on.
Details: Open Monday to Friday 08h30-16h30; Saturdays 09h00-12h00. Phone to book before you visit. Hour-long guided tours are available, and tailored to suit the interests of visitors.
Further information: Durban Unlimited, P O Box 1044, Durban 4000, tel (031) 304-4934.

Killie Campbell, universal woman

There aren't many people who devote their entire lives and fortunes to creating a lasting historical legacy for the future, but Dr Margaret Roach Campbell was one such person.

Daughter of the sugar baron Marshall Campbell, Killie, as she was known by her friends, was irresistibly drawn to treasure-hunting: seeking out objects, artefacts, books and paintings that were relevant to the history of Natal.

An overwhelming influence on her was Dorothea Fairbridge, an expert on all aspects of Cape Dutch settlement, who had inherited a passion for antiquities from her grandfather, the famous bibliophile Charles Fairbridge.

Killie was fired by the older woman's enthusiasm and creative energy, and, with Dorothea as guide and mentor, they explored the Cape's old homes and gardens. It was here that Killie came to fully appreciate local art, architecture and history. She was determined to emulate Dorothea's achievements in the Cape by collecting various cultural and historical treasures of Natal.

On annual trips to Britain with her mother, she frequented antique and second-hand bookshops, and spent all of her clothes allowance on books, manuscripts, maps and so on. This was the start of her magnificent library, which contains more than 1 000 titles found nowhere else in Africa.

Killie Campbell – anthropologist, historian and bibliophile.

DURBAN

LOCAL HISTORY MUSEUMS
Central Durban

Map: page 111, 8E
The Local History Museum (the Old Courthouse) is just behind the City Hall in Aliwal Street. You'll find the Old House Museum at 31 St Andrews Street, and the KwaMuhle Museum at 130 Ordnance Road.
Details: Open 08h00-17h00 throughout the year; closed on Christmas Day and Good Friday. Admission free.
Further information: Local History Museum, Old Courthouse, Aliwal Street, Durban 4001, tel (031) 300-6241; (031) 300-6311 (KwaMuhle Museum); (031) 300-6250 (Old House Museum).

The picturesque and charming Old Courthouse is the appropriate home for this repository of Durban's colonial past. It was the first public building to be erected in Durban, and today enjoys national monument status. Here, old Durban can be explored with the aid of documents, maps and photographs; a variety of household and personal items have been collected and preserved, and the Durban Room on the first floor has replicas of the settler past – Henry Francis Fynn's wattle-and-daub cottage, Miss Fann's Fancy Repository, with essential items of Victorian paraphernalia, an apothecary which gives insight into early medicine, and a sugar mill.

A favourite among the many visitors is the costume room where early clothing, accessories and old uniforms can be inspected in detail.

The Old House Museum is one of the Local History Museum's satellites, and this bungalow with an encircling verandah is typical of the colonial style of the 1840s. Step through the front door, and you are transported back to 19th-century Durban. Much of the furniture and artefacts are the original contents, and many other fascinating old pieces of furniture and fittings are displayed.

One of the newest of the Local History Museum's satellites is the KwaMuhle Museum, which covers aspects of 20th-century industrialization. Housed in the old 'Native Affairs' administration building on Ordnance Road, visitors will also find displays relating to South Africa's past, like the resistance to apartheid, the much-maligned pass laws, trade unions and urban African administration.

The elegant Old Courthouse building – home to Durban's Local History Museum.

MARIANNHILL MONASTERY
Pinetown

Map: page 111, 4A
Mariannhill Monastery is about 25 km west of Durban. From the N3 at Pinetown, travel south for 5 kilometres.
Details: To visit the mission, apply beforehand. Teas and light lunches are available at the Tre Fontane Guesthouse.
Further information: The Superior, Convent, Mariannhill 3601, Pinetown, tel (031) 700-2411.

Once, the Mariannhill Monastery was the largest institution of its kind in the world, and remains Africa's biggest mission station. It was founded in 1882 as a Trappist Monastery by Father Franz Pfanner, an Austrian Trappist, who came to South Africa with a small group of monks at the request of a local bishop. However, the Trappist rule was not conducive to missionary activity and, in 1909, Mariannhill changed from a monastery to a mission institute.

As the years passed, Mariannhill developed into a vast complex of redbrick buildings in the neo-Romanesque style. Most of them were designed and executed by Brother Nivard Streicher, an engineer and architect.

The focal point is the twin-towered cathedral which rises above the surrounding cluster of buildings that include workshops, the Retreat House, the Mission Centre, convent, liturgical vestment department, the Tre Fontane Guesthouse, art studio, schools (both primary and senior), adult education centres, the Jabulani self-help centre and the extensive St Mary's Hospital.

The redbrick campanile at Mariannhill rises from a beautifully arched and colonnaded walkway and a peaceful courtyard.

NATAL MARITIME MUSEUM
Small Craft Harbour

An evocative cocktail of salty sea air and diesel fumes welcomes you to the excellent Natal Maritime Museum which comprises three fascinating vessels, an exhibition hall and a sea-cottage shop. For some, the highlight of the museum is the appealingly squat and sturdy classic steam tug, the *JR More*. This beautifully preserved craft was the last of its kind to be built, and now has the distinction of being the world's last remaining example of the powerful twin-screw model.

Two other vessels which are enjoying a relaxed retirement are the 1927 pilot boat, *Ulundi*, and the mahogany-hulled World War II minesweeper, *SAS Durban*. These three craft offer would-be sailors an opportunity to explore and examine every centimetre from port to starboard, including bridges, galleys, alleyways, decks, cabins and engine rooms.

A glance through the portholes reveals unique views of the harbour, from the far-off container terminal to the forest of masts gently undulating in the nearby yacht basin.

Children love the Pirate Experience: a replica of an old galleon and a simulated cabin where they can enjoy an audio-visual show chronicling the romantic and bloodthirsty history of the pirates who once sailed the seas off the coast of Africa, and among the islands of the Comores and Seychelles.

The exhibition hall has various displays of maritime memorabilia; the sea-cottage shop sells nautical souvenirs to keep memories of your visit alive.

Three old ladies of the sea form the basis of the Natal Maritime Museum.

Map: page 111, 8E
The Natal Maritime Museum is readily accessible, 5 minutes from the city centre at the bay-end of Aliwal Street. From the bottom of Aliwal Street there is pedestrian access via a subway or, if travelling by car, turn right into the Victoria Embankment, and enter the harbour at the Point Yacht Club. Carry on around to the left until you come to the Maritime Museum.

Details: Open Monday to Saturday 08h30-16h30; Sundays 11h00-16h30; closed on Christmas Day and Good Friday. Guided tours, holiday programmes and workshops are available. Ample parking. Refreshments available from shop.

Further information: Maritime Museum, c/o Local History Museum, Old Courthouse, Aliwal Street, Durban 4001, tel (031) 306-1092 or 300-6241.

NEW SMALL CRAFT HARBOUR
Off Victoria Embankment

To experience the hustle and bustle of a busy, working harbour, you can't beat a ride on the harbour ferry. This is the mode of transport used by fishermen and dock-workers who need to get around this enormous port, and what it lacks in luxury it more than makes up for in authenticity.

Aboard the ferry you experience all the romance and excitement of a large port, intensified by the chilly breeze off the water, the tang of the sea and the undulating swell.

While the ferry weaves through the busy maritime traffic, you can view the harbour through the eyes of a sailor: the arrivals and departures of ocean-going vessels, the thrill of being diminished by the vastness of a bulk carrier.

The ferry visits several piers, giving close-up views of the container terminal, the general cargo, the naval base and other spots, as well as rounding the Point, and crisscrossing the harbour entrance.

Map: page 111, 8E
You can catch the harbour ferry in the Small Craft Basin, right next to the Maritime Museum.

Details: The harbour ferry leaves every day at the following times: 05h00, 06h05, 07h05, 10h50, 12h00, 13h10, 14h10, 16h00, 16h30, 16h55, 19h30, 21h00, 23h30, 00h30.

Further information: Durban Unlimited, P O Box 1044, Durban 4000, tel (031) 304-4934.

DURBAN

THE PLAYHOUSE
Smith Street

Map: page 111, 8E
The Playhouse is centrally situated in the heart of Durban, opposite the City Hall in Smith Street.
Details: A variety of productions is produced and presented throughout the year, including special items during school holidays. Consult the local newspapers for details. Refreshments available. Ample parking.
Further information: The Playhouse, P O Box 5353, Durban 4000, tel (031) 304-3639.

Theatre is thriving in Durban, largely due to The Playhouse, an intriguing Tudor-style building that is home to the Natal Performing Arts Council. Don't be fooled by the old-world appearance: behind the quaint façade there are five separate performing venues, all featuring state-of-the-art design and equipment.

Starting as a grand picture palace in 1896, The Playhouse has had many reincarnations over the years. Just some of the international luminaries that have taken the spotlight include Noël Coward, Arthur Rubenstein, Maurice Chevalier, Spike Milligan and Liberace.

After much of the building was devastated by fire, extensive renovations were undertaken with the aim of incorporating as many of the original features as possible – the wooden beam and leaded window façade were retained.

The Playhouse reopened in 1986, quickly re-establishing itself as one of the country's most exciting theatrical centres. With its five main venues, The Playhouse caters for all cultural tastes. For tradition, glamour and opulence, head for The Opera with its original star-spangled ceiling of tiny lights. Well over a thousand patrons can sink into the plush seating and enjoy major operas, ballets, musicals and pantomimes with the benefit of superb visibility and acoustics.

Smaller musicals and plays are performed at The Drama. The Cellar is the popular venue for intimate supper theatre and cabarets. The Loft at the top of The Playhouse is for avant-garde productions, and The Studio features recitals, revues, one-man shows and jazz sessions.

The plushly carpeted grand staircase of The Playhouse. Opened in 1896, this theatre was the scene of the first South African screening of Charlie Chaplin's first comedy.

With its Tudor-style façade reminiscent of the days of William Shakespeare, The Playhouse offers a varied choice of plays, operas, revues and musicals to Durban's theatregoers.

THE WORKSHOP
Aliwal Street

Map: page 111, 7E
The Workshop is centrally situated on the corner of Aliwal Street and Commercial Street.
Details: Open Monday to Friday 08h30-17h30; Saturdays 09h00-17h00; Sundays 10h00-17h00. Closed on Christmas Day. Ample underground and open parking. Excellent security.
Further information: The Workshop, P O Box 1941, Durban 4000, tel (031) 304-9894.

Arguably Durban's most stylish, and certainly most famous, shopping centre is The Workshop, a recent venture which has sensitively preserved Durban's architectural heritage. The name derives from the fact that the centre was originally a series of old steam-locomotive rail workshop sheds. The renovation took place in the mid-Eighties, when the tide had finally turned in favour of preserving rather than wholesale tearing down.

The result is a spacious, bright and airy mall, natural light pouring in from the conservatory-like roof. The Victorian architecture, with its supportive structures and girders, has been retained throughout, and the designers have extended the elegance and grandeur of the Victorian era to the interior, with the style of the shopfronts, details like lampposts, and barrows which stock all kinds of home-industry goods and crafts.

This elegant and up-market mall describes itself as a speciality shopping centre, with 130 shops and 30 barrows spread over two levels. You'll be able to wander at leisure past areas named after old railway platforms, and gaze at a huge cross section of merchandise. Boutiques feature the best local designer clothes, gifts, crafts, curios, books and African art; there are also jewellers, coffee shops, takeaways, restaurants, cinemas, banks, a delicatessen and a supermarket.

Also within the complex is the interesting old stationmaster's house, which is now a national monument that provides a wonderful venue for a restaurant.

Crowned cranes at the Umgeni River Bird Park. These striking birds forage in marshlands and grassveld.

UMGENI RIVER BIRD PARK
Durban North

It's hard to believe that the lush, tropical setting of the Umgeni River Bird Park was once an old, disused quarry. Only 1,5 km from the Umgeni River Mouth, a stone's throw from the heart of Durban, this park is rated among the top three bird parks in the world, and is set against a stunning backdrop of 30-m-high cliffs on three sides. To add to the grandeur, three steep waterfalls run off the cliff faces and tumble into pools surrounded by palms, cycads and other magnificent plants, creating a tropical Eden which is home to over 3 000 exotic and indigenous birds.

Fig parrots, cockatoos, macaws, Amazon parrots, lorikeets, toucans, mynas, hornbills, loeries and pheasants are housed, in pairs, in individual aviaries. There are also four fascinating walk-through aviaries where the birds are exhibited according to geographical distribution or species.

Equip yourself with the park's self-guided tour pamphlet and stroll along the meandering walkways, through small glades and copses, and alongside pools which, apart from the resident flamingoes and cranes, attract large numbers of indigenous birds such as kingfishers, weavers, hamerkops, ibises, spoonbills, ducks and geese. There are comfortable hides for closer inspection, and informative, well-illustrated plaques are in abundance to enable visitors to identify all the birds.

No-one is ever in a hurry to leave this tranquil and exotic sanctuary. Should you get hungry, a thatched rondavel is situated among the trees alongside the park's largest waterfall, where you can enjoy teas and light meals in unsurpassed surroundings.

Map: page 111, 1E
The Umgeni River Bird Park is easy to find in Riverside Road. Heading north from Durban on the Northern Freeway (M4), turn left after the Ellis Brown Viaduct.
Details: Open daily 09h00-17h00. Children's parties and after-hours functions are catered for. School groups and pensioners are admitted at reduced rates. Ample parking.
Further information: Umgeni River Bird Park, P O Box 35205, Northway 4065, Durban, tel (031) 83-1733/4.

An extravagantly plumed macaw, native to the tropics, eyes visitors to the Umgeni River Bird Park.

VICTORIA STREET MARKET
Central Durban

Map: page 111, 7C
You can't miss the Victoria Street Market in the heart of Durban on the corner of Queen and Victoria streets.
Details: Open 7 days a week, Monday to Saturday 06h00-18h00; Sundays 10h00-16h00. Basement parking is available; the entrance is on Queen Street.
Further information: Small Business Development Corporation, P O Box 48882, Qualbert 4078, tel (031) 306-4021/2.

The bright and brash Victoria Street Market has risen from the ashes of that famous Durban institution, the old Indian Market. The change came about when it was decided that the site of the old market was too dangerous for both traders and shoppers, and that a new venue, closer to the main shopping area, was needed. The Small Business Development Corporation provided the modern, three-storey mall which bears the distinction of having no less than 11 different domes, each carefully styled after a public building in India. Although the romance of the old market no longer exists, convenience almost makes up for it, and, thankfully, the Indian spirit still flourishes in this new venue.

Spice and incense permeate the 180 shops, kiosks and stalls that trade here. This is the starting point for anyone seeking value for money – the choice is bewildering. Around every corner are pyramids of richly coloured spices, nuts, pulses, grains, dried beans, fruit and vegetables of every description. From cumin to saffron, tamarind to vanilla pods, you'll find it here.

Hardened carnivores will find the fish and meat market well worth a visit. Apart from pork (the market is halal), there are all kinds of edible flesh, from rabbit and goat meat to the more prosaic lamb and beef; and portioned from every conceivable body part, from chicken feet and necks, to livers and giblets. For seafood lovers, there are mountains of prawns, crabs, mussels and crayfish, as well as a good selection of fresh fish.

A feast for the eyes awaits you in the sari and fabric emporia, Aladdin's caves filled with huge bolts of jewel-bright silks in every colour, from rich magentas to peacock blue, shot through with metallic thread. There are also checked cottons from Madras and sheer voiles, all irresistible. Indian crafts and handiwork are well represented, with plenty of woodcarving, inlaid furniture, brassware and exquisite silver, gold and ivory jewellery. Fortunately, autobanks are conveniently situated nearby, and when you're completely exhausted, you can stagger to one of many restaurants with your purchases, and round off the experience with an authentic Indian meal.

The exterior of the Victoria Street Market belies the bustle of its oriental interior.

VIRGINIA AIRPORT
Durban North

Map: page 111, 1E
Virginia Airport is situated about 12 km north of Durban. Drive north on the N2, and take the Virginia off-ramp. Turn right under the bridge, and you'll see the airport in front of you.
Details: With Mid-East Charters all trips depend on pilot availability. A minimum of 2 hours' notice is required, but it is preferable to book on the day before. Court Helicopters requires 48 hours' notice.
Further information: Africa Airport Consultants, P O Box 22578, Glenashley 4022, tel (031) 84-4144; Mid-East Charters, P O Box 20316, Durban North 4016, tel (031) 83-8505; Court Helicopters, P O Box 22495, Glenashley 4022, tel (031) 83-9513.

It is possible to see most of Durban's major sights in less than half an hour, without paying any entrance fees. However, it's far better to treat yourself to a short air flip as an introduction to the city, to whet your appetite; or as a memorable way of rounding off a visit – a final fling, so to speak.

Virginia Airport, just 12 km from Durban, has a number of companies offering sightseeing trips, in both fixed-wing craft or helicopters. If a bird's-eye view appeals, Court Helicopters will buzz you over the city, harbour and beachfront for 15 minutes, producing the thrilling sensation that only a helicopter can offer.

A wider-ranging trip is available from Mid-East Charters, whose 20-minute flips in a light aircraft are for a maximum of three people, but they are happy to tailor a trip to your needs if you want to spend longer in the air. The standard flip hugs the coast from Umhlanga up to Ballito, back to Durban, and over the beachfront and harbour.

A lot depends on the weather, but there can be few more exciting and rewarding ways of exploring Durban and its surrounds. From this angle you can appreciate the beauty of the coastline, where the colours of the ocean merge, from ink to aquamarine, depending on the depth of the water. Shoals of fish show up as shadows, and schools of dolphins making their way up the coast are a common sight. Finally, a toytown overview of Durban with its enormous harbour makes for an unforgettable experience.

CENTRAL KWAZULU-NATAL

ALBERT FALLS NATURE RESERVE
Near Pietermaritzburg

Map: page 127, 2/3D
From Pietermaritzburg take the R33 towards Greytown for 22 km, until you reach the Albert Falls turn-off. From here follow the signposts to the reserve, 2 km further on.
Details: Open 08h00-13h00, and 14h00-16h30, Monday to Sunday. Overnight visitors must take up accommodation before 16h00 on the day of arrival. No pets. All boats must be registered with the Natal Parks Board.
Accommodation: Two fully equipped, hutted camps: Notuli and Bon Accorde, each with rondavels and chalets. Notuli has a camp site at the water's edge; Bon Accorde has 2 camp sites and squash courts.
Further information: Notuli hutted camp: Natal Parks Board, P O Box 1750, Pietermaritzburg 3200, tel (0331) 47-1981. Bon Accorde chalets, and all camp and caravan sites: The Camp Superintendent, Albert Falls Nature Reserve, P O Box 31, Cramond 3420, tel (03393) 202/3.

Boating, water-skiing, sailing, fishing, bird-watching and game-viewing are just some of the attractions at the delightful Albert Falls Nature Reserve, a half-hour's drive (24 km) from Pietermaritzburg.

The reserve, established in 1975, includes the picturesque Peatties Lake, near Cramond, a popular recreational spot for locals in the Pietermaritzburg area. The lake was expanded to include the 2 274-ha Albert Falls Dam, which serves as a catchment area for the Umgeni, Doornspruit and Nculwane rivers.

There's a little bit for everyone at this reserve: there are several picnic spots in the vicinity of Albert Falls; a 200-ha game park, with a variety of mammals and birds; canoe races, held regularly below the falls; and a national bass tournament held each September. Follow the self-guided, two-kilometre Nyoni Trail, which winds gently through clumps of thorn scrub and open grasslands overlooking the tranquil lake. The trail starts at Notuli Chalet (parking available here), and ends at the Notuli camp site.

Animals here include zebras, impala, blesbok, reedbuck, grey duiker, springbok, bushbuck, red hartebeest and oribi. Fish eagles nest in tall trees in the vicinity of the lake, and along its fringes you can see such water birds as cranes, herons, cormorants and ducks.

The Notuli chalet camp, in the small game park that lies six kilometres from the entrance gate, offers comfortable accommodation in rondavels and chalets, while the Bon Accorde camp has sites for campers and caravanners, as well as 10 five-bed chalets.

Visitors enjoy fireside camaraderie in the Albert Falls Nature Reserve.

Watersports, particularly powerboating, are popular at Peatties Lake.

BAYNESFIELD ESTATE
Near Pietermaritzburg

Map: page 127, 4D
Drive 80 km west from Durban on the N3, then turn onto the R56 (the Ixopo/Richmond road). After 12 km turn left at the T-junction, drive 400 m, then turn right at the Baynesfield sign. The entrance to the estate is 6 km further on.
Details: The house and 2,4-ha garden are open for tours by appointment (minimum 10 people).
Accommodation: The overnight Baynes Cottage has 10 beds, toilet, water, a coal stove, paraffin lamps and cooking equipment. Bring your own food, crockery and sleeping bags. Nearby Pietermaritzburg also offers plenty of accommodation.
Further information: Baynesfield Estate, P O Baynesfield 3770, tel (0332) 51-0043.

A beautiful valley, surrounded by gentle, rolling hills, runs through this estate, in a sylvan setting of open grasslands and forests of indigenous black stinkwood, Cape chestnut and yellowwood trees.

The forests and grasslands provide an ideal habitat for 115 bird species, including the endangered blue swallow, and a thriving community of small mammals such as common reedbuck, blue and grey duiker, bushbuck, Cape clawless otters, genets, vervet and samango monkeys and caracals.

One- and two-day trails wind through the estate, following the old road built by Baynes himself, passing through wetland areas via a rustic bridge, and climbing natural terraces to reach the overnight Baynes Cottage. You bypass the old quarry from which stone was excavated for the original buildings, and a furrow once used to transport water to a turbine. This was one of the first hydroelectric schemes in the country, providing electricity for the house and the creamery.

Baynesfield Estate belonged to farmer Joseph Baynes, son of a Byrne settler, and was left to the State in the 1920s to foster scientific research, create agricultural schools and colleges, and to serve as a public park.

The estate's museum, housed in what used to be the first butter factory in the province, has some compelling exhibits: medals, trophies, books and Baynes's farming diary, whose aged pages record the life and times of the pioneer farmers of 100 years ago.

The museum, along with the main residence, Baynes House, and South Africa's first cattle-dipping tank, has been declared a national monument.

CROCWORLD
Scottburgh

For close encounters of the crocodile kind, there's no better place than this reptilian den, where more than 10 000 of these primeval amphibians wait to impress you with fearsome anatomies and gaping jaws.

Crocworld is not only the largest man-made home for crocodiles on the African continent, it also has the only crocodile aquarium on the continent. Here you can get various thrilling underwater perspectives, not only of crocodiles, but also of catfish and tigerfish, and water monitors as well.

Close-up views of hundreds of giant crocs at feeding time, snapping their jaws and devouring the morsels tossed to them, is an experience you're unlikely to shake off in a hurry.

The crocs range in size from hatchlings (incubated in the sandbanks) to giant antiquarians. Put together on one scale, the combined assembly would weigh about 200 tons.

Other inhabitants you're likely to see at Crocworld are fish eagles, flamingoes, jackal buzzards, bushbabies, and such primates as vervet monkeys.

There are also tropical fish in tanks, mounted butterfly collections, American alligators, dwarf crocodiles, terrapins, lizards and snakes.

The walkways and viewing bridges combine to make a visit to Crocworld a fun safari for the whole family.

The entire park, which is landscaped with indigenous trees and shrubs (most of which are clearly identified), can accommodate up to 8 000 visitors daily.

The large breeding dams, which house more than 300 adult crocodiles, attract a wide variety of birds: hamerkops, water dikkops, weavers and plovers. The icing on the cake is a three-kilometre nature trail through typical KwaZulu-Natal coastal bush where you can see monkeys, small antelope and birds.

Guided tours afford you an in-depth look at the business of crocodile-farming, including farming methods, skinning and meat-processing. There's also a conference and education centre, with video

Map: page 127, 5E
Drive south from Durban on the N2. Between Umkomaas and Scottburgh take the No. 110 off-ramp, and follow the signposts to Crocworld.
Details: Open 08h30-16h30. Restaurant open in the evenings. Feeding times daily at 11h00 and 15h00. Group bookings or private tours by arrangement.
Accommodation: Scottburgh and the KwaZulu-Natal South Coast offer a wide selection of accommodation.
Further information: Crocworld, Old South Coast Road, Scottburgh 4180, tel (0323) 2-1103.

The Nile crocodile, which mesmerizes visitors at Crocworld with its gaping jaws and rows of formidable teeth.

Crocodiles – ancient relatives of the dinosaurs

The giant reptiles you see at Crocworld are among the oldest living relatives of the long extinct dinosaurs, a fascinating, hugely varied order that ruled the earth from 225 million to 65 million years ago, when, for reasons that even scientists have not fully explained, they abruptly disappeared.

Crocworld's inmates are Nile crocodiles, the only kind among the world's 14 species found in the southern subcontinent's inland waters. In the fullness of maturity they can become six-metre monsters, and they account for more human deaths in Africa than any other form of wildlife.

Few grow to that length, however: adults tend to average around five metres, from their horny-plated snouts to the tips of their powerful tails, which they use to propel themselves through the water.

They are extremely strong swimmers. But for much of the day the crocodile remains immobile, basking on the sunlit banks and sand islands of the river (it does this to gain body heat), often with its head raised and its great mouth gaping.

For long periods, too, it lies almost completely submerged, with only its eyes, ears and nostrils above the surface.

A specially adapted fleshy valve, located at the back of the mouth, prevents water from entering the air passages. The nostrils and ear openings, likewise, have valves which close when they're fully submerged. During these motionless periods the log-like presence is barely discernible by the passing parade of animals and birds, and those incautious enough to approach too close are likely to perish in one lightning snap of its massive jaws.

Crocodiles are carnivorous, their diet a varied fare of water birds, fish and small mammals. Occasionally, a larger animal is taken, and, if it proves too bulky to be swallowed, the croc will drag it down to the depths and rotate rapidly until a manageable chunk is torn off.

The female is an excellent parent. She lays between 20 and 50 oval, hard-shelled eggs in a hole or shallow scrape in the drier sand of the river bank. The eggs are covered, and then closely guarded for about 12 weeks – until the squeaks of the 250-mm young signal the beginning of the hatching process.

The mother then guides them (sometimes carries them in her mouth) to the water, where they remain in a kind of 'crèche' for several months. During this most vulnerable time they are fiercely protected by both parents. Nevertheless, the survival rate is low.

Crocodiles are prized for the fine leather they yield and, increasingly, for their meat, and they are intensively farmed in many parts of southern Africa.

In reptilian terms, they have reasonably well-developed brains and, when reared in captivity, they can display some surprisingly advanced behaviour. They are able to relate (though in a very modest way) to humans, adapt to well-established routines, recognize their keepers and, in some instances, tolerate a certain amount of handling.

CENTRAL KWAZULU-NATAL

At Crocworld, a network of paths winds through the bush, revealing reptile-filled enclosures and a varied bird life.

presentations and some very interesting natural-history exhibits providing facts on crocodiles and their evolution.

For children there's a playground, a bunny park and a petting farmyard.

An *a la carte* restaurant (which is also open in the evenings) serves crocodile steaks and kebabs, plus scrumptious fresh cream scones and tea for those with less adventurous palates. A well-stocked curio shop offers books, crocodile-skin belts, bags and purses, fun T-shirts, some attractive ethnic jewellery, takeaway crocodile steaks and biltong.

The fearsome Nile crocodile basks lazily during the day, but usually spends the night partially submerged in water.

HAZELMERE NATURE RESERVE
Near Verulam

Map: page 127, 3E
From the N2 highway take the Mount Edgecombe/Umhlanga turn-off, and turn left towards Mount Edgecombe. Follow the road, ignoring turn-offs, and pass under a large, arched bridge. The first turning signposts the dam.
Details: Open 05h00-19h00, 1 October to 31 March; 06h00-18h00 1 April to 30 September. Admission fee charged.
Accommodation: Twenty-two camp sites, 16 of which have electrical plug points.
Further information: The Officer-in-Charge, Hazelmere Nature Reserve, P O Box 1013, Verulam 4340, tel (0322) 33-2315; Natal Parks Board, P O Box 662, Pietermaritzburg 3200, tel (0331) 47-1981.

This Natal Parks Board resort, just half an hour's drive from Durban, is a 508-ha haven for people who love water and its associated sporting activities: angling, jet-skiing, powerboating, sailing, canoeing and swimming.

The 218-ha dam, which is fed by the Umdloti River, has been zoned into different user areas for barefoot and classical skiing, sailing and powerboating. The Canelands Boating Club has its own private stretch of water here, and there's an attractive swimming area which is demarcated by buoys.

Nature-lovers can also enjoy short rambles or an hour-long trail through the wetlands here. If you're lucky, you may see a reedbuck darting through the undergrowth, or catch a glimpse of a fish eagle as it swoops across the water.

Afterwards you can enjoy a picnic under one of the thatched *lapas* on the grass, or cool off in the water (life-savers are on duty during the holiday periods).

Public access is by road, but a small section is accessible only by boat, adding to the sense of adventure. Fish species include bass, tilapia and scalies. Fishing licences are available from the office.

HOWICK FALLS
Howick

These falls, one of KwaZulu-Natal's truly spectacular sights, are known to the Zulu people as KwaNogqaza – 'the place of the tall one'. Here, from a viewsite above the falls, you can watch the dizzying cascade of the Umgeni River tumbling 95 m into the gorge below.

The falls are situated within the town itself. In the early 1800s the Umgeni River was crossed at a ford at Alleman's Drift, just below the present Midmar Dam wall. By 1850 the ford had been moved to the more convenient, but rather more perilous, site just above the falls. Many people, swept over the rocky ledges, lost their lives in the bubbling cauldron of spume below. One of them, a wagon assistant, was washed over the edge when his employer, a Dutch farmer, ignored the red flag which indicated that the river was in flood (during floods in 1987 the water cascaded over the falls at a rate of 1 000 000 litres per second).

The succession of fatalities included a young student, Charles Booker, who was dared to dive over the falls in 1940, with tragic consequences. Another victim was local schoolmaster James Bell, who is believed to have committed suicide. Today the falls seem less sinister, and are visited by thousands of tourists for the magnificent scenery, and the tranquil country drives in the vicinity.

There's plenty of parking near the falls, plus a tearoom with outdoor seating, a selection of attractive viewsites, and a rambling gorge-walk to the bottom of the falls, where the river continues on its journey to the Indian Ocean.

A spectacular veil of white water plunges into a deep pool at Howick Falls. The falls were proclaimed a national monument in 1951.

Map: page 127, 3C
Drive north from Pietermaritzburg on the N3. Turn off to Howick (26 km from Pietermaritzburg). The falls are to the right, before the central business district.
Details: Open all year around. No admission fee charged.
Accommodation: Ranges from comfortable hotels to simple camp sites. Try the stylish Old Halliwell Country Inn, P O Box 201, Howick 3290, tel (0332) 30-2602 or 30-6800; or the picturesque Fern Hill Hotel, P O Box 5, Tweedie 3255, tel (0332) 30-5071 or 30-2319. There is a caravan park close to the falls. For something completely different, try the Midlands Meander, a route that traverses the heart of the KwaZulu-Natal Midlands, with cosy accommodation *en route*.
Further information: Howick Publicity Association, P O Box 881, Howick 3290, tel (0332) 30-5305.

KRANTZKLOOF NATURE RESERVE
Kloof

Take your binoculars and a pair of hiking boots along when you visit this 535-ha reserve, 27 km from Durban. It's a favourite, easily accessible retreat centred around a well-forested gorge cut by the Emolweni River, and is popular with locals seeking a quiet day in the country, or a ramble by the waterside.

The lovely riverine forest, gorges and grassland are sanctuary to a teeming community of birds – more than 200 species in all.

Discerning bird-watchers are likely to spot crowned eagles nesting high in the cliffs, Wahlberg's eagles, Knysna loeries conspicuous in their metallic green and crimson plumage, purple-crested loeries, sparrowhawks, African jaçanas, helmeted guinea fowls, Narina trogons and scores of smaller species. Mammals include bushpigs, bushbuck, reedbuck, red and blue duiker, vervet monkeys, spotted genets and three species of mongoose.

There's a variety of attractive trails available to hikers. They include the four-kilometre Nkutu Trail, which starts at the Valley Road picnic area, the eight-kilometre Uve Trail, which starts at the Uve Road gate, and shorter rambles to the Kloof Falls and the iPithi Falls.

The trails take you through forest and grassland where you'll see quinine, wild pomegranate and wild banana trees, tree ferns, cycads and three species of protea.

The Nkutu Trail crosses a pleasant stream, follows the edge of the rocky escarpment, then winds down to a large pool at the bottom of the gorge. Take care on the descent (a walking stick for support is advisable), as the route is steep and can be slippery.

The facilities at Krantzkloof Nature Reserve include an interpretive centre, with some natural-history displays, and facilities for film shows. An education centre is nearing completion.

Map: page 127, 3E
The reserve lies 5 km from the centre of Kloof, and 26 km from Durban. From Durban drive west along the R613 to Kloof. Follow the Krantzkloof Nature Reserve signposts along Kloof Falls Road, through Kloof, and make your way to the bottom of the gorge.
Details: Open between sunrise and sunset. Admission free. Visitors should bring insect repellent, as ticks can be troublesome. Swimming is not recommended because of the risk of bilharzia. Booking essential for the education centre.
Accommodation: Day-visitors only.
Further information: The Officer-in-Charge, Krantzkloof Nature Reserve, P O Box 288, Kloof 3640, tel (031) 764-3515.

CENTRAL KWAZULU-NATAL

Map: page 127, 7D
From Durban take the N2 highway south for 118 kilometres.
Details: All-year-round holiday resort. Highest rainfall in March; highest average of sunshine days – April to August; highest temperatures – January to March.
Accommodation: Ranges from 4 hotels to 2 caravan parks, 4 guest lodges and wide choice of holiday flats and villas.
Further information: Margate Today, P O Box 1253, Margate 4275, tel (03931) 2-2322.

MARGATE
KwaZulu-Natal South Coast

Fringing some of the finest bathing beaches in the country, Margate has a casual, sun-soaked village atmosphere, with winding streets, cosy restaurants, lovely art galleries, and a host of tantalizing leisure attractions.

During peak seasons, when the younger set arrive in town, it fairly jumps with light-hearted entertainment such as beauty parades, musical concerts and beachfront competitions. Nightlife often goes on until dawn. Adding to Margate's physical charm is its wealth of lush, subtropical vegetation, and the fact that there's barely a kilometre or two of beach which isn't bisected by a river or stream making its way to the sea.

Margate's main beach is the safest and most popular on the South Coast – a vast area of golden sands and blue water, offering some excellent surfing, fishing and boating. Adding to the various attractions are a beachfront lagoon, a freshwater Olympic swimming pool, a children's pool, grassed terraces shaded by coconut palms, fun slides and an amusement park.

Other sporting activities at Margate include golf at the recently redesigned Country Club (visitors are welcome), scuba diving, squash, tennis and bowling.

The Wildabout Art and Crafts Trail takes in the Margate Reptile and Snake Park, which accommodates a variety of reptiles, including black and green mambas, and rattlesnakes. Shops and studios along the trail display original jewellery, pottery, leatherwork and other indigenous arts and crafts.

There is no shortage of food outlets in the Margate area – 22 in all, offering anything from five-minute takeaways to elaborate curry and crayfish dishes. The cuisine is cosmopolitan, too: Portuguese, Italian, Chinese and a range of local country cooking.

A wider circle of activities radiating from the town includes a stroll through the Uvongo Bird Park, where king hornbills steal the show; a visit to the Riverbend Crocodile Farm, home to more than 200 Nile crocodiles; horse-riding at Round Up Ranch; and a look-in at five nature reserves, including Skyline (an arboretum). Children enjoy visiting African Eden, an Angora rabbit farm located within one of the few remaining KwaZulu-Natal coastal forests.

Margate's annual airshow in May is the largest of its kind in the southern hemisphere, drawing hundreds of aviation enthusiasts from all over the country. Margate Airport, which is KwaZulu-Natal's second-largest, offers microlight flips and formal instruction on how to fly.

Sun-bronzed beaches, washed by the warm waters of the Indian Ocean, are the star attractions at Margate.

A multicoloured hot-air balloon soars skywards at Midmar Dam, a mecca for fun-seekers and watersport enthusiasts from all over KwaZulu-Natal.

MIDMAR DAM
Near Howick

This brilliant sweep of sparkling water, flanked by lush, grassy terraces and emerald hills, is one of Central KwaZulu-Natal's most popular inland venues.

Built in 1961 on farmland 24 km from Pietermaritzburg, the dam offers the full range of watersports – yachting, skiing, windsurfing and swimming. You can even cruise the upper reaches of the dam, where an 820-ha game park, the Midmar Nature Reserve, has been developed. Here you'll probably see red hartebeest, black wildebeest, blesbok, springbok, reedbuck, oribi and zebras, and other mammals grazing on the shoreline. There's also a rich variety of bird life, including giant and pygmy kingfishers, and birds such as Stanley's bustards and secretary birds. Facilities in the reserve include game-viewing trails and comfortable accommodation in chalets.

The Natal Parks Board cares for the recreational section of the dam which is bilharzia-free. There are beautiful rolling lawns and many cosy picnic spots on the water's edge.

Areas of the dam have been zoned off for anglers, and here you may catch carp, bass, and bluegill (licences are available from the Parks Board office).

The entry fee into Midmar includes admission to the Historical Village, one of the area's best-kept secrets. This reconstruction of a turn-of-the-century Natal country village includes a number of relocated buildings, such as the Eston Station, two furnished period houses, Zulu huts and a Shiva temple.

Agricultural machinery and transport vehicles are on display in five exhibition halls, and special exhibits include a Shackleton aircraft, Durban's last steam-driven tugboat, a functional narrow-gauge railway, and an operational water mill. The Plough and Cart restaurant offers light lunches and teas.

Cosy chalets fringed by trees offer visitors comfortable accommodation near the water's edge at the Midmar Nature Reserve, an attractive 820-ha game park.

Map: page 127, 3C
Drive north from Pietermaritzburg on the N3. After 24 km turn left at the signpost reading Howick/Midmar.
Details: Bathing is permitted. A boat shop has bicycles, windsurfers, canoes and yachts for hire over weekends, and daily in peak holiday periods.
Accommodation: Thirty-one fully equipped chalets, include a 6-bed chalet specially equipped for handicapped people. There are also 16 rustic cabins, equipped with fridges and stoves, and communal ablution facilities. Three camp sites, all with water frontage.
Further information: Natal Parks Board, P O Box 1750, Pietermaritzburg 3200, tel (0331) 47-1981; The Officer-in-Charge, Midmar Nature Reserve, Private Bag X6, Howick 3290, tel (0332) 30-2067/8.

NATAL LION AND GAME PARK
Near Pietermaritzburg

This privately owned and beautifully situated park was originally established in 1966 on 240 ha of well-wooded, undulating terrain in the upper region of the Valley of a Thousand Hills.

A leisurely hour-long drive through the park in your own vehicle will bring you eye to eye with lions (there are about 30 of them in the park), giraffes, zebras, impala, nyala and elephants. Apart from the lions, a major attraction is the six Asian elephants, believed to be the only ones of their kind living in the wild on the African continent. The owners hope that the lone Asian bull elephant will start breeding with one or more of the five females. For bird-watchers there are more than 120 species, including black- and yellow-billed kites and sacred ibises.

The Natal Zoological Gardens, 150 m from the gate to, and across the road from, the Lion Park, is home to eight Bengal tigers, a pair of black leopards, spotted leopards (also being bred), orang-utans, water buffaloes and a fine collection of parrots. There is a curio shop that stocks hides, skins and various other souvenirs, and offers light refreshments.

Map: page 127, 3D
The turn-off to the Lion Park is about 18 km east of Pietermaritzburg, on the N3 to Durban. The park's gates are 7 km from the highway.
Details: Open 08h00 to dusk.
Accommodation: The Lion Park Safari Lodge, adjoining the park, offers 10 thatched rondavels spread out on lawns shaded by indigenous thorn trees. Reservations: P O Box 1353, Pietermaritzburg 3200, tel (0331) 50-1104.
Further information: Natal Lion Park, P O Box 36, Umlaas Road 3730, tel (0325) 5-1411; Natal Zoological Gardens, P O Box 36, Umlaas Road 3730, tel (0325) 5-1423.

▶ CENTRAL KWAZULU-NATAL

NATAL SHARKS BOARD
Umhlanga

Map: page 127, 3F
Drive north from Durban on the N2. After 15 km take the Umhlanga turn-off and then turn left. Follow the signposts to the Sharks Board.
Details: Show times: The Natal Sharks Board is open every day for fishing licences, and for those who wish to visit the curio shop. Shows and tours, lasting half an hour, are held Mondays to Thursdays. Please contact the Board *(see below)* to check times.
Accommodation: Nearby Umhlanga Rocks offers a variety of excellent hotel accommodation.
Further information: Natal Sharks Board, Private Bag 2, Umhlanga Rocks 4320, tel (031) 561-1017.

On a hillside overlooking Umhlanga, with sweeping views of the Indian Ocean, is the headquarters of the Natal Sharks Board, one of the world's most effective organizations for minimizing the threat of shark attacks in South African waters.

Few things raise the human hackles more than the thought of suddenly being attacked and savaged by a shark. And there is certainly no greater inducement to avoid the beach than if there are sharks in the water.

Historic attempts to keep sharks at bay include inks, stains, poison gas, sound waves, harpooning and hunting. But way back in 1937 a chance discovery pointed the way to a successful antishark device. An Australian fisherman discovered that many sharks became entangled in his wide, diamond-shaped mesh nets and, without the necessary forward movement to breathe, suffocated and died.

The KwaZulu-Natal coastline, previously ravaged by a series of fatal shark attacks along its popular bathing beaches, was to benefit considerably from the Australian's discovery – but only after the Natal Anti-Shark Measures Board (now known as the Natal Sharks Board) was formed in 1964.

The great white shark, feared predator of the deep, has razor-sharp teeth that are able to bite effortlessly through the largest of prey.

Man's battle against sharks

The very last thing a bather in KwaZulu-Natal's coastal waters would want to see is a triangular dorsal fin cutting through the waves towards him. A shark attack is a terrifying – and potentially fatal – occurrence. Happily, such incidents are now extremely rare. They were common enough in the fairly recent past, notably during the Second World War years, reaching their tragic peak in the late 1950s.

But the introduction of safety nets, and the establishment, in 1964, of the Natal Anti-Shark Measures Board (NASMB) have all but eliminated the hazard.

These primitive, torpedo-shaped, scaleless and cartilaginous fish (their skeletons are of cartilage, not of bone) thrive on the rich marine life of the western Indian Ocean. Many have razor-sharp, serrated teeth. All boast acute eyesight. They do not see in colour, but their vision in the dimness of the depths is more than 10 times as sensitive as a human's.

They also identify objects through a highly developed sense of smell, and an ability to detect vibrations in the surrounding ocean.

A total of 109 species of shark are represented in these southern waters. They range from the small (30 cm) pygmy to the 15-m whale shark. Not all are fearsome hunters of the sea: the massive basking shark, as well as the whale shark, for instance, feed on plankton, and have small teeth.

Most sharks give birth to live young, but some of the smaller ones lay eggs, the clutches encased in horny coverings that are often seen among the washed-up flotsam on the beaches. These are known as 'mermaids' purses'.

Among the more notable species of shark found off the South African seaboard are:
■ The dusky shark *(Carcharhinus obscurus)*, a blunt-snouted fish that grows to 3,5 m and more. Dangerous.
■ The blue shark *(Prionace glauca)*, a four-metre creature more common in deeper offshore waters. Potentially dangerous.
■ The Zambezi (or Van Rooyen's) shark *(Carcharhinus leucas)*, a powerful, broad-headed, wide-mouthed species that haunts estuaries and other shallow stretches of water. Very dangerous.
■ The hammerhead shark *(Sphyrna zyaena)*, a bizarre-looking fish whose eyes are sited on long projections on either side of its head. This shark reaches six metres in length in the tropics, rather less in the south. Aggressive, 'cheeky' rather than dangerous.
■ The ragged-toothed shark *(Carcharias taurus)*, a heavy, three-metre species, with pointed snout and formidable teeth. Favours the shallower waters. Dangerous.
■ The great white shark *(Carcharodon carcharias)*, up to 6,5 m in length, fearless, and responsible for more attacks on humans than other shark species. Dangerous.

Many shark specimens are 'tagged' (for identification and further study) as part of the research programme – an exercise that calls for skilful diving, endurance and courage.

In 1988 two members of the Natal Sharks Board, Bob Wilson and Geremy Cliff, set a world record by tagging 41 ragged-toothed sharks in less than four hours.

The decision to start an association to cater for safe bathing, and to counter the threat of sharks, came after the Black December of 1957, during which seven bathers were attacked (five fatally) on the KwaZulu-Natal South Coast.

By 1994, 379 nets had been installed, protecting 40 beaches in total. In all the waters protected by nets in KwaZulu-Natal, there have been very few attacks.

However, there are some critics who argue that the nets have adversely affected the balance of nature in the sea, not only by killing sharks, but also by trapping other marine species, such as dolphins.

At the Board's premises in Umhlanga, the emphasis today is as much on education as it is on preventing attacks, and there's a lot to be learnt about sharks by visiting the Board.

There are audiovisual presentations showing how boat crews service the nets at sunrise each day, tagging and releasing sharks that are still alive.

There are also various interesting displays featuring the biology of sharks, their acute sense of smell and their sensitivity to electrical impulses.

Some 20 to 35 sharks that are potentially dangerous to man – great whites, tiger and Zambezi sharks – are released alive from the nets each year.

Dead sharks which are found in the nets are brought back and refrigerated for research and public dissection. Stomach contents sometimes reveal items such as cans and other man-made debris. The teeth are used as jewellery, sold in curio shops, and the fins go to the Far East to be used in shark-fin soup.

The tiger shark is a solitary man-eating scavenger, found throughout the warmer seas of the world.

A hiker surveys the spectacle of the Umzimkulwana River as it meanders through the Oribi Gorge. The area hosts a variety of birds and animals.

ORIBI GORGE NATURE RESERVE
Near Port Shepstone

Towering cliffs overlook the deep and bush-covered ravine carved out by the Umzimkulwana River, a tributary of the Umzimkulu, at the heart of the Oribi Gorge Nature Reserve, 21km west of Port Shepstone. Of all the many valleys and gorges carved out by KwaZulu-Natal's mighty rivers on their tumultuous journeys to the sea, perhaps none is more spectacular than this one.

Huge, sun-bleached boulders pave the granite riverbed as it winds gently between cliffs carpeted by indigenous forests. Bushbuck, common reedbuck, blue and grey duiker, vervet and samango monkeys, leopards, and a teeming population of birds, from raptors to sunbirds, thrive beneath the shelter of ancient trees and plumbago bushes. Leopards also occur in the area, and watch out for African pythons and water leguans.

The gorge is known for its rock formations, among them Baboon's Castle, The Ramparts, The Walls of Jericho and The Pulpit. From the Overhanging Rock there are some breathtaking views of a horseshoe bend formed by the river. The contrasting vegetation includes giant stinkwood trees, ferns and mosses, euphorbias, open grasslands and proteas.

Three trails penetrate the forests of the reserve. The nine-kilometre View Trail winds up the escarpment, from which there are exquisite views over the slopes to the valley below. The Hoopoe Falls Trail leads seven kilometres along the banks of the Umzimkulwana River to reach a pretty waterfall, while the shortest, the five-kilometre Nkonka Trail, meanders eastwards from the picnic site to a weir on the Umzimkulwana. Shorter walks are also available to the public.

Map: page 127, 6C/D

The entrance to the Oribi Gorge Nature Reserve is 21 km from Port Shepstone, on the road to Harding.

Details: Open 05h00-19h00 during the summer months (1 October to 31 March), and 06h00-18h00 during winter (1 April to 30 September). Visitors are advised not to swim or paddle in the river because of bilharzia.

Accommodation: A camp at the head of the Umzimkulwana Gorge offers six 4-bed huts with an *en suite* half-bathroom. A 7-bed, self-contained cottage is also available. The Oribi Gorge Hotel is licensed. Write to: P O Box 575, Port Shepstone 4240, tel (0391) 9-1753.

Further information: Natal Parks Board, P O Box 1750, Pietermaritzburg 3200, tel (0331) 47-1981; The Camp Manager, Oribi Gorge Nature Reserve, P O Box 81, Paddock 4244, tel (0397) 9-1644.

PLACES TO VISIT

PIETERMARITZBURG

ALEXANDRA PARK

Map: page 137
From the city centre drive east along Commercial Road (towards Durban). When you cross the bridge over the Msunduze River on the outskirts of the town, turn right for the park.
Details: Open 24 hours a day all year round.
Accommodation: Pietermaritzburg has plenty of accommodation.
Further information: Parks and Recreation Department, P O Box 31, Pietermaritzburg 3200, tel (0331) 42-2970; Pietermaritzburg Publicity Association, P O Box 25, Pietermaritzburg 3200, tel (0331) 45-1348/9.

This 65-ha flagship of the city's parks, lying in a tranquil bend of the Duzi River, was named after Princess Alexandra of Denmark, who later became Queen Alexandra of England.

It was designed as a park where you can relax in the soothing shade on a summer afternoon, and as a venue for more hectic pursuits, such as cycling, soccer, cricket, hockey and swimming in the park's inviting pool.

Not far from the Cape chestnuts and jacarandas, the aloes and the bougainvilleas, is a charming cricket oval, with the gracious Jubilee Pavilions and an adjacent bandstand. This features a rare 'chinoiserie' roof, based on the architectural style of the Far East. A newly designed, informal rose garden features flowers with such evocative names as the Pearl of Bedfordview and the Bushveld Dawn. Keep an eye out for a rare horse trough with a hoof-shaped base.

A lovely display house, which changes weekly, contains orchids and bromeliads. The Percy Taylor rockery has a profusion of succulents, while the Mayor's Garden has two magnificent palm avenues and some formal flowerbeds.

Spring-flowering azaleas are a particular delight. The Pavilion Restaurant between the rose garden and the oval serves light meals.

Visit the park in May, when one of South Africa's largest outdoor art shows is held, attracting artists and art-lovers from across the country.

The tree-fringed Victorian bandstand at Alexandra Park's cricket oval is a reminder of the town's colonial era. The park's gardens provide superb picnic spots in beautiful surroundings.

NATAL NATIONAL BOTANICAL GARDEN

Map: page 137
Off Mayor's Walk, to the southwest of the city centre.
Details: Open all year round 08h00-18h00 daily, except Tuesdays. Entry fee during weekends and holidays. Children should be accompanied, as there are rock outcrops and poisonous or thorny plants.
Accommodation: Pietermaritzburg offers varied accommodation.
Further information: The Curator, Natal National Botanical Garden, P O Box 21667, Mayor's Walk 3208, tel (0331) 44-3585; Pietermaritzburg Publicity Association, P O Box 25, Pietermaritzburg 3200, tel (0331) 45-1348/9.

Fancy a cool stroll through mist-belt forests, where delicate fronds caress you as you pass, and the gentle tinkle of running water is never completely out of earshot? Then visit the Natal National Botanical Garden, where the shady trees part their branches to expose panoramic views across the Swartkops Valley.

Lying on an ancient flood plain and hillside where the Dorpspruit joins the Msunduze River, this 49-ha garden, established in 1874, is a showcase for the indigenous flora of KwaZulu-Natal. It features two sections: the Exotic Garden and the Indigenous Garden, each crisscrossed by a network of paths that lead you on walks through the trees.

The prime objective of the garden was to provide plants for the farms and plantations of the settlers. Over the years it developed into a refuge featuring magnificent southern-hemisphere plants and trees such as swamp cypresses, giant figs, camphor trees, tulips and magnolias. Several of these are the last of their kind in South Africa.

The garden has not been without its critics. The duck-pond development, created by one of the early curators in the relaxed 'English Garden' style, became known as 'Adlam's Folly', since it led to his dismissal.

Showy butterflies, dragonflies and the hummingbird hawk moth make the garden an insect-lover's paradise. More than 100 bird species, including four types of kingfisher and the rare purple heron, have been recorded here. Small antelope, vervet monkeys, mongooses and otters also occur.

This is a garden for all seasons: displays of spring flowers, abundant summer foliage, autumn colour, and beautiful branch patterns in winter. It is also a popular venue for a pipe-band festival. The restaurant is open from 08h30 to 17h00, and offers meals and teas.

MACRORIE HOUSE

The essence of the romantic Victorian era is perfectly captured in this imposing Victorian residence, with its multigabled roof, delicate 'broekie-lace' ornamentation, and its deep, shady verandahs.

The house began life in 1852 as the home of an Englishman, Edward Few, who came to South Africa and established what was to become a prosperous sawmill. Later, in 1873, the house was registered in the name of Agnes Macrorie, wife of the Bishop of Pietermaritzburg. The new owners made considerable changes to their home, adding a double-storey section, the striking cast-iron verandahs and delicately traced iron railings around the garden. Also installed was a miniature Gothic chapel with an altar imported from Bishop Macrorie's old parish church in England, and a beautiful painting on the reredos. The bishop was a man of refinement, and his study, with its beautifully preserved grand piano, bears witness to his gracious lifestyle. The fine examples of the furniture of the time give you some idea of the style in which the Macrorie family lived. In the garden is a summerhouse used for theatrical and other presentations, and a herb garden.

Today the house is maintained by the Simon van der Stel Foundation, which specializes in the restoration of buildings of historical importance.

Map: below
Macrorie House Museum is on the corner of Pine and Loop streets. From the City Hall turn right into Boshoff Street, and right again into Loop Street.
Details: Open 09h00-13h00 Tuesday to Thursday; 11h00-16h00 Sundays..
Further information: The Curator, Macrorie House, 11 Loop Street, Pietermaritzburg 3201, tel (0331) 94-2161; Pietermaritzburg Publicity Association, P O Box 25, Pietermaritzburg 3200, tel (0331) 45-1348/9.

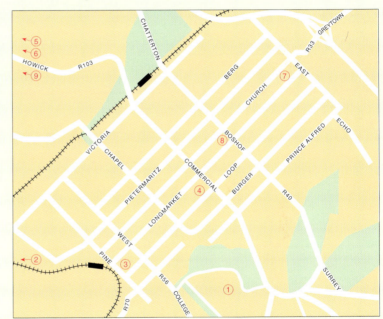

KEY TO THE MAP
1 Alexandra Park
2 Natal National Botanical Garden
3 Macrorie House
4 Natal Museum
5 Green Belt Trails
6 Queen Elizabeth Park
7 Sri Siva Soobramoniar Temple
8 Voortrekker Museum
9 Wylie Park

NATAL MUSEUM

Peer through a peephole in the ocean floor at prehistoric coelacanth and man-eating shark; listen to the shrill, haunting call of the whales.

Take a step back in time, and witness the age of dinosaurs, as their monstrous, 20th-century replicas stalk the silent halls of the Natal Museum. Closer to the present, you may see the rare okapi, square-lipped rhinoceros and the dwarf buffalo, or wander through a fascinating

The exterior façade of the Natal Museum in Pietermaritzburg, which houses a range of fascinating natural-history exhibits.

Map: above
The Natal Museum is at 237 Loop Street, Pietermaritzburg. From the City Hall travel north on Longmarket Street (a one-way street), turn right into Boshoff Street, and right again into Loop Street.
Details: Open 09h00-16h30 Monday to Saturday; 14h00-17h00 Sundays. Admission fee charged.
Further information: The Curator, Natal Museum, Private Bag 9070, Pietermaritzburg 3200, tel (0331) 45-1404/5; Pietermaritzburg Publicity Association, P O Box 25, Pietermaritzburg 3200, tel (0331) 45-1348/9.

Drakensberg cave, and marvel at the Stone-Age art of the San (Bushmen).

There's such a wide choice of historic themes at the Natal Museum, that you'll need a full day to go through it all properly. And the themes are so well presented that it takes some adjustment to move from one time frame to another. You can visit the replica of a Victorian lane, where a horse waits to be shod by a blacksmith, an old woman rocks in her chair, and the governor's wife is preparing tea. Shepstone Place recreates the spirit of 19th-century settler life in Pietermaritzburg, with period rooms, a settler's cottage and a pharmacy. Also on display are the old wooden decks of Portuguese caravels reminiscent of the voyages of intrepid, early mariners.

If your interest is natural history, there are beautiful showcases of mammals and birds, reptiles and insects – among the finest in the country. Africa's heritage of large mammals is fully revealed in an outstanding exhibition of every species of antelope, including such rarities as the bongo, addax and okapi, as well as zebras, lions and other big game.

In the colourful dinosaur gallery – a must for children – terrifying sounds mimic the noises made by *Tyrannosaurus* and *Triceratops* when they roamed the plains of southern Africa about 200 million years ago.

Visitors to Natal Museum can see this gigantic reconstruction of the last wild elephant found in KwaZulu-Natal.

Map: page 137
Daily hiking trails in and around Pietermaritzburg. Various starting points. The trails are located to the west and northwest of Pietermaritzburg. For directions it is best to consult the Green Belt Trails brochure and map available from Pietermaritzburg Publicity Association *(see address below).*
Details: Open all year round. Picnic site and parking facilities at World's View. Watch out for sudden thunderstorms in summer.
Accommodation: Hotel and guesthouse accommodation available in Pietermaritzburg.
Further information: Pietermaritzburg Publicity Association, P O Box 25, Pietermaritzburg 3200, tel (0331) 45-1348/9.

GREEN BELT TRAILS

One of the special features of the city of Pietermaritzburg is its surrounding countryside, and this has been made accessible to the busy city dweller by the introduction of a series of beautiful hiking trails which are known collectively as the Pietermaritzburg Green Belt Trails.

Lush temperate forests, thornveld and grassland, alive with a variety of animals, flowers and birds, make these trails a nature-lover's delight.

The trails pass through a variety of veld types, each with its own special tranquillity and treasure of flora and fauna.

To the northwest of the city the countryside rises to 1 067m above sea level, with misty hills and a high rainfall. To the west, around Queen Elizabeth Park *(see separate entry),* you'll find yourself in undulating, open grasslands, while at World's View, south of Queen Elizabeth Park, you hike below shaded plantations of wattle and pine.

The enticingly cool hills about 12 km northwest of the city offer attractive rambles such as the Ferncliffe Trail system, which explores the secrets of a 250-ha indigenous forest just below the escarpment. Here the flowering Cape chestnut and bush lily compete with ferns, mosses, lichens and exotic plants for a place in the sun.

The main Ferncliffe Trail, Lemonwood (so named for its bounty of lemonwood trees), has six different walks radiating from its winding course. These take you to such romantic places as Sunset Rock, Bat Cave (inhabited by four species of bat) and The Everglades. One of the trails also leads to a crystal-clear waterfall and stream. None of the trails takes longer than an hour to complete.

The Dorpspruit Trail, opened on World Environment Day in 1987, marks the beginning of a series of city spruit trails. Following the banks of the Dorpspruit River, the two-kilometre trail takes you past the Voortrekker Bridge and the remains of the old city quarry, where a branch leads off to link up with the Green Belt Trails at World's View.

The World's View Trail (2,4 km) starts at Voortrekker Road, and snakes through pine and wattle plantations as it follows an old Voortrekker route. The Upper Linwood Trail and the Lower Linwood Trail both start on Celtis Road (a map mounted on a plinth marks the start). The Upper Linwood Trail (2,4 km) follows the path of a now disused railway line established in 1916 to ease the climb out of Pietermaritzburg, passing through a short tunnel *en route*.

The Lower Linwood Trail (4,3 km) is an easy walk through cool, aromatic pine plantations. Note that all the trails are open to hikers and horse-riders only; motor vehicles are forbidden.

Indigenous and exotic plants are just some of the many attractions of Queen Elizabeth Park near Pietermaritzburg.

QUEEN ELIZABETH PARK

This small but enchanting nature reserve on the northern outskirts of Pietermaritzburg also serves as the headquarters of the Natal Parks Board, and as an environmental education centre and outdoor recreational area.

Special attractions at the park are its mammals, which include white rhinos, impala, Burchell's zebras, blesbuck, bushbuck and blue duiker, and its large number of indigenous and exotic plants. Notable among these are the cycad collections in the gardens of the Douglas Mitchell Centre (the Natal Parks Board's offices), the endangered Hilton daisies, and patches of indigenous bush along the drainage lines.

A model 'environmentally friendly' bird garden shows visitors how to attract birds to suburban gardens. Another section shows the work being done in eradicating such undesirable plants as lantana, bugweed, Mauritius thorn and wild ginger.

For strollers there's the circular, self-guided iDube Trail, a viewing hide, as well as attractive picnic spots. Wildlife films and environmental workshops are held throughout the year for schoolchildren and adults.

Map: page 137
Queen Elizabeth Park lies about 8 km from the centre of Pietermaritzburg. Travel north on Commercial Road and when you reach the traffic circle, take the road to Montrose (Duncan McKenzie Drive). This road ends at the park.
Details: Day-visitors only. No camping. Entrance free. Three picnic sites with braai facilities. Curio shop.
Accommodation: Pietermaritzburg offers a wide variety of accommodation.
Further information: The Officer-in-Charge, Queen Elizabeth Park, P O Box 662, Pietermaritzburg 3200, tel (0331) 47-1961.

Mountain-bike trails such as this one at Ferncliffe near Pietermaritzburg enable trailists to cover long distances in quiet country surroundings.

PIETERMARITZBURG

Map: page 137
From the City Hall travel along Longmarket Street (a one-way street) towards East Street. The temple is at 545 Longmarket Street.
Details: Open 07h00-18h00 Monday to Saturday; 08h00-18h00 Sundays.
Further information: The President, Sri Siva Soobramoniar and Marriamen Temples, P O Box 7902, Cumberwood 3235, tel (0331) 42-5430; Pietermaritzburg Publicity Association, P O Box 25, Pietermaritzburg 3200, tel (0331) 45-1348/9.

SRI SIVA SOOBRAMONIAR TEMPLE

Established in 1898 in the South Indian style of architecture, and dedicated to Soobramoniar, one of the sons of Siva, this temple is an oasis of tranquillity in the heart of Pietermaritzburg, and is one of the main places of worship for the city's Hindu population.

Together with the Marriamen Temple, it forms the oldest complex of its kind in the city, and caters traditionally mostly to Tamils. Brightly painted relief figures of Siva and his wife, Parvati, seated on Siva's vehicle, the bull Nandi, decorate the front pediment over the verandah. Also depicted are Siva's sons, Ganesha and Soobramoniar.

Fronting the temple are finely crafted sculpture friezes of some of the Hindu gods, as well as the 'footprint' of Rama, one of the most powerful incarnations of Vishnu, the preserver of the universe.

On the exterior of one of the walls is a popular shrine depicting images of the nine planets (navagraha). Devotees circle these images in the hope of attracting the favour of the planetary gods.

The Marriamen Temple was built in 1924 to honour the Divine Mother of the human race. Crowd-drawing festivals at the complex include the firewalking ceremony, which takes place annually on Good Friday, when some 50 devotees celebrate the end of a 10-day fast by walking barefoot across pits of glowing coals, watched by an admiring crowd.

Also celebrated is the holy festival of Kavadi, when the devotees take their vows and often enter a trance.

The exterior (right) and the interior (inset) of the Sri Siva Soobramoniar Temple in Pietermaritzburg.

Map: page 137
The Voortrekker Museum is at 340 Church Street. From the City Hall, drive north on Longmarket Street, turn left into Boshoff Street, and left again into Church Street. To reach Andries Pretorius's house at 333 Boom Street, continue along Church Street, turn right into Commercial Road, and right again into Boom Street.
Details: Open 09h00-16h00 Monday to Friday; 08h00-12h00 Saturdays. Admission free.
Further information: The Curator, Voortrekker Museum, P O Box 998, Pietermaritzburg 3200, tel (0331) 94-6834.

VOORTREKKER MUSEUM

This museum started out as a tiny church, named the Church of the Vow, which was built by the Voortrekkers in 1841 to commemorate their victory over the Zulus at the epic Battle of Blood River.

It served its original purpose for just 20 years before being converted into a commercial building. Much later, in 1912, it became the home of the Voortrekker Museum.

For true lovers of early South African history there's a treasure chest of historical Voortrekker relics, among them the second-oldest oxwagon in South Africa, flintlock rifles, and Boer leader Piet Retief's prayer book. There are also some showcases of Voortrekker clothes and children's toys.

The bold architecture of the Memorial Church next to the museum symbolizes the struggles of the Voortrekkers in KwaZulu-Natal, and features the words of the vow in which these pioneers pledged that 'should the Lord grant victory (they would) build Him a church to hallow His great name'. The statues of Retief and Gert Maritz, another Boer leader, stand solemnly in the forecourt.

The newest addition to the museum is the thatched, double-storey house of

Commandant Andries Pretorius, who led the victorious commando at Blood River.

Pretorius's house, dating back to 1846, has shale-stone walls, yellowwood ceilings and a tiled floor, all in excellent condition. On display within the house are furniture and household effects dating from 1840. In keeping with the trend of the day, the walls upstairs are pale pink, while downstairs they're pale blue.

Stones at the entrance to the grounds were erected by Pretorius on the banks of the Black Umfolozi River, as a token of peace and friendship between the Zulus and the Boers. You will find Pretorius's house at 333 Boom Street.

WYLIE PARK

This relatively small, charming park was bequeathed to the city of Pietermaritzburg in 1954 by a local citizen, on condition that it be used as a place of quietness and peace.

Nestling in a quiet valley five minutes from the city, Wylie Park has certainly lived up to the precondition, offering visitors a tranquil beauty all year round, but especially in the springtime, when plants such as daffodils, anemones and ranunculi flower amidst hundreds of azaleas, emblem flower of the city. A 10-minute walk is the Azalea Amble.

Two enormous swamp cypresses stand guard over a marshy area where a stream enters the park, trickling past ranks of yellowwoods, oaks and magnolias, before flowing into a quiet pool, and then exiting the park.

Indigenous flora, such as proteas, strelitzias and ericas, interspersed with striking firs and maples, add flowering colour throughout the year. Other attractions are a cycad garden, a clump of bamboo and a perennial garden, always in bloom.

A flamboyant explosion of azaleas blooms in profusion at Wylie Park. These beautiful flowers, the emblem of Pietermaritzburg, are at their best in the spring.

Map: page 137
Wylie Park is in the Pietermaritzburg suburb of Wembley, to the west of the city. Drive north on Longmarket Street from the City Hall. Turn left into Boshoff Street, and left again into Victoria Road. Turn right onto the R103, the Old Howick Road. After about 2,8 km turn left onto Taunton Road.

Details: Open 07h30-16h30 all year round. No admission fee charged.

Further information: Parks and Recreation Department, P O Box 31, Pietermaritzburg 3200, tel (0331) 42-3186.

CENTRAL KWAZULU-NATAL

SILVERGLEN NATURE RESERVE
Durban

Map: page 127, 4E
Follow the N3 leading west from the city centre. After Tollgate Bridge it is 3,2 km to the Outer Ring Road (the N2). Turn south onto the N2 and drive 9,5 km before turning west onto the Chatsworth/Higginson Highway. At the traffic lights turn right onto Higginson Highway. After 2 km, turn left into Havenside Drive, and then fourth left into Silverglen Drive. After 3,5 km turn left again into Lakeview Drive, which leads 600 m to the reserve gates.
Details: The reserve is open at all times, as the road through it is a public thoroughfare. Picnic and braai sites are open 06h00-18h00, 1 October to 30 April, and 07h00-17h00, 1 May to 30 September.
Accommodation: Hotel accommodation available in Durban and Pietermaritzburg.
Further information: The Officer-in-Charge, Silverglen Nature Reserve, P O Box 3740, Durban 4000, tel (031) 21-1303 or 404-5628.

This 220-ha natural oasis between two urban communities supports a wealth of indigenous coastal grassland and trees, ranging from Natal camwood, forest fever berry and marula, to wild plum and velvet bushwillow.

The abundant wealth of plants and trees has attracted some 145 species of bird, including such specimens as green coucals and plum-coloured starlings, which you may be lucky to see along two trails winding through the reserve.

One trail crosses a small stream and enters a patch of riverine bush interspersed with trees such as silver oak and tree fuchsia. The other trail winds through a marshy area and alongside a plantation of gum trees, with sweeping southerly views over Umlazi. Grassland flowers in spring include small pink carnations and everlastings.

If you're an animal-lover, you should keep an eye out for a group of banded mongooses, or more elusive inhabitants such as red or blue duiker or bushbuck. On Boomslang Bend you might even catch a quick glimpse of its potentially dangerous reptilian namesake; and at the Clearwater Dam, look out for fish eagles and Egyptian geese.

A vantage point over the Umgeni Valley shows the winding course of the river through the bush country of the KwaZulu-Natal Midlands.

UMGENI VALLEY PROJECT
Near Howick

Map: page 127, 3C
Leave Pietermaritzburg on the N3, travelling west for about 30 km, then take the Howick/Midmar Dam turn-off. Cross over the freeway and follow the Howick signs through Howick. Immediately after the second set of traffic lights turn right onto the road signposted Karkloof/Rietvlei. Continue for about 1 km, and turn right at the signpost for Umgeni Valley.
Details: Open 08h00-16h30 all year round. Walkers allowed into the reserve from sunrise to sunset. Camps accessible only by foot, so pack lightly. No electricity.
Accommodation: Three fully equipped cottages, sleeping 2 to 6, with views of the valley. Four rustic camps.
Further information: Umgeni Valley Project, P O Box 394, Howick 3290, tel (0332) 30-3931, 30-5721.

Magnificent sandstone cliffs fall sheer from gentle grasslands at the 656-ha Umgeni Valley Project, home of giraffes, zebras, wildebeest, eland, nyala, impala and a variety of other mammals.

Launched in 1976 as an environmental education centre for young and old, this secluded reserve lies just below the Howick Falls, where the Umgeni River is at its spectacular best.

No less than 15 000 students come here every year to participate in adventure programmes, which include abseiling, hiking and bushcraft. A junior hunter's course deals specifically with the hunting and environmental management skills of young students.

Apart from the benefits offered by the training centre, there's plenty to see and do here. Bird-watching, for one, will bring you into contact with many of the 206 species of bird. These range from the tiniest warblers to magnificent black, crowned and martial eagles which soar above the cliffs.

A network of self-guided footpaths traverses the reserve, affording a glimpse of the large mammals, as well as the tinier animals and plants. The most popular trail is a four-day guided hike from the Howick Falls to the Karkloof Falls, through the valley bushveld.

The other, shorter, trails are steep and winding, and require a fair degree of physical fitness. For those who are not so agile, picnic spots have been provided at the top of the valley. There's also a five-kilometre drive up to the viewsite area.

Down in the valley you can swim in the Umgeni and its tributaries after good rains. Canoeing is discouraged because of the steep gradient of the river.

CENTRAL KWAZULU-NATAL

UMTAMVUNA NATURE RESERVE
West of Port Edward

The deep riverine forests and rocky cliffs which fringe the Umtamvuna River (the border between KwaZulu-Natal and Transkei) hold exceptional delights for nature-lovers – particularly those who are interested in indigenous plants.

September bells, everlastings, cycads, tree ferns and 35 types of orchid are just some of more than 100 identified plant species that camouflage an abundant world of birds and animals.

The 250 bird species include breeding colonies of crowned eagles, fish eagles and Cape vultures, as well as a number of smaller species, such as the rare peregrine falcon and Gurney's sugarbird. Mammals here include oribi, bushbuck, baboons, otters, samango and vervet monkeys, water mongooses and porcupines.

Umtamvuna, 3 257 ha in extent, is the most southerly of KwaZulu-Natal's reserves, and runs inland for about 25 kilometres. Proclaimed in 1971, it is the only area in the world conserving North Pondoland coastal highland sourveld.

Self-guided circular trails, all of which are extremely beautiful, vary in length from half a kilometre to eight kilometres. The Lourie and Fish Eagle trails start at the southern end of the reserve, while the others explore the koppies, cliffs and grasslands of the northern section. Report to the game guard at the entrance before starting off. If you prefer a guided tour, book a game guard in advance.

Map: page 127, 7C
From Durban follow the N2 south to Port Shepstone. Just south of Port Shepstone turn onto the R620 for Uvongo and Southbroom, and then the R61 for Port Edward. At the intersection with Owen Ellis Drive in Port Edward turn west onto Izingolweni Road. The reserve is signposted some 8 km along this road.
Details: Open sunrise to sunset all year. Map and information brochure available at the gate, as well as a bird list. Toilet and braai facilities at northern gate.
Accommodation: Day-visitors only; there is plenty of accommodation at all the KwaZulu-Natal South Coast resorts.
Further information: The Officer-in-Charge, Umtamvuna Nature Reserve, P O Box 25, Port Edward 4295, tel (03930) 3-2383.

Wild valleys cloaked in dense, riverine vegetation are a feature of the Umtamvuna Nature Reserve in southern KwaZulu-Natal.

The vistas of mountain and valley seem to go on for ever in the Valley of a Thousand Hills.

VALLEY OF A THOUSAND HILLS
Botha's Hill

A lingering glance across the changing canvas of peaks, slopes and emerald riverbeds of the Valley of a Thousand Hills is enough to transport you back to the Pleistocene Age, about 200 million years in time.

Visually, the landscape has changed little since the Umgeni River and its tributaries sculpted their masterpieces from the sandstone beds of KwaZulu-Natal, leaving the valleys and sandstone hills which gave the area its name.

Today you can drive along the Old Main Road between Durban and Pietermaritzburg (particularly the stretch from Botha's Hill to Cato Ridge), and stop at any one of several vantage points along the way. Notable among these is the Rob Roy Hotel, whose owners will gladly point the way to the most scenic spots to visit.

There are several produce stalls and craft markets along the way, the most attractive of which is PheZulu *(see box: The rich tapestry of Zulu traditions)*, at 168 Old Main Road, an immensely popular simulated Zulu kraal, which gives you an authentic insight into the traditions, customs and crafts of the Zulu people. These traditions go back to the 18th century, when early Nguni clans first settled there.

PheZulu (the name means 'high up') is perched above the valley, with its hazy backdrop of blue-tinged hills. Household routines such as beer-brewing, cooking,

Map: page 127, 3E
On the N3 from Durban go through the Toll and take the Assagay/Shongweni turn-off on the left. Turn right over the bridge, and at the next stop street turn left into Old Main Road, Botha's Hill. The places featured are all on the right, and signposted, 32 km from Durban. From Pietermaritzburg follow the N3 east towards Durban. Where the road divides take the R613, and the first off-ramp to the left. Follow the road to Botha's Hill, and continue following the route from Durban.
Details: There are no tourist facilities in the valley.
Further information: The Information Officer, The Valley Trust, P O Box 33, Botha's Hill 3660, tel (031) 777-1955; PheZulu, P O Box 671, Botha's Hill 3660, tel (031) 777-1000.

The rich tapestry of Zulu traditions

The rural lifestyles on show at PheZulu and other 'living museums' in the Valley of a Thousand Hills illuminate an ancient culture that is crumbling under the onslaught of Western ways. Still, much of it remains – a delight to the eye and a stimulus to the mind.

In traditional Zulu society the women cultivated the fields, cared for the children and generally ran the household. The men served as stockmen and hunters – and also as soldiers in the splendidly bedecked, age-graded regiments created by the great warrior-king Shaka.

The male regalia, still worn on ceremonial occasions (and for the benefit of tourists), is a dramatic melange of oxhide shield, stick (sometimes spear), a kilt of animal-skin 'tails', fur, ostrich plumes on the head and, if the man is married, a head-ring.

Both men and women wear a wealth of beadwork around their ankles, hips, arms and necks. The beads are a relatively recent addition, though – they were introduced to the Nguni people by 19th-century traders. And they have significance as well as charm.

Intricately stitched together, the patterns and colours have taken on symbolic meaning, conveying happiness and sadness, poverty, wealth, and so on. Those of the man serve as a kind of love-letter – they speak subtly of the respect and affection in which he is held by the woman who fashioned them.

Cattle have had a pre-eminent place in the Zulu rural economy. Just how important they were is indicated by the number of words and phrases – more than 100 of them – used to describe the different varieties, and their distinguishing features. Cattle were the subject of praise-poems; they provided the sacrifices through which contact with the deities and ancestors was maintained, and the link (through lobola, or the 'bride price') between families.

Meat, though, was a rare delicacy rather than part of the standard Zulu diet. The cattle kraal was sacred, and the daughters of the house were the only women allowed to enter.

Surrounding the kraal were the family homes, beautifully crafted beehive-shaped structures of saplings thatched with grass.

These are some of the more visible ingredients of a time-honoured tapestry, and they are becoming less prominent with each succeeding generation. More enduring are the folklore and ritual, music (largely created by the cowhide drum and the 'choral band'), dance, epic poetry, customs, manners – the firm bonds of kinship.

In common with other African peoples, the Zulus believe in a Supreme Being, Umvelinqangi ('the first ever to live'), or Nkulunkulu ('creator of all things'). They also believe in their ancestors, and that they are near to them.

thatching, beading and knife-sharpening are interspersed with lively Zulu dancing and drumming.

A traditional kraal reflects the rural lifestyle of the people and typical furnishings of Zulu communities in the country. An open-air theatre offers four shows daily. These feature Ngoma dances, stories on folklore, taboos and rituals, the throwing of bones by a *sangoma* (witchdoctor), and a typical wedding ceremony.

The handsome curio shop features beadwork, sculptures and other crafts. Further up the road is the Assagay Safari Park, with its collection of over 400 crocodiles and snakes, and a natural-history museum. An open-air theatre offers live productions on aspects of Zulu culture. The restaurant is open during the day.

A rich tapestry of Zulu traditions is revealed at kraals such as this in the Valley of a Thousand Hills. Spears, shields, beadwork and other arts and crafts are all part of the Zulu heritage.

VERNON CROOKES NATURE RESERVE
Near Umzinto

Map: page 127, 5D
From Durban head south on the N2. Turn off at the Park Rynie/Umzinto fly-off, then follow the Highflats/Ixopo road. The reserve turn-off is about 3 km past Umzinto, 12,5 km from the freeway. The entrance gate is 6 km further on.
Details: Open all year round, sunrise to sunset.
Accommodation: The rustic Nyengelezi Camp in a forest clearing has all facilities and sleeps 20 people.
Further information: The Officer-in-Charge, Vernon Crookes Nature Reserve, P O Box 10624, Umzinto Station 4201, tel (0323) 4-2222.

Surrounded by sugar-cane fields and lovely softwood plantations, the Vernon Crookes Nature Reserve, lying eight kilometres north of Umzinto, is a 2 189-ha mosaic of rolling grasslands and forest patches, diverse enough to support a wide range of birds and mammals.

You can see more than 310 bird species among the abundant vegetation, which includes wild banana trees, ancient yellowwoods, flowering Cape chestnuts and numerous veld flowers. The variety of indigenous flora is thanks, in part, to the changing altitude within the reserve (from 150 m to 610 m above sea level).

Ten species of cisticola, forest-dwelling broadbills, Narina trogons, crowned and martial eagles, and a host of other birds make this a birder's paradise. Large antelope species such as eland, and zebras and blue wildebeest, congregate with smaller species such as bushbuck, nyala, oribi (rare to the area) and impala.

There's also an abundance of other smaller animals such as vervet monkeys, hyraxes, black-backed jackals, slender and banded mongooses, porcupines and servals, introduced by the Natal Parks Board from the Drakensberg.

Most of the remaining animals were introduced during the 1960s, when the reserve was privately owned.

The reserve offers about 12 km of game-viewing roads, an attractive picnic site and the 20-bed rustic Nyengelezi Camp. Visitors are welcome to walk in the reserve, but remember to take insect repellent – ticks can be troublesome.

DRAKENSBERG

DRAKENSBERG

CATHEDRAL PEAK
Near Winterton

Map: page 145, 3C
Cathedral Peak is reached via Winterton. From Winterton take the road leading southwest to Cathkin and Champagne peaks and follow signposts. The hotel is situated about 42 km further along.

Details: Permits for hiking and camping in the mountains, and for the drive up Mike's Pass, are obtainable from the Natal Parks Board office at the foot of Mike's Pass. Caves must also be booked in advance.

Accommodation: To book a camp site at Cathedral Peak, contact The Officer-in-Charge, Cathedral Peak, Private Bag X1, Winterton 3340, tel (036) 488-1880. Hotel accommodation available at Cathedral Peak Hotel, P O Winterton 3340, tel (036) 488-1888. The hotel is on private property. If you are not a guest at a hotel, you will need to begin your walks at the boom at the end of the Mlambonja River Valley road, or at the camp site.

Further information: Natal Parks Board, P O Box 1750, Pietermaritzburg 3200, tel (0331) 47-1981.

The sweeping vista up to the Cathedral Range, an awesome complex that includes Cleft Peak, The Bell and Cathedral Peak itself.

The blue-grey peaks of the Cathedral Range rise up above the Little Berg, silent, majestic, strangely forbidding, presenting an irresistible challenge to mountaineers. The Cathedral Range is a massive barrier of basalt that thrusts out eastwards from the main wall of the Drakensberg escarpment. Over the aeons the basalt has been eroded to form an impressive bastion of freestanding peaks. The original Zulu name for this ridge is *Mponjwane*, which means 'the place of the little horns'. Among the most imposing pinnacles are Cathedral Peak, the Bell, the Outer Horn, the Inner Horn, the Mitre, and Chessmen. Equally impressive are the peaks of the escarpment wall, such as Cleft Peak and the Mlambonja Buttress. From the summit of any of these peaks hikers are rewarded with awe-inspiring views of the length of the escarpment as it sweeps away to the north and south, fading to the palest blue-grey until it merges with the sky.

The dramatic terrain of Cathedral Peak range has made it one of the country's prime mountaineering areas. But you don't have to be a seasoned climber to enjoy the many delights of this lovely corner of South Africa. Lying in the shadows of the range are the folds of the Little Berg, the transitional zone between the low country of KwaZulu-Natal and the craggy heights of the escarpment. Several deep valleys are carved through the foothills of the Cathedral Peak area. Here walkers are rewarded with magnificent mountain scenery, beautiful indigenous trees, waterfalls, cascades and fern-fringed pools, where trout flick through the shadows.

The Cathedral Peak area is noteworthy for its dense forests, which are the largest surviving indigenous forests in the whole of the KwaZulu-Natal Drakensberg. This region includes the Mdedelelo Wilderness Area, and is administered by the Natal Parks Board as part of the Natal Drakensberg Park, which stretches from Cathedral Peak southwards as far as Bushman's Nek.

A minor drawback of the Cathedral Peak area is the limited choice of accommodation, because there are only two places to stay. Cathedral Peak Hotel is one of South Africa's best-known mountain resorts, a large, traditional establishment that has excellent facilities.

Lower down the scale is a pleasant, treed camp site opposite the guardhouse at the foot of Mike's Pass, south of the hotel.

A network of trails fans out from the Cathedral Peak Hotel, many of them leading into the Mlambonja Wilderness Area, which is administered by the Natal Parks Board. Experienced climbers will find it difficult to resist the energetic 10-km slog from the hotel to Cathedral Peak, or several other epic climbs, while the casual visitor will enjoy the many lovely walks that wind up the Mlambonja and adjoining valleys, leading to natural beauty spots such as Neptune's Pool and Marble Baths.

Those in search of a short hike with alluring scenery should not miss Rainbow Gorge. This undemanding two-hour ramble leads walkers splashing up a steep-sided and shadowy gorge, with an atmosphere of Tolkienesque enchantment: here pools are fringed with ferns and mosses, rainbows shimmer in the gauzy veils of spray and, further along, a giant chockstone is wedged between the gorge walls.

If you intend staying a little longer in the area, it's well worth venturing into the lonely Ndedema Gorge for a few days. This steep-sided valley supports an abundance of plant and animal life, and has many fine pools and cascades, as well as some beautiful pockets of thick yellowwood forest. The valley is famous for being one of the world's most important storehouses of San (Bushman) rock art – there are 17 sandstone rock shelters and caves containing some 4 000 individual paintings, the precious legacy of the ancient Stone-Age people who once lived and hunted in these remote foothills. These national treasures are strictly protected. Visitors may not camp or make fires in caves where paintings are found (some of the finest paintings are not even marked on the maps).

A worthwhile drive for those who lack the inclination to hike is up Mike's Pass, a winding road that takes motorists to picnic sites at the top of the Little Berg.

Many of the caves and rock shelters of the Ndedema Gorge served as 'galleries' for the long-gone San (Bushman) artists.

Hiking in the Berg

On a clear, mild day, the Little Berg presents an inviting and benign face to walkers but, as countless unfortunate hikers have discovered, these mountains can be treacherous, and deserve the greatest respect. Sudden changes of weather are common – terrifying thunder and lightning storms, sudden deluges that burst the banks of rivers, blinding snowstorms, blanketing fogs and bitterly cold temperatures. If you are planning to hike in the Drakensberg, even for a few hours, it is essential to take a number of common-sense precautions. These may well save your life in the event of a change of weather, an accident or a sudden illness.

■ Be sure to obtain the necessary permit before you set off, and always let someone know where you are going and how long you expect to be away. If you intend staying a night or more in the mountains, it is essential to sign the mountain register. People who fail to do so can be held responsible for all the costs incurred during a mountain rescue.

■ Leave early so that you do not have to walk in darkness, and never hike alone. Do not deviate from the paths or take short cuts – not only do you run the risk of losing your way, but you may also cause erosion to paths and thereby damage the environment.

■ Always carry an accurate map; these may be obtained at hotels, Natal Parks Board offices, forest stations and at all good bookshops. The definitive reference to the KwaZulu-Natal Drakensberg is a set of three maps compiled by the Directorate of Forestry, with cartography by Peter Slingsby. Another very useful reference is *Drakensberg Walks* by David Bristow (Struik), which contains maps and descriptions of 120 walks and hikes.

■ Be sure to take along the right equipment. Basic essentials for a hike include a torch, whistle, map, water bottle, first-aid kit, sunscreen cream, paper and pen, and high-energy rations such as chocolates, nuts and raisins.

■ Dress sensibly for the weather. Most of the rain falls in summer, and snow can be expected in winter, with light rain and fog in spring and autumn. Even on short day-hikes wear sturdy boots. Take along a hat and a warm jersey.

CATHKIN PEAK
Near Winterton

Map: page 145, 3C

The Cathkin Peak area is reached via Winterton, which lies 23 km west of the N3, between Pietermaritzburg and Ladysmith. From Winterton drive south on the R600. This tarred road continues for about 30 km, finally ending at Monk's Cowl Forest Station.

Details: Permits to enter the wilderness area are available from the Natal Parks Board at Monk's Cowl Forestry Station: The Officer-in-Charge, Monk's Cowl Forestry Station, Private Bag X2, Winterton 3340, tel (036) 468-1103.

Accommodation: There is a wider choice of accommodation here than anywhere else in the KwaZulu-Natal Drakensberg, ranging from luxury hotels to traditional family resorts and rustic camp sites. The closest hotel to the mountains is the Champagne Castle Hotel, Private Bag X8, Winterton 3340, tel (036) 468-1063. Many of the area's finest hikes begin at Cathkin Park Hotel, Private Bag X12, Winterton 3340, tel (036) 468-1091. Other hotels and resorts include the Drakensberg Sun, P O Box 355, Winterton 3340, tel (036) 468-1000; Champagne Valley Resort, Private Bag X25, Winterton 3340, tel (036) 468-1174; Berghaven Holiday Cottages, P O Box 192, Winterton 3340, tel (036) 468-1212; and The Nest, Private Bag X14, Winterton 3340, tel (036) 468-1068. At Monk's Cowl Forestry Station there is a terraced camp site with basic facilities.

Further information: Natal Parks Board, P O Box 1750, Pietermaritzburg 3200, tel (0331) 47-1981.

A century ago the lonely mountain folds that lie in the shadow of mighty Cathkin Peak were accessible only to those tenacious souls – settlers, woodcutters and mountaineers – who were prepared to make the long trek into the heart of the Drakensberg by wagon. Today, this lovely corner of KwaZulu-Natal is the most popular of all the province's mountain resort areas. Environmentalists may deplore the development that has taken place here in recent years, but there is no doubt that the many hotels and resorts in the Cathkin area have opened up this part of the Drakensberg to casual holiday-makers who appreciate comfortable accommodation and a wide choice of recreational facilities.

The most striking feature of the landscape is Cathkin Peak. This majestic basalt massif stands proud of the main wall of the Berg, its flat-topped, steep-sided bulk dominating the entire range. So formidable is this peak that the Zulus named it *Mdedelelo*, which means 'make way for him', the name usually applied to a bully. Behind Cathkin Peak, forming part of the escarpment, is Champagne Castle, at 3 377 m the second-highest peak in South Africa.

Monk's Cowl lies between the two, a jagged, threatening pinnacle that has claimed the lives of several mountaineers. North of Champagne Castle is the Dragon's Back, which has at its eastern end the Drakensberg's most extraordinary landmark: Ntunja, or Gatberg, a small peak that is neatly punctured by a huge, natural hole, resembling some sinister, unseeing eye.

In the shadow of the mountains the hills and valleys of the Little Berg roll away towards the lowlands of KwaZulu-Natal like the folds of a deep green quilt. The main access road from Winterton follows the course of the Sterkspruit River, and all along its length are camp sites, resorts and hotels. This is also the home of the world-famous Drakensberg Boys' Choir, where youngsters with voices like angels are able to enjoy their school years in the fresh mountain air.

Mountaineers and other keen hikers who visit this area are faced with a number of challenges, among them the trails that wind up to meet the contour path of the Little Berg, passing well-known landmarks such as Crystal Falls, The Sphinx, Jacob's Ladder, Verkykerskop and Stable Cave. Those who would like to strike out from the contour path and attempt the strenuous hike to the summit of Champagne Castle may choose from two routes, one via gruelling Ship's Prow Pass, and the other via Gray's Pass. The contour path continues northwards through the Mdedelelo Wilderness Area, a pristine 29 000-ha sanctuary that stretches as far as the Ndedema Gorge in the north *(see also entry for Cathedral Peak)*. All of the main hikes in this area begin at the Monk's Cowl Forest Station or at the Cathkin Park Hotel (which is private property).

For the casual walker there are many lovely short walks that lead through patches of beautiful indigenous forest, past deep, clear pools and tumbling cascades. Particularly recommended is the walk to Fern Forest, a one-kilometre ramble through sylvan corridors fringed by ferns, lichens and yellowwood trees. Other undemanding walks in the area lead to Sterkspruit Falls, Crystal Falls, the Grotto and to Barry's Grave, a simple sandstone memorial that is a sobering reminder of the heroism of the early mountaineers who tackled the formidable mountains of the Cathkin area. The grave is the final resting place of the talented young climber Dick Barry, who fell to his death on Monk's Cowl in 1938, aged only 22 years.

Another splendid way to explore the area is on horseback. Several hotels in the area have horses for hire.

The beautiful view towards Champagne Castle and Cathkin, a 3 194-m massif which is detached from the main Cathedral formation.

DRAKENSBERG

The attractive Injasuti Camp. From here one can see the splendours of Champagne Castle and the 3 410-m Injasuti Dome.

The reserve's main camp hugs a hillside beneath the snow-clad Giant's Castle buttress.

GIANT'S CASTLE GAME RESERVE
Near Estcourt

The whisper of the wind through pale golden grass and the hushed murmurings of icy waters are the only sounds that sift through the blue-grey silence of the high mountains at Giant's Castle Game Reserve, situated some 65 km southwest of Estcourt. This lovely nature sanctuary, with its vast, rolling expanses of Little Berg, its soaring mountain backdrop and its great diversity of game and bird life, is the ideal holiday destination for nature-lovers who enjoy the peace and solitude of wide-open spaces.

Large numbers of eland graze the grasslands of this part of the Little Berg, and it was in order to protect these fast-vanishing herds that the reserve was originally proclaimed in 1903. The name of the reserve refers to the four-kilometre-long ridge and adjacent peak known as Giant's Castle, which, at 3 314 m, is the fifth-highest peak in the country. Also within the reserve is the highest peak, the 3 409-m-high Mafadi Peak.

In 1980 the reserve expanded to incorporate Injasuti to the north (formerly a private farm called *Solitude*), bringing its total area to 34 638 hectares. The Injasuti Valley has a quiet loveliness all of its own, nestling in the long shadows of some of the most formidable features of the high Berg, among them the Injasuti Triplets, the Greater and Lesser Injasuti buttresses, the Red Wall, and the peak that is picturesquely known as The Old Woman Grinding Corn.

The reserve's two hutted camps are arguably the most beautiful to be found anywhere in the Drakensberg. The stone-and-thatch cottages of the main camp lie among indigenous gardens with views of Giant's Castle, while Injasuti Camp to the north comprises a string of cottages that huddle together on a valley floor, embraced by a glorious amphitheatre of mountains.

The reserve is watered by the Bushmans and Injasuti rivers and numerous branching streams that flow through pockets of tangled indigenous forest, creating numerous small cascades and clear, icy pools that are most inviting on a hot summer's day. The rivers are amply stocked with trout, and fishing in the reserve is permitted.

A network of hiking trails crisscrosses the reserve, ranging from short, pleasant rambles through leafy valleys, to energetic hikes along the Little Berg escarpment, and then on to the top of the escarpment via Langalibalele Pass and Bannermans Pass. Particularly recommended is the Forest Walk, an enchanting 4,5-km round trip along Two Dassie Stream. A pamphlet and map describing features of this and other walks are available from the camps.

Hikers can expect to see more varied game here than anywhere else in the Berg, including eland, blesbok, oribi, klipspringer, grey rhebok, reedbuck and red hartebeest. Over 140 bird species have been identified in the reserve. It is also one of the last strongholds of the endangered lammergeier, or bearded vulture. Lammergeiers are fed in winter

Map: page 145, 3/4C
Giant's Castle Game Reserve is situated 65 km southwest of Estcourt and is well signposted. To reach Injasuti Hutted Camp turn off the N3 freeway at the Loskop interchange and follow the road for 27 kilometres. Turn left at the Injasuti signpost; the camp is 32 km further along. There is no direct road linking the 2 hutted camps.

Details: The reserve is open from sunrise to sunset. Admission charged. Permits to enter the wilderness area may be obtained from the hutted camps and entrance gates.

Accommodation: At Giant's Castle Hutted Camp there is a luxury lodge for 7 people, and self-catering accommodation in cottages and bungalows. The hutted camp at Injasuti accommodates guests in 17 self-contained 6-bed cabins. Visitors may stay overnight at Lower Injasuti Cave and Fergy's Cave (both have basic ablution facilities), but bookings must be made in advance. To reserve accommodation in huts and in caves, write to the Natal Parks Board, P O Box 1750, Pietermaritzburg 3200, tel (0331) 47-1981. The Injasuti camp site accommodates 80 people. To book, contact The Camp Superintendent, Injasuti Camp, Private Bag X7010, Estcourt 3310, tel (036) 488-1050. Hillside camp site accommodates 150 people and caters primarily for horse-riders; horse-trails may be booked. Contact The Officer-in-Charge, Hillside, P O Box 288, Estcourt 3310, tel (0363) 2-4435.

Further information: Natal Parks Board, P O Box 1750, Pietermaritzburg 3200, tel (0331) 47-1981.

149

DRAKENSBERG

Bow-wielding hunters surround a huge bison-like creature on the wall of a Giant's Castle cave. The reserve has two site museums.

at a special 'vulture restaurant'. They and other cliff-dwelling species may be viewed from a stone bird hide.

Many beautiful San rock paintings are concealed in caves and overhangs in the sandstone cliffs of the reserve – it was here that the last Drakensberg Bushman was shot in 1903. An insight into the ways of these ancient hunter-gatherers may be gained by visiting the open-air museum at Main Caves. This archaeological treasure house contains over 700 distinct rock paintings, as well as life-size figures and artefacts. Also worth visiting is Battle Cave in the Injasuti Valley, a national monument that contains a magnificent frieze of a battle scene. Guided tours are offered daily to both caves. Several of the other caves in the reserve can accommodate hikers.

Giant's Castle Game Reserve has a special attraction for horse-riders, who may hire horses at the reserve's Hillside Camp for two- and three-day mountain rides.

LOTENI NATURE RESERVE
Near Himeville

Map: page 145, 4C/D
From the N3 between Pietermaritzburg and Ladysmith turn west onto the R103 at Howick. You reach Nottingham Road after 28 kilometres. Turn east onto the Himeville road. The tarred road ends after 28 kilometres. Continue for a further 32 km until you see the signposted turning to Loteni on the right. The hutted camp is 14 km further along this road.

Details: The reserve is open from sunrise to sunset. Admission charged. Permits to enter the wilderness area are available at the Natal Parks Board office near the hutted camp.

Accommodation: Loteni Hutted Camp has 14 self-contained cottages, and Simes rustic cottage, which sleeps ten. There is also a camp site with 10 stands.

Further information: Natal Parks Board, P O Box 1750, Pietermaritzburg 3200, tel (0331) 47-1981; The Camp Manager, P O Box 14, Himeville 4585, tel (033) 702-0540.

It's a long and twisting road that leads visitors deep into the cool, green embrace of the mountains, but once you reach Loteni you know that the lengthy drive has been worth it. Set in the southern part of the Drakensberg, this wild and secluded mountain sanctuary has a special magic for nature-lovers, and also for anglers who come to enjoy excellent trout-fishing along a 12-km length of the broad Loteni River.

The 3 984-ha reserve forms part of the vast Mkhomazi Wilderness Area, which is bordered by Giant's Castle to the north and Sani Pass to the south. In turn, this area forms part of the larger Natal Drakensberg Park. The high mountain wall in the background lacks some of the drama of the freestanding peaks to the north, but is nonetheless a formidable presence, featuring some of the highest points in South Africa. Among them are The Tent (3 130 m) and Redi Peak (3 314 metres). At the foot of the escarpment are the grassy slopes of the Little Berg, a deep, rich green in summer, fading to burnished gold during the dry winter months. Isolated corridors of indigenous forest are concealed in deep gorges, while the open, grassy slopes are scattered with beautiful everlastings *(Helichrysum spp.)* and ericas. A variety of antelope roams the sour grasslands, including mountain reedbuck, grey rhebok and eland.

The area is particularly noteworthy for its fine caves, two of which (Yellowwood Cave and Ash Cave) are a fairly undemanding three-hour tramp along the Loteni River.

A rustic but comfortable hutted camp lies in splendid isolation on the valley floor, offering fine views of the high Berg. This is a useful base for those hikers who wish to explore the higher reaches of the valley. A small settler homestead situated nearby has been converted into a fine museum, and displays old implements, furniture and utensils.

The rounded green hills of Loteni, a part of the Little Berg known for its bird life, its caves and for the superb trout-fishing along the river.

ROYAL NATAL
Near Bergville

Great patience is needed to obtain a reservation for a holiday in Royal Natal, but it's worth the long wait, because this spellbindingly beautiful mountain sanctuary is one of the finest in South Africa, and certainly the foremost of all the reserves that fall within the Natal Drakensberg Park. Encompassing some 9 000 ha of the Little Berg, the reserve boasts a singularly spectacular scenic backdrop: the mighty Amphitheatre, a towering mountain wall whose formidable buttresses and dizzying pinnacles soar half a kilometre upwards to embrace the clouds.

This gigantic massif, extending for five kilometres north to south in a sweeping arc of volcanic basalt, divides the snowbound plateau of Lesotho from the rolling hills and valleys of KwaZulu-Natal. There are few sights in the whole of southern Africa as awe-inspiring as the Amphitheatre, especially when viewed from the rim of the escarpment. The Eastern Buttress forms its southeastern bastion, concealing the Devil's Tooth and Inner Tower. To the west is the Beacon Buttress and the Sentinel.

The highest peak of the plateau is Mont-aux-Sources, which was named by two French missionaries who trekked to the edge of the escarpment in 1837. More than eight important rivers rise here, including the Tugela, which smokes over the lip of the escarpment in a series of spectacular falls, dropping 850 m before spilling down into Royal Natal's lovely Tugela Valley.

The park was proclaimed in 1916, but earned its royal title in 1947 when it was visited by the British Royal Family. The Amphitheatre is the most notable scenic feature, but even when the mountain wall is obscured by banks of swirling cloud, the reserve is a place of singular beauty. The Little Berg rolls away from the Amphitheatre in a series of velvety folds, its wind-rippled grass slopes spangled with wildflowers, its valleys concealing numerous quick-flowing rivers and streams. The varied topography supports a diversity of plant life, and over 180 species of bird have been identified here, including the rare and majestic lammergeier or bearded vulture.

Over 30 walks and climbs are mapped out in the reserve, ranging from easy rambles through the Little Berg to gruelling hikes that lead backpackers to

The thin ribbon of the upper Tugela hurries down the cloud-wreathed Mont-aux-Sources heights to make its way through the Royal Natal park. One of the river's falls drops sheer for more than 180 metres.

Map: page 145, 2B
The park is situated 48 km along a tarred road west of Bergville (take the R74 and turn left towards the park after 29 km), or 72 km from Harrismith via the Sterkfontein Dam and Oliviershoek Pass.

Details: Tendele Camp and the Royal Natal camp-site gates are open from sunrise to sunset. Admission charged at the entrance.

Accommodation: Tendele Camp has a luxury lodge, bungalows, cottages and self-catering chalets. For reservations write to the Natal Parks Board, P O Box 1750, Pietermaritzburg 3200, tel (0331) 47-1981. To reserve a camp site at Mahai or nearby Rugged Glen, which caters for 45 visitors, contact The Officer-in-Charge, Royal Natal, Private Bag X1669, Bergville 3350, tel (036) 438-6412. The comfortable, privately run Royal Natal National Park Hotel is situated near the Visitors' Centre. To make reservations contact the hotel at Private Bag 4, Mont-aux-Sources 3350, tel (036) 438-6200. Other hotels in the area include Little Switzerland, Private Bag X1161, Bergville 3350, tel (036) 438-6220; The Cavern Berg Resort, Private Bag X1626, Bergville 3350, tel (036) 438-6270; Hlalanathi Berg Resort has chalets and camping sites. Contact the resort at Private Bag X1621, Bergville 3350, tel (036) 438-6308.

Further information: Natal Parks Board, P O Box 1750, Pietermaritzburg 3200, tel (0331) 47-1981.

Horseback riders explore the countryside of the Rugged Glen reserve, virtually part of the Royal Natal complex. The park offers magnificent scenery and beautiful wildflowers.

the very top of the Amphitheatre. One of the most popular is the lovely seven-kilometre walk up the Tugela Gorge, which passes through protea savannah and yellowwood forest into the main gorge, where there are many lovely mountain pools.

Maps may be purchased at the park's Visitors' Centre, which also has some interesting exhibits detailing the history, fauna, flora and geology of the region. Also obtainable here is the informative trail guide for Otto's Walk, a three-kilometre interpretive ramble through forest scrub and indigenous forest.

Many people use the reserve as a base from which to tackle the Sentinel Hiking Trail, a walk that is unique in the Drakensberg, in that it allows hikers to make a very quick ascent to the top of the escarpment. A road leads to a car park at the base of the Sentinel, where the trail begins. From here it is a moderately strenuous two-hour walk to the summit, with the last section involving a hair-raising vertical climb up the famous chain ladders.

Hikers may camp overnight on the Mont-aux-Sources plateau, but it is essential to sign the mountain register and to ensure that you have the necessary equipment *(see box on page 147)* before setting off.

Another excellent way to explore the reserve is on horseback. Horses may be hired from Rugged Glen (adjacent to Royal Natal, and four kilometres from its gate). Trout-fishing in the park's rivers and dam is another attraction. (Rugged Glen also offers trout-fishing.)

The accommodation in the reserve caters to all tastes and pockets. Tendele is a lovely camp that commands some splendid views of the mountains. Mahai camp site has pleasant grassed sites for tents and caravans.

NORTHERN KWAZULU-NATAL

NORTHERN KWAZULU-NATAL

BLOOD RIVER MONUMENT
East of Dundee

Map: page 153, 3B
The Blood River battlefield is about half an hour's drive from Dundee. Take the Vryheid road north, turn right after 21 km, and continue for a further 19 kilometres.
Details: The battlesite museum is open daily throughout the year. There is an admission fee. Of interest are replicas of various guns, as well as life-size bronze wagons.
Accommodation: Hotel, self-catering and caravan/camping facilities are available in and around Dundee.
Further information: Talana Museum, Private Bag X2024, Dundee 3000, tel (034) 2-2654; Pietermaritzburg Publicity Association, P O Box 25, Pietermaritzburg 3200, tel (0331) 45-1348.

Ghosts from a tragically violent past whisper at you from among the great bronze oxwagons that mark the battlesite of Blood River. There are 64 of them, arranged in the precise laager formation contrived by the Voortrekkers, filling the space between the Ncome Spruit – the name, ironically, means 'pleasant stream' – and a deeply eroded gulley, with a clear line of fire to the northwest.

Across this field, on 16 December 1838, the massed ranks of Dingane's warriors advanced, and were slaughtered in their thousands.

The Voortrekkers had suffered grievously during the preceding months. They'd left their homes in the colonial Cape in search of a new land. But early in the year their optimistic dealings with Dingane ended abruptly with the killing of Piet Retief and his advance party on the bloody slopes of Umgungundhlovu. The Zulu impis then attacked the other Trekker groups, inflicting substantial losses on them at Bloukrans, Bushmans River (now called Weenen, or the 'place of weeping') and Moordspruit, before the laagers were strengthened.

In November 1838 Andries Pretorius had been summoned from Graaff-Reinet, far to the west, to lead a large force, named the Wenkommando, in a concerted drive against the Zulus. In the days before the confrontation the Voortrekkers made a vow to (or covenant with) God. This affirmed that, should the Almighty grant them victory, they would build a church in His honour, and for ever observe the date as a Sabbath and day of thanksgiving.

The Wenkommando, augmented by the Trekkers' coloured employees and a group of British settlers from Durban, comprised some 470 men, the Zulu impi over 12 000.

But the huge Zulu numbers, rawhide shields, knobkerries, stabbing spears and courage proved no match for the deadly firepower of muzzle-loaders, flintlocks and three small cannons.

The wagons were lashed firmly together, their wheels joined by wooden

Full-scale replicas of wagons arranged in a laager commemorate the role of the Voortrekkers at the Blood River Monument near Dundee.

palisades or 'veghekke' to present a barrier that the Zulus failed to breach in three suicidal onslaughts.

When they finally retreated, they left 3 000 dead comrades on the field of battle. The Trekker casualties amounted to just three wounded, among them Andries Pretorius.

The Voortrekkers went on to found the short-lived Republic of Natalia, and built the Church of the Vow in Pietermaritzburg, the quiet republican capital.

Dingane was eventually ousted by his half-brother Mpande, and fled to what is known today as Swaziland. Pretorius moved north to fight for Transvaal's independence from the British, and eventually bequeathed his name to a future capital of South Africa.

FORT NONGQAYI
Eshowe

Eshowe's picturesque fort, with its white-walled battlements and three turrets, seems to have leapt from the pages of a P C Wren novel about the French Foreign Legion. It was, in fact, built by the British around 1884, after the Anglo-Zulu War, as a barracks for the Natal Native Police who served as bodyguard to the then resident commissioner, Sir Melmoth Osborn. It now houses the Zululand Historical Museum, which is well worth visiting for its military, British and Zulu royal memorabilia, and artefacts of local interest. Also exhibited are fossils dating back some 60 million years, photographs of the fort and its unique force in action, a splendid Spanish mahogany furniture collection belonging to John Dunn (the famous white Zulu chief), and works by local artists. Local crafts are on sale. The building, a proclaimed historical monument, is surrounded by immaculate lawns and stands of indigenous flora that invite picnickers. An American naval gun, an anchor from the *HMS Tenedos*, and an early sugar-cane wagon are to be seen in the grounds. From the fort, a 20-minute trail leads to the sparkling and lovely Mpushini Falls.

The nearby Dlinza State Forest is one of the few substantial indigenous forest reserves in the world to be embraced by a town. It is 205 ha in extent, and its dense green canopy gives shade to bushbuck, blue duiker, bushpigs, little vervet monkeys, vivid butterflies and a host of birds. Some 180 species of wildflower, including orchids, clivias and delicate ferns, flourish within the reserve.

For visitors, there are footpaths, self-guided trails, a road system and six picnic spots. An attractive natural amphitheatre known as the Bishop's Seat is the setting for Nativity plays every three years.

Map: page 153, 5D
From Durban take the N2 highway or the more scenic M4 as far as Ballito, and then the N2 to Gingindlovu, and turn onto the R68. Continue for 26 km to Eshowe. The fort is on Nongqai Road. The Dlinza Forest Nature Reserve is traversed by both Goatly Road and National Arch Drive.

Details: Museum: Open daily throughout the year 09h00-16h00. Check before visiting on religious holidays. Admission free but donations welcome. Information: Zululand Historical Museum, P O Box 37, Eshowe 3815, tel (0354) 4-1141. Dlinza Forest Nature Reserve: Open throughout the year 05h00-19h00 (October to March), and 06h00-18h00 (April to September). Admission free.

Accommodation: Eshowe and surrounds are well served by hotels, guesthouses, bed-and-breakfast and self-catering facilities, as well as guest farms. There is a municipal camping/caravan park. To the north of Eshowe is Shakaland *(see separate entry)* and, off the R34 to Empangeni (some 35 km from Eshowe), is KwaBhekithunga, a complex of beehive huts offering novel accommodation in a traditional setting.

Further information: Eshowe Publicity Association, P O Box 37, Eshowe 3815, tel (0354) 4-1141; KwaBhekithunga, P O Box 364, Eshowe 3815, tel (03546) 644; Zululand Historical Museum, P O Box 37, Eshowe 3815, tel (0354) 4-1141; Natal Parks Board, P O Box 1750, Pietermaritzburg 3200, tel (0331) 47-1981.

John Dunn, the legendary white chief who lived in Zululand.

NORTHERN KWAZULU-NATAL

HLUHLUWE-UMFOLOZI PARK
North of Mtubatuba

Map: page 153, 3/4E
Hluhluwe-Umfolozi Park is 280 km from Durban, and 60 km north of Mtubatuba. Follow the N2 to Hluhluwe Village, and turn left onto the tarred road stretching 20 km to Hluhluwe's Memorial Gate. For Umfolozi, turn left 3,4 km beyond Mtubatuba, and continue for 27 km, turning off at the signpost. A 13-km road runs through the corridor, linking the Sithole area of Hluhluwe with Umfolozi's Masinda Camp.

Details: Open daily throughout the year. Gate times: 05h00-19h00 (summer) and 06h00-18h00 (winter). Best time to visit is winter, when the wildlife is more concentrated and visible. Entry fee per vehicle and passenger. Literature on the various walks and trails, and on other attractions and amenities, is available from the camp offices.

Accommodation: Umfolozi has 2 main camps (Mpila and Masinda) and 2 attractive bush camps (Nselweni and Sontuli), offering accommodation ranging from fully equipped and serviced chalets to simple 4-bed rest huts with separate cooking and ablution facilities. Hluhluwe's Hilltop Camp is the oldest hutted camp in KwaZulu-Natal, offering self-contained cottages and rondavels with ablution blocks (also braai and freezer facilities). Newly built at Hilltop is a luxurious rest camp boasting an *a la carte* restaurant (venison a speciality), cocktail lounge/bar and fine views. The Hluhluwe section's Mtwazi Lodge and the Muntulu Bush Camp are more intimate.

Further information: Natal Parks Board, P O Box 1750, Pietermaritzburg 3200, tel (0331) 47-1981.

If Africa's fast-shrinking rhino population manages to avoid total eclipse, the credit, or a great deal of it, must go to the Natal Parks Board and its conservation efforts in the Hluhluwe-Umfolozi area.

For almost 100 years following their inception in the late 1890s – they are among the oldest of the continent's conservation enterprises – the two sections functioned as completely separate units, self-contained reserves, separated by a narrow corridor. They were then consolidated to create one of the biggest and finest of the world's game sanctuaries.

The combined 96 000-ha area is warm, well-watered, lush, and it embraces a remarkable diversity of habitats. In the Umfolozi segment, which occupies the fertile countryside between the White and Black Umfolozi rivers, you'll find generous flood plain, well-treed wetland and woodland savannah, dense bush thicket and sweet natural pastures. Hluhluwe is somewhat smaller, hillier, an enchanting mix of misty forest, grassy hill and emerald-fringed watercourse.

The place derives its name from the thick lianas or 'monkey ropes' that entwine the riverine trees.

Between them, the Hluhluwe and Umfolozi are home to more than 1 000 white and about 400 black rhinos. Both animals are classified as endangered, though the smaller, more aggressive 'black' species is especially vulnerable.

Cool morning mists lift to unveil the verdant slopes of the Hluhluwe-Umfolozi Park, still largely untrampled by streams of visitors.

A pair of white rhinos refresh themselves at a muddy water hole at Hluhluwe-Umfolozi Park. The mud insulates their skin against tickbites.

The rhinos, in common with the other herbivores of the region, fell victim to the massive campaign that was launched in the 1920s to eradicate the disease-bearing tsetse fly. Over 100 000 head of game were exterminated before chemical controls replaced the culler's rifle. The few remaining rhinos were cherished, grew in number and, in the 1960s, with the development of drug-darting techniques, small breeding herds were captured and translocated to other reserves to ensure (at least for a time) the survival of the species. At the vanguard of this exercise was the environmentalist Ian Player and his team of Natal Parks Board rangers.

The other game populations also made a good recovery, and today the park is

haven for a stunning variety of wildlife. Mammals alone number nearly 90 species. Elephants, buffaloes, lions and leopards join the rhinos to complete the 'big five' complement. Hippos, giraffes, zebras, wildebeest, cheetahs, hyaenas, wild dogs and an array of antelope add to the splendid parade. The Hluhluwe-Umfolozi Park is also a bird-watcher's delight: over 350 species are represented. Notable raptors include white-backed vultures, bateleurs, Wahlberg's eagles and the rarely seen Narina trogon.

Visitors enjoy self-guided drives along 80 km of game-viewing roads. Especially recommended are the 67-km self-guided Umfolozi Mosaic, and the two Hluhluwe auto trails (detailed booklets available).

Some 24 000 ha of the Umfolozi section are preserved as wilderness, open only to hikers on organized trails. Of these, the five-day White Rhino route, organized by the Wilderness Leadership School, is especially worthwhile.

There are several other interesting hikes and rambles, including short (two-hour) ranger-conducted game walks from the main camps.

A waterbuck cow at Hluhluwe. This graceful, rather shy, antelope is easily identified by the white 'target' ring on its rump.

ITALA GAME RESERVE
Louwsburg

Itala, a 30 000-ha expanse of varied and ruggedly beautiful landscapes, is something of a phoenix among the country's game reserves.

It lies well inland, to the south of the Pongola River, and for much of the century's earlier decades its natural riches were squandered. Rinderpest and, later, a game extermination programme designed to rid the region of tsetse fly, made massive inroads into the wildlife population (indeed, 25 mammal species disappeared altogether). Alien flora corrupted much of the ground cover. Tenant farmers took over, and the land suffered grievously from overgrazing.

Then, in 1973, the area was proclaimed a reserve, and the Natal Parks Board moved in to nurture the veld back to health, and to restock it with its original game animals. In the process, they accomplished an environmental miracle.

Today, Itala is a pristine sanctuary for more than 80 different kinds of mammal, including elephants, white and black rhinos, buffaloes, giraffes, zebras, leopards, cheetahs, hyaenas, the country's largest concentration of klipspringer, and many other antelope.

About 320 bird species have been recorded. Among the high cliffs and wooded slopes of the western parts you'll

Map: page 153, 2D
Itala is located just north of the village of Louwsburg. From Durban take the N2 to Pongola, turn left onto the R66 and drive for 24 kilometres. Turn right onto the R69 and continue for 54 km to Louwsburg. Alternatively, take the route through Eshowe and Melmoth to Vryheid, and then turn east along the R69 for the final 63-km stretch to Louwsburg. The reserve is a 1-minute drive from the village.
From Gauteng take the N2 to Piet Retief, the R33 to Vryheid and continue to Louwsburg via the R69.
Details: Open dawn to dusk throughout the year. Gate times (summer) 05h00-19h00 and (winter) 06h00-18h00. Entry fee per vehicle and passenger. Fuel is available at the main gate. The reserve has a network of gravelled game-viewing roads, viewpoints and picnic sites. The 3-day wilderness trails (book in advance) are conducted from March to October. Guided day-walks are also on offer. Itala has a 1 200-m airstrip for fly-in guests. Private pilots must make prior arrangements with Itala's office.
Accommodation: Ntshondwe Camp has fully equipped, self-catering 2- and 3-bedroom units, an *a la carte* restaurant, takeaway, swimming pool, small supermarket and curio shop. Ntshondwe Lodge offers 3 *en suite* bedrooms, a pool and domestic help. Ntshondwe's conference centre has accommodation for 56 delegates in 28 two-bed rooms. The small, self-catering bush camps – Thalu, Mbizo and Mhlangeni – are sited well away from the main tourist routes (bring your own food).
Further information: Natal Parks Board, P O Box 1750, Pietermaritzburg 3200, tel (0331) 47-1981. To reserve an Itala conference venue, contact Itala Game Reserve, P O Box 98, Louwsburg 3150, tel (0388) 7-5106. To reserve camp sites, contact The Warden, Itala Game Reserve, P O Box 42, Louwsburg 3150, tel (0388) 7-5239.

The black eagle: lord of the skies

If you glance up from the rugged, boulder-strewn slopes of the Itala reserve's western escarpment you're likely to see a black eagle, one of the less common and most striking of southern Africa's birds of prey.

It will be hunting – perhaps in tandem with its mate – for the dassies, or rock rabbits, that make up the bulk of its diet.

These small, rodent-like mammals, whose closest living relative is (of all things!) the elephant, share the black eagle's habitat, living in colonies ranging from a few to several hundred individuals. They're often to be observed basking in the sun among the rocky outcrops. Easy meat, it would seem, for the big birds, but they are sharp-eyed and will emit a high-pitched bark and scuttle into their holes at the first sign of danger.

The eagles can only succeed by surprise attack, swooping around the corner of a cliff. Moreover, they often hunt in pairs, one bird distracting the prey while the other prepares itself for the run-in.

To keep hunger at bay a black eagle two-some needs to catch one dassie every two to three days, more often if the birds have a nestling to rear. They invariably build their nests of sticks and leaves on a cliff ledge, returning to them year after year, repairing and enlarging the structure prior to the protracted winter breeding cycle. The older nests can reach two metres in diameter and an impressive four metres in depth. Some pairs maintain more than one nest, alternating between them seasonally.

The pair produces a clutch of two eggs, the first laid about four days before the second, but cainism – the 'Cain-and-Abel' sequence in which the stronger (first-born) chick kills off its sibling – inevitably takes its toll. Why this should be so remains a mystery. It almost certainly isn't a struggle for limited food supplies, since the nest, in many instances, contains an abundance of dassie carcasses.

Black eagles are large, powerful, noble-looking raptors, weighing up to six kilograms, and their distinctive wings can measure 95 cm from tip to tip. Despite their name they are not a uniform black, though they appear almost so when perched. And even then, at certain angles, you can see the typical V-shaped white lines on their backs.

NORTHERN KWAZULU-NATAL

find breeding pairs of black eagles. Elsewhere, on the open bushveld and in the magically forested river valleys (six rivers make their way through the reserve) there are bat-hawks and martial eagles, brown-necked parrots and Cape eagle-owls.

Itala's 200-guest Ntshondwe is among the finest of rest camps. It nestles beneath the towering cliffs of the western escarpment, and the views from its 39 comfortable chalets and cottages are quite stunning. The thatched buildings, sensitively designed to blend with their rugged, boulder-strewn and euphorbia-graced surroundings, front onto a water hole. The latter is well patronized, and you view the animals from strategically sited walkways and hides. There is also a conference centre.

Higher up the hill is Ntshondwe's luxurious lodge, which boasts its own swimming pool, sundeck and braai area. Each of its three bedrooms is equipped with a bathroom *en suite*. Further away, secluded beside streams in the heart of the reserve, are three bush camps.

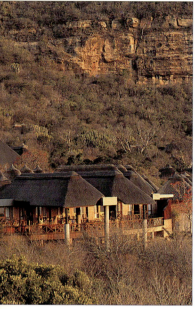

Weatherworn cliffs loom protectively above the thatched restaurant complex at Itala's Ntshondwe Camp.

Itala Game Reserve comprises a rich world of grasslands and dense indigenous bush, crisscrossed by a network of trails and paths.

KOSI BAY NATURE RESERVE
Northeastern KwaZulu-Natal

Map: page 153, 2F
Take the N2 highway to the Jozini turn-off, and bear left at Jozini towards the Ndumo Game Reserve. Pass the Ndumo turn-off to continue through KwaNgwanase (stop at the petrol station to fill up). The tar ends here. Continue straight, and turn right at the store 7 km further on. The Kosi Bay Camp is another 7 km from here.
Details: Open dawn to dusk throughout the year. Entrance fee. The 18-km route from Kosi Bay Camp to the estuary is suitable only for four-wheel-drives, and a limited number are allowed along it each day.
Accommodation: The small and very pleasant Kosi Bay Rest Camp offers 3 fully equipped lodges (sleeping 2, 5 and 6, respectively) and 15 camping sites scattered among the trees. There are also 4 trail camps.
Further information: Department of Nature Conservation, Private Bag X9024, Pietermaritzburg 3200, tel (0331) 94-6696/7/8.

The name is misleading: this entrancing 11 000-ha stretch of coastal countryside is not known for its bay, but for its chain of four lakes. They extend for some 30 km along the northern Maputaland shoreline, their fresh waters separated from the sea by some of the world's highest forested dunes.

Summertime here is hot and humid, and Kosi Bay and its marine extension have enormous appeal for bird-watchers, fishermen, hikers, skin-divers, snorkellers and boating enthusiasts. An early Portuguese explorer described the complex as 'the river of the sands of gold'.

Largest of the lakes is Nhlange. Amanzimnyama is the southernmost. Mpungwini connects with Makhawulani, the northernmost, which drains into a wide, sweeping estuary (the 'bay') that narrows to its sea outlet.

Here, at the northern end, the local Tembe villagers build timber-boomed, twine-tied traps (locally known as fish 'kraals') to guide the fish into smaller enclosures where they are speared. This fascinating technique, like so much else in Maputaland, belongs to the old Africa, a traditional fisherman's craft handed down through countless generations.

For the rest, the Kosi Bay reserve is a wonderland of tropical greenery, the terrain graced by reeds and water lilies, rare orchids, ancient cycads, wild date and ilala palms, giant sycamore figs, mangrove swamp and grassland. All of which attracts regiments of birds, the 300 recorded species featuring palmnut vultures, African fish eagles, herons, kingfishers and flufftails.

Hippos and crocodiles bask in and around the lakes (bathing is forbidden). Duiker, bushbuck and monkeys (including the rare samango monkey) inhabit the woodland areas.

There's excellent fishing in the estuary and lakes (bream, sea pike, queenfish), and, of course, in the sea – both from the shore and further out, among coral reefs whose magical depths attract a galaxy of colourful marine life. If you're skin-diving or snorkelling, though, beware of sharks and such toxic creatures as the scorpionfish and the lethal stonefish.

The seashore also serves as host to the once-endangered giant leatherback and loggerhead turtles, which crawl up the beaches at night to lay their eggs. A Natal Parks Board/Department of Conservation turtle survey team operates from nearby Bhanga Nek.

Terrestrial attractions include some pleasant walks, notably the four-day Kosi Trail (book well in advance) and a scout-guided ramble that beats a sure path through the dense ground cover.

Fishermen at Kosi Bay fashion a trap of branches and poles to tunnel fish into a small enclosure.

LAKE SIBAYA
North of Sodwana Bay

South Africa's largest freshwater lake extends across 77 km² of the tropically humid Maputaland coastal plain north of St Lucia *(see separate entry)*, its clear, placid, blue waters separated from the Indian Ocean by a massive rampart of forested dunes. (These are amongst the highest vegetated coastal dunes in the world.) The separation, though, is fairly recent in geophysical terms.

Sibaya was once a sea estuary, and it is still home to 10 or so species of marine fish that, over millennia, have adapted to their changed environment.

Sibaya is also a natural haven for crocodiles and more than 150 hippos, both of which play their part in sustaining the ecosystem – the former by restricting the number of catfish, the latter by enriching the lake's overall nutrient content with their droppings.

Moreover, the hippos help control reed growth and keep the labyrinthine channels and inlets open.

The lake and its surrounds are sanctuary for reedbuck, side-striped jackals and a host of small mammals, and for a splendid number and variety of birds. Especially prominent among the 250-odd species is the African fish eagle, known for its plaintive call and spectacular hunting routine.

Herons, cormorants (white-breasted and reed) and kingfishers (giant, pied and malachite) also delight the eye.

The lake area, a proclaimed reserve, hasn't yet been extensively developed, and the roads, though passable, tend to be a bit rugged in wet weather. Bird-watching hides and some pleasant walking trails have been established, and visitors have access (by four-wheel-drive) to the adjacent and inviting Nine Mile Beach. Neither the lake nor the sea here is suitable for casual bathing.

Sibaya's attractive Baya Rest Camp is a wilderness venue with reed-and-thatch huts, boardwalk, boma and a pool.

Map: page 153, 2F
Sibaya is 20 km north of Sodwana Bay. From Durban follow the N2 coastal highway to and through Hluhluwe Village and turn off at the signpost. The condition of this gravel access road varies from season to season.

Details: Open dawn to dusk throughout the year. Entry fee per vehicle and passenger. Visitor facilities include bird-watching hides, observation platform and short walking trails. Fishing permitted; boats and coxswains can be hired. Bathing is prohibited. Beware of crocodiles, hippos, malaria (take precautions before arrival) and bilharzia. Bring your own provisions; the nearest shop and petrol outlet are at Mbazwana, about 20 km to the south.

Accommodation: Baya Camp, 150 m from the lakeshore, offers 2- and 4-bed huts with communal bathroom facilities. Visitors either cook their food over the fire or have meals prepared for them by camp staff. There are freezer facilities.

Further information: Department of Nature Conservation, Private Bag X9024, Pietermaritzburg 3200, tel (0331) 94-6696/7/8.

The setting sun casts a purple haze across the reed-fringed waters of Lake Sibaya.

Luxuriant greenery and yellow-barked fever trees envelope Nhlohlela Pan at Mkuzi Game Reserve.

MKUZI GAME RESERVE
East of Mkuze

Map: page 153, 3E
Mkuzi Game Reserve lies about 335 km north of Durban. Follow the N2 highway north through Mtubatuba and Hluhluwe Village. Turn right at the Mkuzi sign 35 km beyond Hluhluwe, and continue on gravel for 15 km, turning off again at the sign for the final 10-km stretch.
Details: Open 05h00-19h00 from October to March and 06h00-18h00 from April to September. Entry fee per vehicle and passenger. Visitor amenities include game-viewing gravel roads, self-guided auto trail (comprehensive brochure available), self-guided and conducted walks of varying lengths, picnic sites and viewing hides. Petrol is on sale at the entrance gate. Take precautions against malaria.
Accommodation: Fully equipped cottages and bungalows, together with simpler rustic and rest huts (communal cooking and ablution facilities), are available at Mkuzi's Mantuma Camp. The attractive Nhlohlela Bush Camp, sited beside Nhlohlela Pan, has 4 very comfortably appointed 2-bed reed-and-thatch huts, linked by a raised boardwalk, which is lit by lanterns at night, and a viewing platform. The camp has a resident game guard and caretaker.
Further information: Natal Parks Board, P O Box 1750, Pietermaritzburg 3200, tel (0331) 47-1981.

Mkuzi is different from the region's other major reserves. Here the terrain is flattish, mostly open, its profusion of game – white and black rhinos, giraffes, wildebeest, warthogs, hippos and crocodiles, and a host of antelope species – easily visible. Leopards and cheetahs are among the more elusive animals, the black-backed jackal being more commonly seen. Mkuzi is generally acknowledged as one of southern Africa's most rewarding game-viewing areas.

Not that there isn't scenic variety. The marine reserve which adjoins the Greater St Lucia Wetland complex *(see separate entry)*, has its dense thickets, its woodland, riverine forest and wetland. Tree-wisterias, scarlet flame-bushes, scented acacias and marulas are among prominent floral species.

Huge sycamore figs, with girths of up to 12 m, embower the fringes of the Mkuze River's mist-wreathed Nsumo Pan, home to fish eagles, pelicans, storks, wild geese and ducks, herons, jaçanas, stilts, ungainly hamerkops and a great many other aquatic birds.

Elsewhere there are honeyguides, bee-eaters, twinspots, plum-coloured starlings and white-backed vultures – more than 400 species in all. Close to the entrance gate, in the KwaMalibala area, is a 'vulture restaurant', where these vulnerable birds are fed a dietary supplement of bones.

To the south of the reserve, across the Mzunduze River, sprawls a beautiful, 4 000-ha controlled wilderness where, in the winter season, sporting hunters help cull animals that are beyond the area's carrying capacity.

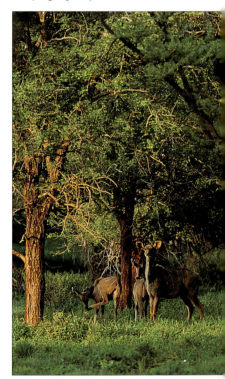

Kudu in the undergrowth at Mkuzi. This elegant buck is known as the high-jump champion of the animal world, being able to clear a 2,5-m fence with the greatest ease.

NORTHERN KWAZULU-NATAL

Ordinary visitors are allowed to make use of the hunting camp and its facilities during the summer months.

Mkuzi encompasses an 80-km network of game-viewing roads, and hides to which the animals come in great numbers. At Nsumo there are two bird-watching platforms and a pleasant picnic site. The recommended self-guided trail – it leads through the fringing fig forest – is only one of a variety of lovely walking options. These range from short, self-guided rambles to one-day conducted hikes, and the Bushveld trails which are arranged according to the needs of the group and the vagaries of the season.

Pelicans dip and dive as the flock takes to the water in search of food at Ndumo Game Reserve.

NDUMO GAME RESERVE
North of Ndumo

A superb selection of birds and scenic variety are the chief drawcards of this wetland paradise.

Ndumo is one of the smaller of KwaZulu-Natal's many reserves: it covers just 10 000 ha of the Pongola River's lush, low-lying flood plain in the far north of the region. Nevertheless it encompasses a quite remarkable diversity of habitats, taking in river and pan, reedbed, marshland, dry sandveld, and patches of woodland and evergreen forest. Wild orchids and lovely impala lilies lend splashes of colour to the verdant landscapes.

About 420 different avian species have been identified within the reserve – almost as many as you will find in the whole vastness of the Lowveld's Kruger National Park. They tend to be concentrated around the lily-garlanded pans, the largest of which is the six-kilometre-long Banzi, and the rather smaller (four-kilometre) Nyamithi, and they include several tropical birds that are at the southernmost extremity of their range.

The latter, though, are the exceptions among the vast concourse. The rich aquatic vegetation of the pans, seasonally exposed by the ebb of the Pongola River, attracts such bird species as pelicans, flamingoes, stilts, storks, egrets (notably black egrets) and herons (the goliath variety is especially prominent), jaçanas, pygmy and Egyptian geese, Pel's fishing owls, African fish eagles and a kaleidoscopic array of small waders.

The woodlands and sandveld, too, have their lively residents. Keep an eye open for the Narina trogon, the yellow-spotted nicator, the brown-headed parrot and the pink-throated twinspot. There are swallows, larks, weavers, shrikes, flycatchers and sunbirds aplenty.

Fewer, but more impressive, are the raptors such as snake eagles, bateleurs, eastern red-footed falcons and others.

Terrestrial wildlife is also well represented. The reserve is sanctuary for both the white and the even rarer black rhinos, buffaloes, giraffes, leopards and various antelope (among them the shy, seldom-seen suni). Noteworthy are the nyala, some of whose distant forebears were taken as prize specimens to London Zoo by the intrepid Victorian hunter and explorer, Frederick Courtenay Selous.

Map: page 153, 1E
From Durban follow the N2 to the Jozini turn-off, about 10 km after the turn-off to Mkuze Village. Continue for 66 km, through Jozini, to the T-junction, turn right and follow the Ndumo signs along 18 km of good sand road.

Details: Open dawn to dusk throughout the year. Entry fee per vehicle and passenger. There's a network of game-viewing roads; game- and bird-watching hides have been established. Open-vehicle tours can be reserved. Informative literature, notably on the self-guided auto trail, is available at the camp office. Best time for bird enthusiasts is midsummer. Nearest shop and fuel outlet are 2 kilometres from the gate, at Ndumo Village.

Accommodation: Ndumo has 1 rest camp, an attractive cluster of comfortable, self-contained 3-bed bungalows on top of a hill. Two rustic bush camps are being developed (1 of them on stilts to view the hippo). There is a caravan/camping facility just outside the reserve.

Further information: Department of Nature Conservation, Private Bag X9024, Pietermaritzburg 3200, tel (0331) 94-6696/7/8.

ONDINI HISTORIC RESERVE
Near Ulundi

Map: page 153, 4D

From Durban take the N2 highway to Gingindlovu. Turn off onto the R68, and drive past Eshowe and Melmoth to the junction with the R66, which leads to Ulundi. Ondini is to the southeast of the town. Follow the signs.

Details: Open daily 09h00-16h00 throughout the year (except Christmas Day). Admission charge. Parking and picnic site with toilets available.

Accommodation: The only accommodation currently available in Ulundi is the smallest Holiday Inn in the world (P O Box 91, Ulundi 3838, tel (0358) 2-1121), and the Umuzi Tourist Camp at the museum.

Further information: KwaZulu Monuments Council, P O Box 523, Ulundi 3838, tel (0358) 79-1854/5; KwaZulu Cultural Museum, P O Box 523, Ulundi 3838, tel (0358) 79-1223.

Ondini, King Cetshwayo's royal residence, and the capital of the Zulu Kingdom from 1873 to 1879, is situated some eight kilometres outside the town of Ulundi. On 4 July 1879 Lord Chelmsford's 5 000-strong force advanced on the Zulu capital, formed a square, and beat off an attack by some 17 000 lightly armed warriors. More than 1 500 Zulus were killed; casualties on the British side numbered just 12 dead. Chelmsford then burned Ulundi to the ground *(see box)*.

Today, the royal section of Ondini has been excavated by archaeologists, and Cetshwayo's spacious (nine-metre-diameter) royal residence, and a kraal of beautifully thatched 'beehive' homes, have been meticulously reconstructed.

Adjacent to Ondini is the KwaZulu Cultural Museum which houses a number of interesting displays on regional history, culture and art.

Also exhibited is a particularly fine display of local beadwork. Audiovisual programmes on the culture and history of the region are held, and education officers are available to assist with school and other educational groups.

Visitors are accommodated in a fascinating tourist 'camp' which has been built on the lines of a traditional Zulu *umuzi* or homestead. However, modern ablution facilities are provided.

Other sites in the area include the Ulundi Battle Monument and Nodwengu (the Zulu capital during the reign of King Mpande from 1840 to 1872). Museum staff will provide information on, and directions to, the less accessible sites such as KwaGqokli Hill, where King Shaka scored his first military success against the powerful Ndwandwe in 1818, and the Emakhosini (place of the kings), where early Zulu kings lie buried. In Ulundi, the Legislative Assembly building is home to a magnificent collection of tapestries depicting Zulu history (visits made by arrangement with the KwaZulu Cultural Museum). The Hluhluwe-Umfolozi Park lies some 30 km to the east of Ulundi.

Near Ondini is the Ulundi Memorial, a building that marks the site of the last battle of the Anglo-Zulu War *(see box)*. Here, the power of the Zulu nation – though not its pride – was finally broken by Queen Victoria's disciplined redcoats.

Ulundi was King Cetshwayo's royal village after he was crowned in 1873, but lasted as such for only six years.

RORKE'S DRIFT
Southeast of Dundee

Map: page 153, 4B

From Dundee take the R68 to Nqutu and follow the signposts to Rorke's Drift. The site lies 48 km from Dundee, 16 of them on dirt.

Details: The museum is open daily 08h00-17h00, except Christmas Day, Good Friday, Easter Sunday and Family Day. Admission is free. The arts and crafts centre is open weekdays 08h00-16h30, and Saturdays 10h00-15h00.

Accommodation: There is no accommodation at the battlesite, but there are a number of private lodges, guest farms and caravan/camping sites in the general area. Fugitive's Drift Lodge, 12 km from the battlesite, has cottages with beautiful views over Isandhlwana and Rorke's Drift. Contact them at P O Rorke's Drift 3016, tel (03425) 843. Dundee has hotel accommodation.

Further information: Rorke's Drift Provincial Museum, c/o Rorke's Drift Arts and Crafts Centre, P O Rorke's Drift 3016, tel (03425) 627/671; Dundee Publicity Association, P O Box 74, Dundee 3000, tel (034) 2-2677; Talana Museum, Private Bag X2024, Dundee 3000, tel (034) 2-2654.

The scene, embracing a small cluster of buildings close to the Buffalo River and the grandeur of the Zululand hills all around, looks tranquil enough today, but a little over a century ago it echoed the sound and fury of one of the Anglo-Zulu War's hardest-fought battles.

On the afternoon of 22 January 1879, a two-regiment impi of Cetshwayo's army, eager after their signal victory over the British at Isandhlwana to the southeast, attacked the 100-strong Rorke's Drift garrison. The bitter fighting lasted through the night, and when the impi's

A tapestry on display at Rorke's Drift highlights various aspects of life in a Zulu kraal.

Captured for ever in brilliant wools, a Zulu herdsman tends his charges near his kraal.

decimated ranks finally withdrew, they left the makeshift British fort badly damaged but still standing, its defenders defiant. Some 300-400 Zulus lay dead on the field.

Seventeen of the British were killed in the fighting. Their two officers, lieutenants John Chard (the senior) and Gonville Bromhead, and nine others were subsequently honoured with the Victoria Cross, Britain's highest military award for gallantry.

The Rorke's Drift site museum, a treasure house of visual information on the Anglo-Zulu War *(see box)*, is especially notable for its model and audio-visual recreations of the various battles. The original thatched mission house, used as a hospital by the garrison, was rebuilt in the 1880s and now serves as part of the Evangelical Lutheran Mission. The old commissariat store has been replaced by a church.

Nearby is the renowned Rorke's Drift Arts and Crafts Centre, started by the Evangelical Lutherans in the 1960s under Swedish tutorship. Here you can buy a wide variety of locally made products, including an enchanting range of karakul wool tapestries and rugs, silkscreen work and pottery.

The war that broke the Zulu nation

'I have done you no wrong, therefore you must have some other object in view in invading my land.'

So wrote Cetshwayo, king of the Zulus, to the Cape's colonial governor in 1879. In January of that year a large contingent of British troops under the command of Lord Chelmsford had marched into Zululand, a neutral territory, for a cynical political reason.

At that time the British were pursuing a 'confederalist' policy in southern Africa, their intention being to impose a loosely unitary system of subcontinental government that fell firmly within the Imperial sphere of influence. The Zulu nation, proud, independent and militarily powerful, was seen as a threat to these cosy plans, and High Commissioner Sir Bartle Frere decided to crush it by force of arms.

Various pretexts were contrived. The Zulus were told to dismantle their traditional military system, to allow white missionaries into their country, to admit a British Resident into the royal court, and so forth. On 11 December 1878 Cetshwayo was presented with an ultimatum, which he rejected, and on 12 January 1879 Chelmsford launched his three-pronged invasion.

His central column, which he accompanied, forded the Buffalo River at Rorke's Drift and encamped on the plain beneath a strangely shaped hill named Isandhlwana. Close by was the main Zulu army, some 14 000 warriors in total, though the redcoats remained serenely ignorant of their presence.

The morning attack came as a complete surprise to the British. Most of their ammunition was still packed away in boxes and, with only bayonets for protection, they were cut to pieces.

By 14h00 no less than 860 soldiers and 470 auxiliaries lay dead on the blood-soaked battlefield. Zulu losses were estimated at about a thousand. Part of the bruised but victorious impi then went on to invest the small British garrison at Rorke's Drift *(see entry)*.

Isandhlwana was the only major Zulu triumph: spears, shields and suicidal valour simply couldn't prevail against the guns and rock-solid discipline of the invaders. The northern column, after experiencing a sharp reversal at Hlobane, took a murderous toll of Zulu life at nearby Nkambule. And, towards the end of March, the southern force, with Chelmsford in command, moved up from the Lower Tugela River, defeated a large Zulu impi at Gingindlovu, relieved Eshowe and finally, on 4 July, fought and won the decisive battle outside the Zulu capital of Ulundi.

NORTHERN KWAZULU-NATAL

SHAKALAND
Near Eshowe

Map: page 153, 4D
Shakaland is 160 km north of Durban. Take the N2 north, and turn left onto the R68 turn-off (just beyond Gingindlovu) leading to Eshowe. Turn left at the Shakaland signpost 14 km beyond Eshowe. Continue for 3,5 km to the entrance.
Details: Open throughout the year. Daily and overnight inclusive rates; special rates for children. Cultural experiences (tours) 09h00-10h30, 11h00-12h30 and 16h30-17h30. Facilities include restaurant, cocktail bar, swimming pool, field trips and visits to traditional villages.
Accommodation: The comfortable beehive huts incorporate bathrooms *en suite*. Telephone and fax at reception.
Further information: Shakaland, P O Box 103, Eshowe 3815, tel (03546) 912.

To pass through the gates of Shakaland is to find yourself in another world, another time. This is part of the old Africa, where the amaZulu ruled unchallenged, a place of beaded headdresses and rawhide shields, beehive huts, *sangomas* and a lifestyle that, although still in evidence in the remoter country areas, properly belongs to the great age of Shaka.

Shakaland nestles among the aloes and mimosa trees of the Mhlatuze River Valley, where the original Zulu clan settled in the 18th century. It is a cultural centre built for very modern purposes. It was created as the film set for the magnificent 1980s docu-drama production of *Shaka Zulu* and later used for two other television spectaculars, *The John Ross Story* and *Ipi-Tombi*.

Overnight guests (day-visitors are also welcome) stay in superbly thatched Zulu huts, cleverly enhanced by modern comforts and, for a day or two, immerse themselves in the intricate, endlessly fascinating traditions of the Nguni people. Morning and afternoon tours introduce you to the arts of spear-making, weaving, beadwork, pottery, beer-brewing, stick-fighting, and to the distinctive ways of

Armed with shields and sticks, hide-clad Zulu men prepare for a ritual dance at Shakaland. In the background is a traditional beehive hut.

the Zulus – their manners, mores, dress, social organization and beliefs.

Mealtimes are rather special. The restaurant, which affords some exceptional views over shimmering lake and hills, offers authentic cuisine, the delicacies ranging from *uphuthu* (maizemeal), *ubhomubhomu* (kidney beans), pumpkin and spinach, to *inyama yenkomo* (stew) or *inyama eyosiwe* (grilled meat).

A Zulu herbalist, surrounded by various herbs and the tools of his trade, awaits patients at Shakaland.

At Shakaland, a young maiden displays the brilliant beadwork for which the Zulu nation is famed throughout the world.

PLACES TO VISIT

ST LUCIA

One of the world's most remarkable, and most fragile, conservation areas sprawls serenely across the Zululand seaboard north of the Umfolozi River's lower reaches.

The recently consolidated Greater St Lucia Wetland Park encompasses a wondrous, 275 000-ha compound of reed-fringed lake linked by a narrow channel to the sea, a pan teeming with a splendid variety of birds, marshland, flood plain and papyrus swamp, palm veld, broad grassland, semiarid savannah, high dune, and a long strip of Indian Ocean, notable for its offshore coral reefs and marvellous marine life.

The area straddles the subtropical and tropical climatic zones, which accounts in part for its extraordinary diversity.

Centrepiece of the complex, which is administered by the Natal Parks Board, is the 36 000-ha 'lake', which is actually a hugely extended, shallow estuarine lagoon system stretching 60 km from Mapelane and the Umfolozi Mouth northwards to the Mkuzi River's soggy flood plain. On the geophysical calendar the system is young: it was formed a mere 25 000 years ago when the sea receded to leave a sandy plain, parts of which retained a mix of salt and fresh water.

The area has been intelligently developed for tourism: visitor amenities – camps, a resort, boat moorings, walking trails – are concentrated at certain points, leaving the greater portion of the wetlands and their surrounds to nature and the conservation authorities.

The most notable of the various components of this beautiful wetland area are described in the following four pages.

Map: page 153, 3/4E/F
From Durban take the N2 highway to Mtubatuba and continue for about 26 km on the R618 to St Lucia Estuary.
Further information: Natal Parks Board, P O Box 1750, Pietermaritzburg 3200, tel (0331) 47-1981. Camp sites are reserved through the relevant local officers-in-charge.

KEY TO THE MAP
1 False Bay Park
2 Mapelane
3 Marine Reserve
4 Mfabeni and Tewate
5 St Lucia Estuary
6 St Lucia Game Reserve
7 St Lucia Park

Sunset at Lake St Lucia outlines billowing clouds and sea gulls searching for marine morsels.

ST LUCIA

Map: page 165
Follow the N2 north from Mtubatuba for 55 km, and turn right for Hluhluwe Village. Continue beyond Hluhluwe, northeast of the railway station, following the signs to False Bay Park.
Accommodation: Apart from the rustic camp, False Bay has no permanent accommodation, but there is a 38-stand caravan/camping site overlooking the lake. Visitors with boats must keep to the various designated areas of the lake to fish, bird-watch or enjoy the scenery. Bait is available. The nearest shop and fuel outlet are at Hluhluwe Village, 15 km to the west, but you can obtain cooldrinks, braai charcoal and odds and ends at the camp.
Further information: The Camp Manager, False Bay Park, P O Box 222, Hluhluwe 3960, tel (035) 562-0425.

FALSE BAY PARK

Red duiker and suni, zebras, impala, reedbuck, nyala, bushbuck, waterbuck, hippos, crocodiles, bushpigs, warthogs and spotted hyaenas are among the residents of False Bay Park. This pristine sanctuary covers 3 200 ha of woodland, thicket, unique sand forest and sweet grassland abutting the northwestern part of St Lucia Lake.

It is also home to nearly 280 different bird species. Paradise flycatchers, purple-crested loeries and golden-tailed woodpeckers are common in and around the sand forest; the woodlands are home to crested francolins and puffback shrikes.

This is bird-watcher's country, but it's also something of a mecca for fishermen, boating enthusiasts, photographers and hikers. Recommended is the three-hour (either seven- or 10-km) Mpophomeni (meaning 'waterfall') Walk. Dugandlovu is a charming rustic camp comprising

Zebras drinking at a water hole. These striking, timid animals will often bolt after slaking their thirst.

Burchell's zebras – beautiful, banded beasts of the plains

One of the most magnificent spectacles to be seen on the open veld of southern Africa is a herd of Burchell's zebras on the run, their striped coats flashing and their hooves thundering as they surge across the grasslands.

These beautiful creatures tend to be gregarious by nature, living in small, compact family groups which, in turn, often combine to form part of a larger herd. Most of the family groups are led by a single stallion. These males tend to stay on the periphery of the herd, their senses acutely tuned to the slightest sign or sound of danger.

In the face of a charge by a predator, such as a lioness or a pack of wild dogs, it is not uncommon for the males to take a protective rearguard position, putting their own lives at risk, while the rest of the herd flees to safety.

The exact purpose of the zebra's eye-catching stripes has not been established beyond all doubt, but there are several theories. Among the most popular of these is the theory that the stripes serve to camouflage their owners; another theory holds that the stripes are a form of identification within the herd, because each set of stripes is unique. Burchell's zebras can be distinguished from other zebra species by the yellowish 'shadow' stripes which are clearly visible between the black on the hindquarters.

Named after a talented Victorian artist, naturalist and traveller, William Burchell, these zebras are the most common of the zebra species found in southern Africa.

Burchell's zebras prefer the open grasslands and lightly treed bushveld vegetation which occur in the northeastern reaches of the subcontinent. They are mainly grazers, having strong upper lips to coax the various grasses between their sharp teeth.

Foals may be born at any time of the year after a gestation period of about 11 months. The mare gives birth to a single foal, which weighs between 30 and 35 kilograms. The offspring live on the fresh dung of the adults during the first precarious week of their lives. Thereafter they start to graze with the parents.

four four-bed huts (bring your own linen). A bucket shower and paraffin lighting add to the bush experience.

You can drive to the camp, but most prefer the open-ended Dugandlovu ('lost elephant') Trail to get there. Loop routes provide walkers with shorter variations on both routes.

Some delightful picnic sites have been laid out along the shoreline. After your outing, sip sundowners on the viewing platform overlooking the western shores of the Greater St Lucia Wetland Park – an unforgettable experience.

MAPELANE

Across the estuary from St Lucia Village, on the south bank of the Umfolozi River, is the little hideaway of Mapelane, southernmost and arguably the most attractive of Natal Parks Board camps. The place has a wild, remote feel about it, even though it's close (as the crow flies) to the busy estuary village, its log cabins and camp sites hidden among thick bush beneath the gigantic coastal dunes.

The bird life here – more than 200 species have been recorded – is especially prolific and visible, and there are some enticing beach and forest walks. Recommended is the short, steep climb to the top of the dunes; the towering Majaka Hill, to the south, is also worth exploring. Fishermen make good catches from rock, beach and ski boat. The shoreline is rich in mussels and crayfish.

Map: page 165
The 45-km approach road from the N2 to Mapelane is sandy and difficult to negotiate in parts.
Details: The nearest shop and petrol outlet are at KwaMbonambi, 40 km away.
Accommodation: The 10 five-bed log cabins are self-contained, each with an equipped kitchen and dining area, and are serviced daily. Bring your own food.
Further information: Log-cabin bookings: Natal Parks Board, P O Box 1750, Pietermaritzburg 3200, tel (0331) 47-1981. Camp-site bookings: The Officer-in-Charge, Private Bag, St Lucia Estuary 3936, tel (035) 590-1407.

MARINE RESERVE

The St Lucia and Maputaland marine reserves, now combined within the Greater St Lucia area, stretch in an unbroken 5,6-km-wide shoreline and ocean belt from just south of Cape Vidal up to the Mozambique border.

The beautiful northern segment is world-renowned for its loggerhead and leatherback turtles, gentle giants of the sea that once faced extinction, but are now back in numbers to lay their eggs on the night-time beaches.

Leisure-bent humans, too, are drawn to the broad golden sands: shell-collectors for their sunny ambience and beautiful cowrie shells; ski-boat anglers and skin-divers for the wealth of tropical fish and the offshore coral reefs. The coastal forest reserve north of Sodwana is run by the Department of Nature Conservation. To the north of Mabibi, no vehicles except those for management are allowed on the beach. A permit is required to drive on the beach south of Mabibi.

Map: page 165
The St Lucia and Maputaland marine reserves extend from 1 km south of Cape Vidal to the Mozambique border. Follow the signs from Cape Vidal.
Accommodation: This is available at Kosi Bay, Sodwana Bay and Lake Sibaya *(see separate entries)*. There are also a number of private resort and fishing camps along the Maputaland coast (contact the Department of Nature Conservation, P O Box X9024, Pietermaritzburg 3200, tel (0331) 94-6696/7/8 for details).
Further information: Natal Parks Board, P O Box 1750, Pietermaritzburg 3200, tel (0331) 47-1981.

The incredible journey of the sea turtle

For more than 60 000 years giant turtles – two-metre-long leatherbacks and their rather smaller loggerhead cousins – have nested in the soft sands of KwaZulu-Natal's beautiful northern shoreline.

These gentle creatures are genetically programmed to seek out that precise stretch of beach on which they themselves were hatched (which in some instances can be decades before), and they travel immense distances through the ocean to do so. Some swim from as far away as East Africa's Mombasa area, 2 500 km to the north, unerringly homing in on their birthplace.

After mating in the offshore waters the female scrambles through the intertidal zone and searches the beach for a special aroma, a scent inextricably linked to her own origins.

When she finds it, she scrapes a hole in the sand and drops her first clutch of about 100 eggs, covers them up, and then wearily makes her way back to the ocean. She will lay perhaps five more clutches during the summer, and will return in future seasons (though not every year) to repeat the cycle.

After 70 days the tiny hatchlings break out of their soft shells to run a gauntlet of ghost crabs on their path to open water. And the sea harbours many more enemies. It is reckoned that only one in about 500 newborn turtles lives to reach maturity.

Turtles are slow-moving, their only means of defence their protective shells. They are also an immensely ancient species, having survived virtually unchanged in form and habit for 100 million years. But their resilience is no match for the greed of man. By the early 1960s the two species had been brought to the brink of regional extinction by human predation, killed off in their thousands for their meat, body oil, eggs, and hard shells that can be fashioned into ornaments.

In 1963 the Natal Parks Board mounted an intensive rescue operation and, with the help of the local villagers, has managed to reverse the trend. The beach breeding grounds are strictly protected and carefully monitored.

Loggerhead turtle hatchlings dig their way out of the sand before scuttling to the water's edge. Sea birds and crabs are a constant threat to their survival.

ST LUCIA

Map: page 165
Take the road north from St Lucia Estuary, passing through the Eastern Shores gate. Cape Vidal is about 30 km further on.
Details: The area is part of the Greater St Lucia Marine Reserve. There are restrictions on vehicle access onto beaches, on bottom-fishing and on other activities.
Accommodation: Cape Vidal Camp has serviced, self-contained log cabins, and a 50-stand camp site. On the shores of Lake Bhangazi there are larger fishing cabins and a tented camp for trailists.
Further information: Natal Parks Board, P O Box 1750, Pietermaritzburg 3200, tel (0331) 47-1981. Camp site bookings: The Officer-in-Charge, Cape Vidal, Private Bag, St Lucia Estuary 3936, tel (035) 590-1404.

MFABENI AND TEWATE

These two areas which were formerly known as the Eastern Shores Nature Reserve and the Cape Vidal State Forest, respectively, are now consolidated and managed as a single unit.

As the name suggests, the former lies to the east of Lake St Lucia, occupying a little over 15 000 ha of precious dune forest and coastal grassland that sustain a huge reedbuck population (more than 6 000 throng the entire Eastern Shores, Cape Vidal and Tewate area).

Here too you'll find buffaloes, kudu, red and grey duiker, waterbuck, side-striped jackals and monkeys (the seldom-seen samango as well as the ubiquitous vervet). Eastern Shores has been the centre of bitter debate between various conservationists seeking to preserve the environment, and businessmen who want to mine the dunes for their wealth of titanium.

Fringing the reserve to the east is the Tewate Wilderness Area, known until fairly recently as the Cape Vidal State Forest, but now under Natal Parks Board control. Most of the 11 000-ha area com-

The graceful impala, seen here at a watering hole, will flee with balletic leaps when startled.

prises fascinating sand-dune forest (the vegetated sand dunes, rising some 180 m above the sea, are the world's highest) and marshy grassland.

Visitor facilities, clustered in and around the Cape Vidal Camp on the coast, include self-contained and serviced five- and eight-bed Swiss-style log cabins, and a 50-stand camp site. There are larger 'fishing cabins' seven kilometres away on the shore of Lake Bhangazi. The area is much favoured by the ski-boat fishing fraternity. Snorkelling and spearfishing are especially popular (and rewarding).

The nearest shop is at the estuary, so visitors should be sure to stock up with enough provisions. Petrol and firewood are available at Cape Vidal.

This is also pleasant walking terrain – the birds of the dune forest are a delight, and the scenery eye-catching. Both can be enjoyed on the self-guided Mvubu Trail. The 22-km Mziki (an overnight trail) starts at Mount Tabor, near a point called Mission Rocks, and leads you through the countryside between Cape Vidal and the estuary. There's also the four-night St Lucia Wilderness Trail.

Tranquil Lake Bhangazi, with its promise of a rich harvest, lures many anglers to its sandy shores.

Map: page 165
St Lucia Estuary is 25 km east of Mtubatuba *(see introductory panel)*.
Accommodation: St Lucia Estuary offers a range of conventional accommodation. Contact the St Lucia Town Board, P O Box 16, St Lucia Estuary 3936, tel (035) 590-1339.
Further information: Natal Parks Board, P O Box 1750, Pietermaritzburg 3200, tel (0331) 47-1981. Camp-site bookings: The Officer-in-Charge, St Lucia, Private Bag, St Lucia Estuary 3936, tel (035) 590-1340.

ST LUCIA ESTUARY

The village of St Lucia Estuary, a busy little centre packed with shops and places to stay, and the gateway to the eastern portions of the St Lucia complex, lies on the eastern bank of the narrow-channelled estuary. It is surrounded by the St Lucia Nature Reserve, an attractive area of caravan parks (three of them), jetties, parking lots, a small game park, walking trails (the Gwalagwala is especially rewarding) and the Crocodile Centre. This last not only houses the giant reptiles of

the Nile, the long-snouted and dwarf varieties – but it also serves as an interpretive agent for the whole St Lucia region, and is well worth a visit for the wealth of fascinating information that it affords. The crocodiles are usually fed on Saturday afternoons.

Other activities include surf-angling, surf-bathing (but be careful: there are no shark nets, and no lifeguards to pull you to safety), deep-sea fishing charters and boat tours of the estuary.

ST LUCIA GAME RESERVE

The reserve – the oldest part of the combined conservation area (it was proclaimed in 1895) – covers the lake itself and its several low-lying islands. For the most part the waters, 30 km at their widest, are not much more than a metre deep, though gullies and channels reach down further.

The myriad species of fish, crustaceans (including sea-born panaeid prawns, which mature in the freshness of the lake) and other creatures attract African fish eagles, great clouds of white pelicans and flamingoes, Caspian terns, a variety of heron species, spoonbills and a vast array of other aquatic birds.

Also prolific are the crocodiles and, especially, the hippos, which are most numerous in the south, around the estuary. You can see the sights from the comfort of the 80-seat *Santa Lucia* pleasure craft, which sets out from St Lucia Estuary bridge jetty.

Map: page 165
Follow the signs at St Lucia Estuary.
Details: The public has free access to the lake, but there are restrictions on boating, fishing, bathing and certain other activities.
Accommodation: Visitors usually stay at Fanies Island *(see accommodation for St Lucia Park).*
Further information: Natal Parks Board, P O Box 1750, Pietermaritzburg 3200, tel (0331) 47-1981; The Officer-in-Charge, St Lucia, Private Bag, St Lucia Estuary 3936, tel (035) 590-1340; *Santa Lucia* launch bookings: Natal Parks Board, Private Bag, St Lucia Estuary 3936, tel (035) 590-1340.

ST LUCIA PARK

The park comprises a narrow strip of dry land running around most of the lake system, taking in the village at the southern end.

The 13 000-ha area is graced by reedbeds and woodland, interspersed with some grassy patches, to provide an impressive variety of habitats for bird and animal. Among the latter are duiker, bushbuck and vervet monkeys. The bird life is magnificent. Several walking routes, designed for bird-watchers and lovers of gentle scenery, have been laid out, among them the five-kilometre Umkhiwane and the shorter (two-kilometre) Umboma trails.

Two pleasant Parks Board camps – Fanies Island and Charter's Creek – have been established on the western side. They offer camp sites and a variety of fully equipped self-catering accommodation, swimming pools (hippos and crocs preclude lake bathing), fishing (bait available), boats for hire (bring your own motor) and the self-guided walks mentioned. Bring your own food.

Hippos occasionally meander through the camps at night. Keep an eye out, too, for crocodiles.

Map: page 165
The park comprises an approximate 1-km trip around the entire lake area. To reach the 2 camps, continue on the N2 through Mtubatuba for 20 km, turn right and drive the 13 km to Charter's Creek. Fanies Island is 11 km further on (follow the signposts).
Accommodation: Fanies Island has 1 seven-bed cottage, 12 two-bed rest huts (with a communal kitchen and ablution blocks) and 20 camp sites. Charter's Creek has a variety of huts and 1 cottage, with a communal lounge, kitchen and ablution blocks.
Further information: Natal Parks Board, P O Box 1750, Pietermaritzburg 3200, tel (0331) 47-1981; Fanies Island camp site: The Camp Manager, Fanies Island, P O Box 201, Mtubatuba 3935, tel (035) 550-1631; Charter's Creek: The Camp Manager, Charter's Creek, Private Bag 7205, Mtubatuba 3935, tel (035) 550-1513 or 550-4180.

Thatched self-catering chalets at Charter's Creek lie in attractive seclusion beneath the scarlet blossoms of shady coral trees.

Dawn breaks to reveal Fanies Island in the heart of Lake St Lucia. Here beds of aquatic plants provide food for a large variety of fish and shellfish.

SODWANA BAY NATIONAL PARK
Northern Zululand

Map: page 153, 2/3F
Take the N2 to a point just north of Mkuze Village, and turn right towards Ubombo. Continue to Mbazwana and then south, following the signposts.
Accommodation: Sodwana Bay's caravan/camping site has 600 stands and a capacity for 4 000 visitors. There's also permanent accommodation in 20 log cabins. The resort has ablution blocks, a supermarket and a community recreation hall. There are fish-weighing points and fish freezers, and boat storage facilities.
Further information: Natal Parks Board, P O Box 1750, Pietermaritzburg 3200, tel (0331) 47-1981; Camp-site bookings: The Officer-in-Charge, Sodwana Bay National Park, Private Bag 310, Mbazwana 3974, tel (035) 571-0051.

Scuba divers prepare to be taken to an offshore reef at Sodwana Bay, reputed to have the richest game-fishing waters in the world.

Among the most popular – that is to say, the most crowded – segment of Greater St Lucia is the small (413 ha) Sodwana Bay National Park, in the marine reserve well north of the lake.

Despite its pressing summertime human presence, though, visitors tend to stay close to the huge camp site and its well-organized community amenities, and much of the park remains largely untouched. The lakelets and the dune and swamp forests are tranquil havens for a great many birds, and for reedbuck, duiker and other antelope. Here, too, you'll find the rare Tonga red squirrel.

The bay itself, its beaches, clear blue waters and the lovely offshore coral reefs, are famed among scuba divers, snorkellers and anglers. Splendid catches of sailfish, blue and black marlin, tuna and other game fish are almost routine among the deep-sea fishing fraternity.

In summer, beaches host the large loggerhead and leatherback turtles *(see box)* that come ashore to nest. Night-time 'turtle tours' are laid on by the Natal Parks Board (December and January) for camp residents only. The two self-guided trails – Jesser and Ngoboseleni – start near the camp.

TEMBE ELEPHANT PARK
East of Ndumo Game Reserve

Map: page 153, 1/2E/F
Tembe lies in the far north of KwaZulu-Natal, on the Mozambique border. From Durban follow the N2 past the turn-off to Mkuze, to the Jozini turn-off. Drive northwards for some 66 km, and turn left at the T-junction. The tarred road stretches about 45 km to the park entrance.
Details: Open dawn to dusk throughout the year. Entrance fee. Self-guided drives along 81 km of sandy roads. Only 4-wheel-drive vehicles are admitted into the park – this area used to be part of the ocean floor, and the roads are very sandy.
Accommodation: One tented camp (with kitchen and ablution facilities), with four 2-bed safari tents. The kitchen has a stove, refrigerator and freezer. A camp cook helps prepare meals. It is an exclusive camp – one party of tourists books the entire camp. The nearest shop and petrol outlet are at KwaNgwanase. Take precautions against malaria.
Further information: Department of Nature Conservation, Private Bag X9024, Pietermaritzburg 3200, tel (0331) 94-6696/7/8.

Civil war and the changing patterns of human settlement during the 1970s and 1980s all but destroyed southern Mozambique's once-great herds of free-roaming elephants.

But some of these animals regularly migrated across this country's border with South Africa, between the Mputo Elephant Park and the forests and swamps of northern Zululand, and a few of these – a bare 100 individuals – have eventually found asylum behind the electrified fences of the 30 000-ha Tembe Elephant Park.

The park is still in its infancy, but signs are that the tuskers have adapted well to their new, rather restricted, home, and their numbers are increasing.

Wildlife also includes black and white rhinos, giraffes, zebras, kudu and other antelope (Tembe has one of the highest populations of suni antelope in southern Africa), leopards, hyaenas and a wealth of birds. The insect life is fascinating; butterfly enthusiasts can look forward to a real field day.

The lazy, ambling gait of the elephant belies the fact that it can run at a speed of some 40 km/hour. Many of Tembe's elephants have crossed into the park from Mozambique.

TRANSKEI

TRANSKEI

AMATOLA HIKING TRAIL
Near King William's Town

Map: page 171, 5B
From King William's Town take the R30 north for 13 km; turn left onto the 10-km secondary road leading to (and signposted for) the Maden Dam. You can also join the Amatola Trail (from its second section) from Stutterheim. Drive west along the R352 for 20 km, to the Dontsa Pass (a steep 1:12 ascent to 1 088 m) and Forest Station.

Details: Open throughout the year. The summer months are best. The weather tends to be unpredictable. Water is usually plentiful, but may be scarce on the first, second and sixth days of the hike. Hiking parties are limited to 16 persons. Take provisions, blanket/sleeping bag, and arrange transport from trail's end.

Accommodation: Hikers overnight in five comfortably rustic huts equipped with bunks and mattresses; braai area (firewood available), toilets, running water. There are hotels in King William's Town and Stutterheim.

Further information: Eastern Cape Tourism Board, P O Box 186, Bisho 5608, tel (0401) 95-2115; or East London Metropolitan Tourism Association, P O Box 533, East London 5200, tel (0431) 2-6015. Map and brochure available.

This hiking trail is among the more strenuous of southern Africa's formal routes. It's also one of the most rewarding. The 105-km, six-day hike leads you over the broad plateaus and through the dense forests – of yellowwoods, sneezewoods, ironwoods and other lofty species – of the Amatola Mountains which border the Amatola region.

The vistas from the high ground, and from openings that suddenly appear through the mantle of trees, enchant the eye, taking in the Great Karoo to the north, and most of the Amatola region, to the Indian Ocean in the south. En route there are fast-flowing, trout-filled mountain streams, spectacular cascades and crystal-clear bathing pools.

The trail begins at Maden Dam, 518 m above sea level, and just over 20 km from King William's Town (the capital town of the Eastern Cape Province), and ends near Hogsback *(see separate entry)*.

Hikers spend their first night in the lovely Evelyn Valley, and thereafter make their way over the rising terrain to the Geju plateau (1 880m), which they reach on the fourth day. The penultimate section takes them along a meandering, pool-flanked contour path, the final one through evergreen woodlands graced by a splendid waterfall.

The full Amatola Trail is designed for the fitter, younger walker. But if you aren't quite up to the mark, or you haven't the time, there are other, less demanding, options. Several link paths lead from the various forest stations to provide shorter routes. Especially recommended are:

■ The lovely two-day Evelyn Loop Trail, which starts at Maden Dam, and then winds for 27 km through the mysterious Pirie Forest.

Fine views unfold from the 1 040-m plateau, and from the old forester's hut where hikers spend the night.

■ The Pirie and Sandile day-walks, also in the Maden Dam area.

The former follows the historic railway line built for the local timber industry; the latter, named in honour of the legendary Xhosa warrior-chief Sandile (1820-78), takes you to the large cavern that served as his hide-out during his last (and fatal) confrontation with British colonial troops.

■ The Zingcuka Loop Trail, at the end of the Amatola route. This is a 36-km

A waterfall drizzles down a rock face, creating a delicately dripping veil to enchant hikers on the popular Amatola Hiking Trail.

circular excursion around the magnificent Hogsback peaks.

At one time the Amatola Mountains were haven to herds of elephants and other large game animals. These have long since gone, shot out by the early hunters. Nevertheless, the region remains rich in wildlife.

Among the mammals you may be lucky to glimpse through the green forest depths (which, because of the thickness of the high, sun-blocking canopy, is surprisingly free of dense undergrowth) are bushbuck and duiker, bushpigs, baboons and samango monkeys, found here at the southernmost limit of their range.

The bird life is both prolific and colourful. Be sure to keep an eye out especially for the various sugarbirds, the green twinspots, the beautiful Knysna loeries and the Cape parrots.

Special residents of the area are the Amatola toad, the Hogsback frog and, most intriguing of all, an earthworm that grows to almost 2,5 m in length.

COFFEE BAY
Wild Coast

This entrancing little village and resort, girded by the mountains and spectacular cliffs that lie between the Bomvu and Nenga river mouths, received its rather exotic name from a disappointingly prosaic incident.

It is believed that an old, 19th-century freighter ran aground at the mouth of the lagoon and spilled its cargo of coffee beans, some of which reached shore, and took root there.

Today, though, the area is entirely devoid of coffee trees. But it does boast an impressive litany of natural assets, among them the magnificent coastal scenery. The most dramatic of the viewpoints involves a fairly steep ascent up a rutted track to Mapuzi ('place of pumpkins'), from which you can see the great sweep of the seaboard and, inland, most of the Transkei region.

Also recommended are various walks to the Umtata River Mouth, just a few kilometres up the coast, and the longer hike to the renowned Hole in the Wall *(see separate entry)*.

The setting sun creates its own symphony of colours over the Wild Coast, near the attractive resort of Coffee Bay.

Other attractions at the resort include fishing, surfing, bathing (the waters are safe), bird-spotting and golf.

The quiet little village of Coffee Bay has a pleasant hotel that overlooks the kilometre-long beach.

Map: page 171, 4E
Drive 20 km south from Umtata on the N2, turn left at Viedgesville, and continue for another 14 km to Mqanduli. Thereafter, follow the signs to Coffee Bay. For light-aircraft owners there's a 750-m landing strip.
Details: Coffee Bay is worth visiting at any time of the year; the springtime months are especially attractive.
Accommodation: Ocean View Hotel, P O Coffee Bay, tel (0471) 37-0254; or Wild Coast Hotels Reservations and Information, Private Bag X5028, Umtata 5100, tel (0471) 2-5344.
Further information: Eastern Cape Tourism Board – Eastern Region, Private Bag X5029, Umtata 5100, tel (0471) 31-2885; or Wild Coast Hotels *(see above)*.

Palms of the Wild Coast

Among the most attractive of southern Africa's seven species of indigenous palm tree is the Pondoland palm *(Jubaeopsis caffra)*, which grows to a modest five metres, and bears an edible fruit that looks like a miniature coconut.

There are over 3 000 species, belonging to 200 genera, in the family of flowering plants known as Palmaceae. The roots grow from the base of the trunk to form a ball of fibre, the long bole shedding its leaves until the tree takes on its classic profile – a straight, bare stem with a splendid crown of foliage. The nature of the foliage, in turn, divides the trees into two broad types – those with fan-shaped (palmate) leaves, and those with feather-like (pinnate) fronds. Many species yield such products as coco, betel nuts, dates, sago, sugar, vegetable oil, wax, coir, starch, vegetable ivory and cane.

Perhaps the best known of the southern African species is the ilala or lala palm. Its large, fan-like leaves are used extensively by thatchers and basketmakers; the sap is fermented to produce a powerful, aromatic wine; the hard, tennis-ball-sized fruits provide elephants and baboons with a favourite delicacy; and the kernels, very much like ivory in appearance, are carved into trinkets.

Also common in KwaZulu-Natal are the clustered wild date palms *(Phoenix reclinata)*, so called because their stems lean away from the centre, and the 20-m-tall *Phoenix canariensis*.

Then there's the tropical African fan palm *(Borassus aethiopum)*, a resident of the Eastern Transvaal Lowveld and regions to the north. This also reaches 20 m in height, but is very slow to mature, producing its flowers only after some 30 years.

Many kinds of exotic palm species thrive in southern African conditions. Among them are the well-known Washingtonias – *Washingtonia filifera* (the cotton palm), and *Washingtonia robusta* (the thread palm) – from Mexico.

DWESA AND CWEBE NATURE RESERVES
Wild Coast and hinterland

Map: page 171, 4/5D/E
From Umtata travel south on the N2 towards Idutywa. For Dwesa: from Idutywa take the road east towards Gatyana (formerly Willowvale), and bear left at the first fork, following the Dwesa signposts. For Cwebe: leave the N2 at the Xhora (formerly Elliotdale) signpost, halfway between Umtata and Idutywa, and continue through Xhora, following the signposts to The Haven.
Details: Open sunrise to sunset throughout the year. Entrance fee charged. Self-guided walks along a network of paths. Fishing allowed only in demarcated areas; no spearfishing.
Accommodation: Dwesa has 4- and 5-bed chalets equipped with gas stoves and refrigerators, and a 20-stand caravan/camping site. Cwebe has no facilities, except for the nearby The Haven Hotel, which offers luxurious lodging in thatched bungalows with *en suite* bathrooms. Also golf course, tennis courts, swimming pool. Petrol and general dealer.
Further information: Rest camps: Nature Conservation Division, Department of Agriculture and Forestry, Private Bag X5002, Umtata 5100, tel (0471) 2-4322 or 31-2711/2. The Haven Hotel, Private Bag X5028, Umtata 5100, tel (0474) 62-0247.

Evergreen yellowwood, ebony and white stinkwood forests, a ruggedly beautiful coast of bluffs and bays, and long swathes of golden sand, are the essential – and most appealing – ingredients of these adjoining conservancies.

The two areas, both very similar in character, are separated by the Mbashe (or Bashee) River.

Mangrove swamps add variety to the shoreline, their fragile habitats sustaining an intricate interdependence of life forms. On the beaches you'll find seashells that would grace any collector's cabinet.

Down at the water's edge, too, the wild animals of the area are seen occasionally – mammals such as blesbok and eland, bushbuck and duiker which quietly wander down from their inland homes to take in the sea air.

Among other wildlife species which have been either introduced or reintroduced into the reserves are buffaloes, blue wildebeest and a small crocodile population. The prolific bird life includes the beautiful Narina trogon and the mangrove kingfisher.

The 3 900-ha Dwesa section, the oldest of the Transkei region's reserves, offers excellent fishing opportunities, both from beach and rock, and in the many small streams that rise in the forests and end in estuaries untainted by pollution. Spearfishing, though, is not permitted.

Dwesa has a small rest camp of self-contained chalets (they are sited 50 m from the beach), a caravan/camping ground and, near the Ingomana River Mouth, a number of private holiday homes, some on stilts.

The smaller, and the more recently developed Cwebe Nature Reserve, which is 2 150 ha in extent, offers similar accommodation, together with the attractive bungalows of The Haven resort hotel, popular for its ocean views.

Cwebe also has an enchanting lagoon (Cape clawless otters and fish eagles are numbered among the resident species) and, on the Mbanyana River, a waterfall of magical beauty.

Both nature reserves provide really fine fishing, especially from a rock formation known as Shark's Island.

Neither of the reserves has an internal road network, but numerous pathways lead from the camps.

Wild seas, craggy bluffs and fauna-rich coastal forests combine to form Dwesa Nature Reserve, a remote nature-lover's wonderland.

EAST LONDON
Eastern Cape coast

For more than a century and a half, East London has drawn fame and fortune from its harbour, which is located around the broad mouth of the Buffalo River.

The city is, in fact, South Africa's only major river port, handling a whopping three million tons and more of cargo annually. For the most part this cargo originates from, or is destined for, the hinterland of the Eastern Cape.

The harbour's chief claim to notability, though, is the 'dolos' system of interlocking breakwater blocks – a technique conceived and perfected by local engineer Eric Mayfield in 1961, and now used in harbours throughout the world.

East London is a substantial centre of some 200 000 inhabitants, a figure heavily augmented by daily commuters from Mdantsane, and other high-density dormitory towns, and by the seasonal influx of tourists.

The latter are drawn to the city and its environs by attractions of the quieter and more family-orientated kind – splendid stretches of bronze sand, a warm sea and its pounding surf, coastal resorts on the seaboard to either side, pleasant parks and gardens, and an inviting spread of hotels and restaurants.

A newly constructed waterfront development in the harbour area, known quaintly as Latimer's Landing, offers restaurants, shops, fleamarkets and a host of other attractions.

Beaches

The city's Indian Ocean shoreline is graced by three broad, white stretches of sand, each with its own character, all highly popular with bathers, surfers and sun-worshippers.

Nearest to the central area is Orient Beach, sheltered in the lee of one of the harbour's two breakwaters.

It takes its name from a Russian sail-rigged steamship that ran aground in 1907, and over which the pier was built (you can still see part of the rusty old hull poking from beneath the concrete).

Orient is well equipped for the leisure-bent visitor. Attractions include two new circular swimming pools, paddling pool and playground, restaurant, kiosks, putt-putt course, a theatre, coloured umbrellas for hire and, of course, the blue sea and its challenging rollers.

Next door is Eastern Beach, especially favoured by the surfing fraternity (who can ride the waves until well after dark– the shore is floodlit), and backed by wooded dunes.

Beyond these you'll find the attractive grounds of the Marina Glen picnic and recreation area.

East London's aquarium, which houses a small, but well-chosen collection of marine and freshwater fish, as well as a group of endearing Cape fur seals, lies between Orient and Eastern beaches.

The third major beach, Nahoon, is adjacent to Eastern Beach, bounded by Nahoon Point and the Nahoon River. The forested dunes and nearby golf course create a refreshing expanse of urban greenery.

Around the estuary are mud flats and mangrove swamps that sustain a fascinating variety of wetland life.

Map: page 171, 6C
Orient Beach is a 15-minute stroll from the City Hall, and accessible from Currie Street. Eastern Beach is reached via Moore Street. The broad, 4-km Esplanade runs along the seafront, connecting the two beaches. Nahoon lies further to the north.
Details: Orient Beach is well served by amenities; Eastern and Nahoon beaches rather less so. All three have change rooms and toilets. City shops and services are within easy walking distance. The Eastern Beach area offers picnicking facilities and a restaurant.
Accommodation: East London is well served by hotels, guesthouses and self-catering facilities.
Further information: East London Metropolitan Tourism Association, P O Box 533, East London 5200, tel (0431) 2-6015.

White-tipped rollers pound the golden beaches at Gonubie, where the Gqunube River spills into an estuary frequented by holiday-makers.

EAST LONDON MUSEUM
Town centre

The building, one of the city's more attractive, enjoys two major claims to fame. It houses both the first specimen of the primitive – and once presumed extinct – coelacanth fish to be identified in modern times, and the only dodo's egg in existence.

Unlike the coelacanth, the dodo, as the cliché has it, is a truly dead species. These flightless, turkey-sized birds, former residents of the Indian Ocean island of Mauritius, were simply too tame for survival, and were slaughtered in their thousands by the early settlers, and by passing ships' crews.

The very last of them were seen in the 1680s, though related species lived on, for about another century, on various other islands.

There is much else to intrigue visitors to the museum, which is ranked among the best of its kind in Africa.

The wide-ranging displays feature humankind through the ages; Xhosa, Mfengu and other traditional cultures; the story of the colonial (and, in particular, German immigrant) settlers; maritime exhibits relating to East London Harbour, and the fascinating fossils of the Karoo system.

Part of the complex is Gately House, a period museum which is beautifully furnished with its original Victorian contents. It was once home to John Gately, East London's first mayor.

Map: page 171, 6C
The main museum is at the upper end of Oxford Street. Gately House is at the bottom of Park Street.
Details: Open weekdays 09h30-17h00; Saturdays 09h30-12h00; Sundays 11h00-16h00. Small admission charge. Parking available. Gately House: open Tuesday to Thursday 10h30-12h30 and 14h00-17h00; Saturdays 15h00-17h00; and Sundays 15h00-17h00; closed Mondays.
Further information: East London Museum, P O Box 11021, Southernwood 5213, tel (0431) 43-0686; East London Metropolitan Tourism Association, P O Box 533, East London 5200, tel (0431) 2-6015.

GONUBIE RIVER MOUTH
North of East London

Map: page 171, 6C
Gonubie is 25 km northeast of East London. Take the N2 and turn coastwards at the Gonubie sign. The road reaches, and then follows, the shoreline for 4 kilometres. Parking is plentiful.
Details: The town has a shopping centre and excellent resort amenities, among them hotels and shady caravan parks. Sporting facilities include golf, bowls, tennis, squash, heavy- tackle angling (at the river mouth), surfing and boating. An attractive boardwalk runs along the seafront, providing a popular venue for walkers and joggers.
Accommodation: There is a choice of fine hotels in Gonubie and East London.
Further information: The Town Clerk, P O Box 20, Gonubie 5256, tel (0431) 40-4000.

The wild bramble berries of the river mouth's immediate hinterland gave their local African name to the Gqunube River, and to the delightfully village-like centre of Gonubie, some way up the coast from East London.

This is a prime recreational area. The river is navigable for four kilometres, and is much favoured by fishermen, boating enthusiasts and picnickers.

Holiday homes cluster on one side of the lagoon-type estuary, dense greenery covers the bluff on the other. Bathers and surfers are drawn to the kilometre-long river-mouth beach and to German Bay further to the south. There is a tidal pool and some fine rock-angling spots.

Gonubie boasts a small nature reserve, whose vleis and marshland sustain more than 130 different bird species. Notables include summer-nesting cranes, jaçanas, moorhens and coots. These and many other species can be seen from established hides, and from the well-laid-out paths.

The reserve also embraces an information centre, and a popular garden of medicinal plants commonly used by African herbalists.

The wide mouth of the Gqunube River loops into the warm waters of the Indian Ocean, flanked by bluffs dotted with holiday homes.

HOGSBACK
See page 178

HOLE IN THE WALL
Wild Coast

Map: page 171, 4E
From Umtata travel south on the N2. After 20 km, at Viedgesville, turn east for Mqanduli, and then follow the sign-posted road to Coffee Bay. After about 54 km, turn south onto the signposted road for Hole in the Wall, at the Ncwanguba trading store.
Details: Angling, walking. Near the hotel, beach leisure, safe swimming, horse-riding and other amenities.
Accommodation: At Coffee Bay, and at the Hole in the Wall Hotel and Holiday Village, 2 km from the cliff. The latter offers *en suite* bungalows and cottages, restaurant, poolside pub, bowling alley, pool room.
Further information: Eastern Cape Tourism Board – Eastern Region, Private Bag X5029, Umtata 5100, tel (0471) 31-2885; Wild Coast Hotels Reservations and Information, Private Bag X5028, Umtata 5100, tel (0471) 2-5344; or write to Hole in the Wall Hotel and Holiday Village, P O Box 17179, Congella 4013, or Private Bag X558, Mqanduli.

A short distance along the seaboard from Coffee Bay is a gigantic detached cliff, perhaps the most visited – and certainly the most photographed – single feature of the entire Wild Coast.

Its flanks are precipitous. Its flat top, broad and large enough to accommodate several football fields, is clothed in a mantle of greenery.

This is the famed Hole in the Wall, named after the river-and sea-eroded, arched passageway that tunnels through the base, and through which the angry ocean rollers thunder with a deep resonance. The locals know the massif as *esiKhaleni*, which means 'place of noise'.

There used to be a pretty little camp site, set in a forest of milkwoods, on the shoreline opposite. But the trees have now been fenced off, and visitors usually stay at the nearby hotel, a pleasant venue of chalets and cottages set in pleasantly landscaped surrounds.

There's excellent fishing in the area around the Hole in the Wall, and some splendid short walks inland, through dense woodlands and over grassy hills, and along the rugged coastline.

Amazing showpieces of the Kaffrarian Museum

In one of the halls here you'll see the glassy-eyed, mounted carcass of a hippopotamus – the mortal remains of an animal with a very special story.

This is Huberta, who captured the headlines in 1928 when she set off from the Richards Bay area to the north, on a three-year, 600-km overland odyssey down the heavily populated seaboard, her every move reported to an enchanted reading public. Her wanderings eventually came to an unhappy end when she was shot by hunters on the banks of the Keiskamma River.

Huberta, prominent though she may be, is just a tiny part of the Kaffrarian Museum's natural-history collection.

A staggering 40 000 mammal items have been gathered together under one roof here since Guy Shortridge, curator during the 1920s, began accumulating specimens.

The vast majority are hidden away in the back rooms, but there's still much to draw the eye, including such rarities as the Namaqualand silver mole, a black lechwe from Zimbabwe, the hero shrew (the smallest mammal found in Africa), and a record 5,5-m-high giraffe.

Dioramas illustrate the veld and its teeming wildlife, before colonial encroachment transformed the land for ever.

The two other major sections include 'Border' militaria, and the story of the area's hardy 19th-century settlers (many of them German immigrants), their lifestyles and fascinating costumes.

Of note are the recreation of an early rural store, and the wagons and carriages that were so skilfully crafted by the frontiersmen.

The Xhosa Gallery hosts fine displays of Xhosa and Khoisan culture, including superbly crafted and brightly coloured examples of traditional beadwork.

Also part of the complex is the Missionary Museum, keynotes of which are the printing presses that helped spread The Word among the indigenous peoples.

The main museum building is worth more than a passing glance: it's an elegantly imposing edifice constructed in 1898, at the high tide of the British Empire. The whispers of tourists and the rustle of bats' wings are the only sounds to be heard in the recesses of the

Behind the dainty façade of the Kaffrarian Museum are numerous exhibits depicting social and natural history, military events, and the full spectrum of Xhosa culture.

Sudwala Caves today, but in earlier times these caverns rang with the clash of spears and the anguished cries of battle.

From about 1815 to 1840, Somcuba, a wily old renegade who was joint regent of the Swazi people after Sobhuza's death, had established a settlement here, and this was where he kept the large numbers of royal cattle he had misappropriated during his reign.

When Mswazi, heir apparent to the throne, came of age, he attempted to recover the stolen cattle. Eventually, Somcuba and several thousand supporters were trapped in the caves by Mswazi and his regiments. Later, Somcuba was relieved by a Boer commando from Lydenburg, with which he had earlier formed an alliance.

Rumour has it that Somcuba stored large numbers of diamonds and other gems in clay pots, and secreted them somewhere in the caves. An equally persistent tale is that the apocryphal 'Kruger Millions' are hidden in their murky depths. This consignment of gold bullion and sovereigns belonging to the old Republic is said to have disappeared between Waterval-Onder and Nelspruit during the Anglo-Boer War. Boer commandos are known to have hidden ammunition for the heavy 94-pounder Long Tom guns in the caves, but no trace has ever been found of the most fabulous golden hoard in South African legend.

The surf-battered arch of the Hole in the Wall is clearly visible from the rocky shore.

PLACES TO VISIT

HOGSBACK

Map: page 171, 5B
Hogsback is accessible both from Alice to the south and from Cathcart to the northeast. From Alice take the R63 towards King William's Town, turn left onto the R345, and continue for 30 kilometres. From Cathcart follow the R345 leading south to Seymour and Hogsback (51 kilometres).

Details: Hogsback is worth visiting at any time of the year, but the spring and summer months are especially inviting. The village has a supermarket, post office, library and craft shops.

Accommodation: Hogsback has 3 hotels and a guesthouse: The Hogsback Inn, P O Box 63, Hogsback 5721, tel (045642) 6 or (045) 962-1006; King's Lodge, P O Hogsback 5721, tel (045642) 24 or (045) 962-1024; Hogsback Arminel Mountain Lodge, P O Box 67, Hogsback 5721, tel (045642) 5 or (045) 962-1005; Amatola Guest House, P O Box 45, Hogsback 5721, tel (045642) 59 or (045) 962-1059.

Further information: Permits for forest walks are obtainable from Hogsback Forest Station, P O Box 52, Hogsback 5721, tel (045642) 55 or (045) 962-1055. As yet, there is no information office in Hogsback, but the booklet *Exploring Hogsback* is widely available locally at shops and hotels. The locals and staff are knowledgeable and helpful.

Evergreen canopy forests, undulating mountains and a really entrancing little village combine to create one of the Southeast Cape's most inviting get-away-from-it-all destinations.

Much of the scenically exquisite countryside is protected within the Hogsback State Forest, the Aukland Nature Reserve, and the beautiful forests of the Tyumie River Valley – areas that are graced with dense spreads of Outeniqua yellowwoods and white stinkwoods, assegai and camdeboo trees, stately Cape chestnuts, sneezewoods, knobwoods, ironwoods and red pears. Beneath them, on the twilit forest floors, are groves of tall ferns and thick tangles of undergrowth through which footpaths wind their intricate way.

This is a quiet world, mysterious and enchanting, the deep silence only occasionally broken by the call of a loerie or the brief chatter of a samango monkey.

The area's rather evocative English name is believed to derive from the three high peaks that tower over the plateau. Seen from certain vantage points they bear a resemblance to a trio of the wild hogs – bushpigs – that root around in the night-time forest depths. Local Africans know the place as Belekazana, which means 'bear on the back' (one of the hills, seen from another angle, is reminiscent of a woman carrying a child). However, whatever disagreements there are about origins, few will deny the beauty and tranquil charm of Hogsback.

The village itself amounts to little more than a scattering of houses and holiday bungalows, three intimate hotels, a guesthouse and a caravan/camping site in an attractively shady setting.

The gardens and immaculate surrounds are bright with a profusion of azaleas, rhododendrons and other northern-hemisphere flora.

Not very far from the village is the Arboretum – a fine showpiece of exotic (mainly European) as well as African tree specimens. Its stand of Californian redwoods is the largest in southern Africa.

To get to the Arboretum involves a leisurely stroll along tree-flanked Oak Avenue, at the end of which is a natural 'cathedral', where open-air services are held at Christmas and Easter (logs serve as benches).

Nearby you'll find the charming little stone church, St Patrick's-on-the-Hill, which is one of the smallest churches in the country.

The Hogsback area is first and foremost walking country. The choice is wide, the routes ranging from three-

The picturesque village of Hogsback nestles in the fertile Tyumie River Valley at the foot of the gentle Amatola Mountain range.

A path winding lazily through the Arboretum epitomizes the intoxicating serenity of walking in the Hogsback.

kilometre rambles through the trees to 20-km hikes up hill and down dale.

Before starting off, get hold of the local booklet *Exploring Hogsback* (informally known as 'The Piggy Book'), a highly informative guide that describes the elaborate system of paths, the 'piggy walks' and 'blue-crane walks', the historic sites (the area is steeped in colonial 'frontier' history), waterfalls, pools and mountain heights.

The paths are also clearly marked with the hog motif, and different colours define the various routes. Many of the walks afford breathtaking views of valley and mountain.

Also recommended is a comprehensive tree list: several of the lofty specimens are numbered for identification.

Among the more rewarding of the outings in the area are:
■ A three- to four-hour ramble from Oak Avenue, along Forest Drive and back on the contour path, digressing to view the breath-taking splendours of the Kettlespout Falls.
■ Through the Aukland Reserve, entering at a point near King's Lodge. *En route* you'll see the 800-year-old, 36-m-high Outeniqua yellowwood known as the Big Tree, and the Tyumie River's lovely Madonna and Child Waterfall. The Bridal Veil Cataract is worth a digression. Allow between two and three hours for the excursion.
■ The short Military Path from the Hogsback Library (housed in a quaint rondavel) through the forest and down to the road that leads to Alice, and the even briefer stroll from the Oak Avenue picnic spot to the lovely 39 Steps Waterfall.
■ Scrambles up the various peaks. Most popular is the ascent of Tor Doone, from whose 1 565-m summit there are some superb 360° views of the surrounding forested countryside.

Others include the climb up Gaika's Kop (1 963m), from where you can see far-off Queenstown in one direction, and the distant Indian Ocean in the other; the Elandsberg (2 017m), and, of course, the three hogsbacks themselves, each of which rises imposingly to more than 1 800 m above sea level.
■ The fairly new Hogsback Hiking Trail, an attractive, 32-km, two-day route that takes in the forest, waterfalls, some rock-climbing and an overnight halt at Gaika's Kop.

The region is no longer famed for its big game (hunters shot it out a long time ago) but on your wanderings you could well glimpse small antelope such as bushbuck and duiker, as well as vervet monkeys, rock dassies and their elusive cousins, the nocturnal tree dassies. And, of course, bushpigs live here too. Jackal buzzards wheel in the sky above.

Festooned on the ground are thick bramble patches of sweet blackberries and, according to the season, delicate harebells and other lovely wildflowers.

The Madonna and Child Waterfall is named after the shape of the rock formation which underlies the falls.

Hogsback's Arminel Mountain Lodge, reclining in the shade of towering trees, reflects the charming ambience of an English country home.

MAZEPPA BAY
Wild Coast

Map: page 171, 5D
Mazeppa Bay is located towards the southern end of the Wild Coast. Leave Butterworth on the N2 travelling north. On the outskirts of the town you cross the Gcuwa River – turn right here for Centane/Kentani. At Centane take the road to Mazeppa and Nxaxo Mouth.
Details: Pleasant to visit at any time of the year, but especially so from October through to May.
Accommodation: Mazeppa Bay Hotel, Private Bag 3014, Butterworth, tel (0474) 3278; or Wild Coast Hotels Reservations, Private Bag X5028, Umtata 5100, tel (0471) 2-5344.
Further information: Camp site: Nature Conservation Division, Department of Agriculture and Forestry, Private Bag X5002, Umtata 5100, tel (0471) 2-4322 or 31-2711/2; or Wild Coast Hotels *(see above)*.

Three wide, golden beaches fringed by wild date palms, an inviting hotel connected to its own island by a (seemingly precarious) suspension bridge, and some of the finest fishing you'll find anywhere – these are among the prime attractions of this lovely resort area.

The Island is a notable deep-water angling spot. Common catches here and elsewhere include shad, musselcracker, queenfish, and such renowned fighting species as the barracuda and the hammerhead shark – which can weigh in at anything up to 450 kilograms. Almost as rewarding are nearby Shark Point and the Boiling Pot.

Stretching north from The Island towards Clan Lindsay Rocks (named after an 1898 shipwreck) is First Beach, perhaps the most enticing to bathers, snorkellers, scuba-divers and sun-worshippers. To the south are Second and Shelley beaches, which are favoured by the surfing fraternity.

This is also splendid walking country. The high dunes of the coastline are decorated by gnarled old milkwood trees. The six-kilometre stroll to the resort at Qora Mouth is recommended.

Mazeppa Bay's hotel is famed for its seafood. The Friday and Saturday buffets are special.

A lone angler waits patiently at Msikaba Lagoon, where indigenous forest plunges to the water's edge.

MKAMBATI NATURE RESERVE
Wild Coast and hinterland

Map: page 171, 3F
From Umtata travel north on the N2 to Brooks Nek (about 162 km north of Umtata, and 13 km south of Kokstad). Turn east onto the road to Bizana. Turn south after 36 km, at Magushani, onto the R61 to Flagstaff. After 29 km turn left towards the Holy Cross Mission, and follow Mkambati signposts.
Details: Open dawn to dusk throughout the year. Entrance fee.
Accommodation: Mkambati Nature Reserve offers comfortable 6- and 8-bed cottages, and 3-bed rondavels, together with a serviced lodge (5 double rooms, guest lounge, resident cook).
Further information: Nature Conservation Division, Department of Agriculture and Forestry, Private Bag X5002, Umtata 5100, tel (0471) 2-4322 or 31-2711/2; Mkambati Nature Reserve, P O Box 574, Kokstad 4700, tel (037) 727-3101; or Keval Travel, P O Box 388, Kokstad 4700, tel (037) 727-3124.

The scenically delightful Mkambati Nature Reserve occupies some 8 000 ha of coastal grassland, incised by perennial streams, and bordered by the deep, densely wooded valleys of the Msikaba and Mtentu rivers.

In the northern parts the countryside takes on a subtropical look. Some of the lower-lying areas are graced by delicately balanced swamp forests. Notable are the Pondoland palms, or 'mkambati coconuts'.

The shoreline beckons the fisherman, the hiker, and those who enjoy lazing in the sun. Take a walk along one of the many inland pathways, and you'll see (though this, of course, depends on the time of the year) some exquisite wildflowers – watsonias and gladioli, daisies in the grassy swathes, ground orchids and many other interesting varieties.

A walk up the Msikaba will bring you to the spectacular Horseshoe Falls, where icy waters tumble and bubble over a series of scenic rapids before falling noisily to the sea below. Also here is a breeding colony of Cape vultures that nests in the flanking cliffs.

Mkambati's wildlife includes zebras, eland, blue wildebeest, gemsbok, hartebeest and blesbok.

The riverine forests are home to an impressive number and variety of birds, including the endangered Cape vulture and the beloved fish eagle.

Among the reserve's visitor facilities are various types of accommodation, and The Club House *a la carte* restaurant, which specializes in venison and seafood.

PORT GROSVENOR
Wild Coast

An optimistic 19th-century attempt to build a harbour on this ruggedly rocky part of the northern Wild Coast came to nothing, and the engineers departed, leaving the lonely shoreline to the sea birds and the turbulent surf.

This failed project is recalled in the first part of the name. The second commemorates one of southern Africa's more notable shipwrecks.

In August 1782 the treasure ship *Grosvenor* foundered off Lambasi Bay, consigning 14 of the people on board to a watery grave.

The remaining 138 set off on the long trek westwards towards the Cape frontier settlements and beyond, to Cape Town.

They had little in the way of food, weapons and trading goods, and only six eventually reached safety. The remainder presumably perished *en route*, though it is thought that some may have abandoned their odyssey to settle among the black communities of the southern seaboard. Only a century later, however, did evidence of the *Grosvenor's* fabulous cargo finally emerge.

Bills of lading unearthed showed she was carrying bullion and, possibly, jewels, coins, plate and other precious items – among which, according to rumours, was the legendary Peacock Throne of Persia. This last belonged to Shah Jehan, the renowned warrior and architect of India's Taj Mahal.

Two years after the first reports appeared, a small fortune in gold and silver coins was washed ashore, and the hunt was on.

Several very ambitious salvage schemes were launched during the following decades, the last one in 1952, but shifting sands, razor-edged rocks and treacherous currents around the wreck site proved too formidable, and each had to be abandoned.

Still, individual divers have come up with a few valuable bits and pieces, and passers-by have stumbled on the occasional small relic.

Today the wreck's precise position is the subject of some debate. But most experts agree that a vast store of wealth lies waiting to be claimed.

Port Grosvenor is worth visiting for the wild beauty of the land and seascapes: ideal country for walking. And for beachcombing – you might, just possibly, spot a gleaming reminder of the fabled riches hidden just beneath the waves.

Map: page 171, 3F
From the N2 make your way coastwards to Lusikisiki (best route is from Brooks Nek, near Kokstad, via Flagstaff). A four-wheel-drive is recommended. The road thereafter runs eastwards from a point just north of Lusikisiki. Drive past the signs to Magwa Falls and, after 7 km, bear right at the fork and continue for 25 kilometres. At the 25-km mark you'll see a track leading towards the sea. Port Grosvenor is 7 km further on.
Details: Best times to visit are the usually dry winter and springtime months.
Accommodation: The nearest facilities are to the south, at the Embotyi River Bungalow Complex (Wild Coast Hotels Reservations and Information, Private Bag X5028, Umtata 5100, tel (0471) 2-5344), and further along, at Port St Johns *(see separate entry).*
Further information: Nature Conservation Division, Department of Agriculture and Forestry, Private Bag X5002, Umtata 5100, tel (0471) 2-4322 or 31-2711/2.

Shipwrecks along a treacherous shore

Many of the 1 300 or so vessels that have come to grief along southern Africa's treacherous shoreline were wrecked along the Transkei region's Wild Coast. Earliest of them were the sailing ships of 16th-century Portugal's great Indies-bound trading fleets.

The navigational kits of the time were simple, even rudimentary, comprising little more than a compass, some crude instruments for gauging degrees of latitude and wind direction, and an astrolabe, which also determined latitude by recording the movement of the midday sun across the meridian.

Maps were both creative and inaccurate. Captains knew little of the Wild Coast's winds, currents, reefs and shoals. And, of course, they had to contend with the savage storms of the southern seas.

The caravels, with their high poop decks, tended to be badly built and difficult to handle in poor weather.

One of the more tragic of the wrecks was that of the *Sao Joao*. She foundered at the Mtamvuna River Mouth in 1552, with the loss of more than 100 lives. The 440 exhausted survivors scrambled up the shore and set off northwards on an overland odyssey plagued by accident, sickness, the predations of wild animals, and hostility from the local people. Eventually, just eight Portuguese and 17 slaves reached Mozambique Island some 1 600 km from their landfall.

Two years later the *Sao Bento* went to her grave off the Mtata estuary, to the south of the Mtamvuna River. Those who reached dry land – there were 323 of them – also decided to head north.

Their epic journey over the wild hills took 72 days. *En route* they came across some of the dropouts from the *Sao Joao* party, survivors who had chosen safety among the African communities. Of the *Sao Bento* group, 62 got to the Maputo River, but it was five months before a rescue ship arrived, and only 24 survived.

Even more heroic, and certainly more successful, were the 285 survivors of the *Santo Alberto*, wrecked near the Hole in the Wall in 1593. Following an inland route (they were the first whites to see the snowcapped Drakensberg), the intelligently led band, which included two women, remained more or less intact until they reached the Portuguese east-coast settlement 88 days later.

A contemporary engraving illustrates in graphic detail the tragic fate of the Grosvenor, which struck a reef and was wrecked in a gully off Lambasi Bay in August 1782.

Map: page 171, 4E
From Umtata take the 91-km R61 route east through Libode, Mhlengana and Ntshimbini to Port St Johns.
Details: Port St Johns is pleasant throughout the year.
Accommodation: Port St Johns offers hotels, bungalows and cottages, as well as caravan/camping facilities. Try the Umngazi River Bungalows, 6 km south of the town, with its luxurious bungalow accommodation; Protea Cape Hermes Hotel, P O Box 190, Port St Johns, tel (0475) 44-1234; Coastal Needles Hotel, P O Box 9, Port St Johns, tel (0475) 44-1031; and Second Beach Holiday Resort, P O Box 18, Port St Johns, tel (0475) 44-1245.
Further information: Wild Coast Hotels Reservations and Information, Private Bag X5028, Umtata 5100, tel (0471) 2-5344; The Municipality, P O Box 2, Port St Johns, tel (0475) 44-1244.

PORT ST JOHNS
Wild Coast

The small town at the mouth of the Mzimvubu River is perhaps the most attractive of all the Wild Coast's destinations. Its setting of deep river-gorge, two massive headlands, evergreen forest, golden sand and blue ocean is quite magnificent, and it has all the amenities the quieter holiday-maker could wish for.

The place is believed to have taken its name from a very famous 16th-century shipwreck *(see panel)*, but the modern settlement began life only in the 1870s, when the British colonial authorities established a garrison and began converting the estuary into a commercial harbour. At that time the hinterland teemed with a variety of wild game (indeed, the local Mpondo inhabitants know the gorge and estuary as 'the home of the hippopotamus'), and there was a brisk trade in ivory and skins.

The river, navigable for some 10 km upstream, is popular among canoeists and boating enthusiasts. Its valley is laced by a fantasia of lush subtropical fruit plantings, and by pathways that take you to some quite enchanting beauty spots. Roadside stalls sell bead- and basketwork, cane products, batiks and bananas, litchis, pawpaws, mangoes and avocado pears.

Three splendid stretches of sand grace the shoreline. First Beach, perhaps the best of the onshore fishing areas (there's also excellent deep-sea angling), is the venue of one of Port St Johns's two pleasant hotels. A leisurely ferry connects First Beach with Agate Terrace, a 'cottage colony' resort just to the north. To the south is Third Beach.

The town and its surrounds have served as permanent home to a lively little community of writers, artists and others in search of the idyllic life. The climate is near perfect, the sea safe (though the occasional shark lurks off the beaches) and warm enough for bathing even in the winter months.

Flanking Third Beach is the Silaka Nature Reserve, a small but enchanting little expanse of wooded valley and grassy hill that sustains blue wildebeest, zebras, blesbok and some lovely forest birds. There are a number of chalets for hire within the reserve.

Port St Johns has a nine-hole golf course, bowling greens, tennis courts, shops, a library, and an intriguing little natural-history museum.

A fisherman, braving the chilly dawn, casts his line into the sea at Port St Johns, one of the more popular Wild Coast resorts.

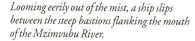

Looming eerily out of the mist, a ship slips between the steep bastions flanking the mouth of the Mzimvubu River.

WILD COAST HIKING TRAIL
Transkei coast

The Transkei region's shoreline is known as the Wild Coast – a name which refers not, as might be expected, to the absence of human settlement (on the contrary, the hinterland is heavily populated), but to its spectacular land- and seascapes, and to the sometimes storm-tossed, always treacherous, sea.

This 280-km maritime strip is a magnificent wilderness of wide beaches and secluded coves, high dunes, dramatic cliffs and rocky reefs that probe finger-like into the sparkling Indian Ocean, forests and mangrove swamps, and patches of graceful Pondoland palms. Further inland there are rolling green hills and stands of dense woodlands.

The full Wild Coast Trail (which is clearly marked by white-painted footprints) takes up to 25 days, and traverses the entire length of the seaboard, from the Mtamvuna estuary close to Port Edward, to the Great Kei River Mouth in the southwest.

Hikers, however, have a number of less demanding options: the route is divided into five shorter (three- to six-day) sections. Secondary tracks link the main coastal road with the trail heads.

Among the myriad features of interest along the trail are the Mkambati, Dwesa and Cwebe nature reserves, the famed Hole in the Wall, enchanting little resort centres and timeless Xhosa villages.

The waterfalls, of which there are many, are especially lovely.

The Mfihlelo Falls to the north cascade over an imposing massif directly into the sea (the drop is a full 160 metres). At the similar but smaller Waterfall Bluff, still further to the north, you can walk between the towering cliff face and the

Map: page 171, 3/5C-F
The N2 highway runs parallel to the coast; secondary roads branch off at regular intervals. The latter can be in poor condition, especially during the rains. Hikers on the full route start at the Mtamvuna River Mouth, and walk southwestwards. The Mtamvuna estuary is reached via the N2 to Port Shepstone, and then the R61 to Port Edward.

Details: Open throughout the year. Best times for the hike are the warmer months; access can be difficult during rainy spells. Maximum of 12 persons per group. Permits required; tide tables recommended. Provisions are obtainable at numerous trading stores along and near the route, but carry a water bottle.

Accommodation: Trailists overnight in traditional Xhosa-style huts sleeping twelve. The huts are equipped with bunks, mattresses and basic furniture. There is running water and fireplaces.

Further information: Nature Conservation Division, Department of Agriculture and Forestry, Private Bag X5002, Umtata 5100, tel (0471) 2-4322 or 31-2711/2.

Waterfalls plunge over steep cliffs into the sea at Mkambati Nature Reserve.

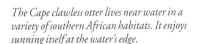

The Cape clawless otter lives near water in a variety of southern African habitats. It enjoys sunning itself at the water's edge.

Graceful hunters of the waterways

Walk along the wooded reaches of any Southeast Cape river, and you could well catch a glimpse of an otter slipping sinuously into the water. These bright-eyed, bristly-whiskered mammals, which are relatives of the weasel, are ranked among the most gracefully accomplished swimmers of the wild kingdom. Their perfectly adapted physique – long, muscular body, short legs, seal-like head, and thick, tapering tail – is beautifully streamlined for the purpose.

They can travel 500 m underwater without coming up for air, at a cruising speed of about 10 km/hour.

For shelter, they burrow into the bank, digging a long, two-entry tunnel rising to a level above the water.

The upper entrance, which is well hidden among the dense riverine foliage, doubles as an air vent, and the shelter is cosily lined with leaves and grass.

Two species are found in southern Africa, both of which are widely distributed. The larger is the Cape clawless otter *(Aonyx capensis)*, biggest of all the Old World members of the family. Adult males reach an average mass of more than 12 kilograms. Females weigh in at two kilograms more.

They are brown (the underparts lighter than the upper), except for the snout, throat, neck and chest, which are off-white. And, as the name suggests, the animal lacks claws, though it has vestigial nails on the third and fourth toes of its hindfeet. By contrast, the webbed toes of the smaller spotted-necked otter *(Lutra maculicollis)* sport short, sharp claws, and it is easily recognized by its white-dappled throat.

The otter is a superb catcher of fish (its staple diet), but will hunt and eat a range of other small creatures – frogs, crabs, rodents, and so forth. The clawless variety is especially indiscriminate: it spends much of its time on dry land, and has been known to raid poultry pens.

Otters at play are a delight to the eye. If you spot a family during your riverside ramble, watch quietly from behind cover and, if you're lucky, you'll see the adults and young sliding down the muddy bank, one after the other, to plunge joyously into the water, emerging time and again to repeat the game.

TRANSKEI

roaring cataract – an other-worldly and memorable experience.

Shipwrecks litter the coastal waters. The birds of the region (fish eagles and white-backed night herons are among the swampland varieties) and the intricate intertidal marine life are sources of endless fascination.

Note: Do not drink water from rivers and streams without purifying or boiling it first. Pilfering can be a problem; keep a careful eye on your possessions at the overnight camps.

Other precautions: ticks are a nuisance (infected ones cause fever); sharks may lurk in the estuaries. When crossing the latter, make your way upstream and take the plunge (pushing your pack in front of you) when the tide is coming in.

WILD COAST SUN
South of Port Edward

Map: page 171, 3F
From Durban travel south along the N2 to Port Shepstone. At the Oribi Toll Plaza turn south onto the R61, which leads for some 44 km to the Wild Coast Sun.
Details: Open throughout the year. The resort is self-contained, offering twin, family, 'executive' and suite accommodation; shops, restaurants; postal telefax and other services. There's a wide range of sporting and leisure activities.
Further information: Sun International, P O Box 784487, Sandton 2146, tel (011) 783-8660; or P O Box 3651, Durban 4000, tel (031) 304-9237.

South Africa's premier coastal hotel and casino resort hugs the shores of a limpid and lovely lagoon on the extreme north of the Transkei region's shoreline, and offers just about everything the heart of the holiday-maker could wish for.

The overall design of the complex is both imaginative and attractive: there's a Pacific Islands-look about the buildings; timber and thatch are prominent; all is light and airy – even, surprisingly, the gaming area. The grounds are lush, terraced in parts, open to superb views, graced by a lovely profusion of plantings.

On offer is the full range of sporting and leisure activities, including golf (the excellent 18-hole course ranks among the country's best), bowls, tennis, squash, swimming (three pools, one of them heated, and the sea), canoeing and sailing at Water World.

Among other water-related sports are jet-skiing, parasailing and windsurfing. Outdoor-lovers who are in search of quieter pleasures take long horseback rides along the golden sands.

Indoors there are lovely restaurants (the Commodore is renowned), cocktail bars, a theatre that plays host to international entertainers, two lively show bars and, of course, the casino, where you can try your luck at the tables or at slot machines that have created an elite group of instant millionaires. The hotel has about 400 rooms, each of which looks out to either ocean or golf course.

The day-visitor centre caters handsomely for nonresidents.

The Wild Coast Sun lures holiday-makers to its bronze beaches and subtropical surroundings from all corners of southern Africa.

SOUTHEAST CAPE

SOUTHEAST CAPE

ADDO ELEPHANT NATIONAL PARK
North of Port Elizabeth

Map: page 185, 5C
From Port Elizabeth drive east along the N2 to the Swartkops River, just outside the city, and then turn left onto the R335 for the 29-km drive to Addo. Continue along the road to Coerney, to reach the National Park 73 km from Port Elizabeth.
Details: Open daily throughout the year 07h00 -19h00.
Accommodation: There are 2 luxury, 6-bed cottages, each with air-conditioned bedrooms and *en suite* bathrooms; 24 air-conditioned chalets with bathrooms and kitchens; six 2-bed huts (no air conditioning) with showers, toilets and refrigerators. There's also an attractive camping/caravan site under trees, with ablution and braai facilities, and communal kitchens.
Further information: The National Parks Board, P O Box 787, Pretoria 0001, tel (012) 343-1991; P O Box 7400, Roggebaai 8012, tel (021) 22-2810.

When an elephant flaps his ears, does it mean he is annoyed? Yes!

Take a tip from the lions – treat an elephant with great respect, for he is the real king of the wilds, quite unafraid of your car. You will have many opportunities to meet elephants at close quarters in the 14 551 ha of undulating valley bushveld that comprises the Addo Elephant National Park, for there are over 200 of them, four times the density of elephants in the Kruger National Park.

The reserve was created in 1931 to protect a small group of elephants – the survivors of a once-enormous population that was virtually exterminated by trophy hunters, farmers and poachers in this part of the Southeast Cape. It is situated in the dense, indigenous bush country of the Sundays River Valley, in the midst of a prosperous farming area, where farmers and hunters had reduced them almost to extinction earlier this century.

The elephants are gregarious, living in family groups led by a cow, and the dominant bull of the reserve does most of the breeding. For many years this was a bull called Hapoor, whose ear had been nicked by a bullet. He was finally deposed in 1968, broke out of the reserve, and was shot. His head is mounted on the wall of the park restaurant.

Besides elephants, you'll see many other mammals in the reserve, including such species as the nocturnal aardvark, duiker, caracals, buffaloes, bushbuck, bushpigs, eland, grysbok, red hartebeest, black-backed jackals and kudu.

The buffaloes are of particular interest, for they are the only Cape buffaloes to have survived, and have changed their habits from herd animals that graze during the day, to solitary animals that browse at night.

Another threatened species which is prospering in the reserve is the East African black rhinoceros. There are also more than 150 bird species, ranging from ostriches to raptors and waterfowl.

The park, an easy drive from Port Elizabeth, offers comfortable sleeping facilities for guests, an excellent *a la carte* restaurant, a swimming pool, braai and picnic facilities, a curio shop and caravan and camping sites.

For nature-lovers and botanists there is the four-hour Spekboom Trail, which lies inside a fenced-off botanical reserve. But for most visitors the elephants are the principal and ever-present attraction.

Two bull elephants wrestle in the Addo Elephant National Park. These pachyderms are usually quite placid creatures, rarely displaying outbursts of aggression.

APPLE EXPRESS
Langkloof

For a unique – and historic – view of the rugged Southeast Cape hinterland and the fertile Langkloof Valley, there's no better way to travel than on the famed Apple Express – a fascinating steam-powered adventure along one of the world's last narrow-gauge railway lines.

To appreciate just how narrow it is, the gauge of the Apple Express railway line is 610 mm, compared with the average international gauge of 1 440 mm, and Transnet's gauge of 1 065 millimetres.

The Apple Express made its first 285-km trip from Port Elizabeth to the

Langkloof Valley in 1906, its mission – to collect agricultural produce and transport it back to Port Elizabeth.

Although the express has not traditionally served as a passenger line, it covers an exceptionally scenic route which includes two main bridges – over the Gamtoos River (washed away in the 1905 floods, and then rebuilt), and the sensational bridge over the Van Staden's Gorge.

The 197-m-long railway bridge over the Van Staden's River was completed in 1904 and still remains the highest of its kind in the world.

Although the Apple Express originally took sightseers as far as the Gamtoos town of Loerie, today the trip is somewhat shorter, taking day-trippers to Thornhill, about 15 km past the Van Staden's River Bridge.

The steam-train trip starts from King's Beach at 10h00 (Saturdays, Sundays and Wednesdays in season), and then passes through six stations before it crosses the Van Staden's River Bridge.

Lunch is available at the Thornhill Hotel, after which the train returns to Port Elizabeth.

Map: page 185, 6C
The Apple Express departs from Humewood Road Station, just south of the city centre.
Details: During the December/January holiday period, trips take place on Saturdays, Sundays and Wednesdays; out of season, one trip per month. The excursion starts at 10h00. At 12h00 you reach Thornhill, where you can enjoy either your own picnic, or lunch at the Thornhill Hotel (P O Box 72, Thornhill 6375, tel (04212) 653). The train leaves at 14h00 and returns to Humewood by 15h30.
Accommodation: You can choose either to overnight at the Thornhill Hotel and return on the train, or you can stay at one of the many hotels, guesthouses or holiday cottages in Port Elizabeth.
Further information: Port Shepstone and Alfred County Railway, P O Box 21847, Port Elizabeth 6000, tel (041) 507-2333; Port Elizabeth Publicity Association, P O Box 357, Port Elizabeth 6000, tel (041) 52-1315.

The Apple Express snakes through fertile countryside between Port Elizabeth and the Langkloof Valley.

BAVIAANSKLOOF
Near Humansdorp

If you are looking for an adventurous trip, a tough drive with outstanding scenery in really wild surroundings, try the dramatic Baviaanskloof.

From Humansdorp leave the N2 and travel along the tarred R332, over the hills for 32 km, to Andrieskraal, where the road intersects the R331. Continue west along the R332 for four kilometres to Heroncliff, where the tar ends. For the next 168 km there are no garages, and petrol is obtainable at only two points.

The gravel road turns north into the mountains, following the course of the Groot River, the road sandwiched between the river and the cliffs. After 12 km on gravel you will pass Goede Hoop Church settlement. The road crosses and recrosses the Wit River, passes the Cockscomb Forest Station (here you must turn left at the fork), and ascends a steep mountain pass, arriving on a broad escarpment 27 km from Heroncliff.

As you continue westwards, the road descends to the Bukkraal River, 170 m above sea level, then dips into a meshwork of rolling hills. The road meanders through the hills, clinging to the edge of sheer drops as it rises for seven kilometres from the valley, up the main Baviaanskloof Pass. Drive carefully – the gravel is dangerous.

At Coleskeplaas, 72 km past the end of the tarred road, the kloof starts to open out, and the road runs alongside the river. On both sides are the mountain peaks, seldom less than 300 m and often more than 700 m above the river. Twenty kilometres further on is Kleinpoort (where you can buy petrol), and another five kilometres further on is the police post at Studtis. This is where the Baviaanskloof Forest Reserve is situated.

Beyond Studtis the river gorge narrows, and the road winds between tall peaks for seven kilometres to Beacon's Nek, where the kloof widens into the Verloren River Valley. Another 28 km brings you to the foot of the third and last pass, Nuwekloof.

The scenery here is majestic, with steep krantzes flanking the narrow kloof. The pass is only three kilometres long and emerges onto the Karoo. The road to Willowmore, 33 km away, marks the end of this journey of discovery.

Map: page 185, 5B
Follow the N2 westward from Port Elizabeth for 88 km to Humansdorp. Turn north along the R332, past Andrieskraal, Heroncliff, Goede Hoop, Coleskeplaas, Kleinpoort and Studtis, to Willowmore.
Details: The Baviaanskloof may be closed temporarily by heavy rainfall, or by the rise of river levels. Enquire at (04942) 469.
Accommodation: At Geelhoutbosch in the Willowmore district there are 5 fully equipped 6-bed bungalows.
Further information: Cape Nature Conservation, Private Bag X1126, Port Elizabeth 6000, tel (041) 390-2179; Gamtoos Agricultural Route, P O Box 206, Patensie 6335, tel (04232) 3-0437.

PLACES TO VISIT

GRAHAMSTOWN

THE ALBANY MUSEUM COMPLEX

Map: below
The Albany Museum and History Museum are at the western end of the town, on the corner of Somerset Street and Lucas Avenue.

Details: Open Monday to Friday 09h30-13h00 and 14h00-17h00; Saturdays and Sundays 14h00-17h00. Closed Christmas Day, New Year's Day, Good Friday and Workers' Day.

Accommodation: Grahamstown offers accommodation, ranging from hotels to guesthouses. Try the Cathcart Arms Hotel, P O Box 143, Grahamstown 6140, tel (0461) 2-7111; Graham Protea Hotel, 123 High Street, Grahamstown 6140, tel (0461) 2-2324; Settlers Inn, P O Box 219, Grahamstown 6140, tel (0461) 2-7313.

Further information: Albany Museum, Somerset Street, Grahamstown 6140, tel (0461) 2-2312; Grahamstown Publicity Association, 63 High Street, Grahamstown 6140, tel (0461) 2-3241.

An important drawcard for visitors to Grahamstown is the Albany Museum Complex, which has five fascinating museums under its umbrella: the Albany or Natural Sciences Museum, the History Museum, the Observatory Museum, the Provost Prison, which stands on Lucas Avenue, and Fort Selwyn, guarding the entrance to the 1820 Settlers National Monument above the city.

The imposing façade of Grahamstown's Albany Museum, home to a variety of cultural, geological and traditional displays.

Albany Museum

An Egyptian mummy, depictions of the life of early man, artefacts and showcases of animals and birds are just some of the delights of the Albany Museum, the second-oldest museum in South Africa.

Other attractions are displays of traditional Xhosa dress and beadwork.

Apart from its displays, the museum also specializes in the study of geology, freshwater fish, insects and archaeology.

The museum was founded in 1855 by the Eastern Province Literary, Scientific and Medical Society, and its first collection was housed in the home of the geologist Andrew Geddes Bain.

History Museum

This section of the museum houses a wide variety of important relics of the 1820 Settlers – their jewellery, furniture, porcelain cooking utensils, toys, clothing and military memorabilia. And for those interested in genealogy, the museum also displays the records and family trees of the settlers, as well as offering a genealogical service to the public. There are also three permanent art galleries.

KEY TO THE MAP
1 Albany Museum
2 Observatory Museum
3 Anglican Cathedral
4 1820 Settler National Monument

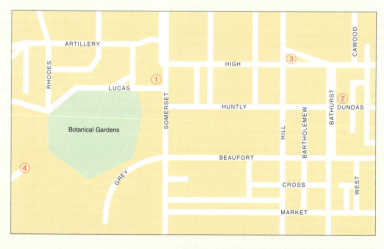

Map: above
The Observatory Museum is in Bathurst Street, just off Church Square.

Details: Open Monday to Friday 09h30-13h00 and 14h00-17h00; Saturdays 09h00-13h00.

Accommodation: See Albany Museum Complex.

Further information: Albany Museum, Somerset Street, Grahamstown 6140, tel (0461) 2-2312.

OBSERVATORY MUSEUM

The Observatory Museum was originally a 19th-century shop and home designed and owned by jeweller Henry Carter Galpin, who lived in Grahamstown from 1850 until 1886. The building was restored by De Beers Consolidated Mines Limited, because the very first diamond found in South Africa was identified in this house in 1867 by Dr W G Atherstone – a local medical doctor.

In the topmost turret of the museum Galpin constructed a camera obscura – the only one in the southern hemisphere that is still in perfect working order. Here you can marvel at the miniature moving reflections of the scenes outside. Also to be seen are the Meridian Room, where Grahamstown time was first set, the open clockworks, rooms containing Victorian furniture and a nostalgic curio shop.

ANGLICAN CATHEDRAL

The stately 45-m bell tower and spire of the Cathedral of St Michael and St George – reputedly the tallest in the country – dominate the skyline in the City of Saints.

Work on this Anglican church, built in early English Gothic style, began in 1824, and was finally completed 128 years later, in 1952. The south wall is part of the original church, making it the oldest surviving church structure in South Africa.

During the frontier wars the cathedral was used as a depot for the distribution of arms and ammunition, as well as a refuge and officers' headquarters.

For some years there was a split in the Anglican community of the town, when the dean excluded the bishop from St George's Church. The split was healed in 1885, after the death of the dean, and the cathedral's name marks the amalgamation of the two communities.

There are several memorials inside the cathedral, including one to Joshua Davis Norden, thought to be the only memorial erected in an Anglican cathedral in memory of a contemporary Jew.

In the belfry is the first full complement, and the heaviest, of eight bells on the African continent. They were cast in London in 1878, and include the metal from the first three bells that hung in the tower.

Map: page 188
The cathedral stands in Church Square, occupying the middle of High Street in the city centre, and visible from every direction.
Details: The cathedral is open on weekdays 08h30-16h30, and on Saturdays 08h30-11h00.
Accommodation: See Albany Museum Complex.
Further information: The Cathedral of St Michael and St George, P O Box 102, Grahamstown 6140, tel (0461) 2-2445.

1820 SETTLERS NATIONAL MONUMENT

This monument is not a memorial shrine, but was built to commemorate the contribution made by English-speaking South Africans in the development of the country. Opened in 1974, it stands on a hill overlooking Grahamstown.

The Grahamstown Foundation manages and promotes its use as an educational, cultural and conference centre.

The most important such conference is the annual National Arts Festival, which is the largest cultural event in Africa, attracting thousands of performers and visitors to Grahamstown. The programme includes cabaret, drama, dance, films, music, exhibitions and lectures. It takes place in early July each year.

The focal point of the building is the Fountain Foyer, in which you can see the bubbling Millstone Fountain, a soaring yellowwood sculpture by local artist Cecil Skotnes. From the foyer, entrances lead to the impressive Monument Theatre, which has 900 seats and excellent stage facilities. Conference halls, lounges and open areas are equipped for a wide variety of functions. Enjoy a stroll around the art gallery, with its changing display by local and international artists, or enjoy a meal in the pleasant Monument Restaurant, with panoramic views across the city.

Indigenous flora fills the flowerbeds outside, and the gardens are dotted with fine bronze and stone statues.

Map: page 188
The monument stands on Gunfire Hill, southwest of Grahamstown, overlooking the Botanical Gardens.
Details: Open throughout the year.
Accommodation: See Albany Museum Complex.
Further information: Grahamstown Foundation, P O Box 304, Grahamstown 6140, tel (0461) 2-7115; Grahamstown Publicity Association, 63 High Street, Grahamstown 6140, tel (0461) 2-3241.

Hardships of the 1820 Settlers

'I stood for a minute thinking of my dying child, my blasted crops, my scattered and ruined flock. I have need of fortitude to bear up against such accumulation of misery. Farewell ...'

So wrote the unfortunate Captain Thomas Butler, one of thousands of British settlers who were brought in by Lord Charles Somerset to 'civilize' the Zuurveld – the Albany district of the Southeast Cape – in 1820.

In the months that followed, the immigration scheme seemed destined for disaster as the newcomers struggled to come to terms with a strange land, and its often hostile people. Over the previous decades hardy white frontiersmen had steadily pushed the borders of the colonial Cape eastwards. And in doing so, they encroached ever further into Xhosa territory, provoking a succession of 'frontier wars'.

The first had erupted in 1779, to be followed by eight more major confrontations during the succeeding century.

Somerset, first of the London-appointed Cape governors after the imposition of Crown Colony status in 1814, was convinced that only large-scale immigration could bring peace to the troubled region – by providing a buffer between the Xhosa people and the more settled white communities to the west.

In 1919 the Westminster parliament voted to sponsor the scheme, and 4 000 applicants were selected.

The next year 21 ships, bearing English, Irish, Welsh and Scottish families, sailed into Algoa Bay.

The settlers were taken inland to their prescribed allotments, some of which were a two-week journey away, over formidably wild terrain. The first seasons were indeed hard. The allotments were very small, their implements few. Locusts and drought played havoc with their harvests. And the Xhosa, deeply resenting the mass intrusion, posed a constant threat.

The monument to the settlers.

SOUTHEAST CAPE

GREAT FISH RIVER RESERVE
Near Grahamstown

Map: page 185, 5D
From Grahamstown travel northwards along the R67 leading to Fort Beaufort. The turn-off to the reserve is 28 km from Grahamstown. The reserve is situated 3 km further on.
Details: The reserve is open 06h00-18h00, although the gates may be closed temporarily during wet weather.
Accommodation: A variety of options is available, ranging from camping facilities and self-catering cottages to luxurious lodge accommodation.
Further information: The Officer-in-Charge, Andries Vosloo Kudu Reserve, P O Box 1006, Grahamstown 6140, tel (0461) 2-7909.

The Great Fish River Reserve is a newly formed conservation area consisting of the Andries Vosloo Kudu Reserve, the Sam Knott Nature Reserve and the Double Drift Reserve. The total size of this impressive area is 45 000 hectares.

All three of the reserves included in the complex are joined by a circular drive which makes it easy for day-trippers to view the game. Here populations of Cape buffalo, black rhino, hippo, eland, red hartebeest, springbok, warthog and leopard make their home. And the trees are alive with birds – over 220 species have been recorded. The separate Inyathi Game Camp, which is located inside the reserve, is host to an even wider range of game, including white rhinos, giraffes, zebras, bontebok, waterbuck, gemsbok, blue wildebeest, impala and elephants.

There are picnic sites on the banks of the Fish River, where keen anglers may fish. Several other picnic sites throughout the reserve offer spectacular views of the Fish River Gorge. Hunting packages are offered in the Double Drift Reserve during winter, and some excellent hiking trails are open all year.

The reserve is situated on the traditional boundary between Settler and Xhosa communities – once the scene of fierce conflict between the two groups. Evidence of these conflicts remains today in the forts, signalling towers, farmsteads, barracks and graves in the area.

This white rhino is one of a large variety of game to be seen in the Great Fish River Reserve between Grahamstown and King William's Town.

JEFFREYS BAY
West of Port Elizabeth

Map: page 185, 6B
From Port Elizabeth take the N2 westward over Van Staden's River Bridge, past Thornhill (47 km) and over the Gamtoos River. Not far beyond (about 75 km from Port Elizabeth), several side roads turn off to Jeffreys Bay.
Details: During the summer holiday season the resort is very crowded. Reserve accommodation in advance.
Accommodation: Beach Hotel, P O Box 1288, Jeffreys Bay 6330, tel (0423) 93-1104; Jeffreys Bay Youth Hostel, 12 Jeffreys Street, Jeffreys Bay 6330, tel (0423) 93-1379; Jeffreys Bay Caravan Park, P O Box 21, Jeffreys Bay 6330, tel (0423) 93-1111; Kynaston Bed and Breakfast, P O Box 111, Jeffreys Bay 6330, tel (0423) 96-1845; The Savoy Protea Hotel, P O Box 36, Jeffreys Bay 6330, tel (0423) 93-1106.
Further information: Jeffreys Bay Publicity Association, P O Box 460, Jeffreys Bay 6330, tel (0423) 93-2588.

Between May and August each year the low-pressure systems that move across the Cape generate a swell that rolls round the headland of Cape St Francis, and into Jeffreys Bay, making it one of the best surfing areas in the world. Enthusiasts from as far afield as Australia and the United States make pilgrimages to Jeffreys Bay to surf there.

That is Jeffreys Bay's claim to fame. It was named after a trader who established a post here in 1849. Before the surfers discovered it, the village was a quiet little seaside resort, with a large beach and safe bathing. It is known for the variety of seashells from which lovely ornaments are still made by local residents. Another drawcard is the good fishing at nearby Gamtoos River Mouth.

The lighthouse at Cape St Francis serves as a warning to mariners plying the treacherous coastline of the Southeast Cape.

KOWIE CANOE TRAIL
Port Alfred

You can hear the haunting cry of hadedas (glossy ibises) echoing across the still waters of the Kowie River, watch the tails of spotted grunter send circles spinning towards lazy sandbanks, or lie back in your canoe, and relax as the current takes you gently upstream. Such are just a few of the sensory delights that await you on the Kowie Canoe Trail.

The trail starts at the Riverside Caravan Park in Port Alfred, and follows the Kowie River upstream for some 18 km to Horseshoe Bend, in the Waters Meeting Nature Reserve near Bathurst. On the way you'll glimpse euphorbia-laced banks, sun-soaked valleys, and rural communities tending stock on emerald hills. At the Waters Meeting Nature Reserve you can choose to overnight in a four-roomed chalet camp, with very basic facilities (bunks, fresh water, braai wood), or you may obtain a permit to sleep in the forest. You may also follow an interesting six- to eight-kilometre hiking trail, which starts at the picnic spot some two kilometres from the entrance to the reserve. Here in the forest the only sounds you hear are the crackling undergrowth beneath your feet, the chattering of birds, the humming of insects, and the river as it glops and ripples at your side.

Port Kowie was established as the official port for Grahamstown in 1821. It failed to live up to expectations, however, because of very narrow channels and treacherous currents, and would have died altogether, but for the efforts of William Cock, who changed the course of the river in the 1830s. In 1860 it was renamed Port Alfred in honour of Prince Alfred, and struggled on until the 1930s, when the port was abandoned. Today the Kowie River has become a major venue for watersport enthusiasts, and shelters a sizable fleet of river and deep-sea craft which engage in fishing expeditions.

Map: page 185, 5E
Take the N2 northwards from Port Elizabeth for 80 km to Ncanaha; turn onto the R72 and follow it through Alexandria and Kenton-on-Sea to Port Alfred. The trail starts at the Riverside Caravan Park on the west bank.

Details: Canoes are obtainable from the caravan park, but you must carry all your own equipment should you wish to overnight at the Horseshoe Bend hut. The hut is for canoeists only.

Accommodation: There are several places to stay, including The Halyards (on the Royal Alfred Marina), P O Box 208, Port Alfred 6170, tel (0464) 4-2410; Hotel Kowie Grand, P O Box 1, Kowie West 6171, tel (0464) 4-1150; Hotel Victoria, P O Box 2, Port Alfred 6170, tel (0464) 4-1133; Riverside Caravan Park, P O Box 217, Port Alfred 6170, tel (0464) 4-2230.

Further information: Port Alfred Publicity Association, P O Box 63, Port Alfred 6170, tel (0464) 4-1235.

Port Alfred, a tranquil haven for holiday-makers on the banks of the Kowie River, is the starting point of the Kowie Canoe Trail.

Living fossils of the Southeast Cape

If you walk along any of the Southeast Cape river banks, you may spot, here and there on the flanking hillsides, palm-like plants among the dense mantle of bush vegetation.

These are cycads, 'living fossil' descendants of immensely ancient seed-bearing species that have changed little in structure and habit for 150 million years and more. The plants were at the peak of their ascendancy in the hotter, drier regions between 60 and 50 million years ago.

Individual cycad specimens live for hundreds if not thousands of years. In some respects they are similar to ferns. In others they are like the conifers: they bear cones.

The largest cone produced by any living plant is that of *Encephalartos caffer* – which can weigh in at 40 kilograms.

Altogether about 100 species of cycad are found in the tropical and subtropical parts of the world. South Africa is home to two genera. The larger, *Encephalartos*, embraces 28 species of widely differing appearance, each growing in a belt that extends from the Soutpansberg, near the Limpopo River, down to Swaziland, KwaZulu-Natal and the Southeast Cape. Their stems, protected by tightly packed, swollen leaf-bases, vary from the undetectable to monsters about 13 m tall.

The latter, *E. transvenosus*, can be seen at their most splendid at the kraal of Modjadji, the Rain Queen, in the Duiwelskloof area of North Transvaal. There, thousands of these 'Modjadji palms' flourish in a forest that is regarded as one of Africa's botanical wonders.

The *Encephalartos* cycad is also known as the bread-palm, a reference to early travellers' records of the crude bread made from the starch of the stem-pith. However, this is really a misnomer, since it is not a palm and, moreover, most of the species are poisonous.

Cycads are protected in South Africa, and there are heavy penalties for removing them. Nevertheless, many plants are illegally traded, and lost to the country, each year.

SOUTHEAST CAPE

MOUNTAIN ZEBRA NATIONAL PARK
West of Cradock

Map: page 185, 4C
From Cradock drive north and then, after 6 km, turn west along the road to Graaff-Reinet. After 5 km take the road to your left. The reserve is well signposted, and is about 27 km from Cradock.

Details: Gates open between sunrise and sunset throughout the year. The autumn months (March to May) are the most comfortable for visiting the park.

Accommodation: Apart from the trail huts, the rest camp has fully equipped, 2-bed chalets, camping/caravan sites, a swimming pool, restaurant, shop, petrol station, and picnic and braai areas.

Further information: The National Parks Board, P O Box 787, Pretoria 0001, tel (012) 343-1991; P O Box 7400, Roggebaai 8012, tel (021) 22-2810.

There are three species of zebra – Grevy's (the biggest), Burchell's (the most numerous), and the Cape mountain zebra (the smallest, and one of the rarest living mammals). In 1937 there were only a few dozen Cape mountain zebras left in the world, and the Mountain Zebra National Park was created for six of them. It was only in 1950, with the introduction of further mountain zebras, that the herd began to multiply. Today there are over 200 of them, enough to share with other reserves.

But it's not just the mountain zebras that make this reserve a special place: by South African standards the populations of other animals are fairly large – there are about 150 eland, just as many black wildebeest, more than 400 reedbuck and nearly 300 springbok. There are also plenty of blesbok, red hartebeest, kudu, klipspringer and gemsbok. You will also find caracals, ostriches, baboons, bat-eared foxes, silver jackals, African wild cats and aardwolfs.

A hot, dry summer and a clear, cold winter provide grazing and browsing enough for all. There are over 200 bird species in the reserve, including ostriches, Cape eagle owls and a pair of Verreaux eagles. Another unusual inhabitant is the giant earthworm – a four-metre monster with a girth of some 20 mm, that surfaces after heavy rains.

Although there is a good game-viewing road through part of the reserve, the only way to appreciate the park fully is to explore it on foot. The principal trail is the Mountain Zebra Trail, a 31-km-long, three-day hike, that is crisscrossed with game tracks and illuminated with San (Bushman) paintings. Charming stone huts provide rustic accommodation for the two overnight stops.

For the less energetic, accommodation is provided in charmingly furnished, fully serviced cottages, each sleeping four people. Or you may choose to hire the delightful Doornhoek Guest Cottage, a restored Victorian house.

Cape mountain zebras wander freely throughout the Mountain Zebra National Park, where they are usually found in herds of up to 12 animals.

PLACES TO VISIT

PORT ELIZABETH

CAMPANILE

For a panoramic view of Port Elizabeth and Algoa Bay, you can huff and puff your way up the 204 steps of the Campanile's spiral staircase, to a superb viewing platform at the top.

Standing more than 51 m high, the Campanile is one of those landmarks that find their way into just about every tourist brochure written about South Africa. Modelled on the Italian campaniles, this square, redbrick bell tower, at the entrance to the Port Elizabeth docks in Jetty Street, was erected to commemorate the landing of 4 000 British settlers in 1820.

The commemorative stone was laid by the then governor general, Prince Arthur of Connaught, on 9 April 1921, and the work was completed in 1923.

When originally constructed, the Port Elizabeth Campanile had a fine all-round view, but the surrounding buildings now partially obscure the view of the city.

In the Campanile is a carillon of 23 bells, which ring out their chimes daily, the bells being operated by electronic means. Six of the bells carry memorial inscriptions to the 1820 Settlers.

KEY TO THE MAPS
1 Campanile
2 Feather Market Hall
3 Fort Frederick
4 Happy Valley, Humewood Beach, King's Beach
5 Horse Memorial
6 Museum Complex
7 Snake Park
8 Oceanarium

Map: below
The Campanile is situated just below the Market Square, at the entrance to the docks in Port Elizabeth. To gain access you must pass under the paved deck in front of the Norwich Union Building, and beneath the freeway.
Details: Open weekdays 09h00-13h00, and 14h00-16h00; Wednesdays and Saturdays 08h30-12h30. Closed Sundays, Christmas Day, Good Friday, Day of Goodwill and New Year's Day. Entrance fee charged.
Accommodation: There's a variety of hotel and other accommodation in Port Elizabeth.
Further information: Port Elizabeth Publicity Association, P O Box 357, Port Elizabeth 6000, tel (041) 52-1315.

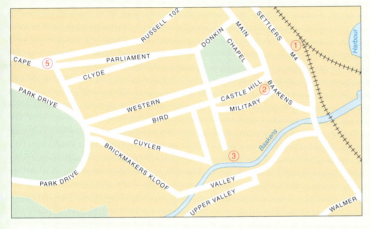
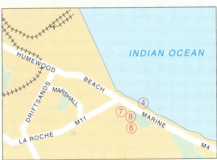

FEATHER MARKET HALL

The gracious ostrich feather, so popular 100 years ago, has left us a charming reminder by way of the Feather Market Hall at Port Elizabeth. This edifice was completed in 1885 as a market for the auction of feathers.

Due to the collapse of the ostrich feather industry at the outbreak of World War I, the Feather Market performed its original function for only a few years. During this time it was used as a wool auction room.

It became a venue for indoor sports competitions such as boxing, wrestling and gymnastics, with several international competitions being held there.

It is pleasing to note that, instead of being demolished, the Feather Market has been beautifully renovated, and was reopened in 1993 as a convention centre.

It offers a function hall with a stylish foyer and private rooms, and also contains a large organ which is often used for performances of oratorios.

Map: above
The Feather Market Hall is located in the centre of Port Elizabeth, in Baakens Street, just off the Market Square.
Details: Open all year for visits and functions.
Accommodation: There's a variety of hotels and guesthouses in Port Elizabeth.
Further information: Feather Market Centre, P O Box 374, Port Elizabeth 6000, tel (041) 55-5514; Port Elizabeth Publicity Association, P O Box 357, Port Elizabeth 6000, tel (041) 52-1315.

Once the scene of vigorous trade, the Feather Market Hall has now been restored as a venue for public events.

PORT ELIZABETH

FORT FREDERICK

Map: page 193
Drive up White's Road from the Market Square. At the top of the road turn left into Belmont Terrace. Continue southward down the road, past the Athenaeum, to reach Fort Frederick.
Details: The fort is a national monument maintained by the City Council, and is open to visitors daily.
Accommodation: There's a wide variety of hotels and guesthouses.
Further information: Port Elizabeth Publicity Association, P O Box 357, Port Elizabeth 6000, tel (041) 52-1315.

It was Frederick, the noble Duke of York ('he had 10 000 men...'), who left us his name in Fort Frederick, the first structure built in Port Elizabeth.

Erected in 1799 by the Argyllshire Highlanders and the 8th Light Dragoons on the eminence overlooking Algoa Bay, at the mouth of the Baakens River, the fort was intended to prevent both foreign invasion and local rebellion.

The first commander of the fort was Major Edward Lemoyne, who was posted there in 1800, with 350 soldiers and an armament of two eight-pounder cannons on the fort, and two three-pounders on the nearby blockhouse.

The Batavian Republic, in its turn (1803-1806), kept a garrison at Fort Frederick – 150 men under Major Carl van Gilten and Captain Ludwig Alberti. The landing of the 1820 Settlers at Port Elizabeth was supervised by Captain Francis Evatt, who commanded Fort Frederick at the time. The grave of Captain Evatt lies to the north of the fort.

After 1868 the fort was not occupied, and in 1889 it was transferred to the City Council. It was used temporarily during World War II but was thereafter thoroughly renovated and returned to the City Council. It has been a national monument since 1936.

HAPPY VALLEY, HUMEWOOD BEACH AND KING'S BEACH

Map: page 193
Follow the M4 (Settlers Way) southwards past the city centre to where Walmer Boulevard turns west. The M4 then becomes an ordinary highway, which you follow along the coast for a short distance to reach King's Beach on the left. For Happy Valley continue round the S-bend, and follow the Humewood beachfront to the far end. Happy Valley lies to the right, and beyond Humewood is Summerstrand.
Details: All the beach facilities are concentrated at King's Beach and Humewood, and many other tourist attractions are to be found nearby, including the museums, the Oceanarium and the Snake Park.
Accommodation: Port Elizabeth has a wide variety of hotels and guesthouses.
Further information: Port Elizabeth Publicity Association, P O Box 357, Port Elizabeth 6000, tel (041) 52-1315.

Shrieking with delight, children slip and slide down the water chute at King's Beach, while their parents laze on its golden sands.

Happy Valley, with its gentle lawns, lily ponds, and beautiful gardens, is a mere amble away from Humewood Beach – one of the finest bathing beaches in Port Elizabeth.

In summer the gardens are illuminated by a large, colourful display of lights and various nursery-rhyme characters. You can have a game of chess on a giant chessboard (pieces available from the beach manager's office), or enjoy a snack at one of the restaurants nearby.

Situated on the Shark River, Happy Valley experienced a traumatic time in the great flood of 1968, when most of its contents were washed out to sea. However, it was soon rebuilt to its present charming status, and now serves as a strollers' retreat, or a place to picnic in the shade of trees.

Nearby King's Beach (so named because King George VI bathed there in 1948) is a popular recreational area, with excellent bathing, pools, water chutes, a delightful minigolf course, supertube and a quaint miniature train to keep the children happy.

HORSE MEMORIAL

Map: page 193
From Main Street turn left up Russell Road, and follow it to its junction with Cape Road and Doncaster Street. The memorial stands near this junction.
Further information: Port Elizabeth Publicity Association, P O Box 357, Port Elizabeth 6000, tel (041) 52-1315.

The death of 326 073 British horses during the Anglo-Boer War of 1899-1902, as well as the loss of innumerable horses by the Boer forces, moved a Port Elizabeth woman so much that she conceived the idea of a memorial to the dead horses.

As a result of her ceaseless efforts, the Metropolitan Drinking Fountain and Cattle Trough Association in London eventually commissioned a sculptor named Joseph Whitehead to execute a sculpture of a horse drinking from a bucket held by a British soldier.

The inscription on it reads: 'The greatness of a nation consists not so much in the number of its people, or the extent of its territory, as in the extent and justice of its compassion.'

The sculpture, with a drinking trough, was originally erected in 1905 at the junction of Rink Street and Park Drive. In 1957, due to increasing traffic dangers, it was moved to its present site in Cape Road, Port Elizabeth, near the junction with Doncaster Road.

At the time it was erected it was the only horse memorial in the world.

PORT ELIZABETH

MUSEUM COMPLEX
Humewood

From various historical relics to soaring dolphins, from invertebrate fossils to slithering snakes – all are on show within Humewood's Port Elizabeth Museum Complex. Situated on the beachfront, the complex is one of the leading tourist attractions in the Port Elizabeth area. Varied entertainment is offered by the Port Elizabeth Museum, the Snake Park, the Tropical House and the Oceanarium – all of which form part of the complex.

Various Khoikhoi implements, San (Bushman) rock art, African beadwork and weapons are some of the fascinating items on display in the Port Elizabeth Museum. You can also visit the Marine Hall, with its exhibits of shipwrecks, cannons, copper ingots, old porcelain and pieces of eight – all bringing to life an age when hosts of sailing ships plied the southern African waters. Also on display here is a collection of finely crafted models of sailing ships.

For the fashion-conscious, there is a beautiful array of period costumes dating from the 19th century.

The rest of the museum is devoted to the wonders of nature, with exhibits detailing marine mammals, the skeleton of a whale, local fish species and birds, fossils and early man, and the famous Kritzinger collection of seashells from Jeffreys Bay.

The Port Elizabeth Museum originated in the City Hall, then moved twice, before it was transferred to Humewood in 1961.

Equally attractive (to the children, that is) is the nearby ice-cream parlour and gift shop.

Snake Park
More than 1 000 live snakes, poisonous and nonpoisonous, from adders to huge pythons, writhe around their enclosures in the Port Elizabeth Snake Park, an integral part of the Museum Complex. While the keepers have tried to make the enclosures reflect the natural habitats as closely as possible, nearby open pits give views of crocodiles, lizards and tortoises.

The Reptile Rotunda is a fascinating educational centre where special exhibitions explaining these creatures and their habits are held.

Attached to the Snake Park is the Tropical House, where you can wander through luxuriant vegetation, with birds flying freely around you.

The success of the Port Elizabeth Museum and its relationship to the Snake Park and Oceanarium are largely due to Frederick William Fitzsimons, the man who identified the Boskop Skull, and who was director of the museum from 1906 to 1936. He was always interested in snakes, and while the museum was still in the Market Buildings he began exhibiting live snakes.

In 1919 Fitzsimons established a snake park, the first in Africa, and the second in the world. In 1925 he created a larger and more elaborate park, to which Johannes Molikoe was appointed snake attendant.

Molikoe exhibited snakes to visitors, and became world-famous. Fitzsimons published a series of press articles about the Snake Park, and it became a major tourist attraction in South Africa. When the museum moved to Humewood, the Snake Park did so too.

Fitzsimons's purpose in creating the park was not only to familiarize people with snakes, but also to obtain their venom. He became an international authority on snake venom.

Map: page 193
The Oceanarium, Snake Park and Museum are situated at Humewood, which you will find by following the M4 southeastwards from the city centre. Keep along the coast – beyond the S-bend is the suburb of Humewood. At the far end lies Happy Valley. The Museum Complex is situated between the Holiday Inn Garden Court and Happy Valley.
Details: Open daily throughout the year 09h00-13h00 and 14h00-17h00; closed on Christmas Day. The Oceanarium provides dolphin shows daily at 11h00 and 15h00.
Accommodation: There's a wide variety of hotel and guesthouse accommodation in the city.
Further information: Port Elizabeth Publicity Association, P O Box 357, Port Elizabeth 6000, tel (041) 52-1315.

The Port Elizabeth Museum, with its fine displays of local history and natural wonders, attracts thousands of visitors each year.

A thirsty puff adder (Bitis arietans) heads for the pool at Port Elizabeth's Snake Park.

PORT ELIZABETH

Oceanarium

Like black, sky-bound missiles the dolphins of Port Elizabeth's Oceanarium hurtle from the surface of their spacious pool in Humewood, entertaining crowds with unimaginable acrobatics.

Breathtaking somersaults, prodigious leaps into the air, and unrestrained races around the pool leave their sedentary human counterparts awed and humbled by the magic of it all.

This twice-daily performance by the dolphins, started in 1963 by a pair of dolphins which became affectionately known as Dimple and Haig, has underscored the overwhelming success of the Oceanarium, which attracts more than 100 000 visitors every year.

Other attractions at the Oceanarium are the mischievous Cape fur seals, which climb out of the water and start to waddle around the pool, and an underwater observatory from which you can watch the dolphins in their element.

In the aquarium two fish tanks reveal a dim, submarine world of silent cruisers: sharks, rays, turtles and fish, and a host of multicoloured subtropical fish.

It was Frederick William Fitzsimons who took the first steps towards establishing an Oceanarium, little knowing how popular it would become.

In 1930 a Marine Hall was added to the Museum, and in it he exhibited a collection of whale skeletons and other marine objects.

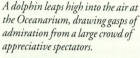

A dolphin leaps high into the air at the Oceanarium, drawing gasps of admiration from a large crowd of appreciative spectators.

The acrobatic skills and exuberance of the dolphins at the Port Elizabeth Oceanarium are a major attraction for visitors to the city.

SOUTHEAST CAPE

RHODES
East of Aliwal North

In the bad old days of the 1880s, when the village of Rhodes was known as Rossville (after the local Dutch Reformed minister), it was customary to enter the local pub on horseback and order your drink from the saddle.

The cowboys of those times really enjoyed their liquor – understandably, when you consider that barrels of it were dragged over the mountains to the old Horseshoe Inn.

Today Rhodes (renamed in honour of Cecil John Rhodes in 1893) is known not for the rowdy nights, gambling evenings and raunchy barn dances of its early years, but more for its crisp mountain air, trout-fishing and skiing possibilities in winter (the highest peak in the area is Ben MacDhui, at 3 001 metres).

Its pretty main street is shaded by a number of stone pines presented by Cecil John Rhodes – the whimsical cause of the town's name change.

The bar of the old Horseshoe Inn, now known as the Rhodes Hotel, still sports the horns of Wydeman, the strongest of the oxen that drew the liquor wagons across the mountains.

Map: page 185, 2F
From Aliwal North go eastward along the R58 for 122 km to Barkly East; here turn east along the scenic R396 to Naude's Nek, passing Moshesh's Ford (34 km) to reach Rhodes, about 25 km further on.
Details: If you're visiting Rhodes in winter, be prepared for the icy weather.
Accommodation: Rhodes Hotel has 12 rooms, mostly *en suite*, so booking is essential. Annexed to the hotel are 4 houses for rent, while the municipal camping site offers camping facilities.
Further information: Rhodes Hotel, P O Box 21, Rhodes 5582, tel (04542) 21.

SHAMWARI GAME RESERVE
East of Port Elizabeth

You need not risk malaria, nor travel to the Kruger National Park to see the Big Five – you can go to Shamwari.

Stretching along the Bushmans River, 72 km from Port Elizabeth, Shamwari has reintroduced many of the mammals that were virtually hunted out of the Southeast Cape. Here, amongst other animals, you will see lions, white and black rhinos, elephants, buffaloes, leopards and hippos in the Bushmans River. Because the reserve lies in an area where various ecosystems overlap (forest, fynbos, Karoo and savannah), it is able to accommodate browsers, grazers and mixed feeders.

As a result, there is a wide variety of antelope, ranging from such species as eland, kudu, gemsbok and bontebok to red hartebeest, blesbok, springbok and black springbok. There are also a number of zebras and a multitude of smaller game, as well as over 300 bird species.

You may enjoy a game drive in an open vehicle, accompanied by experienced game rangers, or you may prefer to get closer to nature on a walking safari or even a night-drive.

A bonus to travellers wishing to visit Shamwari is the fact that they can ride there on the *African Safari*, a train that commutes between Johannesburg and Port Elizabeth. Special railway carriages bring you to a siding near the reserve, where you transfer to Land Rovers.

Map: page 185, 5D
You can reach Shamwari either by the *African Safari* (from Johannesburg), or by car, following the N2 eastwards from Port Elizabeth, and then the N10 northwards to Paterson. From here follow the turn-off leading east along the Sidbury road. The park is signposted along this road.
Details: Gates open all day.
Accommodation: There is a choice between traditional thatched chalets, and refurbished old houses that belonged to settlers a century ago.
Further information: Shamwari Game Reserve, P O Box 7814, Newton Park 6055, tel (042) 851-1196.

VAN STADEN'S RIVER BRIDGE
West of Port Elizabeth

The pedestrian walkway along the Van Staden's River Bridge is not for those who suffer from vertigo. Peer over the bridge's railing, and you'll see a drop of 125 m ending in the bottom of the gorge below.

The bridge, which spans 340 m, and rests on a concrete arch 25 m wide, was constructed simultaneously from opposite banks, and opened in 1971. Then it was the second-largest arch in the world.

The construction of the new bridge 37 km west of Port Elizabeth was a massive boon to traffic which, before its completion, had to descend into the quite precipitous Van Staden's Gorge before climbing out of it through a series of sharp curves and hairpin bends.

The old bridge at the bottom of the gorge is still there, and you can still drive through the pass and see the Van Staden's Wildflower Reserve *(see separate entry)*.

Crossing the new bridge provides magnificent views down into the Van Staden's Gorge, and across the plain that tilts away from the Gamtoos River.

The Van Staden's Pass was named after Marthinus van Staden, who farmed in the area in 1744.

Map: page 185, 5C
From Port Elizabeth take the N2 westward to reach the bridge (37 km). Apart from stopping to admire the view from the bridge, you might like to visit Van Staden's River Mouth. This is reached by a side road 15 km long, turning off the national road east of the bridge, and winding through attractive wooded country, down valleys and along hilly coastline to the river mouth.
Details: Take the road over the old bridge, which crosses the Van Staden's River at the bottom, if you wish to stop and admire the scenery.
Accommodation: At Van Staden's River Mouth there is a resort with 11 cottages and 13 rondavels – contact Van Staden's River Mouth Resort, P O Box 141, Greenbushes 6390, tel (0422) 955-5990; for caravan sites contact Van Staden's Caravan Park, P O Box 318, Port Elizabeth 6000, tel (041) 776-1059.
Further information: Port Elizabeth Publicity Association, P O Box 357, Port Elizabeth 6000, tel (041) 52-1315.

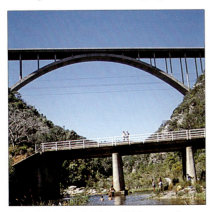

The new Van Staden's River Bridge soars above the old one, providing splendid views down into the gorge.

SOUTHEAST CAPE

VAN STADEN'S WILDFLOWER RESERVE
Van Staden's River Mouth

Map: page 185, 5C
From Port Elizabeth take the N2 west for 35 km until you reach the R102 side road. Turn left along this road and drive until you see a turn-off on the right to the Wildflower Reserve.
Details: Open sunrise to sunset all year (except during heavy rains).
Accommodation: The reserve is close to the Van Staden's River Mouth Resort, full details of which appear under 'Van Staden's River Bridge'.
Further information: Van Staden's Wildflower Reserve, c/o Algoa Regional Services Council, P O Box 318, Port Elizabeth 6000, tel (041) 955-5649; Van Staden's River Mouth Resort, P O Box 141, Greenbushes 6390, tel (0422) 955-5990.

People who scratch their names on natural objects are never popular: in the 1780s the names of several such gentlemen appeared on a tree in the indigenous forest near Van Staden's Pass. A subsequent traveller (no friend of tree-scratchers) had painted a gallows above their names and the tree (in fact the entire area) became known as the Galgenbosch.

Today this area is famous for another reason – it is the site of the beautiful Van Staden's Wildflower Reserve. This 500-ha reserve is bisected by the N2, which divides it into southern wooded slopes and a plateau on the north. The southern forest is classified as 'Alexandria Forest veld type' and includes Cape chestnuts, black ironwood, cabbage trees, bastard saffron, Cape fig, white pear, wild elder and yellowwood trees.

The plateau is covered with fynbos, which has been reinforced by planting massed proteas, ericas, everlastings, pelargoniums and orchids.

This is a 'walkabout' reserve, with several small picnic sites, and a large one just north of the N2 bridge.

ZUURBERG NATIONAL PARK
North of Port Elizabeth

Map: page 185, 5C
From Addo Elephant National Park continue for 12 km northward along the R335 until you reach the Zuurberg National Park.
Details: Open daily throughout the year from sunrise to sunset.
Accommodation: Kabouga Guesthouse, P O Box 52, Addo 6105, tel (0426) 40-0556; Zuurberg Inn, P O Box 12, Addo 6105, tel (0426) 40-0583.
Further information: The Park Warden, Zuurberg National Park, P O Box 76, Addo 6105, tel (0426) 40-0581; National Parks Board, P O Box 787, Pretoria 0001, tel (012) 343-1991; P O Box 7400, Roggebaai 8012, tel (021) 22-2810.

This 24 683-ha wildlife retreat in the Winterhoek Mountains, 12 km north of Addo Elephant National Park, offers panoramic views of the surrounding countryside, and an opportunity to see a startling variety of animals and birds.

Kudu, grey rhebuck, bushbuck, mountain reedbuck and grey duiker may be seen in the company of the rare blue duiker and mountain zebra. In addition there are bushpigs, baboons, vervet monkeys, caracals and jackals. Among the 150 or so species of birds in the forested ravines are Knysna loeries, and both black and crowned eagles.

Two circular trails, one covering 12 km (four hours), and the other covering 2,5 km (one hour), take you through wild, broken countryside comprising kloofs, ravines and pools, where you may see rare plants such as the Zuurberg cushion bush and the Zuurberg cycad. Of special interest to botanists are the three types of vegetation within the park – false fynbos or heathland, evergreen coastal forest, and valley bushveld, with its low, thorny shrubs and euphorbias.

Other attractions include horse-riding, tennis, swimming, bowls and minigolf.

You may stay at the newly opened, serviced Kabouga Guesthouse, shaded by a canopy of yellowwood and fig trees, or at the Zuurberg Inn which lies adjacent to the park.

These apparently arid mountains will surprise you with the richness and variety of their wildlife.

Because of the Zuurberg's elevation (most of the range is above 700 m, with the highest peak at 988 m) early travellers battled to cross it, until 1850, when the Zuurberg Pass was completed.

One of the more colourful inhabitants of the Zuurberg National Park is the Knysna loerie. This bird of the evergreen and riverine forests is quite easily spotted because of its brightly coloured plumage and growling calls.

GARDEN ROUTE

GARDEN ROUTE

BARTOLOMEU DIAS MUSEUM
Mossel Bay

Map: page 199, 1D
Mossel Bay is linked to Cape Town, 390 km to the west, and Port Elizabeth, 360 km to the east, by the N2 highway. The museum complex is signposted from the town's main intersection.

Details: Open throughout the year, Monday to Friday 09h00-13h00, and 14h00-17h00 (but all day during school holidays); Saturdays 10h00-13h00; Sundays 14h00-17h00. Ample parking available. Admission free, but donations are welcome.

Accommodation: Mossel Bay has excellent hotel, guesthouse, self-catering and caravan/camping facilities.

Further information: Information Centre, Bartolomeu Dias Museum, Private Bag X1, Mossel Bay 6500, tel (0444) 91-1067.

Five centuries of European exploration and colonial settlement are celebrated in the scatter of buildings and relics that comprise Mossel Bay's museum complex.

The museum, which was developed over a number of years, opened with a flourish in 1989, one year after the 500th anniversary of the arrival of Bartolomeu Dias, first European in modern history to touch South Africa's shores.

Among the museum's components are:
■ The reception and information area in Market Street, housed in a reconstruction of a granary built by the Dutch East India Company in 1786;
■ The Post Office Tree (Grave Street). The enormous, venerably gnarled milkwood, embraced by a paved walkway, is a national monument;
■ A replica of a padrão, or stone cross, erected on the exact spot on which Dias is thought to have stepped ashore;
■ The Maritime Museum (Market Street). Centrepiece of the exhibition here is a full-size replica of Dias's caravel. Visitors can clamber aboard, and explore the broad-beamed little vessel with its high poop deck and lateen rig (triangular sail). Three striking stained-glass panels, early maps, shipwreck salvage, coins, gemstones and other reminders of early exploration and trade also draw the eye;
■ The perennial spring so prized by the early navigators still produces clear, sweet water, but it now makes its way into a small dam. This pleasant area is part of the museum's nature reserve, noted for its indigenous plants. Many of the species have been reintroduced. Wild olives, milkwoods and aloes feature prominently. Pathways lead you to attractive viewsites;
■ The Shell Museum next door contains a large and enchanting selection of local seashells;
■ The local History Museum (situated in Market Street), whose two buildings – a solid Victorian edifice and its much smaller Karoo-type annexe, erected in 1858 to serve as the first municipal centre in Mossel Bay – house an evocative array of exhibits, among them fascinating replicas of early shops, and displays nostalgically recalling the heyday of the Union Castle mailships;
■ Munroeshoek Cottages (Santos Road), a cluster of three small houses, dating from the 1830s, one of which functions as an arts and crafts centre. A tearoom serves refreshments.

The Dias Monument in Mossel Bay is a tribute to the man who led the first European navigators.

A beautiful replica of the caravel used by Bartolomeu Dias to cross the Atlantic more than 500 years ago graces the interior of the Dias Museum.

DIEPWALLE STATE FOREST
North of Knysna

Diepwalle's dense growths of canopy-forming hardwood trees, which combine with the adjacent woodlands to form one of the country's best-preserved expanses of natural forest, serve as a refuge to the remnant of the famed Knysna elephant herd.

At the last count, only three of the pachyderms were still alive (though there have been proposals to augment the tiny group, and so expand its gene pool), and you'll be lucky indeed if you manage to spot one in the depths of this great forest. But there's other wildlife to see and enjoy, including bushbuck, baboons, vervet monkeys, a host of small forest mammals and some lovely birds, among them colourful Knysna loeries, crowned eagles, gymnogenes and Narina trogons. And then, of course, there are the trees themselves: magnificent white and red alder, Cape beech, ironwood, white pear, stinkwood, yellowwood and many other handsome species.

The forest can best be explored along the noted Elephant Walk, a nearly 20-km, eight-hour hike made up of three interconnecting circular routes.

Map: page 199, 4C/D
From Knysna follow the N2 eastwards for 7 kilometres. Turn left onto the R339 and follow the Diepwalle signs for 16 kilometres.
Details: Open throughout the year 06h00-18h00. Entrance fee payable at the Diepwalle Forestry Office. Picnic spots. Permits required for the Elephant Walk and its subsidiary routes.
Accommodation: Hotel, guesthouse and caravan/camping facilities are available in and around Knysna.
Further information: The Officer-in-Charge, Chief Directorate of Forestry, Southern Cape, Private Bag X12, Knysna 6570, tel (0445) 82-5466.

Monarchs of the forest

The King Edward VII Tree in the dense canopy forests north of Knysna is a giant yellowwood, thought to be about 600 to 800 years old. It is nearly 39 m tall, measures six metres in circumference and is one of the best-known 'big trees' growing in the great indigenous forests that stretch along the Garden Route, from the town of George to the Tsitsikamma area in the east.

These are the largest of South Africa's remaining indigenous forests, home to handsome stinkwoods, moss-garlanded white and red alders, pink-flowered Cape chestnuts, assegais and majestic yellowwoods.

King of the glades is undoubtedly *Podocarpus falcatus*, the Outeniqua yellowwood, which can grow to 60 m in height and is found in the southern woodlands. It is also found in montane forests as far north as the Lowveld and Escarpment and Mozambique. Like others of the genus (which belong to the same order that includes the pines, cedars and the great redwoods), it is an evergreen species with narrow leaves and a long, tapering bole. Both the male and the female produce cones (the male's ones are smaller) but the seed is borne only by the female.

More modest in size, more numerous but just as attractive, is the upright yellowwood, *Podocarpus latifolius*. It has also proved more vulnerable to man's depredations, serving as the main source of timber for the early Cape colonists. The wood is lighter than the now-fashionable Oregon pine, but finer grained, tougher, smoother and capable of taking a high polish.

Prized by skilled cabinet-makers for the mature timber of the older trees, the real yellowwoods were chopped down in their thousands to be converted into ships' fittings and elegant Cape furniture, and into the wide floorboards, the great beams and heavy doors of the classic Cape Dutch homesteads.

Later, with the advent of the railways, the timber was fashioned into sleepers. The Lowveld and Escarpment forests, too, were quickly denuded of their yellowwoods and used, with almost unbelievable alacrity, for pit props and the other timber needs of the youthful mining industry. Today all four species of South African yellowwood are protected in their various forest habitats.

Within the past few decades the species have become popular as ornamental trees, gracing private estates and city gardens such as Kirstenbosch on the Cape Peninsula.

Forest giants tower above a rolling canopy of green near Nature's Valley. These dense forests, with their liana-draped trees, are home to a variety of colourful birds.

GARDEN ROUTE

GEORGE MUSEUM
Courtenay Street

Map: page 199, 2C
George is 436 km from Cape Town in the west, and 330 km from Port Elizabeth in the east. Take the N2 to the signposted turn-off onto the N9, 10 km west of Wilderness, and continue along the short (3 km) stretch into town. The museum is in Courtenay Street at the top end of York Street.
Details: Open throughout the year, Monday to Friday 09h00-16h30; Saturdays 09h00-12h30; Sundays 09h00-13h00. Open also on public holidays, except Christmas Day and Good Friday. Admission free. Parking. Gift shop and coffee bar on premises.
Accommodation: George and its surrounding area offer a variety of hotel, guesthouse, self-catering and caravan/camping facilities.
Further information: George Museum, Private Bag X6586, George 6530, tel (0441) 73-5343; George Tourism Association, P O Box 1109, George 6530, tel (0441) 74-4000.

A fine array of antique musical appliances – music boxes, polyphones and early gramophones – is perhaps the most eye-catching display in a museum noted for its delightfully divergent mix of exhibits. Another display that entrances all visitors is the exhibition of fairy paintings by local artist Ruby Reeves.

Notable, too, is the building itself, which began its chequered career in 1812 as the local drostdy, or magistrates' court and residence, serving as such for 14 years until it burned down. It was rebuilt as a private home, and then changed its character yet again to function as the renowned Victoria Hotel. After careful restoration and renovation, it opened its doors to the museum-going public in 1992.

Much of the space is devoted to the story of the region's early timber enterprises – yellowwoods, stinkwoods and other local hardwood trees were used in the manufacture of everything from furniture to ships' fittings, and the industry has played a prominent part in George's history. Other exhibits take in two rooms, furnished in 19th-century style, a selection of old-fashioned printers' equipment, and an evocative gallery of photographs showing the town in its earlier days and after, a place that visiting Victorian novelist Anthony Trollope described as 'the prettiest village in the world'.

There is also a fast-growing section researching the local indigenous forests and timber industry. Research into 'early Outeniqualand' and its inhabitants is also under way. The newly opened 'discovery room' is a refined re-creation of George's first small museum.

GOUKAMMA NATURE RESERVE
Near Knysna

Map: page 199, 3D
The Goukamma Nature Reserve lies south of the N2 highway, between Sedgefield and Buffels Bay. Take the N2 westwards from Knysna. After 16 km, turn left towards Buffels Bay. The entrance to the reserve is 6 km on.
Details: Open daily throughout the year 08h00-18h00. A small entry fee is charged during the months of December, January and April. Visitors can only explore on foot (there are no internal roads). Toilet facilities available at the main picnic site.
Accommodation: There is a self-contained double rondavel for 6 people, and a bush camp on the shores of Groenvlei, which accommodates 4 people. Knysna, Wilderness, Sedgefield and the surrounding areas are well served by hotels, guesthouses, self-catering units and caravan/camping facilities.
Further information: The Officer-in-Charge, Goukamma Nature Reserve, P O Box 331, Knysna 6570, tel (0445) 83-0042; Knysna Publicity Association, P O Box 87, Knysna 6570, tel (0445) 82-5510.

The enchanting 2 230-ha Goukamma Reserve includes coastal fynbos terrain, an offshore marine sanctuary, and a shimmering expanse of fresh water known as Groenvlei, easternmost of the Wilderness lakes *(see separate entry)*.

Here botanists and bird-watchers, ramblers and beach-anglers can enjoy true tranquillity in pristine surroundings.

Among the numerous attractions of the area are the Goukamma River and its estuary, the dunes, a 14-km stretch of coastline interspersed with rocks and sandy coves, a strip of Indian Ocean extending one nautical mile outwards from the high-water mark, and the narrow promontory ending in Walker Point. To the east is the sweep of Buffels Bay and its magnificent beach.

The marine reserve is a monitored sanctuary for most sea-living species. Visitors may not remove or disturb any organism, collect bait, use casting nets, or fish from a ski boat or with a spear. A formidable enough litany of don'ts, perhaps, but there's still plenty that you can do. Canoeing, boating, boardsailing, rod-and-line fishing (from the shore; permits required) and swimming (in the river; sea-bathing is hazardous) are popular pastimes. Picnic spots and braai sites have been developed around the estuary and, for strollers, some 35 km of pathways have been established.

Among the reserve's many residents are Cape grysbok, bushbuck, blue and common duiker, bontebok and a variety of smaller mammals, including such interesting species as vervet monkeys mongooses, caracals, badgers, otters, bushpigs and others. About 210 bird species have been recorded.

A suspension bridge spans the inviting waters of the Goukamma River, linking hiking trails on either side. The reserve's scenic delights draw nature-lovers from all corners of the country.

KAAIMANS RIVER AND FALLS
Near George

For more than two centuries the surging tide of the Kaaimans estuary, the cliff-flanked gorge through which the river flows, the magnificent waterfall upstream, and the woodland splendour of the surrounding countryside, have drawn admiration from explorers, travellers and nature-lovers.

Today the lower reaches of the river still present some of the most dramatic vistas of the Garden Route, enjoyed by passengers on the Outeniqua Choo-Choo steam train *(see separate entry)* that puffs its way over the curved, concrete bridge straddling the river mouth, by canoeists paddling upstream to the waterfall, and by motorists driving along the scenic stretch of the N2 between George and Wilderness.

Both the waterfall and the most striking section of the gorge are actually on the Swart River, just before its confluence with the Kaaimans River, and can easily be reached from the highway. The increasing number of visitors, however, has had its price.

Roadbuilders, completely disregarding the pristine beauty of the natural environment, have dumped rubble into the river and its waterfall basin; commercial traffic noisily plies the twisting route down to the gorge, and developers have cleared away forest stands to make room for boat-trailer parks.

Map: page 199, 2D
The Kaaimans lies astride the N2, between George and Wilderness.
Details: The area can be explored on foot and by boat. The river, its sandy estuary and the offshore waters are popular among watersport enthusiasts.
Accommodation: Self-catering and caravan/camping facilities are available in and around Victoria Bay. Both George and Wilderness offer a wide range of accommodation.
Further information: George Tourism Association, P O Box 1109, George 6530, tel (0441) 74-4000.

A steam train billows smoke as it crosses the Kaaimans River Bridge near Wilderness, offering passengers breathtaking views of mountain and sea.

The Kaaimans River has sculpted deep, forest-fringed ravines all along its course through the undulating hills of the Wilderness.

PLACES TO VISIT

KNYSNA

Knysna is one of the Cape's premier resort centres, drawing holiday-makers, boating enthusiasts, second-home owners and affluent retired people from afar.

The area's popularity is a relatively recent phenomenon. Not much more than a century ago the *Cape Almanac* condemned the access roads and terrain as 'the most difficult of description ... a country known only to a few hunters, and abounding in elephants and buffalo'. Now the N2 highway linking Cape Town and Port Elizabeth runs right through it.

Knysna was founded by George Rex, one-time marshal of the British Admiralty's High Court in Cape Town, and said by some to be the unrecognized son of England's King George III. Rex arrived at Knysna in 1804, built a magnificent homestead close by the lagoon, farmed the land and lived, with his two common-law wives and growing progeny, the life of a feudal lord until his death in 1839.

Today Rex's 12 000-ha estate forms part of the Knysna lake area, the lagoon and the fringing evergreen woodlands.

The pristine beauty of Knysna's watercourses, and the lush vegetation of the surrounding countryside are major reasons for the town's rapid growth.

Map: page 199, 4D
Belvidere Estate is on the southern shore of Knysna Lagoon. Turn right off the N2 before it crosses the water, and follow the signs to Brenton; turn left after 2 kilometres.
Details: Visitors are welcome at the church. No admission charge, of course, but donations (to parish funds) are gladly received. Services are held on the first and third Sundays of the month at 07h30 and 09h00.
Further information: Knysna Publicity Association, P O Box 87, Knysna 6570, tel (0445) 82-5510.

BELVIDERE CHURCH
Belvidere Estate

On the banks of the lagoon to the west of Knysna town stands a faithful replica in miniature of a 12th-century Norman chapel. This is the Church of the Holy Trinity, measuring just 5,56 metres across the nave, seating about 60 parishioners, and built in 1855 by Lieutenant Thomas Duthie, who some years before had married the daughter of Knysna's flamboyant founder, George Rex. It is an exquisitely cosy little building, perfect in all of its proportions, and a splendid example of Victorian romanticism at its most tasteful.

Masterpieces in stained glass impart an air of graceful tranquillity inside Belvidere Church, west of Knysna.

FEATHERBED NATURE RESERVE
Western Head

Champagne and fresh oysters for breakfast, stunning views of sea, lagoon and mountain, and rambles through pleasant fynbos countryside are major drawcards of this private sanctuary set atop the western of the two great sandstone cliffs known as The Heads.

The Featherbed Nature Reserve's 70-odd ha, a declared National Heritage Site, are home to about 100 different species of bird (some of them are classified as threatened), and to bushbuck, red duiker and the country's largest breeding stock of blue duiker.

Arriving guests are ferried to Featherbed Bay Beach in a comfortable barge and then, after refreshments, are taken up the mountain in a four-wheel-drive vehicle. They are then conducted along the 2,2-km Bushbuck Trail, a scenically charming route shaded for much of its course by milkwood trees. There are brief visits to the old rocket station, to the ancient strandloper ('beach-ranger') caves; to a spectacular coastal feature called Nature's Arch, and to Coffee Bay, whose 'amazing secret is only revealed to those who come and see'.

Map: page 199, 4D
A chartered ferry takes guests across Knysna Lagoon to the trailhead at Featherbed Bay Beach.
Details: The reserve is open 7 days a week throughout the year; the day-visit package includes transport, and either a guided walk or conducted drive (each component is costed separately). The Tavern caters for the evening trade and for special functions.
Accommodation: No guest accommodation within the reserve. Knysna and surrounding area are well served by hotels, guesthouses, self-catering units and caravan/camping facilities.
Further information: Featherbed Nature Reserve, P O Box 750, Knysna 6570, tel (0445) 2-1693/2-1697.

Hewn granite memorials in fields of green lend dignity to the grounds of the Church of the Holy Trinity near Knysna.

The church, designed by Sophy Gray, wife of the then Anglican bishop of Cape Town, is constructed almost entirely of local materials. Notable among its stained glasswork is the rose window, made from shattered pieces salvaged from English churches destroyed during the 'Blitz' of the Second World War. Included are fragments from bombed-out Coventry Cathedral.

Centrepiece of Belvidere Estate is Belvidere itself, a pleasing Georgian Colonial house that now serves as a country lodge, floored in yellowwood and graced by fine antiques. Its guests are accommodated in 22 nearby Victorian cottages. Much of the estate consists of a sensitively designed residential area of some 160 homes and a retirement village.

The remarkable Sophy Gray

The charming little Church of the Holy Trinity near Knysna is just one of more than 50 churches in South Africa designed by Sophia, wife of Robert Gray, Cape Town's pioneering Anglican bishop.

Sophy, a tall, handsome, forceful Yorkshirewoman with burnished brown hair and hazel eyes, arrived at the Cape with her husband in 1848 to establish the Church of the Province of South Africa, and to maintain the independence (from the State) of the new diocese. The couple were in the prime of their lives – she was 34 at the time, he six years older – and they set about their task with boundless energy. Robert immediately embarked on the first of his many journeys into the still-raw interior to inaugurate mission stations and parishes. He soon became known as the 'post-cart bishop'.

Sophy, an excellent horsewoman and talented artist, accompanied him on many of his expeditions, filling her sketchbooks with a vivid visual account of their travels. More prosaically, she had a talent for organization and, over the years, administered his episcopal see.

She also helped him found a number of educational institutions. The Grays had settled on Protea Farm (now Bishopscourt) – in part of Cape Town's Constantia-Newlands area. Sophy ran the farm and started a small school. This later became the noted Diocesan College for Boys, informally known as Bishops.

It is as a church architect, though, that Sophy will be best remembered. Her designs, romantic in the Victorian Gothic tradition, were transformed into bricks and mortar in parish after parish as the diocese grew to maturity. The building in Knysna's Belvidere area is typical of her style. Among others are the Anglican cathedrals in George and Pietermaritzburg, and St Saviour's in Cape Town's Claremont suburb.

KNYSNA

LAGOON AND HEADS
Knysna

Map: page 199, 4D
Knysna is on the N2, 493 km from Cape Town and 259 km from Port Elizabeth.
Details: Access to the lagoon is restricted to demarcated areas, and fishing, bait-collecting, boating and other activities are regulated by the National Parks Board, from which a comprehensive brochure is available. The Board runs an office on Thesen's Island, tel (0445) 2-2095.
Accommodation: The area is well served by hotels, self-catering and bed-and-breakfast accommodation, and caravan/camping facilities.
Further information: Knysna Publicity Association, P O Box 87, Knysna 6570, tel (0445) 2-1610.

The expanse of water stretching to the south of Knysna is one of the country's largest and loveliest tidal lagoons. It is fed both by the Knysna River and by the sea, which enters through two cliffs known as The Heads, and its surface reflects the tall trees of the forests and the mountains behind. Like the Wilderness lakes to the west, the lagoon and its surrounding area are a conservation area, administered by the National Parks Board.

Among the lagoon's many precious natural assets is its treasure chest of marine life, which includes Knysna oysters, fish, crabs, prawns, sea-urchins and the rare sea horse, *Hippocampus capensis*.

Knysna, nestling along the lagoon's north shore, is noted for its brewery (superb draught ale), pubs, coffee houses, restaurants, craft and speciality shops, and for the local produce – ham, cheese, honey, trout and, of course, oysters.

The western Head accommodates the private Featherbed Nature Reserve. More accessible to the general public is the eastern bluff, easily reached by road, and from which there are splendid views of the sea on one side and, on the other, the town across the water, and the forests and mountains beyond.

The lagoon area offers some enticing beach, forest and waterside walks and, for those who prefer finding their way around by water, cabin cruisers and powerboats for hire.

Undulating hills shear off to a rocky shore and the warm waters of the Indian Ocean on a farm near the Knysna Heads.

MILLWOOD HOUSE AND MILLWOOD MINE
Queen Street

Map: page 199, 4C/D
Details: From February to November the museum is open 09h30-12h30 Monday to Saturday; in December and January 09h30-12h30 and 14h30-16h30. Admission free, but donations are welcome. On-street parking usually available.
Accommodation: Knysna offers a variety of hotel, guesthouse and other accommodation.
Further information: Millwood House Museum, Queen Street, Knysna 6570, tel (0445) 2-2133; Knysna Publicity Association, P O Box 87, Knysna 6570, tel (0445) 2-1610.

This building right in the centre of Knysna started life 32 km away, among the dense undergrowth of Millwood, which, improbable though it may sound, witnessed one of South Africa's earliest gold rushes.

The attractive house was prefabricated, in 1886, of wood and corrugated iron, ornamented with the fashionable fretwork of the era. Later, long after the alluvial deposits ran out, it was moved piecemeal to its new location.

The place is filled with various fascinating relics of the fortune-seeking days, and paintings, photographs and other exhibits tell the interesting story of the wider Knysna region.

Next door is the iron and yellowwood Parkes Cottage, also translocated from the goldfields, and behind it stands Parkes Shop, where a display illustrating Knysna's timber industry can be found.

There's little enough to see at Millwood itself, although in its early days it was a substantial settlement supporting hotels, bars and commercial enterprises.

All that now remains are some excavations and a 160-m tunnel. The old Bendigo Mine is currently being restored, and visitors can see the old cemetery and the graves of some 100 people.

Millwood House is in the town of Knysna. To get to the goldfields, turn north from the N2 highway two kilometres west of the lagoon bridge, pass through Rheenendal, turn right onto the Bibby's Hoek road and pass the Goudveld Forest Station. Follow the signs for Jubilee Creek and then those for Millwood. Both sites are worth visiting.

LAKES DISTRICT
Wilderness to Knysna

For sheer beauty, few parts of the exquisite Garden Route can compare with the lakes area that extends eastwards along the coastal terrace, from Wilderness to Knysna.

This watery world, a declared national park of some 2 500 ha (with a further 10 000 ha of adjoining land proclaimed for conservation), encompasses five lakes, two estuaries and nearly 30 km of enchanting Indian Ocean shoreline. Inland, wooded slopes sweep up to the Outeniqua Mountains, part of the southern Cape's splendid coastal rampart. The lakes and their surrounding area are a magnet for holiday-makers in search of gentle relaxation, for watersports enthusiasts, swimmers, hikers, anglers and, along the shoreline, surfers and sunbathers.

The tourist infrastructure is, predictably, well developed. Visitors have an indulgent choice of hotels, resorts, guesthouses, chalets, time-share units, caravan parks and eateries. There are recreation facilities aplenty, the roads are excellent, and the crowds keep coming.

All of which amount to a major, potentially critical, dilemma for the National Parks Board, who must ensure that a reasonable balance is maintained between tourism and conservation in this very special corner of the country. Compounding the problem are a patchwork of public and private boundaries, the demands of local-interest groups, pressure from developers and their clients, an expanding residential community (a lot of affluent retirees and others either want to settle or maintain second homes here), confrontations over water resources, and various proposals for a new freeway.

Still, South Africa's Lakes District remains as close to paradise on earth as you're likely to find.

Among its components are, from west to east, the Touws River estuary, also referred to as Wilderness Lagoon; the Serpentine, a broad and meandering channel connecting the lagoon with Island Lake (Eilandvlei), the first of the lakes proper and much favoured by windsurfers, water-skiers and boaters; Langvlei, Rondevlei, Swartvlei (one of the largest saltwater lakes in South Africa, and the venue for major sailing regattas), and Groenvlei.

Curiously enough, although these lovely expanses of water are close neighbours, they weren't all formed by the same physical process. Swartvlei, for example, is an old river valley, and Rondevlei an eroded basin (both were submerged by the ocean). Groenvlei is separated from the sea by a barrier of dunes, but its waters are relatively fresh.

Although all the vleis fall under the control of the National Parks Board, Rondevlei and Langvlei form the core of

Map: page 199, 3D
The Wilderness area is reached via the N2 (the reserve lies on either side of the highway).

Details: Public access is unlimited, although watersports are permitted within zoned areas. Boats are available for hire. Restricted swimming and fishing.

Accommodation: The National Parks Board runs two camps (the Ebb and Flow, and the Wilderness), accommodation ranging from simple 2-bed huts with shower and toilet, to fully equipped, self-contained 6-bed cottages. Caravan/camping facilities are also available.

Booking: National Parks Board, P O Box 787, Pretoria 0001, tel (012) 343-1991; National Parks Board, P O Box 7400, Roggebaai 8012, tel (021) 22-2810. The greater George-Wilderness-Knysna region is well endowed with hotel, resort, lodge, guesthouse, self-catering and caravan/camping facilities.

Further information: Wilderness Information Centre, Wilderness Station, Wilderness 6560, tel (0441) 77-0045. The Centre is open weekdays and on Saturday mornings in season.

Water-skiing, sailing, canoeing and swimming are some of the attractions offered to holiday-makers on the Touws River near Wilderness.

GARDEN ROUTE

the conservation effort, serving as a major bird sanctuary. The sedge and reedbeds provide habitats for about 80 different kinds of waterfowl, including the rare osprey.

A special section has been set aside for the protection of bontebok, while duiker, bushbuck and grysbok can be spotted.

You can, of course, drive through the Wilderness Lakes District, but it is probably best explored on foot. Five trails have been established, ranging from three to 10 km, the longest being the Pied Kingfisher, a circular route (part of it on the lakeside boardwalk) along the Touws River and Serpentine. The Giant Kingfisher takes you through forest to a charming waterfall. The Brown-headed Kingfisher winds up the Duiwe River Valley to another cascade (lovely views on the way). The Half-collared Kingfisher tracks the river's western bank. The Cape Dune Molerat goes through the sandy reaches of bird-rich Rondevlei. In spring the countryside is ablaze with flowers.

Maps and information are available from the Parks Board's Wilderness camp and the Rondevlei office.

Boardwalks such as this offer hikers access to the bird life and natural wonders of the Wilderness Lakes District. They also protect the shoreline from being damaged.

NATURE'S VALLEY
Near Plettenberg Bay

Map: page 199, 5D
Nature's Valley lies to the south of the N2 highway. Drive 26 km to the east of Plettenberg Bay, and turn right at the Nature's Valley sign.
Details: Nature's Valley and the De Vasselot section of the Tsitsikamma National Park are accessible throughout the year. De Vasselot has a camping site with ablution facilities.
Accommodation: Plettenberg Bay offers a wide variety of hotel, guesthouse, self-catering and caravan/camping facilities. For accommodation in Plettenberg Bay, contact the Plettenberg Bay Publicity Association, P O Box 26, Plettenberg Bay 6600, tel (04457) 3-0465/6.
Further information: See Tsitsikamma National Park.

Drive up to the summit of the Groot River Pass, and a beautiful vista unfolds: of the river and its deep gorge; of dense, green forests, their trees festooned with thick lichen; and, on the shoreline three kilometres away, a limpid lagoon girded by a scatter of attractive holiday homes. This is Nature's Valley, one of South Africa's most enchanting resort areas.

Developers have had to keep their distance, and the valley remains entirely unspoilt. It is surrounded on three sides by the Tsitsikamma National Park *(see separate entry)*, whose De Vasselot section offers some 30 km of short walks through a countryside of forest and fern, coastal heath, hill and steep ravine.

The renowned Tsitsikamma Hiking Trail crosses a section of the De Vasselot, and the Otter Trail ends here.

The National Parks Board has issued a sketch map of the various walks, which range from one to four kilometres. To get the most out of your day's outing, you can try several of them in sequence.

For the rest, there's bathing in lagoon and warm ocean, sunworshipping on the broad sands, and bird-spotting. About 280 bird species have been identified here, 25 of them sea birds. Cape gannets, giant kingfishers and black oystercatchers can be observed along the coast, with Knysna loeries, paradise flycatchers and olive woodpeckers in the forest.

Nature's Valley, with its tranquil lagoon, sweeping bronze beaches and cluster of seaside homes, reflects the slumbering solitude and charm of the Garden Route.

OTTER TRAIL
Tsitsikamma National Park

The first, and still among the most popular, of South Africa's organized hiking trails leads you through the magnificent coastal and forest terrain of the Tsitsikamma National Park *(see separate entry)*, from Storms River Mouth westwards to the Groot River estuary and Nature's Valley. The five-day, 42-km trail has been charted, and is run by the National Parks Board.

The route is broken up into fairly easy stages – the longest day's walk covers just 14 km – but the going is tough in some of the stretches, and others demand a good head for heights.

For most of the way hikers follow the shoreline, scrambling up to the coastal plateau 200 m or so above the sea, along the more rugged, cliff-obstructed parts. The terrain variously includes steep slopes, dense forest canopy (handsome yellowwoods, alders, Cape beeches, white milkwoods, stinkwoods), swift-running streams, a few golden beaches and lovely tidal pools. Moreover, the pace is slow enough to allow you to study the plant and bird life at leisure (over 280 species of the latter have been identified), enjoy the breathtaking scenery, and spend time snorkelling in the pools.

Resident wildlife includes leopards, bushpigs, bushbuck, duiker, baboons, vervet monkeys and, in the marine section, seals and dolphins. Whales come close inshore to breed and calve during winter. Special features along the route include strandloper (early Khoisan) middens, the spacious Guano Cave, and some entrancing waterfalls.

Hikers overnight in rudimentary cabins maintained by the National Parks Board. The trail is a perennial favourite with the walking fraternity, so book well in advance.

Map: page 199, 6D

The Otter Trail begins at Storms River Mouth Rest Camp. Take the N2 to a point 4 km west of the village of Storms River. Turn south through the Tsitsikamma National Park, following the signs to Storms River Mouth.

Details: The trail is in use throughout the year. A maximum of 12 trailists start each day, though they may set off in smaller numbers. Overnight huts must be used in route sequence (to avoid confusion). The huts usually stock firewood, but include a camp stove in your backpack, and take along a water bottle. Provisions (bread, fresh meat, canned goods, long-life milk) are available at Storms River Mouth, which also has a takeaway outlet and *a la carte* restaurant. Before starting out, hikers must obtain a permit from reception, and sign in at the information centre at Storms River Mouth.

Accommodation: There is a selection of conventional accommodation (hotels, self-catering units) and caravan/camping facilities in the general Storms River/Tsitsikamma area.

Further information: Chief Director, National Parks Board, P O Box 787, Pretoria 0001, tel (012) 343-1991; National Parks Board, P O Box 7400, Roggebaai 8012, tel (021) 22-2810.

Tidal pools offer hikers cool relief along the Otter Trail, which tracks the coastline between Storms River Mouth and Nature's Valley.

GARDEN ROUTE

Map: page 199, 3C
George lies 3 km off the N2, 432 km from Cape Town and 320 km from Port Elizabeth.
Details: The train runs daily except Sundays and certain public holidays, departing George Station at 08h45, arriving in Knysna some two-and-a-half hours later. The return journey starts at 13h35 and ends at 16h15. Refreshments available on board, and souvenirs are sold at both George and Knysna stations. Special package tours, offered during the Christmas holidays, take in a Knysna lagoon cruise and lunch. Also available are occasional holiday trips to places as distant as Mossel Bay. Another special is a double-headed locomotive train that sporadically conveys passengers from Mossel Bay to Knysna. Tickets, and details of all excursions, are obtainable at George Station. Bookings can be made at either the George or Knysna station, or telephone George Station on (0441) 73-8202/73-8288.
Accommodation: The George, Knysna and Wilderness areas are well served by hotel, guesthouse, self-catering and caravan/camping facilities.
Further information: George Tourism Association, P O Box 1109, George 6530, tel (0441) 74-4000; Knysna Publicity Association, P O Box 87, Knysna 6570, tel (0445) 82-5510.

OUTENIQUA CHOO-CHOO
George to Knysna

The handsome, squeaky-clean Class 24 locomotive, with its characteristic barrel-shaped tender attached, and its timber-fitted, leather-scented old carriages, is the very last of the scheduled South African steam railway services to have survived the onslaught of diesel traction and electrification. It plies daily between George and Knysna, and you don't have to be a railway enthusiast to be touched by its enchantment. Even the halts along the way have a musical ring to their names – Table Top and Fairy Knowe, Serpentine, Duiwe River, Rondevlei, Dennebos, Lake Pleasant, Belvidere (among others).

Essentially a working freight-train with provision for up to 300 passengers, the Choo-Choo starts its journey from George, and puffs its way through woodlands and fern forest to meet the sea at Victoria Bay, a magical little cove. It then passes through a series of tunnels, and negotiates the long, scenically stunning sweep of the Kaaimans River Bridge to enter Wilderness, and emerges to follow the chain of lakes and the steep incline of the Goukamma Valley, before descending to Knysna. Here it skirts the western shore of the lagoon before finally crossing a long, low-level bridge.

At Knysna there's time enough for a pleasant pub lunch or picnic before the return trip begins. Alternatively, take a one-way ticket only and drive back, so you can see a bit more of the Knysna area.

The driver of the Outeniqua Choo-Choo takes time off for a quick cuppa, before setting off on the trip from George to Knysna.

The romance of rail

Tourist interest has prompted a revival of steam travel around South Africa, but the 'Outeniqua Choo-Choo', linking George and Knysna, is the country's last 'genuine' survivor from the great age of rail.

This began in Durban in 1860, when a fanfare of trumpets launched the first steam train on its way from the city to the Point, just over three kilometres away.

Proposals for a commercial Cape railway, however, had been submitted as early as 1845, though these came to nothing. It wasn't until the late 1850s that a contract was awarded for the inaugural Cape line, between Cape Town and the Winelands centre of Wellington. The project was plagued by incompetence and various mishaps, and the 34-km track to Eerste River, vanguard of what was soon to become a sophisticated countrywide network, was completed in 1862.

There was little further progress for the remainder of the decade, but the discovery and exploitation of Kimberley's fabulous diamond fields by prospectors and entrepreneurs in the 1870s and, more significantly, of the Witwatersrand's goldfields, gave powerful impetus to railway development.

So, too, did fierce competition – between the British colonies of Natal and the Cape on the one hand, and Paul Kruger's Transvaal on the other – to connect the goldfields with a seaport. By the end of the century an impressive 7 000 km of track linked the subcontinent's major centres.

Today the national railways stretch over 36 000 km, of which 20 000 have been electrified. Much of the network comprises the 'Cape gauge' (3ft 6in, or 1 065 mm). Initially the standard 1,5-m British gauge was adopted, but it proved rather too broad to cope with the gradients and twisting curvatures of the great mountain rampart between Cape Town and the interior.

Indeed a number of minor lines – for instance the Apple Express between Port Elizabeth and Avontuur in the enchanting Long Kloof – are known for their even narrower (610 mm) gauges.

An Outeniqua locomotive lends a special old-world charm to the countryside as it rumbles across a bridge spanning the Touws River at Wilderness.

OUTENIQUA HIKING TRAIL
Outeniqua Mountains

The Outeniqua is among the toughest of the country's better-known trails, a seven-day odyssey through some of the most beautiful scenery of the Southern Cape. The itinerary is demanding. It starts from Beervlei in the Bergplaas State Forest, north of Swartvlei Lake, and makes its 90-km way over lovely, well-watered mountain fynbos and woodland terrain, eastwards to the Harkerville Forest Station.

En route you're treated to stunning views across the tree-covered hills and valleys of the Garden Route, and the blue waters of the Indian Ocean beyond. The plant life – ericas, proteas, flame-red aloes, lilies, wild orchids, pincushions and much else – is at its colourful best from early- to midsummer (October to January). The latter part of the trail runs through splendid forest country, where many of the more striking trees are labelled with their national tree list numbers. At the middle of the hike, near Millwood, you'll come across relics of the early gold diggings.

The area enjoys rainfall throughout the year, snow and frost sometimes cover the wintertime uplands, and the countryside is often mantled in seductive mists. Trailists overnight in fairly basic but spacious huts – there are eight altogether – equipped with bunks, mattresses, fireplaces and firewood.

For those who don't have the time (or energy) for the full route, there are several shorter variations, including a number of day-walks, and the two-day trail that follows a scenic path from the Goudveld Forest Station to Millwood and back. There's also the celebrated Elephant Walk through the Diepwalle Forest.

The awesome turrets of the Outeniqua Mountains rise above blankets of low-lying clouds. This is one of the spectacular panoramas that unfold to travellers on the Outeniqua Pass.

Map: page 199, 2/3C
Take the N2 to Wilderness. Turn onto the Hoekwil Road, opposite Wilderness Holiday Inn. Follow the signs to the Beervlei Forest Station (19 km from Wilderness).
Details: The trail is open throughout the year.
Accommodation: Overnight huts, each accommodating 30 people, are provided with bunks, mattresses and firewood. Trailists must provide their own bedding and provisions. The full range of conventional accommodation is on offer in and around Knysna and Wilderness.
Further information: The Department of Water Affairs and Forestry, Southern Cape, Private Bag X12, Knysna 6570, tel (0445) 82-5466. A brochure and detailed map are available.

ROBBERG NATURE RESERVE
Plettenberg Bay

Robberg, the 'mountain of seals', is a scenic, four-kilometre promontory of red sandstone that probes finger-like into the blue waters of the Indian Ocean at the southern end of Plettenberg Bay. This high headland is valued by locals and visitors alike for its part in keeping the westerly winds away from the bay's golden sands.

But it has other assets. The whole of the peninsula – 240 ha of it in all – is a proclaimed nature reserve, notable for its rich intertidal and bird life, and for the caves that once sheltered communities of strandlopers ('beach-rangers').

The floors of most of these caves contain strandloper middens – deposits of shells that indicate the nature of their marine diet. Almost sheer cliffs dominate the northern section of the reserve. The southern slopes are gentler, and you reach the principal archaeological site, Nelson's Caves, via a leisurely walk along a ridge that offers fine views of sea and rocky shore. Other walks, which start from the car park, follow the old fishermen's paths to some splendid viewsites. The round trip from the car park to the point is about three hours. The surrounding sea is a proclaimed marine reserve.

Map: page 199, 5D
Plettenberg Bay is just off the N2, roughly midway between Cape Town and Port Elizabeth. From town take the airport road and follow the Robberg signs.
Details: Open daily throughout the year 07h00-17h00 (20h00 from 1 December to 15 January). Parking available. Entrance fee per person and vehicle. Entry permit obtainable at the gate. Picnic and braai sites at the car park.
Accommodation: Plettenberg Bay offers a wide selection of hotel, self-catering and camping facilities.
Further information: The Officer-in-Charge, Robberg Nature Reserve, Private Bag X1003, Plettenberg Bay 6600, tel (04457) 3-2125/ 3-2185.

GARDEN ROUTE

TSITSIKAMMA NATIONAL PARK
Near Nature's Valley

Map: page 199, 6D
The park lies to the south of the N2 highway. There are two access routes. For the De Vasselot (western) section, take the Nature's Valley turn-off, 26 km east of Plettenberg Bay. The Storms River Mouth turn-off is 60 km east of Plettenberg Bay.
Details: The park is open throughout the year. Admission charge for day-visitors.
Accommodation: Caravan and camp sites available (running water, ablution blocks, fireplaces), as well as forest cabins. The Storms River Mouth camp offers fully equipped, self-catering log cabins and 'oceanettes', a shop, takeaway and *a la carte* restaurant. At De Vasselot there is a caravan and camping site 3 km from the shop in Nature's Valley.
Further information: National Parks Board, P O Box 787, Muckleneuk, Pretoria 0001, tel (012) 343-1991; or The Park Warden, Tsitsikamma National Park, P O Storms River 6308, tel (042) 541-1607/541-1651.

One of the country's longest, narrowest and loveliest parks encompasses nearly 80 km of the Cape's coastal strip – from the Groot River and Nature's Valley eastwards along the southern Cape coast. It is also noted as the first marine park to be proclaimed in Africa, its boundary extending five kilometres seaward to take in a treasure-trove of ocean life.

A number of rivers and streams cut through deep ravines before discharging into the Indian Ocean. Here there are cliffs, caves, golden sands and a myriad rock pools alive with marine creatures. Dolphins and whales can regularly be spotted beyond the rollers.

The land is well watered and richly endowed with plants such as proteas, ericas, pincushions, sugarbushes, everlastings and other fynbos species, ferns, aloes, wild orchids and many kinds of lily. There are also some majestic stands of indigenous forest, especially in the De Vasselot section in the extreme west. Notable of these are Outeniqua yellowwoods, Cape chestnuts, stinkwoods and white milkwoods.

This botanical diversity attracts nearly 280 bird species, special among which are Knysna loeries, paradise flycatchers and slim-lined forest canaries. Other wildlife includes bushbuck, blue duiker and grysbok, baboons, vervet monkeys and Cape clawless otters.

The Tsitsikamma area is splendid walking country. The Otter Trail *(see separate entry)* runs along the western half of the national park. From Storms River Mouth there are numerous day-walks, such as the Loerie and Mouth trails, and there is also an underwater trail for qualified scuba divers, although competent swimmers can snorkel in the sheltered bays.

The dense forests of the Tsitsikamma National Park conceal a host of scenic delights, such as this tranquil pool surrounded by trees and ferns.

YSTERNEK MOUNTAIN FYNBOS AND FOREST NATURE RESERVE
Near Knysna

Map: page 199, 4C
The Ysternek Reserve is part of the Diepwalle State Forest. From Knysna take the N2 east for 7 kilometres. Turn left onto the R339 to Uniondale. The road becomes gravel after 6 kilometres. Continue for some 20 km, and look for the Diepwalle Forest Station turn-off.
Details: Open dawn to dusk throughout the year. No permits required for entry. No admission fee.
Accommodation: At the Diepwalle Forest Station there is a hut for hikers on the Outeniqua Hiking Trail.
Further information: The Officer-in-Charge, Chief Directorate of Forestry, Southern Cape, Private Bag X12, Knysna 6570, tel (0445) 82-5466.

This is a perfect spot to spend a quiet hour or two away from the busier tourist lanes. The Ysternek reserve, part of the Diepwalle conservation area *(see separate entry)*, was created to preserve the region's heath-type montane fynbos, but it's also a sanctuary for a fern-graced patch of evergreen natural forest that encloses an exquisite little picnic site. Prominent among the trees are red and white alder, stinkwood, white and hard pear and other canopy-forming species.

From the picnic area, known as the Valley of Ferns, a road takes you up to an observation point from which you can see the panoramic Buffelsnek woodlands, the Outeniqua Mountains, Tsitsikamma highlands, and the dense, deep-green mantle of the Knysna forests.

The whole Ysternek Reserve is a bird-watcher's delight, especially in springtime, when flowers are abundant. With a little patience, you may be lucky to spot the colourful Knysna loerie and the entrancing Narina trogon among the high foliage. Protea seed-eaters, mountain buzzards and Cape eagles inhabit the more open spaces. The reserve is also home to a number of animals, including bushbuck and leopards.

SOUTHERN CAPE

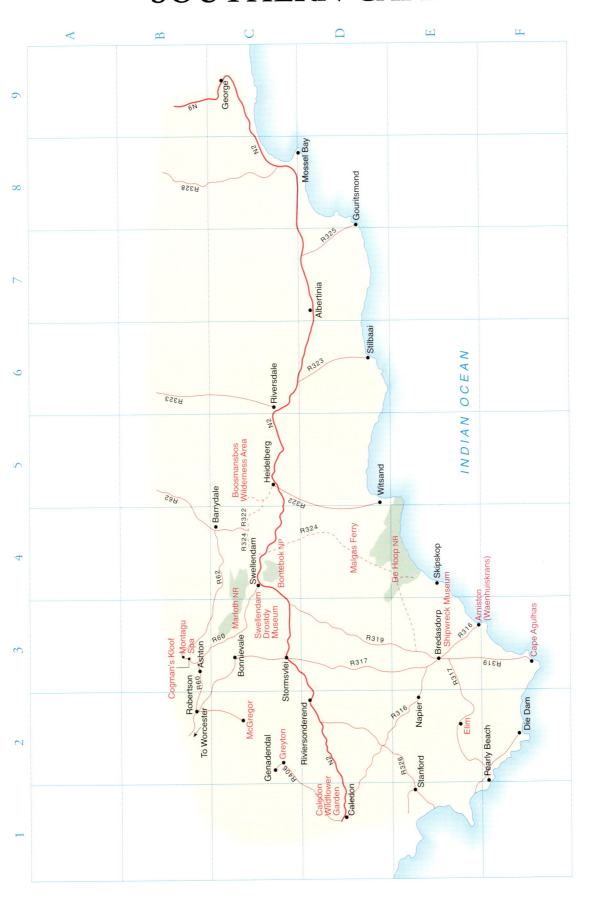

SOUTHERN CAPE

ARNISTON
Near Cape Agulhas

Map: page 213, 3E
From Cape Town take the N2 east to Caledon. Turn onto the R316 through Bredasdorp, and on to Waenhuiskrans. Bear in mind that the village is also known as Arniston, and may be sign-posted as such.
Details: Activities include angling, boating, bathing, walking, sunbathing and generally relaxing. The summer months are the best.
Accommodation: Excellent hotel, self-catering and caravan/camping facilities are available in and near the village.
Further information: Suidpunt Publicity Association, P O Box 51, Bredasdorp 7280, tel (02841) 4-2584.

This entrancing little fishing village on the shores of Marcus Bay is popular among weekenders in search of the picturesque: the prettily thatched and limewashed cottages that huddle around the shoreline would fit happily into the most romantic of Victorian paintings. Many are notable for their huge baking ovens. The coastline is well worth exploring, and there's plenty of local colour: noisily cheerful commercial fishermen hawk their catches (which include fine, fresh oysters), and their young sons snare huge octopuses in the rock pools.

The place takes its English name – it is officially known as Waenhuiskrans – from one of the most tragic shipwrecks of the south coast's notoriously treacherous waters. In May 1815 the laden British troopship *Arniston*, swept inshore by wind and current, foundered in the bay with the loss of 372 servicemen, civilian passengers and crew. Only six of those on board managed to struggle to safety.

The village's Afrikaans name is a reference to the enormous sea-cavern, gouged from the nearby cliffs, which the early settlers in the area thought quite big enough to serve as a coach-house (known as a 'waenhuis') accommodating several wagons and spans of oxen. The cave, which is only accessible at low tide, is the product of an erosive process that has carved many weird and wonderful rock formations along the coast. Also of interest are the prehistoric stone fish traps which were built by the 'Strandloper' people of precolonial days.

The general area boasts some lovely bays, beaches, walks and drives.

Local fishermen and helpers cluster around their sturdy, salt-stained boats on Arniston's beach. The village, though a fashionable vacation venue, has retained its picturesque old-world charm.

BONTEBOK NATIONAL PARK
Near Swellendam

Map: page 213, 4C
From Cape Town, take the N2 east, through Caledon, to Swellendam. Turn right at Swellendam's eastern end and follow the gravel road for 6 km to the park's entrance. The route is well signposted.
Details: Open throughout the year October to April 08h00-19h00; May to September 09h00-18h00. Information centre, shop (nonperishable groceries, soft drinks, gift items), all-weather gravel internal roads, walking trails; swimming and fishing in the Breede River. Parking available. Entrance fee. Best months to visit: September to December.
Accommodation: Caravan/camping stands with ablution facilities; fully equipped caravans available for hire. Nearby Swellendam has 3 hotels and self-catering accommodation.
Further information: The Park Warden, Bontebok National Park, P O Box 149, Swellendam 6740, tel (0291) 4-2735. Advance booking: National Parks Board, P O Box 787, Pretoria 0001, tel (012) 343-1991; or P O Box 7400, Roggebaai 8012, tel (021) 22-2810.

Few enterprises can claim such decisive and lasting success in fulfilling their prime purpose as the Bontebok National Park, a 2 800-ha expanse of attractive heath country flanking the Breede River.

The bontebok, a medium-sized, dark brown antelope with distinctive white markings, once roamed the southern Cape plains in their thousands, but by the 1930s hunters and the growing number of encroaching farmlands had reduced the species to the point of extinction. Then local landowners then came to their rescue, safeguarding a number large enough to sustain the gene pool, and paving the way for the creation of a

One of the park's 200 or so bontebok, pulled back from the brink of extinction by the efforts of local farmers. These graceful, lyre-horned antelope are mainly grazers, though they will sometimes eat the leaves of shrubs.

national park – finally established in the Bredasdorp area in 1931, with a breeding herd of just 22 of the animals.

Thirty years later the reserve was moved to its present location, and is now sanctuary to a thriving population of about 200 bontebok (surplus animals are regularly translocated to other reserves and to game farms), together with Cape mountain zebras and a scattering of other antelope such as grysbok, grey rhebok, duiker, red hartebeest and steenbok. The park is also notable for its 200 or so different kinds of bird, and for its floral wealth: wild olive, yellowwood and milkwood trees grace the Breede River's banks; blood-red aloes bloom in June and July; many-coloured wildflowers decorate the fynbos countryside during the springtime months.

All this can be seen and enjoyed at ease: the park has a 25-km road network and, for the slightly more energetic, there are two short walking trails. Other visitor facilities include an information centre and shop (near the main gate), various picnic and braai sites, and a camping ground beside the river.

The bluebuck: death of a species

Like the bontebok, the imperilled bluebuck once roamed the hills and plains around Bredasdorp, Caledon and Swellendam. But it proved even more vulnerable to human encroachment and the hunter's bullet, and has long been extinct: the very last recorded specimen was shot in South Africa around 1800.

The species *Hippotragus leucophaeus*, a relative of the roan and sable antelope, derived its name from the blue-grey colour of its coat, though it had other markings – an off-white underbelly and brown forehead. Among other distinguishing features were its vestigial mane and rather handsome swept-back horns. Little is known of its habits except that, judging from the habitat, it's almost certain to have been a browser rather than a grazer.

Physical evidence of the bluebuck's existence is limited: just four mounted specimens have been preserved, all in Europe (kept at museums in Paris, Vienna, Stockholm and Leyden). A pair of horns that could possibly have belonged to the animal is on view in Grahamstown's Albany Museum.

BOOSMANSBOS WILDERNESS AREA
Langeberg

The pristine, 14 200-ha wilderness which sprawls across the southern slopes of the Langeberg is rather remote, little publicized but well worth getting to know for its high peaks, deep gorges, spectacular views, its botanically important montane fynbos (heath) and swaths of deep green natural woodland.

The area is part of the Grootvadersbos Nature Reserve. Its 70 km of tracks are essentially functional, constructed for the forest patrols, but the more adventurous hikers may stray from the beaten path in search of real interest. Recommended routes are the scrambles to the top of the Grootberg (1 637 m), Horingberg (1 496 m), the Noukrans peak (1 452 m), and the longer (27 km) trail starting from the campsite and overnighting at the Helderfontein Huts – two old stone 'management' cottages – on Grootberg's southwestern side.

This route zigzags down alongside the dark, mist-wreathed, magical canopies of stinkwood and yellowwood, white and red alder, Cape holly, beech and candlewood. You'll also see, on an adjoining ridge, a patch of mountain cypress.

Bird life includes olive woodpeckers and martial and booted eagles. Mammals here tend to be elusive but you could spot bushbuck, grey rhebok, grysbok and, possibly, leopards. More easily seen are the baboons and rock-rabbits (dassies).

The rounded hills and far horizons of the Boosmansbos Wilderness Area beckon hikers and bird-watchers all over South Africa. Evergreen trees grace the valleys; higher up are patches of yellowwood, stinkwood and red alder.

Map: page 213, 5C
Turn off the N2 at Heidelberg, westwards on the R322, and drive for about 12 kilometres. Turn onto the signposted gravel road leading to the Grootvadersbos Nature Reserve.

Details: Open sunrise to sunset throughout the year. The nature reserve office is open 08h00-16h00 Monday to Friday (excluding public holidays). Permits required. Entry on foot only. Maximum of 12 persons admitted per day. Hikers are advised to book (by telephone) 3 months in advance.

Accommodation: Two trail-hut shelters for hikers, and a camp site at the entrance to the reserve. Conventional hotel, guesthouse, self-catering and caravan/camping facilities available in and around Swellendam; Heidelberg has a hotel, caravan park and a nearby guest farm.

Further information: The Nature Conservator, Grootvadersbos State Forest, P O Box 109, Heidelberg 6760, tel (02934) 2-2412.

SOUTHERN CAPE

CALEDON WILDFLOWER GARDEN
Caledon

Map: page 213, 1D
Signposted off the N2 at Caledon.
Details: Open daily throughout the year 07h00-19h00. Small admission charge. Spacious parking. The springtime months (August to October) are the best.
Accommodation: Caledon has hotels, a guesthouse and farm accommodation.
Further information: Caledon Publicity Association, Caledon Municipality, P O Box 258, Caledon 7230,
tel (0281) 2-1511.

In springtime, nature-lovers beat an enthusiastic path to the local reserve, officially known as Victoria Park and famed for its splendid displays of wildflowers – Namaqualand daisies, gazanias, *Arctotis*, *Dorotheanthus*, the beautiful Caledon bluebell (*Gladiolus spathaceus*), about 135 species of protea and much else.

The reserve extends across 214 ha of Swartberg hillside, within which there's a 56-ha cultivated section that has been masterfully landscaped. Here you'll find charming pathways and wooden bridges, lawns, picnic spots, an ornamental lake, handsome indigenous trees, shrubs, a prolific bird life and, of course, the flowers themselves. The cultivated area hosts the annual and hugely popular Caledon Wildflower Show, held in mid-September.

Beginning and ending at the garden is an enticing 10-km, three- to four-hour walk that traverses the wider area, leading hikers through rich fynbos terrain to the summit of the hill (834 m), from which there are panoramic views of the surrounding countryside. At the top, too, you'll see a fascinating rock formation known as The Window.

The garden's cosy tearoom provides refreshments during the spring flower season. Visitors can buy ericas, mesembryanthemums (vygies) and other plants from the nursery.

A Taiwanese trawler, victim of high wind and treacherous current, lies aground off Agulhas.

CAPE AGULHAS
South of Bredasdorp

Map: page 213, 3F
Turn off the N2 at Caledon, south onto the R316 to Bredasdorp. From Bredasdorp, take the signposted Agulhas road.
Details: Lighthouse Museum open Tuesday to Saturday 09h30-16h45; Sunday 10h30-13h30.
Accommodation: There are hotels at Struisbaai, Bredasdorp and Arniston. L'Agulhas has caravan/camping facilities.
Further information: Cape Agulhas Lighthouse Museum, P O Box 235, Bredasdorp 7280, tel (02846) 5-6078. Suidpunt Publicity Association, P O Box 51, Bredasdorp 7280, tel (02841) 4-2584.

You'd expect something special from the southernmost point of Africa, and the meeting place of two great oceans (the Indian and the Atlantic), but Cape Agulhas has little of the spectacular about it. Here the inland plain, after the mild interruption of some small hills, slips quietly under the sea to become the shallow, 250-km-wide Agulhas Bank, most extensive part of southern Africa's continental shelf and one of the richest fishing grounds in the world.

There is, though, one prominent feature: the distinctive Cape Agulhas lighthouse, built in 1848 (it's the country's second-oldest) in the style of the great Pharos light-tower outside Alexandria in ancient Egypt. This stretch of the southern coast is notorious for its reefs, currents and offshore winds. The lighthouse – its original 4 500 candlepower (fuelled from oil extracted from the tails of the local sheep) has been upgraded over the decades to 12 million – has proved a lifesaving boon to seafarers for the past century and a half.

Inside the tower is a unique lighthouse museum – the only one of its kind in Africa – telling the story of lighthouses generally and this one in particular (the exhibit forms part of the Bredasdorp Shipwreck Museum).

There's also a tearoom. The immediate surroundings are modestly decorated by an indigenous garden. At the southernmost point, about a kilometre walk beyond the lighthouse, a monument was erected in 1986.

Agulhas's odd-sounding name is derived from the Portuguese word for 'needle', a reference not to any physical feature but to a particular navigational curiosity: early mariners coming down this coastline found that, off the Cape, their compasses were unaffected by magnetic deviation and bore 'directly upon the true poles of the earth'.

The cape's village, which was formally known as L'Agulhas, comprises little more than a scatter of holiday homes and a caravan park.

The shoreline is rocky, but there are two tidal pools for bathing, Struisbaai's enticing 14-km beach is nearby, and, if you have the time to spare, the walk eastward to De Mond makes a pleasant enough outing. The nearest urban centre of note is Bredasdorp.

The historic Agulhas lighthouse, friend to seafarers for more than 150 years, stands sentinel over Africa's southernmost point.

COGMAN'S KLOOF
Near Caledon

The road linking the Breede River Valley with the Klein Karoo (and, more immediately, the towns of Ashton and Montagu) makes its way over Cogman's Kloof, a winding 10-km pass built by renowned road engineer Thomas Bain in 1877. The route is a scenic delight, the views of the surrounding and distinctively hued mountains breathtaking. At the summit there's a small Anglo-Boer War fort built in 1899.

Cogman's Kloof cuts through the lovely Montagu Mountain Nature Reserve, a 1 200-ha sanctuary for the scarlet aloes, the succulents, fynbos and other precious plants of the Langeberg range's northern parts. This is superb walking country, much favoured by nature-lovers, ramblers and hikers. Charted trails range from 12 to 15,6 km, the longest leading to Blou Pont, from which you can see five towns. There are also a number of gentler walks in the vicinity of Montagu.

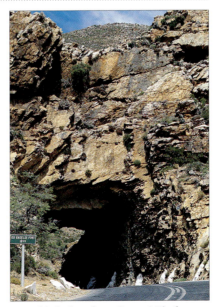

Part of the high road over Cogman's Kloof passes through a tunnel. Stunning views of mountain and valley unfold along the rest of the way.

Map: page 213, 3B
Leave the N1 at Worcester and continue east on the R60, through Robertson to Ashton. Turn north over the pass towards Montagu.

Details: The road is in excellent condition at all times of the year. It's worth exploring both Montagu *(see separate entry)* and the Ashton area. The latter is renowned for its rose nurseries and thoroughbred stud farms. Montagu Mountain Nature Reserve is open throughout the year. There is no entrance fee. Hikers have the use of two 6-bed cabins with cooking and ablution facilities.

Accommodation: Hotel and self-catering accommodation is available in and around Montagu.

Further information: The Town Clerk, Montagu Municipality, P O Box 24, Montagu 6720, tel (0234) 4-2471; Montagu Tourism Information Bureau, P O Box 24, Montagu 6720, tel (0234) 4-2471.

SOUTHERN CAPE

DE HOOP NATURE RESERVE
East of Bredasdorp

Map: page 213, 4E
Turn off the N2 at Caledon, onto the R316 to Bredasdorp. Turn northeast on the R319 for 9 km, and then turn right (signposted De Hoop) onto a gravel road. Continue for 34 km and turn right again onto the final 7-km stretch to the reserve's entrance.

Details: Open daily 07h00-18h00. There is a shop and petrol pump at Ouplaas, 15 km away.

Accommodation: Cottages to hire. Camping site, picnic sites. Hotel accommodation and caravan/camping facilities are available in Bredasdorp and Arniston.

Further information: The Officer-in-Charge, De Hoop Nature Reserve, Private Bag X16, Bredasdorp 7280, tel (0922) 782/700; The Director, Department of Nature and Environmental Conservation, Private Bag 9086, Cape Town 8000, tel (021) 45-0227.

De Hoop Nature Reserve, one of the Cape's most important and attractive reserves, is a nature-lover's paradise. Here you will feel the stresses of city life slip away as you immerse yourself in the unspoiled beauty and tranquillity of this 36 000-ha Eden – home to about 1 500 species of lowland fynbos.

The adjacent marine reserve, stretching five kilometres out to sea, is one of the world's great sanctuaries and breeding grounds of southern right whales, once hunted almost to extinction.

From May to December these huge, gentle creatures come to the warm waters of De Hoop to calve, and, when the sea is calm, you can see them cruising off the coast with their newborn. The marine reserve also hosts a great variety of fishes.

De Hoop is also home to the last breeding colony of rare Cape vultures in the Southwest Cape.

De Hoop encompasses a large vlei, limestone hills, massive sand dunes and part of the Potberg Mountain range. Originally established as an experimental wildlife farm, the reserve is still haven for an impressive number of wildlife populations, including such mammals as bontebok, Cape mountain zebras, grey duiker, steenbok, eland, klipspringer, black-backed jackals and baboons.

More intriguing, perhaps, are the smaller creatures: mongooses, angulate tortoises, mountain agamas, puff adders, cobras and other snakes. There are 86 species of bat at De Hoop. The *Windhoek* guano cave is home to about 150 000 bats belonging to five species.

De Hoop accommodates no less than 250 species of bird, many of which make their homes around the vlei.

The farm *De Hoop*, originally owned by the Dutch East India Company, was

The moody magic of the De Hoop coast at sunset. Scenic beauty and a rich plant life are major drawcards.

More than 200 different kinds of resident and migratory bird frequent De Hoop's marshland.

Wonders of the Cape's floral kingdom

The famed heath-type fynbos vegetation of the Southwest Cape covers less than one-fiftieth of one percent of the earth's land surface, but it is so rich in plant life, and so unusual in its origins, that botanists have classified it one of the world's six 'floral kingdoms'.

In scientific terms, it thus enjoys equal status with the great Boreal Kingdom that extends over parts of North America and much of Asia and Europe.

This extraordinary diversity of hardy, generally low-growing, evergreen shrubs – which is technically classed as Cape macchia – flourishes in habitats ranging from coastal sands to sub-alpine mountain slopes. Most of the 8 600 species (compared to 15 000 in the whole of the vast landmass of Australia) are small-leafed plants such as the beautiful proteas and ericas, the almost leafless reed-like restios and a huge number of corms and bulbs.

Of the 989 different genera, nearly 200 are unique to a particular area. Many species are restricted to just a few scattered microhabitats. Some parts of the countryside sustain an incredibly varied floral population (as many as 121 species have been recorded within a single patch measuring 10 square metres).

Fynbos is well adapted to soils poor in nutrients and to the onslaughts of summer droughts, high winds and periodical veld fires – attributes essential to survival after the Cape's climate began to change (from the subtropical to the harsher, drier, colder 'Mediterranean' type) about 12 million years ago.

It has been the region's dominant vegetation for about four million years, managing to withstand the lesser but frequent climatic changes by 'migrating' either up or down the mountains as temperature, moisture and other conditions have dictated.

purchased by the Department of Nature Conservation in 1956. A nearby farm, *Windhoek*, was added in 1957, and the two areas joined by further land acquisitions. The De Hoop Marine Reserve was proclaimed in 1986 to help aid the recovery of the overexploited coastal environment and ecosystems.

The emphasis in the reserve is on education and nature-orientated outdoor recreation. To this end, hiking trails, a mountain-bike trail, walks and a circular drive for vehicles have been provided.

There are impressive displays of local ecology at the De Hoop office and at Potberg, and school groups are welcome at the environmental education centres at Potberg and Koppie Alleen, where a fascinating 1000-ha shifting dune system may be observed. This is the largest dune system protected within a nature reserve in the country.

The De Hoop Mountain Bike Trail in the eastern sector of the reserve is very popular. Amateurs be warned, though: many parts of the trail cross rugged and challenging terrain. If you are a novice, play it safe and leave the challenge to more experienced bikers.

The bike trail starts at the Potberg Environmental Education Centre and heads for Cupidoskraal, where you will find a comfortable overnight hut. Day-rides fan out from Cupidoskraal to the coast, along demarcated tracks.

Trails are limited to 12 cyclists a day, and permits are required. Be sure to wear helmets, and take along emergency kits. Swimming on the 12-km coastline is extremely dangerous and is not advised.

An old farm-wagon, long put out to pasture, complements Elim's charm. Villagers still draw profit from the wildflowers of the countryside.

ELIM
West of Bredasdorp

Perhaps the most attractive of the Cape's 19th-century Moravian mission stations, and the least affected by the passage of time, Elim was founded in 1824 and has changed little since.

Beautifully thatched, white-walled little cottages, charmingly varied in their rooflines and the styles of their eaves and windows, face onto a furrowed and fig-tree-lined main street, at one end of which is a gabled church. Inside this building, all is light: walls and pews are painted white, the hanging lamps gilded and ornamented with flying angels. The church's German-made clock, set in the main gable, first started ticking in 1764 and remains faithful to the hours. Nearby is the historic water mill, oldest of its type in the country (it was built in 1828) and now a national monument.

The countryside around Elim is famed for its springtime display of *Helichrysum* and *Helipterum*, the distinctive and beautiful 'everlastings' that find their way to gravesides the world over.

At one time the villagers used to pick, dry and market about 70 000 kg of the blooms each year, but the trade has fallen off to some degree in recent years. You can see the industry at its busiest on the nearby farm *Phesanthoek*.

Map: page 213, 2E
Turn off the N2 at Caledon, onto the R316 to Bredasdorp. Take the Agulhas road (R319) and turn right onto the R317 at the Elim sign. Alternatively, take the more scenic coastal route (R43) via Hermanus and Gansbaai, turning inland just beyond Pearly Beach.
Details: Elim, though no longer in the care of German fathers, still functions as a mission station. Courtesy requires that you contact the local church authorities (the pastor or the council of wardens) before any detailed exploration.
Accommodation: The village has no hotel, but there's a pleasant guesthouse. Hotel accommodation is available in Bredasdorp.
Further information: Mr Paul Swart, P O Box 20, Elim 7284, tel (02848) 705; Suidpunt Publicity Association, P O Box 51, Bredasdorp 7280, tel (02841) 4-2584.

SOUTHERN CAPE

GREYTON
East of Genadendal

Map: page 213, 2C
Turn off the N2, 3 km east of Caledon, onto the R406 to Greyton.
Details: The area is at its visual best in spring and early summer (September to November). The reserve is open sunrise to sunset throughout the year. Admission free.
Accommodation: Hotel and caravan/camping facilities are available in and near the village.
Further information: The Town Clerk, Greyton Municipality, P O Box 4, Greyton 7233, tel (028254) 9620.

The village, with its oak-lined main street, its charming hotels and pleasant setting beneath the heights of the Riviersonderend ('river without end') range, is among the Cape's more stylish weekend destinations. It's also home to a coterie of artists, writers and other free spirits who value tranquillity and have been attracted by the gentle, rather old-fashioned, character of the place. Greyton has antique shops, a pub, some delightful little cottages and a vaguely Victorian atmosphere. One of the hotels, The Post House, was built in the 1860s in English country style (antiques, log fires, rose garden), and still presents itself as 'purveyor of food and lodging to the gentry'.

Close-by Greyton Nature Reserve is worth exploring: it covers 2 220 ha of rugged mountain slopes that rise, at their loftiest, to 1 565 m above sea level. This is a splendid area for walking, especially in springtime when the wildflowers are in bloom. Sharp-eyed visitors will be able to spot klipspringer, grey rhebok, grysbok, duiker and baboons among the montane fynbos ground cover. Part of the challenging Boesmanskloof Hiking Trail passes through the reserve.

The sturdy, whitewashed elegance of The Post House, one of Greyton's cosy hotels. The village is popular among artists and holiday-makers.

MALGAS FERRY
Malgas, south of Swellendam

Map: page 213, 4D
Turn south off the N2, onto the R324, 17 km east of Swellendam. After 22 km turn right and continue for 15 km to Malgas.
Details: The ferry operates throughout the year. Continue along the road past Malgas and you'll skirt the northern boundary of De Hoop Nature Reserve *(see separate entry)* and eventually arrive at Bredasdorp.
Accommodation: Swellendam has hotel, self-catering and caravan/camping facilities.
Further information: Swellendam Publicity Association, P O Box 396, Swellendam 6740, tel (0291) 4-2770.

Malgas, once one of South Africa's very few inland ports and site of the last of the country's vehicle ponts (or river ferries), lies on the Breede River 50 km upstream from its south coast estuary.

Local entrepreneur Joseph Barry broke new trading ground when, in 1822 – before the advent of the railway and when overland routes were still appallingly rugged – he brought freight to the village by sea. Barry's coaster negotiated the dangerous bars at the river mouth to make its slow way to what was then known as Malagaskraal. Thereafter, the Barry family's vessels, notably the 158-ton *Kadie*, regularly plied the route carrying out the region's wheat, wool and, later (from the Little Karoo), ostrich-feather exports, and bringing in general supplies, mostly for the Barrys' own commercial enterprises.

Little of Malgas's past glory remains, though the setting is as peaceful and beautiful as ever. And the pont has survived. For many years it was powered by Oom Moxie Dunn, who harnessed himself to the cable and 'walked' the ferry across. The job is now handled by two men, though still for a modest enough fee. Differential rates apply to cars, farm vehicles, bicycles, wheelbarrows, horseback riders, pedestrians, donkeys, cows and so forth.

Malgas's pont about to off-load. The ferry was once a boon to local traders.

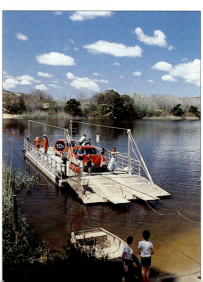

MARLOTH NATURE RESERVE
Swellendam

High mountains, deep ravines, mysterious evergreen forests of yellowwoods and stinkwoods cut through by clear, cold streams, a profusion of wild gardenia and almond, of proteas and other fynbos plants. These are the principal assets of the Marloth Nature Reserve, a sanctuary for animals and plants covering about 11 300-ha on the slopes of the Langeberg range near the town of Swellendam.

This mountain paradise is home to leopards, seldom-seen antelope, baboons and a number of small animals, reptiles and amphibians, including the rare ghost frog. The bird life, too, is prolific, and includes black eagles.

The Langeberg's most eye-catching physical features include the Clock peaks, a series of heights whose summits cast shadows from which, it is said, you can tell the approximate time of day.

More than anything else, though, this is a place for keen hikers. The 74-km Swellendam Trail, which is one of the most attractive segments of the National Hiking Way system and the first to follow a full 360° circular route, crosses the reserve. The complete trail takes seven days but there are shorter variations; explorers can digress down paths leading into cool, luxuriantly green kloofs and ravines such as Duiwelsbos, Koloniesbos and Wamakersbos.

There are many attractive picnic sites at Duiwelsbos and Hermitage Kloof. Walkers spend the night in huts. The nearest formal accommodation is in the town of Swellendam.

Map: page 213, 3/4C
Turn off the N2 into Swellendam. Follow Main Road to the traffic lights. Turn towards the mountain into Andrew Whyte Street and look for the Marloth Nature Reserve signpost.
Details: Open throughout the year, sunrise to sunset (except public holidays). Entry by permit only. Admission charge.
Accommodation: Swellendam has hotels, self-catering accommodation and a caravan/camping ground.
Further information: The Manager, Marloth Nature Reserve, P O Box 28, Swellendam 6740, tel (0291) 4-1410. Hiking trail information and bookings: Tel Cape Town (021) 402-3043/ (021) 402-3093.

MONTAGU SPA
Montagu

The town of Montagu has been famed for more than a century for its warm and soothing mineral springs, located in the Badkloof just north of the central area. You can reach them either by road or along a shady footpath known as Lovers' Walk. The latter meanders through a cliff-flanked ravine rich in colour and lively with the sound of birdsong. There is another hot spring on the farm *Baden* four kilometres away.

The springs were grievously assaulted by severe floods in 1981 but have been pleasantly redeveloped as a resort. The site of the genteel old Montagu Baths Hotel is now occupied by the stylish Avalon Springs, built at the foot of a sheer cliff face beside the welling spring. To immerse yourself in the waters under a clear and brilliantly starlit night sky is pleasure indeed. The hotel has three *a la carte* restaurants, an indoor warm-water

Map: page 213, 3B
Turn off the N1 at Worcester. Continue east on the R60, through Robertson to Ashton. Turn north and drive over Cogman's Kloof *(see separate entry)* to Montagu.
Details: The springs can best be enjoyed as a guest of either hotel or resort.
Further information: Avalon Springs Hotel, P O Box 110, Montagu 6720, tel (0234) 4-1150; Montagu Springs Resort, P O Box 277, Montagu 6720, tel (0234) 4-1050; Montagu Tourism Information Bureau, P O Box 24, Montagu 6720, tel (0234) 4-2471. Visitors to the Montagu Springs Resort and other establishments pay an admission fee to use the springs.

One of several bathing pools fed by the Montagu Spa's health-giving springs. The mineral waters bubble up at a temperature of 43°C.

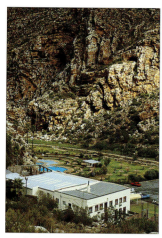

Avalon Springs and its very popular therapeutic pools huddle beneath a towering cliff face.

mineral pool, cold-water plunge pool, three outdoor mineral pools, health spa, sauna, steam bath, spa bath and other health-giving attractions.

Next door is the more family-orientated Montagu Springs complex, which is set in parkland bisected by the Keisie River. Some lovely trees and shrubs grace the grounds.

Ducks, geese and swans float, wander and waddle at will. There are attractively designed and very comfortable chalets, cottages and villas, all privately owned but available for hire. Guests have the use of three lovely swimming pools, tennis courts and many of next-door Avalon Springs' facilities.

Montagu itself has its distinctions. It's set in a bountiful region of fruit farms and vineyards that produce, among other things, richly flavoured muscadels and fortified wines (the town hosts the annual Muscadel Festival).

To the north is an area known as the Koo, a rugged countryside that sustains fine orchards of apple, pear, peach and apricot trees. A popular attraction is the tractor/trailer ride that carries guests to the summit of the Langeberg Mountains every Wednesday and Saturday, and on public holidays.

Montagu's wildflower garden, formally named the Centenary Nature Reserve, embraces South Africa's largest concentration of mesembryanthemums, commonly called vygies, and from the middle of June to the end of October, on Tuesdays at 10h00, local ladies entertain visitors here to tea and cake.

Though founded less than a century and a half ago (in 1851), the town boasts an impressive 23 buildings proclaimed as national monuments, 14 of them in Long Street alone.

The oldest of these monuments, Joubert House, is part of the museum whose main section is located in what was once the mission church.

It now houses local-interest displays, among them a fine collection of herbs (these are for sale) and a gruesome relic of a murder long ago.

The exterior of Bredasdorp's Shipwreck Museum, which graphically records maritime tragedies along the South African coastline.

SHIPWRECK MUSEUM
Bredasdorp

Map: page 213, 3E
Turn south off the N2 at Caledon, onto the R316 to Bredasdorp (75 km). The museum is in the centre of town, close to the distinctive N G Church.
Details: Open Monday to Thursday 09h00-16h45; Fridays 09h00-15h45; Saturday 09h00-12h45; Sundays 11h00-12h30. Parking plentiful. Small admission charge.
Accommodation: Bredasdorp has hotels, a guesthouse and caravan/camping facilities.
Further information: Bredasdorp Shipwreck Museum, P O Box 235, Bredasdorp 7280, tel (02841) 4-1240; Suidpunt Publicity Association, P O Box 51, Bredasdorp 7280, tel (02841) 4-2584.

About 250 seagoing vessels have come to grief in the Cape south coast's moody waters since records were first kept, a litany of disaster graphically recounted in Bredasdorp's Shipwreck Museum.

Three of the oldest buildings in town have been beautifully renovated to serve as the museum complex. One of them, the Old Rectory, is a typical 19th-century Strandveld dwelling, though its individual components vary in character.

The bed and sitting rooms are simply appointed with, among other things, relics (washstand, medicine chest, wine cabinet and so forth) from the wrecks of the *Clan MacGregor* and the *Queen of the Thames*. The dining room is opulently Victorian. The quaint Strandveld Coach House next door sports an antique fire engine and various farm implements and farm vehicles.

Also adjoining the Old Rectory is the large Cape Dutch Gothic Church building that has worn several hats (bazaar, cinema, roller-skating rink as well as place of worship) over the decades since admitting its first congregation in 1868. It now functions as the Shipwreck Hall, centrepiece of the museum. Recorded sound effects, scale models and a poignant array of salvaged items immerse you in the doomed world of the *Birkenhead*, the *Arniston* and other casualties of the cruel sea.

SWELLENDAM

One of South Africa's oldest towns, Swellendam is home to a number of impressive historic features, among them the splendid Drostdy. The edifice, which originally served as the landdrost's (magistrate's) court and residence, is now the centrepiece of the Drostdy Museum, a cluster of charming buildings which together provide an intriguing insight into Swellendam's graceful, though occasionally turbulent, past.

The town began life in 1743 in what was then the far extremity of colonial encroachment, developing peacefully enough until the mid-1790s, when the local burghers started to rebel against the gross corruption of the officials of the ruling Dutch East India Company, and set up their own national assembly.

The rebels managed to hold out for three months before submitting to the new British military regime installed in Cape Town. Thereafter, Swellendam behaved itself impeccably, growing into the farming and commercial capital of the Overberg ('across the mountain') region, its long main street ranking among the busiest and most handsome of the 19th-century Cape's thoroughfares.

PLACES TO VISIT

Map: page 213, 4C
Swellendam is just off the N2, 227 km from Cape Town. Leaving the N2, turn left at the first intersection (Station Street), which arches around to become Swellengrebel Street.

Details: The Drostdy Museum is open Monday to Saturday 08h00-13h00 and 14h00-17h00. Admission charge. Plentiful parking.

Accommodation: Swellendam has 3 hotels (all within walking distance of the museum complex), self-catering accommodation and a caravan/camping park, delightfully set on the banks of the Cornlands River.

Further information: Swellendam Publicity Association, Oefeningshuis, P O Box 396, Swellendam 6740, tel (0291) 4-2770; The Town Clerk, P O Box 20, Swellendam 6740.

Swellendam's museum complex, set against a lovely mountain backdrop. The town, among South Africa's most historic, was once the capital of a short-lived 'republic'.

THE DROSTDY

Completed in 1747, the white-walled, thatched building originally conformed to a T-shape but was later (in 1813) enlarged to its present size. A small wine cellar ornamented with finely crafted plaster relief work was added around 1825. The Drostdy served as a model for many houses in the town. The Drostdy now houses some fine 18th- and 19th-century Cape furniture, and a collection of old animal-drawn vehicles can be seen in the barns.

The graceful symmetry of the 18th-century Drostdy, now a repository of Cape furniture and an intriguing exhibition of early wagons.

SWELLENDAM

Light from the dapple-shaded garden illuminates Mayville's charming entrance hall. House and furnishings reflect the lifestyle of a prosperous 19th-century country family.

THE AMBAGSWERF (CRAFTS GREEN)

This building behind the Old Gaol was constructed in the 1970s to exhibit the tools and equipment used by artisans and craftsmen of the past – blacksmiths, coppersmiths, millers, coopers and wainwrights (Swellendam was an important wagon-building centre in Victorian times). The water mill (originally part of the Drostdy property and re-created near its original site), horse mill and threshing floor represent the importance of wheat-farming in earlier times. Visitors can buy flour ground by the old water mill.

ZANDDRIFT

An old (1757) Cape Dutch farmhouse, that once stood near Bonnievale, was pulled down and reconstructed in the museum's grounds. It now functions as a restaurant.

MAYVILLE AND ITS ROSE GARDEN

The cottage is a delightful example (it dates from 1855) of transitional Cape Dutch-Georgian architecture, a theme carried through to its furnishings, the whole reflecting the comfortable lifestyle of a prosperous mid-Victorian platteland bourgeois family.

Pride of place, though, is taken by the enchanting Victorian-style rose garden, which comprises a duet of rectangular enclosures linked by various archways, a gazebo, and a lovely array of plants so arranged that you can follow changing tastes and trends among rose gardeners from the 17th to the 19th centuries. Some of the species are both rare and beautiful; the garden is in full bloom in the latter part of October.

THE OLD GAOL

Diagonally opposite the Drostdy, in Swellengrebel Street. The thatch-roofed Gaoler's Cottage next door also served as the post office (the man did double duty as postmaster). The apartment in front of the gaol became home to the local deputy sheriff and, in 1813, the complex was extended to provide a wing for the landdrost's secretary.

The Swellendam Museum's Ambagswerf (Crafts Green), a showplace of the crafts that sustained a self-sufficient frontier community.

SOUTHWEST CAPE

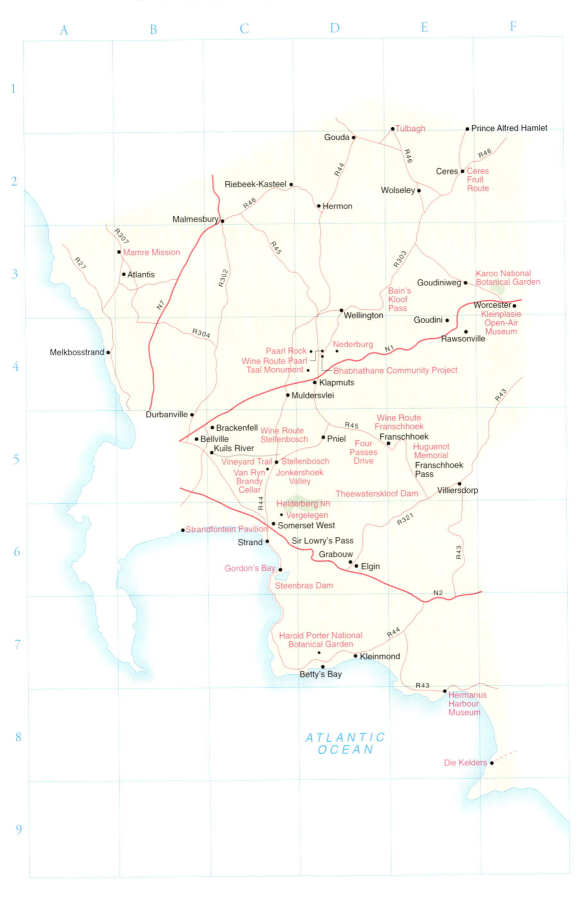

BAIN'S KLOOF PASS
Near Wellington

Map: page 225, 3D

From Cape Town take the N1 to the Klapmuts/Franschhoek off-ramp. Turn left on the R44 (Agter-Paarl), and continue to Wellington. Turn left into Retief Street and right into Church Street. Continue straight on to Bain's Kloof. Alternatively, take the N1 to Paarl and, from Main Street, follow the signposts to Wellington. Turn right into Church Street and continue straight on to the pass.

Details: September to November brings lush, green vegetation.

Accommodation: Hotel, self-catering and caravan/camping facilities are available in and around Wellington and Paarl.

Further information: Wellington Publicity Association, P O Box 695, Wellington 7655, tel (02211) 3-4604; Paarl Publicity Association, P O Box 47, Paarl 7622, tel (02211) 2-3829/2-4842. The Tweede Tol camp site (open 1 September to 15 May) has ablution facilities. Reservations: Cape Department of Nature Conservation, Private Bag X14, Paarl 7622, tel (02211) 61-1535 or their office in Elgin, tel (0225) 4301.

A winding wonderland of rock formations, mountain tops and tumbling water opens up as you drive the historic Bain's Kloof Pass, between the Boland town of Wellington and the Breede River Valley.

This dramatic 30-km pass between the Slanghoekberge and the Limietberge was built in the 1850s by Andrew Geddes Bain, the doyen of 19th-century road builders in southern Africa, and functioned for almost a century as the main route between the southwestern Cape and the interior. Apart from its tarred surface and a few reinforcing features, the road is much the same today as it was then, winding between rugged sandstone buttresses to the 579-m summit, where one may stop at Eerste Tol to have a

Bain's Kloof Pass, one of the greatest engineering feats of Andrew Geddes Bain, soars above the Witte River Gorge, with its lush, green vegetation and scattered boulders.

The Bains: road builders of the 19th century

In the annals of civil engineering in South Africa, the two Bains, Andrew Geddes and his son Thomas, enjoy an unprecedented pre-eminence. Between them these masterminds cut some of the most important and most challenging routes through the country's formidable southern coastal rampart, to create highways into the interior that are still very much in use today.

Andrew, a fun-loving Scot, had no formal training. He arrived at the Cape in 1816 to work as a saddler, and spent part of his young adulthood exploring trading possibilities in Tswana country (now Botswana). He also fought in the Eastern Cape's Frontier War of 1834/35. But he had a natural gift for engineering, took an interest in road-building and, in 1836, was awarded a medal for 'gratuitously superintending the construction of Van Ryneveld's Pass' in 1834. After some years, during which he farmed and built military roads on the Frontier, he went on to carve out roads over Mitchell's Pass (Ceres), Gydo Pass, and reconstructed Karoopoort. The precipitous Katberg Pass near Fort Beaufort was built shortly before his death in 1864.

The elder Bain had other talents too. He was an accomplished writer of popular verse in his lighter moments and, in more serious vein, he was a pioneering geologist, whose *Geology of South Africa*, published in 1853, broke new scientific ground. He was also an expert on palaeontology, unearthing a number of previously unknown fossil species.

His son Thomas was just as versatile. The Southern Cape's famed Prince Alfred's, Robinson, Garcia's and Swartberg passes, Cogman's Kloof, the George-Knysna road and the lovely drive from Cape Town's Sea Point, south to Hout Bay, all featured among his projects. In all, he built 24 passes (compared to his father's eight). He was also a surveyor of railway lines and served as District Engineer for the Railways, building the Roodezand (Nieuwekloof) Railway Pass near Tulbagh.

He also investigated the Orange River's potential for irrigation (now being profitably realized), the mineral resources of the Eastern Cape and Namaqualand, and the Free State's coal deposits. Like his father, he was an avid geologist and palaeontologist.

It must also be remembered that all of the Bains' road-building was achieved using unskilled convict labour – these forgotten miscreants must share in the glory of these monuments to engineering.

picnic and enjoy the scenery (no fires). Here a plaque records the construction of the pass. The views on your way up and from the top are spectacular, taking in the rich mosaic of the Berg River Valley, Paarl Mountain, Paardeberg, the wheatfields of the Swartland and Table Mountain. Two attractive hiking trails start from the Eerste Tol point.

The northern side of the pass follows a distinctive cleft through the mountains leading to the Witte River Valley – a steeply sided, boulder-strewn gorge filled with lush greenery and wildflowers, cascades and pools, giant boulders and such imposing features as the Montagu Rock, Bells Rock (named after colonial surveyor Charles Bell) and the huge overhang of Dacres Pulpit. Part-way down is the Tweede Tol camp site and picnic ground, starting point of a circular hike through the Wolwekloof. Several other charted walks, ranging from a gentle ramble to a strenuous hike, crisscross the wider area. Best known, and certainly one of the most challenging, is the 37-km two-day Limietberg Trail (a section of the popular Boland Hiking Trail) that leads from the Hawequas Forest Station, near the foot of Du Toit's Kloof Pass, to the upper slopes of the 1 174-m Limietberg, and then down to Tweede Tol. The views *en route* are stunning.

A detailed map of the various walks and hikes is available from the Tweede Tol camp manager, and you'll need a permit before setting out. The pass was declared a national monument in 1980.

Hikers in the Bain's Kloof area penetrate magnificent scenery, including dramatic rock formations, breathtaking mountain views and abundant plant life.

BHABHATHANE COMMUNITY PROJECT
Near Paarl

The Xhosa name *Bhabhathane* means 'butterfly', which illuminates the transition this self-help weaving centre has undergone, from its modest beginnings to confident and colourful maturity.

The project was launched in 1987 by the local Lutheran minister and a small group of women from Mbekweni, Paarl's adjacent township, in an effort to do something positive about the area's appalling unemployment problem. It turned out to be a highly successful effort.

The workshop is now producing a delightful range of hand-woven carpets, tapestries, runners and cushions made from a 60:40 blend of double-spun karakul wool and mohair.

The designs are attractive and varied, though if you feel you can do better, just give the craftspersons a sketch and they'll translate it faithfully into the finished product. The bright, washable, cotton rag-rugs are also a popular line.

Visitors can call at either the workshop in Paarl's Drommedaris Street or at the shop in the Ikhwezi Community Centre on the farm *Vlakkeland*, between Paarl and Wellington. *Bhabhathane* is an attractive destination, offering charm and originality.

Map: page 225, 4D
Take the N1 to Paarl. Workshop: SBDC Hive, Drommedaris Street, Dal Josafat 7646. Shop: Ikhwezi Community Centre, Farm *Vlakkeland*, just off the Van Riebeeck road (R303), between Paarl and Wellington.
Details: Open Monday to Friday 08h30-17h00; weekends and public holidays by appointment, tel (02211) 68-1393/68-2611.

SOUTHWEST CAPE

CERES FRUIT ROUTE
Ceres basin

Map: page 225, 2E
Take the N1 to Klapmuts. Bear left for Wellington and Gouda on the R44, and follow the signs to Ceres. Alternatively, branch off onto the R303 at Wellington, following the signs to Ceres.
Details: Best months are November (cherry-picking) to April.
Accommodation: The region is well served by hotel, self-catering and country-lodge accommodation, and by caravan/camping facilities.
Further information: Captour Information Bureau, P O Box 863, Cape Town 8000, tel (021) 418-5214; Ceres Publicity Association, P O Box 563, Ceres 6835, tel (0233) 6-1287; Wellington Publicity Association, P O Box 695, Wellington 7655, tel (0211) 3-4604; or Tulbagh Valley Publicity Association, P O Box 277, Tulbagh 6820, tel (0236) 30-1348.

This leisurely and interesting journey introduces you to the charming little town of Ceres and its very tranquil surrounding countryside.

The name, taken from the Roman goddess of agriculture, aptly depicts one of South Africa's richest and most beautiful deciduous fruit-growing regions. The Ceres basin, flanked by the high mountains of the Witzenberg, Hex River and Skurweberg ranges, yields nearly 12 percent of all the apples and 40 percent of the peaches grown in the country, 60 percent of its export pears and, for good measure, cherries, nectarines, plums, grapes and vast quantities of onions and potatoes. One of the largest cold-storage complexes in the country is situated in Ceres, which is also regarded as the fruit-juice capital of the country.

Farms, co-operatives, farm stalls, packing houses and others have combined to provide a comprehensive insight into the industry. A variety of special fruit tours, organized both locally and from Cape Town, runs from December through to April, and may last anything from one hour to two days.

Included in the various options are good, old-fashioned farm hospitality for overnighters, an orchard trail, and interesting trips around the harvesting and packing processes.

These are the formal tours, but you may prefer to go it alone along one of the recommended routes. These average a 275-km round trip from Cape Town.

Once you are in the area, there's a choice of itinerary. For example, you could begin at Wellington and enter the Ceres basin by way of Bain's Kloof Pass *(see separate entry)*, or drive from Gouda over Nieuwekloof Pass. Both routes turn off the N1 at Klapmuts, and then follow the R44 through the lovely orchards and vineyards around Agter-Paarl.

Alternatively, travel via the Huguenot tunnel and Du Toit's Kloof Pass. Whichever way you approach, you'll pass through three growing areas: the Warm and Koue Bokkeveld area around Ceres, Tulbagh and Wolseley.

Take your time, make a day of it, two days, even a week. The region has a selection of excellent hotels, guesthouses and self-catering chalets. If you do decide on a self-drive outing, though, contact one or more of the local Publicity Associations for guidance on the specifics: where to go, where to stay, sights to see, recommended walks and guided tours. Check the appropriate telephone directory for numbers of these associations. Remember also the Ceres Festival, which takes place every May and includes a half-marathon, cycling and other activities.

Ceres is only one of several fruit routes; also highly recommended are the Four Passes *(see separate entry)* and Breede River itineraries.

Winter snows cover the ground in Ceres which, in springtime, thaws out to become one of the richest fruit-producing areas in the country.

SOUTHWEST CAPE

Sturdy steps lead down the steep cliffs to Die Kelders, where underground waters rise up to form pools of clear water in the sandstone hollows.

DIE KELDERS
South coast

Lady Anne Barnard, renowned diarist of the first English occupation of the Cape, once enjoyed a dip in the deep, crystal-clear pools of 'the cellars', a string of underground caverns through which a warm and slightly saline stream flows. That was in 1798, when the waters had already gained their reputation as a curative agent for rheumatism and other ailments. However, records show that early farmers in the area knew of the existence of the pools as early as 1712.

The setting, in a cliff overlooking the broad sweep of Walker Bay and its fringe of rolling white dunes, is spectacular. On the heights above, there's an attractive little hotel from which you can watch southern right whales cruising along the coast between August and December.

Nearby is the cosy fishing hamlet of Gansbaai, a pleasant village with a photogenic harbour. A little further along, at the eastern end of Walker Bay, the sea washes with deceptive smoothness over the reefs and sunken rocks of Danger Point, one of the southern shoreline's most hazardous features.

It was off the point that the British troopship *Birkenhead* came to grief in 1852, with the loss of 445 lives, most of them soldiers. Heroes to a man, they stood to rigid attention on the tilting decks as the civilian passengers were ferried to safety. Some of the survivors settled in the area to merge comfortably into the local farming community. Their descendants, though they bear English surnames, are almost exclusively Afrikaans-speaking.

Map: page 225, 8F
From Cape Town take the N2 to Botrivier. Turn off south on the R43 and follow the coastal road through Hawston, Hermanus and Stanford to a point about 5 km from Gansbaai. Die Kelders (signposted) is on your right.
Details: The caves are closed to the public.
Accommodation: Apart from De Kelders Hotel, Gansbaai also has a hotel, together with caravan/camping sites.
Further information: De Kelders Hotel, P O Box 80, Gansbaai 7220, tel (02834) 4-0421.

The Southwest Cape is a treasure-trove of colourful fynbos. Here fluffy white blooms of Metalasia densa are flanked by the vivid yellow bietou and the deep pink Erica irregularis.

SOUTHWEST CAPE

FOUR PASSES DRIVE
Winelands-Overberg

Map: page 225, 5/6C/D/E
Take the N2 from Cape Town and branch off on the R310 through Stellenbosch and the Helshoogte Pass, to the R45 junction. Turn right (signposted Franschhoek) and follow the R45 to its junction with the R321, close to Theewaterskloof Dam. Follow the R321 over Viljoen's Pass to Grabouw. Turn right onto the N2.
Details: Road conditions are excellent throughout the year, though Sir Lowry's Pass can test the nerves on a windy day. The scenic drive is at its best in the dry months. Plenty of pleasant stops along the way, including farms on the wine routes.
Further information: Captour Information Bureau, P O Box 863, Cape Town 8000, tel (021) 418-5214; Stellenbosch Tourist Information Bureau, P O Box 368, Stellenbosch 7600, tel (021) 883-3584; *Franschhoek Vallée Tourisme*, P O Box 178, Franschhoek 7690, tel (02212) 3603; Elgin/Grabouw Municipality, P O Box 32, Grabouw 7160, tel (024) 59-2501; Gordon's Bay Municipality, P O Box 3, Gordon's Bay 7150, tel (024) 56-2135; and Somerset West Municipality, P O Box 19, Somerset West 7129, tel (024) 852-2421.

This circular route, ranking among the country's most splendid scenic drives, takes you from Cape Town through the winelands (Stellenbosch is your first port of call), over the Franschhoek mountains and into the Overberg. It then returns through the fruit-growing areas of Elgin and Grabouw, the lofty Hottentots-Holland mountain range and the coastal centres of Gordon's Bay, Strand and Somerset West.

The four passes in the name are Helshoogte, Franschhoek, Viljoen's and Sir Lowry's, each of which gives breathtaking views of this loveliest of regions. Among highlights along the way (travelling clockwise from Somerset West) are:

From the Helshoogte Pass, there are panoramic views of the carefully manicured vineyards of Stellenbosch.

■ **The Bottelary road,** (R44) on the way to Stellenbosch: a delightful drive through vineyards and orchards.
■ **Stellenbosch:** a town of grace, charm and historical interest *(see separate entry).*
■ **The Helshoogte Pass,** which links Stellenbosch with the lovely Drakenstein Valley. Pine plantations obscure the view along some stretches, but the route is still strikingly scenic. Look out for the high Simonsberg (1 390 m) on your left. On the other side of the pass, before the road (R310) joins the R45, are the Rhodes fruit farms, still among the most productive of the country's growing areas. They were bought on behalf of financier-politician Cecil John Rhodes, and are now run by the Anglo-American group. Also close by is Boschendal, the lovely Cape Dutch-style manor house and wine estate *(see page 256).*

The apple orchards: South Africa's gardens of plenty

The road leading eastwards over spectacular Sir Lowry's Pass takes you down to the charming orchards of Elgin and Grabouw, among South Africa's top three apple-growing areas (the others are the Ceres district, and the Eastern Cape's Long Kloof).

The fruit made its first appearance in the country in 1654, when Jan van Riebeeck, ever the enterprising horticulturist, introduced seedlings from the island of St Helena and nurtured five of the trees on his farm *Bosheuvel*. The Cape's first crop, though, consisted of small, tart 'wine apples' grown in the Company's Garden from stock brought in from Holland. It was harvested on 17 April 1662.

Today, over 12 million apple trees grace the three districts, most reaching maturity after eight years, and remaining productive for upwards of thirty.

The modern industry began in the early 1900s when Sir Antonie Viljoen experimented in the Elgin area with the well-known English Cox's Orange Pippin. The variety didn't flourish, but the test-runs provided valuable data for future plantings of more suitable types. Apples that now thrive include the ever popular Granny Smith (imported from Australia), Golden Delicious, the superb Red Delicious (from America), White Winter Pearmain, York Imperial, and such relative newcomers to the scene as Top Red and Gala.

■ **Franschhoek** ('French Corner'), the home of the early Huguenot immigrants, and now a pleasant little town set in the splendid Franschhoek Valley. The town and surrounds are known for their superb restaurants.

■ **Franschhoek Pass**, finished in 1825 to link hitherto isolated Franschhoek with the wider world. The unusually long bridge, 13 km from town, is an attractive example of dressed-stone masonry.

■ **Theewaterskloof Dam**, a large and rather inviting stretch of water that serves as both a reservoir and a playground for watersport enthusiasts.

■ **Viljoen's Pass**, which cuts through the imposing Groenland Mountains, offers a number of exceptional views over the Riviersonderend Valley to the east. The pass was named after Sir Antonie Viljoen, who pioneered the local apple industry way back in the early 1900s.

■ **Grabouw and Elgin**, twin centres of the country's premier apple-growing region, producing superb crops of Golden Delicious, Granny Smith and other varieties. Visitors are welcome, but don't just pop in during the frenetically busy harvesting season. Contact the local information office about laid-on tours.

■ **Sir Lowry's Pass**, named in honour of Sir Galbraith Lowry Cole (Cape governor, 1825-33), cuts through the Hottentots-Holland mountain range to open up awesome vistas of ocean, coastal plain, and rugged uplands. A digression at the base of the pass will lead you through Gordon's Bay, and then on to the Strand and Somerset West urban complex, before rejoining the N2 for Cape Town.

GORDON'S BAY
East of Cape Town

Little wonder that Gordon's Bay ranks among the region's most popular holiday and retirement centres. The scenically superb marine drive through the Hottentots-Holland Mountains looks down on a picture-postcard village and harbour that have slept soundly in the sun since the later 17th century, when Simon van der Stel governed the Cape. In those days it was known as Visch Hoek, later renamed in honour of Robert Jacob Gordon, the Dutch colony's last military commander (Gordon explored the coast in the 1770s, and died – by his own hand – after the 1795 British occupation).

The harbour in its present form, though, is a relatively new feature: it was built just after the Second World War and served for three decades as base for the South African merchant navy's Louis Botha Training College. Now it's given over entirely to commercial fishing boats and, more noticeably, to a fleet of elegant leisure craft.

Gordon's Bay offers sailing, safe bathing (at Bikini and Main beaches; the rock pools are ideal for children) and watersports. There are numerous attractive fishing spots along the coast, or you can hire a deep-sea boat and try your hand at tuna and marlin-fishing.

The waters around Gordon's Bay are home to both Indian and Atlantic Ocean species. Be careful when fishing from the rocks: freak waves are common.

There's plenty laid on for visitors: pleasure cruises, paddle-skis for hire, bowls, tennis, squash, golf; restaurants (predictably, seafood features prominently); a top-rate hotel; supermarket, boutiques, speciality shops (selling crafts and gifts, hand-knitted carpets and fishing bait, amongst other things); three holiday resorts with chalets and caravan/camping facilities, and a private fun-park.

There are some lovely, scenic drives in the area, both along the coast and inland, among the mountains and apple orchards. It is also within easy reach of the winelands. For strollers, there's a beach-front flanked by lawns and paving, and Milkwood Park, whose pathway also runs along the shoreline. Slightly more demanding is the 7-km Danie Miller Hiking Trail across the mountain slopes (superb views).

Also in Gordon's Bay is the new Harbour Island development, consisting of an attractive small-boat harbour, inland waterways, housing and waterfront business premises.

Map: page 225, 6C
The N2 from Cape Town will take you towards Somerset West and Strand. Turn right onto the coastal road (R44) just before you get to Strand, and continue for 5 km along the marine drive to Gordon's Bay.
Details: The harbour is open to visitors at all times.
Accommodation: Excellent hotel; three resorts offering self-catering facilities and caravan/camping sites. The municipal holiday resort, Hendon Park, is situated next to the sea, and from here the main bathing area can be reached easily.
Further information: Gordon's Bay Municipality, P O Box 3, Gordon's Bay 7150, tel (024) 56-2135.

The new harbour development at Gordon's Bay – a popular venue for watersport enthusiasts.

SOUTHWEST CAPE

HAROLD PORTER NATIONAL BOTANICAL GARDEN
Betty's Bay

Map: page 225, 7D
Turn off from the N2 to Gordon's Bay, about 60 km from Cape Town. Continue through Gordon's Bay, following the coast to Betty's Bay (42 km). The garden's entrance is a short drive to the north. The access route is clearly signposted.

Details: Open daily throughout the year 08h00-18h00; tearoom 08h30-17h30. Picnic site, toilets and parking at entrance. Entrance fee charged. Comprehensive brochure and trail guide available. Selection of fynbos plants available for sale to the public.

Accommodation: None within the reserve, but Kleinmond, on the coast just to the east, has hotel and caravan/camping facilities.

Further information: Harold Porter National Botanical Garden, P O Box 35, Betty's Bay 7141, tel (02823) 2-9311.

Watsonias, gladioli, everlastings and many other plants of the hugely diverse and botanically fascinating Cape floral kingdom are the stars of this scenically attractive little reserve, just off the coastal road leading east from Betty's Bay. The flowering season lasts from October through to February, though the lovely nerine lily blooms in March. Look out for the red disa in December and January, and especially for the ericas, 50 species of which grow in this one small area which has the biggest number of plant species in a single location in the world.

Five of the Harold Porter's 188 ha are cultivated (the plants are labelled), the rest given over to heath-type macchia vegetation, or fynbos, and crisscrossed by a contour of mountain walks. The routes are designed for all ages and fitness levels. The Rod Smitheman Interpretive Trail focuses on plant identification and the varied nature of the landscape. Highest point is the Platberg Peak (917 m above sea level), and the most scenic spot is Leopard's Kloof, access to which requires a special permit from the curator.

About 60 species of bird are attracted by the multicoloured floral displays, among them ground woodpeckers, Cape thrushes, sugarbirds and sunbirds. Resident mammals include buck, baboons and such small species as porcupines, mongooses and spotted genets.

The garden's tearoom serves English and continental breakfasts, light lunches and tea-time fare.

The Harold Porter National Botanical Garden (above) offers walks winding into the ravines, revealing a bounty of indigenous fynbos.
Right: A ramble in the wilds holds the promise of great adventure for these two youngsters and their furry friend.

A swathe of glowing watsonias illuminates the foothills of the Helderberg Nature Reserve.

HELDERBERG NATURE RESERVE
Somerset West

Magnificent scenery, a rich bird life, fine walking trails and a wealth of proteas, ericas, pelargoniums and bulbous plants are the drawcards of this 363-ha sanctuary on the outskirts of Somerset West. The high, and often cloud-wreathed, Helderberg peak, part of the Hottentots-Holland range, provides an impressive backdrop. The reserve stretches about halfway up its slopes.

A number of colour-coded circular walks, lasting from half an hour to three hours, start from the entrance area, the longest leading you to Disa Gorge where, from December through to March, you'll find eye-catching displays of wildflowers, among them the 'Pride of Table Mountain' *(Disa uniflora)*.

Here, too, are a charming waterfall and indigenous stands of stinkwood, yellowwood and ironwood trees. Longer and more strenuous hikes have been charted along the Helderberg's upper slopes, others below the rugged krantzes. The peak itself is only for competent climbers. The vistas from the summit, embracing the sea and shoreline, the mountains to the north and the Cape Peninsula to the west, are breathtaking.

The area's bird life, some of which is unique to the region, includes Victorin's scrub warblers, black eagles and mountain buzzards. Within the oak-shaded picnic site is a herbarium, as well as a field museum/information centre.

Map: page 225, 5/6, C/D
Follow the N2 east from Cape Town to Somerset West. Take the turn-off onto the R44. Turn right into Main Street at the first set of traffic lights on the R44. At the second set of traffic lights, turn left into Lourensford Road and follow the Helderberg signs through the suburbs. Turn left into Hillcrest Road, right into Reservoir Road, and left into Verster Street.

Details: Open throughout the year. April to October 07h00-18h00; November to March 07h00-20h00. Parking available. Entrance free. A tearoom opens for business seven days a week. No dogs, cycles or fires are permitted.

Accommodation: Hotel, guesthouse, self-catering and caravan/camping facilities are available in and around Somerset West.

Further information: Information Bureau, P O Box 19, Somerset West 7129, tel (024) 51-4022; or Helderberg Nature Reserve, P O Box 19, Somerset West 7129, tel (024) 51-6982.

HERMANUS HARBOUR MUSEUM
Hermanus

Map: page 225, 8E
Hermanus is 120 km from Cape Town via Botrivier. Take the N2 east to either Botrivier or Caledon, turning south to the coast on either the R43 or R320. Alternatively, take the coastal route (R44) leading from the outskirts of Strand past Gordon's Bay, Pringle Bay and Kleinmond, to join the R43 (157 kilometres). The Old Harbour is on Hermanus's Marine Drive.

Details: Open Monday to Saturday throughout the year 09h00-13h00 and 14h00-17h00; closed Sundays and public holidays.

Accommodation: There are excellent hotels, guesthouses and self-catering accommodation in and around Hermanus. There are caravan/camping facilities available nearby, and at Onrus (7 km along the coast) and in the Salmonsdam Nature Reserve.

Further information: Hermanus Publicity Association, P O Box 117, Hermanus 7200, tel (0283) 2-2629; also Old Harbour Museum, P O Box 118, Hermanus 7200, tel (0283) 2-1475; Photographic Museum, tel (0283) 70-0418.

The evocative, open-air museum focuses on a cosy little natural harbour that functioned as the centre of a thriving fishing industry for over a century.

Hermanus, set between grand mountains and the sea, started life in the 1830s as home to an independent-minded teacher and shepherd named Hermanus Pieters and, over the following decades, attracted an increasing number of commercial fishermen, whalers and lime-makers (the coast here is rich in seashells). Lately, these have been joined by an increasing number of sporting anglers, holiday-makers and affluent retirees.

The Old Harbour, too small to cope with the number of working and leisure craft that were pressing in, was eventually superseded by a fine new marine complex, and now serves as both a showcase of nostalgia and a tacit memorial to the hardy fisherfolk of yesteryear.

The Old Harbour's work-worn but carefully restored little boats date from between 1855, when they were powered by sails and oars, and 1961; their gunwales are scarred by the action of countless fishing lines. Look inside the earlier ones, and you'll see the wooden partitions that separated the crew members' catches. On the rocks above the harbour are the 'bokkem' stands, used for wind-drying the fish.

Scenes of the old days – boats off-loading, women and children crowding round – are time-frozen in an exhibition of sepia photographs inside a small stone annexe to the museum.

The building, located behind Lemm's Corner, originally served as the Dutch Reformed Church's local Sunday school, and was moved stone by stone from its original site. Among other preserved structures are a number of the original fishermen's cottages, including the oldest house in town (now a coffee and curio shop). Other cottages serve as a florist's and restaurant/tapas bar. Lemm's Corner is also the scene of a colourful weekend craft market, which helps raise funds for the museum's upkeep.

Once bristling with fishermen, the Old Harbour at Hermanus is now preserved as a museum, and is the venue for a variety of maritime festivals and happy summer-holiday picnics.

SOUTHWEST CAPE

HUGUENOT MEMORIAL
Franschhoek

Franschhoek's imposing, but delicately graceful monument, set against a stunning mountain backdrop, honours the memory of the French Protestant immigrants who settled in the area during the late 1680s and 1690s. Though few in number, they had a salutary effect on the local scene, bringing with them not only badly needed skills (farming, viticulture, building), but also some of the cultural refinements of Europe.

The memorial incorporates a lot of symbolism. Dominant features are the three elegant arches, representing the Holy Trinity, surmounted by a small golden sun (Righteousness) and a plain cross (Faith). Standing before the arches is a female figure holding a Bible in her right hand and a broken chain (Religious Liberty) in her left; *fleurs-de-lis* decorate her dress (Nobility); she straddles the earth (Freedom of Spirit), and she is casting off her cloak (Oppression). Other symbols include a harp (the Arts), a sheaf of corn and a vine (Agriculture), and a spinning wheel (Industry).

Alongside the memorial is the Huguenot Memorial Museum, a building modelled on, and incorporating parts of, an elegant, now demolished Cape Dutch mansion called *Saasveld*. The mansion was designed by French architect Louis Thibault and erected in 1791 on Cape Town's Kloof Street.

Map: page 225, 5E
From Cape Town take the N1 towards Paarl. Just before Suider-Paarl, turn right onto the R45, which will take you to Franschhoek. You'll find the monument and museum on Lambrechts Street.
Details: The complex is open Monday to Saturday 09h00-13h00 and 14h00-17h00, and Sundays 14h00-17h00; closed Christmas Day and Good Friday. Guided tours in spring and summer. Small admission fee. Parking available.
Accommodation: Franschhoek and its surroundings offer plenty of hotel, country-lodge and self-catering accommodation. Caravan/camping facilities are available in the general area. The local restaurants are renowned; the farm stalls especially inviting.
Further information: Huguenot Memorial Museum, P O Box 37, Franschhoek 7690, tel (02212) 2532/2673; or the *Franschhoek Vallée Tourisme*, P O Box 178, Franschhoek 7690, tel (02212) 3603.

The foyer of the Huguenot Museum, with its gleaming floors and fine furniture, preserves part of the rich heritage of the Huguenots.

Graceful gables of the Cape

The first thing you associate with Cape Dutch architecture is the gable, the decorative upper part of the wall – most prominently above the front door, often at the rear as well, sometimes at the ends.

The first gables were simple affairs: a mere break in the thatch of a sharply steeped roof to make space for a window into the loft. But later, in the skilled hands of European craftsmen and slaves imported from the East, the feature became more ornamental, and in some cases, highly elaborate. A number of distinctive types evolved, the most common perhaps the 'holbol', which had alternate convex and concave curves that took on, over the years, curlicued edge-mouldings and intricate patterns of scallop-shells, stars, birds, stylized feathers and the like.

The Cape's earliest surviving gable (on Joostenberg, near Paarl, and dated 1757) is of the similar-sounding 'bolbol' variety, which has a series of convex curves on each side of its rounded apex. Later designs from around 1790 onwards featured more classical elements, with columns, fluted pilasters and triangular pediments. The related 'halsgewel' is seen perhaps at its most attractive in Cape Town's magnificent Constantia Manor House.

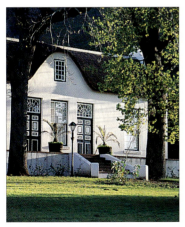

The Cape Dutch style of architecture is unique to South Africa. Typical of the style is the gable, ranging from the simple dormer gable of the thatched home on the left, to the carved and moulded example on the right.

SOUTHWEST CAPE

Jonkershoek Valley lies hemmed in below ancient slopes, covered here with a profusion of spring flowers.

JONKERSHOEK VALLEY
Near Stellenbosch

Map: page 225, 5C
Take the Jonkershoek road out of Stellenbosch. Follow the signs. Jonkershoek begins about 10 km from the town centre.
Accommodation: Stellenbosch offers an extensive range of accommodation, from camping sites to luxury hotels.
Further information: Stellenbosch Tourist Information Bureau, P O Box 368, Stellenbosch 7600, tel (021) 883-3584.

Scenic splendour and a wealth of sightseeing interests are the enticements of the valley, which lies to the east of Stellenbosch. Here the Eerste River rises to make its way through the green and pleasant countryside, at one point cascading over a waterfall.

To the south are the towering heights of the Stellenboschberg and Haelkop, to the north a dramatic twosome known as The Twins of Jonkershoek.

The main features of interest include:
■ **Neil Ellis Wines**. Based on the farm *Oude Nektar*, one of the two historic homesteads in the valley, which was built in 1815 (though the land was granted to and farmed by freed slaves way back in 1692). It is notable for its dignified Cape Dutch frontage and intricate gable. Restaurant facilities. Wine-tastings and sales Monday to Friday 09h00-16h30 (and Saturdays 09h00-12h30, October to April). Contact Neil Ellis Wines, P O Box 917, Stellenbosch 7599, tel (021) 887-0649 for details.
■ **The neo-Classical splendour of Lanzerac**, completed in 1830 and now one of South Africa's most elegant country hotels. Some of Lanzerac's outbuildings are much older than the main house; the original wine cellar serves as the reception area and restaurant, various outhouses as bedrooms, the stables as a cocktail bar. The grounds, shaded by oaks and plane trees, are beautiful. Contact Lanzerac Hotel, P O Box 4, Stellenbosch 7600, tel (021) 887-1132.
■ **Assegaaibosch Nature Reserve**, on the northern slopes of the Stellenboschberg, and adjacent to the Jonkershoek State Forest. The 168-ha reserve is primarily a sanctuary for mountain fynbos (heath) and its rare proteas. For visitors, there are short walks, the most pleasant perhaps being a 2,5-km circular trail leading up the hillside. Picnic and braai spots near the entrance, and a 5-ha wildflower garden with labelled specimens. The Jonkershoek State Forest offers longer trails. Permits are obtainable from Cape Nature Conservation, Private Bag X1, Uniedal 7612, tel (021) 886-5858, or at the entrance to the forest.
■ **The Jonkershoek Fisheries Station**, one of the country's oldest and largest hatcheries, breeds trout for distribution

Delicately decorated with garlands, the gable of the Oude Nektar farmhouse rises above its beautifully tended gardens.

to rivers and dams throughout southern Africa, and they're open to the public. Bass, tilapia (bream) and other freshwater fish are also nurtured; the station's aquarium is stocked with such local species as yellowfish and Cape kurper, and exotics such as bluegill sunfish and banded bream. There's a range of informative literature available at the reception area. Open Monday to Friday 08h15-16h30. For more information contact Jonkershoek Nature Conservation Station, Private Bag 5014, Stellenbosch 7599, tel (021) 887-0184.

■ **Hottentots-Holland Nature Reserve** is a magnificent 26 000-ha stretch of rugged mountain slope and deep, thickly wooded valley, gorge and precipitous cliff. Many watercourses rise in the area. The reserve is known for its scenery, its bird life (110 species), and especially its floral wealth. More than three dozen plant species found here are classed as threatened. Visitors can drive as far as the Jonkershoek State Forest (or, from the opposite direction, the Grabouw and Nuweberg nature conservation stations off the R321) but will then have to proceed on foot along part of the challenging Boland Hiking Trail. Open throughout the year, but accessible only via the Boland Hiking Trail. Contact Cape Nature Conservation, Private Bag X1, Uniedal 7612, tel (021) 886-5858. There are picnic spots in the adjacent Jonkershoek, Nuweberg and Grabouw state forests.

Jonkershoek Trout Hatchery, established in 1893, is one of the oldest fish-breeding centres in the Southwest Cape. Tours of the hatcheries and the aquarium can be arranged.

A flamboyant blanket of gazanias cloaks the veld in the Karoo National Botanical Garden.

KAROO NATIONAL BOTANICAL GARDEN
Worcester

A wealth of unusual plants draws visitors to the 154-ha Karoo National Botanical Garden, just one hour's drive to the north of Worcester.

The garden lies within South Africa's winter rainfall area, and boasts a varied and colourful plant population.

The best time to visit is in springtime, when the Namaqualand daisies, mesembryanthemums (vygies), gazanias, ursinias and felicias are at their best.

Spring bulbs include such varieties as freesias, tritonias, lachenalias, drosanthemums and bulbinellas.

Autumn, spring and early summer are the best times to walk the garden's many natural trails, which take you into the heart of this natural flower display.

Summers are hot and the winters are cool and wet, with occasional snowfalls on the Brandwacht Mountains north of the garden.

Early winter sees the blooming of colourful oxalis, while later in winter, beautiful flowering aloes start making their appearance.

Map: page 225, 3F
Three kilometres north of Worcester on the N1 you'll see the Botanical Garden sign on your right.

Details: Open daily 07h30-16h30. Admission fee during peak flowering season only (free for all educational groups). Parking, toilet and lecture-hall facilities. Kiosk open 10h00-16h00 during peak periods. Guided tours can be arranged at the office.

Accommodation: Hotel, self-catering accommodation and camping/caravanning facilities available in and around Worcester.

Further information: Karoo National Botanical Garden, P O Box 152, Worcester 6849, tel (0231) 7-0785.

SOUTHWEST CAPE

KLEINPLASIE OPEN-AIR MUSEUM
Worcester

Map: page 225, 3F
Kleinplasie lies on the outskirts of Worcester. Travel east on High Street, turn southeast onto the R60 for Robertson. Follow the signs to Kleinplasie on your left.
Details: Open Monday to Saturday 09h00-16h30; and on Sundays 10h30-16h30.
Accommodation: Self-catering chalets in the complex. Contact the Worcester Agricultural Society, P O Box 59, Worcester 6849, tel (0231) 7-0091.
Further information: Kleinplasie Open-Air Museum, P O Box 557, Worcester 6849, tel (0231) 2-2225/6; Worcester Publicity Association, 75 High Street, Worcester 6850, tel (0231) 7-1408.

The lifestyles of the early Cape Dutch farmers are vividly portrayed at the Kleinplasie Open-Air Museum, on the outskirts of Worcester. Replicas of the houses and buildings they lived and worked in create an authentic spirit of their times.

The daily activities of this 'living' museum introduce you to the homely arts of bread-baking, tobacco-twisting, candle-making, wheat-milling, iron-forging, and other self-reliant disciplines. Special activities include the roasting of coffee beans, distilling of the fiery alcoholic brew, 'witblitz' (white lightning), jam-making, soap-making, the plucking of down, and the traditional baking of farm delicacies such as milk tart. There is also a variety of seasonal presentations, such as grape-pressing, sheep-shearing, plants of the veld and dairy month.

The museum has a tearoom and a restaurant where traditional lunches are served. There is also a museum shop where visitors can buy farm products. The baked goods, jams, chutneys and, of course, the heady witblitz are worth sampling. Nearby is the KWV's Wine House restaurant and wine cellar (the heart of the Worcester Wine Route).

An old train takes visitors on a nostalgic trip to the new extension, which has on display agricultural equipment and tools used until the 1940s. On the drawing board is a replica of an early rural village, which will include buildings such as a cartwright's shop, a roller-mill, church, general dealer, school and hotel.

An employee of the Kleinplasie Open-Air Museum shows visitors how early Cape Dutch cooks baked their bread on an open fire.

MAMRE MISSION
Mamre

Map: page 225, 3B
Turn right off the R27 north of Cape Town onto the R307, to skirt the industrial town of Atlantis. Mamre is about 5 km further on. Alternatively, carry on along the R27 for a further 9 km and turn right (signpost Mamre). The village is 10 km further on.
Details: The water mill is open on weekdays 09h00-12h00 and 13h00-17h00; and the church may be visited with prior permission from the Moravian Mission.
Further information: Moravian Church, P O Box 2, Mamre 7347, tel (0226) 6-1117.

A beautiful little church, its gabled parsonage and a cluster of picturesque, whitewashed, black-thatched cottages greet you as you proceed down Mamre's Main Street.

The village, some 55 km north of Cape Town, off the R27 coastal route, was founded in 1808 when Governor the Earl of Caledon urged the German Moravian Church to start a mission settlement for the impoverished Khoikhoi people of the area.

Mamre was then known as Groene Kloof, a bleak place that originated over a century earlier as a military outpost, and then as a cattle post. The Moravians and their new flock gave it a fresh face, a new purpose and a new life. The intention from the beginning was to create a productive, self-supporting community, its

Gently framed by autumn leaves, the attractive water mill at Mamre was restored by the Rembrandt Group in 1973 as a museum.

SOUTHWEST CAPE

members living by Christian precepts and working as farmers and craftsmen, and it proved gratifyingly successful.

Wheat-growing and market-gardening provided the impetus, but the men were also trained in bricklaying and carpentry, tanning and smithing, the women in hat-making – skills that brought some prosperity and a lot of respectability and self-esteem.

The church was dedicated in 1818; a horse-drawn mill made its appearance in 1830, to be replaced in 1844 by a fine new water mill which, though it fell prey to neglect, has been carefully restored and is now something of a showpiece. In 1854 Groene Kloof was renamed from a Biblical passage: 'Then Abraham removed his tent, and came and dwelt in the plain of Mamre.'

Today Mamre is a much bigger residential centre, many of its inhabitants commuting daily to work in Cape Town and its industrial northern suburbs, but the mission still enjoys a pre-eminent place in the community – and the legacies of a charmingly well-ordered past remain intact.

NEDERBURG
Paarl

Arguably the most important event on the South African wine calendar is the April Nederburg Wine Auction – where case lots of the Cape's finest wines are offered for sale to merchants, aficionados, collectors, investors and private buyers. They come from all corners of the world to enjoy the sales and the convivial atmosphere, the tasting, food stalls and fashion parade.

The Nederburg homestead, set in the wide sweep of the Klein Drakenstein countryside, belongs to the Stellenbosch Farmers' Winery (SFW) group, serving as an 'official' building and something of a showcase, but for most of its 200-year lifespan it was the lived-in, much-loved home of a succession of dedicated wine-farming families.

Nederburg's origins were humble enough. In 1791 the land was granted to Philippus Wolvaart, whose immigrant father had worked as a stable hand and later as a tanner in the rugged young Cape Colony. Philippus named his new farm after Sebastiaan Nederburgh, commissioner-general of the Dutch East India Company at the time, and nine years later erected a fine manor house, whose exterior, until well into the 20th century, remained unchanged in form and character – an unusual occurrence in the annals of Cape Dutch architecture.

The homestead was built to the classic Cape-country, H-shape floor plan, with

Map: page 225, 4D
Turn left off the N1 onto the R101 – the Dal Josafat road – near Paarl. Turn left at the stop sign. Drive for about 5 kilometres. The signposted Nederburg turn-off is on your left.
Details: Wine-tastings and sales Monday to Friday 08h30-17h00; Saturdays (November to March) 09h00-13h00. Weekday cellar tours by appointment include wine-tasting. Picnic lunches 1 November to 1 March (booking essential).
Accommodation: For details contact the Paarl Publicity Office, P O Box 47, Paarl 7622, tel (02211) 2-4842.
Further information: Nederburg, Private Bag X3006, Paarl 7620, tel (02211) 62-3104.

The imposing entrance to Nederburg, the world-famous home of the annual Nederburg Wine Auction. Wines from this estate have won over 950 medals locally and abroad.

The brewer who turned to wine

The sparkling reputation of Cape wines owes not a little to the efforts of a man who trained, not as a wine-maker, but as a brewer.

Johan Graue was a prosperous emigré who left Hitler's increasingly dangerous Germany in the 1930s to settle in the Cape. He used the money he had earned brewing beer in his native land to purchase the Nederburg estate – and immediately set about improving the standard of the Cape's wines. 'Good wine', he said, 'starts in the vineyards,' and he began by culling plantings of inferior quality, introducing new ones, and keeping a meticulous record of each vine.

After the Second World War, he and his son Arnold developed the revolutionary 'cold' technique of fermenting white wine, a method that effectively countered the Cape's often too-hot summers. This, together with Arnold's technical skill and a heavy investment in sophisticated production processes, swiftly elevated Nederburg to the top rank of local producers.

A year later Arnold Graue died in an air crash, and his father, burdened with personal loss and the demands of an expanding enterprise, gradually withdrew from the scene (he died in 1959). Nevertheless, Nederburg's newly acquired reputation was maintained, even enhanced, over the following years by the genius of Gunter Brozel, Johan Graue's successor at the helm. Among other things, Brozel continued the practice of buying and blending grapes grown by other farmers under the best soil and microclimatic conditions and, in many cases, from vines originally nurtured on Nederburg itself. Newald Marais is currently cellar-master and chief oenologist (wine expert).

239

an elaborately gabled front entrance leading into the traditional screened 'voorkamer', the whole girded around by a stoep of russet-coloured flagstones. The interior suffered at the hands of its Victorian occupants, but one of Nederburg's later owners, Henry Currey (Cecil John Rhodes's private secretary from 1884 to 1893), did much to restore the beauty of the original around the turn of the century. Later still, a double-storey wing was added to create a more comfortable, but perhaps less visually pleasing, home.

For all its vulnerability to changing domestic fashion over the decades, Nederburg remains a magnificent homestead. Its neat, beautifully proportioned rooms, filled with fine furniture, can be viewed only by appointment but, on certain winter evenings, young musicians play chamber music for the public, filling the house with the poignant sounds of older, perhaps more civilized, ages.

The rounded granite surfaces of Paarl Rock have been worn smooth by aeons of exposure to the elements. Paarlberg (Paarl Mountain) is estimated to be 500 million years old.

PAARL ROCK
Paarl

Map: page 225, 4D
Paarl lies just off the N1 from Cape Town. Take the R45 exit and make your way along Main Street. Turn left after a few blocks, at the Paarl Mountain Nature Reserve sign, and follow Jan Phillips Drive. There's a second entry at the northern end of town.
Details: The reserve is open throughout the year, 08h00-18h00 in winter 07h00-19h00 in summer.
Accommodation: There are numerous hotel, country-lodge, self-catering and caravan/camping facilities in and around Paarl.
Further information: Paarl Publicity Office, P O Box 47, Paarl 7622, tel (02211) 2-4842.

Dominating the winelands centre of Paarl is the domed Paarlberg, with its three rounded outcrops known as Paarl Rock (the lowest and largest), Bretagne Rock and Gordon's Rock. From their summits there are superlative views of the town below, the splendid Berg River Valley, its flanking ranges and, in the distance, the ocean and the distinctive bulk of Table Mountain.

It was from these granite outcrops that Paarl derived its name. When the early explorer Abraham Gabbema saw them in 1657, on a morning when the dew glistened on their mica-studded surfaces, the heights reminded him of a 'diamandt-ende peerlberg' ('diamond and pearl mountain').

You reach them from town by way of Jan Phillips Drive, a circular and scenic road that takes you to the Mill Water wildflower garden, a wonderland of proteas and pincushions, gazanias and ericas – about 200 indigenous species in all. In the months of August and September the slopes are mantled by dense carpets of yellow, red and orange springtime blooms. The garden's picnic area is set beside the old mill stream.

About three kilometres beyond a feature called Breakfast Rocks, you take a footpath up to the summit of Paarl Rock, where there are a beacon, an old cannon, a tumble of boulders and a large cave. The path which takes you to Bretagne and Gordon's rocks is half a kilometre further along the road; the former is easily climbed with the help of a chain, the latter poses more of a challenge.

Some 200 ha of the surrounding area is taken up by the Paarl Mountain Nature Reserve and its mountain peak, its proteas, aloes, wild olives and its stands of natural forest, among them a patch of lovely silver trees. This last is the largest member of the protea family, growing to 16 m in height (reputedly only within sight of Table Mountain, though it's been successfully cultivated overseas). Paths meander along the slopes; picnic and braai sites have been laid out.

Fishermen favour the several dams for their trout and black bass, said to be the country's biggest.

SOUTHWEST CAPE

Sunlight is reflected off the wind-whipped waters of Steenbras Dam above Gordon's Bay.

STEENBRAS DAM
Near Gordon's Bay

Surrounded by tall stands of pine forest and flanking mountains, Steenbras Dam looks more like a Scandinavian fjord than the prosaic series of reservoirs it is, supplying a small proportion of Cape Town's water needs. The dams stretch 10 km over a catchment basin bounded by the Kogelberg (near Gordon's Bay) and Hottentots-Holland ranges, its northeastern reaches accessible by way of the spectacular Sir Lowry's Pass – a setting of almost unrivalled beauty.

Much of the dams and their surroundings are out of bounds to the general public (it's a municipal conservation area), but close to the wall at the Gordon's Bay end is a fairly large recreation area with basic bungalows, picnic spots and terraced rock gardens. The dams sustain rainbow and brown trout and are much favoured by keen anglers, even though the conservation rules forbid them to wade into the water.

The gum-shaded, tarred road that meanders through the surrounding fynbos countryside offers an inviting day-drive; bird-lovers can spot the occasional African fish eagle, as well as the Egyptian goose and many others. Hikers visiting the area have access to the Steenbras River Valley from two sides: either the western side below the dam wall, or from the southern side (starting at the Steenbras River Mouth), off the R44. Permits are required for walking this trail and hikers are restricted to not more than 30 persons per day.

The Egyptian goose is easily recognizable by the distinctive brown patch on the centre of its breast, and by its hoarse call.

Map: page 225, 6C
There are two entrances: For the northern entrance, turn off the N2 east of Sir Lowry's Pass, following the signs. For the southern entrance, turn off the N2 west of Sir Lowry's Pass, pass through Gordon's Bay on the R44 coastal road, and look for the Steenbras sign on your left.

Details: The dams are accessible throughout the year, 08h00-19h00 October to April; and 08h00-17h00 May to September. Small entrance fee. Best fishing months: September and October.

Accommodation: The bungalows in the recreation area are equipped with 4 beds, a table and 2 benches. For permits to enter the area and bungalow reservations, contact the Civic Amenities Office, City Administrator's Department, P O Box 298, Cape Town 8000, tel (021) 400-2507. Day-entry permits can also be obtained from municipal offices in Somerset West, Gordon's Bay and Grabouw during office hours.

Further information: Permits for the Steenbras River Trail are obtainable from the Parks and Forest Branch, City Engineer's Department, P O Box 1694, Cape Town 8000, tel (021) 400-3269.

PLACES TO VISIT

Map: page 225,5C

STELLENBOSCH

South Africa's second-oldest town lies in the valley of the Eerste ('first') River, a place that has grown gracefully over the centuries since it was originally founded in 1679 as a farming outpost, and named in honour of the innovative governor of the Cape, Simon van der Stel.

The first townsfolk planted avenues of oak trees that were to reach splendid maturity, created open spaces and built charming little lime-washed homes with extra-thick walls and thatched roofs. Today the oaks still embower the thoroughfares, and much else of the past still remains – particularly in Dorp Street, lined by the country's longest row of historic buildings, and around Die Braak, the town square. Stellenbosch is

Saxonhof, on Dorp Street, started life in 1704 as a Cape Dutch home. Later additions included an upper storey and the elegant verandah above the front door.

Dorp Street has the longest row of historic buildings in South Africa. Most of these stately edifices have been tastefully restored.

STELLENBOSCH

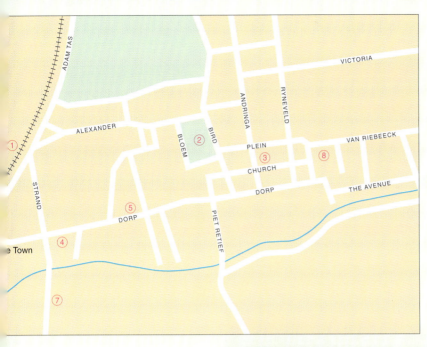

KEY TO THE MAP
1 Bergkelder
2 Die Braak
3 D'Ouwe Werf
4 Libertas Parva
5 Oom Samie se Winkel
6 Oude Libertas Centre
7 Oude Meester Brandy Museum

also home to one of South Africa's leading universities – a lively, 12 000-student institution integrated into the town and which, for decades, functioned as the intellectual nursery of Afrikanerdom. The university's museum, its lovely botanical garden, and, especially, its conservatoire, are renowned. Stellenbosch is also the fast-beating heart of the country's wine industry.

One of the ornate gables of the University of Stellenbosch's Eben Dönges Centre, home of the Sasol Art Museum.

BERGKELDER

Some of South Africa's finest wines mature in the coolness of a large and labyrinthine cellar cut into the slopes of Stellenbosch's Papegaaiberg ('parrot mountain', so called because Van der Stel, while camping in the area, amused himself by shooting at wooden targets shaped like parrots). Visitors wander through cloister-like chambers lined to their arched ceilings with candle-lit bottles; ranks of small, hand-built French oak casks rest on polished stone floors.

The Bergkelder belongs to Distillers Corporation, which built the cellars in 1968 to serve as a maturation, bottling and marketing centre for its own wines, including Fleur du Cap, the Stellenryk 'Collection', J C le Roux and the Grunburger range – and to make its advanced technology and many distribution skills available to other producers in the region. About a score of independent estates have joined the scheme.

Part of the complex is taken up by the Vinoteque, a special cellar in which special lots of individually owned wines are matured under ideal conditions. Temperature, humidity and light levels are closely monitored by the cellarmaster. Wine-lovers who have 'bought forward' (invested in young wines) receive regular reports until the vintages, their value and their quality enhanced, are ready for release.

Tours of the Bergkelder begin at the massive mountainside doors and proceed through dimly lit corridors and caverns to a room where the cellar's wines may be sampled. Wines may be purchased in a separate shop on the estate.

Map: above
The Bergkelder is on the mountainside behind the Stellenbosch Railway Station.
Details: Tours daily at 10h00, 10h30 and 15h00 Monday to Friday throughout the year. Admission charged; booking essential.
Further information: Bergkelder, P O Box 184, Stellenbosch 7599, tel (021) 887-3480.

STELLENBOSCH

Map: page 243
Bloem Street.
Details: VOC Kruithuis: Open Monday to Friday 09h30-13h00 and 14h00-17h00; closed Saturdays, Sundays, Good Friday, Christmas Day. Admission fee charged.
Burgerhuis: Open Monday to Friday 09h00-12h45 and 14h00-17h00; Saturdays 10h00-13h00 and 14h00-17h00. Admission charged.
Further information: Stellenbosch Tourist Information Bureau, P O Box 368, Stellenbosch 7599, tel (021) 883-3584.

DIE BRAAK

Stellenbosch's town centre, following European rural tradition, is a spacious village green that once hosted meetings and festivals, feasts and games and, though its most energetic figures today are leisurely strollers, it still has much of the charming past about it.

Die Braak was set aside in 1703 as a parade ground for the Cape settlement's burgher militia, and for many years its military origins were emphasised by the firing of cannon from the nearby Kruithuis. This was the VOC (Dutch East India Company) arsenal or powder magazine, built in Bloem Street in 1777 and now a national monument housing antique firearms, sharp-edged weapons and sundry VOC memorabilia. The building is a simple, two-storey affair with a barrel-vaulted roof and attractive bell tower. Security and safety were as important then as now, and the whitewashed, mud-plastered stone walls are nearly 70 cm thick, the high, surrounding wall graced by handsome, arched gateways.

Almost as old is the Burgerhuis, one of several elegant local residences built by Anthonie Fick. It was completed in 1797 and served for a time as the local landdrost's home, but over the years suffered tasteless alterations and, latterly, neglect as well, but enough was known of the original to enable the Municipality of Stellenbosch to restore it to its former grace. Today it functions as the head-

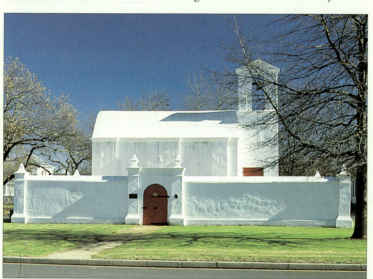

The old VOC Kruithuis on Die Braak was used for a short while as a shelter for the local fire brigade.

An aerial view of Die Braak, once a military parade ground, but now the peaceful centre of a country town.

quarters of the Historical Homes of South Africa Society, and as a museum. When you visit, take special note of the main gable, a fine example of neo-Classical decoration.

Among the various other buildings of interest in this part of town are St Mary's-on-the-Braak, a cosy and attractive little thatched-roof Anglican church; and the Rhenish Mission complex – a rather spacious (1 200 capacity) church which also serves as a parsonage.

Lord Charles Somerset attended the church's inauguration in 1824. Its pulpit, the work of master cabinet-maker Simon Londt, is a magnificent example of the 19th-century wood-carver's craft. The craftsmanship of the gable is also eye-catching. St Mary's is the only building on De Braak itself; the others are nearby.

The Burgerhuis on Die Braak was built in 1797, and now serves as headquarters for the Historical Homes of South Africa Society.

The solemn exterior of the Rhenish Church opposite Die Braak houses an elaborately carved pulpit.

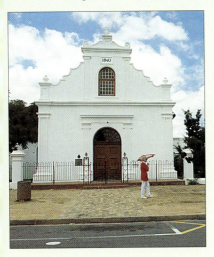

D'OUWE WERF

The name means 'the old yard' and it is thought to be South Africa's most venerable inn, a magical little hostelry that has provided passing travellers and traders with comfort and good cheer for close on two centuries.

The site, in the older part of town, was originally occupied by the Cape Colony's first church, which was destroyed by fire in 1710. Some 90 years later, after the land had been deconsecrated, Wouter Wium opened an inn, which enjoyed an excellent reputation among Victorian visitors. This, too, burned down (by slaves who were later publicly hanged), and the place was rebuilt in larger and more elegant guise, boasting a second storey, superbly proportioned raftered rooms and two staircases. The thatched roof was destroyed in a third fire, and the charred door and window frames are still visible. Today D'Ouwe Werf has 25 rooms, some of which are furnished with sumptuous four-poster or canopy beds, rich fabrics and antiques.

Downstairs is a courtyard in which visitors can take tea or light meals, or simply relax with a good book in the dappled shade provided by vine-bedecked pergolas.

Map: page 243
30 Church Street.

Further information: 30 Church Street, Stellenbosch 7600, tel (021) 887-1608/ 887-4608. Tours of the town and its wine route can be arranged at the reception desk; a helicopter is available for trips further afield.

The cosy interior of D'Ouwe Werf, a luxurious hideaway in the heart of Stellenbosch.

STELLENBOSCH

Libertas Parva, the graceful home of the Rembrandt van Rijn Art Gallery.

Map: page 243
31 Dorp Street.
Details: The gallery and museum are open Monday to Friday 09h00-12h45 and 14h00-17h00; Saturdays 10h00-13h00 and 14h00-17h00; Sundays 14h30-17h30; closed Good Friday and Christmas Day. Admission free. Parking available.
Further information: Stellenbosch Tourist Information Bureau, P O Box 368, Stellenbosch 7599, tel (021) 883-3584.

LIBERTAS PARVA

The elegant, gabled, H-shaped, Cape Dutch mansion was once the home of the Krige family, whose daughter Sybella ('Issie') met and married Jan Christiaan Smuts while he was a student lodging at the nearby Akkermannhuis. It also hosted such luminaries as Cecil Rhodes, the brilliant 'Onze Jan' Hofmeyr, and Cape premier John X Merriman. Today the complex, its period character preserved, houses an art gallery and museum.

The Rembrandt van Rijn Art Gallery is a must for anyone interested in South African art: on display are works by the eccentric and greatly talented Irma Stern, Anton van Wouw and his godson Jacob Pierneef, who for much of his painting career portrayed the solitude and beauty of the Highveld landscape in detailed, rather stylized fashion.

In an adjacent area (the original cellar) is the Stellenryk Wine Museum, its huge, old vats, its presses and implements telling the story of wine-making through the ages. Among the rarer and more eye-catching exhibits are a wine jug from biblical Israel, Greek and Roman amphorae, a Scandinavian beaker, and some fine examples of early furniture and glassware, including bottles (some with the original labels intact) from the Dutch-ruled Cape of the 18th century.

Map: page 243
84 Dorp Street.
Details: Oom Samie se Winkel: Open Monday to Friday 09h00-18h00; Saturdays 09h00-17h00; tel (021) 887-2612. Cafe Filipe (restaurant and tea garden): Open Monday to Sunday 09h00-17h00; (same address as Oom Samie se Winkel), tel (021) 887-2710. Street parking only.
De Akker Country Pub Restaurant and its tasting centre are open 7 days a week.
Further information: 90 Dorp Street, Stellenbosch 7600, tel (021) 883-3512.

OOM SAMIE SE WINKEL

The scents of tobacco and dried fish, of spices and fruit and freshly tanned leather mingle together to produce sharp pangs of nostalgia for the good old days before supermarkets, an era when your local corner shop was crammed to its low eaves with everything you could possibly need and much that you didn't, and where the aproned proprietor served you personally, and sometimes passed the time of

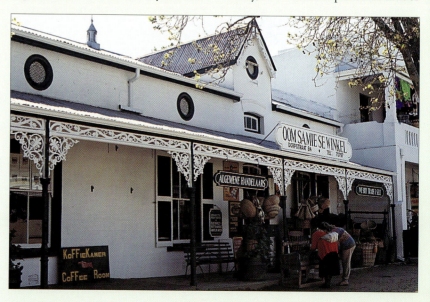

Oom Samie se Winkel, where the air is pungent with the aromas of sweets, tobacco, spices and dried fish.

day with you. Oom Samie se Winkel (Uncle Sammy's Shop) was among the first of Stellenbosch's trading stores and it's never been out of business, though it has changed over the years. Later renovations gave it an attractive Victorian face-lift. The exterior, with its pavement stoep and delicate wrought-iron tracery, is charming.

The inside also belongs to yesteryear, and there's a bewildering range of goods on sale, including some delicious homemade preserves, as well as a variety of curios, household goods, bric-a-brac – and some excellent wines of origin.

The Victorian Wine Shop, which is part of the overall premises, specializes in unusual releases and really exceptional vintages, and will make up (and send) gift packages for you. At the back is a delightful tea garden.

Nearby, on the corner, you'll find De Akker, a pub much favoured by local students, and a wine-tasting centre. Here you can sample the region's wines, and read all about them in the house library.

OUDE LIBERTAS CENTRE

Sunday evening twilight concerts, held in the centre's 430-seat amphitheatre, are magical affairs: you sit in the enclosure, which is cleverly sheltered from the southeaster, or bring along a picnic hamper, eat, sip wine and laze on the lovely lawns as the light fades and the music washes over you.

The complex, built on the slopes of the Papegaaiberg by Stellenbosch Farmers' Winery (SFW), comprises an underground cellar and restaurant – and the amphitheatre, modelled on the ancient Greek auditoria of Athens and Epidauros. It was inaugurated with a flourish, in 1977, with a performance by celebrated Russian pianist Vladimir Ashkenazy.

Drama and ballet feature on the seasonal programme, which extends from December to March, but the venue is best known for a mixed bag of musical evenings that range through the spectrum, from free-form funk, trad jazz and the joyous sounds of Africa, to Mendelssohn and Mozart. In the intervals you're served complimentary glasses of good wine and grape juice. Wine and light meals can also be purchased; the concerts begin at 20h15.

The centre is on the outskirts of Stellenbosch, on the R310 to Cape Town. Concerts are held on Sunday evenings from December to March (see the press for details). Bookings for the amphitheatre are made through Computicket, tel (021) 21-4715. In the event of bad weather, the venue will either be changed or the performance cancelled (and your money refunded or used as credit for another evening). For updates on weather conditions, tel (021) 808-7474 or (after hours) 808-2380. You needn't book for a place on the lawns, but there's a small admission charged.

Map: page 243
Adam Tas Road, opposite Stellenbosch Farmers' Winery.
Details: Tours of the wine centre are made by appointment.
Further information: Stellenbosch Farmers' Winery, P O Box 9, Stellenbosch 7599, tel (021) 808-7911.

A jazz ensemble performs beneath the oaks at the Oude Libertas Centre, the popular venue for a wide variety of twilight concerts.

OUDE MEESTER BRANDY MUSEUM

Stills, bottles and glassware are among the 1 000 and more exhibits that, together, give you an intriguing insight into the world of brandy, past and present.

The premises originated as a collection of turn-of-the-century labourers' cottages – rather special ones. They were designed by the architect Herbert Baker, creator of Cape Town's Groote Schuur and Pretoria's Union Buildings – and rescued from demolition when the Distillers Corporation bought them in 1976. They were then restored by Historical Homes of South Africa.

Displays lead you through a continuous sequence, from the time brandy was first distilled in South Africa (1672) to modern production methods. Of particular note are the Victorian period room, the old cooperage, and an 1818 brandy still on loan from Richelieu et Cie, of Cognac, France. Some of the other brandy stills, fashioned by Cape coppersmiths, are almost as impressive.

Map: page 243
Old Strand Road.
Details: Open Monday to Friday 09h00-12h45, 14h00-17h00; Saturdays and public holidays 10h00-13h00, 14h00-17h00; Sundays 14h00-17h30. The museum is closed on Good Friday and Christmas Day.
Further information: Stellenbosch Tourist Information Bureau, P O Box 368, Stellenbosch 7599, tel (021) 883-3584; or Oude Meester Brandy Museum, P O Box 13, Vlottenburg 7604, tel (021) 881-3785.

PLACES TO VISIT

Map: page 249
18 Ryneveld Street.
Details: Open Monday to Saturday 09h30-17h00; Sundays and religious holidays (excluding Christmas Day and Good Friday) 14h00-17h00. Admission charged.
Further information: Village Museum, c/o Stellenbosch Museum, Private Bag X5048, Stellenbosch 7599, tel (021) 887-2937. The Research Centre for Historical Archaeology is located in the Old Agricultural Hall, on The Avenue, Stellenbosch. Visits by appointment, tel (021) 887-2937.

STELLENBOSCH VILLAGE MUSEUM

Historic houses dating from a number of eras cluster together within the bounds of a single museum complex to lead you on a fascinating journey through the past.

The buildings, straddling the decades between 1709 and 1850, have been beautifully restored to their original character and condition. Each is furnished in the appropriate period style, and its garden filled with the kind of decorative, medicinal and culinary plants, such as herbs and fruit trees, that would have adorned the home in its heyday.

The historical divisions aren't rigid, of course, since styles overlapped, and different fashions were popular at the same time but, nevertheless, the houses strikingly illuminate changing domestic tastes within the Cape's 'Stellenbosch Colony' over almost three centuries.

The route through the museum follows a chronological sequence. Have a close look at the scale model at the entrance, and then wander through at a leisurely pace. The restorers have paid meticulous attention to detail and there's a great deal to be seen.

To date, the Village Museum covers 5 000 square metres and boasts four homes, but restoration work is ongoing, and two more will be open to the public in due course to reflect the Edwardian and 1920s periods.

Associated closely with the enterprise, and worth a visit (by appointment only) is the nearby Research Centre for Historical Archaeology.

The museum's administrative offices at 37 Ryneveld Street are housed in a dignified Cape Victorian edifice which was built in about 1880, the Erfurthuis. Of special interest is the double-storey wood-and-iron balcony which surrounds the house, and the formal, but elegant, dining room within.

The interior of Blettermanhuis displays the furniture of a prosperous family living in Stellenbosch during the late 18th century.

The interior of Grosvenor House is decorated with classical borders around the cornices and doors, and houses fine pieces of period furniture.

STELLENBOSCH VILLAGE MUSEUM

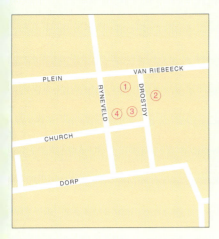

KEY TO THE MAP

1 Blettermanhuis The handsome, classically H-shaped, six-gable house was originally home to Hendrik Bletterman, the last landdrost (magistrate) of Stellenbosch to be appointed by the Dutch East India Company, and a man who fully expected to live in a grand manner (he moved in shortly after the British occupation, and bitterly resented the new regime).

The house was completed in about 1789 – the exact date isn't known – and after Bletterman died in 1824 it became government offices, while the barn next door functioned successively as a school for slaves, a theatre, a pox hospital and as the local police headquarters from about 1880 to 1979. The architecture of the main house, and especially the splendid frontage, are typical of the late 18th-century Cape style; furniture and effects are those of an affluent country-town family of the period 1750-80.

2 Grosvenor House Perhaps the most elegant of the museum's components, the house was built in 1782, and extended over the following years to reach splendid maturity by 1803. It has been preserved as one of the finest examples of the double-storey, flat-roofed town homes favoured by patrician Cape families of the early 1800s. Decorating the classical façade are fluted pilasters supporting a prominent cornice; the interior belongs to the period 1800-30. The garden gallery beckons browsers with occasional temporary exhibitions.

3 Home of O M Bergh This was originally an H-shaped, thatched and gabled building, but it underwent radical alteration during the mid-19th century, while the Bergh family – descendants of the Swedish adventurer Olof Bergh and his wife Angela, a freed slave – were in residence. The rather sombre, richly wallpapered and heavily furnished interior indicates the prevailing taste of this era. You'll also see an unplastered room in the grounds that tells you something about the nature of early construction and the way restorers set about their research.

4 Schreuderhuis This is the country's oldest restored town house, built in 1709 – just 30 years after Stellenbosch itself was established – by Sebastian Schreuder, a humble Saxon soldier employed by the ruling Dutch East India Company. Architecture, decor and appointments are simple, with thick, limewashed walls supporting reed ceilings and thatched roofing. Windows are tiny and only those in the front of the house are glazed (the rest are covered with waxed cotton). The floor is of simulated clay (the original would have been of clay earth). Strings of herbs, onions and salted fish hang from the roof beams, the kitchen has a homely, open hearth, and the furniture is Spartan, comprising a few rare and charmingly rough-hewn early (1690-1720) Cape pieces.

Contrasting with the simplicity of the interior of Grosvenor House, Bergh House is filled with the cosy clutter of an affluent mid-19th-century family.

The exterior of Grosvenor House, bought by the Dutch Reformed Church in 1942, to become the first of the Stellenbosch house museums.

SOUTHWEST CAPE

The huge tidal pool at Strandfontein Pavilion, with its gently lapping waters, offers safe swimming to summer visitors and their children.

Map: page 225, 6B
From central Cape Town take the M5 to Muizenberg. Turn eastwards along the coast on Baden Powell Drive (R310) and follow the signs.
Details: Pavilion: open all year, 07h00-20h00 during summer, and 08h00-17h00 during winter. Entrance fee charged. There's a large car park adjacent to the pavilion.
Further information: Civic Amenities Office, City Administrator's Department, P O Box 298, Cape Town 8000, tel (021) 400-2507.

STRANDFONTEIN PAVILION
False Bay

The pavilion, rising like some giant, geometrically designed sand castle above the broad white reaches of Strandfontein Beach, is the focal point of one of greater Cape Town's most popular leisure areas, a magnet for the multitudes who live on the adjacent and rather bleak Cape Flats. It was built, in the bad old days of racial segregation and 'separate but equal' amenities, to rival Muizenberg's older and more famous pavilion just up the coast. Now, of course, its restaurant, refreshment kiosks and other facilities can be enjoyed by all.

Next door is Africa's largest tidal pool – a boon to families with children, because the beach here falls away rather sharply. The backwash is strong, and sea-bathing has its risks. Other drawcards include a king-size water slide, and landscaped terraces that are sheltered from the south-easter and pleasant for picnicking.

Along the shoreline to the east is Mnandi Beach, often crowded at weekends, which also has its own pavilion, palm-fringed pool, water chutes and picnic area. You can reach it after a lengthy stroll along the sands or, from the west, via the coastal drive. A number of minor roads lead seawards from the latter to give access to the popular Blue Waters Beach and to lonelier parts of the shoreline.

Map: page 225, 4D
Paarl lies just off the N1 from Cape Town. Take the R45 exit leading along Main Street. Turn left after about 500 m, at the monument sign.
Details: The monument is open throughout the year 09h00-17h00. No admission charged. Parking available when gates are open. Kiosk at the monument sells refreshments. Museum: open weekdays 09h00-13h00 and 14h00-16h30.
Further information: Paarl Publicity Association, P O Box 47, Paarl 7622, tel (02211) 2-4842.

TAAL (LANGUAGE) MONUMENT
Paarl

Three linked columns, a fountain and a spire that soars 57 m above the heath and woodland slopes of Paarl Mountain commemorate the long and often bitter campaign to have the Afrikaans language officially recognized in South Africa.

Each of the monument's elements symbolizes the massive debts which are owed by the language – to the Western world, to the Africa of Khoisan and Xhosa, and to the Malay-speaking people who were brought to the Cape as slaves from the various Indonesian islands and elsewhere. Visitors can enjoy panoramic views of the valley and surrounding heights. Pleasant walks lead from the monument through the Paarl Mountain

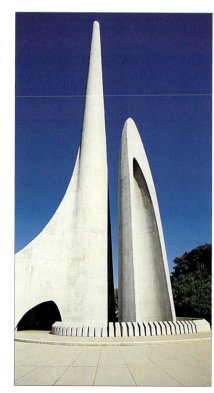

The Taal Monument soars skywards on the southern slopes of Paarl Mountain, commemorating the people of South Africa and their languages.

The struggle of a language

Afrikaans is rooted in the High Dutch of Zuid Holland (South Holland). It was spoken by the early European settlers, but took on new words from English, French and German immigrants, and from the vocabularies of the indigenous peoples. As the centuries rolled by, and the colonists became more isolated from their homeland and from the principal Cape settlement, the language lost the rigidity of its parent, and took on a new character.

Formal Dutch continued to be used in public affairs and in schools until 1828, when the new British regime proclaimed English as the sole official medium. But the Netherlandic language survived, rescued from oblivion by the granting of press freedom in the late 1820s.

Meanwhile, Afrikaans, which was spoken privately but virtually unwritten for nearly two centuries, had slowly started to mature, producing its first printed expression in 1856 in the form of a religious book for Cape Malays. This was followed in 1861 by the publication in book form of a series of lighthearted vernacular sketches that first appeared in *The Cradock News*.

Thereafter the campaign to promote Afrikaans rapidly gained momentum. The South African War elevated it on a patriotic ground swell. The language, Afrikaner leaders insisted, was inseparable from national identity. The moving spirit behind the struggle was the Afrikaner Bond, backed by such periodicals as *Die Afrikaanse Patriot* and, later, J H 'Onze Jan' Hofmeyr's *Ons Land*.

A second language movement took up the cudgels after the war, driving its points home in the years leading up to Union in 1910. At its vanguard were Hofmeyr, Marie Koopmans-De Wet, the mystic genius Eugene Marais, the editor Gustav Preller, Totius (J D du Toit) and C J Langenhoven, who, among many other things, wrote the words to *Die Stem*.

As a consequence the status of Dutch was constitutionally entrenched by the Act of Union, and 10 years later – on 8 May 1925 – Afrikaans became recognized as the country's second official language. The two were joined by nine other official languages in the early 1990s, when South Africa was on its way to a full democracy.

Nature Reserve and up to Paarl Rock and its neighbouring outcrops.

Paarl played a key role in the language movement, serving as the stamping ground of such hardy campaigners as the Hollander Arnoldus Pannevis, who taught at the Paarl Gymnasium, and his student, the brilliant Stephanus Jacobus du Toit. The town also produced the first Afrikaans newspaper, *Die Afrikaanse Patriot* (1876). On Pastorie Avenue is Gideon Malherbe House, a museum devoted to the history of the language and named after one of the eight original pioneers of the movement. Its 1870s period character has been preserved in the five ground-floor rooms. The upper storey contains historical exhibits, among them the press on which *Die Afrikaanse Patriot* was printed.

TULBAGH
See page 252

VAN RYN BRANDY CELLAR
Vlottenburg

The attractive blue-and-white complex off the R310 at Vlottenburg, outside Stellenbosch, ranks among South Africa's largest distilleries and maturation cellars. It also turns out some of the country's best-known brandies, which you can see being made on your tour of the complex. Especially eye-catching are the bubbling copper stills and a timber-lined maturation cellar scented by 'angel's share' (the heady fumes of evaporating brandy). Cooperage demonstrations give you an insight into an ancient craft; tastings introduce you to the various brands.

The cellar also runs brandy courses, and there's the occasional and delightfully sociable musical evening, which involves a recital, followed by an audio-visual presentation, cocktails and dinner.

Map: page 225, 5C
From Cape Town take the N2 east, turning left onto the R310 to Stellenbosch. The cellar complex is on your right.
Details: Guided tours Monday to Thursday 10h30 and 15h00, Friday 10h30. Closed weekends and public holidays. Entrance fee charged.
Further information: Van Ryn Brandy Cellar, P O Box 13, Vlottenburg 7604, tel (021) 881-3875.

Among the demonstrations held at the Van Ryn Brandy Cellar is the ancient craft of cooperage, practised since the early days of wine-making.

PLACES TO VISIT

Map: page 225, 1E
From Cape Town take the N1 to Klapmuts. Turn left on the R44 and drive past Paarl and Wellington to Gouda. Turn right on the R46, then bear left at the Tulbagh signpost.
Accommodation: The Tulbagh area is well served by hotel, self-catering and country-lodge accommodation, and by caravan/camping facilities.
Further information: Tulbagh Valley Publicity Association, P O Box 277, Tulbagh 6820, tel (0236) 30-1348.

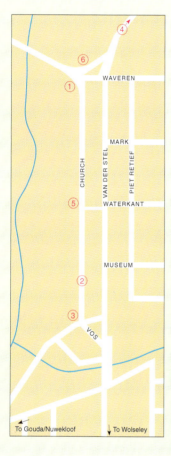

TULBAGH

It's not often that earthquakes do more good than harm – but this was certainly true of the earthquake that struck Tulbagh on 29 September 1969, at least for the historic buildings of the town. Although many were badly damaged, they had been sadly neglected over the decades, the lovely façades ruined by insensitive 'improvements', balconies added, gables removed, to make way for new rooflines and so forth.

Only when renovations began – and plaster was stripped away to reveal the variegated brickwork, the old door and window openings and the original gables – did a full picture of past splendours emerge. A restoration committee was convened, historians and other knowledgeable people got their heads together and, in due course, the eminent architect Gabriel Fagan and his wife Gwen were commissioned to devise a full reconstruction programme. Today, visitors can revel in the results of this ambitious project. A stroll down Church Street leads past 32 listed homes – all in pristine condition.

The town lies in a basin of the Little Berg River in a charming region of fertile valleys and high hills (the Winterberg and Witzenberg ranges), of fruit orchards and rolling vineyards and villages that were once at the cutting edge of Dutch colonial expansion.

Tulbagh originated in 1699 as a farming outpost called Roodezand – the general area was then known as The Land of Waveren, after a prominent Netherlands family – but the town proper began to take shape only in the mid-1790s, after the Old Church was completed. It was renamed in 1804 in honour of the enlightened Cape governor, Ryk Tulbagh.

The noble homes of Church Street, Tulbagh, were painstakingly restored after the earthquake that rocked their foundations in 1969.

KEY TO THE MAP

1 Ballotina, on the west side opposite the Parsonage (see opposite), dates back to the early 1800s, when it was home to the local minister's widow. It's a smallish, charming house which may well have been designed by the architect Louis Thibault in experimental mood. The front gable, wide, flattened and topped by a segmental pediment, is particularly unusual. It is not open to visitors.

2 Church Street The thoroughfare extends for less than a kilometre, but you'll need at least a morning to explore it properly – even though most of the buildings are private homes, a few of which are open to the public. Others function as shops and restaurants.

3 De Oude Kerk Volksmuseum Tulbagh has combined four of its most historic buildings – located in Church Street – into a 'people's museum'. Seen together, they give you a rounded view of the town's past. They include:

The Old Church Museum. Tulbagh's first church

was erected in the 1740s to serve what, in Cape governor Baron Gustaav von Imhoff's estimation, had become a 'blind, heathen community' too far removed from a place of worship (the nearest was in distant Stellenbosch). It was a modest, cruciform building to begin with, but later acquired a new wing, a beautifully ornamented gable, a decorative encircling wall, and a freestanding bell tower. Inside are galleries of stinkwood and yellowwood, 18th-century and Victorian furniture, and paintings by the talented artist Thomas Baines.

Mon Bijou (generally known as De Wet House). A gracious two-storey, flat-roofed building designed by Louis Thibault and completed in 1816. Now the home of a leading collector, it is filled with antiques and works of art and, unfortunately, is not open to the public.

The Victorian House, Van der Stel Street: an elegant 19th-century edifice furnished and decorated in period style.

4 Old Drostdy Just four kilometres outside the town. Yet another neo-Classical Thibault creation. The seat of the old magistracy, with its three-arched, gabled portico, its finely proportioned, high-ceilinged interior and magnificent woodwork, is

The Old Church Museum has served as a church, a billet for British soldiers during the Anglo-Boer War, a concert hall, and a venue for church bazaars.

The interior of the Old Drostdy gleams with burnished wood. On display is a particularly fine collection of porcelain.

now both a museum housing paintings, early Cape furniture and household items, and the headquarters of a well-known wine company. Visitors are amiably received, and can taste a fine range of wines in the old jail. Cellar tours, audiovisual presentations, tastings Monday to Saturday 10h00-12h50, 14h00-16h50; Sundays 14h30-16h50, tel (0236) 30-0203.

5 Paddagang, or 'frog alley', is reputed to have been named after the hordes of frogs that used to pass by on their way to and from the nearby river. The long, low, thatched and white-walled edifice (No. 23, about halfway up and set back from Church Street) has uncertain origins, but a mid-Victorian photograph shows it was venerable even then. The garden, with its herbs and old-fashioned roses, is lovely. Paddagang is now a restaurant where wines can be sampled and home-style dishes enjoyed. The interior has been decorated by local artists.

6 Parsonage The house, at the northern end of the street, is very typical of the Cape Dutch style: U-shaped, thatched and elaborately gabled, and with a pleasing symmetry about it. Here, too, is a delightful garden. The Parsonage is not open to visitors.

Set in beautiful gardens on the banks of the Klip River, Paddagang was once used as either a store or as slave quarters.

SOUTHWEST CAPE

VERGELEGEN
Somerset West

Map: page 225, 6C
On Lourensford Road. Turn northwards off the N2 at Somerset West, onto the R44, and follow the sign to Vergelegen.
Details: Open seven days a week 09h30-16h00. Admission charged. Gift shop. Parking available. Visitors have access to part of the homestead, and to the library, wine-tasting room and interpretive centre, and the Octagonal and Rose gardens. Refreshments and light lunches are served in the tea garden. Guided walks through the estate on Tuesdays and Saturdays. Three daily tours of the winery by appointment, Monday to Saturday. Special activities include the Sappi Horse Trials in November and carols by candlelight in December.
Accommodation: Somerset West offers a wide variety of accommodation, from hotels and guesthouses to camping sites. Contact Somerset West Information Bureau, P O Box 19, Somerset West 7129, tel (024) 514-0221.
Further information: Public Relations Manager, Vergelegen, P O Box 17, Somerset West 7129, tel (024) 51-7060.

One of the oldest, and certainly the grandest, of the Cape's historic estates, long closed to the public, now welcomes visitors to its broad acres at the foot of the Hottentots-Holland Mountains.

Vergelegen – the name means 'faraway place', which speaks of its one-time remoteness from Cape Town – is a classic example of Cape Dutch architecture at its youthful best, and it should have been the pride of the early colonial settlement, but its appearance on the scene in 1701 was greeted by a storm of protest from a community appalled by the extravagance of the enterprise.

Conceived and owned by Willem Adriaan van der Stel, the profligate Cape governor of the time, it was established at enormous cost, with the aid of Dutch East India Company money, material and slaves. More provocatively, the estate, with its beautifully laid out vineyards (half a million vine stocks had been planted by 1706), its fruit orchards, orange groves, reservoirs and 18 cattle posts, was about 10 times larger and a lot better founded than the average freeburgher's farm, which gave Van der Stel an unfair trading advantage.

The upshot was a petition to have the governor removed from office, and he was forced to leave for Amsterdam in 1708, to explain his abuse of authority. The resentful burghers also insisted that the land be divided up and the house demolished, but the new owner (Barend Gildenhuys) was understandably reluctant to destroy the lovely homestead, and prevaricated, eventually pulling down only the rear portion.

Vergelegen passed through a number of different, and often careless, hands over the centuries, but was eventually restored to its early glory by Randlord Sir Lionel Phillips and his wife Florence, who bought the property in 1917. It later passed to the Barlow family, who hosted the British Royal Family on their 1947 tour ('Never did I hear Their Majesties express such pleasure,' a member of the entourage recalled), and now belongs to the Anglo-American group.

The grounds are a joy, their centrepiece the Octagonal Garden, originally built to confine Simon van der Stel's sheep and cattle and now a delightful mix of wide, herbaceous border, wrought-iron trellised ambulatory, and more than 300 species of flowering plant, such as hollyhocks and azaleas, delphiniums, japonicas, hellebores and much else.

Other parts of the grounds feature a 'white' garden graced by limpid ponds, a rose garden, a herb and vegetable garden, and the Lady Phillips Tea Garden.

Especially lovely are Vergelegen's trees, among them five magnificent camphors planted by Van der Stel in 1700 (they're

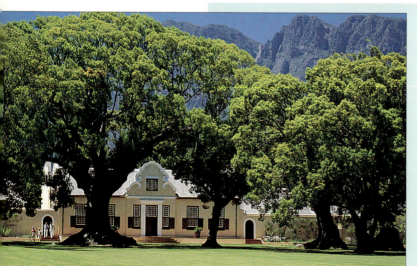

The historic Vergelegen homestead is guarded by a row of beautiful camphor trees.

The camphor: tree for all seasons

The stately camphor trees that grace Vergelegen's spacious grounds and some of the region's other grand gardens, are native to China and Japan, although nowadays they are cultivated for ornamental purposes throughout the world. They are especially popular in the sunnier American states: California and Texas, for instance, and Florida (where they are occasionally found growing wild).

Cinnamomum camphora, which belongs to the laurel family, is an evergreen, densely crowned, shiny-leafed aromatic species that reaches about 12 m in height.

It's a handsome tree – but it has a lot more than good looks going for it. The wood retains its scent for years, and is much favoured by cabinet-makers for their finer work. From its sap, camphor is extracted (usually by steam distillation). This is widely used orally for the relief of breathing and circulation problems, as a carminative (flatulence reliever) and expectorant. Its other medical uses are as an antiseptic, and as a balm to soothe.

It also has its commercial uses, playing a significant part in the manufacture of plastics, varnishes, lacquers, explosives, drugs and cosmetics, and as a moth repellent. These days, though, little of the industrial world's camphor comes from the camphor trees themselves. It can be produced more cheaply, in greater quantities and in a more environmentally friendly fashion by synthetic means.

national monuments). There's also an oak that is reputed to be South Africa's oldest, a rare dawn redwood, once thought to be an extinct species, and a gnarled, old mulberry, relic of Van der Stel's abortive silk-making venture. An avenue of almonds, chestnuts and oaks is being developed to replicate that planted in 1707.

The homestead was originally built to a double-H plan, the two sections connected by a gallery. Its splendidly gabled walls and thatched-roof exterior look much as they did in the governor's day, although the eastern gable is a later addition, and two wings were added by the Phillipses (these blend in well). Inside, all is light and grace. Of note are the teak and yellowwood screen and the fine furniture. The old wine cellar – an outbuilding dating from 1816 – was converted into a library to house Sir Lionel's book collection.

The winery is a new addition, and unlike any other in the country. It is an octagonal, four-level structure set on the hillside, its roof garden affording splendid views over the estate, the surrounding mountains and the sweep of False Bay. The emphasis throughout is on simplicity (for a productive unit, it's remarkably uncluttered) and, in wine-making terms, on time-honoured craftsmanship. New vines were planted in 1989, and their first wines released in 1992.

Graceful urns and annuals flank the walkway to the Octagonal Garden at Vergelegen, filled with a profusion of flowers and herbs.

VINEYARD TRAIL
West of Stellenbosch

This rambling one-day hiking trail over 24 km, through some of the lovelier parts of the wider Stellenbosch area, provides an energetic alternative to the drive-yourself wine route.

The route leads you from the Oude Libertas Centre *(see under Stellenbosch)* through forest plantations, swathes of emerald-green vineyards, and the olive groves and orchards of the fertile and splendidly scenic Bottelary farmlands, to Kuils River in the west. That's the full itinerary, but if you haven't the legs or the time for the longer haul, you can turn off after seven kilometres, and make your way down the exquisite Devon Valley, or at the 14,5-km mark, both of which take you back to Stellenbosch.

There are highlights aplenty along the hike, among them the views from Papegaaiberg, Protea Heights and Bottelarykop, the flora of the fragile Renosterveld vegetation, and the charming wine farms of Koopmanskloof and Rozendal. All in all, this makes a fine day's outing in an especially inviting part of the region.

Map: page 225, 5C
The Oude Meester Centre's amphitheatre, starting point of the trail, is on the R310 on the outskirts of Stellenbosch.
Details: Best months for walking are September to March. If you choose the full 24-km route, you'll have to be dropped off at the Oude Libertas Centre and met at Kuils River. Alternatively, take the train from Cape Town to Stellenbosch Station, and the train back from Kuils River afterwards.
Further information: Map, permit and guidance on picnic spots, refreshment outlets and so on are available from the Stellenbosch Tourist Information Bureau, P O Box 368, Stellenbosch 7599, tel (021) 883-3584.

The Vineyard Trail winds between verdant hills and pretty farms, leading you deep into the fertile heart of the winelands.

PLACES TO VISIT

WINE ROUTE: Franschhoek

Map: page 225, 5D/E
For more details contact *Vignerons de Franschhoek*, Franschhoek Vineyards Wine Centre, P O Box 280, Franschhoek 7690, tel (02212) 3062 mornings only.
Further information: Franschhoek Vallée Tourisme, P O Box 178, Franschhoek 7690, tel (02212) 3603.

The 16 venues on this wine route grace the Franschhoek Valley, first settled by the French Huguenot immigrants in the later years of the 17th century. All belong to the *Vignerons de Franschhoek*, a fairly exclusive association of growers formed in 1984 to promote the fine wines of the area. It's a beautiful, fertile valley, buttressed on three sides by soaring mountain slopes. Some of the estates are very old, most bearing romantic-sounding names that evoke their founders' exotic origins.

Of the route's 16 members, four are estates, five are private wineries, one a co-operative and the remainder are farms that have their grapes processed (or 'vinified'), according to their own specifications, in a central winery.

Not all the cellars are open to the public at set hours. Several offer tours and tastings by appointment only, but a selection of the wines can be sampled at the Franschhoek Vineyards Co-operative's wine centre in town, at the nearby Wine House (which dates from 1688), and at several of the area's most inviting hotels and restaurants.

KEY TO THE MAP
1 Bellingham, on the road to Paarl (R45), west of town. An old (1693) farm that fell upon hard times, but has risen, Phoenix-like, during the past few decades to become one of the region's leading wine producers, renowned for its dry whites. Attractions include an impressive cellar complex, and a small (90-seat) natural amphitheatre, where musical shows are sometimes staged. Cellar tours Monday to Friday (December to April), tastings and sales Monday to Saturday (November to April). Closed on public holidays. Light lunches December to April. Facilities for the disabled.
Further information: Bellingham, P O Box 13, Franschhoek 7690, tel (02211) 4-1011.
2 Boschendal, on the R310, close to its junction with the R45. A fine, Cape Flemish-style mansion on land farmed since 1685. The house is a museum, as well as focal point of the splendid vineyards. The old wine house and tap house now function as a gift shop and tasting parlour, respectively. The restaurant is renowned for its traditional Cape buffet lunches. Picnic lunches offered November to April, light meals and teas available at *Le Cafe*. Vineyard tours by appointment; audiovisuals in cellar. Tastings and sales Monday to Saturday.
Further information: Boschendal, P O Groot Drakenstein 7680, tel (02211) 4-1031 [4-1252 for restaurant and picnics]; 4-1152 for *Le Cafe*; 4-1034 for tours.
3 Dieu Donne, on the Uitkyk road north of Franschhoek. Superb views from the higher vineyards. Cellar tours by appointment. Tastings and sales Monday to Saturday (December and January), Monday to Friday (February to November).
Further information: Dieu Donne, P O Box 94, Franschhoek 7690, tel (02212) 2493.
4 Franschhoek Vineyards Co-operative, on the R45 as you enter Franschhoek. Known for its *La Cotte* range (some of the co-op's profits paid for the restor-

Lying in the sheltering crook of pine trees, this homestead is a fine example of the beautiful wine-farm manors found in the Franschhoek Valley.

WINE ROUTE: FRANSCHHOEK

ation of historic *La Cotte* Mill, which dates from 1779), produced from grapes supplied by its 120 members. Some of the beverage, though, is bottled under individual labels. Cellar tours by appointment. Tastings and sales at the Franschhoek Vineyards Wine Centre, Monday to Saturday throughout the year.
Further information: Franschhoek Vineyards Co-operative, P O Box 52, Franschhoek 7690, tel (02212) 2086/7.

5 La Provence, on the R45, close to Franschhoek. An enchanting estate whose history dates from 1694. Overnight accommodation available in historic cottage on the estate. Cellar tours by arrangement. Wine-tastings and sales Monday to Saturday throughout the year.
Further information: *La Provence*, P O Box 393, Franschhoek 7690, tel (02212) 2163; *La Provence* Guest Cottage, tel (02212) 2163/2315.

6 L'Ormarins, off the R45, close to Bellingham. An exceptionally attractive, gabled homestead fronted by a placid pond. The old cellar has been meticulously restored and equipped with the latest technology. Cellar tours and tastings Monday to Saturday throughout the year.
Further information: *L'Ormarins*, P O Groot Drakenstein 7680, tel (02211) 4-1026.

7 Mouton-Excelsior, off the R45, south of Franschhoek. The original 19th-century building features 'Die Binnehof' wine house, where the best Franschhoek wines can be sampled. Charming setting for picnics. Light lunches served daily at Die Binnehof. Book in advance for picnic lunches. Fireside bistro meals served in winter. Tastings and sales Tuesday to Sunday (closed Mondays).
Further information: *Mouton-Excelsior*, P O Box 290, Franschhoek 7690, tel (02212) 3316.

The second Manor House at Boschendal has a sophisticated interior with a louvred screen dividing the main rooms.

Glowing woodwork, brass candelabras and richly painted walls combine to create an air of opulence within Boschendal's gracious buildings.

The timeless art of making wine

The essentials of wine-making haven't changed a great deal over the centuries. The grapes are still hand-picked from the vines by small armies of field workers in the clear, scented air of a late Cape summer. The lusciously ripe fruit is then hauled by truck or tractor-trailer to the pressing rooms, where the stalks are extracted, and crushers grind the grapes into a dense soup of skin, flesh and juice called 'must'.

Treatment thereafter depends on the basic type of grape used. For a white-wine end product, the skins are removed (and re-pressed to squeeze out the last drop), the must clarified to get rid of foreign bodies and other impurities, and yeast added to boost fermentation, which takes place in the cellars under controlled conditions (temperature – usually 15-18°C – and humidity). During the process, the natural sugar in the grapes is slowly converted into alcohol and the carbon dioxide escapes. When the quantities of these latter elements are just right, the temperature is abruptly lowered to stop the action of the yeast.

Red wines require a different approach. Here the skins, which determine colour and flavour, are left in the must to ferment, and when the sugar content reaches its optimum level, the wine is poured into wooden (or, increasingly, stainless steel) casks or vats. These aren't completely airtight, the atmospheric gases filtering through to react in subtle fashion with the wine. Most red wines take at least three years to mellow, some less, others more, many reaching their full maturity in the corked bottle.

These are the main stages of wine production, but the procedure is a lot more complicated than the outline may suggest. A myriad considerations, from the nature of the cultivar to market niche, introduce innumerable variations and refinements. The process is full of nuances and subtleties that demand years of experience, a sense of exactitude and an almost instinctive skill.

PLACES TO VISIT

WINE ROUTE: Paarl

Map: page 225, 4D
For more details contact the Paarl Wine Route Publicity Association, P O Box 46, Paarl 7622, tel (02211) 2-3605; or Paarl Publicity Office, P O Box 47, Paarl 7622, tel (02211) 2-4842.

The route, which meanders through the entrancing valley of the Berg River, is smaller than that of the better-known Stellenbosch area, but nevertheless covers the full spectrum of wines, from light whites to full-bodied reds, rich ports and nutty sherries.

Paarl was founded in 1720 as a farming and wagon-making centre, and is today an attractive and substantial town, its jacaranda and oak-lined main street running a full 10 km from end to end. Prominent on the local calendar is the annual Paarl Nouveau Festival every April, a fun-filled celebration, during which the region's wine-makers deliver the season's first fresh products to waiting crowds on the summit of Paarl Mountain in a large variety of conveyances. Food and other stalls – and wine, of course – are among the drawcards; booking advisable.

A bucolic character pays tribute to Nederburg's glorious wines.

The oak-shaded homestead at Laborie dates back to the late 18th century.

The distinctive goats' tower at Fairview, known for its award-winning, delicate wines and wide variety of goat's-milk cheeses.

KEY TO THE MAP (OPPOSITE PAGE)

1 Backsberg, Simondium road, on the lower slopes of the Simonsberg. Especially attractive tasting parlour. Self-guided cellar tours (with the aid of closed-circuit TV demonstrations). Small wine museum. Tastings and sales Monday to Saturday.
Further information: Backsberg Estate, P O Box 1, Klapmuts 7625, tel (02211) 5141/2.

2 Fairview, south of Paarl Mountain. Fine estate goat's-milk and sheep's-milk cheeses to complement the wine. A goat tower captures the attention; among other farmyard residents are sheep, pigs, chickens, guinea fowl, pheasants, quails and peacocks. Cellar tours by appointment. Tastings and sales Monday to Saturday.
Further information: Fairview Estate, P O Box 583, Suider-Paarl 7624, tel (02211) 63-2450.

3 KWV, an abbreviation of Ko-operatiewe Wijnbouwers-Vereeniging, the largest wine co-operative in the world, has its headquarters in Paarl. The administration is housed in La Concorde, a splendid neo-Classical building on Main Street. The enormous cellar complex is in Kohler Street. Cellar tours (audiovisual presentation, a walk through the sherry and export sections) and tastings Monday to Saturday. No purchases (wines are for export only). Sales at KWV-owned Laborie wine house.
Further information: KWV, P O Box 528, Suider-Paarl 7624, tel (02211) 7-3007/8.

4 Laborie, on the slopes of Paarl Mountain. Owned by KWV; known for its *a la carte* and buffet lunches (traditional dishes) as well as its attractive selection of wines. Cellar tours. Tastings and sales Monday to Saturday.
Further information: Laborie Estate, P O Box 632, Suider-Paarl 7624, tel (02211) 7-3095.

5 Landskroon, south of Paarl Mountain. Like Fairview *(see bottom left)*, famed for its cheeses (but from the estate's prize-winning Jersey herd, not from goats). Vintner's platter November to April; cheese-tasting Monday to Saturday; cellar tours on request. Tastings and sales Monday to Saturday.
Further information: Landskroon Estate, P O Box 519, Suider-Paarl 7624, tel (02211) 63-1039/59.

6 Nederburg, a superb Cape Dutch mansion near Paarl, and venue of the country's premier wine auction *(see separate entry)*.

7 Paarl Rock Brandy Cellar on Drommedaris Street. This internationally famous cellar, host to the

annual Nederburg wine auction, holds informative cellar tours during which visitors can view the entire production process. The enterprise was founded in 1856, and there's still an old-world charm about the place. Audiovisual presentation. Museum. Tastings and tours Monday to Friday at 11h00 and 15h00. Chamber music concerts in winter. Facilities for the disabled.
Further information: Nederburg Wines, Private Bag X3006, Paarl 7620, tel (02211) 62-3104.

8 Rhebokskloof, just north of Paarl Mountain. Three restaurants (traditional Cape cuisine, *a la carte*, buffet and light meals). Shop. Estate tours in four-wheel-drive vehicle available. Jazz concerts during summer. Open seven days a week.
Further information: Rhebokskloof Estate, P O Box 7141, Noorder-Paarl 7623, tel (02211) 63-8386.

9 Villiera, on the Old Paarl road southwest of town. Specializes in the production of sparkling wines. Picnic facilities available. Cellar tours by appointment. Art exhibitions during winter. Sparkling wine breakfasts during summer. Tastings and sales Monday to Saturday.
Further information: Villiera Estate, P O Box 66, Koelenhof 7605, tel (021) 882-2002/3.

10 Zandwijk, on the slopes of Paarl Mountain. South Africa's only kosher winery. Donkey-cart rides for children during school holidays. Cellar tours by appointment. Jazz concerts held regularly. Tastings and sales Monday to Friday.
Further information: Zandwijk Wine Farm, P O Box 2674, Paarl 7620, tel (02211) 63-2368.

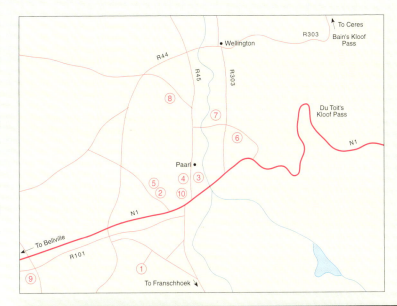

Redolent with the heady aroma of fine wines, the famed cellars at KWV offer daily tours to guests visiting the estate.

Guests at Rhebokskloof can enjoy excellent cuisine on the terrace, while soaking in the tranquil setting of cool gardens and a shimmering lake.

PLACES TO VISIT

Map: page 225, 5C/D

For more details contact the Stellenbosch Wine Route Office, P O Box 204, Stellenbosch 7599, tel (021) 886-4310; or Stellenbosch Tourist Information Bureau, P O Box 368, Stellenbosch 7599, tel (021) 883-3584.

WINE ROUTE: Stellenbosch

The Stellenbosch wine route is the oldest, the largest, and probably the most visited of the Southwest Cape's wine routes. Modelled on the famed *Routes de vin* of France, and the German *Weinstrassen*, it was established in April 1971, and now encompasses five co-operative wineries and 22 private cellars and estates. Many of the estates are very old, their gabled, whitewashed Cape Dutch homesteads, rolling vineyards and their shade-dappled grounds lovely beyond measure. All of the 27 venues are within a 12-km radius of town.

The routes are clearly signposted with their individual emblems. Visitors are encouraged to sample the wines: there's no limit to the number you're permitted to try, though you're usually charged a small fee per glass. Most of the places offer tours (at set times), during which you may see something of the bottling and labelling processes, view the casks tiered in the coolness of a wine- and wood-scented cellar, and talk to people who know all the secrets and subtleties of wine craft. A number of the estates serve 'vintners' platters' and tasty country-style meals, a few run superb restaurants, and you'll occasionally come across one that maintains a small museum, an art gallery or a farm stall selling local specialities.

Blaauwklippen's museum houses a large collection of furniture and kitchen equipment.

The vineyards of Delheim produce wine renowned throughout the world.

WINE ROUTE: STELLENBOSCH

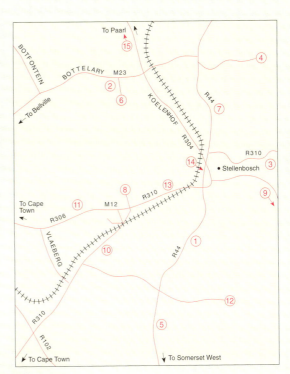

The 300-year-old homestead at Morgenhof lies tucked into the sun-washed south-western foothills of the Simonsberg.

KEY TO THE MAP

1 Blaauwklippen, on the R44, close to Stellenbosch. Attractions include a museum exhibiting coaches and carriages (coach rides around the vineyards October to April), early Cape furniture and utensils. The shop sells local produce, preserves and souvenirs. Coachman's lunch Monday to Saturday (booking essential). Cellar tours Monday to Friday; tastings and sales Monday to Saturday.
Further information: Blaauwklippen, P O Box 54, Stellenbosch 7599, tel (021) 880-0133/4.

2 Bottelary Co-operative Winery, off the M23, northwest of Stellenbosch. Known for its annual Harvest Day (last Saturday in February), when visitors can help with the picking and pressing of grapes and join in the festivities. Tastings and sales Monday to Saturday.
Further information: Bottelary Co-op Winery, P O Box 16, Koelenhof 7605, tel (021) 882-2204.

3 Delaire, on the Helshoogte Pass, is worth visiting for its magnificent views as well as its wines. Picnic lunch offered in summer (or bring your own and eat on the lawns). Tastings and sales Monday to Saturday.
Further information: Delaire, P O Box 3058, Stellenbosch 7602, tel (021) 885-1756.

4 Delheim, off the Klapmuts road (R44), high on the slopes of the Simonsberg. Superb views across to Table Mountain, best enjoyed over an alfresco vintner's platter on the umbrella-shaded lawn. The tasting room is especially enchanting, the wines superb. Cellar tours, tastings and sales Monday to Saturday.
Further information: Delheim, P O Box 10, Koelenhof 7605, tel (021) 882-2036.

5 Eikendal, between Stellenbosch and Somerset West, on the slopes of the Helderberg. Swiss-owned. Undertones of Continental Europe in both the character of the wines and the hospitality. Summertime Swiss country lunches, hot meals May to September, cheese fondues Friday evenings. New vintage celebrated in party style each April. Playground. Tractor rides through vineyards November to February. Cellar tours, tastings and sales Monday to Saturday.
Further information: Eikendal Vineyards, P O Box 2261, Stellenbosch 7601, tel (024) 55-1422.

6 Hartenberg Estate, off the Bottelary road, in the enchanting Devon Valley. Tranquil park-like setting; vintner's platter lunches offered throughout the year (outside in summer, and in the tasting room in winter). Cellar tours, tastings and sales Monday to Saturday.
Further information: Hartenberg Estate, P O Box 69, Koelenhof 7605, tel (021) 882-2541.

7 Morgenhof, on the Klapmuts road (R44). The farm dates from 1692, the homestead from 1820, and the complex is among the region's most prominent tourist venues. Attractions include historic buildings (visitors may wander freely), museum cellar (demonstrations of 19th-century wine-making), extensive herb garden, and the restaurant's simple but sustaining lunches. No cellar tours (although there is a viewing platform). Tastings and sales Monday to Saturday.
Further information: Morgenhof, P O Box 365, Stellenbosch 7599, tel (021) 889-5510.

8 Neethlingshof, Vlottenburg Road (near Stellenbosch, off the R310 to Cape Town). A splendid mansion and one of the region's showpieces. Superb visitor amenities, among them the Lord Neethling Restaurant (Oriental specialities;

The lovely gardens at Neethlingshof, which was first farmed in 1692.

261

WINE ROUTE: STELLENBOSCH

The stately homestead at Uiterwyk still has its original hand-hewn yellowwood floors and ceilings, mellowed by time to a delicate honey colour.

the restaurant belongs to the prestigious *Confrerie de la Chainä des Rotisseurs*). Light meals at Palm Terrace restaurant November to April. Rooms beautifully furnished with antiques. Cellar tours, tastings and sales Monday to Sunday.
Further information: Neethlingshof, P O Box 104, Stellenbosch 7599, tel (021) 883-8988.
9 Neil Ellis Wines on the historic farm *Oude Nektar*, in the scenic Jonkershoek Valley *(see separate entry)*. Has been upgrading its vineyards – noble cultivars like Cabernet Sauvignon have been planted. Picnic lunches December and January, booking essential. Tastings and sales Monday to Friday, Saturdays October to April.
Further information: Neil Ellis Wines, P O Box 917, Stellenbosch 7599, tel (021) 887-0649.
10 Spier, on the Cape Town-Stellenbosch road (R310). Known for its two excellent and popular restaurants – traditional Cape cooking in one,

simple country-style fare enjoyed on the oak-shaded terrace of the other. Also its Ou Kelder art school and gallery (the original wine cellar). Cellar tours Monday to Friday. Tastings and sales Monday to Saturday.
Further information: Spier Estate, P O Box 28, Vlottenburg 7604, tel (021) 881-3808.
11 Uiterwyk, up Stellenbosch Kloof, off the R310. Elegant manor house on land farmed by the same family since 1682. Cellar tours on Saturdays. Tastings and sales Monday to Saturday.
Further information: Uiterwyk, P O Box 15, Vlottenburg 7604, tel (021) 881-3711.

OTHER PLACES OF INTEREST

12 Dombeya Farm, off the R44, close to Rust-en-Vrede estate. A craft workshop producing attractive fabrics (mainly wool, also mohair and cotton), hand-knitted jerseys, shawls, mats. Beautiful setting. Tea garden and indigenous rock garden. Open Monday to Saturday.
Further information: Dombeya Farm, Annandale Road, Strand Highway, Stellenbosch 7600, tel (021) 881-3746.
13 Jean Craig Pottery, on the Devon Valley road (off the R310), just outside Stellenbosch. Visitors can observe the whole pottery process from a central viewing platform. There's a wide selection of products on sale, ranging from the charmingly rough to the sophisticated. Open Monday to Sunday.
Further information: Jean Craig Pottery, P O Box 1250, Drostdy Hof Centre 7599, tel (021) 883-2998.

14 Simonsberg cheese factory, Stoffel Smit Street, on western outskirts of Stellenbosch. Tours. Factory shop. Open Monday to Friday.
Further information: Simonsberg Cheese, 9 Stoffel Smit Street, Stellenbosch 7600, tel (021) 883-8640.
15 Wiesenhof Wild Park, 12 km from Stellenbosch, on Paarl road (R44). Free-roaming animals fed daily 11h00-12h00. Boating on the lake. Picnic and braai facilities. Coffee bar; light refreshments. Closed Mondays.
Further information: Wiesenhof Wild Park, P O Box 50, Klapmuts 7625, tel (02211) 5181.

The five-pointed Castle of Good Hope has been painstakingly restored to its former splendour.

CASTLE OF GOOD HOPE
Buitenkant Street

Map: page 263, 5D/E
From Adderley Street, turn right into Strand Street (towards the southern suburbs). Turn right again at the second set of traffic lights. You will see the Castle on your left.
Details: The museum area is open between 09h30 and 16h00. The Castle is closed on Christmas and New Year's days, Good Friday and Easter Sunday. There are daily conducted tours at 10h00, 11h00, 12h00, 14h00 and 15h00. Admission charged.
Further information: The Curator, The Castle, P O Box 1, Cape Town 8000, tel (021) 469-1160.

A cannon at the Castle bears the inscription of the Vereenigde Oost-Indische Compagnie.

How did well-heeled Capetonians live a hundred years ago? Two hundred? Three hundred? You'll learn some of the answers at the Castle, South Africa's oldest occupied building and one of Cape Town's prominent landmarks, where a number of rooms are fitted out in the styles dating from the 17th century to the mid-19th century.

It was in April 1652, just two days after the arrival of the first European settlers, that work began on Cape Town's first defensive structure – a rather modest earth-and-timber fort on the site of the present Parade. This fort, however, had shortcomings, and the local settlers complained to the Dutch East India Company's directors in Amsterdam, known as the Lords Seventeen. They, in turn, devised a plan which would allow for a castle large enough to hold and safeguard all the farmers and others within the walls. The blueprint was for a pentagonal structure, typical of the Dutch military fortifications of the day, with bastions at each of the five corners.

The outbreak of war between Holland and Britain lent urgency to the project and work began in 1665 under Ijsbrand Goske, a military engineer who was later appointed commander at the Cape. By the end of the year the site had been levelled, a church built and the great stone walls were about to rise from their foundations. However, construction stopped two years later, when Dutch naval victories removed the immediate threat of invasion, and restarted in 1671.

Today you can still see a difference in the colour of the stonework between the two periods. The Castle was completed in 1679. Its five bastions were named after titles held by Prince William of Orange: Nassau, Oranje, Leerdam, Buren and Catzenellenbogen.

In due course Governor Simon van der Stel closed the sea entrance to the Castle because spring tides habitually inundated the area. It was replaced with the present entrance, features of which are the Clock Tower and a carved coat of arms.

After the British took over at the end of the 18th century, they continued to use the area as focal point of Cape Town's social life. Less glamorous are the cells beneath Nassau, used as a torture chamber known as the Black Hole.

The changing of the guard and ceremony of the keys can be viewed once a day on weekdays (sometimes the Friday sequence is a full-dress affair, complete with military band). On display behind the Kat balcony are the paintings of the William Fehr collection, together with fine furniture, carpets and tapestries dating from the 17th-to-19th centuries.

A new collection has been started by the William Fehr Collection Museum, to furnish newly restored rooms and display artefacts discovered during restoration of the Castle. Completed now, and open to the public, are the period rooms in the house of the Secunde (second most senior official at the Cape), which also boast the remains of a number of murals and a unique, painted floor.

COMPANY GARDENS
See page 266

CULTURAL HISTORY MUSEUM
Adderley Street

A mini world-tour awaits visitors to Cape Town's Cultural History Museum, where each room reveals a different culture from the past – ranging from ancient Egyptian to European classical times. On display are porcelain, textiles, silverware, pottery and religious items from China, Japan, India, Tibet and Indonesia.

Many of the exhibits have been selected for their influence on South Africa's cultural heritage. Eye-catching exhibits include European, local and Oriental ceramics (some of these last date from the Chinese Han dynasty), and an intriguing mock-up of a 19th-century Cape chemist's shop. Fascinating, too, are the displays of exquisite glassware, antique weaponry, musical instruments, coins and stamps. Also on display are old postal stones, which served as 'letter boxes' for the early Dutch ships that beat their way around the desolate Cape of Storms.

In the museum's courtyard are the tombstones of Dutch colonial pathfinder Jan van Riebeeck and his wife Maria. The couple had in fact departed the Cape's shores 10 years after the first landing to settle in Batavia (Indonesia), but are best remembered now for the part they played in bringing the first white settlers to South Africa.

The graceful building in which these treasures are housed started life in 1679, as the governing Dutch East India Company's single-storey Slave Lodge. It also served, less formally, as the local brothel. When the iniquitous slave trade began to wilt under the onslaught of the abolitionists the lodge was extended in masterful fashion by the celebrated architect Louis Thibault (1750-1815) and the builder Herman Schutte (1761-1844). From 1810 it functioned as the Supreme Court and, variously, as post office, public library and government offices.

Map: page 263, 5C
Follow Adderley Street towards the mountain. Where it turns to the right at the entrance to Government Avenue, the museum is on your left.
Details: Open Monday to Saturday 09h00-16h30; closed on Sundays, Christmas Day and Good Friday. Admission charged.
Further information: The Curator, SA Cultural History Museum, P O Box 645, Cape Town 8000, tel (021) 461-8280.

At the Cultural History Museum the ornamentation on a pediment, carved by local sculptor Anton Anreith, bears a royal coat of arms watched over by a unicorn.

GOLDEN ACRE
Adderley Street

Central Cape Town's premier shopping venue is a glittering, cosmopolitan complex of cavernous 'foyer' department stores, speciality shops, restaurants, coffee houses, cinemas and offices, which forms part of an even larger concourse running beneath Adderley and adjacent thoroughfares. Among points linked by the bustling and largely subterranean passages are the railway station, the coach and air terminals, the sky-scraping Cape Sun Hotel, two parking garages and, across the square from the station, the Captour, Satour and National Parks information centres.

The Golden Acre is thought to occupy the site of the primitive, leaky-walled fort built in the early 1650s by the first Dutch settlers, though nothing remains of the structure. A small reservoir, or dam, dating back to the commandership of Jan van Riebeeck's successor, Zacharias Wagenaer, was uncovered during building excavations for the modern centre, and the thoughtful architects redrew their plans to retain the relics *in situ*. They're now attractively displayed behind glass.

Just up the street from the Golden Acre are Cape Town's famed and rather raucous flower-sellers, who will (after a little haggling) sell you exquisite blooms for next to nothing.

Map: page 263, 4D
The Golden Acre is clearly visible on the corner of Adderley and Strand streets.
Details: Open during shopping hours. Consult the newspaper for cinema times.
Further information: Captour, P O Box 863, Cape Town 8000, tel (021) 418-5214.

The harvest of Adderley Street's flower-sellers blankets the pavement with a riot of colour and the heady perfume of exquisite blooms.

PLACES TO VISIT

COMPANY GARDENS

Map: page 263, 5B/C

Emerald lawn and birdsong, fountain and lily-mantled pond, stately tree, exotic shrub and flowering plant, and a maze of meandering pathways that beckon the stroller and the lover of tranquillity in the loveliest of surroundings – all this you'll find within a stone's throw of Adderley Street's roaring traffic.

Cape Town's Gardens, more correctly known as The Company Garden, has a direct line of descent to the earliest settler days, when the captains and crews of Holland's great maritime empire were desperate for 'the means of producing herbs, flesh, water and other needful refreshments' on the long and dangerous haul between Europe and the Indies. Indeed it was one of Van Riebeeck's very first tasks to plant a vegetable patch,

An aerial view of the gardens shows the Natural History Museum and Planetarium in the background.

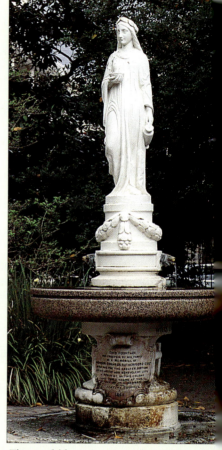

This graceful fountain was erected in 1864 in memory of businessman Howson Rutherfoord. It was later moved to the Company Gardens.

though the project was plagued by setbacks in the harsh winter of 1652.

Eventually, though, after crop disease and the elements had done their very worst, his field began to yield its rich bounty of radishes, lettuces, peas, beans, fennel and endives.

Just 10 years after the Dutch landing, the area was already hinting at its future, less functional, character: it covered an impressive 18 ha, and vines, oaks and ashes, apple, pear, citrus, cherry and olive trees shaded its more mundane plants – among which sweet potato, maize and tobacco were now prominent.

A pleasure lodge made its appearance in 1680 (intended for entertaining visitors excluded from the Castle), a structure later rebuilt to become Tuynhuys, the residence today of South Africa's state president. Further additions to the area included a Slave Lodge, now the Cultural History Museum *(see page 265)*, and a hospital. Governor Simon van der Stel enhanced the Garden's beauty – one French visitor remarked that it would have fitted well into a corner of Versailles – and set aside a section for the cultivation of rare plants. His son, the extravagant W A van der Stel, created a small zoo, or menagerie, at the mountain end.

Bisecting the garden at this time was the principal south-north thoroughfare (known today as Government Avenue), an extension of the Heerengracht that led up from the harbour and, in the early 1700s, was fringed by a number of lemon and orange trees.

Smaller walkways were flanked by trees bearing apples, apricots, pears, quinces, pomegranates and maturing chestnuts. Other plots were planted with the fruits, shrubs and flowers from various other continents. Some were boxed in by 'high hedges of a kind of laurel locally called wild peach'.

Among special delights were a winding stream and its delicate Chinese bridge, a maze of oak trees, and two lion-flanked gateways near the menagerie and aviary.

'A modest Vauxhall' is how Captain Cook described the area in 1777. The north-south thoroughfare was finally completed in 1804.

During succeeding decades the garden was reduced substantially – from its original 18 ha to today's six ha – by the encroachment of a long line of splendid buildings on the eastern side. But the area is still spacious, and as entrancing as ever. More than 3 000 varieties of tree, shrub and flower, most of them exotic species, grace the grounds.

The oaks along Government Avenue, a favourite among visitors, are home and playground to little grey squirrels, whose ancestors were brought from America by Cecil John Rhodes; close by are an aviary bright with bird life, and a tranquil tea garden, as popular for its dapple-shaded surroundings as its modest fare.

Shaded by trees, this elegant gateway in the Company Gardens serves as a tribute to the considerable talent of the versatile sculptor Anton Anreith.

A statue of Sir George Grey, Governor of the Cape from 1854 to 1861. His collection of Africana is housed at the South African Library in the Gardens.

The tearoom at the Company Gardens tempts visitors to take a welcome break within its tree-shaded, tranquil surroundings.

GREENMARKET SQUARE
City centre

Map: page 263, 4C
Greenmarket Square is in the central city area, bounded by Shortmarket, Long and Longmarket streets.
Details: The Market is open from Monday to Saturday. The Old Town House is open from Monday to Friday 10h00-17h30; Saturdays 10h00-13h00; Sundays 10h00-17h00.

Arguably the most pleasing of the city's several piazzas, this cobbled, shade-dappled, animated place is usually filled to overflowing with street-traders' stalls laden with craftwork, costume jewellery, leatherware and creative clothing.

Hidden away in the bric-a-brac is the occasional bargain antique – although the chances of finding the genuine item are a lot better at the nearby indoor antique market in the upper part of Burg Street (opposite Newspaper House), or in the Church Street antiques mall.

Trade was the original function of Greenmarket Square and the Parade. Other squares were used for outspanning ('parking') oxen. Growers of fruit and vegetables would haul their wagonloads of produce from their farms in the upper Table Valley. With the advent of the internal combustion engine, however, most became sterile parking lots – a fate happily now avoided in Greenmarket Square when it reverted to its role as a market, to add colour and life to the city scene.

Numbered among the more impressive buildings fringing the square are the Gothic-revival Metropolitan Methodist Church, which Victorian Capetonians (the foundation stone was laid in 1876) at one time regarded as the country's most splendid place of worship, and the Old Town House.

This latter, completed in the 1750s, was designed as an imposing symbol of Dutch colonial law and good order, and in the early days housed both the Burgher Senate (the civic council) and the Burgher Watch, a kind of combined police force and fire-fighting squad.

The 18th-century populace was summoned to the square by the tower's bell to hear proclamations read from the elegant balcony. A circle set into the floor of the entrance porch marks the spot from where all distances from the city are measured. The building's interior was later remodelled (the star-spangled dome, the double staircase and the rich appointments are notable features) to serve as an art gallery, and now displays some magnificent works, including nearly 100 Dutch and Flemish masterpieces donated by the financier Sir Max Michaelis.

On the area's western side is the former Shell House, modelled on the London Thames Embankment's well-known Shell Mex House, and now operating as the Holiday Inn's Garden Court Inn on the Square, a pleasant and conveniently situated hotel. The Inn's terrace is a popular rendezvous; patrons tend to linger, sipping long drinks, soaking in the ambience, enjoying the sunshine and the kaleidoscope of the market and its polyglot throng.

The surrounding Art Deco buildings are also well worth mentioning (the city's finest concentration of Deco architecture) – in particular Market House, with its indigenous floral and wildlife decorations, Namaqua House, and the recently extended Sun Assurance building (now called Protea Assurance).

Fleamarket stalls cover the cobblestones like brightly coloured toys below the imposing edifices flanking Greenmarket Square.

Local musicians, traders and vivid wares blend in exuberant harmony at Greenmarket Square's fleamarket.

CAPE TOWN

GROOTE KERK
Adderley Street

The 'Great Church', parent venue of the Dutch Reformed Church (NGK) in southern Africa, is the oldest of the country's formal places of worship: the present building was consecrated only in 1841, but the soaring steeple belongs to its thatched and gabled predecessor, whose first stone was laid in 1678.

Inside, you'll see a fine wooden pulpit with a pedestal of carved lions (also belonging to an earlier period – the feature is the work of sculptor Anton Anreith and carpenter Jan Jacob Graaff), a vast roofspan with vaulted teak-and-pine roofing, and a number of old gravestones, some of which serve as paving slabs, others as wall insets.

Map: page 263, 5C
The Groote Kerk is at the top of Adderley Street, on the left as you face the mountain, and also fronts onto Adderley Street.
Details: Open Monday to Friday 10h00-14h00; Sunday services 10h00 and 19h00.

The ornate pulpit, created by Anton Anreith for the Groote Kerk, has graced this beautiful building since its instalment in 1779.

HARBOUR
Foreshore

There is much more to Cape Town's harbour than the alluring Waterfront development *(see separate entry)*. The harbour is also a fascinating kaleidoscope of sounds, sights and sensations from around the globe. Cape Town's port, the country's second-biggest after Durban, is a lot quieter than it was in the heyday of passenger steamers, but the working section still hosts ships from the world's seafaring nations – as a stroll along the quayside will attest.

Notable features include the vast pre-cooling stores that handle the Western Cape's export-fruit harvests, the pleasure craft of the Royal Cape Yacht Club basin and the glamorous cruise ships that disgorge their millionaire passengers into sightseeing buses alongside.

The city was known as 'The Tavern of the Seas', owing its prominence and prosperity over the decades to its strategic position astride the ocean lanes, and to its harbour – although it was a long time

Map: page 263, 2E
There are two main entrances to the harbour area: via Oswald Pirow Street on the Foreshore, and through the Waterfront access via Dock Road. However, instead of carrying on into the Waterfront complex, turn right along the Duncan Dock road towards the Royal Cape Yacht Club and its small-craft harbour.
Details: Specific Waterfront venues are clearly signposted near the harbour entrance.
Further information: Victoria and Alfred Waterfront Information Office, P O Box 50001, Waterfront 8002, tel (021) 418-2350.

A luxury liner berths below Cape Town's modern high-rise skyline and the sandstone massif of the city's beloved Table Mountain.

CAPE TOWN

before the latter amounted to very much. The first jetty made its appearance in 1656, but it wasn't until the latter 19th century – after ships and lives by the hundred had been lost to the Cape's notoriously vicious storms – that any real development took place. In 1860 Prince Alfred tipped the inaugural wagonload of stone for a new harbour (its inner basin was named in his honour, the outer one after his mother, Queen Victoria). Later projects, which reclaimed the present Foreshore from the sea, created the huge Duncan Dock, the 442-m Sturrock Dry-Dock, and the Ben Schoeman dock, with its container terminal.

A seaside city that lost its sea

For the past half-century and more, until the imaginative new Waterfront made its appearance *(see page 278)*, Capetonians were cut off from their once much-loved city seafront. Gone are the leisure beaches that sloped down into Table Bay not far from today's railway station, the old harbour, and the splendid promenade pier at the end of Adderley Street. Today they are all covered over by the broad avenues and tall buildings of a 145-ha segment of the northern city known as the Foreshore.

The area was reclaimed from the sea during the harbour reconstruction work of the 1930s and 1940s, when massive quantities of sand and silt, dredged up from what was to become the giant Duncan Dock, were dumped on the landward side of the project.

Running up from the new harbour is the Heerengracht, a wide thoroughfare flanked by office blocks, its central island an attractive compound of lawn, ornamental pond and fountain, palm trees (transplanted survivors of the harbour building operations – they once lined the graceful Marine Parade beachfront), and pieces of sculpture. These last – the war memorial, and statues of Cape Town's founder Jan van Riebeeck and his wife Maria – survey what used to be Roggebaai, or 'rocky bay'. A short distance to the east, along Hertzog Boulevard, is the impressive Nico Malan Theatre complex.

For many Capetonians, however, concrete and glass are a sterile substitute for what author Lawrence Green remembered as 'the liveliest corner of the waterfront ... a beach of oars, tackle boxes and snoek kerries, anchor ropes and stone anchors. It was a memorable sight when the whole fleet put to sea under spitsails and jibs, and the scene on their return was even more vivid. For then, all the old Malay priests and grey-bearded hadjis in Cape Town, all the bright-skirted Malay womenfolk and fezzed small boys seemed to be waiting on the sand. Then the fish carts were piled high and the fish-horns sounded triumphantly ....'

'Holiday Time in Cape Town in the Twentieth Century', portrayed by artist James Ford in the 1890s.

HELIPORT
Waterfront

Map: page 263, 2C
The two helipads open to tourists are along East Pier, on the Victoria Basin's Quay 7, and on Bay Road, beyond the main harbour's Ben Schoeman Dock, facing onto Table Bay.
Details: Contact Court Helicopters, P O Box 2546, Cape Town 8000, tel (021) 25-2966 (Waterfront base) or (021) 25-5900 (Bay Road base). Civair Helicopters, also based at the Waterfront, offers a wide range of tour options – write to P O Box 120, Newlands 7725, or tel (021) 948-8511.

For the best of bird's-eye scenic views, there can't be much to beat a helicopter flip over the city and Cape Peninsula. High mountains, wooded valleys, shimmering blue sea, picturesque harbour villages and the bustling city – they're all there, unfolding before you like an exquisite tapestry.

Chief among several helipads operating in and around Cape Town is an especially busy one at the Victoria and Alfred Waterfront, from where you're borne aloft on a four-seater for anything from a ten-minute hop around the City Bowl and Table Mountain to an hour's jaunt to Cape Point in the far south. On the latter trip you're flown out along the Atlantic seaboard, past the wide, white beaches of Clifton and Camps Bay and the imposing Twelve Apostles massifs, over the pretty seaside centres of Llandudno, Hout Bay and Kommetjie. After circling Cape Point – the grandest of sights on a clear summer's day – you return along the False Bay coastline, catching your breath as you swoop over the edge of Table Mountain to land back at base.

Somewhere between these two options are a number of other Peninsula itineraries, plus a range of tours that fly you further afield on morning, all-day or even longer package excursions.

JEWISH MUSEUM
Gardens

Flanking Government Avenue in the lovely Gardens area are the imposing Great Synagogue, a domed and twin-towered building in the Renaissance style and, next door, the Old Synagogue, which is designed in the Egyptian revival style that caught the mid-Victorian imagination for a short time.

The latter, South Africa's first really permanent Jewish place of worship, was consecrated in 1863 and houses the treasures of the Jewish Museum, such as textiles, documents and artefacts of ceremonial significance.

The Cape's first Jewish congregation had assembled some years before, at Yom Kippur in 1841. The Cape Jewish Board of Deputies was formed in 1904, and merged with the other provincial bodies to become a national body when Union was founded. But the Jewish role in southern Africa goes back to much earlier days: Jewish mapmakers aided the early navigators, Jewish pilots helped guide Da Gama to India, Jewish merchants helped create the Dutch maritime empire, and a number of Dutch pioneers were of Jewish origin. Much later, after Britain occupied the Cape, Jewish immigrants began to arrive in greater numbers (the majority from Lithuania), the rate increasing significantly after the Kimberley diamond fields were opened in the 1870s and the gold-rich Witwatersrand in the 1880s.

Map: page 263, 6B
84 Hatfield Street, Gardens. From Orange Street, turn away from the mountain into Hatfield Street.
Details: The synagogues are open from Tuesday to Thursday 14h00-17h00; Sundays 10h00-12h30; and also Wednesday mornings in December, January and February. Closed on Jewish and public holidays. Admission free.
Further information: The Curator, Jewish Museum, 84 Hatfield Street, Gardens 8001, tel (021) 45-1546/ 434-6605.

The twin-steepled Great Synagogue abuts the Jewish Museum, repository of some fine artefacts significant to the Jewish community.

KOOPMANS-DE WET HOUSE
Strand Street

The classical façade of Koopmans-De Wet House, with its fluted columns and tasteful pediment, conceals large, luxuriously furnished rooms.

Map: page 263, 4C
Koopmans-De Wet House is on your left as you drive up Strand Street towards Sea Point.
Details: Open Thursday to Saturday 09h30-16h30. Children under 12 must be accompanied by an adult. Admission charged.
Further information: The Curator, Koopmans-De Wet House, 35 Strand Street, Cape Town 8001, tel (021) 24-2473.

A rare glimpse into the fashionable home environment of a well-to-do Cape family in the final years of Dutch rule awaits visitors to Koopmans-De Wet House – one of the most elegant of the city's historic homes, and a showcase of the arts.

The late 19th-century socialite, Maria Koopmans-De Wet, moved into her parents' stylish town house shortly after their death. She launched herself enthusiastically onto the Cape social scene, and immediately started entertaining such luminaries as Cecil Rhodes, Sir Henry Bartle Frere, the liberal Afrikaner J H Hofmeyr, and republican presidents Brand, Reitz, Steyn and Kruger, at her soirees and chamber concerts.

More seriously, she campaigned passionately for the preservation of the Dutch heritage and recognition of what was to become the Afrikaans language. During the South African War of 1899-1902, she was placed under house arrest for her efforts to help the Boers of the infamous concentration camps.

The neoclassical building, completed in 1701 and enlarged several times by its various owners, is regarded as a fine example of late 18th-century Cape domestic architecture. The façade is thought to be the work of the eminent architect Louis Thibault and the sculptor Anton Anreith. Among the more interesting exhibits are rare Arita dishes that bear the 'VOC' (Vereenigde Oost-Indische Compagnie, or Dutch East India Company) monogram, the yellowwood and stinkwood furniture, the Dutch and German glassware, the Nanking porcelain and the restored murals.

LONG STREET
City centre

Map: page 263, 5B
Follow Adderley Street towards Table Mountain. At the entrance to Government Avenue, Adderley Street becomes Wale Street, which then intersects Long Street.
Details: The SA Sendinggestig is open Monday to Friday 09h00-16h00; and on Saturday mornings 09h00-12h00 during school holidays. Admission free, but donations welcome.
Further information: 40 Long Street, Cape Town 8001, tel (021) 23-6755.

The SA Sendinggestig was erected by two local craftsmen, whose contracts still exist in the mission's records.

Junk shops, takeaways and bars, boarding and bawdy houses and second-hand clothes shops line a thoroughfare that not too long ago functioned as the fast-beating heart of central Cape Town. In the earlier years of the century, Long Street was the place to shop, socialize and be seen.

Time and the tide of fashion have taken their toll and the street is more ordinary now, even dilapidated in parts, but lively enough and still worth an exploratory stroll.

Bargain hunters are drawn to the antique shops and second-hand bookstores that rank among the best in the country. Others are attracted by the charmingly filigreed late-Victorian edifices starting at Strand Street. Most of these are at the mountain end (the Blue Lodge is an especially eye-catching example). Many of the venues are getting face-lifts, though the work falls short of full restoration – 'façadism', which involves gutting the interior and constructing a new structure behind or within the existing façades, as has been done at Winchester House on the corner of Long and Shortmarket streets. Passersby can't tell the difference, and the visual results are delightful.

Also of note are the beautiful little Palm Tree and Dorp Street mosques, both above Wale Street. About halfway along the street, on your right as you face the mountain between Castle and Hout streets, is the Sendinggestig, or missionary meeting house, one of the Cape's most elegant early church buildings. Its neoclassical façade features Corinthian pilasters, moulded cornice and a gable decorated with urns. Inside is a handsome hall with its galleries, an imposing pulpit and a pipe organ. The Sendinggestig, completed in 1804, initially served as a centre of education for slaves. It is now a museum housing valuable documents relating to the early missionary work of the various churches in South Africa.

MALAY QUARTER
Wale Street

Hugging the slopes of Signal Hill, on the fringes of the city, is a dense cluster of picturesque, flat-roofed houses dating from the late 18th and early 19th centuries. This is the so-called Malay Quarter, or, more correctly, Bo-Kaap ('Above-Cape'), quaint and narrow-alleyed home to part of a large Islamic community that has its origins in the slaves imported in the early colonial days by the Dutch East India Company.

Until recently the area, a collective national monument, was a bit run-down, and some parts still are, but the buildings are gradually donning new coats of plaster and paint.

In fact, the first of the Cape's Muslims, far from being a slave, was Sheik Yusuf, a revered spiritual leader, aristocrat and feisty rebel against the Company's often harsh rule in Batavia (Indonesia), who was exiled to the Cape as a 'political prisoner' in 1694. Yusuf was followed by a steady stream of folk from the islands of the East – Java, Bali, Timor, the Celibes – and from Ceylon (Sri Lanka). Some of these people spoke Malay (which became a kind of *lingua franca*) and brought with them their craftsmen's skills, their customs and religion. With the abolition of slavery in the early 1800s many of these newly liberated and highly respected people moved to the western part of town, into houses vacated by European immigrant artisans.

There was little intermarriage with other groups and the community remains close-knit and devout, its members regularly attending the city's several attractive little mosques. Members of this community regularly make pilgrimages to Mecca (which is required of every Muslim who has the means), and to the six local kramats, the tombs of holy men. The original language is no longer spoken, but much else has survived time and translocation, including the Khalifa, a trance-like sword dance that once featured in religious ceremony, but which is now performed only as a spectacle. More enduring have been the Malay culinary delights: the exotic foods introduced from the East have evolved into a cornucopia of classic Cape dishes, among them such well-known delectables as bredie (a spicy meat and vegetable stew), bobotie (a sweet curried dish made from mincemeat, topped with egg) and blatjang (chutney).

Cape Town's extensive Muslim heritage is best seen in the Bo-Kaap Museum at 71 Wale Street, a small period house dating from 1763. This is the oldest of the city residences to have survived in its original form. It is thought to have belonged to the celebrated Abu Bakr Effendi, a respected religious leader and academic who came from Turkey to start an Arabic school. Effendi wrote one of the first books to be published in Afrikaans – a bilingual work, in Arabic script, entitled *Bayad-ud Din*, meaning 'Explanation of the Faith'. The museum is furnished as a typical 18th-century Muslim home. Traditional copper and brass utensils decorate the kitchen.

Map: page 263, 4B
Follow Adderley Street towards the Gardens. Here it turns right to become Wale Street. Bo-Kaap is at the top end of Wale Street.
Details: Bo-Kaap Museum is open Tuesday to Saturday, and public holidays 09h30-16h30. Closed Good Friday and Christmas Day. Children under 12 must be accompanied by an adult.
Further information: Captour, P O Box 1403, Cape Town 8000, tel (021) 418-5214.

The Malay Quarter in the Bo-Kaap sprawls in pretty pastel shades up the slopes of Signal Hill.

Pioneer of Islam at the Cape

Hallowed among Cape Town's Muslims is the memory of Sheik Yusuf, 17th-century holy man, insurrectionist, honoured exile and brother of the Sultan of Macassar (who also ruled the East Indian state of Goa).

As a 20-year-old, Yusuf travelled to Java to spread the Islamic faith, but eventually took up arms against the all-powerful Dutch East India Company, leading his insurgent forces in a year-long guerrilla campaign before he was forced to surrender.

The Dutch initially locked Yusuf up in the Castle of Batavia, on Java, and then banished him to Ceylon (Sri Lanka), but the fiery rebel enjoyed rather too big a following for their peace of mind. Threats of a Macassarese invasion to liberate Yusuf forced the Dutch to exile him to their young Cape colony across the Indian Ocean in 1694. Yusuf, his family and retinue, 49 followers, 2 wives and some servants, were settled on the shores of False Bay, near the Eerste River Mouth. Today's Macassar Beach and the adjoining suburb of Macassar are among some of the local place-names that commemorate his sojourn.

There were a number of Muslims at the Cape before Yusuf's arrival, and thousands more were to follow during the succeeding decades, most of them slaves, but some of them spiritual leaders of distinction. Yusuf, however, is regarded as the founder of the region's Islamic community and is venerated as such. His tomb, or kramat, is close to the town of Faure. It is one of six such holy places – five on or near the Peninsula and one on Robben Island – which together form a 'sacred circle', within which those who live enjoy special protection from the elements. The tombs are meticulously maintained, brightly decorated with fine fabrics, and visited by the devout.

CAPE TOWN

NICO MALAN THEATRE CENTRE
D F Malan Street

Map: page 263, 4E
Follow Adderley Street towards the sea. Turn right into Hertzog Boulevard and left into D F Malan Street.
Details: Tours backstage: Wednesdays and Fridays at 11h00, plus Mondays during December.
Further information: Nico Malan Theatre, P O Box 4107, Cape Town 8001, tel (021) 21-5470. Show bookings: Computicket offices, tel (021) 21-4715. Credit-card holders can make reservations at the theatre, tel (021) 21-7695.

The focus of Cape Town's mainstream entertainment, and the country's first large multi-use centre for the presentation of the performing arts is housed in a strikingly modern building on Cape Town's Foreshore. At the heart of the 'Nico', as locals call it, is an impressive 1 200-capacity opera house used for ballet, opera, musicals, symphony concerts and other lavish productions. There is also a 570-seat theatre and a smaller theatre, the Arena, which entertains its 120-strong audiences to intimate and, occasionally, experimental shows.

The design is a pleasant blend of the grand and the cosy, with Italian crystal chandeliers gracing the spacious foyer of the main auditorium. The calendar, which takes in opera, ballet, oratorio, drama and lighter productions, is lively and full (up to 600 performances a year, excluding the children's shows in the foyer). The Nico also has a restaurant, the Café de la Opera.

Soaring columns flank the immense doors leading to the hallowed chambers of Cape Town's Parliament.

PARLIAMENT
Government Avenue

Map: page 263, 5C
Follow Adderley Street towards Table Mountain. The Parliament buildings are on your left as you reach the entrance to Government Avenue.
Details: Guided tours: Monday to Thursday 11h00 and 14h00; Fridays 11h00 during recess periods (usually July to January), but not during Easter recess. The gallery is open during parliamentary sessions; tickets available from Room 12.
Further information: Houses of Parliament, P O Box 15, Cape Town 8000, tel (021) 403-2911 before arrival. Jackets and ties required in the gallery.

Stately home to South Africa's lawmakers, the white-and-red-trimmed edifice, which faces onto the lovely city Gardens, was built for the old Cape colonial legislature in 1885 and variously described by contemporaries as 'palatial', 'magnificent' and 'stunning', though the first members were known to complain of the draughts, the poor acoustics and the inferior lighting. The stately interior, decorated in traditional reds and greens, is certainly spectacular.

The building was enlarged at Union in 1910, extended again several times in the decades that followed, and adapted in the 1980s to accommodate P W Botha's controversial three-chamber parliament. Of special note is the original House of Assembly, which now serves as the dining room, and the opulently Edwardian wing that the distinguished architect Sir Herbert Baker designed around the later House of Assembly. The Library (which contains the superb 50 000-volume Mendelssohn collection of Africana) and the Parliamentary Museum are accessible to visitors, as is the public gallery.

PLANETARIUM
Queen Victoria Street

Sound and light combine to produce a memorable other-worldly sensation as projectors probe the southern heavens, displaying the star-crusted constellations of the past, present and future on a domed ceiling.

The principal instruments, similar to those used by NASA trainees, can reproduce the night sky at any stage of a 26 000-year period – 13 000 years either side of modern times. In fact, the planetarium has a total of 12 projectors, which can simulate terrestrial, as well as celestial, horizons.

You can learn about the changing state of the night sky above southern Africa by attending the regular 'The Sky Tonight' show on the first Saturday of each month at 13h00. Other shows change regularly.

Map: page 263, 6B
The Planetarium is part of the South African Museum complex in Queen Victoria Street, on the southern fringes of the central area. Follow Adderley Street towards the Gardens. After Adderley swings right to become Wale Street, turn left into Queen Victoria Street.
Details: Shows on Tuesdays and Thursdays 13h00; Tuesday nights 20h00; Saturdays 12h00 and 14h00; Sundays 14h00 and 15h30. Extra daily shows during school holidays. Admission charged.
Further information: The Planetarium, P O Box 61, Cape Town 8000, tel (021) 24-3330.

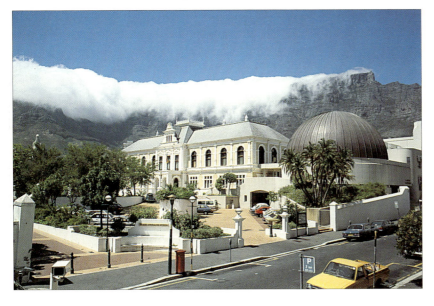

The South African Museum and its domed Planetarium lie beneath the cloud-covered curve of Table Mountain.

The ornate carvings that embellish the doorways and balcony of Rust-en-Vreugd are attributed to Anton Anreith.

RUST-EN-VREUGD
Buitenkant Street

This 18th-century house on the eastern fringes of the city contains some of the finest items in the celebrated William Fehr collection of historic watercolours, drawings and prints, and Africana such as oil paintings, furniture, ceramics, glass and metalware are on display in the Castle *(see separate entry)*.

The building itself, which dates back to about 1778, is the finest example of an 18th-century Cape town house. It was originally the home of the disreputable (disliked by the colonists) Willem Cornelis Boers, an official who amassed a fortune through shady dealings and extortion. Architecture at the time was much influenced by the young and talented Louis Thibault, who had arrived from Europe full of fresh ideas. It is thought that the prolific Anton Anreith created the baroque carvings that decorate the façade's doorways and balcony.

Map: page 263, 6C
From Adderley Street, turn towards the Grand Parade via Darling Street. Turn right into Buitenkant Street.
Details: Open 09h30-16h00 (weekdays only). Admission charged. Organized school groups free.
Further information: The Curator, Rust-en-Vreugd, 78 Buitenkant Street, Cape Town 8001, tel (021) 45-3628.

CAPE TOWN

An exhibit at the South African Museum illustrates the lifestyle of the San, who mastered the art of survival in the harsh Kalahari environment.

Map: page 263, 6B
Follow directions as given for the Planetarium.
Details: Open daily 10h00-17h00. Closed Good Friday, Christmas Day. There is an admission charge for adults; free entry on Wednesdays. Lectures and videos on a regular basis.
Further information: The South African Museum, P O Box 61, Cape Town 8000, tel (021) 24-3330.

SOUTH AFRICAN MUSEUM
Queen Victoria Street

Eerily realistic plaster casts of San (Bushmen), together with displays of San rock art, are among the fascinating variety of exhibits on show at the South African Museum. The casts, created from living subjects by artist James Drury in the early years of this century, complement the so-called 'images of power' – artefacts with deep mystical significance for the early San.

Of special interest too are the dioramas of the fossil-rich Karoo and the reptiles, many with disproportionately large craniums (these were the *dinocephalians* or 'fearful-heads') that roamed the then-fertile plains 200 million years ago. The Karoo in fact recounts a great many chapters of the evolutionary storybook, from the time the first amphibians crawled out from the primordial sea, to the emergence of the first mammals.

The museum was founded in 1825 by Governor Lord Charles Somerset, who intended it as a centre for the 'reception and classification of objects of the animal, vegetable and mineral kingdoms which are found in South Africa' – a brief it has followed with precision and integrity. One of the earliest of the 'receptions' is the skull of an enormous, now-extinct buffalo, with a curved span of horns measuring an intimidating 2,5 metres.

The place houses much else in the fields of natural history (notably birds and fishes), geology, archaeology and the study of man. The Whale Well (four levels high) is certainly worth a visit; slightly at variance with the main themes is the section devoted to the history and nature of printing.

Whales of the southern seas

One of the most spectacular exhibits at the South African Museum is the Whale Well – containing plaster casts of some of the largest mammals on the planet.

That these great sea mammals once lived on land is evident from their minute residual hindlimbs (the forelimbs evolved into flippers), and from their need for air – some submerge to depths of 1 000 metres and more but have to surface every half-hour or so. Otherwise, they are wholly adapted to life beneath the ocean waves, moving over immense distances, interacting with each other and communicating in their own 'language' according to intricate patterns that scientists don't yet fully understand.

Their order, *Cetacea*, is divided into two groups: the baleens or whalebacks, which feed by filtering plankton and other tiny marine organisms through the baleen plates in their mouths, and the carnivorous toothed whales. Fish, octopus, squid and even sea birds feature in the latter's diet, though the only type that preys on other mammals is the relatively small killer whale, which has been known to lunge up onto coastal rocks to snap up a fat seal.

Among species that inhabit South African and neighbouring waters are the southern right, pygmy right, the finback, the humpback, the 30-m blue whale, largest of all earth's animals (all these are baleens), the killer whale and the great sperm whale, which has been hunted to the brink of extinction for its blubber.

A whale skeleton hangs suspended above visitors to the South African Museum's Whale Well.

SOUTH AFRICAN NATIONAL GALLERY
Gardens

Over 6 500 works are housed in the gallery, some of the finest donated by Abe Bailey, turn-of-the-century Randlord, politician, rebel (against Paul Kruger's Afrikaner-run Transvaal republic), husband of famed aviatrix Mary Bailey, sportsman, and patron of the sports and of the arts.

The largest of the attractive building's halls is used for a frequently changing exhibition of modern South African art. There is also a touch gallery for the blind, and film shows and lectures are presented throughout the year. Of note are the carved main doors, which depict the wanderings of the Jewish people.

Nearby is a magnificent statue of Jan Smuts – soldier, statesman, philosopher, naturalist and among the most revered of South Africans. The work of British sculptor Sydney Harpley, it was erected in 1964 and immediately provoked a public outcry: critics considered it a grotesque parody of a great man, but it radiates power and personality, conveying the essence of this colossus that dominated the South African political arena during the century's first five decades. Taken aback by the uproar, the city fathers hurriedly commissioned a blander version of the subject, and this, a 5,3-m bronze work by Ivan Midford-Barberton, stands at the northern end of Government Avenue.

Map: page 263, 5C
The gallery is off Government Avenue, in the Gardens area. Follow Adderley Street towards Table Mountain. Where it turns into Wale Street, Government Avenue is directly ahead of you.
Details: The National Gallery is open Mondays 13h00-17h00; Tuesday to Sunday 10h00-17h00; closed Christmas Day, Good Friday. Admission free.
Further information: The Curator, South African National Gallery, P O Box 2420, Cape Town 8000, tel (021) 45-1628.

'Christ Head', painted in 1952 by local artist Alexis Preller, is on display in the South African National Gallery.

Stroll along brick-paved walkways and enjoy a cup of tea below leafy saplings in St George's Mall.

ST GEORGE'S MALL
City centre

For city strollers with time on their hands and a little money in their pockets, this is probably the most inviting of the city's thoroughfares. The mall used to be a 10-block, traffic-congested street until a few years ago, when the civic planners blocked it off for the near-exclusive use of pedestrians. The entire length is attractively brick-paved and embowered; at the bottom end is Thibault Square. Shops and arcades, including the up-market Stuttafords Town Square, run up either side, and there are umbrella-shaded bistros, kiosks and street stalls along the central pavement area, giving serendipity shoppers space to move and some intriguing wares to choose.

Buskers, some more talented than others, entertain passers-by.

Map: page 263, 4C
The Mall runs between Adderley and Burg streets, from Thibault Square in the north up to Wale Street in the south.

PLACES TO VISIT

VICTORIA AND ALFRED WATERFRONT

Map: page 263, 1C

From Adderley Street drive towards the sea and turn left into Coen Steytler Avenue. You can reach the Waterfront via Dock Road, which leads off Coen Steytler. From the Atlantic suburbs (Sea Point, Green Point) you can reach the Waterfront via Beach and Portswood roads.

Details: A shuttle bus plies between the Waterfront and the city's Tourist Information Bureau on Adderley Street, close to the railway station. A bus also links the Waterfront with Sea Point (via Beach Road). No admission charge. Parking space is plentiful. Hotel accommodation *in situ*.

Further information: Captour, P O Box 863, Cape Town 8000, tel (021) 418-5214; Victoria and Alfred Waterfront Information Office, P O Box 50001, Waterfront 8002, tel (021) 418-2350. The latter's service includes advice, directions, bookings for tours and walks, guidance on activities and events, and a continuous audiovisual presentation. Wheelchairs available.

Adding a flavour of San Francisco to Cape Town, the vibrant, thoroughly cosmopolitan Waterfront development at Table Bay Harbour clings to the water's edge, a glittering wonderland reclaimed from the sea.

Watched over by the brooding massif of Table Mountain, the Waterfront has become the Western Cape's premier entertainment and shopping complex, offering theatres, cinemas, restaurants and fast-food outlets, and a fascinating variety of speciality shops, galleries and craft markets. Here the tang of the sea is immediate, the hustle and bustle of Table Bay's boats and ships ever present. Not for nothing is this part of town known as 'The Tavern of the Seas', a place where visitors may relax in convivial surroundings and replenish sagging spirits.

KEY TO THE MAP

1 The SA Maritime Museum houses a model of Table Bay as it was constructed in 1897 by convicts. Before that, in 1860, all there was to protect visiting ships from the full force of winter's northwesterly gales was a breakwater, which was inaugurated by Prince Alfred, son of Queen Victoria. The original harbour basin was named in his honour. Also on display is a model showing future developments within the complex, as well as South Africa's largest collection of model ships open to the public. Open daily 10h00-17h00 (except Christmas Day and New Year's Day). Entrance fee charged. For further details contact the museum at (021) 419-2505.

2 The Telkom Exploratorium uncovers the history of communication throughout the ages with exhibits ranging from the oldest of telephones to the latest in space-age technological developments. Contact the Exploratorium at (021) 419-5957 for details.

3 The Dock Road Complex comprises a theatre, Dock Road Cafe, the Pumphouse pub, and the Dock Road Venue which is used for conferences, public and private functions, and exhibitions. The complex is housed in the old Electric Light and Power Station,

The Waterfront from the air. The long building on the left is the luxurious Victoria and Alfred Hotel, renowned for its fine accommodation.

The Waterfront, sheltered beneath the silent monolith of Table Mountain, combines effervescent trade with bustling port activity.

This vividly restored figurehead, just below the Port Captain's building, braves the elements.

and has been imaginatively restored, in keeping with its workmanlike origins. For details, telephone the complex at (021) 419-7722.

4 The unique indoor Arts and Crafts Market has more than 140 stalls offering goods ranging from clothing, toys and jewellery to art, ceramics, porcelain, furnishings and woodwork. Many of the goods on sale are made on the spot, and stallholders are happy to discuss their crafts with you. Open daily during December, January and the Easter holidays between 09h30 and 18h00. At other times between 10h00 and 17h00. Entrance free.

5 Helicopter rides offer high-flyers a spectacular bird's-eye view of the Peninsula. You can take an hour-long tour around the Peninsula or a scenic flip along the coast to Hout Bay and back. Flights to the winelands can also be arranged. Contact Court Helicopters at (021) 418-2369, Civair Helicopters at (021) 419-5182 or Sport Helicopters at (021) 434-4444 for details.

Those wishing to cross Victoria Basin may use the Penny Ferry, which has been in operation for over a century.

VICTORIA AND ALFRED WATERFRONT

A glassblower practises his ancient craft, using nimble fingers and a delicate touch to fashion ornaments.

The Red Shed, where a cornucopia of crafts is made, exhibited and sold. An added bonus is being able to chat to the craftspeople themselves while admiring their wares.

6 The Penny Ferry was established over 100 years ago to transport seamen. Today it offers landlubbers a chance to test their sea legs on a four-minute trip between the Pierhead and South Quay. Other boat trips, including romantic sundowner cruises, are also available.

7 The Amphitheatre, on the Market Plaza in the heart of the Waterfront development, is the venue for concerts and shows, from children's choir festivals to pop concerts. The Cape Town Symphony Orchestra also performs here on occasion.

8 The Two Oceans Aquarium on Dock Road is a marine emporium of stunning proportions.

9 The new BMW Pavilion at the Portswood Road entrance features the fascinating IMAX cinema, designed to dazzle with images projected onto a screen five storeys high. After the show you may choose to wander around the showroom filled with luxury vehicles and motorcycles. For further details contact the IMAX Theatre at (021) 419-7340.

10 The *SAS Somerset* (formerly the *HMS Barcross*, built in 1944) is moored in the Alfred Basin in front of the Victoria and Alfred Hotel. So, too, is the steam tug *Alwyn Vintcent*, built in Venice in 1954, for the then South African Railways and Harbours. You may board the vessels to see how they were used in their heyday. Contact the SA Maritime Museum *(see page 278)* for details.

For more information about any of the facilities, exhibitions, shops or activities, contact the Victoria and Alfred Waterfront Information Office, P O Box 50001, Waterfront 8002, tel (021) 418-2350.

The Amphitheatre is the setting for many musical events. Here the Cape Town Symphony Orchestra performs an open-air concert before an enthusiastic audience.

CAPE PENINSULA

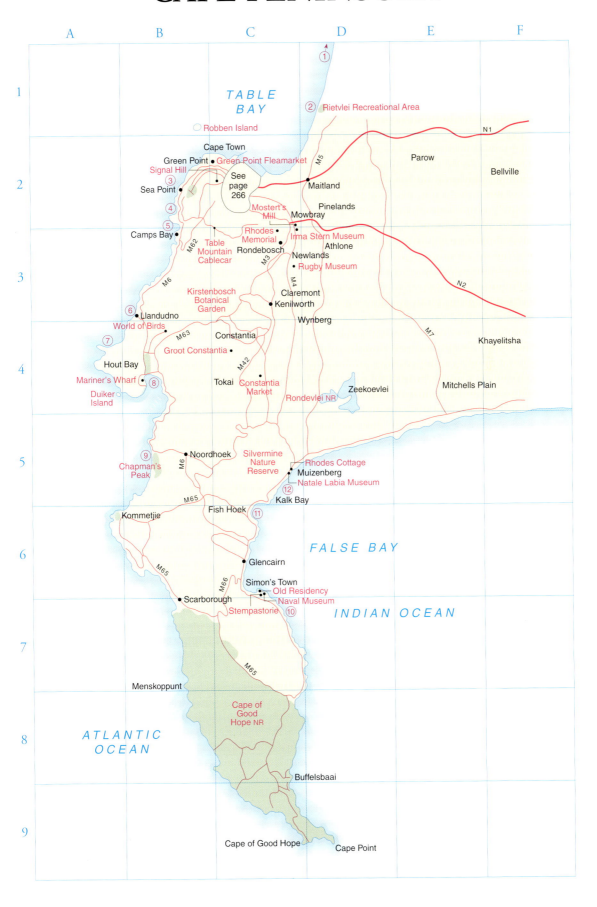

PLACES TO VISIT

Beaches around the CAPE PENINSULA

Sun, sea and sand rank high among the Cape Peninsula's drawcards, but these pleasures are by no means uniform along its 150-km coastline: a quirk of nature has endowed the eastern and western seaboards with entirely different personalities. The former tends to be windy but with warm water, the latter pleasantly sheltered from the southeasterly wind but with almost freezing water – thanks to the cold Benguela Current sweeping northwards from the South Atlantic.

Generally speaking, bathing around the Cape Peninsula is safe, and there are plenty of opportunities for boating, windsurfing, paragliding, scuba-diving and snorkelling off most of the wide, sandy beaches. In some spots, however, there are backwashes and rip currents, so be sure to ask locals about the bathing conditions before you venture into the water. Stick to the popular areas, which are patrolled by beach constables and manned by lifeguards.

The famous, flat-topped heights of Table Mountain provide a striking backcloth to Bloubergstrand's broad beach. The resort village, noted for its fine restaurants as well as its sands, is becoming increasingly popular.

KEY TO THE MAP, page 281
1 Bloubergstrand is well north of the city and not strictly part of the Peninsula, but there's a splendid view of Cape Town and Table Mountain from its two bays. Big Bay is for surfers and paddle-skiers, Little Bay for families. Nearby Table View is similar; the bathing is safe, the southeaster usually strong, and the water cold.
2 Milnerton offers eight kilometres of golden sands, and is popular with anglers and surfers; canoeists enjoy paddling on Milnerton Lagoon; golf and horse-racing are among the local attractions.
3 Sea Point. High-season holiday-makers crowd this cosmopolitan suburb, and its seafront is a favourite among strollers. The shore is rocky and the small bays form pocket beaches which are well patronized. Tidal pools are much used at Saunders Rocks, Sunset Beach and Milton Road. There's a magnificent saltwater pool at the Sea Point Pavilion.
4 Clifton has four fine, wind-free and fashionable beaches, each divided from the next by large granite boulders. Families tend to gravitate to Fourth Beach, and the trendy young to the other three. The sea is invariably calm, blue and very cold. Yachts anchor offshore, backdropped by the grand massifs of Lion's Head and the first of the Twelve Apostles that form the western coastal rampart. Just south of the main Clifton beaches is Maiden's Cove, a popular recreational spot with picnic sites and braai facilities.
5 Camps Bay has a magnificent wide, white beach, and, together with its palm-lined promenade, azure blue sea and stunning mountain backdrop, has become one of Cape Town's leading beaches. It is readily accessible, and the pavement cafés, bars and restaurants, together with magnificent late sunsets, make this beach the place to be for fun-seekers. There are also a tidal pool and picnic area at the southern end of the beach.
6 Llandudno has perhaps the loveliest of all seaside settings, bounded on three sides by precipitous mountainside, and on the fourth by an enchanting little beach. The surf, though, can be rough and there are dangerous crosscurrents at times.
7 Sandy Bay. There's more than bare bottoms at South Africa's best-known nudist beach. It is marvellously secluded, framed by fynbos-covered mountain slopes and the rocky Oude Schip peninsula in the south. The line of its beachfront is broken by boulders that afford welcome privacy. On most days, even in high summer, the water's very cold.

CAPE PENINSULA BEACHES

Fashionable Clifton, on the Atlantic seaboard close to the city, has four secluded beaches that beckon the beautiful people.

Camps Bay, just to the south of Clifton, is geared to family outings. Swaying palms, shops and pavement bistros line the attractive beachfront.

8 Hout Bay has one of the Peninsula's best walking beaches – against the magnificent backdrop of Chapman's Peak and The Sentinel. Easy parking makes it a favourite with holiday-makers – so get there early.

9 Noordhoek. For much of the time the Peninsula's longest stretch of sand is virtually deserted. There aren't any facilities, the area tends to be blustery and the currents strong, but it's a fine venue for long walks and gentle horseback rides.

10 Boulders, just north of Simon's Town on the False Bay shore, is an attractively secluded haven which comprises a tumble of huge, round rocks on a sandy shore. The granite boulders are ideal vantage points for watching the antics of jackass penguins, or for sunning yourself above the sea. You can swim in the small bays here, although the water can be cold at times. Other pleasant spots in the vicinity are Seaforth just south of Simon's Town, Froggy Pond, and, further south, Miller's Point, which has a tidal pool, a neat little caravan park and a restaurant.

11 Fish Hoek's beachfront offers gentle surfing and safe bathing in water that is substantially warmer than that on the west coast. Nearby St James boasts a small, sheltered beach and a tidal pool.

12 Muizenberg. This is perhaps the finest and most popular of all the Peninsula's beaches. The sands stretch 15 km, merging in the east with Sunrise, Strandfontein and Mnandi beaches. Muizenberg's seafront is lined by a grassy embankment and raised promenade. Its sunken-gardens complex incorporates a swimming pool, boat-pool, water slide, kiosks, restaurant and putt-putt course. Adding a charming splash of colour to the scene are Victorian-style bathing boxes.

Muizenberg beach is indeed lovely, and often wind-blown, stretching 15 km southwards from the charming town.

A thriving colony of quite endearing and endangered jackass penguins – so named for their braying call – occupies the Boulders area near Simon's Town.

283

CAPE PENINSULA

CAPE OF GOOD HOPE NATURE RESERVE
Southern Peninsula

Map: page 281, 8C

Take the M4 or M5 south to Muizenberg and then along the False Bay shoreline, following the signs. The alternative route – along the Peninsula's west coast (M65) from Sea Point to Hout Bay, and over Chapman's Peak and through Kommetjie and Scarborough – is longer but scenically rewarding.

Details: Open throughout the year: November to April 07h00-18h00; May to October 07h00-17h00. There's no public transport to the reserve, but coach tours set out from Cape Town each day. Admission is charged per person and vehicle, and there are entrance fees to picnic areas such as Buffels Bay and Bordjiesdrif.

Accommodation: Hotels around the Peninsula offer comfortable accommodation, with easy access to Cape of Good Hope Nature Reserve. There are also several caravan parks and camping sites.

Further information: Cape of Good Hope Nature Reserve, P O Box 62, Simon's Town 7995, tel (021) 780-1100; Captour, P O Box 1403, Cape Town 8000, tel (021) 418-5214/5.

The massive headland of Cape Point falls almost sheer to waters wreathed in legend – a wild, mystical place filled with the constant roar of surf and the scream of whirling sea gulls.

Cape Point is the highlight of the Cape of Good Hope Nature Reserve. Nearly 8 000 ha of indigenous fynbos (fine bush) cover the reserve. In spring, this natural garden bursts into bloom in a surge of colour. About 1 200 plant species have been recorded in the area.

Fauna includes the once-threatened bontebok and other antelope, mountain zebras, caracals and Cape foxes, about 160 species of bird (including ostriches, black eagles and pelagic species such as albatrosses and cormorants), and several troops of baboons. These baboons are believed to be the only primate groups in the world (excluding man) that subsist on the fruits of the sea, which they scavenge at low tide. They tend to become overfamiliar with visitors and are persistent beggars of food. To avoid any confrontation with the baboons, do not feed them under any circumstances, and keep your car doors closed if you happen to have any food in the car.

There is a network of roads and paths that crisscrosses the reserve. These lead to viewsites, braai areas and picnic spots.

Cape Point probes like a giant, hooked finger into the sometimes placid, often turbulent, southern ocean. The headland is an integral part of the reserve.

Three tidal pools and some pleasant stretches of beach beckon bathers and sun-seekers. Buffels Bay, with its neatly terraced lawns and idyllic picnic spots, has a slipway for small craft and access to some excellent snorkelling and scuba-diving areas (marine life here is varied and plentiful).

On your way in or out of the reserve, stop off at the old homestead which serves as a restaurant and kiosk.

Cape Point is the southwesternmost point and inspirational tip of Africa. For sheer majesty and excitement, no visit to the Peninsula would be complete without a trip to Cape Point. To reach the

The sociable residents of Cape Point

The dog-faced baboons that entertain and sometimes pester you at Cape Point are chacmas, found over many parts of southern Africa.

They are sociable, inquisitive, intelligent and very agile creatures that have adapted remarkably well to life in open country. Though fairly large – a full-grown male can weigh up to 40 kg – chacmas sometimes fall prey to leopards and other big carnivores.

They roam the open veld or mountain ranges in troops of up to 100 individuals, retiring into a 'laager' when danger threatens. The males will fight to the death, if need be, to protect the females and young members of the troop.

Baboons cover a lot of ground in their foraging forays, feeding on roots, fruits, bulbs, certain kinds of succulent leaf, insects, scorpions, lizards and even birds and small mammals. The baboons of the Cape of Good Hope reserve routinely scavenge the shoreline at low tide, and are known to eat certain species of shellfish.

Chacma baboons roam parts of the Cape of Good Hope Nature Reserve.

viewsite above Cape Point, you can either take a shuttle bus to the top of the massif or climb the steps. Once you reach the base of the old lighthouse (built in 1857), you're rewarded with magnificent vistas, taking in the whole of False Bay and the distant Hottentots-Holland Mountains, Danger Point (80 km away) and the ocean all around.

Legend has it that a ghost ship, the 17th-century *Flying Dutchman*, sails the seas off Cape Point, her torn sails and tattered rigging flapping in the wind.

The summit of Cape Point commands memorable vistas over the ocean and sweeping shore. After Cape Agulhas this is the second most southerly point of the African continent.

CHAPMAN'S PEAK
Hout Bay

The tortuous 10-km road along the sea-flanking mountainside between Hout Bay and Noordhoek is one of the world's most spectacular scenic drives. The road bisects yellow, red and brown layers of Table Mountain sandstone, as it winds 600 m up to the highest point. Along the way are plenty of picnic spots from which you can survey the shimmering beauty of Chapman's Bay, the tranquil harbour and beach of Hout Bay and the imposing mountain known as The Sentinel. Take a camera along – the photographic opportunities are excellent.

As you descend from the crest of Chapman's Peak Drive, another stunning vista unfolds before you – the broad, white sands of Noordhoek washed by breakers rolling in from the South Atlantic. In the distance you will see Slangkop Lighthouse and the pretty little village of Kommetjie. Try to make the trip just before dusk, when the dying sun caresses the hills, and the lights of Hout Bay village and harbour begin to twinkle.

Chapman's Peak and Bay are thought to have been named after John Chapman, an English mariner who came ashore in 1607 to explore Hout Bay.

Motorists face dizzy heights, steep gradients and sharp bends along Chapman's Peak Drive.

CONSTANTIA MARKET
Constantia

On many Saturdays of the year an Aladdin's cave of handiwork entices browsers and buyers to Constantia's upper Kendal Road, venue of the oldest, and arguably the best, of the Peninsula's half-dozen or so craft markets. The wares on display are refreshingly original, ranging from beautiful yellowwood furniture from Knysna, home of the hardwoods, to hand-blown glassware, basketry and innovative jewellery. There are also carpets and tapestries, trendy and sophisticated clothing, pottery for Africa, and a fair sprinkling of the unusual – delicate handmade dolls, for example. Tea and pancakes (and boerewors rolls), on sale in the shady grounds, sustain shoppers and strollers.

Nearby are the vineyards and architectural splendours of *Groot Constantia* (see separate entry), in whose grounds a second market is held occasionally on Sundays. Here the stalls are fewer but the occasion is more geared to the family outing. Pony rides and strolling musicians (flutes and recorders are usually in evidence) are among the attractions.

Map: page 281, 4C
Take the M3 to the Kendal Road turn-off. Turn right at the stop street. The market is on your left. There is plenty of parking available.
Details: The market is usually held once a month throughout the year, 08h00-13h00, but weekly in December. A calendar is available from Captour.
Further information: Constantia Craft Market, 22 Woodside Drive, Pinelands 7405, tel (021) 531-2653.

CAPE PENINSULA

DUIKER ISLAND
Hout Bay

Map: page 281, 4A
Enter Hout Bay Harbour at the Mariner's Wharf sign; the *Circe* takes on passengers a little further along the quayside.
Details: Circe sails at 10h30 every day from October to April, and at 10h30 on Saturdays and Sundays from May to September.
Further information: Circe Launches, P O Box 26290, Hout Bay 7872, tel (021) 790-1040.

In midsummer a noisy congregation of more than 4 000 Cape fur seals suns itself on this small, 1 500 m² rocky island just to the southwest of Hout Bay's strikingly prominent Sentinel massif. Keeping the seals company is a mixed community of sea birds, including sea gulls, terns and Bank cormorants, a species which is more or less restricted to the Western Cape and Namibian seaboards.

The seals are perhaps too common for their own good: commercial fishermen in South African waters tend to resent (and sometimes persecute) these large and voracious aquatic mammals for the inroads they make on marine resources.

Only *bona fide* researchers, suitably armed with permits, may set foot on Duiker Island, but ordinary visitors can experience close encounters with the wildlife from the deck of the launch *Circe*, which sets out from Hout Bay every morning during the season and every weekend in the winter months. Other launches also ply the sightseeing route, but only in summer.

A dense mass of Cape fur seals blankets tiny Duiker Island near the Peninsula fishing harbour of Hout Bay. For centuries these ocean mammals have been prized for their pelts, meat and blubber.

GREEN POINT FLEAMARKET
Green Point

Map: page 281, 2C
Take either Western Boulevard (M6) or Somerset Road (via Strand Street) westwards, past Signal Hill on your left, to the traffic circle. You'll see the stadium, its car park and the market on your right.
Details: The market is open 09h00-17h00 on Sundays and public holidays throughout the year.

The fleamarket held on the Green Point Stadium's parking area is the largest of the country's weekend venues, a pleasant enough place for loitering on a sunny Sunday morning, and ambling between the rows of stalls. Not much craftwork is on display – you'll have to visit the craft market at the nearby Waterfront *(see separate entry under Cape Town)* for the individual touch – but there's plenty of fossicking interest among the bric-a-brac and books, jewellery, factory goods, used hardware and other items from cleared-out lofts and garages.

The scene is busy and colourful, and among the food outlets there's a fully fledged and excellent fish-and-chip stall. Proceeds from the running costs of the market are divided among 34 charities in the greater Cape Town area.

GROOT CONSTANTIA
Constantia

Map: page 281, 4C
Turn off the Blue Route (M3) onto the M41, signposted 'Constantia', and follow directions to Hout Bay. After 3 km, turn left onto a tarred road signposted 'Groot Constantia'. This access road is 2,5 km long.
Details: Open daily except Christmas Day and Good Friday 08h30-18h00. Small entrance fee. Guided tours of the cellar hourly 10h00-16h00; wine sales 10h00-17h00. Parking available. Visitor amenities include a gift shop and two restaurants. You can take along picnic baskets and relax on the shady lawns.
Further information: Groot Constantia Trust, Private Bag, Constantia 7848, tel (021) 794-5128.

A long avenue of oaks links the ornamental pool, where Cape Town's high society once disported itself, with the manor house of Constantia, perhaps the stateliest of all the country's historic homesteads, and a prime destination for locals and tourists.

It is in the general area of the pool that several startled visitors have, over the years, reported seeing the ghost of Simon van der Stel, the outstanding Cape governor who built the original house and lived there until his death in 1712. Van der Stel also planted the first of the vineyards for which Constantia became renowned, the sweet, rich red wines eventually finding their way to the aristocratic tables of Europe. Among those they seduced was King Louis Philippe of France, who sent a representative to the Cape to buy a consignment.

Constantia achieved the height of its wine-making fame, and of its architectural glory, during its occupation by the Cloete family from 1778 to 1885. The gracious single-storey, beautifully thatched homestead, which conforms to the classic U-shape of the Cape Dutch style, was all but destroyed by fire in 1925, but meticulous restoration has preserved its

CAPE PENINSULA

Grecian myth and 18th-century Gallic artistry come together beautifully in the elaborately carved pediment of Groot Constantia's double-storey wine cellar.

grandeur. Its gable is unusually large, and in its niche stands a statue of *Abundance* bearing a cornucopia. Inside you'll find some superb period furniture, tapestries and paintings, and delicate antique porcelain from Holland, the Rhineland, China and Japan.

Elsewhere in the grounds is the *Jonkershuis*, the house which was traditionally built for the eldest son of the family, and a two-storey cellar that is thought to have been designed by French architect Louis Thibault. The cellar's exquisite pediment, the work of Anton Anreith, features a fine stucco relief of *Ganymede*, youthful cupbearer of the Grecian gods, surrounded by romping cherubs. And if you're fascinated by the story of wine and wine-making over the centuries, the museum next door is well worth an hour of your time.

Groot Constantia is one of the Constantia Valley's three functioning wine farms – its neighbours are the more modest *Buitenverwachting* and *Klein Constantia* – which together form the Peninsula's only wine route.

The elegant Cape Dutch manor house of Groot Constantia. Here visitors may view the beautifully furnished interior, a wine museum, a cellar and two restaurants.

IRMA STERN MUSEUM
Rosebank

A carefully chosen selection of dedicated works by one of South Africa's most talented and controversial artists is on display at her former home in the southern suburb of Rosebank.

Between 50 and 100 of Irma Stern's works are on view, together with sculptures and her splendid collections of ancient treasures, antique furniture, Congolese and other African artefacts, and *objets d'art*. Her studio is just as it was during her lifetime (she died in 1966).

Trouble dogged Irma Stern in her early career. The exuberant, prolific and innovative painter, born in 1894 into a wealthy German-Jewish farming family in what is now the North-West Province, travelled widely in her youth, holding the first of her great many one-person shows in Berlin in 1919. When she returned to her native land a year later, though, her oils were dismissed by some as 'revolutionary', and the police went so far as to investigate charges of immorality.

In the beginning, Irma Stern found it extremely difficult to sell her work in South Africa, despite her ever-increasing international popularity.

Eventually, however, she gained local acceptance: her numerous exhibitions (63 in South Africa alone, each of which featured over 80 works), her tireless wanderings through the subcontinent, and her portrayal of the Africans she encountered, gave her white peers a striking insight into, and understanding of, the lives and ways of their fellow countrymen. Among many honours bestowed on her was the Guggenheim International Art Prize (1960).

Map: page 281, 3C
The museum is in Cecil Road, Rosebank. Leaving the city, turn left off the M3 at the windmill, towards Mowbray. Take the first turning on the right and watch for the sign 'Irma Stern Museum'.
Details: Open Tuesday to Saturday 10h00-17h00; closed 13h00-14h00. Closed on Sundays, Mondays and public holidays. Admission charged.
Further information: The Curator, Irma Stern Museum, Cecil Road, Rosebank 7700, tel (021) 685-5686.

KIRSTENBOSCH BOTANICAL GARDEN
Kirstenbosch

Map: page 281, 3B/C
From Cape Town, take the M3 to its intersection with Rhodes Avenue (signposted 'Hout Bay'). Turn right and continue for about a kilometre. You'll see Kirstenbosch on your right.
Details: Open April to August 08h00-18h00; September to March 08h00-19h00. Admission and parking fees are charged. Free entry to pensioners on Tuesdays. Information kiosk open daily 10h00-16h30. Conducted group tours from the restaurant terrace on Tuesdays and Saturdays at 11h00. Guides are available for parties at other times, by prior arrangement.
Further information: National Botanical Institute, Private Bag X7, Claremont 7735, tel (021) 762-1166.

Kirstenbosch sprawls over 528 ha of the steep, well-watered slopes of the Table Mountain range, from Newlands up to Maclear's Beacon. It ranks among the most impressive of Africa's botanical gardens, because of the variety of indigenous plants nurtured in its cultivated area. Here, over an area of just 36 ha, are about 6 000 species of indigenous plant, including proteas, ericas, mesembryanthemums (or 'vygies', as they are generally known in South Africa), cycads and a host of others. Pelargoniums, also known as geraniums, have been hybridized to decorate the world's window boxes.

The Cycad Amphitheatre is sanctuary to most southern African varieties of this ancient floral family. Known as the 'living fossil' of the plant kingdom, the cycad first made an appearance about 150 million years ago, reaching its ascendancy 80 million years later. Also of note is the J W Matthews Rock Garden (succulents) and, higher up, the Protea, Erica and Restio (reed) gardens in which, amongst other plants, the lovely silver tree *(Leucadendron argenteum)* flourishes in abundance.

The cultivated area is arranged logically, carpets of related plants radiating out from a central point. In between are pathways that offer delightful strolls. Expert guides are available to conduct visitors around the grounds. For the visually disadvantaged, there are a perfume garden and a Braille Walk.

Serious research and documentation – Kirstenbosch leads the field in these respects – are conducted in the Compton Herbarium, a vast data bank of over 250 000 specimens.

Some of these are now extinct: they belong to the South African Museum's collection, which dates from 1825 and is on permanent loan to the herbarium.

The rest of the 528-ha property remains in its natural forested state, though two gravel routes lead to the upper parts. One leads you through Skeleton Gorge

Kirstenbosch in wintertime (above). Each season has its grace. Spring and early summer, when the hillside is a riot of colour, are especially inviting months.

Most of South Africa's more than 300 protea species can be seen at Kirstenbosch.

The fynbos kingdom: a fantasia of flowers

The tough, evergreen, mostly low-growing and small-leafed plants you see growing wild on the Peninsula, and in cultivated form at Kirstenbosch, are known locally as fynbos (fine bush), and together they comprise one of the wonders of the botanical world.

The Peninsula is part of a floral zone that extends across the winter rainfall parts of the Southwest and Southern Cape, a region that covers less than one-fiftieth of one percent of the world's land surface, yet has been given equal ranking with the great Boreal Kingdom covering North America and a substantial part of Europe and Asia.

The generally low-nutrient soils of the Cape's mountain slopes and sandy coastal fringes support about 6 000 hardy species, compared with 15 000 in the whole of Australia, which is a hundredfold bigger in size. Many species are confined to one particular small, and often crowded, area – up to 120 different plants have been identified within a single 10 m² patch. More than a third of all fynbos species are found on the Cape Peninsula itself.

Among the best-known and brightest members of this unique floral tapestry are the ericas (600 varieties) and proteas (368). Perhaps the best known of the proteas is South Africa's lovely national flower, the king protea.

These plants and the wealth of bulbs, corms and many others are mostly ancient ones, which have survived the geophysical upheavals of millions of years by 'migrating' either up or down the hillsides, according to the dictates of climate. But the habitat is now under unprecedented pressure from human encroachment, alien shrubs and tussock grasses. Other threats are sweeping fires and the Argentine ant, which has largely supplanted the local ant, so disrupting the delicate process by which protea seeds are distributed.

to the top of Table Mountain, and the other through lovely stands of yellowwood and ironwood trees. Three forest trails of varying length also lead through this natural reserve.

The abundant bird life includes such species as paradise flycatchers, sugarbirds and sunbirds (including the malachite and orange-breasted sunbird). Features of special interest include a small segment of Jan van Riebeeck's wild almond hedge, planted in 1660, and a natural spring lined with Batavian bricks, known as Colonel Bird's Bath. There's also an avenue of massive fig and camphor trees, which Cecil Rhodes commissioned in the late 1890s. Kirstenbosch was one of several tracts of real estate Rhodes owned and bequeathed to the nation.

An attractive restaurant within the grounds serves breakfast, tea and lunch, and is open every day except Christmas Day. There's also a garden shop, which has an array of books and gifts, and the plant sales nursery, with an outstanding range of indigenous plants.

MARINER'S WHARF
Hout Bay

A complex of waterfront and marine-orientated gift shops – together with a fresh-fish outlet, seafood bistro and restaurants – draws tourists to Hout Bay's harbour. Here you can dine on fish straight out of the sea, or savour the taste of rock lobster freshly plucked from holding tanks and cooked to your requirements.

Other culinary delights on sale at the market include oysters (any pearls you find are yours to keep), calamari and smoked snoek.

Elegant yachts and battered working craft huddle side by side along the dockside moorings. These are presided over by Hout Bay's 'republican navy' – a one-time minesweeper christened *SAS Pretoria*. The minesweeper (formerly *HMS Dunkerton*) was one of some 120 'ton'-class vessels built for the Royal Navy in the 1950s. Visitors are welcome aboard.

Other attractions include the *Circe* boat trips which offer regular trips to view the seal colony on Duiker Island *(see separate entry)*, and the much longer 'champagne sunset' cruises to Cape Town Harbour; the helicopter excursions that are sometimes on offer; Hout Bay Beach, which is quieter than most Cape beaches; the local museum; and the World of Birds *(see separate entry)*.

If you're in the Peninsula area during June/July, make a point of attending the popular Snoek Festival. The Hout Bay Festival is held in spring (September).

Hout Bay's charming, hill-flanked harbour serves as headquarters of the Peninsula's crayfishing fleet. Great quantities of snoek are also caught, and sold on the quayside.

Map: page 281, 4B
Take Victoria Drive (M6) from Sea Point, past the Llandudno turn-off and down the hill to the traffic lights. Cross straight over and continue towards the bay until you see the harbour, and the Mariner's Wharf sign, on your left.
Details: Mariner's Wharf is open daily throughout the year. *SAS Pretoria:* Saturdays and Sundays 12h00-17h00; daily 10h00-17h00 during school holidays; small admission charge.
Further information: Mariner's Wharf (Pty) Ltd, P O Box 26101, Hout Bay 7872, tel (021) 790-1100.

MOSTERT'S MILL
Mowbray

There's a touch of old-world Holland in the graceful lines of the old windmill, or 'horse mill' as it was technically known, below the University of Cape Town's campus – an unmistakable landmark which you see as you motor out of town along Rhodes Drive.

The area was intensively farmed in the days of Dutch rule at the Cape. Sybrandt Mostert, who bought the farm *Welgelegen* from his father-in-law Gysbert van Reenen, built the mill in about 1795 in order to grind wheat. Much later the mill and the farm formed part of Cecil Rhodes's vast property empire.

It was restored to its original condition with financial help from the Netherlands government in 1936 and declared a national monument four years later. The machinery is in full working order but no longer serves its original purpose, though there are tentative plans to get it going again – and one may yet see the great sails answer the southeaster's call.

Map: page 281, 2C
Take either Eastern Boulevard (N2) or De Waal Drive (M3) out of Cape Town. The two highways come together at 'Hospital Bend'. Follow the M3, whose next section is Rhodes Drive. Mostert's Mill is on your left, reached by turning left (down Rhodes Street) just before you come abreast of it.
Details: Open daily and on public holidays 09h00-15h00; self-guided tours only. Admission free.
Further information: Friends of Mostert's Mill, P O Box 5132, Rondebosch 7700, tel (021) 761-6102.

Fine art on show: the entrance to the Natale Labia Museum's gracious drawing room.

NATALE LABIA MUSEUM
Muizenberg

Fine furniture and an impressive art collection are housed in what used to be called *The Fort*, former home to Prince Natale and Princess Ida Louise Labia, and now a satellite museum of the South African National Gallery.

Prince Natale was a between-wars Italian diplomat who worked tirelessly to promote trade and cultural links between his country and South Africa. But Mussolini's invasion of Abyssinia in the mid-1930s put an abrupt end to his work. He died of a heart attack in 1936. His widow, daughter of the powerful, wealthy and widely unpopular randlord, J B Robinson, loaned her father's collection of old masters to the South African National Gallery. A small part (27 works) of the loan was later converted to an outright gift by her son. These, together with some of the original furniture, now fill the ground floor of the museum. The upper floor has been skilfully converted into a temporary exhibition space, lecture room and offices.

Map: page 281, 5C
The museum is at 192 Main Road, Muizenberg. To get there from Cape Town: take the M3 highway to the T-junction. Turn left onto the M64. Turn right onto the M4, which takes you into Muizenberg as Main Road.
Details: Open Tuesday to Sunday 10h00-17h00; closed on Mondays. The museum's restaurant, Café Labia, is closed during August. Admission free. Special exhibitions, concerts, lectures, poetry readings, drawing classes for adults and children, and pottery classes are held throughout the year.
Further information: Natale Labia Museum, 192 Main Road, Muizenberg 7951, tel (021) 788-4106/7.

NAVAL MUSEUM
Simon's Town

The story of Simon's Town's illustrious naval tradition is told at the Naval Museum, situated in the Masthouse, West Dockyard. The town was the Southern Atlantic station of Britain's Royal Navy from 1814 to 1957, and headquarters of the South African Navy to the present day. Among the exhibits are photographs tracing the development of the naval installations over the decades, personality portraits, and some fascinating items transferred from Green Point's Fort Wynyard Museum, which focused on coastal defence.

The previous home of the museum – the nearby Martello Tower – now houses artefacts and displays about the local dockyards. The simple two-storey building, featuring a parapet and platform on top, is the oldest surviving British structure in the country: it was built by the newly arrived occupation forces in the mid-1790s to protect the powder magazine, and as a lookout. It commands a fine view of False Bay and its approaches.

Map: page 281, 6C
From Cape Town take the M3 highway to the T-junction. Turn left onto the M64 and right onto the M4 to Muizenberg. Continue through Muizenberg and along the coastal route (still the M4) to Simon's Town. Access to the naval museum, on the West Dockyard, is via Court Road, past the Simon's Town Museum.
Details: The Naval Museum is open Monday to Friday 10h00-16h00; on weekends in December and January only; closed Christmas Day, New Year's Day, Good Friday. Those wishing to visit the Martello Tower should enquire at the museum.
Further information: SA Naval Museum, Private Bag X1, Simon's Town 7995, tel (021) 787-3657.

OLD RESIDENCY
Simon's Town

Over the centuries this handsome, many-roomed house, built as a winter residence for the governor in 1777, has served as magistrates' court, slave quarters and prison, naval hospital, customs post and government offices. Today it contains the many and absorbing exhibits of the Simon's Town Museum.

On view are such intriguing items as an archaeological excavation, a 19th-century 'rocket wagon', mementos of Admiral Lord Nelson (who recuperated from an illness here), various uniforms, ships' badges, logbooks and a mock-up of a 1939-45 wartime pub. The displays are collectively entitled 'Simon's Town: Events and People'.

Here, too, you'll see reminders of *Just Nuisance*, the renowned Great Dane which befriended British sailors during the Second World War. The naval base's surgeon-captain was at *Just Nuisance's* deathbed in 1944, and the giant dog was buried with full military honours on a hill overlooking Simon's Town. A white ensign covered his coffin, and 200 officers and men stood to attention as the last post sounded and the firing party's farewell volley rang out. A bronze statue of the much-loved animal stands in the town's Jubilee Square.

Map: page 281, 6C
From Cape Town, take the M3 highway to the T-junction, turn left onto the M64 and then right onto the M4 that takes you through Muizenberg. Follow the coast road (still the M4) to Simon's Town. The Old Residency is situated in Court Road.
Details: Open Monday to Friday 09h00-16h00; Saturdays 10h00-13h00; closed on Sundays and public holidays. Admission by donation. The museum also houses the area's information centre.
Further information: Simon's Town Publicity Association, 118 St George's Street, Simon's Town 7995, tel (021) 786-2436.

Lady Eleanor, phantom of the Old Residency

Take a night-time stroll through the Residency's high-ceilinged corridors and you may just glimpse the ghost of a pretty young girl. This is Eleanor, 14-year-old daughter of Lord George McCartney, who served as the Cape's first British governor and used the house as a retreat in 1798. Eleanor's best friends were the children of the local fishermen. She liked to play with them on the beach – a habit that earned the stern disapproval of her aristocratic parents. They locked her away in one of the Residency's rooms, but she soon discovered a secret passage and quietly slipped away again to be with her friends – only to catch pneumonia and die. Today, it is said, her spirit simply refuses to leave the family home.

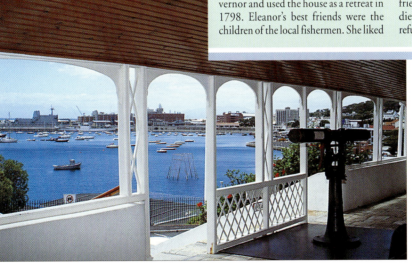

The verandah of the historic Old Residency, which now functions as the Simon's Town Museum, overlooks a part of the harbour, bright with leisure craft.

RHODES COTTAGE
St James

'White as the sands of Muizenberg, spun before the gale,' wrote Rudyard Kipling, who loved this blustery, sunlit segment of the False Bay coast with its warm waters, wide, white beaches and hill-graced hinterland. So too, did his great friend Cecil Rhodes, who spent his declining years here, often alone with only his memories of grandeur gone. Rhodes died in 1902, in a fairly unpretentious thatch-roofed, stone-walled hideaway called Barkly Cottage, now known as Rhodes Cottage, a small museum housing an intriguing selection of photographs and personal memorabilia relating to the controversial financier, politician and empire-builder.

Map: page 281, 5C
Take the M3 to Muizenberg. Drive through town along Main Road (M4), past the railway station on your left. You'll see the cottage on your right, about half a kilometre further on.
Details: Open Tuesday to Sunday 10h00-13h00 and 14h00-17h00; closed on Christmas Day.
Further information: The Curator, Rhodes Cottage Museum, 246 Main Road, Muizenberg 7945, tel (021) 788-1816.

The snug thatched cottage at St James, near Muizenberg, where Cecil John Rhodes spent the last years of his life.

RHODES MEMORIAL
Rondebosch

Map: page 281, 3C
Take the M3 out of Cape Town, which becomes Rhodes Drive, and follow the signs to the 'southern suburbs'. Continue for a kilometre past the University of Cape Town (you'll see the upper campus on your right) to the Rhodes Memorial signposted turn-off on your left. Follow the road that winds up behind the university to the memorial's car park.

Details: Open during daylight hours Tuesday to Sunday throughout the year; closed on Mondays. Access is free. The tearoom closes at 17h00.

○○High up on the slopes of Devil's Peak stands architect Herbert Baker's columned, white-granite memorial to his great friend and patron, Cecil John Rhodes – a place for quiet contemplation in the tomb-like but oddly comforting silence, and for recalling the grand, if arrogant, days of *Pax Britannica* in Africa.

The memorial is an imposing structure, a kind of 'temple' which is designed in neo-Classical style and unashamedly imperialistic in concept. It commemorates a man who, undeniably, was a powerful force in the shaping of events in 19th-century southern Africa. It features an eye-catching equestrian work by the sculptor George Watts, aptly entitled 'Physical Energy', and eight great stone lions. There's also a bust of Rhodes with this moving inscription by Rudyard Kipling: 'The immense and brooding spirit still shall quicken and control.

Granite pillars support the Rhodes Memorial, which overlooks the Cape Flats and the distant peaks of the Hottentots-Holland Mountains.

Cecil Rhodes: the colossus that crumbled

For sheer meteoric quality, few careers have managed to match that of Cecil John Rhodes, the visionary, tycoon and arch-schemer who strode so imperiously across the southern African stage in the latter 19th century.

Rhodes, the fourth son of a Hertfordshire parson, was an unexceptional and rather frail teenager when he arrived at Kimberley, perhaps the world's toughest mining community, in 1872. But within a decade his steely determination, his capacity for a hard day's work and ever-present instinct for a good opportunity had brought half of the fabulous diamond fields within the ambit of his highly successful company (the future De Beers).

Rhodes made a second fortune on the golden Witwatersrand. Then he gained control of the Kimberley fields, buying the remaining half from Barney Barnato with a cheque for 5 338 650 pounds. Rhodes founded the British South Africa Company as a first step on the road to pan-African dominion. He then took over the premiership of the Cape Colony, pushed through the rail link to the Highveld, and dispatched his Pioneer Column to carve out a brand-new country – Rhodesia, now Zimbabwe – beyond the Limpopo. In the end, though, corrosive ambition was to prove his downfall. It led to the Jameson Raid, an almost comic-opera attempt to seize the gold-rich Highveld, to his demise as a credible political leader, and, indirectly, to the hugely destructive Anglo-Boer War.

For all that, though, dignity attended Rhodes in his passing. After his premature death at Muizenberg in March 1902, his body was taken north by train, along part of his dreamed-of Cape-to-Cairo route, into the territory that bore his name. His last resting place is a grave he had chosen among the boulders of his beloved Matobo Hills in Zimbabwe.

Living he was the land, and dead, his soul shall be her soul.'

Panoramic views extend from this high vantage point – over the Cape Flats to the blue-hazed Hottentots-Holland Mountains in the distance. You can savour the view, and the delicious scones and cream, from the terrace of the nearby tearoom.

Access to the memorial is either by car or on foot. The gentle walk starts from the university campus area and meanders through the oak-shaded paddocks of Groote Schuur Estate, where you might see fallow deer browsing.

RIETVLEI RECREATIONAL AREA
Milnerton

A spectacular world of birds makes its home at the Rietvlei wetlands, just north of Cape Town city. It includes flamingoes, pelicans, Egyptian geese, ducks, coots, stilts, black-backed gulls, fish eagles, Arctic terns and a host of other birds.

Rietvlei is one of the Cape's most extensive waterfowl breeding areas. It lies on a coastal vlei that is nurtured by the Diep River, and connected to the sea by a tidal lagoon (a popular recreational area amongst the locals). There are large feeding water pans which draw migrant birds from Europe in late spring.

The Coastal Bird Conservation Council runs a 'hospital' here for contaminated and injured sea birds, many of them jackass penguins (so named for their braying call) which have been fouled by oil pollution.

A large lake to the north of the wetlands is used for such watersports as powerboating, water-skiing, canoeing and boardsailing.

Map: page 281, 1D
Take the R27 out of Cape Town (Marine Drive, becoming Otto du Plessis Drive), past the marshlands and lagoon on your left. After the lagoon, Marine Drive appears again (as the M14) on your left. Continue on Otto du Plessis Drive, passing 2 lakes on your right. Go through 1 set of traffic lights, and turn right at the next into Blouberg Road. At the next set of lights, turn right into Pentz Drive, then take a right at Grey Avenue to reach the recreational area.
Details: Open daily 08h30-17h30. Admission fee charged for motor vehicles and boats.
Further information: Milnerton Municipality, P O Box 35, Milnerton 7435, tel (021) 550-1111.

ROBBEN ISLAND
Table Bay

The oval-shaped island, clearly visible from the shores of Table Bay and the seaside suburbs of Green Point and Sea Point, gained worldwide notoriety as 'South Africa's Alcatraz', a prison that included Nelson Mandela (for 27 years) among its more illustrious inmates.

These days, though, Robben Island has a different and kindlier image: since 1991 it has been embraced by the South African National Heritage Programme, which seeks to preserve it as a breeding ground for Damara and Caspian terns, jackass penguins and nearly 30 other species of bird.

These and the rugged coast and offshore marine life, the arum lilies and the splendid views across the bay to Table Mountain, put it among the upper echelons of the Cape's tourist venues.

Among the 574-ha island's more prominent buildings is the old Residency, one-time home to the local commissioner, and the square-towered Church of the Good Shepherd, designed by turn-of-the-century architect Herbert Baker, and centrepiece of the tiny village (bank, post office, general dealer's store). There are also a lighthouse, built in 1864 and much needed both then and now – at least 22 wreck sites have been charted on and close to the shore – and an attractive small harbour at Murray Bay.

Map: page 281, 1B
Robben Island lies in Table Bay, 9 km from the nearest bay shore and just over 12 km from the Atlantic suburb of Green Point.
Details: For tours to the island contact The Commander, Public Relations, Private Bag, Robben Island 7400, tel (021) 411-1006.

Captain Cook's unwanted gift

Among Robben Island's more dubious claims to distinction is the reputed part it played in the infamous rabbit infestations that have plagued Australia. Jan van Riebeeck introduced these fast-breeding leporids onto the island in 1654 in an effort to supplement the Cape settlement's production of food. With good pasturage and no carnivores to keep their numbers down, the rabbits thrived.

When Captain Cook visited Robben Island a century later, he was much impressed by the 'pretty rabbits' which seemed to abound there, and took a number of them on to Australia's eastern coastal region, which Britain formally 'annexed' in 1770. They were, so far as is known, the ancestors of the vermin that were later to completely devastate many of Australia's farmlands.

Typical of Robben Island's unpretentious buildings is the colonial-style primary school, used by the children of prison staff.

Rondevlei's marshlands are home to a host of aquatic birds. Animal life includes a group of hippos.

RONDEVLEI NATURE RESERVE
Zeekoevlei

Map: page 281, 4D
The Rondevlei Nature Reserve is at Fisherman's Walk, Zeekoevlei. From the city take the M3 then the M5, which becomes Prince George Drive. At the intersection with Victoria Road, there is a sign for Rondevlei. Turn left, and follow the road until you reach Fisherman's Walk. Turn right; the entrance is ahead of you.
Details: Open daily 08h00-17h00. Best months to visit are January through to April.
Further information: The Warden, Rondevlei Nature Reserve, Fisherman's Walk, Zeekoevlei 7945, tel (021) 706-2404.

Hippopotamuses are unlikely residents in the Cape Peninsula, so far from their usual home to the north. However, you'll find them here – but only if you're patient. They like to bury themselves among the reeds and are rarely seen by visitors. In fact, hippopotamuses – known as 'sea cows' to the early colonists – were once commonplace all over southern Africa. But the last of these great semi-aquatic mammals were shot out of the Cape region a century and more ago.

Rondevlei, however, is really for the birds. Its large vlei, or shallow lake, girded by the coastal dunes of the False Bay area south of the city, is home to about 225 species of bird. Most of these are waterfowl – ducks, grebe, coots, Caspian terns and fish eagles, but there are also dry-land species, including martial eagles. On an average day you can expect to spot in the region of 50 different species, rising to perhaps 70 during favourable summer spells. Also present is a small but intriguing array of animals – species such as mongooses and genets, Cape hares, porcupines and dune molerats.

To preserve the fragile mixed sandveld and coastal fynbos environment, visitors are restricted to the vlei's northern shore, along which a waterside path meanders. Here there are benches, a hide and strategically sited viewing points. Two lookout towers (telescopes *in situ*) enable you to scan the entire reserve and its surroundings. A small museum displays Rondevlei's fauna and flora, and audio-visuals are presented (to groups) in a 50-seat lecture theatre.

RUGBY MUSEUM
Newlands

Map: page 281, 3C
Take the M3 from Cape Town. Turn off at the Groote Schuur/Newlands turn-off. Continue until you reach the T-junction with Main Road. Turn right. After 500 m turn left into Boundary Road.
Details: Open weekdays 09h30-16h30, and on those Saturdays for which big matches have been scheduled.
Further information: The Curator, SA Rugby Museum, P O Box 99, Newlands 7725, tel (021) 685-3038/686-4939.

The first recorded adult rugby match played in South Africa took place on Cape Town's Green Point Common on 23 August 1862, between a military and a civilian team. Four decades later, the legendary Paul Roos led a national side, known for the first time as the Springboks, on a triumphant tour of Britain to inaugurate a half-century of near-dominance in the international arena.

Much of the story is told in the South African Rugby Museum – arguably the largest of its kind in the world – at Newlands Stadium, historic home of the Western Province Rugby Union. Blazers, badges, jerseys, boots and caps worn by the greats of the green-and-gold are on display, together with nearly 2 000 photos and a wealth of other memorabilia.

SIGNAL HILL
Cape Town

For the best view of Cape Town at night, head for Signal Hill – one of a trilogy of physical features surrounding the landward side of the city.

The hill is connected to the more imposing Lion's Head peak by a saddle, which, together, are said to resemble the shape of a lion in repose. A road leads from Kloof Nek to the 'lion's rump', from where there are splendid views of the city, mountain, harbour and, to the west, Cape Town's 'Riviera' suburbs, and Robben Island beyond. Sunset is probably the best time to make the trip.

Each day at noon an artillery piece fires a single blank round from near the top of the hill – a signal that it is precisely midday and, less generally known to those within earshot, a sign of respect to those who fought and died in the great wars of the century.

The hill's name derives not from the noonday signal, but from earlier times, when the 350-m-high crest hosted a semaphore station for communicating with ships standing out to sea.

Only on rare occasions does a conventional artillery troop now do duty at the gun emplacement: the firing pin is activated by remote control from the South African Astronomical Observatory in the southern suburbs.

Map: page 281, 2C
Drive up Kloof Nek (M62) towards Table Mountain's lower cable station. Turn right into the Signal Hill (signposted) road at the top.

The Silvermine Reserve, whose terrain is covered by heath-type fynbos vegetation, is superb walking country. Its higher parts take in magnificent views of two oceans.

SILVERMINE NATURE RESERVE
Near Noordhoek

This magnet for hikers, picnickers and lovers of tranquillity covers just over 2 000 ha of unspoilt Steenberg mountain wilderness, stretching across the narrow waist of the Peninsula, from Muizenberg and Kalk Bay in the east to Noordhoek Peak in the west.

Way back in 1687 Dutch settlers were convinced the ground here held a lode of precious silver, but the signs were illusory and nothing of value was found at the time (though later prospectors unearthed workable manganese deposits). Silvermine does have its treasures, but they're of a different and more lasting kind: its terrain is a natural wonderland of plateau, pinnacle and hill, clear upland stream (the Silvermine River), waterfall, valley, forested gorge, huge cave and a remarkable floral richness.

The heath-type fynbos vegetation – proteas, ericas, leucadendrons – attracts sugarbirds and sunbirds, Cape robins and many other birds. Animals include steenbok, grysbok and grey rhebuck, and smaller mammals such as caracals, porcupines and genets.

Various walks, taking from half an hour to half a day, have been charted and a number of viewsites, picnic and braai spots established. You can drive to many of the viewsites, but the best of them – the heights above the reservoir – are accessible only on foot. The vistas from the latter, taking in False Bay and Hout Bay, are memorable.

There is also a mountain-bike route, signposted from the main gate on the Kalk Bay side.

The reserve is bisected by the scenically enchanting Ou Kaapseweg (Old Cape Road), which runs from Westlake through the Steenberg, to descend into the Fish Hoek Valley.

Map: page 281, 5C
From Cape Town, take the M3 highway south towards Muizenberg (this becomes the Simon van der Stel Freeway just before you get to the Wynberg off-ramp). Turn right at the T-junction (Westlake intersection), onto Steenberg road, past Westlake suburb (and hospital) on your right. Bear left onto Ou Kaapseweg (M64), along which are the two signposted Silvermine entry points.

Details: Open daily throughout the year 08h00-19h00 in summer, 08h00-18h00 in winter. An admission fee is charged. A comprehensive map, available *in situ* and from Captour, describes the walking routes, including the popular 7-km hike from the parking area (near the reservoir) to Noordhoek Peak and back. Braai sites have been laid out; bring your own firewood; portable braai equipment is not allowed for fear of fires.

Further information: The Forester, Silvermine Nature Reserve, P O Box 30223, Tokai 7966, tel (021) 75-3040/1/2/3.

STEMPASTORIE
Simon's Town

Map: page 281, 6C
You get to Simon's Town from Cape Town via the M3 and the M4, which takes you through Muizenberg. Follow the coast road (still the M4) into Simon's Town. The Stempastorie is on Church Street (No. 2).
Details: Open Monday to Saturday 09h00-16h30; closed Sundays, Good Friday and Christmas Day. Admission charged. Limited parking. Tours offered daily. Reservations in advance required for large groups.
Further information: Simon's Town Publicity Association, 118 St George's Street, Simon's Town 7995, tel (021) 786-2436.

Flags, national anthems and the other paraphernalia of nationhood form the core of an unusual museum housed in Simon's Town's original Dutch Reformed church parsonage.

The choice was no coincidence – it was here that Dominee M L de Villiers composed the music for 'Die Stem van Suid-Afrika'. The words were written by the Afrikaans author and politician C J Langenhoven in 1918. Dominee De Villiers's piano is an exhibit. You'll also find a history of the search for a national flag at the beginning of the century.

On display too is South Africa's coat of arms, an intriguing melange of images representing the four provinces established at Union in 1910. The Lady of Good Hope was chosen to illustrate the Cape, an oxwagon the Transvaal, two wildebeest Natal, and an orange tree the Orange Free State. The images are embellished by a wavy line, symbolizing the Orange River, and two flanking animals, a springbok and a gemsbok.

Among other emblems are South Africa's national flower, the king protea, the blue crane and the yellowwood tree.

Symbols that stirred both anger and pride

After Union in 1910 various quarrelsome factions, ranging from die-hard Afrikaner republicans to true-blue British loyalists, argued bitterly and sometimes violently about a national flag.

Several designs were produced over the years – including one that sparked a number of demonstrations in Durban. Eventually, in 1927, a compromise was agreed.

The new emblem displayed the colours of the original *Prinzenvlag*, flown by the United Netherlands in the 1650s. It incorporated a small central motif, comprising the Union Jack and the ensigns of the old Transvaal and Orange Free State republics. The standard was raised for the first time in 1928 – in Cuba of all places – together with the British flag. This dual approach lasted until 1957.

Less contentious (at least in origin) was the springbok, South Africa's national mammal, which served for more than eight decades as a symbol of sporting prowess.

The animal was taken from the 19th-century Orange River Colony's coat of arms and introduced, without fuss, during South Africa's inaugural rugby tour of Britain in 1906. Various names had been bandied about in dressing rooms and press columns. One British sportswriter even suggested the unmanly *Mimosas* as the collective epithet – before team captain Paul Roos finally settled on *De Springbokken*.

Until the later years of the apartheid era, only white South Africans were entitled to wear the springbok badge, an exclusiveness that prompted demands for change.

TABLE MOUNTAIN CABLE CAR
Table Mountain

Map: page 281, 2C
To reach the lower cable station, leave the city on Buitengracht Street, which leads on to Kloof Nek (M62). Turn left at the top of the hill (Kloof Nek), following the signs for the Cableway.
Details: The cable car operates daily throughout the year, weather permitting. Times vary with the seasons: May to October 08h30-18h00; November to April 08h00-22h00. Advance reservations can be made at the cableway booking office, Captour Information Bureau, Adderley Street (next to the railway station), tel (021) 418-5214. Tickets can also be purchased at the cableway station – but beware of long queues in season (December and January).
Further information: The Director, Table Mountain Aerial Cableway Company Ltd, P O Box 730, Cape Town 8000, tel (021) 24-8409.

The ride lasts just five minutes, but at the end you've been transported into a different world: the mountain's precipitous northern face rises, sheer, for more than a kilometre above the sea.

From its summit there are the most stunning views – of the narrow finger of land running down to Cape Point in the south, of the blue-hazed mountains of the hinterland, of the flanking Devil's Peak and Lion's Head sentinels on either side, of the ocean all around, and the city and its harbour far below.

The flat-topped crest of the sandstone massif measures some three kilometres from end to end. It can be seen 200 km out to sea on a clear day, though often the sandstone ramparts are obscured by the 'tablecloth', a white mantle of wind-driven cloud that swirls across the plateau and then dives down in a continuous and spectacular cascade.

CAPE PENINSULA

The familiar 'tablecloth', product of the Cape southeaster, tumbles over the mountain's rim in a continuous cataract. The massif is among Africa's best-known landmarks.

At these times the mountain is closed to sightseers. The cable car is the most popular means of access for visitors. If you're fit and adventurous, you can climb to the top, using charted paths that range from the undemanding to the strenuous and highly dangerous.

Treat the mountain with great respect, and don't try routes you know nothing about. Despite constant warnings, many people have died or been injured in falls from the more unfamiliar paths on Table Mountain. The gradients, the hidden hazards, and changeable weather call for the utmost caution. Before attempting your climb, get hold of a good guidebook or contact the Mountain Club of South Africa for advice. Then tell someone where you are going and when you expect to be back. Better still, make the climb with someone who knows the terrain.

You make the ascent principally for the magnificent vistas that unfold, but the summit has other attractions, too. These include a modest restaurant and souvenir shop from where keepsake letters (postmarked Table Mountain) can be sent, and a souvenir certificate obtained. Informative wall-charts give details of the nature reserve, the plant life of the well-watered central plateau, and the short walks leading from the cable station. The Table Mountain Reserve sustains nearly every one of the Peninsula's 3 000-odd floral species, many of them lovely, some of them rare. Look out for the shimmering silver tree *Leucadendron argenteum*, tallest of the proteaceae of southern Africa (it can grow up to 16 m), and the red disa *(Disa uniflora)*, a wild orchid also known as 'Pride of Table Mountain'.

The best time to ride to the summit is late afternoon – so that you can see Cape Town both in daylight and, after a spectacular sunset, at night.

Most visitors ascend the mountain by cable car. At the top there's a restaurant, and pathways that lead to splendid viewing points. The heights are part of a nature reserve.

As the Portuguese explorer Vasco da Gama and his mariners approached the Cape in December 1497, 'a sable cloud, which in thick darkness did the welkin shroud' appeared over their heads and assumed a monstrous human shape that warned the intruders off its territory, threatening 'shipwrecks and losses of each kind and race'.

This was the first European sighting of Table Mountain and its equally famous tablecloth – an extraordinary geological and climatic freak that has given rise to a host of myths and legends that have been passed down through generations.

Three myths of the mountain

Da Gama's report prompted the Portuguese poet Luis de Camoes to link the mountain with a hideous mythical phantom called *Adamastor*. Legend has it that *Adamastor* tried to topple the Grecian gods, failed to do so, and was turned into a mountain. For his pains he was set to watch over the southern seas.

The legend is enshrined in a book of poetry called *Lusiad*. It holds that *Adamastor's* spirit survives in the swirling clouds of Table Mountain and its southern extension – the Cape of Good Hope, known also as the Cape of Storms.

Another better-known myth is the story of *Jan van Hunks*, a one-time seafarer, who retired to take his ease on the hillside. *Van Hunks* supposedly challenged the devil to a pipe-smoking contest (which produced the 'tablecloth' that often mantles the summit).

Even more intimidating is the tale of a little creature named *Aintje Somers*, a gnome-like prankster of undetermined gender, who dresses up as a woman to deceive, assault, rob and strip those who happen to stray from the beaten path. *Aintje* inhabits the lower slopes, and there's enough of the modern mugger about him/her to indicate that he/she was once a very real person.

297

CAPE PENINSULA

Colourful parrots are among the exotic, sometimes rare, and often exquisite, species on view in the walk-in aviaries at the World of Birds, South Africa's largest bird park.

WORLD OF BIRDS
Hout Bay

Map: page 281, 4B
Take Victoria Drive (M6) from Sea Point to the traffic lights at the bottom of the hill that descends into Hout Bay. Bear left at the lights, and then take Valley Road, the first turning to your left. Turn left yet again at the first stop street and follow the signs.
Details: Open daily throughout the year 09h00-17h00, except Christmas Day and Good Friday. Admission charged.
Further information: The Director, World of Birds, Valley Road, Hout Bay 7800, tel (021) 790-2730.

A walk through Hout Bay's World of Birds is truly a walk through nature – a fascinating glimpse into the private lives of about 450 different bird species.

The 100 or so aviaries are large and cleverly landscaped to reproduce the natural habitats of the birds – feeding, building nests, incubating eggs, socializing as if you weren't even there. Swans, cormorants, herons and egrets make their home among the willow-shaded ponds.

The sanctuary also serves as hospital and orphanage, caring for injured birds and animals. Especially endearing are the monkeys (including rare varieties) and the meerkats, which belong to the mongoose family. Of the two types, the suricate is the smaller, and is often seen balanced upright on its hindlegs surveying the world with wide-eyed wonder. The general setting, in Hout Bay's sylvan valley, is lovely.

KAROO

299

KAROO

ARBEIDSGENOT MUSEUM
Oudtshoorn

Map: page 299, 5D
Arbeidsgenot is in Jan van Riebeeck Road, Oudtshoorn, and is prominently signposted.
Details: Open weekdays 09h00-12h30 and 14h00-17h00; Saturdays 09h00-12h30. Closed Sundays, public and religious holidays.
Accommodation: A variety of hotels, farms and guesthouses offer excellent accommodation in and around Oudtshoorn.
Further information: Klein Karoo Marketing Association, P O Box 1234, Oudtshoorn 6620, tel (0443) 22-6643.

For lovers of Afrikaans literature, a visit to Arbeidsgenot, former home of celebrated South African author C J Langenhoven, must rank high on places to visit in Oudtshoorn. The house where Langenhoven found much of the inspiration for his works bears testimony to his love of hard work and discipline.

Langenhoven (1873-1932) was a true 'son of South Africa', who became a writer, poet, lawyer, senator and champion of the Afrikaans language. He is, perhaps, best known for having written one of the country's national anthems, *Die Stem van Suid-Afrika*.

Many of Langenhoven's personal belongings have been tracked down, and are on permanent display at the museum.

The building was bequeathed to the people by his widow, and her clothing still hangs in the cupboards as it did at the time of her death.

Poignantly, there are many beautiful carvings of Herrie the Elephant, an imaginary creature the author invented. Langenhoven's readers were so fond of the elephant that they sent him figurines and carvings of it throughout his life.

You can also see many examples of Langenhoven's own craftsmanship, particularly his woodwork. He also designed an attractive garden sundial which was installed at Arbeidsgenot in 1926.

The Swartberg Mountain range

The Swartberg (Black Mountain) range, one of the most beautiful massifs in southern Africa, provides a 200-km-long barrier between the Klein and Great Karoo. At its foothills lie the legendary Cango Caves, a mecca for thousands of tourists every year.

The range was traditionally known to the San (Bushmen), its early inhabitants, as the *Kango*, which means 'water mountains', so called because of the many streams originating on its slopes.

The Seweweekspoort Mountain, at 2 326 m above sea level, is the highest point in the Swartberg. Despite its name, the Swartberg range is coloured by red sedimentary sandstone, and brilliant yellow lichens clinging to the precipitous rock faces.

The Swartberg is also home to a reclusive community living at Gamkas Kloof, also known as Die Hel (The Hell), situated in an almost inaccessible valley. The community was started by a trekboer at the beginning of the 19th century, when the valley was uninhabited, and was only discovered during the Anglo-Boer War by a band of Boer guerrillas who were fleeing from the British.

As the Boers reached the bottom of Die Hel's ravine around sunset, they were approached by a bearded man dressed in animal skins, who introduced himself as Cordier – a descendant of the trekboers who had arrived there earlier. Numerous cave paintings and wooden peg ladders reaching up rock faces to wild beehives indicate that the San once lived in the valley prior to the advent of the Dutch.

Die Hel's inhabitants live entirely on the produce generated by their small farms, mainly Hanepoot grapes, which are dried and sold for export. The only means of reaching the valley is via a winding road, built in 1962.

Leopards still roam the heights, preying on the dassies, baboons and antelope that live there. Aloes proliferate on the slopes, interspersed with tall watsonia species. In addition, there is a variety of heaths, and over 150 species of gladioli. In the aftermath of frequent fires in the area, masses of fire lilies spring from the soil.

If you're in the area, consider a visit to Toorwaterpoort (Pass of Enchanted Water) in the eastern Swartberg range. Here a hot spring, said to have medicinal properties, bubbles to the surface. Legend has it that an ailing San (Bushman) was left at the spring to die, but recovered miraculously from his illness after drinking the water.

Simple accommodation, consisting of a few rondavels, is available at Toorwaterpoort, and there's a pleasant camping area. About 200 000 litres of water reach the surface every day, at a cosy temperature of 54°C. Toorwaterpoort is about 73 km from De Rust.

Lush pastures and picturesque farm buildings bask in the foothills of the mighty Swartberg massif. Winter in the Karoo can be bitterly cold, and snowfalls often occur.

BEAUFORT WEST MUSEUM COMPLEX
Beaufort West

The century-old pear trees which line the streets of Beaufort West are always a welcome sight for weary travellers commuting on the N1 between Cape Town and Gauteng Province. It's certainly worth stopping here – if only to visit the Beaufort West Museum Complex in Donkin Street.

The museum comprises a trio of historical buildings: the Stadshuis, the Sendingkerk and the old Sendingpastorie.

Construction on the Stadshuis, designed by James Bisset, was completed in 1867. It was the first city hall to be built in the Karoo, and sports a gleaming façade and moulded plaster decorations.

The people of Beaufort West are proud of their sons. To celebrate the achievements of famous former inhabitants of the town, exhibitions here highlight the feats of heart surgeon Chris Barnard and the late Foreign Affairs Minister, Eric Louw.

The Chris Barnard Exhibition boasts more than 1 000 exhibits, most of them awards and gifts received by the surgeon after he performed the world's first heart transplant in 1967.

On display are tributes from foreign governments, works of art, letters from grateful patients, and unusual offerings such as home-brewed medicines.

The Sendingkerk, built in 1872, features the town's church history, and houses a display of antique clothing.

The Sendingpastorie is the restored birthplace of Chris Barnard and his brother, Dr Marius Barnard. Their father, the Rev A H Barnard, settled in the town in 1913. The building contains family possessions and a fine collection of guns used in earlier South African times.

Map: page 299, 4D
The Beaufort West Museum Complex is on the right-hand side of Donkin Street, at the second set of traffic lights.
Accommodation: There is a wide selection of hotels, guesthouses and private homes in Beaufort West.
Further information: The Curator, Beaufort West Museum Complex, P O Box 370, Beaufort West 6970, tel (0201) 4082; Beaufort West Publicity Association, Private Bag 582, Beaufort West 6970, tel (0201) 2121.

The Chris Barnard collection is housed in this building – a section of the Beaufort West Museum. Exhibits outline the early life and career of this pioneering heart surgeon.

BRANDVLEI
Northwest of Carnarvon

The hamlet of Brandvlei has more to recommend it than the friendliness of its local inhabitants, although that alone is a strong reason to visit this hospitable Karoo hamlet.

Brandvlei shot to world prominence in 1929 when racing driver Sir Malcolm (Donald) Campbell broke the world speed record at Verneukpan, the long salt pan just outside the town, in his famous speed machine, 'Bluebird'. Sir Malcolm's achievement was soon bettered, but for Brandvlei it established a major talking point for years to come, and a permanent niche in history.

Small as it is, Brandvlei has its own airstrip, used by businessmen, and for medical emergencies. The town has an attractive, historic Dutch Reformed Church, which is worth a visit, and nearby you may see intact Bushman rock paintings. You may also stumble across relics of the Boer War littering the veld.

Plentiful summer rains bring bursts of vibrant colour to the area with an astonishing range of Karoo wildflowers. A variety of unusual birds, including the rare coral snakebird, is to be seen within a 100-km radius of Brandvlei, and the area offers excellent hunting on private farms.

Map: page 299, 2B
Take the N1 from Cape Town, bypassing Malmesbury, Moorreesburg, Piketberg, Citrusdal, Klawer, Van Rhynsdorp and Calvinia, to reach Brandvlei.
Accommodation: Brandvlei Hotel, and guesthouses on a number of farms.
Further information: Brandvlei Tourism Board, P O Box 63, Brandvlei 7020, tel (02702) 112; The Town Clerk, P O Box 12, Brandvlei 7020, tel (02702) 28.

CALITZDORP
West of Oudtshoorn

Map: page 299, 5C
The town is on the R62, about 52 km west of Oudtshoorn. From Cape Town take the N2 to Worcester and then follow the R60 east to Ashton. Turn north through Cogman's Kloof to Montagu and continue eastwards on the R62 through Barrydale and Ladismith. Alternatively, drive to Barrydale via the N2 past Swellendam, turning off on the R324 to negotiate the Tradouw Pass.
Accommodation: Fully furnished, equipped 4- and 6-bed chalets available at the Calitzdorp Spa.
Further information: The Town Clerk, Private Bag X02, Calitzdorp 6660, tel (04437) 3-3312; Calitzdorp Spa, P O Box 127, Oudtshoorn 6620, tel (04437) 3-3371; Boplaas Estate, P O Box 156, Calitzdorp 6660, tel (04437) 3-3326/3-3397; and Die Krans Estate, P O Box 28, Calitzdorp 6660, tel (04437) 3-3314/3-3364.

Honeyed wines, delicious dried fruit, lazy hours in warm mineral-spring water and scenic drives. These are some of the attractions offered by the charming town of Calitzdorp in the Gamka River Valley.

Using Calitzdorp as a base, take advantage of one of the excellent guesthouses in the area and make day-trips to historic Matjiesfontein, Oudtshoorn (the 'feather capital' of the Karoo) or the scenic Karoo mountain passes – Meiringspoort, the Seweweekspoort Pass, Swartberg Pass and Montagu Pass.

Calitzdorp, heralded as the port capital of South Africa, is known for its fine wines, among them Hanepoot and Muscadel, and has its own wine route.

Wines may be tasted and bought from Mondays to Saturdays at the local co-operative winery, as well as at Boplaas and Die Krans estates.

Country cuisine is served at the Boplaas restaurant from 5 December to 10 January, and for two weeks at Easter.

At Die Krans Estate you may take a 20-minute, self-guided vineyard tour along meandering paths among the vines, where cultivars are clearly marked.

Southeast of Calitzdorp lies the well-stocked Gamka Mountain Nature Reserve *(see separate entry).*

The local history museum is worth visiting, and a scenic route through Buffelskloof and Kruisrivier to the Cango Valley offers enthralling views of red hills with tunnels right through them.

The Calitzdorp Spa, 22 km outside town on the old road, is popular, especially in winter, when the 35°C water in the swimming pool is particularly enticing. The water is rich in minerals and said to have medicinal properties.

Scenic drives of the Karoo

A sun-burnished buttress soars above succulent Karoo flora near De Rust, the village which serves farmers in the Olifants River district.

There are a number of scenic drives traversing the jagged mountains that separate the Karoo from the lower-lying coastal terrace and the Indian Ocean.

The Robinson Pass, built in 1886 by famous road engineer Sir Thomas Bain, climbs beyond Ruiterbos to the 860-m summit of the Outeniqua Mountains before making its meandering way down to the coastal town of Mossel Bay.

The Outeniqua Pass (799 m), linking Oudtshoorn to George, descends sharply on the southern side of the Outeniquas, along which there are many spectacular viewing points. The railway line follows the same route as the road.

The Swartberg Pass was used by the early Voortrekkers as a way across the steep Swartberg range into the interior of the Karoo. The present pass, opened in 1886, offers splendid views and tempting picnic spots. Several kilometres from the summit, a road branches off to Gamkas Kloof (Die Hel), a deep valley inhabited by descendants of early pioneers.

About 35 km east of Oudtshoorn is the picturesque village of De Rust. This little town lies at the entrance to Meiringspoort, which is characterized by rugged precipices and soaring rock faces, and serves as the chief link between the Klein and Great Karoo. There's a beautiful, 60-m-high waterfall about three kilometres along the road.

The Koos Raubenheimer Dam, on the road to the Cango Caves, affords a delightful picnic spot under historic oaks. Further along the same road is the signpost to Rust-en-Vrede, from where a short walk leads to the 74-m-high Rust-en-Vrede Waterfall.

CANGO CAVES
Near Oudtshoorn

Without a doubt, the Cango Caves are one of the great natural wonders of the African continent.

As you leave daylight and enter the yawning mouth of the caves, a fantasy world of dripstone formations greets you. Spectacular stalactites, formed by calcite deposits from dripping water, hang like icicles from the ceiling, sometimes joining upward-growing stalagmites to form imposing columns.

A herdsman named Klaas Windvogel stumbled on the series of caves in 1780, and reported his find to local teacher Barend Oppel, who in turn contacted a local road builder named Van Zyl. Van Zyl's wonder must have been just as great as he lowered himself on a leather thong into the entrance to the first immense cave – Van Zyl's Chamber, a gallery 98 m long, 49 m wide and 15 m high.

Cleopatra's Needle is the next thrill – a nine-metre-high pillar 150 000 years old. Nearby is Botha's Hall, with its beautiful 'petrified waterfall'.

The main passage leads you through the Rainbow Room to the Bridal Chamber with its stalagmite four-poster bed.

The Drum Room boasts a crystal formation resembling a drum which reverberates when struck. You have to walk down the 220 steps comprising Jacob's Ladder to reach the Cango's longest chamber, the Grand Hall (107 metres). In Lot's Chamber, marvel at calcite figures frozen since time immemorial.

Lumbago Alley is very appropriately named: you have to stoop double down the 24-m-long corridor.

Further on, in King Solomon's Mines, sparkling helictites snake away in all directions, and the Devil's Chimney poses a real challenge – even if you're fit. A circular detour leads you away from this wonderland of dripstone formations and back to the starting point.

In 1972 two professional cave guides discovered an exciting new extension of the Cango Caves, Cango 2, massed with delicate crystalline sculptures. Cango 3, 4 and 5, which were discovered more recently, are said to be even lovelier than Cango 2, but these are closed to the public for the time being.

The Cango Caves Main Hall, a fairyland of artful lighting and breathtaking rock formations, attracts thousands of visitors every year.

Map: page 299, 5D
To reach the Cango Caves, follow Langenhoven Road from Oudtshoorn. The road becomes Baron Van Rheede Street, which leads directly to the caves, 30 km north of the town.
Details: During the December school holidays and the Easter weekend, tours are conducted every hour on the hour from 08h00 to 17h00. For the rest of the year, tours are conducted every hour on the hour from 09h00 to 16h00. The caves are open every day of the year, except Christmas Day. Attractions include a museum, restaurant and shop. There are also a crèche and kennels.
Accommodation: De Hoek Holiday Resort, 7 km from the caves on the road to Prince Albert, offers 4- and 6-bed chalets, and camping sites with braai facilities and a swimming pool. Cango Mountain Resort, 10 km from the Caves, also offers 4- and 6-bed chalets with braai facilities, television and swimming pool. Camping is allowed.
Further information: Klein Karoo Marketing Association, P O Box 1234, Oudtshoorn 6620, tel (0443) 22-6643; Cango Caves, P O Box 255, Oudtshoorn 6620, tel (0443) 22-7410.

Cango Crocodile Ranch and Cheetahland

Rows and rows of gaping jaws, glinting eyes and several tons of uncompromising menace greet you at the Cango Crocodile Ranch and Cheetahland, not far from Oudtshoorn, a great place to stop over on your way to the Cango Caves.

Guided tours, conducted every half-hour, give visitors a fascinating introduction to some 300 crocodiles, jaguars, cheetahs and lions. The crocodile collection – the crocs range from 50 cm to over four metres – is the largest of its kind in the country.

After touring the crocodile enclosure, you may browse through the well-stocked snake park and crocodile museum. There are a number of tame animals for the children to befriend, including Winston the Warthog, Claude the Camel, a dwarf goat, some miniature horses, a wallaby and an otter.

Cheetahland, built in 1988, offers a novel viewing experience for big-cat fans. Cheetahs, jaguars and lions are on view in naturalistic enclosures connected by elevated walkways. This affords excellent photographic opportunities. Guides offer demonstrations from within the enclosures. The walkway leads visitors along a monkey walk, bird park and water cascade.

Refreshments are available at the 'hot croc café', and a curio shop stocks a wide selection of souvenirs.

The ranch, which is signposted from the Oudtshoorn/Cango Caves road, is open 08h00-17h00 in peak season, and 08h00-16h15 out of season.

For further information contact The Manager, Cango Crocodile Ranch and Cheetahland, P O Box 559, Oudtshoorn 6620, tel (0443) 22-5593/22-5596.

C P NEL MUSEUM
Oudtshoorn

Map: page 299, 5D
The museum stands on the corner of Baron Van Rheede and Voortrekker streets, Oudtshoorn.
Details: The C P Nel Museum and its annexe, the Dorphuis, are open Monday to Saturdays 09h00-13h00 and 14h00-17h00. Closed Sundays (unless by prior arrangement), public and religious holidays.
Further information: The Curator, C P Nel Museum, P O Box 453, Oudtshoorn 6620, tel (0443) 22-7306; Klein Karoo Marketing Association, P O Box 1234, Oudtshoorn 6620, tel (0443) 22-6643.

The town of Oudtshoorn has enough of interest to keep you occupied for a week or more, but your visit will not be complete without dropping in at the C P Nel Museum.

The museum is housed in the premises of the former Boys' High School, and is named after Colonel C P Nel, a local businessman and town councillor who collected a fascinating array of weaponry, early motorcars and war medals. These are displayed at the museum, together with memorabilia relating to the history of the ostrich-farming industry and the growth of Oudtshoorn.

There is an intriguing section reserved for the fashions of the feather-boom era, complete with furniture and porcelain of that period.

A collection of local antiques, including one of the finest collections of old bottles in the world, mirrors the town's history. There is also a fine shell collection bequeathed by the late C P Nel.

The Jewish religion, culture and history, and the contribution of the Jewish community to the development of the town, are depicted in the Jewish Gallery, complete with a synagogue dating back to 1896, which is still in use.

Other attractions are a collection of transport vehicles, dolls in national costume, a charming, old-fashioned grocer's shop, a display of firearms, and a reconstruction of an early 20th-century pharmacy. There are also dioramas devoted to the wildlife of the Klein Karoo.

The extravagantly furnished Dorphuis in High Street, an annexe to the museum, is a fine example of an ostrich palace, with original carpets and wallpaper. It was one of the first houses in Oudtshoorn to have an indoor bathroom, and one of the first to be electrified.

A pair of Cape mountain zebras in the Gamka Mountain Nature Reserve. Once threatened by extinction, these animals are coming into their own again.

GAMKA MOUNTAIN NATURE RESERVE
Southwest of Oudtshoorn

Map: page 299, 5C
To get there, take the Calitzdorp road from Oudtshoorn. After 10 km turn left onto the old concrete road to Calitzdorp. This will bring you to a sign reading 'Uitvlugt'. Take this route to the reserve.
Details: The reserve is open daily 07h00-17h00. Parking at the information centre.
Accommodation: A rustic tented camp is available in the reserve (12 people maximum). Calitzdorp Spa, 10 km further on, offers a restaurant, chalets, caravan park and swimming pool.
Further information: The Officer-in-Charge, Gamka Mountain Nature Reserve, Private Bag X21, Oudtshoorn 6620, tel (04437) 3-3367.

The Gamka Mountain Nature Reserve is not well developed to cater for the tourist trade, but what it offers in natural beauty is ample compensation.

The 9 400-ha reserve, situated on the slopes of the rugged Gamka Mountain southwest of Oudtshoorn, is home to the Cape mountain zebra, which came close to extinction in the 1930s, but whose numbers are increasing steadily. The scenery here is stunning, and the view exceptional from Bakenskop (1 099 m), the reserve's highest point.

Four of the 70 major veld types identified in southern Africa to date flourish in the reserve. They are succulent Karoo, false macchia, succulent mountain scrub (or spekboomveld) and renosterbosveld. There is also a profusion of flowering plants in the reserve.

Roaming freely alongside the zebras are klipspringer, grey rhebok, grysbok, duiker, caracals, steenbok, dassies and baboons. Leopards are seen occasionally.

Spring – when wildflowers bloom in dizzying splendour – is the best time to plan a visit to this interesting spot.

The ideal way to sample the delights of the reserve is on foot. There are six short walking trails, as well as the six-hour Tierkloof Trail and a two-day conducted trail. Bookings for the two-day trail and for educational tours (in vehicles) must be made in advance.

GRAAFF-REINET
See page 306

KAROO NATIONAL PARK
Near Beaufort West

The Karoo National Park covers an area of 44 000 ha just north of Beaufort West. Proclaimed in 1979, it offers unique vegetation, a wealth of animal and bird life, and the unusual fossil treasures for which the central Karoo is famed. It is an ideal stopover point for weary travellers, and offers a relaxing holiday for those with more time to spare. Tourist facilities include charmingly thatched, self-catering chalets, a shop, restaurant, information centre and swimming pool.

Some 64 species of mammal inhabit the park, including black rhinos, mountain zebras, eland, gemsbok, red hartebeest, black wildebeest and springbok. Smaller mammal species include caracals, seldom-seen African wild cats, bat-eared foxes, Cape otters, aardwolfs, suricates and striped polecats.

The 196 bird species in the park include saddlebilled storks, crowned hornbills, bateleur eagles and some jackal buzzards. In addition, the park has seven species of frog, 44 reptile, 32 lizard and 19 snake varieties.

There are a number of trails of varying duration and difficulty. The Fossil Trail (one-day) takes you past the fossilized remains of mammal-like reptiles which lived 240 million years ago.

The Bossie Trail, also an interesting one-day ramble, leads through a collection of some 60 Karoo plants – all labelled and listed in a brochure. The three-day, 26,5-km Springbok Hiking Trail is more challenging, leading to the top of the Nuweveld Mountains, from which there are panoramic views of the Karoo. For off-road enthusiasts, the Karoo 4x4 Trail leads 80 km through indigenous veld. Alternatively, you can survey the night sky on a guided drive.

The Karoo National Park's Fossil Trail highlights a vital passage of evolution – from the origin of fishes to the era of the dinosaurs.

Map: page 299, 4D
The turn-off to the park is just north of Beaufort West on the N1 between Cape Town and Johannesburg.
Details: Gates open 05h00-22h00.
Accommodation: Fully equipped chalets and camping sites at the main complex. A small rest camp on the Nuweveld Mountain plateau offers rondavels with beds. Two huts at Kortkloof cater for those on the Springbok Hiking Trail and the Karoo 4x4 Trail.
Further information: National Parks Board, P O Box 787, Pretoria 0001, tel (012) 343-1991; P O Box 7400, Roggebaai 8012, tel (021) 22-2810; The Park Warden, Karoo National Park, P O Box 316, Beaufort West 6970, tel (0201) 5-2828.

MATJIESFONTEIN
West of Laingsburg

You could almost drive past Matjiesfontein without knowing it's actually there. The tiny settlement, consisting of no more than a handful of dwellings, is just off the N1, some 250 km northwest of Cape Town.

Small as it is, though, Matjiesfontein has some delightful surprises in store for those who've never been there.

The first is the Lord Milner Hotel, with its exquisitely furnished bedrooms, elegant sitting rooms and library overlooking spacious inner courtyards.

The Lord Milner is famous for its handsome English, buffet-style breakfasts, relaxed Sunday luncheons and dinners, for which jacket and tie are strictly *de rigueur*.

Next door to the hotel is the Lairds Arms, a Victorian-style bar. Further down Logan Street is a pretty trio of semi-detached buildings. In the centre is the Post Office, flanked on one side by Olive Schreiner House. On the old station is the Marie Rawdon Museum and the Railway Museum.

Nearby is the Coffee House, where you can enjoy light refreshments. At the Losieshuis, which is affiliated to the Lord Milner, you will find reasonably priced family-style accommodation.

From its rather lowly beginnings as an insignificant railway siding, Matjiesfontein gained prominence due to the efforts of Scotsman James Logan, who saw the inherent potential of the hamlet.

In the early days, an ant-like stream of travellers passed through the town, bound for the Kimberley diamond fields. Accommodation and food were scarce. Seeing his chance, Logan acquired the concession to run a refreshment station at Matjiesfontein. Before the outbreak of the Anglo-Boer War in 1899, he devoted himself to turning Matjiesfontein into a popular resort. Subsequently, it became a favoured holiday place for Cecil John Rhodes, Lord Randolph Churchill and authoress Olive Schreiner.

After a slump in the 1950s, the town enjoyed a revival and is still very popular, particularly among Capetonians.

Map: page 299, 5B
To reach Matjiesfontein, follow the N1 from Cape Town, via Worcester. The town is situated between Worcester and Laingsburg, at the Sutherland crossroads (27 km before Laingsburg). Be on the lookout for the signpost on the right-hand side, as it is indistinct.
Accommodation: There are 36 suites and family rooms at the Lord Milner Hotel and the Losieshuis.
Further information: Lord Milner Hotel, Matjiesfontein 6901, tel (02372) 5203.

PLACES TO VISIT

GRAAFF-REINET

Map: right
Located in Church Street, facing Parsonage Street.
Further information: Graaff-Reinet Publicity Association, P O Box 153, Graaff-Reinet 6280, tel (0491) 2-4248.

DROSTDY

Like the good burghers of 19th-century Graaff-Reinet, you too may complain at having to travel for a month if you wanted to marry, enlist in the army or attend a court case in the Cape.

To placate the citizens, Landdrost Moritz Otto Woeke, of Stellenbosch, decreed that a Drostdy be built in the town to deal with these contingencies, and in 1806 the building was duly erected.

Designed by the well-known architect Louis Thibault, the Drostdy was the hallowed residence of the magistrate and often served as a guesthouse for visiting dignitaries. In 1847 it was sold, together with a large tract of land, and in 1878 it became a hotel.

Early this century, it sported a double-storey Victorian façade, but this was removed in 1975, restoring the building's graceful Cape Dutch proportions.

Today the Drostdy is a luxurious hotel with very carefully selected antiques and paintings that radiate an atmosphere of gracious ease appropriate to the period.

Stretch's Court, behind the Drostdy Hof building, serves as an annexe to the hotel. The restored labourers' cottages now sport shutters, flower tubs and antique lampstands.

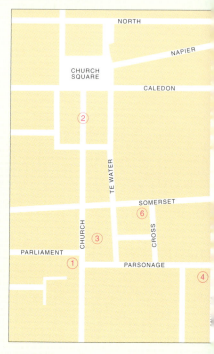

KEY TO MAP
1 Drostdy
2 Dutch Reformed Church
3 Hester Rupert Art Gallery
4 Old Residency
5 Reinet House
6 St James Anglican Church
7 Urquhart House

Monuments at Graaff-Reinet

A monument honours the soldiers who fought during the Anglo-Boer War.

The town of Graaff-Reinet has an impressive collection of monuments mirroring the history and achievements of the people of the area.

Pride of place goes to the Graaff-Reinet War Memorial in front of the Town Hall. This monument, fashioned by well-known London sculptor H C Fehr, features an imposing bronze figure of the Victory Peace Angel mounted on a high pedestal.

The monument honours victims of the two world wars, including local citizens who died in World War II.

The Anglo-Boer War Memorial at the corner of Somerset and Donkin streets was erected on a small plot donated by the late Mr Jurie Laubscher, a citizen of the town. The design of the marble monument, which was made in Italy, is said to have been based on photographs of Boer soldiers.

The Andries Pretorius Monument, about two kilometres outside the town, features an imposing statue of Pretorius gazing towards the north, with his left hand atop a wagon wheel.

The Gideon Scheepers Memorial on the Murraysburg road honours a signaller in the Transvaal Artillery, who was executed by the British after forming his own commando during the Anglo-Boer War. The memorial comprises three rocks supporting a stainless-steel needle, symbolizing the spirit of faith and hope.

The Union Monument, a compelling stone pyramid erected on Magazine Hill, commemorates the union of the four provinces in 1910. Each side of the structure displays a marble tablet bearing the name of a province.

One of the most interesting of Graaff-Reinet's monuments is that built as a tribute to the Jewish pedlars who once canvassed the Cape Colony's interior. The monument consists of a boulder on which a bronze plaque is mounted.

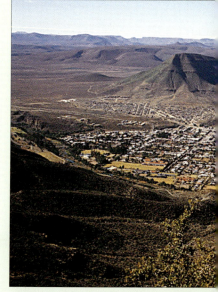

Rocky hillsides overlook Graaff-Reinet, which nestles in a bend of the Sundays River.

DUTCH REFORMED CHURCH

All that glitters isn't necessarily gold, but it might be silver! If you have an interest in Cape silver, you should visit the Dutch Reformed Church at Graaff-Reinet.

This graceful sandstone edifice known as the 'Grootkerk' has a large collection of rare Cape silver, including a silver basin and four silver cups made by the famous silversmith, J C Lötter. There are also a silver baptismal font donated by a parishioner in 1839, and a collection of plates which were made by the British firm Mapin Brothers.

The 'Grootkerk' was built in 1885 to take the place of the so-called 'Klein Kerkie', which had become too small for the congregation at the time of the Rev Charles Murray, son of Presbyterian minister Andrew Murray, who played an important role in the cultural history of Graaff-Reinet.

Both resided in the parsonage (now known as Reinet House, site of the Graaff-Reinet Museum). The Reverend Murray did not live to see the church completed, but his wife attended the laying of the cornerstone in April 1886.

Graaff-Reinet's imposing Dutch Reformed Church, a fine example of Victorian Gothic architecture, was built from local sandstone.

Map: page 306
Located at the head of Church Square, Church Street, Graaff-Reinet.
Details: Open Monday to Friday 08h00-12h00 and 14h00-16h00. Closed on Saturdays, Sundays and public holidays.
Further information: Graaff-Reinet Publicity Association, P O Box 153, Graaff-Reinet 6280, tel (0491) 2-4248.

HESTER RUPERT ART GALLERY

This lovely art gallery in the Old Library Building, just a stone's throw from the popular Drostdy Hotel, is well worth a visit even if South African art is not your speciality. The attractive building, built originally in 1821, houses the work of over 100 leading artists.

The building housing the gallery was originally the Dutch Reformed Mission Church, where missionaries preached the Gospel to the coloured community for over a century.

It was saved from demolition by the Graaff-Reinet-born magnate Dr Anton Rupert in 1965, and named after his mother, Hester.

The building has solid walls typical of the period, culminating in four graceful gables, and a thatched roof supported by a framework of yellowwood beams.

When the roof had to be replaced, fundraisers went to the Transvaal, where President Kruger was persuaded to make a donation to the fund.

Map: page 306
Located in Church Street, opposite the Post Office, Graaff-Reinet.
Details: Open 10h00-12h00 and 15h00-17h00 weekdays, and 10h00-12h00 on Saturdays, Sundays and public holidays.
Further information: Graaff-Reinet Publicity Association, P O Box 153, Graaff-Reinet 6280, tel (0491) 2-4248.

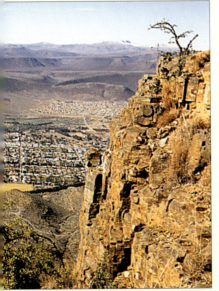

OLD RESIDENCY

This well-preserved national monument diagonally opposite Reinet House was a private residence until 1916, after which it was acquired by the State for use as the residence of the Graaff-Reinet magistrate. It remained so until 1978, when it became the annexe to Reinet House *(see next page)*.

The Residency houses the remarkable Jan Felix Lategan Memorial gun collection – one of the finest collections of sporting rifles in the country. Dr Felix Lategan, a leading authority on historic firearms, presented the museum with a collection of sporting rifles in memory of his young son, Jan Felix Lategan, who died in a mountaineering accident.

The Old Residency also houses some interesting regimental memorabilia of the Midlands Regiment, and various musical instruments.

Map: page 306
The museum is situated on the corner of Parsonage and Murray streets, obliquely opposite Reinet House.
Details: Open 09h00-12h00 and 15h00-17h00 weekdays, and 09h00-12h00 on Saturdays. Closed Sundays and public holidays.
Further information: Graaff-Reinet Museum, P O Box 104, Graaff-Reinet 6280, tel (0491) 2-3801.

GRAAFF-REINET

Map: page 306
In Murray Street, facing the Drostdy Hotel at the bottom end of Parsonage Street.
Details: Open weekdays 09h00-12h00 and 15h00-17h00; Saturdays 09h00-12h00; Sundays and public holidays 10h00-12h00. Closed on Good Friday and Christmas Day.
Further information: Graaff-Reinet Museum, P O Box 104, Graaff-Reinet 6280, tel (0491) 2-3801.

REINET HOUSE

This house, a fine example of 18th-century Cape Dutch architecture in the traditional H-shape, is raised on a podium with arched openings. It has a thatched roof and gables, the front gable adorned with an hourglass.

Behind the whitewashed house is the cobbled courtyard, a paved garden and the famous Black Acorn grapevine planted by Rev Charles Murray in 1870.

The house was built between 1806 and 1812 as a Dutch Reformed Church parsonage, and was occupied by a series of ministers, including Rev Andrew Murray and his son Charles, who together stayed there for 82 years.

After Charles's death in 1904 the building became a hostel, and was later vacated. In 1952 Reinet House was declared a national monument, and later painstakingly restored. In 1956 it opened its doors to the public.

Part of the building and its priceless antique contents were destroyed by fire in 1980. However, reconstruction, financed by donations from townsfolk, began soon afterwards.

The magnificent, gabled Reinet House stands high above Murray Street. Its broad stoep shelters arcaded basements which were once used for storage and as slave quarters.

Map: page 306
The church is situated in Somerset Street, on the corner of Cross Street, in the historic core of Graaff-Reinet.
Further information: Graaff-Reinet Publicity Association, P O Box 153, Graaff-Reinet 6280, tel (0491) 2-4248.

ST JAMES ANGLICAN CHURCH

The most striking feature of St James Anglican Church, an attractive neo-Gothic stone building, is its jewel-like stained-glass windows, casting multi-coloured light onto the pews within.

The belfry is housed in the sturdy entrance porch, added to the church in 1874. Originally, services were announced by the splendid ringing of six bells, but in 1894 these were recast into the existing single bell.

Anglicans wanting to marry in Graaff-Reinet last century first had to approach the resident minister of the Dutch Reformed Church for permission to hold their nuptials in his church. This unusual state of affairs was remedied when the St James Anglican Church opened its doors in 1850. Many couples have married within its portals since.

The first Anglican congregation at Graaff-Reinet dates back to 1845, when the Rev William Long was appointed Colonial Chaplain.

In 1848 Bishop Robert Grey visited Graaff-Reinet whilst touring his diocese on horseback. He encouraged members of the congregation to raise funds to build their own church

The thatched-roof building was ceremoniously consecrated on Bishop Grey's next visit. In 1868 a chancel (the area reserved for the choir and clergy) and sanctuary were added.

Map: page 306
Urquhart House stands on the corner of Market Square and Murray Street, adjoining the Reinet House garden.
Details: Open weekdays 10h00-12h00 and 15h00-17h00, and Saturdays 10h00-12h00. Closed on Sundays.
Further information: Graaff-Reinet Museum, P O Box 104, Graaff-Reinet 6280, tel (0491) 2-3801.

URQUHART HOUSE

Named after Herbert Urquhart, a popular local businessman and mayor, who lived here during the first half of the century, Urquhart House is now owned by the Graaff-Reinet Trust.

Displayed within is a fascinating collection of Victorian furniture, including many Cape Dutch antiques. An unusual feature of this rather attractive Cape Dutch building is a ship's anchor on the gable. It is said that its builder introduced the motif in honour of an ancestor who had been an admiral.

MEIRINGSPOORT
Near De Rust

Separating the fertile Klein Karoo from the Great Karoo is the 200-km-long Swartberg range, a magnificent chain of jagged peaks rising to a height of 2 133 metres. Traversing this formidable barrier are some of the country's most spectacular mountain passes. One of them is Meiringspoort Pass.

The southern entrance to Meiringspoort is at the attractive hamlet of De Rust. From here the pass twists and turns across the eastern fork of the Swartberge for about 21 km, crossing the Meirings River 32 times.

Hemmed in by gigantic precipices of twisted rock, at each bend the road reveals a scene more beautiful than the last. Wildflowers abound at the roadside and the pass teems with dassies.

Fourteen kilometres from the southern entrance there's a memorial to Herrie the Elephant, the well-known literary character of the well-known Afrikaans poet and author C J Langenhoven. Further ahead, a 61-m-high waterfall plunges into a clear mountain pool.

Meiringspoort was conceived by road engineer Andrew Geddes Bain as a link between the Klein and Great Karoo.

Map: page 299, 5D
Take the R29 from Oudtshoorn in a northerly direction towards De Rust and Beaufort West. Meiringspoort is clearly signposted.
Accommodation: Options available are Oulap Guest Lodge (25 km from the Poort), P O Box 77, De Rust 6650, tel (04439) 2250; De Rust Tourist Resort, P O Box 18, De Rust 6650, tel (04439) 2104, which has camping and caravan sites; Meiringspoort Guesthouse (which also has caravan facilities), 15 Le Roux Street, De Rust 6650, tel (04439) 2217.
Further information: Klein Karoo Marketing Association, P O Box 1234, Oudtshoorn 6620, tel (0443) 22-6643.

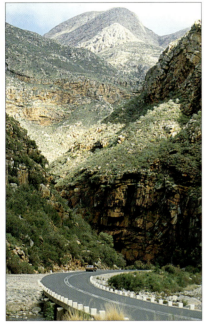

Meiringspoort Pass forges its way through the Swartberg, exposing strata of folded rock. These twisted layers were pushed to the surface millions of years ago by forces beneath the earth's crust.

Montagu Pass winds below the dizzying Outeniqua Pass, exposing at each bend a new vista across the fertile valleys below.

MONTAGU PASS
Near Oudtshoorn

For a relaxing, scenic drive close to nature's outdoor masterpieces, the old Montagu Pass, just a stone's throw away from the newer Outeniqua Pass, between George and Oudtshoorn, is the perfect choice for travellers.

Opened in 1848, about a quarter of the 20-km pass had to be blasted out of bedrock using gunpowder and fire, a feat never before undertaken in South Africa.

While many indigenous trees have been replaced by exotics such as pine and acacia, you can still see a number of majestic stinkwood trees at the aptly named Stinkhoutdraai (Stinkwood Bend), where the railway viaduct, built in 1910, crosses the roadway.

Expertly laid dry-stone embankments are to be seen most of the way up to the summit. Quaint names abound. At Die Noute (The Narrows), cliffs soar to dizzy heights above the road. Just beyond is Moertjiesklip – a reference to a huge rock reputed to have crushed a man who tried to dislodge it.

You can picnic at the Tollhouse (about seven kilometres from the turn-off at Blanco), the Keur River Bridge, with its mossy ferns and cascading water eight kilometres from the Blanco turn-off, at Old Smithy, the 10,5-km stop where the remains of the blacksmith's shop may still be seen, and at Stinkhoutdraai with its five-span arch bridge.

Map: page 299, 5D
To reach Montagu Pass from Oudtshoorn turn south from the R62 onto the gravel road signposted 'Herold' and 'George via Montagu Pass', about 9 km east of the junction with the R29.
Accommodation: Camping sites or chalets at George Tourist Resort, P O Box 772, George 6530, tel (0441) 74-5205.
Further information: Montagu Information Office, P O Box 24, Montagu 6720, tel (0234) 4-1112; The Curator, George Museum, Private Bag X6596, George 6530, tel (0441) 73-5343; George Tourism Association, P O Box 1109, George 6530, tel (0441) 74-4000.

NIEU-BETHESDA
Near Graaff-Reinet

Map: page 299, 3F
A good gravel road branches off the main tarred road to Middelburg, 27 km from Graaff-Reinet.
Details: Open weekdays 09h00-12h00 and 14h00-16h00; Saturdays 09h00-12h00. Closed on Sundays and public holidays. Admission charged.
Accommodation: The only accommodation available in Nieu-Bethesda is that provided by private home-owners.
Further information: The Town Clerk, Nieu-Bethesda 6286, tel (04923) 712; Graaff-Reinet Publicity Association, P O Box 153, Graaff-Reinet 6280, tel (0491) 2-4248.

The charming village of Nieu-Bethesda, 50 km from Graaff-Reinet, might have languished in obscurity, were it not for one lonely woman with a vision of beauty that led her to transform her mundane existence into a wonderland of light and colour. Come and share the radiant dream of the late Helen Martins at The Owl House, immortalized by playwright Athol Fugard in his play *Road to Mecca*.

As you enter Nieu-Bethesda, there's a profusion of pear and quince trees set against a tranquil blue mountain backdrop. On your way to The Owl House, visit the town's Dutch Reformed Church. It has finely carved pews and a unique set of chandeliers.

Near The Owl House, where the road crosses over the Gats River to the western bank, is a water mill more than 130 years old. The village cemetery contains tombstones hewn from solid rock, dating back to 1786.

From a distance, The Owl House resembles a typical Karoo cottage on a handkerchief-sized plot. However, when you enter the cramped building, Helen Martins's peculiar genius is immediately apparent: the walls, ceilings and doors are liberally decorated with coloured ground glass. A myriad mirrors reflect the light from lamps and candles in every room.

The enigmatic 'Miss Helen', as she was known to townsfolk, devoted the last 20 years of her life to what she termed 'the search for light and brightness' and this quest is apparent everywhere.

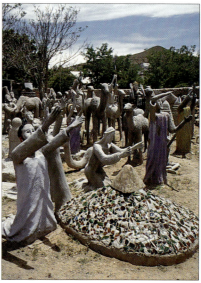
A host of biblical characters enchant visitors at Nieu-Bethesda's well-known Owl House.

In the 'Camel Yard' at the rear of the house, hemmed in by a high stone wall, hundreds of cement figures vie for attention. Camels, owls, peacocks, mermaids, lambs and sphinxes gambol, preen, trot and writhe together – all the marvellous handiwork of Helen and helper Koos Malgas. Eastern philosophy and religion, Christianity and the stellar system also feature prominently in this lovely garden of delights.

Helen Martins died by her own hand in 1976, but she left a rich and compelling legacy of original art.

The simply decorated interior of a church in Nieu-Bethesda offers a warm welcome to worshippers.

OUDTSHOORN OSTRICH PALACES
See page 312

PRINCE ALBERT
South of Leeu-Gamka

Map: page 299, 5D
There are two turn-offs to Prince Albert from the N1 highway, between Cape Town and Johannesburg. The first (R328) is at Prince Albert Road Station, about 83 km from Laingsburg. This tarred road stretches 45 km to the town. The second (R353), 29 km further along at Kruidfontein, is untarred.
Accommodation: The historic Swartberg Hotel (which also has self-catering rondavels) and several guesthouses offer comfortable accommodation in the town.
Further information: Prince Albert Publicity Association, P O Box 109, Prince Albert 6930, tel (04436) 366.

This peaceful town at the foot of the Swartberg range features well-conserved examples of 19th-century Victorian, Cape Dutch and Karoo-style architecture. You'll see them specifically at No. 5 Deurdrift Street, Nos. 1, 5 and 23 Church Street, and Nos. 8 and 12 De Beer Street.

Founded in 1762, Prince Albert enjoyed a brief 'gold rush', but the mine was not viable, and the prospectors left as quickly as they had arrived.

Mementos of the gold frenzy are on display in the Fransie Pienaar Museum, along with a variety of artefacts portraying the rich history of the people of this area. Also on display is a 30-cm-long coffin which was found in a local loft, and, as the legend goes, has never been opened. Other attractions in the town include a large, privately owned mineral collection, a hand-weaving factory, a tannery, a pottery and a jewellery workshop specializing in precious and semi-precious stones.

The town is proud of its authentic water mill which is one of its best-known landmarks. Such water mills played an important role in the life of small towns in bygone days. Sadly, few remain, and therefore the one at Prince Albert is of considerable historical significance.

Three scenic out-of-town drives lead through Scottzkloof, Weltevrede and De Gang, one of the most prolific fruit-growing areas in this region.

SEWEWEEKSPOORT PASS
North of Ladismith

The Seweweekspoort (Seven Weeks Poort) Pass is an intriguing place of mystery and legend, dominated on the east side by the 2 325-m Seven Weeks Poort Mountain, the highest peak in the Swartberg range. Colossal, orange-coloured sandstone cliffs overhang the road, which crisscrosses the river on its way through a 15-km gorge.

One explanation for the unusual name is that brandy-smugglers, taking their wagons from the Cape to Beaufort West, avoided revenue officers by travelling through the pass, a return journey which took seven weeks. Another explanation is that the name comes from the everlasting flowers (known as Seven Weeks) which flourish there.

The ruins of the old tollhouse, built in 1862, still stand, and it is said the tollkeeper's ghost wanders around on stormy nights, swinging his lantern in an attempt to flag down motorists.

The area provides demanding climbs, during which you may spot the rare *Protea aristata*. There are some attractive picnic sites in the kloof.

Aloes flank the dusty passage of the Seweweekspoort Pass as it weaves its way between the wild, weatherworn cliffs of the Swartberg.

Map: page 299, 5C
From the south take the N2, and then the R323 north from Riversdale to Ladismith. At Ladismith, turn east onto the R62. After 21 km turn on to a well-signposted gravel road leading north. The pass begins 5 km from the turn-off.
Accommodation: There are hotels, guest farms, caravan and camping grounds, and self-catering cottages in the Ladismith area.
Further information: Ladismith Municipality, P O Box 30, Ladismith 6885, tel (028) 551-1023; Ladismith Publicity Association, P O Box 390, Ladismith 6885, tel (02942) ask for 4903, or (028) 551-2128.

SWARTBERG PASS
South of Prince Albert

The mighty Swartberg Pass was built by the distinguished road engineer Thomas Bain, more than 100 years ago. A talking point in its day, the pass was opened to the public in 1886.

Convict labour was used to good effect in the difficult construction of the pass, and the ruins of some of the workers' cottages can still be seen.

Built to link Oudtshoorn and the Klein Karoo with Prince Albert in the Great Karoo, this 24-km-long engineering feat still takes away the breath of jaded travellers as it cleaves the Swartberg range at a height of 1 585 metres.

This was the route used by the Voortrekkers in the 19th century on their way to the interior. They, too, must have enjoyed the splendid views as they outspanned after their arduous climb.

The road construction and colourful rock formations make this one of South Africa's most impressive mountain passes. During heavy winter snowfalls the pass is sometimes closed to traffic.

Several kilometres from the summit a road branches off to Gamkas Kloof (Die Hel), a deep, narrow valley, inhabited for several generations by descendants of early pioneers.

The road rises over 1 400 m between steep rock faces, and zigzags its way to the summit. On its descent, it crosses several small streams. Shady picnic spots offer a place to relax and contemplate both natural and man-made marvels.

Map: page 299, 5D
From Cape Town take the N2 east and the N12 north to Oudtshoorn. Continue north along Baron Van Rheede Street (which becomes the R328) towards Schoemanspoort and the Cango Caves. The pass starts 46 km north of Oudtshoorn.
Accommodation: See the entry on Oudtshoorn for accommodation details.
Further information: Klein Karoo Marketing Association, P O Box 1234, Oudtshoorn 6620, tel (0443) 22-6643.

PLACES TO VISIT

OUDTSHOORN OSTRICH PALACES

Map: page 299, 5D
The two show farms, *Highgate* and *Safari*, are on the road to Mossel Bay, between Oudtshoorn and the Robinson Pass.
Details: Both are open every day (excepting Christmas Day). At *Highgate*, tours depart approximately every 15 minutes between 08h00 and 17h00, and last an hour and a half. The *Safari* tours depart every 30 minutes between 08h00 and 17h00 (during Cape school holidays), and 08h00 and 16h30 for the rest of the year. Duration is an hour and a half.
A third ostrich farm, the *Cango Ostrich Farm*, is similar to the other two, and has a wine house as an added attraction. It is situated halfway between the Cango Caves and Oudtshoorn. Tours are conducted every 30 minutes between 08h00 and 17h00 (Cape school holidays), and 08h00 and 16h30 for the rest of the year. Duration: 45 minutes.
Accommodation: Oudtshoorn offers a wide range of accommodation, from luxury hotels to guesthouses, cottages, and camping/caravan sites.
Further information: Highgate Ostrich Show Farm, P O Box 94, Oudtshoorn 6620, tel (0433) 22-7115/6; *Safari Ostrich Show Farm,* P O Box 300, Oudtshoorn 6620, tel (0443) 22-7311/2; Klein Karoo Marketing Association, P O Box 1234, Oudtshoorn 6620, tel (0443) 22-6643.

Do ostrich feathers conjure up an image of garishly coloured fluffy feather dusters? Had you been in the forefront of fashion earlier this century, ostrich feathers would have had very different connotations.

For more than 20 years no woman of style would appear in public without a feather somewhere in her ensemble – be it headband, handbag, fan, cape or boa. Ostrich feathers were literally worth their weight in gold during the feather boom, and, as a result, life was very good for some in the Klein Karoo.

The reason for the upsurge in the popularity of these large, decorative feathers was the introduction of the so-called *Art Nouveau* movement overseas.

Designers everywhere turned to natural forms for their inspiration, and employed flowing, organic lines in their designs. Ostrich feathers fitted the bill perfectly. The money gained from the worldwide demand for top-quality feathers financed an affluent society in the Klein Karoo.

The houses built at that time reflect the prevailing prosperity then. Designed by architects to please clients from simple, rural backgrounds, each building was more extravagant than its predecessor.

When the market collapsed, these palatial homes could no longer be maintained, and became neglected monuments to ostentation. Fortunately, you can now visit some that have been restored to their former glory.

Ostrich rides and races are major attractions at Oudtshoorn's farms.

The multihued sandstone of the Klein Karoo suited the exuberant *Art Nouveau* style perfectly. It was easy to work with, and readily available. Lured by the promise of riches, 12 major architects established themselves in the area.

Chief among them was Charles Bullock, a British emigrant specializing both in public buildings and private residences. Among his best creations were the celebrated Olivier Towers, a private mansion with octagonal rooms and a tower (sadly no longer in existence); Gottland House; and Rus in Urbe (popularly known as 'Foster's Folly'), a 20-roomed mansion with a vast wine

A male ostrich performs a ritual designed to impress its prospective mate. A breeding male has up to three females in his harem, each of which lays three to eight eggs in a communal nest.

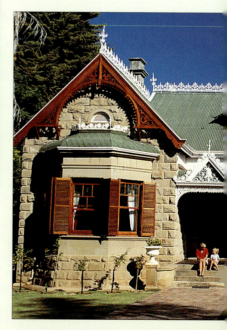

Mimosa Lodge is typical of the eccentric homes built in the Oudtshoorn area after the turn of the century. Its walls of ochre sandstone display turrets, iron lacework and fretwork.

cellar, teak panelling and French stained-glass windows; and the luxurious Le Roux Town House, built for the Le Roux family of Bakenskraal.

Another notable example of Bullock's style is the former Boys' High School, built in 1906 – now the site of the C P Nel Museum. One of Bullock's most exquisite designs, a town house of sandstone in full *Art Nouveau* style, known as the Dorphuis, now forms part of the C P Nel Museum in Adderley Street. It sports outstanding wrought-iron and stained-glass work and is furnished in the opulent style of the feather-boom era.

The most renowned of the various ostrich palaces, Pinehurst, is a private home and is no longer open to the public.

Oudtshoorn is not called the 'feather capital' of the world for nothing. The town is synonymous with ostriches. Nowhere else are the giant birds raised so successfully. Whilst the industry is considerably smaller now than it was prior to the World War I boom period, it still meets a steady demand.

There are currently some 90 000 ostriches in Oudtshoorn, which represents 99 percent of the country's total. Ostriches farmed exclusively for their feathers are plucked every nine months or so – a painless procedure which yields about one kilogram of feathers per bird.

Ostriches may live as long as 40 years. They are extremely powerful, and the males have a lethal kick. Adult birds are capable of attaining speeds of up to 60 km/hour.

Besides feathers for the ubiquitous dusters and fashion accessories, the hides are used for handbags, shoes, belts, wallets and briefcases, and command high prices. Biltong is made from the meat, which is also used for delicious savoury dishes. A single egg, weighing just over one kilogram, makes an omelette equivalent to 24 regular hen's eggs. The shells of ostrich eggs are used for beads or painted lampshades and ornaments.

At the farms *Highgate* and *Safari* you will be taken on a very interesting tour covering most aspects of ostrich-feather production. During the tour you can enjoy the exhilarating thrill of watching an ostrich race, or, if you dare, ride one yourself. The two show farms are on the road to Mossel Bay, between Oudtshoorn and the Robinson Pass.

Highgate has over 100 years of experience with ostriches, and is still run by the same family. A grand tour is conducted by multilingual guides, and ends with a traditional lunch where you can sample ostrich meat. There is a large curio shop.

Safari farm also offers guided tours, and has a showroom featuring ethnic art and products related to the industry. The gracious homestead, Welgeluk, is a national monument.

The grand entrance of Pinehurst, a feather palace built in 1911, leads into an opulent 20-room mansion with a sweeping staircase.

VALLEY OF DESOLATION
Near Graaff-Reinet

The bleak beauty of the aptly named Valley of Desolation has an allure unmatched by any scenery in the 15 000-ha Karoo Nature Park.

Here, the gradual erosion of sedimentary beds has left dolerite pillars rising to heights of 90-120 m above the windswept valley.

A tarred road winds 14 km up the mountain to sites that provide breathtaking views of the ravaged valley, the distant Plains of Camdeboo to the south, and the town known as the 'Gem of the Karoo' below. On your return to the town, stop at the koppie known as the 'Lookout' and climb the short distance to the summit where a toposcope indicates the geographical features, and from where there are fine views. The summit of Compasberg on the horizon is 2 504 m, the highest point in the Sneeuberg range.

A short walk from the car park leads to the edge of the plateau that drops into the valley. Many hiking trails, including the 1,5-km Valley Trail along the mountain top, afford magnificent views.

Map: page 299, 4F
The valley is 14 km from Graaff-Reinet by road. Take the R63 to Murraysburg from Graaff-Reinet. After passing the Van Ryneveld Pass Dam, turn left at the signposted fork 5 km from town. This road takes you to the top of the mountain.

Further information: Department of Nature Conservation, P O Box 349, Graaff-Reinet 6280, tel (0491) 2-3453; the Graaff-Reinet Publicity Association, P O Box 153, Graaff-Reinet 6280, tel (0491) 2-4248.

The dolerite dome of Spandau Kop rises abruptly above the Valley of Desolation's bleak, weather-worn jumble of craggy rocks.

WEST COAST

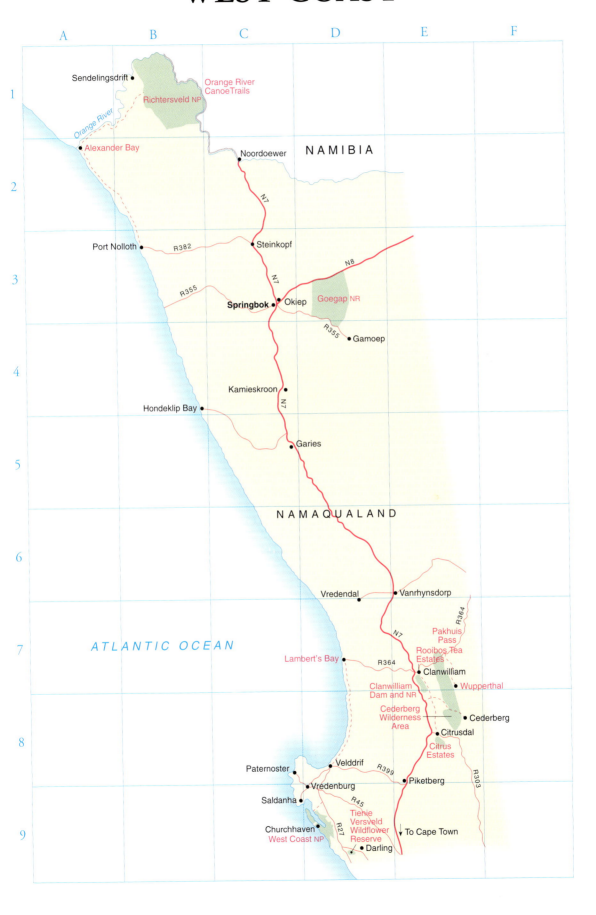

ALEXANDER BAY
Near Orange River Mouth

Map: page 315, 2A
Turn off the N7, 52 km north of Springbok, onto the R382 to Steinkopf. Drive for 93 km to Port Nolloth. Drive north along the 85-km coastal road to Alexander Bay.
Details: Tours of the diamond mine on Thursdays at 08h00. Permits and tour bookings must be organized at least 24 hours in advance.
Accommodation: Hotels in Springbok and Nababeep; caravan and camping sites in Springbok, Port Nolloth and Alexander Bay.
Further information: The Public Relations Officer, Alexkor, Private Bag X5, Alexander Bay 8290, tel (0256) 330.

If diamonds are a girl's best friend, then Alexander Bay, at the centre of South Africa's largest alluvial diamond diggings, ought to be the friendliest place on earth. Unfortunately, however, it's a long way from anywhere – on the desolate seaboard just to south of the Orange River mouth. As you'd expect in a place where diamonds are reputed to line the seabed, you need a permit to get in.

The diamonds were washed down over millennia by the river, to be distributed among the gravels of the seabed, beach and hinterland. To get them out, gigantic earthmovers cut the ground away with almost surgical precision, gouging straight-edged trenches measuring up to 30 m deep and 100 m wide. This is the first step in a process that will yield trayfuls of glittering diamonds destined for the world's vaults, jewellery boxes and, of course, beautiful women.

Local security is tight – as it is in all diamond areas, but especially so in those where the stones lie close to the surface. The controlling company is happy to receive visitors, will readily issue permits, and arranges tours of the mining processes. These include the removal of the overburden by bulldozers and scrapers, the sweeping and sifting, crushing, washing, separation and rough sorting of the stones. It's all done on a grand scale, and it is spellbinding to watch. Visitors are also shown the seal colony and oyster farm.

A two-carat diamond glows with pale fire in its West Coast limestone bed. The diggings around Alexander Bay are among the world's biggest.

Diamonds of the desert

Fabulous diamond deposits were discovered in the bleak desert terrain north of the Orange in 1908, but it wasn't until 1925 that Jack Carstens, a young Port Nolloth soldier on leave from India, made the first big find on the southern coastal strip that started a wild rush for instant wealth.

Prospectors, lured by the promise of instant wealth, converged on the area from far and wide. A few made fortunes, among them the geologist Hans Merensky, who uncovered 12 500 carats within six weeks in 1926, in the Alexander Bay area. Some of the cannier diggers followed the so-called 'oyster line', an oddity of natural science that served as a beacon to the richest treasure-troves. Simply put, the diamonds lay in gravels containing the shells of an extinct warm-water oyster, the two quite different elements brought together by some ancient seismic upheaval that changed the ocean currents.

But it was by no means an idyllic scene: men competed ferociously for the most promising claims, law and order disintegrated completely, and at one point the unruly fortune-seekers threatened to take over the fields by force of arms.

In 1928 Port Nolloth, Alexander Bay and the coveted diamond strip in between were declared State Alluvial Diggings and remained so until 1989, when they were taken over by private enterprise.

CEDERBERG WILDERNESS AREA
Citrusdal

The high and scenically stunning mountain range that rises to the east of Citrusdal and Clanwilliam is a magnet for hikers, ramblers, rock climbers, photographers and nature-lovers. But be warned: visitors aren't restricted to set trails or compulsory overnight stops. You're on your own, and you'll need a detailed map to find your way through the vast wilderness area.

It's a huge area, nearly 72 000 ha in extent, distinguished by pinnacles and deep ravines, splendid vistas, cliffs and caves, clear mountain streams, pools, cascades, and what must be some of the country's weirdest rock formations. Among these are the imposing Maltese Cross and the Wolfberg Arch. Sneeuberg, at 2 027 m above sea level, is the loftiest of the peaks. Snow mantles the range's upper slopes in winter.

The Cederberg mountains are also a botanist's delight. They are named after the Clanwilliam cedar *(Widdringtonia cedarbergensis)*. This handsome tree – found only on this mountain range – just managed to survive man-made fires lit to improve livestock pasture, and the woodman's axe (to harvest the tree's valuable and durable wood). The remaining specimens, confined to rocky outcrops, are now strictly protected.

A 5 000-ha cedar reserve has been set aside for the planting out of nursery-reared seedlings. Another rare resident is the snow protea *(Protea cryophila)*, which clings to life above the snow line. This protea is found only on a few mountain peaks. The flora, which is predominantly mountain fynbos, includes the large red disa, the rocket pincushion, and a small number of eye-catching indigenous trees in the wetter kloofs.

The uplands are well watered and there's wildlife aplenty, but much of it tends to be small and elusive, lost in the rugged vastness. Steenbok, klipspringer, grysbok, duiker, grey rhebok, baboons and African wild cats are among its 30 or so species of mammal. The entire wilderness is a refuge for leopards. Some splendid birds of prey wheel and swoop in the sky above, among them black eagles and jackal buzzards.

Walkers may wander at will and for as long as they please, the only limitations imposed being the amount of food taken along and the hikers' degree of fitness. But there are rules specifically aimed at protecting the natural environment: carry a valid permit; don't light fires (bring a gas stove for cooking); don't pollute the water with soap, and remove all your litter.

Long-distance hikers overnight at the rudimentary mountain huts or in the caves. Most day-visitors stay at Algeria Forest camp site, which caters for caravanners and campers, and is located roughly in the centre of the reserve. Further north, the Kliphuis camp site also has caravanning and camping stands. Neither site has electricity.

The starkly distinctive Wolfberg Arch – one of many strangely sculpted features carved from the Cederberg's rock by the relentlessly erosive action of wind and water.

Map: page 315, 8E
Turn off the N7, 27 km north of Citrusdal eastwards towards Algeria. Follow the signs for Cederberg Wilderness and Algeria. The road crosses the Olifants River and cuts over the scenic Nieuwoudt Pass before reaching Algeria.
Details: Open throughout the year. Small entry charge per person and vehicle. Permits from the Reservation Officer, Cederberg Wilderness, Private Bag X1, Citrusdal 7340, tel (022) 921-2289. Office hours at Algeria: daily 08h00-16h30. The office will provide a map of the area. Picnic sites at Algeria (very attractive) and at Kliphuis on the Pakhuis Pass *(see separate entry)*.
Accommodation: Algeria has a caravan/camping site (ablutions with hot water, a swimming hole, braai sites and a public telephone) and 2 bungalows. Private accommodation available on farms in the area, and at hotels in Citrusdal and Clanwilliam.
Further information: Clanwilliam Tourism Association, P O Box 5, Clanwilliam 8135, tel (027) 482-2024.

WEST COAST

CITRUS ESTATES
Citrusdal

Map: page 315, 8E
Turn off the N7 to Citrusdal.
Details: For in-season tours, contact the Citrusdal Information Centre, Private Bag X5, Citrusdal 7340, tel (022) 921-3210; Goede Hoop Citrus Co-operative, Private Bag X11, Citrusdal 7340, tel (022) 921-3609.
Accommodation: Protea Hotel, Citrusdal; caravan/camping facilities. Chalets, flats, rooms and caravan/camping stands (known as the Baths) 18 km from town.
Further information: The Baths, P O Box 133, Citrusdal 7340, tel (022) 921-3609.

Groves of citrus trees – navel and Valencia oranges, lemons, grapefruit and such easy-to-peel hybrids as Satsuma and Clementine, tambar and minneola – mantle the fertile valley of the Olifants River around Citrusdal. From March through to September, about 6 000 workers harvest, sort and pack the golden fruit, and the air is heavy with its scent.

This is South Africa's third-largest citrus-growing area (after the north-eastern Highveld's Zebediela and the Eastern Province's Sundays River estates), but arguably the foremost in terms of product quality. Long, hot summers yield up to 10 hours of sunshine a day, and winter rains and sandy soil combine to produce as large and sweet a fruit as you'll find anywhere.

It is also by far the oldest growing area. Jan Dankaert trekked north in 1660 and named the valley after a herd of 300 elephant he saw by the river. The inaugural orchards were planted with seedlings taken from Jan van Riebeeck's Boskloof estate (located around today's Claremont suburb). One especially venerable tree, on the farm Groot Hexrivier, began its life about 250 years ago, and is still producing its seasonal bounty.

The local Goede Hoop Citrus Co-operative's 200 members grow about 90 000 tons of fruit a year, of which nearly three-quarters are exported. The co-op organizes tours, by appointment, of its giant pack-house in Citrusdal.

CLANWILLIAM DAM AND NATURE RESERVE
Clanwilliam

Map: page 315, 7E
Turn off the N7 onto the R364, following the signs to Clanwilliam. The dam and reserve are a short distance to the southeast; the road out of town is well signposted.
Details: The dam is accessible throughout the year, but the reserve is closed at weekends out of the flower season. Open 08h00-17h00.
Accommodation: The Clanwilliam Dam Public Resort has self-catering chalets and caravan/camping stands.
Further information: Clanwilliam Tourism Association, P O Box 5, Clanwilliam 8135, tel (027) 482-2024.

Discerning water-skiers reckon that the 18-km dam, whose northern extremity nudges the town of Clanwilliam, is the finest in South Africa. It is certainly one of the country's most beautiful: the ice-blue stretch of water, siphoned from the Olifants River, is girded by vineyards and fertile fields of wheat, lucerne and vegetables, and overlooked by the rugged Cederberg range to the east. Yachtsmen, boardsailors, powerboaters and all manner of other watersport enthusiasts are also drawn to the area, mostly during the annual regatta in November. The concrete wall at the northern end is 236 m long and 31m high. When the reservoir overflows – a rare occurrence in these often drought-plagued times – the artificial waterfall presents a spectacular sight.

Flanking the northeastern corner of the dam is the Ramskop Municipal Nature Reserve, a 54-ha expanse of dryish terrain mantled by a mix of fynbos and Karoo succulent vegetation. This is a transitional zone, which is famed for its late-winter and springtime wildflowers.

It also has its great scenic splendour. Make your way along the circular route to the higher ground and you'll be entranced by the vistas – of town and dam close by, the Olifants River running away into the distance, of the Pakhuis Pass to the northeast, and of the Cederberg's peaks. It also has a network of footpaths.

Enclosed within the reserve is the 7,5-ha Clanwilliam Wildflower Garden, created by a group of enthusiastic local women in the 1960s. Against considerable odds they managed to install an irrigation system beneath a site that 'looked like something between a quarry and an archaeological dig', covered the rocky ground with tons of soil, and went cheerfully off to Kirstenbosch to solicit seeds. Well over 700 indigenous species now flourish in the cultivated section.

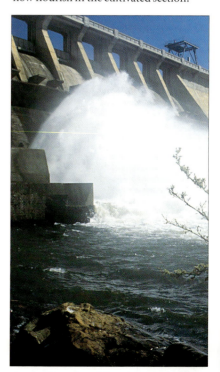

A staggering variety of flowering plants is to be found in the vicinity of Clanwilliam Dam, particularly in the Ramskop Municipal Nature Reserve, a major tourist attraction.

WEST COAST

GOEGAP NATURE RESERVE
Springbok

A stark and, in places, strikingly beautiful landscape, seasonal displays of wildflowers, and the Ian Myers Nature Walk, are the main attractions of the Goegap Nature Reserve near the far-northern town of Springbok.

The sanctuary, formerly known as the Hester Malan Nature Reserve, covers 15 000 ha of rugged Namaqualand countryside – much of it a jumble of gigantic, dome-shaped granite hillocks. In late winter a profusion of spectacular flowers bursts into bloom, covering the countryside in all the colours of the rainbow. Kokerbooms, or quivertrees (a species of aloe from which the Khoisan once fashioned quivers for their arrows), are a feature of the hills; labelled samples of the local flora, mainly succulents, are on display at the reserve's office.

The 45 species of mammal include springbok, gemsbok (both reintroduced to the area), klipspringer, steenbok, mountain zebras, Cape foxes, baboons, aardwolfs and honey badgers. Stately ostriches patrol the plains, and black eagles soar in the skies above. Karoo korhaans, ground woodpeckers and spotted dikkops are commonly seen.

Much of the reserve is inaccessible to visitors, but there are short walks, including the Myers route, which cross the western section. There are also picnic and braai facilities, and an attractive circular game- and flower-viewing drive on a good gravel surface.

Map: page 315, 3D
From the main road in Springbok, take the turn-off to the N7 (marked Cape Town, Airport, Goegap). At the T-junction, turn, following the signpost to the Goegap Nature Reserve. After 4 km you'll see the reserve's entrance gate on your left.
Details: Open throughout the year, daily 08h00-16h00. Admission fee.
Accommodation: Springbok has hotels and a caravan/camping ground.
Further information: The Officer-in-Charge, Goegap Nature Reserve, Private Bag X1, Springbok 8240, tel (0251) 2-1880; Namaqualand Regional Tourism Information Office, P O Box 5, Springbok 8240, tel (0251) 2-2011.

After good rains in late winter and early spring, wildflowers such as these spring from the ground, and form swathes of dazzling colour in the Goegap Nature Reserve.

LAMBERT'S BAY
West Coast

Map: page 315, 7D
Lambert's Bay is 280 km from Cape Town. There are 2 routes: the R27 coastal road through Langebaan, Velddrif (crossing the Berg River mouth) and Elands Bay; and the N7 inland highway to Clanwilliam, and then west on the R364.
Accommodation: Marine Protea Hotel and Raston Gastehaus, as well as self-catering and caravan/camping facilities.
Further information: Lambert's Bay Tourism Association, P O Box 245, Lambert's Bay 8130, tel (027) 432-2335.

A picturesque harbour crammed with work-worn boats and an inviting, if somewhat windswept, beach tempt visitors to the small fishing village of Lambert's Bay. Visitors also come for the crayfish that can be caught along the rugged shores, and tasted at the open-air, delightfully atmospheric, little eateries for which the area is known.

Lambert's Bay is the headquarters of the region's thriving fishing industry, with an enormous commercial catch of anchovies, pilchards, round herrings, Cape hake, kingklip, snoek, monkfish, squid, mackerel and, most profitably, crayfish (rock lobster).

Competing for the fish is a wide variety of sea birds – many of them congregating on the bay's island, which can be reached via a short walk along the harbour breakwater. Huge numbers of birds pack together on the rocky surface with scarcely a wingspan of space between them. Most numerous among the 150 species are the Cape gannets (January is the breeding season), cormorants, jackass penguins, sea gulls and 'sterretjies'.

At one time the birds were regarded as unwelcome competitors, pirates who pilfered the fruits of the sea from under the noses of the hard-working fishermen. In fact they add to, rather than deplete, local coffers by depositing great quantities of guano, a valuable source of fertilizer. Keen birders are also drawn to the nearby Langvlei River where, after good rains, the flamingoes gather in their multitudes, and at the Wadrif salt pan, along the coast to the south.

Lambert's Bay is also the site of the Sandveld Museum, which tells the story of Lambert's Bay and its surroundings. The village's hinterland is famous for its spring displays of wildflowers.

Canoeists paddle an adventurous course through the Orange River's challenging 'Rocket Man' rapids.

ORANGE RIVER CANOE TRAILS
Northern Cape

Map: page 315, 1/2 B/C
Access routes depend on starting points; the safari operator will give directions.
Details: Canoeing, camping and provisions are supplied; bring everything else you need. Since you'll enter Namibia along some of the stretches you'll need a passport and, depending on your nationality, a visa. Take anti-malaria precautions before departure.
Further information: Felix Unite, P O Box 96, Kenilworth 7745, Cape, tel (021) 762-6935; River Rafters, P O Box 14, Diep River 7856, Cape, tel (021) 72-5094/5; and P O Box 68132, Bryanston 2021, Transvaal, tel (011) 792-2353; Aquatrails, 8 Oak Farm Crescent, Constantia 7800, Cape, tel (021) 794-5808; River Runners, P O Box 583, Constantia 7848, Cape, tel (021) 762-2350.

The most adventurous way of getting to know South Africa's premier watercourse is by canoe, kayak, raft or 'rubber duck' inflatable, as a member of a water safari group led by an expert. Attractions include rugged scenery, personal challenge, physical exertion, thrills without spills and a close-up view of the wilderness.

The Orange, known to the Khoisan people as the Gariep, or 'Great River', rises in the Maluti Mountains of Lesotho and makes its way westwards across the central plains, before plunging through the Augrabies gorge on its journey to the Atlantic, 2 250 km from its source.

Most popular of the river-runs is through the moonscape of the northern Richtersveld. The trails, mostly between Noordoewer on the main-road crossing, and the Fish River junction, yield excitement without danger. Rapids, graded from 1 to 6 (that is, from the gentle up to those impossibly difficult ones which you skirt on foot), reach only grade 2 along this stretch. Indeed, the sun poses more of a risk than the waters: a strong barrier cream is a vital part of your kit.

Safaris range from three to six days, covering about 20 km a day; group sizes vary from 15 to 30, camping out beneath the stars at night. The operators supply life jackets and other safety equipment, and instruction. Some cater for all age groups. Generally speaking, though, group members should be good swimmers and reasonably fit.

WEST COAST

PAKHUIS PASS
Clanwilliam

A quiet headstone in the rugged grandeur of the Pakhuis Pass in the northern Cederberg marks the final resting place of writer Louis Leipoldt. The memorial is a fitting one. He loved this majestic wilderness – seeking solitude and peace among the startling rock formations and hidden valleys.

Leipoldt's ashes were interred in a Bushman shelter you'll see on your left, some 5 km to the west of the 905-m summit of the pass. Next to the grave-site is a parking area and a lovely picnic spot.

Built by the renowned engineer Thomas Bain in 1887, the Pakhuis ('pack-house') Pass cuts through the scenically splendid northern Cederberg range, leading to the springtime flower wonderland of the Biedouw Valley and the mission hamlet of Wupperthal. Here there are Bushman rock paintings (rather faded ones) and a path that winds down to a perennial stream and its jumbled valley of sandstone boulders – a fine place for walking, rock-scrambling and taking in the grandeur of far horizons.

Map: page 315, 7E
From Clanwilliam, follow the R364 eastwards. Leipoldt's grave is 17 km from town; the summit of the pass is 5 km further on.

Details: Apart from the picnic site, there are no visitor facilities. Entry to the grave-site is free.

Accommodation: There are self-catering chalets and caravan/camping stands at the Clanwilliam Dam Public Resort.

Further information: Clanwilliam Dam Public Resort, Private Bag X2, Clanwilliam 8135, tel (027) 482-2133.

A good gravel road leads travellers through the soaring sandstone hills that flank Pakhuis Pass. Beyond lies the Biedouw Valley where wildflowers bloom in wondrous profusion.

Leipoldt: writer for all seasons

Clanwilliam's most illustrious son was C Louis Leipoldt, poet and writer, surgeon and connoisseur of fine Cape food, who emerged from the biblical severity of a Rhenish mission environment at the end of the last century to charm the world with words.

Leipoldt's early career in journalism – he was a war correspondent during the Anglo-Boer conflict – ended abruptly in 1901 when the British closed down the pro-Boer *South African News*, and he spent the next 13 years abroad, studying for a medical degree (at London's Guy's Hospital), working as a doctor, and travelling. His journeys were adventurous and occasionally eccentric. He once spent six months aboard a luxury yacht as personal physician to the larger-than-life American publisher Joseph Pulitzer, who wanted someone 'tall, with a good reading voice, literary tastes, a knowledge of languages, placid, never seasick and, if possible, musical'. Leipoldt met all these requirements and, for good measure, could also claim to be a passable doctor. His medical distinctions included gold medals and a Fellowship of the Royal College of Surgeons.

During all this time the words were flowing freely, mostly in Afrikaans, but sometimes in English, and he returned to South Africa, in 1914, as a poet of national stature. His brilliance, though, was to shine over a far wider field: he produced novels and memoirs, short stories, plays, historical works, volumes on wine-making, on the supernatural, and on food. *Kos vir die Kenner*, which appeared in 1933, became a classic Afrikaans cookbook; Leipoldt's *Cape Cookery*, written in English and published nearly 30 years after his death in 1947, endures as a treasure-trove of culinary delights and stylish recipes.

WEST COAST

RICHTERSVELD NATIONAL PARK
Northern Cape

Map: page 315, 1B
Leave the N7 at Steinkopf, westwards onto the R382 to Port Nolloth. At Port Nolloth head north to Alexander Bay and then northeast along the Orange River to Sendelingsdrift/ Reuning. The park's Helskloof entrance gate (the more southerly of the two) is about 350 km north of Springbok and 100 km from Alexander Bay. The main Parks Board office is at Sendelingsdrift, on the Orange River, further to the north.

Details: The park is open from dawn to dusk; movement is prohibited after dark. Permits available from The Park Warden at Sendelingsdrift. Information and bookings: National Parks Board, P O Box 787, Pretoria 0001, tel (012) 343-1991; Cape Town: P O Box 7400, Roggebaai 8012, tel (021) 22-2810. Maps and information from The Park Warden, Richtersveld National Park, P O Box 406, Alexander Bay 8290, tel (0256) 506. Take everything you need, including water, fuel and spares. Nearest shops and petrol at Alexander Bay.

Accommodation: There is a fully equipped, 6-bed guesthouse at Sendelingsdrift. Visitors must take their own provisions and firewood. Contact The Park Warden *(address above)* to make a reservation. The nearest hotels are at Springbok and Nababeep. Caravan/camping sites at Springbok and Port Nolloth.

Further information: Namaqualand Regional Tourism Information Office, P O Box 5, Springbok 8240, tel (0251) 2-2011.

This wild, arid, lonely region – bounded in the north and east by the great loop of the lower Orange River – is intimidating in its vast emptiness, its northern parts distinguished by jagged mountain ranges and galleries of weird, wind-sculpted rock formations that combine to create landscapes of haunting beauty.

All visitors to the park have to obtain a permit at Sendelingsdrift. Hikers who wish to explore this desolate wilderness are accompanied by an official guide. Horizons are far, routes ill-defined, and the tracks are suitable only for high-clearance and four-wheel-drive vehicles. Those determined on going it alone, whether on foot or by 4x4, should plan their routes carefully and advise National Parks Board officials of their itinerary. Better still, join one of the Parks Board guided groups.

Despite its bleakness, however, the Richtersveld is astonishingly rich, its sandy soils sustaining about a third of all known mesembryanthemum species. Also among its more common plants, many of them highly specialized succulents, is the bizarre desert-adapted *halfmens* ('half-person') or elephant-trunk tree, the kokerboom, and the maiden's quivertree. There's not much to see in the way of wildlife, though you come across the occasional klipspringer, grey rhebok, kudu and Hartmann's mountain zebra.

The area is a photographer's dream, with its constantly changing scenery and unspoilt beauty. The park, covering 162 000 ha, belongs to a new generation of southern African sanctuary. More of a community enterprise than a classic wilderness reserve, it was established in 1991 as a 'contractual park' after marathon negotiations (they were spread over 18 years) between the government and the local Nama pastoralists. Today the Nama continue to live and to graze their cattle, sheep and goats on the land, but the National Parks Board manages the environment. The Nama also benefit directly from the jobs created and the inflow of tourist funds.

Until formal hiking and 4x4 trails are established, one of the best ways to see the park is through an Orange River canoe trail *(see separate entry)*. There's good angling in certain parts of the Orange River, especially for giant catfish (or barbel, which can weigh up to 25 kg) and large-mouth yellowfish.

Strangely shaped kokerbooms dot the dry plains of the Richtersveld, a region that is remarkably – and unexpectedly – rich in plant life. The kokerboom is also known as the quivertree.

ROOIBOS TEA ESTATES
Clanwilliam

The future looks rosy for the tea-farmers around Clanwilliam, and with good reason: take a leaf that contains hardly any tannin and no caffeine, has a pleasant scent and taste and a reputation for easing ailments such as bronchitis, and you have a beverage that is bound to climb the popularity charts in this health-conscious age.

The needle-leafed rooibos tea shrub *Aspalathus linearis* is indigenous to large parts of the Western Cape but is at its happiest on the slopes of the Cederberg, the only area in the world where it is systematically grown.

The plant has always been prized by the local Nama and by the European farming families who began to settle in the region two centuries ago, though its potential has been exploited only since the early 1900s. Best known of the several varieties is *Northier*, named after a local medical doctor and nature-lover who did much to put the industry on a sound commercial footing during the 1930s. Since then its cultivation has become a booming and well-organized business. Seedlings are planted out in June and July and harvested during the following year's summer months.

The leaves are then cut, trimmed and left to ferment in heaps before being sun-dried, graded and packed for countrywide distribution and, increasingly, for export. Among foreign customers are the Japanese, probably the world's most discerning tea-drinkers.

Visitors are shown an audiovisual presentation that explains the cultivation, grading and versatility of the leaf. A free booklet gives you the nutritional facts and some intriguing recipes (soup, curry, home-made bread, drinks and punches); visitors are served refreshments that include rooibos tea. A tour of the estates and the factory can be arranged on request.

Map: page 315, 7E
The rooibos industry is based in Clanwilliam. Turn off the N7, eastwards onto the R364 into Clanwilliam, just beyond the dam.
Details: Tours on weekdays at two-hourly intervals; groups of 15 and more should book in advance.
Accommodation: Hotel and guest-houses in and around Clanwilliam. Contact the Clanwilliam Tourism Association, P O Box 5, Clanwilliam 8135, tel (027) 482-2024.
Further information: Rooibos Tea Natural Products Limited, P O Box 64, Clanwilliam 8135, tel (027) 482-2155.

The magic of the rooibos plant

The rural folk of the Western Cape (and others much further afield) endow the rooibos leaf with all manner of medicinal properties, but not all the claims belong in the realms of myth.

A hot cup of the aromatic tea – taken daily by thousands of South Africans, particularly in the Western Cape – really does have a soothing effect, and there are valid reasons for believing that it can relieve such ailments as insomnia and stomach cramps, colic in babies and, when directly applied, nappy rash and other skin disorders. Rooibos also seems to be effective in the management of nervous tension and certain allergies.

The Orange River borders the Richtersveld's northern section, creating a slender strip of greenery in an otherwise desolate region.

TIENIE VERSVELD WILDFLOWER RESERVE
Darling

Map: page 315, 9D
Take the R27 north from Cape Town. Turn east on the R315 towards Darling. You'll see the Tienie Versveld reserve on your right.
Details: Open 24 hours a day throughout the year, though it's really worth visiting only during the wildflower season of August and September.
Accommodation: Darling has a hotel and 2 guesthouses. Contact the Darling Information Bureau, P O Box 5, Darling 7345, tel (02241) 3361 for details.
Further information: Captour Tourist Information Bureau, P O Box 863, Cape Town 8000, tel (021) 418-5214/5; the National Botanical Institute, Private Bag X7, Claremont 7735, tel (021) 762-1166.

A tiny but typical fragment of the briefly beautiful sandveld flora is preserved within this 22-ha sanctuary near the town of Darling.

The reserve, named after a local farmer (who donated the land to what was then the National Botanical Gardens in 1956), is renowned for its spectacular springtime show. Apart from a network of footpaths, there are no visitor facilities.

The most prominent of the residents are the bulbous plants; particularly attractive are multicoloured babianas and lachenalias (both belong to the lily family, of which there are about 900 South African species, and both grace formal gardens in Europe and America); the *aandblomme*, or 'evening flowers', whose sweetly scented blooms are at their best at dusk and during the night; and the insectivorous Sundew *(Droscera)*, which has showy flowers of purple, red, yellow or white, and whose sticky leaf surfaces act as flypaper-like traps for the passing parade of small creatures.

Among the loveliest of all are the chincherinchees, whose curious name derives from the sound made when the stems are rubbed together. There are 60 or so members of this large genus of lily, nearly all of them with white, yellow-green or orange blooms that make for an exquisite cut flower. *Ornithogalum thyrsoides*, perhaps the most popular, is exported in large quantities.

Incidentally, the wider Darling area is famed for its commercially cultivated lupins as well as chincherinchees, and the country's largest orchid nursery is in the vicinity, on the farm *Oudepost*.

WEST COAST NATIONAL PARK
Langebaan

Map: page 315, 9D
Langebaan is 122 km from Cape Town. Take the R27 coastal road north for some 110 km, turn left at the sign and continue on the last stretch to the lagoon and its lodge. Access routes are tarred, but some of the internal roads are gravelled, their condition dependent on the weather. To get to the Postberg, turn left off the R27 at the Donkergat signpost, 85 km from Cape Town, and left again at the Churchhaven/Donkergat sign.
Details: The park is open throughout the year; there's no entrance gate, and no entry charge. Summer is the best time to visit. The Postberg section, however, is accessible only during the wildflower season (August and September) 09h00-17h00, and there is a small entrance fee. The information centre and a gift shop are located in the foyer of Langebaan Lodge.
Accommodation: Langebaan Lodge has *en suite* accommodation, *a la carte* restaurant, cocktail bar and coffee shop. Langebaan has beach bungalows and a caravan/camping site.
Further information: Langebaan Municipality, P O Box 11, Langebaan 7357, tel (02287) 2115; National Parks Board, P O Box 787, Pretoria 0001, tel (012) 343-1991; Cape Town: P O Box 7400, Roggebaai 8012, tel (021) 22-2810; local address: The Park Warden, West Coast National Park, P O Box 25, Langebaan 7357, tel (02287) 2-2144.

Each August about 60 000 migrant wading birds – curlew sandpipers, knots and sanderlings for the most part – leave the Siberian and other Arctic breeding grounds on their long, and often final, journey to take up summer residence in and around the shallow waters of Langebaan Lagoon, without doubt one of the finest of Africa's wetlands.

The lovely lagoon, a narrow 16-km southward projection of Saldanha Bay, is the centrepiece of the fairly recently established and still developing West Coast National Park.

The park stretches across the rather bleak Strandveld (much of it owned by farmers contracted to the National Parks Board), from the Langebaan area to the little seaside village of Yzerfontein in the south. Within its bounds are a section of the bay's rocky shoreline and the little islands of Schaapen, Malgas, Jutten and Marcus. These are virtually separate sanctuaries that provide predator-free roosts and nesting sites for upwards of 750 000 sea birds (the general public isn't allowed to land and walk about on them). Schaapen is home to the biggest-known colony of kelp or southern black-backed gull; others support jackass penguins, cormorants and densely packed breeding colonies of gannets.

Springbok, bontebok, eland and other antelope species roam the Postberg section, an integral 1 800-ha part of the park whose treeless terrain, like that of the wider region, is briefly but magically transformed by the wildflowers of springtime. For the rest of the year, the windblown countryside shows a duller face: ground cover comprises succulents and succulent-type plants, dwarf bushes, sedges, and coastal heath or fynbos. Note that Postberg is open only during August and September.

Most visitors make for Langebaan Lodge, park headquarters, information centre and National Parks Board Lodge all rolled into one. It's a pleasantly informal place whose terrace and windows afford splendid views over the lagoon. The foyer displays give you an insight into bird migration and the marine ecology, and short, guided walks lead from the lodge to the salt marshes and driftsand areas.

Also on offer are three-day, 13- to 16-km educational trails, but here you put up at *Geelbek*, an old homestead now restored to its 1860 dignity. The Postberg section has picnic/braai sites (with toilet facilities) and a gravel network of flower- and game-viewing roads. Tours to the bird islands, together with canoe and horseback trails, are also available.

The lagoon is a magnet for yachtsmen, powerboat enthusiasts, boardsailors and anglers; boats may be launched from Langebaan Yacht Club or directly from Langebaan Beach, and there is a variety of bathing beaches at Langebaan and at nearby Kraalbaai.

Langebaan Village hugs the placid waters of the lagoon, centrepiece of the West Coast National Park. The African black oystercatcher (inset left) is prominent among the sea birds.

The marvel of Langebaan's migrants

Most of Langebaan's summertime wading birds, notably its multitudes of curlew sandpipers, follow the shortest route on their annual 20 000-km flight from the breeding grounds in the tundra wastelands of Siberia – over central Russia and the Middle East and then down along the Great Rift Valley that slices through Kenya, Tanzania and Malawi. Others, like the knots and sanderlings, fly across or around the bulge of Africa. All are genetically programmed to seek the warmth and shelter of the lagoon and its immensely well-stocked larder of marine algae, tiny snails and other mud-loving organisms.

The mud of the lagoon and its marshes is unbelievably rich in nutrients. Scientists reckon that each cubic centimetre may contain as many as 60 million bacteria. By the time the birds are ready to start on their autumn return flight they have, between them, made their way through about 150 tons of minute organisms, and each individual is a lot heavier and healthier than when it arrived in early summer (a sandpiper will almost double its weight). They also leave almost 50 tons of droppings behind on the salt marshes, which helps replenish the larder for the following year's migrant invasion.

The extra store of fat is vital to their survival on the challenging homeward journey – or at least part of it. Close to the equator they will take a two-week break to rest and feed at a wetland lay-by, and repeat the process some thousands of kilometres further north (exactly where is not yet known), before taking off on the last leg of their great odyssey.

PLACES TO VISIT

Map: page 327

Further information: Captour Tourist Information Bureau, P O Box 863, Cape Town 8000, tel (021) 418-5214/5; or contact Flowerline, P O Box 6209, Welgemoed 7538, tel (021) 418-3705.

WILDFLOWER WONDERLAND

For most of the year the Western Cape's coastal strip is a region of windblown sandveld that seems unable to support any but the toughest and most enduring forms of life. The northern section – that part which lies beyond the Olifants River and is known as Namaqualand – is especially captivating in its barren harshness. Surface water is almost nonexistent here and the rainfall poor, ranging from some 280 mm a year to a pitiful 80 mm in places.

Yet the land has its bounty, and its beauty. The soils here, and those of the even more arid Hardeveld to the east of the Atlantic seaboard, sustain 4 000 and more floral species. These are mostly cream, orange and yellow daisies, and mesembryanthemums (which are locally known as 'vygies'), but there's also a profusion of flowering aloes, sorrels, flax, nemesias, lilies (including the enchanting chincherinchees), perennial herbs and a host of others.

They are small, hardy, low-growing plants, well adapted to drought conditions, their seeds lying dormant over the long, dry months. But then, after the modest winter rains, when they sense the warming of the earth and the coming of the pollinators – and before the onset of summer's searing breezes – they germinate, grow and bloom in a matter of days to cover the countryside in an exquisite coat of many colours.

This splendid show is not confined to Namaqualand proper: sandveld flowers mingle with the ericas, proteas and pincushions of the Cape floral kingdom to sustain the magic far to the south of the Olifants.

Namaqualand usually reaches the height of its glory around mid-August, but different species in different areas have their own timetables. The white daisies and oxalis in its many forms are early bloomers (August); others are much later. Nearly all the flowers, however, are at their best between 11h00 and 15h00, turning their faces towards the sun – which, for optimum viewing, you should keep at your back. On very overcast days the blooms remain closed.

It's difficult to specify the most rewarding areas: they vary from year to year, depending on the subtle interplay of local temperature, wind and rainfall. Oddly enough, though, what in normal times are the most arid, desolate-looking places seem to produce some of the finest displays. That said, certain localities consistently feature on the annual flower-viewing itinerary.

WILDFLOWER WONDERLAND

Wild irises, of which there are a great number of different species, add their delicate beauty to the springtime show.

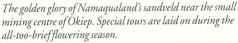

The golden glory of Namaqualand's sandveld near the small mining centre of Okiep. Special tours are laid on during the all-too-brief flowering season.

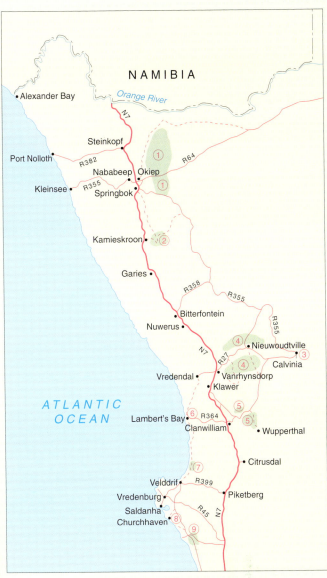

KEY TO THE MAP

1 Springbok area, 553 km from Cape Town; drive in almost any direction from town during the season and you'll see floral wealth. The Goegap Nature Reserve *(see separate entry)* is famed for its succulents and kokerboom trees.

2 Skilpad Wildflower Reserve, 510 km from Cape Town. From the N7, take the turn-off to Kamieskroon. Pass the Kamieskroon Hotel, continue for 2 km to a fork. Take the left fork to Wolwepoort, and follow the Skilpad signpost.

3 Akkerendam Nature Reserve, Calvinia, 421 km from Cape Town. Take the N7 to Vanrhynsdorp, turn off to Nieuwoudtville and continue to Calvinia. Mainly Karoo scrub species.

4 Vanrhynsdorp area. The entire route to Calvinia runs through wildflower country, at its most charming in the early spring. Closer to Vanrhynsdorp are the mesembryanthemums of the Knersvlakte and, to the southeast, a mass of yellow and orange ursinias, bush vygies, lachenalias and dark orange gazanias.

5 Clanwilliam area, 225 km from Cape Town. Always worthwhile, often garlanded when other areas have little or nothing to show. Specific destinations include the Biedouw Valley, over Pakhuis Pass *(see separate entry)* on the way to Wupperthal, and known for its nemesias, blue wild-flax flowers, gazanias and golden ursinias; the Ramskop Municipal Nature Reserve, and the Cederberg Wilderness Area *(see separate entry)*.

6 Lambert's Bay area, especially renowned for its wildflowers.

7 Rocher Pan Nature Reserve, down the coast and inland, 25 km north of Velddrif; take the R27 from Cape Town. The 900-ha reserve comprises a pan and wetland, water birds (165 species) and Strandveld flora. Open daily 07h00-18h00; admission fee.

8 West Coast National Park. A joy in springtime; the flowers of the Postberg peninsula are especially prolific.

9 Darling area, about 70 km from Cape Town, with the Tienie Versveld Wildflower Reserve *(see separate entry)*, the Contreberg Reserve, the flora reserve on *Waylands Farm* and the popular Oudepost Reserve, all on the R307. Admission free.

WEST COAST

WUPPERTHAL
Cederberg

Map: page 315, 7E
Turn off the N7 at Clanwilliam, eastwards onto the R364. Follow the R364 over the Pakhuis Pass for 40 km. Turn off to the Biedouw Valley, which you reach after 10 km. Wupperthal lies 20 km further along this road.

Accommodation: Wupperthal has a guesthouse and camping sites which are made available to visitors by the Moravian Church. Enquire at the mission office or phone (02682) and ask for Wupperthal 4. A number of the area's farms rent out rooms on a bed-and-breakfast basis. Hotels available in Clanwilliam.

Further information: Clanwilliam Tourism Association, P O Box 5, Clanwilliam 8135, tel (027) 482-2024.

As you descend the rugged road from the high Koueberg into Wupperthal you enter a time warp. The village, on the banks of the Tra-Tra River, has been frozen in the early 19th century, its terraced cluster of whitewashed, black-thatched cottages, its church and parsonage just as they were 150 years ago. Donkey-carts still ply the winding streets, the old mission school now does duty as the village store, and the smithy is among several of the original craft premises that have been preserved.

Wupperthal, described by one writer as 'a small fragment of Europe lost in the mountains', began life in 1829 when two Rhenish (German Rhineland) churchmen trekked into the remoteness of the northern Cederberg – an area known as the Hantam – to found a Christian mission among the local Khoisan. The settlement proved remarkably successful and when the abolition of slavery in the latter 1830s prompted an influx of newly freed families in need of work – the mission trained a steady stream of carpenters and masons, bricklayers, blacksmiths, thatchers, tanners, hat-makers and shoemakers.

It became especially famous for its veldskoene, or veld-shoes. Output at one point reached an impressive 700 pairs a week. Ageing machinery led to a slow decline in production, but these tough, all-leather shoes, fashioned without the aid of glue or nails, are still a local, much sought-after speciality.

The best time to visit Wupperthal is in the spring when wildflowers carpet the countryside. Winters can be very cold, summers very hot.

Veldskoene on parade in Wupperthal's craft factory. These stout leather shoes enjoy enduring popularity for the walking comfort they provide. Other local products include tobacco and fragrant rooibos ('red bush') tea.

Wupperthal's terraced cottages overlook the quaintly named Tra-Tra River. The picturesque village has hardly changed in appearance since it began life a century and a half ago.

THE INTERIOR

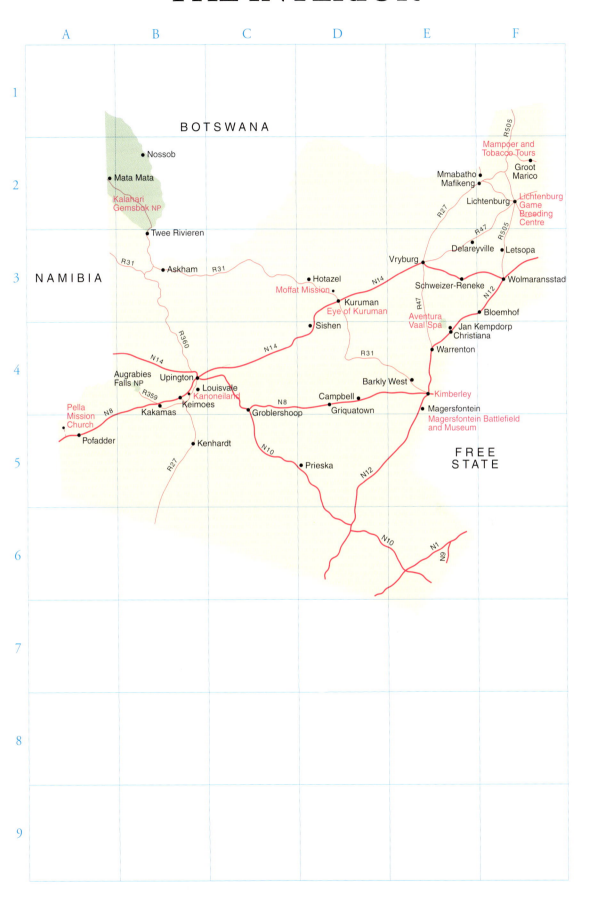

THE INTERIOR

AVENTURA VAAL SPA
Near Christiana

Map: page 329, 4E
The Aventura Vaal Spa is situated 3 km north of Christiana, on the N12 main route, also known as the R29. A comfortable 3- to 4-hour car trip from Johannesburg or Pretoria.
Details: There is a landing strip for light aircraft. *A la carte* restaurant facilities, medical and banking services, shop, riverside *lapa* available. Petrol at main entrance. Public telephones.
Accommodation: Aventura Vaal Spa offers accommodation in modern, comfortable, air-conditioned chalets. The caravan park offers 400 stands, 83 with power points, in a well-laid-out area under shady trees.
Further information: Aventura Ltd, P O Box 19, Christiana 2680, tel (0534) 2244 or (05373) 2244/5/6; The Town Clerk, P O Box 13, Christiana 2680, tel (0534) 2206/7/8.

The Aventura Vaal Spa is an oasis in the heart of the North-West Province. It rests in lush green seclusion on the banks of the Vaal River. At this popular family getaway, a world of comfort and relaxation awaits you.

It is hard to imagine a more perfect point at which to interrupt a journey between the Cape and Gauteng Province. From the outset, the sparkling water and shady trees in the court of the main complex invite you to relax and make yourself at home.

Features of particular interest include a Diggers Museum, where digging implements and equipment may be seen, along with an interesting collection of photographs of a bygone era. A 2 300-ha game reserve serves as a sanctuary to eland, black wildebeest, blesbok, impala, red hartebeest and springbok. There are also large numbers of zebras, giraffes and white rhinos.

The Spa is renowned for its mineral baths, and affords excellent freshwater angling opportunities. It offers several swimming pools, two fun bubble-jet baths and eight private baths for relaxing away from the crowd. The mineral water is heated to a relaxing 36°C in these and the Hydro Spa.

If aquatic activities pall, try a round of minigolf, a spot of horse-riding or a game of outdoor chess.

Aventura Spa is close to Christiana, where you may visit the Ouma Plaas Doll's House, a restored homestead housing a rare collection of handcrafted porcelain dolls in antique-filled rooms. A delightful tea is served on request.

EYE OF KURUMAN
Kuruman

Map: page 329, 3D
The Eye is situated on the town's main road.
Details: The park surrounding The Eye has plenty of picnic sites and a drive-in tearoom with toilets.
Accommodation: There's a motel (Eldorado Motel), hotels and a caravan park to choose from.
Further information: Information Office, Kuruman Municipality, P O Box 4, Kuruman 8460, tel (05373) 2-1095 extension 243.

The town of Kuruman, with its numerous parks, trees and beautiful gardens, is a popular stopover point for travellers on the main routes between the northern and southern parts of the subcontinent.

The remarkable Eye of Kuruman is situated in the town's main street, drawing thousands of visitors annually to its shady banks. This seemingly inexhaustible dolomite spring delivers approximately 20 million litres of crystal-clear water daily, more than enough to cater for the domestic and industrial needs of the town.

The biggest natural fountain in the southern hemisphere, its flow has not been known to diminish, even during the severe droughts experienced periodically in the Kalahari.

The grounds around The Eye have been converted into a beautiful pleasure garden. The pool itself is studded with lily pads and lotus blooms, set among graceful willows and palms.

Fish are plentiful, and include goldfish, carp and blue kurper. Several years ago, members of the Ichthyology Institute at Rhodes University, Grahamstown, discovered an endangered species of fish, *Pseudocrenilabrus philander*, which had made the natural fountain its breeding ground.

Many years ago the Tswana people christened the fountain *Gasegonyane*, which means Little Water Calabash, or Place of Water. The Eye was accorded national-monument status in 1992.

The first European to see the Eye of Kuruman was Samuel Daniel during an expedition into the interior in November 1801. The graceful willows surrounding the fountain were planted by the first magistrate of the town, one Mr Schulz, in 1881. Relics at the site include an old sundial dating to 1831.

Meticulously maintained parklands at The Eye, nourished by the mineral-rich waters, are popular with locals and visitors to the area.

A lion walks along a dry riverbed in the Kalahari Gemsbok National Park. Lions are the largest carnivores on the continent.

KALAHARI GEMSBOK NATIONAL PARK
Far Northern Cape

If you yearn to experience the unspoilt beauty of Africa, to hear the nocturnal calls of wild animals stalking their prey, and be in at the kill with Kalahari lions, then this national park is the perfect holiday destination.

For more than 60 years the park, controlled by the National Parks Board of South Africa, has afforded visitors a glimpse of a world that was almost lost to poaching. It covers an area of 36 000 square kilometres and is one of the last intact ecosystems on the continent.

The park adjoins Botswana's Gemsbok National Park. Together the parks form one of the largest game sanctuaries in South Africa.

The Kalahari Gemsbok Park is a harsh and waterless sea, its waves the frozen, rolling dunes, and its spray the gritty dust, whipped about by the winds.

Two dry riverbeds wind their way through the park. They are the Auob or 'bitter' and the Nossob, or 'treacherous', and their dry beds are tinged with green, the flag marker of Kalahari life. Where roots twist their way to underground water, game will find it too, and so will birds and insects and, eventually, man.

Here, even man's roads follow the rivers, tracing the edges of this great reserve, and linked by the 55-km dune road between Kamqua and Dikbaardskolk. You'll find that names in the Kalahari are as varied and as fascinating as the landscape and its creatures.

Twee Rivieren is an easy one. This is down south at the confluence of the beds of the Auob and the Nossob, and site of the park's administrative centre and main rest camp.

The game drives start here. The longer route leads to Nossob Rest Camp, about 170 km to the north, with the option of pressing on from Nossob for a further 120 km to reach Union's End, which must surely be the most comprehensively remote point in the whole country.

That's part of its attraction; the other is the adventure of the journey that takes in over 20 water holes, each one the favourite of some species. Springbok, for instance, have been seen at Rooiputs in numbers that recall magical scenes of the mass migrations of *trekbokken*.

Only a short distance to the north, gemsbok, and especially red hartebeest, keep a wary eye on opportunistic spotted hyaenas, while leopards – silent and solitary – may appear and disappear at almost any time or place.

The road is sometimes in the riverbed, sometimes beside it, and never far from the wildlife. Lions are said to be plentiful north of Nossob, especially near Kwang, a water hole that draws great numbers of antelope. There's a picnic site at Union's End, and a particular satisfaction in

Map: page 329, 2A/B
The park lies in the far Northern Cape, between Namibia and Botswana. To get there from the south, take the R360 from Upington, following the route marked 'Askham'. The road forks after 88 kilometres. Keep right until you reach a T-junction 64 km on. Turn right, back onto the R360, and follow the road until it forks. Keeping left on the R360, you will pass the Motel Molopo. Twee Rivieren is 62 km further on.
From the north, travel via Kuruman, 540 km from Johannesburg. The tar ends at Hotazel. From there the R31 heads west for 263 km before joining the R360 near the Motel Molopo.
Details: Open throughout the year, but the best game-viewing months are February through May.
Accommodation: All 3 camps offer family cottages, self-contained huts and ordinary huts. Each camp has a caravan/camping site.
Further information: National Parks Board, P O Box 787, Pretoria 0001, tel (012) 343-1991 or P O Box 7400, Roggebaai 8012, tel (021) 22-2810.

A hungry black-backed jackal waits in rigid anticipation for its unseen quarry to betray its hiding place.

THE INTERIOR

The greatest trek of all

'Gregarious' describes the springbok fairly well, but there were times when the term seemed inadequate. Travellers in the 19th century told of densely packed herds of these gazelles literally covering the countryside as far as the eye could see. The massed columns took many hours to pass by and, when they had gone, no blade of green was left in their wake. Food, it is thought, was the spur to these migrations, the packed *trekbokken* – or at least some of the leaders – seeming to know instinctively the direction in which the most abundant supplies lay.

Normally fairly shy and unaggressive, springbok on trek kept relentlessly to their course, disregarding any humans, predators and even some towns and villages they passed through, destroying fences and gardens as they marched. Those animals at the front of the mass that hesitated for any reason – when crossing ravines, for instance – were simply crushed underfoot by the huge pressure from behind.

Antidorcas marsupialis to science, springbok is the common name for this athletic, seemingly joyous creature that executes, for no obvious reason, those bouncing, stiff-legged leaps that the Dutch called 'pronke' or showing off. A purposeful leap, distinct from the balletic, may clear 3,5 m, while a bound at speed – anything up to 90 km/h – may cover 15 metres.

Both grazers and browsers, springbok will dig with their small, sharp hooves for roots and, especially, for succulent bulbs. In the rainy season, when food is plentiful, herds of several hundred springbok are common, and often associate with other species, such as blesbok, wildebeest and even ostrich. The rainy season, too, is lambing time, when grass and bush are green and tender, and provide cover for the day or two that the newborn lamb is almost motionless, soon thereafter to gather strength and speed.

Young springbok rams lock their horns in combat. Such fights are sometimes fatal.

making use of it – it's never known to be crowded. The shorter route from Twee Rivieren is northwest to Mata Mata, some 130 km along the Auob, a riverbed reputed to be the finest place in the world to watch cheetah on the hunt. There are old, abandoned farmhouses along here, built in the years before the park was proclaimed in 1931, by hardy people who, much as they loved their farming, must have valued the wonderful solitude of the Kalahari even more.

KANONEILAND
Near Upington

Kanoneiland, the largest island in the Orange River, is full of unexpected surprises. The hospitable island dwellers will enjoy introducing you to the highlights of their unusual home.

The name Kanoneiland (Cannon Island) at first seems something of an anomaly in this peaceful environment, with the rather lazy waters of the Orange River lapping the fertile banks of the well-cultivated fields that make up most of the island.

It is derived from the small cannon used by the forces of the Cape Colony to bombard the Koranna, led by Klaas Pofadder, during the Second Northern Border War of 1789. By all accounts, the cannon did little to curb the Koranna, but it may be viewed nevertheless in front of the old stone school building on the island. Despite the overwhelming heat, Kanoneiland is intensively farmed. More than half the surface area of the island is devoted to the cultivation of a variety of crops, including grapes, corn, lucern, cotton and pecan nuts.

Delicious fish are also bred for sale. On a visit to the island's catfish farm this delicious smoked delicacy can be ordered in advance, and served, Kanoneiland-style, beneath the spreading branches of an enormous camelthorn tree. Typical fare includes braaied sheep, home-baked bread, traditional desserts and a choice of local wines. Just the thing to conclude a visit to this fertile island paradise.

Map: page 329, 4B
From Upington, on the south bank of the river, a tarred road leads to Louisvale (15 km), and then reaches a turn to the bridge linking Kanoneiland to the banks of the river (26,5 km from Upington).
Details: Shops and petrol facilities easily accessible. Public telephones available.
Accommodation: Kanoneiland Accommodation, on the premises of the old stone school building, offers fully equipped, 2-bed units. Self-catering. Stands for 12 caravans; braai facilities.
Further information: Kanoneiland Accommodation, P O Box 6, Kanoneiland 8806, tel (054) 491-1223 (office hours) or (054) 491-1147 (after hours); Upington Tourist Bureau, Private Bag X6003, Upington 8800, tel (054) 2-6911.

PLACES TO VISIT

KIMBERLEY

ALEXANDER McGREGOR MEMORIAL MUSEUM

The fascinating Alexander McGregor Memorial Museum, or 'Old Museum' as it is known by the local population, was originally built in 1907 by Mrs Margaret McGregor, in memory of her husband, Alexander McGregor, a well-known and respected pioneer of the diamond fields, and former mayor of Kimberley. This museum houses a variety of displays which feature the prehistory and history of the Northern Cape Province, as well as a number of rocks and minerals imported from all corners of the globe. Fashions of past decades are also on show. Every Wednesday a free film is shown between 13h00 and 14h00.

Details are available from the museum. The museum shop stocks souvenirs.

Map: page 334
Situated in Chapel Street, Kimberley.
Details: Open Monday to Friday 09h00-17h00; Saturdays 09h00-13h00; Sundays 14h00-17h00; public holidays 10h00-13h00, 14h00-17h00. Closed on Good Friday and Christmas Day. Admission fee charged.
Further information: Old Museum, P O Box 316, Kimberley 8300, tel (0531) 3-2645/6.

DUGGAN-CRONIN GALLERY

Turn-of-the-century night watchman and keen amateur photographer Alfred Duggan-Cronin escaped the monotony of his job by assembling a remarkable collection of photographs of the indigenous peoples of southern Africa. These and other curiosities are on view at the Duggan-Cronin Gallery in Kimberley. Also on display are examples of traditional African crafts and dress, weapons, household effects and rock engravings.

Between 1919 and 1939 Alfred Duggan-Cronin worked his way through southern Africa, photographing indigenous tribesfolk. There are more than 8 000 photographs in his collection. Most depict members of the indigenous population in traditional dress. These are irreplaceable historical treasures, as the majority of the subjects have subsequently adopted Western dress codes and cultural habits.

Duggan-Cronin's collection is housed in the gallery of what was originally a guest lodge built by John Blades Curry in the 1880s. The lodge has a corrugated iron roof, some gracious old high pressed ceilings and lovely, wide verandahs. The old building was declared a national monument in 1985.

Recently, Aubrey Elliot, a citizen of the town, left a magnificent collection of ethnic beadwork and photographs to the museum to augment the Duggan-Cronin collection.

An additional drawcard is the Pickering Memorial Garden, which greatly enhances and softens the formal lines of the building.

Map: page 334
The museum is located at No. 12 Egerton Road, Kimberley, next to the McGregor Museum.
Details: Open Monday to Friday 09h00-17h00; Saturdays 09h00-13h00; Sundays 14h00-17h00; public holidays 10h00-17h00. Closed on Good Friday and Christmas Day. Parking available. Small admission fee charged. Free access to museum on Mondays. The gallery has a small museum shop where keepsakes may be purchased.
Accommodation: There's a wide variety of hotel and guesthouse accommodation in Kimberley. The Big Hole Municipal Caravan Park in West Circular Road, Kimberley, offers 46 caravan sites with power points, an ablution block and swimming pool. The Riverton Pleasure Resort has 40 stands with a power supply, and a number of chalets and bungalows.
Further Information: Duggan-Cronin Gallery, P O Box 316, Kimberley 8300, tel (0531) 3-2645/6; Tourist Information Office, P O Box 1976, Kimberley 8300, tel (0531) 2-7298/9; SA Tourism Board, Private Bag X5017, Kimberley 8300, tel (0531) 3-1434/ 2-2657.

Alfred Duggan-Cronin travelled 128 000 km in southern Africa, photographing the people and their customs. His collection is an evocative essay of his travels. Shown (above) is 'African Manhood', and 'Xhosa Women' (right).

KIMBERLEY

Map: below
From the centre of town travel west onto Bultfontein Road. Turn off onto either North Circular Road or South Circular Road, and follow the signs to the museum (on Tucker Street).
Details: Open daily 08h00-18h00; closed Good Friday and Christmas Day. Guided tours are available on request through tour operators. Entrance fee charged. Facilities include a tearoom and gift shop.
Further information: Kimberley Mine Museum, Tucker Street, Kimberley 8301, tel (0531) 3-1557/8.

KIMBERLEY MINE MUSEUM

Modern Kimberley may disappoint first-time visitors in search of the rip-roaring mining camps that sprang up a century ago. However, there is one place where you can recapture the spirit of early Kimberley – the famous Kimberley Mine Museum.

In the early 1950s De Beers Consolidated Mines decided to establish a museum at the site of the Kimberley Mine, commonly known as the 'Big Hole'. The mine produced 14,5 million carats of diamonds before its closure in 1914. The fascinating Cultural History Museum was officially opened in 1969.

The museum's aim, to preserve as much as possible of Kimberley's past, has been admirably realized. You don't need much imagination to transport yourself into the bustling throng of mining folk going about their daily business, dressed in the fashions popular a century ago.

The museum, South Africa's largest full-scale open-air museum, has some 48 reconstructed historical buildings which authentically re-create the atmosphere of the bustling mining centre of yesteryear.

From an observation platform adjoining the museum, you may view the immensity of the Big Hole, the largest man-made hole in the world.

The first dwellings in Kimberley in 1871 were all built of canvas, wood and corrugated iron, because the owners didn't expect the mining boom to last long. Little did they guess that the diamond mines would last more than a century, and that Kimberley would develop to become the centre of the world diamond-mining industry.

Among the treasures at the Kimberley Mine Museum is the diamond city's first 'house', a prefabricated wooden structure imported from England in 1877, and transported by oxwagon from the coast. Next to it is the oldest existing church in Kimberley, built in 1875.

As confidence in the town's future grew, traders and merchants began to invest in more permanent structures, no doubt spurred on by a freak cold spell in 1876, when the town was blanketed in snow for two weeks.

Diamond-digging is very thirsty work. Legend holds that in Kimberley's heyday there was a bar on every corner. One such bar, reconstructed in the Kimberley Mine Museum, was 'Diggers' Rest', where miners whiled away their time with games of poker and faro. Fortunes were

The Big Hole in Kimberley, once the scene of a feverish quest for diamonds, is now the focal point of the Kimberley Mine Museum.

Amongst the old shops at the Mine Museum are a 19th-century tobacconist and music shop.

KEY TO THE MAP
1 Alexander McGregor Memorial Museum
2 Duggan-Cronin Gallery
3 Kimberley Mine Museum
4 Kimberley Tram
5 McGregor Museum
6 Pioneers of Aviation Memorial
7 Sister Henrietta Stockdale Chapel

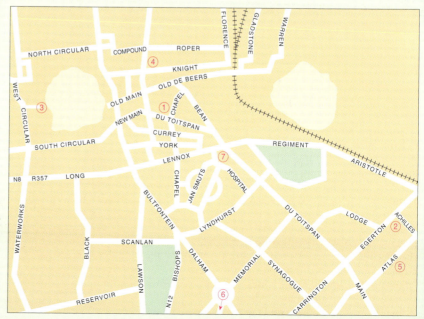

made and lost fast in Kimberley. Mr A Ciring's pawnbroker's shop is testament to the precarious life of the early diggers.

For some, life on the profits generated by diamonds was sweet. At the Mine Museum you can board the De Beers Directors' Private Coach, built in 1897. It includes a bathroom and wine store.

Further evidence of the comfortable lifestyle enjoyed by mining magnates such as Cecil John Rhodes and Barney Barnato is to be found in the ornate Victorian furnishings of the house occupied by managers of the Kimberley Mine.

In the Transport Hall there's a gleaming 1901 Panhard and Levassor motor

A replica of the farmhouse originally owned by the De Beers brothers. The discovery of diamonds increased the value of their farm 120-fold.

A tranquil street scene at the Kimberley Mine Museum belies the rough-and-tumble of early diamond-digging days.

carriage, which belonged to the first general manager of De Beers. Another exhibit is a 1906 Columbia electric Victorian Phaeton.

Exhibits in the Mining Hall show the development of mining in Kimberley and the uses of diamonds in industry.

Genuine diamonds may be seen in the Diamond Pavilion. Here you will marvel at the dazzling variety of colours, cuts and geological peculiarities which make each gem unique. Included in the collection is the first diamond discovered in South Africa, the 10,73-carat *Eureka*, and the largest uncut diamond in the world.

To experience the unusual thrill of prospecting, join a 'Diamond Dig'. You can get a licence from the Claims Officer at *Engelsman's Prospect,* which entitles you to operate the original digging machinery used in the early days at the Big Hole. Next, move to the sorting table to sift through the contents.

You are unlikely to find any real gems to take home as souvenirs, but the sparkle of the rough diamonds which came from the original Kimberley blue ground is bound to lure you back for a second visit. Complete a visit to old Kimberley by taking a ride from the Mine Museum to the City Hall on a restored 1900s tram.

KIMBERLEY

This dignified old electric tram, the last of its kind in the country, ferries commuters between the City Hall and the Mine Museum.

KIMBERLEY TRAM

Map: page 334
The tram route runs between the City Hall and the Kimberley Mine Museum.
Details: Board the tram at either the Kimberley City Hall, or the Big Hole in Tucker Street. Departure times: from the City Hall every hour daily, from 09h15 to 16h15; from the Big Hole every hour daily, from 09h00 to 16h00.
Accommodation: There is a wealth of accommodation in Kimberley, ranging from luxury hotels and motels to guest-houses and caravan parks.
Further information: Tourist Information Office, P O Box 1976, Kimberley 8300, tel (0531) 2-7298/9; SA Tourism Board, Private Bag X5017, Kimberley 8301, tel (0531) 3-1434/ 2-2657.

To sample the traditional method of transport favoured by the prospecting pioneers of yesteryear, you shouldn't miss the chance to ride the Kimberley Tram.

This rubber-wheeled tramcar replica, mounted on a bus-style chassis, closely resembles the original models which plied the streets at the beginning of this century. But today's version is powered by batteries, and offers a 'silent ride', unencumbered by rails and overhead poles and wires.

The livery of the tramcar duplicates the yellow and black of the original Kimberley electric railway.

The tram service, reintroduced in 1985, operates between the City Hall and the Mine Museum. The route from the museum is via Tucker Street, in the centre of the road, to the intersection with North Circular Road. Having passed the substation, the line continues on a roadside reservation beside North Circular Road, as far as Pniel Road, which it crosses. From Church Street and Market Street the line finally reaches the Market Square.

A trendsetter in its heyday, Kimberley was the first town in South Africa to have electric street-lighting, and the first to introduce to its inhabitants the exhilaration of riding an electric tram.

The Kimberley Tramways Company was formed in 1880, with many early diamond-fields personalities on the committee, including Cecil John Rhodes. It wasn't until 1887, however, that construction on the first tramline began.

The tramway linking Kimberley to nearby Beaconsfield was just over 3,5 km long. Despite a somewhat inauspicious start – when one of the first tramcars was derailed – the tramways were extremely popular for over 50 years.

However, during the 1930s when the service became too costly to maintain, some trams were replaced by buses.

Although the town eventually had to abandon its tram service after World War II for various economic reasons, the Kimberley Publicity Association reintroduced the service in 1985.

McGREGOR MUSEUM

A life-size replica of Cecil John Rhodes shaking hands with the British hero of the Siege of Kimberley, General J D P French, in the drawing room of the Kimberley Sanatorium, is just one of several fascinating exhibits housed in the McGregor Museum.

Other galleries feature the military history of Kimberley – and include well-preserved items of military dress, firearms, flags and photographs of events that shaped the area, particularly during the last 100 years.

The museum's geological collection consists of local rock varieties, fossils and minerals, supplemented by specimens from the rest of the African continent and abroad.

A lovely chapel, built in the time of the Sisters of the Holy Family, has been converted into the Hall of Religions, where exhibits pertaining to the five major religions are included. Themes are Ancient Beliefs, The Living Religions, Biblical Biology, and History of Religion on the diamond fields. The hall is dominated by a radiant Tree of Life mosaic.

The Environment Hall depicts the interaction between the Karoo, Kalahari and Grasslands systems which converge in the Kimberley area. Access to the displays on the Northern Cape Environment, the Siege, Kimberley Regiment and the History of Griqualand West is via the lofty entrance hall, with its huge double staircase and painted ceiling.

With the acquisition in the 1960s of the botanical records, and the recollections of the Griqua chief, Jan Pienaar, a fully fledged History Department was established at the museum. Collections of documents and photographs of early Kimberley are expanding rapidly.

The McGregor Museum is housed in the original Sanatorium which was built by Rhodes to serve as a hotel and health resort for the well-heeled in the city.

Designed by G W Greatbatch, and built in 1897, the Sanatorium enjoyed a brief flush of popularity. Rhodes occupied a comfortable suite on the ground floor during the four-month Siege of Kimberley. The rooms he used have been furnished in correct period style.

The Sanatorium was later converted into the Hotel Belgrave. In 1933 it was taken over by the Sisters of the Holy Family, a Catholic order, and served as a convent. The McGregor Museum made the building its headquarters in 1973, when the increase in the number of its collections required additional premises.

Models clad in regimental uniform, and relics left behind on the battlefield, are among the exhibits displayed at the McGregor Museum.

Map: page 334
Located at 2 Atlas Street, Kimberley. From the City Hall, drive south on Jones Street, turn east into Lennox Road, then right into Dutoitspan Road, and left into Atlas Street.
Details: Open Monday to Friday 09h00-17h00; Saturdays 09h00-13h00; Sundays 14h00-17h00; closed Christmas Day and Good Friday. Museum shop open daily. Small admission charge on certain days; free access on Mondays to McGregor Museum and Alexander McGregor Memorial Museum.
Accommodation: A variety of hotel and guesthouse accommodation is available in Kimberley.
Further information: McGregor Museum, P O Box 316, Kimberley 8300, tel (0531) 3-2645/6; Tourist Information Office, P O Box 1976, Kimberley 8300, tel (0531) 2-7298/9.

The headquarters of the McGregor Museum are situated on a large estate which is surrounded by beautiful gardens and lawns.

KIMBERLEY

Map: page 334

Situated in General Van der Spuy Drive, 11 km out of town and 3,5 km beyond the Kimberley Airport, at Alexandersfontein, on the road to the Danie Theron Combat School.

Details: Open weekdays 09h00-13h00, 14h00-17h00; Saturdays 09h00-13h00; Sundays 14h00-17h00; public holidays 10h00-13h00, 14h00-17h00. Closed Christmas Day and Good Friday. Admission fee charged.

Accommodation: Selection of hotels and guesthouses in Kimberley.

Further information: McGregor Museum, P O Box 316, Kimberley 8300, tel (0531) 3-2645/6.

PIONEERS OF AVIATION MEMORIAL

As you stand beside the flimsy biplane at the Pioneers of Aviation Memorial near Kimberley, you wonder just how South Africa's intrepid pathfinders managed to get their flying machines off the ground. Or where they got the courage to climb behind the controls for a flight of uncertain destination.

The courage of these magnificent men in their flying machines is appropriately commemorated at the aviation memorial with this lifelike reconstruction of the Compton-Paterson Biplane used at South Africa's first flying school.

The biplane is housed in a hangar reconstructed from the original one built at the school. Here there's also an exhibition of photographs depicting the proud history of the Air Force, and a striking monument in stone, resembling the wings of aircraft soaring into space.

Kimberley became the home of the first flying school in southern Africa – the Aviation Syndicate School of Flying – in 1912. On a small aerodrome near Alexandersfontein, early aspiring pilots were taught to fly in a box-like contraption used as a flying machine by their instructor, Cecil Compton-Paterson.

In effect, aviation history at Kimberley dates back to 6 June 1911, when John Weston made the first flight in the city. Before an admiring crowd of hundreds, he established a South African nonstop flight record of eight and a half minutes in his Weston-Farman biplane.

Unfortunately for the intrepid pilot, he was unable to obtain permission to open a flying school in the town. This privilege eventually fell to the African Aviation Syndicate.

Captain Guy Livingstone, Cecil Compton-Paterson and 'Bok' Driver arrived in Cape Town in December 1911 to give a series of demonstration flights, which resulted in the establishment of the training school at Alexandersfontein.

The school's first flying machine was imported from England, but it crashed with the future Major-General K van der Spuy, then a keen pupil, on board. Fortunately, he was unscathed, and his enthusiasm for flying was undiminished.

During World War I, the first military pilots – members of the newly formed South African Aviation Corps – were trained at the school, and went on to acquit themselves admirably in combat.

Map: page 334

The Henrietta Stockdale Chapel is situated on the Dutoitspan Road, in the grounds of the Provincial Hospital, bounded by Lyndhurst, Dutoitspan and Memorial roads, and located near the Civic Centre.

Details: The chapel can be visited during the week by contacting the housekeeper on duty at the nurses' home, which is to the left of the hospital, tel (0531) 802-2125.

Accommodation: There's a variety of hotels and guesthouses in Kimberley.

Further information: Tourist Information Office, P O Box 1976, Kimberley 8300, tel (0531) 2-7298/9.

SISTER HENRIETTA STOCKDALE CHAPEL

The attractive chapel in the grounds of the Provincial Hospital (formerly the Kimberley Hospital), is a concrete reminder of the life and work of a remarkable woman, Sister Henrietta Stockdale, who did as much for the nursing profession as the legendary Lady of the Lamp – fellow Englishwoman Florence Nightingale.

Built in 1887, the stone chapel seats 100 in its hand-carved pews, dappled with coloured light from the beautiful stained-glass windows above. The ceiling is supported by massive wooden beams, a theme echoed in the sturdy altar railings. Candles in brass sconces line the walls, and a handsome organ is still used for services and the occasional wedding. There is a separate vestry, and plaques commemorate the dedicated lives of the nuns who served at the hospital.

Sister Henrietta Stockdale, an Anglican nursing sister of the Order of Saint Michael and All Angels, arrived in Kimberley in 1876, fresh from a stint at a Bloemfontein hospital, to work at the Carnarvon Hospital on the diamond fields. She had not been in the area long when she contracted typhoid fever, which was rife in hospitals at the time, and had to spend a period of convalescence in England.

Upon her return she became the first hospital matron in the Northern Cape, with her appointment as such at the St George's Hospital in Kimberley.

After the amalgamation of the Carnarvon and Diggers Central hospitals, Sister Henrietta became matron of the Kimberley Hospital, where she established the first nurses' training school in the country, observing the methods taught her by Florence Nightingale.

The chapel was built at her behest in 1887. It has subsequently been made a national monument.

A statue of Sister Henrietta was sculpted by artist Jack Penn, and erected in front of the nearby St Cyprian's Cathedral. It is the only known statue of a nun in the world. Sister Henrietta is buried in the Dutoitspan Cemetery.

Sister Henrietta Stockdale, pioneering nurse.

THE INTERIOR

The llama is a domesticated South American camel used as a beast of burden, and valued for its shaggy coat.

Originally from Asia, this magnificently horned sambar stag feeds on grasses, leaves and fruit, and grows to a height of 1,4 metres.

LICHTENBURG GAME BREEDING CENTRE
Lichtenburg

The lumbering, heavy-shouldered American bison is a familiar sight in cowboy and Western films, but something of a rarity outside its country of origin. Now you can see one in the flesh at the Lichtenburg Game Breeding Centre in the North-West Province. Watch the creature rub its powerful shoulders with daintier ones of almost 50 other local and exotic breeds of animal.

The 6 000-ha centre, established to assist the National Zoological Gardens of South Africa, also provides opportunities for ongoing research into animal behaviour. Among the animals that roam and breed freely in this protected natural paradise are Indian buffaloes, Angolan sable oryxes, lechwe from Zimbabwe, sambar deer from Asia, Indian nilgai, Sardinian moufflons, llamas from South America, Central African dwarf hippos, white rhinos from KwaZulu-Natal, and the rare Pere David deer.

Pride of place in the breeding centre, however, goes to the growing cheetah population. To accommodate these lithe creatures, an additional 2 000 ha of land, known as the 'Fred Brand Camp', were added in 1978. You may view the cheetahs at close quarters from one of the reserve's well-designed roads.

A special feature at Lichtenburg is the wetland environment which was formed by several permanent fountains. Here dwarf hippos wallow happily, surrounded by a wealth of bird life. Enjoy a meal in the outdoors at the well-developed picnic-cum-braai area, and keep your binoculars handy for viewing breeding pairs of flamingoes, wild ducks, coots, spoonbills, ibises and finches.

There's an Olympic-sized swimming pool at the shady caravan park near the entrance to the reserve.

Besides watersports, the town of Lichtenburg offers facilities for golf, tennis, cricket, basketball, badminton and target-shooting. It also has a socio-historical and an agricultural museum, as well as a public library and an art gallery.

Map: page 329, 2F
The centre is 4 km north of the heart of town. Lichtenburg itself is about 220 km from Johannesburg, and 60 km from Mmabatho, the capital of the North-West Province.
Details: Open every day 08h00-18h00 (summer) and 08h30-17h30 (winter).
Accommodation: There's a caravan park at the entrance of the breeding centre. Lichtenburg has one hotel with all facilities.
Further information: Lichtenburg Municipality, P O Box 7, Lichtenburg 2740, tel (01441) 2-5051.

THE INTERIOR

MAGERSFONTEIN BATTLEFIELD AND MUSEUM
Magersfontein

Map: page 329, 4E
The Magersfontein Battlefield and Museum lies 31,5 km south of Kimberley. To reach the museum, drive down Oliver Road, past the airport turn-off, the Aviation Memorial and the Danie Theron Combat School. At the entrance to the Jack Hindon Officers' Club, turn right onto a signposted gravel road.
Details: There are picnic sites with refuse bins, but fires are prohibited. Tearoom open during museum hours. Admission fee charged.
Open every day 08h00-17h00 all year round. Closed Christmas Day and Good Friday.
Accommodation: There are hotels, guesthouses and the Big Hole Municipal Caravan Park, West Circular Road, Kimberley 8301, tel (0531) 80-6322.
Further information: Tourist Information Office, P O Box 1976, Kimberley 8300, tel (0531) 2-7298/9; SA Tourism Board, Private Bag X5017, Kimberley 8300, tel (0531) 3-1434/ 2-2657; The Military Historian, McGregor Museum, P O Box 316, Kimberley 8300, tel (0531) 3-2645/6; The Magersfontein Caretaker, tel (0531) 2-2029.

No less than seven memorials, dominated by a Celtic Cross, loom above the windswept countryside of Magersfontein Battlefield and Museum, site of one of the most decisive battles of the Anglo-Boer War (1899-1902).

It was here, at dawn on 11 December 1899, that British troops advancing across the plains were met by a devastating barrage of gunfire from the Boer trenches at the base of Magersfontein Hill. After resisting the initial onslaught, the British troops retreated with heavy casualties, particularly among the Highland Brigade.

Today Magersfontein is hallowed ground, a place of quietude and remembrance, where memorials stand tribute to Scottish Highlanders, members of the Black Watch and Guard Brigades and Scandinavian and Boer soldiers.

Magersfontein is one of South Africa's most famous battlesites, a place where men of conviction fought and perished for their beliefs during the so-called Black Week of the Anglo-Boer War.

The area of greatest tactical importance, where the heaviest fighting took place, is now a national monument which is owned and administered by the McGregor Museum. Visitors are free to walk around, or drive to the museum buildings and grave-sites.

With a little imagination it's easy to re-create the atmosphere of the battle, as most of the original defences can still be located, and the veld itself remains unchanged. Sections of the Boer trenches and their system of defence are still visible from the viewing post.

An observation post overlooks the main Magersfontein battlefield, and the museum houses an interesting collection of war relics, such as uniforms, equipment, weapons and graphic photographs of that fateful December day. The battle is depicted on a relief map indicating troop and gun positions, and on a detailed scale model.

In all, the battlefield covers 428 ha, including the museum and seven memorials to fallen soldiers of various regiments. It is not uncommon to find relics of the battle strewn about the veld. These may not be removed, but should be left in position and reported to the caretaker at the McGregor Museum.

The Magersfontein Monuments are located south of the city on sites along the Modder River Road. Regiments which are honoured here include the Highland, Black Watch and Scandinavian corps. There are two British grave-sites as well. The British Garden of Remembrance occupies part of the West End Cemetery, off Green Street, Kimberley.

MAMPOER AND TOBACCO TOURS
Groot Marico

Map: page 329, 2F
From Johannesburg take the R27 via Magaliesberg, Koster, Derby and Swartruggens. From Pretoria the road passes Rustenburg and Swartruggens before reaching Groot Marico.
Details: The tours leave from the Groot Marico Information Centre at 10h00 on the last Saturday of each month. Book in advance. You travel in your own vehicle.
Accommodation: You can stay at farms or game farms in the vicinity. Catered or self-catering accommodation can be arranged through the Groot Marico Information Centre. The Groot Marico Hotel, P O Box 176, Groot Marico 2850, tel (014252) 45, has rooms with or without *en suite* bathrooms.
Further information: Groot Marico Information Centre, P O Box 28, Groot Marico 2850, tel (014252) 85.

To sample the unique hospitality and generosity of Groot Marico residents, eulogized so often by author Herman Charles Bosman, there's nothing to beat these two fascinating tours. As a bonus, you'll get an introduction to the evocative beauty of this part of the Bushveld.

The Mampoer Tour begins at the Groot Marico Information Centre at 10h00 on the last Saturday of each month (preceded by tea and light snacks). Additional tours may be organized for parties of 15 or more.

Vehicles depart in convoy and follow the course of the Groot Marico River to its source, winding through kloofs that bisect the undulating landscape.

At a large natural fountain called Kaal-oog (Naked Eye), you may refresh yourself with a dip in the crystalline depths.

Then it's back to the meandering kloofs, and a stop at the farm *Draaifontein*, where you will be offered large helpings of farm cooking and bread fresh from the *bakoond* (oven). With a little coaxing, your hosts may be encouraged to demonstrate the old craft of plaiting a whip from strips of dried animal skin.

The final stopover is a few kilometres further on, at *Knoffelfontein*, where your hosts continue the old Marico tradition of distilling mampoer, a potent alcoholic brew made from peaches. Sample this elixir, and depart with rosy memories.

Tobacco Tour
The Tobacco Tour also requires pre-booking, and departs at the same time from the same venue. This time round, the convoy makes its way to Doringkraal for a leisurely, late breakfast.

Amply fuelled, you will wind your way to the Marico Bushveld Dam for a short sightseeing excursion. Next it's the *Schuinsdrif* tobacco farm, where a guide will introduce you to the intricacies of producing the perfect tobacco leaf. Refreshments will be served to quell any hunger pangs brought on by the fresh air, before you depart for Enzelsberg for a drop of mampoer in convivial and spirited surroundings.

THE INTERIOR

MOFFAT MISSION
Kuruman

A feeling of deep serenity pervades the stone church, schoolroom and the quaint houses at the Moffat Mission at Seodin, outside Kuruman.

The buildings of the original mission complex, built by the famous missionary Robert Moffat, have been carefully restored. Surrounded by irrigated fields fed by the Eye of Kuruman four kilometres away, they are set beneath magnificent shade trees, including syringa, fig, pear, pomegranate and almond.

Here Moffat and his wife Mary worked among the Batswana people for 50 years.

The Moffat homestead is the oldest building north of the Orange River. Part of it houses a small museum, and the rest a shop and post office. A letter posted here will receive a special franking.

In the nave of the church built with their own hands, Moffat translated and printed the Bible in Tswana. It was the first time the book was printed in Africa, and in a hitherto unwritten African language. The press is housed in the Kimberley Public Library.

The church was designed to seat 800 people. It is built in the traditional manner, with walls over 60 cm thick. Heavy, hand-hewn timbers support the reed-thatch roof.

A simple, and rather unpretentious structure without a steeple or gallery, the mud-floored church does have some outstanding acoustic qualities. Services are still held periodically.

Map: page 329, 3D
Situated in Thompson Avenue, Kuruman. As you leave Kuruman on the road to Hotazel in the north, turn right at the signpost, 5 km outside town.
Details: Souvenirs are available at the bookshop at the Moffat Mission. Refreshments available at shop.
Accommodation: There are various hotels in Kuruman, a municipal caravan park, with 90 sites, and the Second Eye Holiday Resort, P O Box 4, Kuruman 8460, tel (05373) 3-0114.
Further information: Moffat Mission, P O Box 34, Kuruman 8460, tel (05373) 2-2645/8 or 2-1352; The Town Clerk, P O Box 4, Kuruman 8460, tel (05373) 2-1095/6/7.

The Moffat Mission Church at Kuruman, which is still used for church services.

PELLA MISSION CHURCH
Pella

Pella is the perfect oasis, set in the middle of a sandy pan, vividly coloured by minerals in the soil. Standing in the walled garden at the mission, a grove of date palms about you, and figs, grapes and pomegranates in abundance, you could be in the heart of Arabia.

At night the air is perfumed with a variety of subtle odours emanating from the wildflowers and aromatic shrubs in the area. Dates from Pella have a unique flavour and are mailed in wooden boxes to customers all over the country.

Adjoining the garden is the church, a cool haven from the searing heat outside.

The Pella Mission Church was built by Catholic missionaries with the assistance of local residents. None of those involved had any prior architectural or building experience, yet they managed to create a church of great beauty, which stands as a testament to their faith. With its graceful

Map: page 329, 5A
The main tarmac road (N8) from Pofadder reaches the Pella turn-off after 24 kilometres. The mission station is 3 km along this gravel road and then a further 9 km down a second turn-off.
Accommodation: The Pofadder Hotel, P O Box 3, Pofadder 8890, tel (02532) 43; self-catering accommodation at the Pofadder Overnight Chalets, P O Box 119, Pofadder 8890, tel (02532) 19/39/111; Rus-'n-Bietjie Caravan Park, P O Box 99, Pofadder 8890, tel (02532) 36.
Further information: The Town Clerk, P O Box 108, Pofadder 8890, tel (02532) 46.

The magnificent Roman Catholic church at Pella, built by mission fathers equipped with a handful of tools and an encyclopedia.

supporting arches, buttresses and rose-design windows, the church is an eye-catching structure.

There is a clearly chiming bell in the bell tower and a great clock set into the church spire, a gift from a wealthy monk, Father Brisson, which survived many mishaps to arrive safely from England.

The church inside boasts a magnificent altar and a life-sized crucifix, backed by a series of graceful arches.

The church rivals some of the most beautiful country churches in France, whence the monks hailed. When, in 1914, it began to show signs of wear, parts of the roof and pillars were reconstructed and reinforced. The interior was also completely refurbished, in keeping with modern Catholic liturgical trends.

Pella was founded in 1814 by the London Missionary Society, and named after the town which provided refuge for Christians in Macedonia in biblical times. The mission was taken over by the Catholic Church in 1878. Work began on the existing church in 1886.

The Roaring Sands near Postmasburg

The Roaring Sands are famed for their range of unusual acoustics, which include moans and grunts.

One of the strangest geological phenomena in the country, these so-called 'Roaring Sands', which lie on the western side of the Langeberg Dunes in The Interior, form part of a white island of dunes that are 12 km long and three kilometres wide. These dunes are in marked contrast to the red dunes of The Interior, which surround them.

If you disturb the surface of the sand on the western side of the dunes, you will be startled to hear a sound that varies from a low hum to a powerful roar.

Whereas the dry, surrounding red sands are coloured by their high content of iron oxide, the white dunes are peculiar for the quantity of water they contain. The white dunes are believed to have been formed as a result of freshwater springs which over the years leached out red iron oxides.

This freedom from foreign matter, combined with the dry atmospheric conditions, and uniformity of size of the individual sand grains, caused by constant wind movement, provides an explanation for the roaring effect they produce.

The sliding of one's fingers through the sand produces a sound akin to the grunting of a pig, or loud snoring. Scooping up a handful of the strange grains will create a booming noise. Walking on the sand makes a roaring sound, which can be amplified by sliding down the dunes. A person sliding down the dunes can be heard more than 100 m away.

At night the wind creates an eerie moaning effect over the dunes. The sound is markedly louder on the southern face.

Local inhabitants claim that the dunes roar loudest during months with the letter 'r' in them. In truth, the sands know no calendar – they roar when it is dry, and weather conditions are suitable.

The driest months are from May to October. The summer months are extremely hot, with frequent thunderstorms which subdue the sound of the Roaring Sands for several days. Periods of extreme cold also have the effect of diminishing the noise.

Apart from their acoustic properties, the dunes are also known for the presence of fulgurites, caused by flashes of lightning which strike and fuse the sand. These threads of fused sand, glazed and mirrored in parts, are up to two metres long.

You may want to put a sample of the sand in a jar as a keepsake of the Roaring Sands. Try putting the sand in a pair of jam jars attached lid-to-lid, with a finger-sized hole between the two. The device will resemble an egg-timer.

If the jars are upended, the sand will make its roaring sound as it runs between them. Make sure the jars are tightly sealed, however, for if the sand comes into contact with humid air after leaving its place of origin, it will absorb moisture and become mute.

The Roaring Sands are located in the vicinity of the Padkloof Pass. The road is in reasonable condition, but should be negotiated in daylight, as signposts may be missed in the dark.

You can stay at The Witsand Holiday Resort, P O Box 327, Postmasburg 8420, tel (0591) 7-2373. Contact The Town Clerk, P O Box 5, Postmasburg 8420, tel (0591) 3-0343.

FREE STATE

PLACES TO VISIT

BLOEMFONTEIN

FIRST RAADSAAL

Map: below, right
Situated in St George's Street, between President Brand and Green streets.
Details: Open weekdays 10h00-15h00; Saturdays, Sundays and public holidays (excluding Christmas Day, New Year's Day and Good Friday) 14h00 -17h00.
Accommodation: There is a wide selection of hotels in Bloemfontein, as well as caravan/camping sites.
Further information: Bloemfontein Publicity Association, P O Box 639, Bloemfontein 9300, tel (051) 405-8490.

Turning into Bloemfontein's St George's Street, you will come across a humble, one-roomed, thatched-roof building. Quaker-like in its severity of line and lack of embellishment, the solidly built, whitewashed structure has dung floors and small, low windows set into thick walls.

Despite its unassuming character, the First Raadsaal has housed nearly every civilian institution imaginable. It is the oldest existing building in Bloemfontein, and also the cradle of government, the church, and education in the Free State.

Constructed in 1848 by Major Henry Douglas Warden, the First Raadsaal has served as a political assembly, a school, and a utility hall for social gatherings. It is proudly preserved today as the only remaining example of the unique pioneer building style in Bloemfontein.

In 1854 it became the first meeting chamber of the Free State Volksraad, and was used as a school and a Dutch Reformed Church thereafter, until the National Museum was initially established in the building in 1877.

KEY TO THE MAP
1 First Raadsaal
2 Fourth Raadsaal
3 Naval Hill
4 Old Presidency
5 War Museum of the Boer Republics
6 National Women's Memorial

A statue of Boer general Christiaan de Wet, sculpted by local artist Coert Steynberg, stands in front of the handsome Fourth Raadsaal.

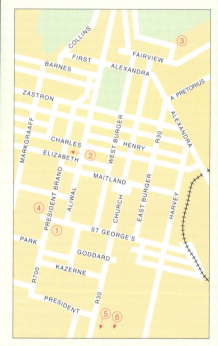

FOURTH RAADSAAL

Map: opposite
Situated in President Brand Street, opposite the Court of Appeal.
Details: The Raadsaal can only be visited by appointment, tel (051) 47-8898.
Accommodation: There is a wide selection of hotels in Bloemfontein, as well as caravan/camping sites.
Further information: Bloemfontein Publicity Association, P O Box 639, Bloemfontein 9300, tel (051) 405-8490.

The domed tower and magnificent Doric columns of Bloemfontein's Fourth Raadsaal have an air of precious austerity that seems to justify its reputation as the Jewel of the Free State.

In fact, this fusion of Greek, Roman and Renaissance-style architecture seems almost out of place, except for the sandstone and redbrick components so characteristic of the Free State building style of a century ago.

The doors of the Fourth Raadsaal were opened by President Frederik Reitz on 5 June 1893, and the parliamentary building was meant to usher in a new era for the 'model' Afrikaner Republic of the Free State.

Shortly afterwards, however, in March 1900, British forces invaded the town, converted the building into a hospital, and removed much of the furniture.

After the South African War, when Union was declared, the building finally reverted to its intended political function, becoming the debating chambers of the Free State Provincial Council.

The building was designed by Lennox Canning, and the cornerstone was laid by President Reitz on 27 June 1890. The building was completed three years later.

The original benches which were used by the Volksraad still remain. The busts of the six former presidents of the Free State Republic adorn the walls. Behind the seat of the Chairman you will see the original coat of arms of the Free State, skilfully carved in wood.

BLOEMFONTEIN

NAVAL HILL

There is no better vantage point from which to view the attractive city of Bloemfontein than Naval Hill. From here visitors get sweeping views of the layout of the city and of the Highveld plains beyond. You can enter close to the city centre on Union Avenue, and enjoy a leisurely drive, or stroll around the flat-topped hill so rich in history.

The name Naval Hill dates back to the Anglo-Boer War (1899-1902), when British forces set up their ship's cannon on the hill. The navy had come to Bloemfontein as part of Lord Roberts's force, and their headquarters were located on the koppie, with its strategic view over the town.

The Wiltshire Regiment of the British Navy used the hill as a depot for fresh horses, and they left evidence of their stay by marking out a huge white horse in stone, as a beacon for the British cavalry returning from the plains.

Naval Hill is now home to the wild animals of the Franklin Nature Reserve, run as a joint venture of the municipality and Bloemfontein Zoo. Several of the buildings used in the Anglo-Boer War, and later World War I, are still standing, and serve as the offices of the Franklin Nature Reserve.

The 251-ha reserve is populated by springbok, blesbok, Burchell's zebras, eland and other indigenous game species.

At the summit of Naval Hill the old Lamont Hussey Observatory, an astronomical observatory which was built and run by the University of Michigan in order to observe binary (double) star systems, has now been converted into a theatre and cultural centre.

Map: page 344
Drive north along West Burger Street, straight into Union Avenue, then right into the reserve at the bottom of Naval Hill.
Details: Open 24 hours a day. Visit by day for animal-viewing; by night for seeing the city lights.
Accommodation: For hotels in Bloemfontein, contact the Publicity Association, P O Box 639, Bloemfontein 9300, tel (051) 405-8490.
Further information: The Department of Parks and Recreation, P O Box 3704, Bloemfontein 9300, tel (051) 405-8786 or 405-8124/5.

The dignified façade of the Old Presidency. The foundation stone of this baronial home was laid by President J H Brand in May 1885.

OLD PRESIDENCY

The Old Presidency in President Brand Street, Bloemfontein, is an interesting example of the Scottish baronial style popular among Victorian architects. The building is a national monument, and enjoys a prime position, just opposite the magistrates' court.

The stately structure, designed by architect Lennox Canning, was completed in 1886. Due to financial constraints, Canning had to trim his original design somewhat, producing a simpler effect than he had planned.

The Old Presidency is so called because it was the official residence of the last three presidents of the old Republic of the Free State.

The building has been restored to pristine condition, and functions today as a very popular museum. The various exhibits depict the respective terms of office of President J H Brand (1864-88), President F W Reitz (1888-95) and President M T Steyn (1896-1900).

Until as recently as 1910, the Old Presidency was occupied as a dwelling – that of Sir Hamilton Goold-Adams, Lieutenant-Governor of the Orange River Colony. Today it is used as a cultural centre for art exhibitions, small theatre productions, musical evenings, and for conferences.

Map: page 344
Located on the corner of President Brand and St George's streets, Bloemfontein, diagonally opposite the magistrates' court.
Details: Open Tuesday to Friday 10h00-12h00, 13h00-16h00; Saturdays and Sundays 14h00-17h00. At the back of the Old Presidency, the stables have been converted into a restaurant where tea and light meals are served.
Accommodation: There is a selection of hotels to choose from in Bloemfontein, as well as camping/caravan facilities.
Further information: Bloemfontein Tourist Information Bureau, P O Box 639, Bloemfontein 9300, tel (051) 405-8490; SA Tourism Board, Private Bag X20543, Bloemfontein 9300, tel (051) 47-1362.

BLOEMFONTEIN

Map: page 344
Both the War Museum of the Boer Republics and the Women's Memorial are located in Memoriam Road, south of central Bloemfontein, and west of the Church Street extension that becomes the N6 to Reddersburg.
Details: Open 09h00-17h00 Monday to Saturday; 12h00-15h00 Sundays. Small admission fee. Admission to grounds and memorial free of charge.
Accommodation: There are many reputable hotels in Bloemfontein, also caravan parks and camping sites. Contact Bloemfontein Publicity Association, P O Box 639, Bloemfontein 9300, tel (051) 405-8490.
Further information: The Director, War Museum of the Boer Republics, P O Box 704, Bloemfontein 9300, tel (051) 47-3447.

WAR MUSEUM OF THE BOER REPUBLICS

The Anglo-Boer War was a time of great patriotism, camaraderie and heroism. It was also a period of appalling suffering, and a source of bitterness that would be passed down the generations.

The War Museum of the Boer Republics in Bloemfontein mirrors this period of upheaval, and is well worth visiting to gain an insight into the well-documented Afrikaner struggle for total independence from British imperialism.

The emphasis at the museum is strongly partisan, but the exhibits are many and varied. Situated at the National Women's Memorial, the museum houses war artwork, weaponry, fascinating items made by Boer prisoners of war in 48 camps scattered across the globe, exhibitions depicting the way of life of those in prisoner-of-war camps, and the concentration camps where women and children were interned.

There is also an extensive collection of furniture and artefacts from typical Boer dwellings of the period. In addition, the personal effects of former Free State President M T Steyn, and those of General Christiaan de Wet, have found a home at the war museum.

Gun enthusiasts will find plenty to interest themselves in the fascinating rifle collection – there are Mausers and Martinis, Metfords, Enfields, Guedes and the Krag and Wesley Richards, all in their restored splendour.

In the Christiaan de Wet Hall, the diorama of a lonely Boer soldier in the vastness of the African veld strikes a poignant note. A fascinating collection of tiles dating to 1900, discovered recently in a semidemolished building in Holland, depicts momentous battles and personalities of the war.

The Kestell and Hobhouse galleries are adorned with paintings and sculptures by Anton van Wouw and other noted artists.

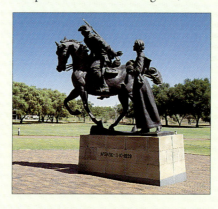

An Afrikaner woman bids her husband farewell as he gallops off to the front.

NATIONAL WOMEN'S MEMORIAL

Two women and a dying child symbolize the suffering of the innocent victims of war.

The National Women's Memorial stands sentinel on a commanding site adjoining the war museum. The celebrated work of South African sculptor Anton van Wouw inspires awe with its powerful simplicity and dignity.

The stark 36,5-m sandstone obelisk commemorates the death of 26 370 Afrikaner women and children during the Anglo-Boer War. A mother holds her dying infant in her arms, while another gazes out over the Free State plains, beyond the spectator, into the past, or perhaps the future.

The ashes of the British camp reformer Emily Hobhouse are buried right at the foot of the monument, honouring her enormous contribution in helping to alleviate the suffering of those incarcerated in the concentration camps during the war.

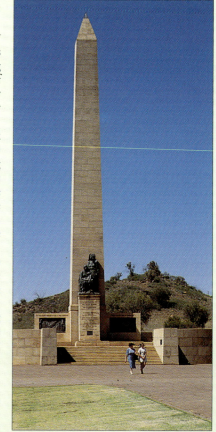

A sandstone obelisk pays tribute to the thousands of women and children who died during the Anglo-Boer War.

AAN ONZE

BLOEMHOF DAM
Bloemhof

The U-shaped Bloemhof Dam just outside the town of Bloemfontein offers excellent game-viewing and fishing opportunities for nature-lovers. Located just below the confluence of the Vaal and Vet rivers, the dam's impressive five-kilometre-long dam wall is one of the longest in the country.

In the 14 000-ha Bloemhof Dam Nature Reserve, on the northern banks of the dam, you may see black wildebeest, eland, red hartebeest, blesbok, springbok, zebras, ostriches and white rhinos, among other indigenous game species.

If game-watching is your mission, enter the reserve through the Verlatenkraal or Bamboesspruit gate, along the road between Bloemhof and Wolmaransstad. A third gate gives access to the reserve at Hopetown Bridge (on the R34, five kilometres from Bloemhof).

If it's good fishing you're after, there can be few better-stocked dams in the area to indulge your passion.

Between the two arms of the Bloemhof Dam is another reserve, the Sandveld Nature Reserve, a sanctuary for red hartebeest, eland, giraffes, springbok, duiker and more than 170 bird species.

Map: page 343, 2B
From Bloemfontein travel northwest on the R64, then north on the R59 to Hertzogville. Continue on the R59 to Hoopstad, and turn west onto the R34 to Bloemhof (40 km). The reserve flanks the road as you enter Bloemhof.
Details: Open daily 08h00-18h00.
Accommodation: Camping/caravan facilities are available.
Further information: Angling: Free State Angling Association, P O Box 377, Welkom 9460, tel (0171) 5-1431. Hunting: Free State Hunters' and Conservation Association, P O Box 428, Bloemfontein 9300, tel (051) 47-1337; The Officer-in-Charge, Bloemhof Dam Nature Reserve, Private Bag X7, Bloemhof 2660, tel (01802) 3-1706.

Gariep Dam – a popular venue for holiday-makers and watersport devotees.

GARIEP DAM
Norvalspont

There's a sense of awe as you stand and view the immensity of the Gariep Dam, which covers an area of 374 square kilometres. At its highest point the retaining wall is an incredible 90,5 m, and the overall width is 914 metres.

But, perhaps more importantly, the dam is capable of holding back 6 000 million cubic litres of water – making it an integral part of the massive Orange River Development Scheme, the largest water-supply scheme on the African continent.

The scheme was developed to provide hydroelectric power and irrigation to land in the Karoo and Eastern Province.

Two hydro power stations – Vanderkloof (220 MW) and Gariep (320 MW) – have been erected at the Vanderkloof and Gariep dams. Apart from the two great dams, there are the Vanderkloof canal system, Fish-Sundays canal system, Welbedacht Dam and the 82-km-long Orange-Fish River tunnel.

The dam wall offers panoramic views all along its length.

Within the wall, an auditorium has regular audiovisual shows outlining the construction of the dam and its excellent safety record.

In times of heavy rains the water cascades down six spillways. A concrete 'apron' has been constructed beneath the overspill to prevent the water from eroding the rock at the base of the dam.

On the northern banks of the dam lies the Gariep Dam Nature Reserve, home to the largest springbok colony in the country, black wildebeest, red hartebeest and ostriches. Adjoining the reserve is the Aventura Midwaters public resort, which provides wonderful views of the shimmering water and the islands.

Also on the banks of the dam is the attractive Oviston Nature Reserve, which offers a guided overnight trail through some beautiful, untouched wilderness. Reservations may be made by contacting The Officer-in-Charge, Oviston Nature Reserve, P O Box 7, Venterstad 5990, tel (0553) 50-0000.

Map: page 343, 5/6B/C
The dam is located 177 km south of Bloemfontein off the N1, and 4 km south of the town of Hendrik Verwoerd.
Details: Aventura Midwaters offers a swimming pool, tennis courts, golf course, bowling green, miniature golf course and horses. Powerboating and yachting on the dam.
Accommodation: Chalets are available at Aventura Midwaters, each with room for 7 people in 3 bedrooms (1 double bed, 5 singles). Lounge-cum-dining room, bathroom, kitchen, carport. Smaller, fully equipped 2-bedroomed units sleep five. Camping/caravan site with 107 stands. The Verwoerd Dam Motel – P O Box 20, Gariep Dam 9922, tel (052172) ask for 60 – is fully licensed and offers modern, luxurious accommodation in 23 rooms with *en suite* bathrooms.
Further information: Aventura Midwaters, Private Bag X10, Gariep Dam 9922, tel (052172) ask for 45.

FREE STATE

GOLDEN GATE HIGHLANDS NATIONAL PARK
Bethlehem

Map: page 343, 3E
The Golden Gate Highlands National Park is 58 km from Bethlehem. The best route is from Durban via Winterton, Bergville and the Oliviershoek Pass. The road traverses the QwaQwa National Park, and passes the Lesotho Open-Air Museum (a great tourist attraction) to reach the Golden Gate.
Details: Open 24 hours a day throughout the year.
Accommodation: Brandwag Camp offers single or double rooms in the main complex, with lounge, bathroom and television. The adjoining chalets offer 4 beds, bathroom, kitchen, television and braai facilities. The camp also offers a restaurant, coffee bar, ladies' bar, curio shop, laundromat and information centre. Glen Reenen Camp offers rondavels with bathroom and kitchen facilities. A spacious caravan park offers 80 stands, bathrooms, kitchens, scullery and braai facilities.
Further information: Golden Gate Highlands National Park, Private Bag X03, Clarens 9707, tel (058) 256-1471; National Parks Board, P O Box 787, Pretoria 0001, tel (012) 343-1991.

The spectacular attractions of the Golden Gate Highlands National Park are virtually unequalled anywhere in the country, and place this reserve at the top of the holiday list for anyone who revels in nature's unspoiled beauty.

Named after the varying shades of gold cast on the sandstone cliffs by the sun, the park nestles in the foothills of the breathtaking Maluti Mountains.

The Golden Gate itself is formed by two huge, russet-burnished rocks 76 m high. The park embraces some 10 000 ha of spectacular scenery, where the only permanent inhabitants are the animals: grey rhebuck, oribi, blesbok, springbok, black wildebeest, eland and Burchell's zebras. Among the smaller mammals that find sanctuary in the park are such nocturnal creatures as African wild cats, aardwolfs and porcupines.

More commonly seen are the marsh mongooses, Cape grey mongooses, large-spotted genets, striped polecats, Cape clawless otters, chacma baboons and black-backed jackals. If you scan the skies you may see one or more of a variety of raptors, ranging from such species as bearded vultures and black eagles to jackal buzzards. On the ground you're likely to see blue cranes, secretary birds, rock pigeons and guinea fowl.

Eroded by wind and rain, the multicoloured sandstone cliffs of the Rooiberge rise above the Golden Gate Highlands National Park.

Clarens – unspoilt artists' haven

If you've ever been to the Free State hamlet of Clarens, you'll wish that it could remain just your private domain – a little bit of heaven at the gateway to the Golden Gate Highlands National Park. If this is a first visit, there's an unforgettable experience in store.

There is arguably no earthly spot more lovely than Clarens in the first light of an autumn morning, when the Lombardy poplars blaze a rich gold. It is easy to see what has drawn various artists and photographers to this spot for decades.

The entrance to the town is guarded by The Titanic, a colossal rock formation in the shape of the doomed ship. The stream that meanders lazily through the town is fringed by graceful willow trees.

Clarens has riches beyond her natural beauty. The town is dotted with beautiful homes; galleries are crammed with *objets d'art*, the mountain water is sweet, and hiking trails reveal the beauty of the Maluti Mountains.

Fewer than 300 people enjoy the privilege of calling this exquisite mountain village home. Many of these are creative individuals who have sought out Clarens for the qualities of peace and space they need to fuel the creative process.

Potters, musicians, painters, sculptors and actors live together in an informal community. Sculptor-painter Martin Wessels was largely responsible for initiating Clarens's artistic growth.

The artistic tradition is not one of recent vintage in Clarens. Numerous fine examples of San rock art are to be found in the area.

Flurries of snow are a feature of winters in the Golden Gate Highlands National Park, when waterfalls freeze in spectacular fan-like formation, and the hills are cloaked in blinding white.

In spring great numbers of indigenous herb and bulb varieties, including watsonias, fire lilies, arum lilies and red-hot pokers, colour the countryside.

Make the most of the superior riding, climbing and walking opportunities in the area. If you prefer sedentary viewing, there's a good network of roads in the park. Alternatively, try one of the walks, which range from a one-hour ramble to the two-day Rhebuck Hiking Trail.

The trail crosses mountain streams, hills and mountains to reach an overnight hut where there are cooking facilities, firewood and drinking water.

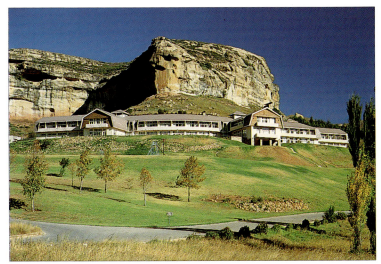

The luxurious Brandwag Camp lies wedged beneath a sandstone fortress known appropriately as The Sentinel.

MARIA MOROKA NATIONAL PARK
Thaba Nchu

The Maria Moroka National Park offers 3 400 ha of enchanting scenic beauty. Its wide-open plains are cupped in a natural amphitheatre formed by the majestic Thaba Nchu (Black) Mountain, and other smaller hills.

The Maria Moroka National Park features a wide variety of game, from springbok to eland, blesbok, zebras, steenbok, black wildebeest and red hartebeest. In all, there are well over 1 000 head of typical Highveld game in the reserve. Enjoy game-watching under your own steam, or enquire about a game-spotting drive with one of the park's rangers.

Bird-watchers, too, will find plenty to occupy themselves at Maria Moroka. Over 200 species of bird have been identified in the area.

Anglers may bag a good catch at the Groothoek Dam, where fishing is restricted to residents of the luxurious Thaba Nchu Sun Hotel. Transport is provided by the hotel. Boat trips across the dam are also an option.

The Maria Moroka National Park offers two hiking trails for the keep-fit fraternity. The Eland Trail takes four to five hours, and snakes through densely vegetated ravines teeming with bird life. It passes the ruins of an old kraal, and scales a steep hill, affording an excellent view of the amphitheatre and its plains.

The two-hour Volstruis (Ostrich) Hiking Trail is a comfortable walk for the less energetic. It crosses the same kloof as the first trail, passes the kraal, and doubles back to the Groothoek Dam.

The park takes its name from the late Maria Moipone Moroka, longtime chief of the local Morolong community. Many old kraal sites remain in the area. The village of Thaba Nchu lies squarely at the foot of the Black Mountain. Founded in 1873, the village still functions as the administrative and trade centre of the Tswana people.

In Thaba Nchu you may see several well-preserved buildings of historical interest. A favourite spot with the art cognoscenti is the beautiful church at the St Francis Catholic Mission, built and decorated by the priest/artist, Father Frans Claerhout.

After a day exploring Maria Moroka's delights, visitors can take the chill out of the evening mountain air with a beautiful hand-knitted Aran jersey produced by the local women.

Map: page 343, 4C
The park is a mere 10 km from the town of Thaba Nchu, and 60 km east of Bloemfontein.
Details: Open sunrise to sunset throughout the year.
Accommodation: The sumptuous Thaba Nchu Sun Hotel and Casino, with all the luxurious facilities you need, is the only accommodation in the reserve.
Further information: Thaba Nchu Sun Hotel and Casino, P O Box 114, Thaba Nchu 9780, tel (05265) 2161.

At Maria Moroka grassy slopes sweep down from the brooding heights of Thaba Nchu Mountain to the waters of Groothoek Dam.

FREE STATE

QWAQWA CONSERVATION AREA
Southwest of Harrismith

Map: page 343, 3E
From Harrismith take the N5 west to Bethlehem for 8 km, then turn left onto the tarred R712 to Phuthaditjhaba.
Accommodation: Eerstegeluk Farm Guesthouse in the QwaQwa National Park offers accommodation for 10 people in self-catering double rooms. Pony rides, golf, tennis, trout-fishing, game-viewing and bird-watching are offered. The Fika Patso Mountain Resort offers self-catering chalets. Restaurant and pub available, as well as conference facilities. The QwaQwa Hotel, P O Box 5581, Phuthaditjhaba 9866, tel (058) 713-0903, offers comfortable accommodation.
Further information: Witsieshoek Mountain Resort, Private Bag 828, Witsieshoek 9870, tel (058712) 5; Fika Patso Mountain Resort and Conference Centre, P O Box 17673, Witsieshoek 9870, tel (058) 789-1733/4; Tourist Information Centre, Division of Ecotourism, Highlands Development, Private Bag X826, Witsieshoek 9870, tel (058) 713-4444/713-0576; QwaQwa National Park, P O Box 403, Kestell 9860, tel (058652) 2102.

Splendid mountain vistas, forested ravines and undulating grasslands offer outdoor-lovers the holiday of a lifetime in the QwaQwa Conservation Area, 30 000 ha of some of the most picturesque parts of the country.

The world-famous Amphitheatre of the Drakensberg Mountains, spearheaded by the imposing Sentinel Peak, is one of the many drawcards in the area.

Bordered by the Royal Natal National Park in the east, Lesotho to the south, and the Free State to the west, the QwaQwa Conservation Area consists of mainly short grasslands, interspersed with ravines of yellowwood trees and tree ferns, and many species of protea.

Typically, most of the animals found here are mountain-living species such as grey rhebuck, mountain reedbuck, baboons and rock hyraxes.

The many bird varieties include jackal buzzards, rock kestrels, black harriers, white-necked ravens, black crows, scarce bearded vultures (lammergeiers), Cape vultures, black eagles, bald ibises and wattled cranes.

A variety of aquatic birds breeds at the Fika Patso Dam in the Namahadi River, 17 km from Phuthaditjhaba, the capital of QwaQwa. The Swartwater Dam southeast of Phuthaditjhaba is a trout-fisherman's dream. You can get fishing permits from the Tourist Information Centre in Phuthaditjhaba.

QwaQwa offers a number of marvellous hiking trails, such as the Metsi Matsho Hiking Trail, which starts and ends at the lovely Witsieshoek Mountain Resort, and affords spectacular vistas of parts of the KwaZulu-Natal and QwaQwa mountains on either side.

A base camp, 60 m from the Witsieshoek Mountain Resort (where you collect the key), sleeps 24, and has hot and cold water and toilet facilities. Trailists overnight in two thatched stone huts (some 13 km from the mountain resort)

Ficksburg's bounty from the earth

Ficksburg is a cornucopia that spills its riches across the country, and lures thousands of visitors annually to enjoy its ample bounty. Cherries, cling peaches, apricots and plums ripen in the balmy air of this eastern Free State town which nudges Lesotho and the majestic Maluti Mountains.

In the second week of November, Ficksburg residents take to the streets to celebrate nature's generosity with the famous annual cherry festival. This tradition has been celebrated by the locals for 20 years, and shared by visitors from around the world.

This, regarded as South Africa's largest and oldest harvest festival, has drawn an estimated 300 000 people to date.

There are street parades led by the beautiful Cherry Queen, groaning tables laden with speciality foods, fine wines and music. Tours are available to the cherry orchards and to the cherry research station some three kilometres outside the town.

If you want a still closer look at the intricacies of cherry production, you may visit the General J I J Fick Museum, a lovely building on the town square, made of local sandstone.

Currently, Ficksburg produces more than 90 percent of the country's cherry crop. In spring, there can be few sights more beautiful than the drifts of pale, moth-like blossoms swathing the town.

Summer comes a close second, however, when golden fields of maize ripple in the slightest breeze. In autumn trees dazzle with burnished foliage, and in winter the Malutis wear their glistening, frozen mantle.

Ficksburg is almost as well known for its asparagus as it is for the more decorative cherry. The area boasts two of the largest asparagus-canning factories in the country. Soil and climatic conditions are extremely favourable for the cultivation of this exotic crop, which is harvested and canned in spring and early summer, from September to December.

sleeping a total of 24 people. Toilets are available. Take your own gas stove.

The Sentinel Trail begins at the Sentinel Car Park, at an altitude of 2 540 metres. There are no overnight facilities on the plateau, so you'll have to bring a tent if you wish to spend the night. There is, however, a basic overnight hut at the Sentinel Car Park.

There are a number of walks in the vicinity of the Fika Patso Dam. These range from relaxing one- to two-hour rambles, to more strenuous two- to three-day hikes. Make sure you're in good physical condition before you embark on any of the overnight hikes. The Fika Patso Hiking Trail begins and ends near the Fika Patso Mountain Resort, where there is an overnight hut which is capable of accommodating 132 people.

The attractive Spelonken Trail in the QwaQwa National Park, adjoining the Golden Gate Highlands National Park, offers a pleasant two-day hike (27 km), and overnight accommodation at two restored farmhouses.

The Sterkfontein Dam Nature Reserve follows the gentle curves of the 19-km-long Sterkfontein Dam.

STERKFONTEIN DAM
Southwest of Harrismith

The Sterkfontein Dam near Harrismith has an important function – ensuring that the supply of water in the Vaal Dam is always equal to the demands made on it. It has several interesting features, including the second-largest earthen wall in the world.

The dam is 19 km long and six kilometres wide, with a maximum depth of 82 metres. At its highest point the dam wall is an impressive 93 m, and at full capacity the waters of the dam sprawl across 6 940 hectares.

It is encircled by the 4 530-ha Sterkfontein Dam Nature Reserve, which provides an ideal habitat for bearded and Cape vultures. Bushman paintings are to be seen at many places in the reserve.

The dam is an ideal venue for water-sport enthusiasts, and powerboating, yachting and water-skiing are all permitted here. Regular sailing regattas draw crowds of spectators to this scenic spot. In addition, the dam offers superb trout- and yellowfish-angling.

Permission may also be obtained to fish in several smaller dams and streams in the vicinity.

Neatly stacked bales of hay await collection beneath a dolerite-topped buttress near Harrismith.

Map: page 343, 3E
The Sterkfontein Dam lies 25 km southwest of Harrismith, off the Harrismith/Oliviershoek road.
Accommodation: Ten self-catering chalets, a farmhouse and a caravan park with ablution and laundry facilities are available, and camping is permitted on the water's edge. Facilities for boaters include slipways, boathouses and a clubhouse. Hotels in Harrismith include the Grand National Hotel, Warden Street, Harrismith 9880, tel (05861) 2-1060; Holiday Inn Garden Court, P O Box 363, Harrismith 9880, tel (05861) 2-1011; and Sir Harry Motel, P O Box 100, Harrismith 9880, tel (05861) 2-2151.
Further information: The Nature Conservation Officer, Sterkfontein Dam Nature Reserve, P O Box 24, Harrismith 9880, tel (05861) 2-3520; The Town Clerk, P O Box 43, Harrismith 9880, tel (05861) 2-1061.

FREE STATE

WILLEM PRETORIUS GAME RESERVE
Winburg

Map: page 343, 3D
From the N1 take the turn-off to the east, 32 km north of Winburg. The Willem Pretorius Game Reserve is located 9 km along this road. It lies to the east of the N1, on the trunk road between Ventersburg and Winburg, 17 km from Ventersburg.

Details: Aventura Aldam has a supermarket for essential supplies, a licensed restaurant and a spacious recreation hall. Fuel available. Swimming pool, tennis courts, bowling green, trampoline, nine-hole golf course available.

Accommodation: Choice of fully equipped rondavels, family cottages or luxury flats. Take extra blankets in winter. Luxury rondavels and flats have own cooking utensils, crockery, cutlery. Cooking facilities and ablution blocks for campers. The Education Centre offers 10 luxury chalets, a hall and conference centre, restaurant, shop, swimming pool, tennis court and caravan sites.

Further information: The Resort Manager, Aventura Aldam, Private Bag X06, Ventersburg 9450, tel (05777) 4077; The Manager, Education Centre, Private Bag X07, Ventersburg 9450, tel (05777) 4003/4.

The Willem Pretorius Game Reserve is regarded as the Free State's prime reserve. Named after Senator Willem Pretorius, of the Free State Executive Committee, who played a pivotal role in its development, the reserve lies in the verdant central Free State grassland area, at the summit of the Doringberg.

The dense vegetation and grassy flats provide an excellent habitat for the indigenous animals that have been painstakingly reintroduced to the area over a period of years. These include large numbers of springbok, black wildebeest, white rhinos, zebras, giraffes, blesbok, buffaloes and impala. The terrain is broken in the north by the Doringberg range, where densely wooded ravines, crisscrossed by watercourses, teem with inquisitive baboons.

The Aventura Aldam public resort is situated on a koppie on the western side of the reserve, and there is a small rest camp and education centre just across the dam, run by the local Department of Nature Conservation.

At maximum capacity, the dam covers 2 771 of the reserve's 12 005 hectares.

Fishing is permitted, and offers the opportunity to land carp, Orange River mudfish, sharp-toothed catfish and yellowfish. A Free State angling licence may be obtained from the resort office. Fishing is limited to the demarcated area. Other watersports include sailing, canoeing and water-skiing.

Martial eagles and fish eagles breed in the protection of the reserve. Other species among the 200 bird species here include herons, Egyptian geese, owls, ibises, cranes and cormorants.

Thirteen kilometres from the resort, next to the N1, is a monument which commemorates the signing of the Sand River Convention on 16 January 1852, whereby the Transvaal was eventually granted independence.

The white rhino is a gentle giant, preferring to amble off rather than confront danger.

Eland graze contentedly on the grassy banks of the Allemanskraal Dam at the Willem Pretorius Game Reserve.

LESOTHO

CENTRAL HIGHLANDS SCENIC DRIVE
Maseru to Thaba Tseka

Map: page 353, 3B/C/D

Accommodation: Old Toll House offers caravan and camping sites, and a refreshment kiosk. Other accommodation includes: Molimo Nthuse Mountain Lodge (60km from Maseru), P O Box 212, Maseru 100, tel 31-2922; Senqunyane Lodge (at Marakabei), P O Box 7423, Maseru 100, tel 31-2601, is fully licensed. Cooking facilities provided (bring your own food). Swimming, horse-riding, fishing. At Thaba Tseka contact The Accommodations Registrar, Agricultural Training Centre, P O Box 125, Thaba Tseka, tel 90-0304.

Further information: Lesotho Tourist Board, P O Box 1378, Maseru 100, tel 31-2896.

A seemingly endless rumble-tumble of dark mountain ridges stretches to the horizon as you take the roller-coaster ride along Lesotho's Central Highlands Scenic Drive.

Here stately pinnacles of rock, like the spires of some ancient cathedral, reach skyward, accentuating the grandeur of this mountain kingdom.

A rich legacy of rock art lies in the caves and other craggy shelters – the only reminder that this used to be the kingdom of the San (Bushmen) who once roamed freely between the rocky turrets. There's also a fascinating bounty of fossil remains, which suggests that dinosaurs lived here thousands of years ago.

From Maseru – the capital and principal town of Lesotho – you take the road to Mafeteng, where a memorial commemorates soldiers of the Cape Mounted Rifles who fell here during the Gun War of 1880. After some 14 km turn left for Roma and Thaba Tseka. From this point on the lowlands you look east towards the distant Maluti Mountain range – its mist-shrouded peaks inviting exploration.

You drive through farmlands and simple homes scattered higgledy-pig-gledy among the foothills, then turn left at a signpost for Thaba Tseka – some 30 km from Maseru. Here the road starts its steep ascent, and the montane panorama unfolds, dominated by the 2 884-m-high Machache Peak.

Nine kilometres later you pass a signposted road leading to the Ha Baroana (Ha Khotso) rock paintings *(see separate entry)*. Shortly afterwards you pass through Ha Ntsi, home of the local breweries, and the Old Toll House, where a small caravan and camping site, and kiosk, offer weary travellers a chance to relax and refresh themselves.

From this point you start the ascent of Bushmen's Pass, the first (and the lowest) of six spectacular passes that wind through the Maluti Mountain range to Thaba Tseka. Bird-watchers should take their binoculars out here: resident bird species include rock jumpers, ground woodpeckers, malachite sunbirds and bearded vultures or lammergeiers.

The road winds gently through rugged terrain to the very summit of the pass (2 268 m), then descends steeply to the east of the first range, to a lush valley watered by the willow-lined Makhaleng

Sparkling and rippling below hazy hills, the Senqunyane, or Little Orange, River separates the Maseru and Thaba Tseka districts.

River. Be sure to drive carefully along this section, and be particularly alert on the blind corners.

After a further three kilometres you reach the Molimo Nthuse ('God help me') Mountain Lodge. Huddled in a swathe of greenery alongside a cascading stream, the lodge's restaurant overlooks the road, and offers a magnificent view across the Makhaleng River Valley.

Climbing steeply, the road now winds up the Molimo Nthuse Pass, its summit marked by a small pyramid peak. Here the tarred road ends, and extra care must be taken on the gravel. The Basotho Pony Project, which offers various trails into the mountains on sturdy Basotho ponies, has its headquarters here.

The road drops sharply into another fairly long, willow-lined valley (the road surface changes to tar again here) before it starts winding its way up the Blue Mountain Pass, penetrating scenery that becomes more dramatic and stark with every bend encountered.

Sparsely grassed hills and gaunt, basalt rock faces, blanketed thickly with snow during the winter (May to July), strain towards the sky, their gorges and valleys deeply shaded. Stop at the windy summit of the pass (2 634 m) for superior views of soaring peaks and magical, misty valleys. The tar ends here, although particularly steep sections further on have been tarred for safety purposes.

The road now follows the curves and gulleys for some 12 km before dropping sharply to pass the rural mud-and-stone settlement of Likalaneng, perched on a rocky outcrop whose surrounding countryside has been ravaged by soil erosion. Here you may be startled to see a number of luridly coloured coffins, ranging from pink and red to brilliant lime green, upended against a shop wall. The Basotho apparently like a vivid coffin to brighten the darkness of their burial ground.

A bridge announces the start of the Likalaneng Pass, piercing mountainsides that are covered in summer with red-hot pokers, their petals ablaze in the rarefied mountain air.

From the summit (2 620 m) the road falls gradually to the Senqunyane (Little Orange) Valley, and the small village of Marakabei (food and fuel available). Senqunyane Lodge lies two kilometres further on, and offers comfortable accommodation for a maximum of 10 people.

Cross the seven-span bridge over the Senqunyane River, and begin the almost sheer climb (700 m in nine kilometres) to the summit of Cheche's Pass (2 560 m), which reveals yet another vista of endless misty mountains rolling towards the horizon. Not for nothing is Lesotho called the 'Mountain Kingdom'!

You descend through a narrow valley to reach Mantsonyane, which has two shops (fuel available). From Mantsonyane the road becomes a narrow track, descending over a bridge, and crisscrossing a series of valleys, before climbing to the tiny hamlet of Ha Letuka.

For four kilometres the road climbs once more to reach the flat moorland of the Maluti's central range, used by the locals for summer grazing. This is a lonely and remote stretch, culminating in the Mokhoabong Pass (2 860 metres). Winters here are bitter, but the days are generally sunny, and you should have uninterrupted views across the snow-blanketed peaks.

Leaving the summit behind, the road drops to the valley floor, reaching Thaba Tseka after some 23 kilometres.

Thaba Tseka, which was established in 1980 as the administrative centre for the central regions of Lesotho, is also the centre for a rural development project. There is no formal tourist accommodation here, but for a basic place to stay you may overnight in the Agricultural Training Centre, which has bunk beds, clean linen (on request) and kitchen facilities. You may also ask permission at the police station to camp in the small forest adjacent to the village.

Molimo Nthuse Mountain Lodge, with its thatched dining room and bar, perches on a verdant, forested slope overlooking the Makhaleng River Valley.

HA BAROANA CAVE
Maseru

Map: page 353, 3B
From Maseru follow the Roma road, and turn left onto Mountain Road after 25 kilometres. Continue for 14 km to reach the signpost to the rock paintings. A good gravel road leads 3 km to the village of Ha Khotso, and ends after a further 2,5 kilometres. From here you walk to the caves.
Details: Open 09h00-17h00. Entrance fee. Craft shop. Site museum.
Accommodation: Nearest accommodation is the camping site at Old Toll House. Contact Lesotho Hotels, P O Box 212, Maseru 100, tel 31-2922; or try the Molimo Nthuse Mountain Lodge (P O Box 212, Maseru 100, tel 37-0211). More sophisticated lodgings may be found in Maseru, including the luxurious Lesotho Sun Hotel and Casino, Private Bag A68, Maseru 100, tel 31-3111.
Further information: Lesotho Tourist Board, P O Box 1378, Maseru 100, tel 31-2896.

Across the length and breadth of Lesotho are relics of the San (Bushman) people, whose existence can be traced back about 50 000 years. They lived among the rocks and caves, recording with remarkable precision their daily lives in hues derived from nature. Soils, clay, plants and even blood from the animals they killed were used to colour their work. Scenes depicted illustrate hunting expeditions, battles and dances.

By far the largest gallery of San rock paintings is at Ha Khotso, some 46 km east of Maseru. A footpath winds down to the curator's hut where tickets to enter the caves may be purchased.

You will be given a guided tour of the rock paintings. There are drawings of the hunt – one showing a lioness, just pierced by the deadly tip of an arrow, and her triumphant hunter. There are also illustrations of people in huts, and of dancers. Human figures, their legs decorated with white markings, share the rock walls with an assembly of wild animals, including such species as eland, lions, hartebeest, leopards, guinea fowl and blue cranes, all indicative of the wide variety of wildlife that once lived in the region.

Ha Khotso, also known as Ha Baroana, is a national heritage site, which falls under the auspices of the Protection and Preservation Commission of the Government of Lesotho. Unfortunately, passing tourists have had little respect for this national treasure, but you can still feel the presence of the yellow-skinned people who lived there thousands of years ago.

LE BIHAN FALLS
Semonkong

Map: page 353, 4C
Semonkong lies 113 km from Maseru, with access to the falls on horseback. The road is suitable only for the more rugged family car. Alternatively, you can fly to a nearby airstrip from Maseru (a 30-minute trip), and then ride 4 km to the falls.
Accommodation: Semonkong Lodge is self-catering, and has hot and cold water, bedding, linen, crockery, cutlery and cooking equipment.
Further information: Semonkong Lodge, P O Box 243, Ficksburg 9730, tel (05192) 2730/3106; The Manager, Fraser Lodge System, P O Box 5, Maseru 100, tel 32-2601; Lesotho Tourist Board, P O Box 1378, Maseru 100, tel 31-2896.

The harsh call of the bearded vulture is the only sound that punctuates the roar of the Le Bihan Falls as they plunge over the edge of a cliff into a frothy pool at the base of a rugged and shady ravine.

For many years the San regarded the falls as their own secret place, but later it was visited regularly by the Basotho people. The first European to visit the falls was Father Le Bihan, a French missionary who stumbled across them in 1881. These falls are the highest in southern Africa, tumbling a sheer 192 m into the pool below. They are also called the Maletsunyane Falls, after the river that flows above them, and are best seen after the summer rains.

On the Maletsunyane's banks is the self-catering Semonkong Lodge, which provides horses for those wishing to visit the falls. If you enjoy hiking, take the two-hour trip to the top of the falls, or the trip to the bottom of the gorge to see the falls and their rainbow brightening the deeply eroded cliffs.

Not far from the waterfall, and on the mountains to the west of Semonkong ('place of smoke'), you can see the rare and lovely spiral aloes which are endemic to this region.

Majestic and mighty, the Le Bihan Falls are a splendid sight as they tumble over a sheer cliff into a deep pool below.

LESOTHO HORSE TRAILS
Maseru

With its myriad shady gorges, sheer mountain peaks and winter blanket of snow, Lesotho is a land that is not always kind to motorized vehicles. But there is an exceptionally good alternative – the tough mountain pony, which is such an efficient climber that it can reach isolated mountain villages inaccessible to any other vehicle.

The Basotho pony is a sturdy little creature descended from the Indonesian horses that were originally imported to the Cape in the early years of the 19th century. Interbreeding with Arab stallions (imported for stud purposes) provided these strong, sure-footed ponies with a number of extraordinary qualities, among them the ability to withstand the harsh climate. Another quality is the pony's sweet-tempered and reliable nature.

There are two main centres from which pony treks begin: the Basotho Pony Trekking Centre, 60 km east of Maseru, at the summit of the Molimo Nthuse Pass; and the Matelile Pony Owners' Association in the Mafeteng district, some 80 km south of Maseru. Both offer treks that vary in length and difficulty, ranging from one-hour jaunts for the faint-hearted, to hardy seven-day excursions into the mountains, sleeping in Basotho villages at night.

From the Basotho Pony Trekking Centre you can visit the Leboela Falls (two hours) and the Qiloane Falls (four hours). Alternatively, you can take the seven-day trek southwards, through sheep and goat country to the mighty Maletsunyane, or Le Bihan, Falls *(see separate entry)*.

Two annual events that take place from the Basotho Pony Trekking Centre in May are the Triple Race and the Endurance Race – both of which attract farmers from all over Lesotho.

From the Matelile Pony Owners' Association Centre, pony treks include a four-hour trip to the Botsoela Falls, a two-day excursion to the Ribaneng Falls in the Thaba Putsoa Mountains, and a special four-day outing that takes in some of Lesotho's wonderful waterfalls at Ribaneng, Ketane and Le Bihan.

There are stops along the way to see San paintings, swim in rock pools, and to visit local villages. You overnight in Basotho rondavels, and your pony takes you through breathtaking passes and areas so remote that you may see no-one but the odd shepherd for hours on end. Here in the mountains the silence is intense, broken only by the clip-clopping of the horses, the barking of an inquisitive troop of baboons, or the screech of a lammergeier soaring above the cliffs.

Various pony trails are also offered by Semonkong Lodge and Malealea Lodge. From Semonkong you can explore the Maluti Mountains, and visit the Le Bihan Falls, trot around the small but bustling village of Semonkong, or follow a two-day course that winds along Lesotho's rutted roads and bridle paths to reach the remote Ketane Falls, where you camp overnight (food provided).

Malealea Lodge is the base for treks lasting from one hour to six days. Basic accommodation in huts is provided for the longer trails.

No experience is necessary to embark on a pony adventure, but be sure to remember that the terrain is rugged, and the facilities are few and far between. The intimacy of viewing Lesotho from the back of a horse is unforgettable, and well worth your courage! Remember also to ask permission before taking photographs, and you may be expected to tip. Do not photograph government and military buildings.

Map: page 353, 3B
The Basotho Pony Trekking Centre is at the summit of the Molimo Nthuse Pass. From Maseru follow the road east into the Maluti Mountains – the centre is some 60 km from the capital. Matelile Pony Owners' Association has its premises 84 km southeast of Maseru. Follow the main road south to Motsekuoa, and turn left for Ha Seeiso and Malealea. The first 50 km are tarred.
Details: Guides are optional on all trails offered. Most tours cater for a minimum of three persons, and a maximum of thirty.
Accommodation: Malealea Lodge has comfortable rooms, some *en suite*, with their own kitchens, and others sharing communal kitchens. There are also six rondavels and a large dormitory with ablution blocks and kitchen facilities. A large recreational/dining room caters for group bookings. Contact Malealea Lodge, P O Makhakhe, Lesotho 922, tel 78-5727/78-5336/78-5264. Semonkong Lodge has self-catering cottages, a bar and a restaurant. Book at P O Box 243, Ficksburg 9730, tel (05192) 2730/3106.
Further information: Basotho Pony Trekking Centre, P O Box 1027, Maseru 100, tel 31-4165; Matelile Pony Owners' Association, c/o Lesotho Tourist Board, P O Box 1378, Maseru 100, tel 31-2896; The Manager, Fraser Lodge System, P O Box 5, Maseru 100, tel 32-2601.

Sure-footed Basotho ponies ease their way across a shallow stream in the mountains of Lesotho.

MOKHOTLONG VILLAGE
Eastern Lesotho

Map: page 353, 3E
From Maseru drive northeast to Butha Buthe (124 km). Continue along the Roof of Africa Drive, following the main road to Mokhotlong (182 km from Butha Buthe).
Details: Bring your own food if you intend staying at the mountaineers' chalet (wine and beer available there).
Accommodation: The Senqu Hotel (P O Box 23, Mokhotlong, tel 92-0330) offers *en suite* accommodation and two bars; the Sani Top Chalet (sleeps 22) is located 8 km on the Lesotho side of the Sani Pass. The chalet has a dining area, hot showers, bedding, shop nearby.
Further information: Himeville Arms Hotel, P O Box 105, Himeville 4585, tel (033) 702-1303, or (033) 702-1305; Lesotho Tourist Board, P O Box 1378, Maseru 100, tel 31-2896.

With the dubious reputation of being the driest, coldest and most remote place in the whole of Lesotho, Mokhotlong is situated in the east, in a valley dominated by Thabana Ntlenyana which, at a height of 3 482 m, is southern Africa's highest 'beautiful little mountain'.

The town originated as a police post in 1905, and for many years was accessible only after several days on horseback from KwaZulu-Natal via the Sani Pass, some 56 km to the southeast. In spite of this, the town grew and became an administrative centre, with goods and materials transported in by packs of donkeys and ponies. One district commissioner even had his wife's beloved piano transported across the Sani Pass by bearers, who then had to repeat the process when his spell of duty was complete.

Radio links were established with Maseru shortly after World War II and, in 1948, an airstrip was built. Roads link it with Butha Buthe to the north, and KwaZulu-Natal to the east. The precipitous road to the Sani Pass is, however, accessible only on horseback, on foot or by four-wheel-drive vehicle.

Mokhotlong means 'place of the bald ibis', its name taken from the greenish, red-headed bird that may still be spotted along the trout-filled Mokhotlong River.

There is a wild and woolly atmosphere about this frontier town, which now has some 75 000 residents. Shops, government offices and a hospital cater for the needs of the villagers, and nearby is the small hamlet of Salang, where King Moshoeshoe II was born in 1938.

The area is excellent for climbing, skiing and walking. A two-day hike leads to the Sani Pass. There are no facilities along the way, and the going is rugged, but the local villagers will usually help you stay on the right path. At the summit of the pass (2 860 m) a chalet offers respite for the foot-weary hiker. Less energetic people can walk along the willow-clad banks of the river which winds between steep cliffs.

The age-old excellence of Lesotho crafts

In common with most other African races, the people of Lesotho are talented and experienced crafters, fashioning a wide variety of clothing, utensils and novelties from the materials readily available to them.

Vividly coloured rugs rub shoulders with mohair shawls and intricately crafted jerseys, while local basketwork and leather goods are hard to beat. Craft centres have been established in many of the towns and villages to ward off the ever present threat of poverty, and many of these operate on a co-operative system, where workers can pool their resources and knowledge, and sell their wares.

In the frozen depths of winter, when the remotest parts of the kingdom are severed from civilization by snow, the village women spin the raw, untreated wool of their sheep and goats, and create intricate jerseys, cardigans and shawls, which are then sold in spring.

More sophisticated knitwear is found in the larger centres. Outlets include Mohair Cottage at the Maseru Sun Cabanas, Lesotho Hand Knits, 75 km north of Maseru, and Butha Buthe Woollen Factory, P O Box 433, Butha Buthe, tel 46-0638.

Fine weaving is another distinctive Lesotho trademark. Originally created to help withstand the icy mountain temperatures, the bright blankets are a distinctive feature of many Lesotho wardrobes. Handcrafted mohair and woollen rugs, tapestries, wall hangings and carpets are popular – and long-lasting – mementos of a trip to the kingdom. At Thorkild Handweaving in Maseru you can watch the weavers work from the design stage through to dyeing and weaving. Mohair Cottage in Maseru also produces a variety of handwoven curtains, blankets and rugs.

Another weaving centre worth a visit is Helang Basali Crafts at the St Agnes Mission at Teyateyaneng, 40 km north of Maseru. Open seven days a week, this interesting centre sells colourful rugs and decorative tapestries.

Basotho grasswork is highly intricate and masterly. The conical hat can be bought from street hawkers, as well as from curio shops. The Basotho Hat Curio Shop (P O Box 148, Maseru 100, tel 32-2458) is built in the shape of its namesake, and offers a wide range of grasswork, from baskets and place mats, to floor mats and flower holders.

Traditional jewellery, once made of clay, copper and beads, is difficult to find, now that westernization has seduced the locals with metallic ornamentation. But in the more remote areas in the southeast you may stumble across ethnic necklaces and bracelets on sale in a rural village. A very popular drawcard for visitors is Beadazzled Jewellery at Kolonyama, where traditional beads are crafted into intricate ethnic and modern necklaces and bracelets.

Remember that prices in the major centres are higher than those in the outlying regions. Haggling is not permissible in the city centres, but quite acceptable in country villages.

In the more mountainous regions you may be able to trade warm clothing for traditional Basotho trinkets – with both buyer and seller making a useful deal. Happy trading!

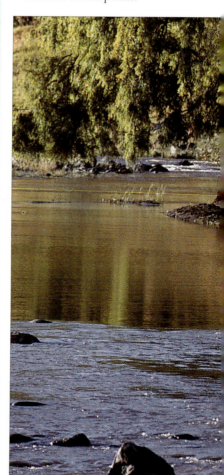

ROOF OF AFRICA DRIVE
Butha Buthe to Sani Pass

Curving and climbing in a series of loops and bends, with a new and breathtaking view unfolding around each corner as you ascend the Maluti Mountains, the Roof of Africa road is the setting for one of the most demanding – and dizzying – motor rallies in Africa.

Here rally drivers pit their skill and endurance in an annual race that starts at Butha Buthe, and zigzags dizzily to finish at the Sani Pass.

Your journey also starts at Butha Buthe, 124 km north of Maseru. Leaving the town, you travel southeastwards across the basalt plateau until, after 15 km, you reach a junction at the village of Ha Marakabei. Continue straight, following the lush green Hololo River. Eight kilometres further on the scenery starts to change, with the rocky massif looming ahead. The peak of Khatibe (2 750 m) rises sharply above the plains.

You wind gently through the rural Hololo Valley, tracing the river's path through poplar groves and beneath rocky outcrops, then loop and weave around hilly slopes to the head of the valley.

At this point the road begins to climb. With the mountain slopes starting to close in around you, you eventually reach the Roof of Africa, and, from this point onwards, your altitude never drops below 2 000 metres.

Some 57 km after Butha Buthe you reach the summit of Moteng Pass, at 2 840 m a spectacular rocky sight. This is the first and the lowest of the passes you cross on the route. However, the road has been improved to allow bus services to Mokhotlong and, if your vehicle has good ground clearance, it is possible to travel to Sani Pass.

The road then drops gently into the Tsehlanyane Valley where the locals make their living by selling beer to passing travellers. You now negotiate the hillside above the 'Oxbow' – a steep-sided loop in the Malibamatso River, and the location of the New Oxbow Lodge (192 km from Maseru; the tar ends here). Nearby, below the confluence of the Malibamatso and the Tsehlanyane rivers, is the site of the mammoth Lesotho Highlands Water Project which, on its intended completion in 2019, will 'ensure a continuous flow of water from Lesotho into South Africa's industrial heartland'.

Leaving the valley behind, you now ascend to the summit of the Mahlasela Pass, passing on the way the Club

Map: page 353, 1D/E, 2E, 3E/F, 4F
The Roof of Africa drive is from Butha Buthe to Sani Pass.
Details: Skiing, hiking, riding, fishing and swimming are popular pursuits in this part of Lesotho.
Accommodation: Butha Buthe has 2 hotels: Moteng Lodge, P O Box 526, Butha Buthe, tel 46-0350; and Crocodile Inn, P O Box 72, Butha Buthe, tel 46-0223. Alternatively, try the New Oxbow Lodge, P O Box 43, Maputsoe, tel Ficksburg (05192) 2247/3434. The Sani Top Chalet sleeps 22 in bunk beds. Hot showers available.
Further information: Sani Top Chalet: Himeville Arms Hotel, P O Box 105, Himeville 4585, tel (033) 702-1303/5; Lesotho Tourist Board, P O Box 1378, Maseru 100, tel 31-2896.

A lone horseman crosses the Senqu River near Mokhotlong. The Basotho pony is well adapted to cope with the sudden storms and regular snowfalls that occur here.

Maluti Ski Chalet (accommodation at this chalet is for members only, non-members can arrange ski trips at the New Oxbow Lodge).

At 3 220 m, Mahlasela ('the place of the attackers') was once the site of red-hot feuds over mountain grazing rights. If you leave your car at the last drivable point, and attempt the breathless 100-m climb to the summit of the pass, you will be rewarded with a spectacular view of the surrounding plateau of the Roof of Africa.

All around are craggy peaks and mysterious valleys, bisected by streams that sparkle as they reflect the sun. Between May and October the mountains are covered by a mantle of crisp, white snow and, even during the summer months, a light dusting of snowflakes on the peaks is not uncommon.

Back on the road you loop and drop into the upper reaches of the Motete Valley, passing ski slopes. You then climb through the harsh mountain slopes of the Pass of Guns, at 3 240 m the scene of yet another grazing-rights battle. This pass is the boundary between the Butha Buthe and Mokhotlong districts.

Climbing still further above the valleys you reach Tlaeeng Pass (3 275 m), estimated to be the highest road pass in southern Africa, dramatically surrounded by bare mountain peaks and an icy, whistling wind.

You now descend in a series of loops and curves, passing an old diamond mine

Hikers often thread their way beneath the Three Bushmen peaks at Sehlabathebe National Park. The nights here can be dangerously cold for hikers.

Rock paintings – legacy of an ancient race

Decorating the maze of caves that crisscrosses the mountains of Lesotho is a magnificent gallery of rock paintings – their colours still vivid and clear – that records the existence and daily lives of the nomadic San who once roamed this mighty plateau.

Many years before the arrival of the Basotho, these nomadic people followed the roving animal populations in their search for food and clothing. They made their homes in caves and rocky overhangs, decorating the walls with illustrations of events that took place in their daily lives, ranging from the animals they saw and hunted with home-made bows and arrows, to dancing figures and traditional ceremonies.

The paints they used were often a combination of clays, soils, plant leaves and roots, water and even blood. Animals were a favourite topic for the artist, especially eland (the largest of the antelope), baboons and lions.

Hippopotamuses are also very skilfully portrayed – sometimes browsing, sometimes pursued by stealthy hunters. Fishing scenes are common, including one which features a hunter using a long, narrow spear aimed carefully from a canoe-shaped boat.

There are an estimated 5 000 rock-painting sites in Lesotho, but not all are accessible to the public. Finding one is indeed a most rewarding experience. The best-known and most visited site is the Ha Baroana Cave *(see separate entry)* which has a superb gallery of paintings.

It is believed that the paintings illustrate stories handed down from generation to generation around the evening fire. The artist was either a member of the clan, or a migratory painter, who specialized in recording events which were of special significance to the group.

Today these paintings survive to immortalize the lives of a plucky race who once lived among the peaks and in the valleys of Lesotho.

at Letseng-la-Terae, and the new De Beers-owned mine-workings on your left-hand side.

From here it is 73 km to Mokhotlong, as the road winds through villages and hamlets, with curious schoolchildren and amused locals watching your progress.

From Mokhotlong it is 56 km to the top of the Sani Pass, and 80 km to the first petrol station on the KwaZulu-Natal side of the pass. Difficult to negotiate at the best of times, this road is impassable in winter, when snowdrifts block the path to all but the most determined motorists.

SEHLABATHEBE NATIONAL PARK
Southeastern Lesotho

Bristling peaks surge skyward above the valley floor in the Sehlabathebe National Park, one of the highest and most remote in Africa. Stark and uncompromising, exposed to the elements, and far from any human settlement, its very isolation is a lure to nature-lovers and hikers seeking solitude on the high ground.

Covering some 7 500 ha, Sehlabathebe ('plateau of the shield') National Park lies in a valley in the eastern highlands of Lesotho, dominated by three peaks which are known by some as Baroa ba Bararo ('the Three Bushmen') or, more descriptively, 'the Devil's Knuckles'.

It was established in 1970 and is the only protected area in the kingdom. In 1974 a research station was established to study the flora and fauna of the area.

The park is always green, because of the summer mists. Natural sandstone arches and caves are found throughout the park, and there are several small lakes forming the headwaters of the Tsoelike River. The Tsoelike and the Leqooa rivers are home to an abundance of rainbow trout, as well as the *Oreodaimon qathlambae*, a tiny fish species.

Sehlabathebe Lodge sprawls at the base of the three peaks. From it you can walk at random along the plateau, dominated by the rugged peaks of the Drakensberg to the east. A gravel road leads northwest to northeast, fording tree-lined rivers that run between rocky outcrops dating back to the Triassic and Lower Jurassic ages.

You may climb the Three Bushmen, a steep ascent of four to five kilometres from the lodge, but well worth the effort for the magnificent views that unfold as you emerge above the early-morning mists that cloak the valley floor.

Look east across the hills and valleys to Bushman's Nek – the border post with KwaZulu-Natal. Snow is common here and the higher peaks are often dotted with white, long after the cold season has passed. Hikers must beware the flash floods that sometimes follow summer rains, hindering east-west progress through the park. Be on the lookout also for mountain adders, which temporarily blind their victims with a discharge of neurotoxic venom.

Although there is not an abundance of wildlife, you may see an occasional troop of baboons – the babies hitching a ride on their mothers' furry backs. Other animals include grey rhebok, oribi, eland and wild cats. The peaks and gulleys are home to a variety of mountain birds, and the cries of rock kestrels, jackal buzzards and black eagles may be heard echoing from the cliffs. You may even be lucky enough to spot the rare lammergeier.

Near the park headquarters in the west, and linked by a nine-kilometre gravel road to the lodge, is a shelter with more than 130 San paintings depicting hunting scenes, tribal rituals and events from daily life.

Once back at the lodge after a day in the crisp mountain air, you can spend the chilly evenings around a crackling log fire, with gas lamps adding a friendly hiss to the cosy atmosphere.

Map: page 353, 4E/F
The park lies 500 km southeast of Maseru. You can reach it by road in about 2 days. The route from Bushman's Nek in KwaZulu-Natal can be made in 5 to 6 hours on foot or horseback (bring a passport). Arrangements can be made for a guide to meet you at Bushman's Nek. Alternatively, a 1-hour flight from Maseru lands at a small airstrip at Ha Paulus, 12 km from the entrance to the park.

Details: Nights bitterly cold, with storms common all year. No fuel available – the nearest is at Qacha's Nek, 105 km to the southwest. Only cash payments accepted in park.

Accommodation: Sehlabathebe Lodge accommodates 12 self-catering visitors. Communal ablution facilities and bedding provided, but bring your own food. A small hostel near the lodge sleeps 6 people, and has water and cooking facilities. Booking recommended, but people are never turned away. Camp anywhere in the park.

Further information: Sehlabathebe Reservations, Lesotho National Park, Ministry of Agriculture, P O Box 92, Maseru 100, tel 32-3600/32-2876.

Almost indiscernible from its surroundings, a rock lizard creeps out of its shelter to sun itself at Sehlabathebe National Park.

The Basotho blanket is the best protection against icy winds that blow down the mountains.

THABA BOSIU HIGHLANDS
East of Maseru

Map: page 353, 3B
Thaba Bosiu is 29 km east of Maseru. Follow the main road to Roma, and turn left at Makhalanyane's Store, 19 km from Maseru. Continue straight until you reach Thaba Bosiu Mission.
Details: You must hire a guide from the Tourist Information Centre in Thaba Bosiu to visit the mountain. Most people visit Thaba Bosiu from Maseru.
Accommodation: Lesotho Sun Hotel, Private Bag A68, Maseru 100, tel 31-3111; Maseru Sun Cabanas, Private Bag A84, Maseru 100, tel 31-2434 or (011) 783-8660; Melesi Lodge at Thaba Bosiu (P O Box 2039, Maseru 100, tel 35-7215/6 or 31-4033).
Further information: Lesotho Tourist Board, P O Box 1378, Maseru 100, tel 31-2896/32-3760.

This mighty mountain, looming silently above the surrounding plateau, gives no hint of the volatile events that took place there early in the 19th century, events that heralded the birth of the Basotho nation.

In the 1820s, in an attempt to consolidate and increase the size of his empire, the Zulu king, Shaka, began a series of attacks on clans living to the east of the Drakensberg range.

The Amahlubi, caught in the path of this onslaught, fled west into the area now known as the Free State, just to the north of Lesotho. For want of food they were forced to turn to cannibalism – commemorated in the name Malimong ('place of cannibals') given to the myriad rock shelters that pepper Lesotho.

The principal chiefs of Lesotho fled to the mountains to escape the marauding parties, and created almost impenetrable fortresses from their very steep heights. Moshoeshoe first occupied the buttress of Butha Buthe but, after being the target of constant harassment, moved southwards to Thaba Bosiu.

Aeons of erosion had worn away its summit, but the flat-topped, sheer landmark was watered by no less than 11 springs, and was ideal for grazing.

On the very night of their arrival, Moshoeshoe's warriors erected a stone wall across the steep entrance pass to the summit, and its remains can still be seen today. Moshoeshoe called his new home Thaba Bosiu, the 'mountain of night', because he and his people arrived in the evening and spent the night strengthening its fortifications.

Until his death in 1870, Moshoeshoe and his warriors repelled a number of attacks, including those of surrounding clans and, later in the 1850s, even attacks from British forces which tried to overthrow the warrior king.

Between 1865 and 1868 Boer forces, lured by the promise of lands owned by Moshoeshoe, attempted to scale the fortress. But their attempts ended in disaster when one of their senior leaders, Commandant Wepener, was killed from a vantage point on a pass known as the 'route of the brave'. His final resting place is still marked.

On the flower-dotted summit your guide will explain the layout of the fortress, and you will be invited to say a prayer to the great king. A tumble of ruins can be seen, including Moshoeshoe's burial-site, and his spirit is said to linger on the summit overlooking the plains below, where he once held such sway. There are clear views from all sides – note especially the Qiloane (Pinnacle), which stands sentinel over Moshoeshoe's mountain fortress.

The magical Maluti Mountains dip and roll into the distance in a series of irregular ridges. Three-quarters of Lesotho is covered by mountains.

SWAZILAND

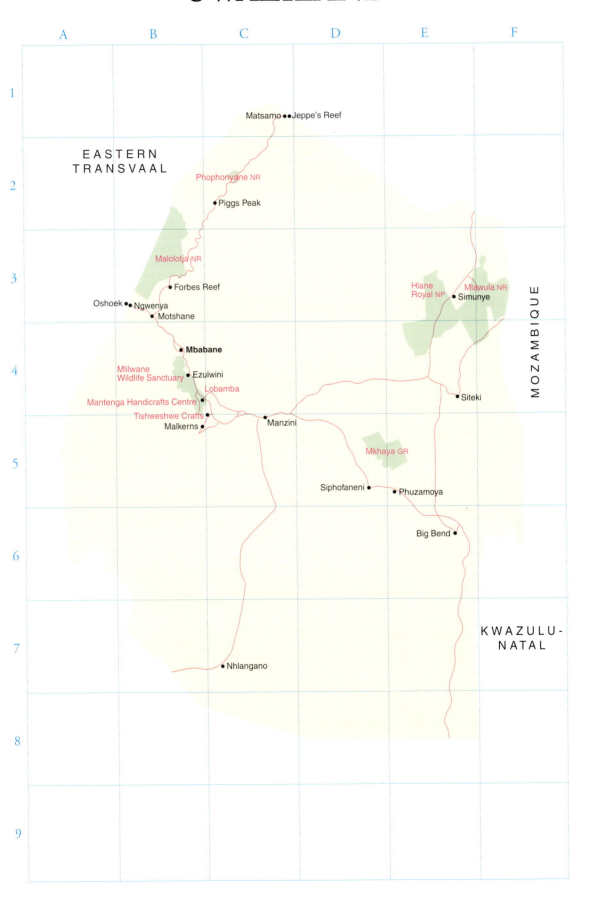

SWAZILAND

HLANE ROYAL NATIONAL PARK
Eastern Swaziland

Map: page 363, 3/4E
From Manzini, take the main tarred road east to Simunye, and follow the Hlane signposts from there. The park is situated 67 km from Manzini.
Details: Gates open sunrise to sunset throughout the year. Day-visitors are welcome. The park is strictly self-catering. The nearest shop is 10 km from the Ndlovu gate. This is a malaria area, so take precautions, as well as supplies of insect repellant. Game-walks with a ranger may be arranged.
Accommodation: In addition to the two rest camps, there are camping/caravanning facilities at Ndlovu Rest Camp.
Further information: Hlane Royal National Park, Central Reservations Office, P O Box 234, Mbabane, tel (09268) 4-8613/4 or 6-1591/2/3 (after hours).

Elephants crash through the bush, and the more silent hunters of the night scuffle through the undergrowth just metres from your chalet in Hlane Royal National Park.

This 30 000-ha sanctuary – the largest in Swaziland, and home to the greatest herds of game in the kingdom – is the king's very own park. It was at the instigation of King Sobhuza II, who was so inspired by the success of the newly formed Mlilwane Wildlife Sanctuary near Mbabane, that this park was established. Today his son, Mswati III, personally oversees its affairs.

The park is home to a teeming world of animals, notably lions, white rhinos, warthogs, impala, kudu, nyala, waterbuck and some of the country's largest herds of wildebeest and zebras. Hlane also serves as a refuge for the world's most southerly colony of marabou storks.

The dense bush and low shrubland at Hlane (the Swazi word for wilderness) attract a splendid variety of bird life, including such species as lilac-breasted rollers, glossy starlings, shrikes, hornbills and the country's biggest population of vultures. Ostriches brazenly stroll into the camp, entrancing you with their preening and sinuous dancing.

A marabou stork on its twig nest at Hlane, home of the most southerly nesting colony of these ungainly birds.

Culling is illegal in this vast reserve, which straddles the main road that runs from the town of Siteki to Mhlume, *en route* to Mozambique.

In the 1960s some of Hlane's animals, including zebras, blue wildebeest and impala, were used to stock Mlilwane Wildlife Sanctuary, which had been the victim of senseless poaching. Today the favour has been returned – Mlilwane game has been used to restock Hlane.

Other attractions within the reserve include the beautiful Mtfombotsi Forest, home to trees more than 1 000 years old, the hippo colony at Mahlindza, and Hunter's Rock, where King Sobhuza II saw his last lion.

A network of roads crisscrosses the reserve, and visitors are encouraged to follow these self-guided trails, using maps provided at the gate.

The condition of the roads deteriorates after heavy rains, and can be difficult to negotiate at these times.

Hlane is the perfect refuge for those people looking for a peaceful wilderness interlude – the two rest camps are small, and provide secluded and comfortable accommodation.

Ndlovu Rest Camp has two rondavels with ablution facilities. Bhubesi Rest Camp, overlooking the Mbuluzi River, offers three self-contained cottages, each with two bedrooms and a shady verandah leading onto a footpath which takes you to the water's edge.

LOBAMBA
Royal Village, Mbabane

Map: page 363, 4B
From Mbabane follow the main road east into the Ezulwini Valley. Lobamba lies about 20 km from Mbabane.
Details: Open daily 08h00-17h00. Guided tours of the museum and village are offered (book in advance).
Accommodation: There's a variety of accommodation in the Ezulwini Valley, ranging from the Royal Swazi Sun to motels and caravan/camping facilities. Hotel accommodation is also available in Mbabane itself.
Further information: Department of Tourism, Ministry of Broadcasting, Information and Tourism, P O Box 338, Mbabane, tel 4-4556; Southern African Regional Tourism Council (SARTOC), P O Box 600, Parklands 2121, tel (011) 788-0742. For museum tours contact The Curator, Swaziland National Museum, P O Box 100, Lobamba, tel 6-1151/6-1178 or 6-1179. Permission to photograph traditional ceremonies may be obtained from the Government Information Service, P O Box 338, Mbabane, tel 4-2761.

This village, the spiritual home of the Swazi nation for 150 years, is flanked by rolling green hills in the heart of the Ezulwini Valley. Clusters of beehive-shaped huts – the traditional shape favoured by the Swazis – form the home of the queen mother (Ndhlovukazi – 'the female elephant') and her attendants. She is an extremely influential person, sharing political authority with her son, the Swazi king (Ingwenyama – 'the lion'). While his powers are far-reaching within his territory, the queen mother controls her own regiments, and her kraal at Lobamba is regarded as inviolate – even to her son.

To the inexperienced eye the simple reed-encircled huts might seem humble, but this village is the pulse of the kingdom. It is the principal royal kraal, and the site of some of the most meaningful of the Swazi's traditional ceremonies. Here you can witness first-hand the colourful spectacle of the Ncwala or 'Festival of the First Fruits', held annually in December and January to renew the strength of the king and his nation for the coming year.

One of the Ncwala festival's highlights is a 40-km march by a group of young Swazi warriors to collect branches of the lusekwane shrub to build a bower for the king. The festival is a moving experience, with sacred songs, mystic rituals, dancing and jubilant feasting.

Visitors are allowed to witness parts of the ceremony, but photography and the recording of sacred rituals are prohibited.

The royal village also serves as a centre for the Umhlanga or Reed Dance, which takes place at the end of August or in early September. Here Swazi maidens gather at the queen mother's residence and set out in parties to gather reeds with which they later repair the windbreak around her homestead. The ceremony culminates in a beautiful, rhythmic 'reed dance', performed by the young maidens in their sumptuously designed costumes.

Near the royal village is the Swaziland National Museum, where you can trace the evolution of the art and craftsmanship of the Swazi people.

Displays here focus on Stone-Age implements, the history of the lavishly coloured traditional dress, and the richness of Swazi traditions and customs. Adjacent to the museum complex is an original Swazi homestead and cattle enclosure, the latter an intricately crafted, laced-wood wall.

Also in Lobamba are the impressive white-walled Houses of Parliament where you can follow proceedings from the public gallery. The buildings may be photographed (from the outside only).

Somhlolo Stadium is a very popular venue for local soccer matches, concerts and the rousing annual Independence Day celebrations.

The Embo State Palace at Lobamba, which is generally used as the official welcome centre for visiting dignitaries and statesmen, may not be approached or photographed without the proper official authorization.

The sacred Festival of the First Fruits

The most important festival of Swazi life is the Ncwala Festival of the First Fruits, which celebrates the arrival of the new harvest, and is intended to renew the strength of the king and his nation for the coming year.

Shrouded in time-honoured Swazi myth and legend, this moving festival is held at the end of December each year.

Swazi officials begin the event by visiting all the main rivers of Swaziland and then moving off to the nation's ancestral headquarters (near Maputo, on the shores of the Indian Ocean) to gather sea water.

As the new moon makes its appearance in the night sky, the water collectors return to the king's residence.

On arrival there they are commanded to march some 40 km to gather the branches of the lusekwane tree, with which they must return the following morning. Only then are the weary footsoldiers allowed to rest.

The next day the branches are used to build a boma (lodge) for the king. Officials and dignitaries arrive, bringing with them the water that has been gathered from the rivers and the sea. The king himself makes an appearance, and the festivities begin.

Ritual songs fill the air, an ox is slaughtered and the warriors begin to dance. A crescent of young men, the colours of their costumes bright against the red dust of the kraal, surge to and fro in waves, chanting their mysterious and magical songs.

On the fourth day, the entire Swazi army assembles in the royal kraal where they are inspected by their king. He leads them in a frenetic, foot-stomping dance.

Later, in the privacy of his boma, the king tastes the newly harvested fruit, signalling the official start of the harvest. The following day is set aside for peace and meditation.

On the final day of the ceremony the warriors march into the hills behind Lobamba where they collect firewood to be used for a huge sacrificial bonfire within the enclosure. They sing and dance around the flames, exhorting their ancestral spirits to send rain to extinguish the flames, and thereby show their favour for the coming year.

The ritual and traditional rites continue until their favour has been won. The Ncwala ends with singing, hand-clapping, dancing and a sumptuous feast.

Resplendent in their ceremonial finery, a Swazi couple prepare to celebrate Ncwala, the sacred Festival of the First Fruits.

MALOLOTJA NATURE RESERVE
Forbes Reef

Map: page 363, 3B
From Mbabane follow the main road northwest to the Ngwenya border post. At Motshane, about 15 km from Mbabane, turn onto the road to Piggs Peak. The entrance to the reserve is on the left, about 18 km from Motshane, and 35 km from Mbabane.

Details: The reserve is open 06h00-18h00 in summer, and 06h30-18h00 in winter. A number of self-guided backpacking trails, ranging from 2 to 7 days, are offered. Backpacking permits, brochures, maps, a hiking and backpacking guide, bird, mammal, amphibian and reptile and flora check lists are available at the reserve. Permits are not necessary for day-walks. Trout-fishing is allowed (a permit is needed).

Accommodation: There are 5 fully furnished log cabins, each sleeping 6 people. The main camp near the entrance has an A-frame hut sleeping 3 people, as well as camping facilities. There is an ablution block with hot and cold water. Bring your own food (shop at entrance). Facilities along the trails are basic. Camping sites have been cleared for a maximum of 2 or 3 small tents each, and only 1 group is booked into a camp at a time. A minimum of 2 and a maximum of 10 people may go on a trail at any time. Visits to the Ngwenya Mine and Lion Cavern must be booked in advance.

Further information: Bookings: Malolotja Nature Reserve, P O Box 100, Lobamba, tel 6-1151, 6-1178/9 or 6-1516; or The Senior Warden, Malolotja Nature Reserve, P O Box 1797, Mbabane, tel 4-3060.

Lush green mountain slopes, verdant river gorges, cascading waterfalls and sheer vertical cliffs combine to make Malolotja Nature Reserve, in the northwestern corner of Swaziland, a nature-lover's dream.

Regarded as one of the last unspoilt mountain wilderness areas in southern Africa, this remote sanctuary (just 35 km north of the Swazi capital, Mbabane) is reserved almost exclusively for hikers, who can savour the magnificence of its rugged beauty in solitude. Some 200 km of trails lead through countryside that ranges from cool, tree-lined valleys to precipitous mountain terrain.

The 18 000-ha reserve, situated in the Highveld along the South African border, was founded in 1972 by the Swaziland National Trust Commission, and was named after the 90-m-high Malolotja Falls – Swaziland's highest. The Nkomati River runs west to east through the reserve, leaving through an impressive gorge. Hikers wishing to explore the northern side of the gorge have to take to the water and ford the river.

Also worth seeing are the Mahulungwane Falls (to the northwest of the Malolotja Falls), the tree-fern-bedecked Mhlangamphepha Valley in the southwestern corner, and two of the highest peaks in Swaziland – Ngwenya (1 829 m) and Silotwane (1 680 metres).

Trails lead to the summit of these peaks which – once you have regained your breath – offer exceptional views of the dramatic scenery in the reserve.

There's no shortage of game in this magnificent reserve. You'll find leopards, servals, aardwolfs, oribi, red hartebeest, grey rhebok, mountain and common reedbuck, warthogs and bushpigs.

Herds of blesbok, blue wildebeest and zebras graze undisturbed in the lush grasslands. Malolotja is also home to more than 280 species of bird, including blue swallows, bald ibises, blue cranes and Stanley's bustards.

An attraction of a totally different kind is the old Ngwenya iron-ore mine and the Lion Cavern in the southwestern corner of the reserve. Haematite and specularite, minerals used for cosmetic and ritual purposes, were mined at Lion Cavern some 41 000 years ago, making it the world's oldest mine.

About 200 km of fascinating trails offer hikers a large variety of challenges: the terrain includes mountains and marshes, riverine forests and open grasslands, and bare outcrops of rock.

However, be sure to refer to your trail map constantly – the trails are marked by cairns only (backpacking camps are numbered). Although these trails require you to be in good physical condition, there are other day-walks that are less taxing. Backpackers must pitch their tents in the designated areas, which have been cleared of bush and are located near water. No fires are allowed on the trails, so remember to pack your camping stove.

The road weaves and dips below crumpled green slopes at Malolotja, exposing a continuous pageant of unspoilt wilderness at each bend.

MANTENGA HANDICRAFTS CENTRE
Ezulwini Valley

A tour of Swaziland would be incomplete without visiting the Mantenga Handicrafts Centre – the largest of its kind in the country. Lying deep in the heart of the Ezulwini Valley, this centre, which has its humble beginnings in some old stable buildings, now consists of a group of workshops dedicated to creating and preserving Swazi crafts.

Here you can catch the real essence of Swazi crafts in the heady scents of grass and clay, the colourful array of patchwork quilts and carpets, the careful details of carved wooden or stone figures, and the perfect symmetry of woven grass bowls.

Everything here is handmade – workshops show the art of hand-printing on greetings cards, and the manufacture of shirts, fabrics and stationery.

Jewellers openly display their valuable wares: there are dazzling gold, silver and ethnic pieces, inlaid with precious and semiprecious stones.

You'll also see the ingenuity behind the making of handwoven rugs, handbags, place mats and fabric cushion covers.

And if that's not enough to get you tugging at your purse strings, there are beautiful clay dishes, embellished with skilfully worked traditional designs, as well as lovingly crafted wooden toys.

Also in the centre is a retail outlet for St Joseph's Mission, where many disabled adults are trained to make various crafts. The products they make at the mission, and later at home, are sold for their own benefit on the open market.

Nearby are the lovely Mantenga Falls, where the Little Usutu River tumbles over weathered rocks into a shimmering pool. Below the falls, young girls bathe and wash themselves in the cool, tree-fringed waters of the river in preparation for the annual Reed Dance.

Map: page 363, 4B
From Mbabane, take the main road to Manzini. The turn-off to Mantenga is on your right after about 18 kilometres. The craft centre is on the road to the Mantenga Falls.
Details: Open daily 08h00-17h00.
Accommodation: The Ezulwini Valley offers a wide range of accommodation, ranging from the sumptuous Royal Swazi Sun to various motels and caravan/camping facilities. Nearest to the Mantenga Handicrafts Centre is the Mantenga Falls Hotel, one of the oldest (and smallest) hotels in Swaziland.
Further information: Department of Tourism, Ministry of Broadcasting, Information and Tourism, P O Box 338, Mbabane, tel 4-4556; or Southern African Regional Tourism Council (SARTOC), P O Box 600, Parklands 2121, tel (011) 788-0742; Mantenga Craft Centre, P O Box A5, Swazi Plaza, Mbabane, tel 6-1136; Mantenga Falls Hotel, P O Box 15, Ezulwini, tel 6-1049.

Deft fingers knot and weave intricately designed bags and garments at Mantenga Handicrafts Centre, where visitors can linger over the abundance of local goods.

Swaziland – a kingdom of master craftsmen

Of all the crafts practised in Swaziland, none surpasses that of grass-weaving. It is a time-honoured culture that produces baskets – so important for carrying and storing grain – bracelets for wearing on arms and legs, mats for the homes of plebeians and princes, beer strainers and bowls in an endless assortment of shapes and sizes.

One type of basketwork is so closely woven that liquids may be stored in it. The basket itself absorbs some of the fluid, keeping its contents cool by evaporation.

Today some of the grasses used traditionally in weaving have been replaced by plastic, but the techniques remain much the same, and the finished product is still impressive.

The Swazis are not only master grass-weavers – their decorating techniques are among the most colourful in Africa.

Specialist shops and roadside markets throughout the kingdom, especially in the Ezulwini Valley, display a vivid variety of locally made wares, and sell quality handicrafts honed to perfection by the combination of the best of traditional design and modern techniques.

Other excellent examples of Swazi craftsmanship are the traditional domed huts, of the type found in the royal village.

Although these interesting beehive-shaped huts have been largely replaced by wattle-and-daub or stone-walled dwellings, they are still found in parts of Swaziland and Northern KwaZulu-Natal.

The construction of these huts is uncomplicated: saplings are laced together by the men to form a semicircular framework. The women then tie thatch to the framework, using ropes made of plaited grass.

Once completed, the huts are quite strong enough to protect the occupants from the harshest weather conditions. They're also cool enough to store perishable food in summer, and to keep their occupants warm during the cold winter months.

SWAZILAND

MLAWULA NATURE RESERVE
Northeastern Swaziland

Map: page 363, 3E/F
The reserve lies between Lomahasha in northeastern Swaziland, the Mozambique border in the east, and Siteki in the south. From Mbabane, travel east towards the Mozambique border. About 13 km before Siteki (about 90 km from Mbabane), turn north onto the road to Lomahasha. The turn-off to Mlawula lies about 42 km along this road, on your right.
Details: The reserve is open 06h00-18h00. Information centre at the gate. Guidebook available. Land Rover tours can be booked. Permits needed for fishing and canoeing. Visitors are urged to take precautions against malaria, and to bring their own food, tents and bedding. Firewood and braai facilities are available.
Accommodation: There are 3 camps within the reserve *(see entry)*.
Further information: Mlawula Nature Reserve, P O Box 100, Mbabane, tel 6-1151 or 6-1178/9.

This reserve, covering about 18 000 ha of typically rugged bushveld terrain on and around the Lebombo Mountains in northeastern Swaziland, is a true bird-watcher's paradise. Here the sparkling waters of the Mbuluzi River hurtle through precipitous ravines and forests full of birds. There are more than 350 species in the reserve, including African finfoot and the spectacular Narina trogon, and you'll find a large number of them on the recommended drive through the Mbuluzi Gorge and Valley (home of the reserve's ironwood forests).

The ironwood trees shelter rare species of cycads, succulents and climbers, and provide a safe refuge for a variety of mammals, including warthogs, kudu, impala, blue wildebeest, oribi, duiker, baboons and samango monkeys.

An unusual feature of Mlawula is the 'vulture restaurant' where the carcasses of game and stock are deposited for the indigenous birds of prey to pick clean. You may watch these mighty birds at their meal from the nearby Emangceni Hide. Book in advance.

You'll get a good chance to see white rhinos crashing through the bush in the wide Siphiso Valley (on the western flank of the Lebombo Mountains), where there are about 50 km of game-viewing drives waiting to be explored.

Bird, mammal and tree check lists, as well as information regarding the trails, can be obtained at the reserve's gate.

Archaeologically, Mlawula also has lots to offer. Early Stone-Age tools, dating back one million years, have been found along the riverbeds of the Lebombo Mountains and, to the west, relics of Middle Stone-Age civilization occur. These sites are protected, but guided archaeological trails are being planned.

There are three camps within the reserve. To the north, on the banks of the Mbuluzi River, is the Mbuluzi camp site, with a reed-enclosed hot-water shower and a thatched shelter.

To the south, alongside the Siphiso Stream (usually dry) is the Siphiso Camp – a large area with facilities for camping and caravanning. The ablution block has hot and cold water, and there are washing-up facilities. The most westerly of the camps, Mlawula offers overnight accommodation for hikers, with three 2-bedded tents equipped with bedding, towels, crockery, cutlery, cooking and ablution facilities.

MLILWANE WILDLIFE SANCTUARY
Ezulwini Valley

Map: page 363, 4B
From Mbabane follow the road southeast to Manzini. After about 15 km take the signposted turn-off to Mlilwane.
Details: The reserve's gates are open from dawn to dusk, but 24-hour access is available. Guided game drives. Swimming pool with braai facilities, shop and restaurant. Mountain bikes can be hired. Function facilities are available, with warthog on the spit and Sibhaca dancing (performed energetically by Swazi warriors in bright traditional outfits).
Accommodation: Wooden and thatched huts, traditional beehive huts, a stone cottage, dormitory accommodation and camping facilities.
Further information: Mlilwane Wildlife Sanctuary, P O Box 234, Mbabane, tel (09268) 4-4541. After-hours calls can be made to 6-1591/2/3.

This, the mother of Swaziland's game reserves, lies about 20 km south of Mbabane, on the gentle slopes of the Ezulwini 'heavenly place' Valley. Its existence is due largely to the efforts of King Sobhuza II, who ruled this tiny kingdom from 1921 until his death in 1982, and Ted Reilly, a local farmer and nature-lover, whose father came to Mlilwane ('little fire') at the turn of the century, and made his home in this magnificent country.

Reilly was so alarmed at the thoughtless destruction of land by money-hungry developers, and the typically short-sighted strategies of the colonial government which had resulted in rapidly dwindling numbers of game, that he turned his family farm into a reserve. Today Mlilwane Wildlife Sanctuary straddles about 5 000 ha of the Swaziland middleveld in a lush and fertile valley that is fed by no fewer than four rivers. It supports an impressive variety of game, including hippos, zebras, eland, nyala, blesbok, waterbuck, duiker, steenbuck, blue wildebeest, buffaloes, warthogs, giraffes and crocodiles.

Self-guided trails wind through dappled glades, shaded valleys and fertile mountain slopes at Mlilwane Wildlife Sanctuary.

Bird life is plentiful (over 200 species), and visitors are treated to friendly visits by various tame animals that are allowed to wander freely through the rest-camp grounds. In grim contrast is the exhibition, at the rest camp, of thousands of wire snares which have been collected over the three decades of the sanctuary's existence – testimony to the harsh reality of poaching.

A network of game-viewing roads crisscrosses the reserve, offering intimate views of the animals, and a visit to a hippo pool and heronry (nesting colony).

For something completely different, visitors can take a guided horse-ride, following the bridle trails that bisect the very heart of game country.

There are several self-guided trails, including the Macobane Mountain Trail, which meanders through breathtaking mountain scenery. When you return, you can plunge in to a natural river pool, before settling down to a first-class meal in the reserve's restaurant, which overlooks the hippo pool and heronry.

This lovely sanctuary is only minutes away from the Royal Swazi Sun Hotel

and Casino, a delightful entertainment complex which is open 24 hours a day.

A reed-fringed dam at Mlilwane, where visitors may observe the bird life.

PHOPHONYANE NATURE RESERVE
Piggs Peak

The lush coolness of a darkened forest, the icy tinkle of the Phophonyane Falls plunging over lichen-encrusted rocks, the whole punctuated by the carolling of scores of tropical birds – that's the attraction at Phophonyane, a secluded and idyllic retreat on the northwestern Swaziland escarpment.

Here Highveld mountains drop away sharply, giving way to forested ravines, which flatten into undulating valleys clothed in lush, subtropical vegetation.

There are panoramic views across the rivers, forests and valleys to the east, and guests are encouraged to walk away the stress of city life along Phophonyane's maze of trails. Along these, you will be entertained by the calls of the myriad bird species that dwell in the forest.

A romantic tale is attached to the dramatic falls at Phophonyane. It is reputed that a beautiful Swazi maiden once waited here for her warrior lover who had arranged to present her with a leopard hide as a pledge of betrothal. Unfortunately her young swain was captured by witches, and she cried so much that her tears formed a waterfall.

For attractions of a different sort, you can visit the nearby Protea Piggs Peak Hotel and Casino, one of the most successful of its kind in Swaziland. Indulge yourself in the pampering luxury of the gymnasium, sauna, swimming pool and floodlit tennis courts.

By night the glittering casino and sophisticated restaurant and entertainment areas lure the socialites.

Map: page 363, 2C
Phophonyane Nature Reserve lies 14km north of Piggs Peak, on the road to Matsamo and Jeppe's Reef.
Details: Gates open sunrise to sunset throughout the year.
Accommodation: Phophonyane Lodge offers thatched cottages, a guest suite and an exclusive tent camp, all of which are fully serviced and equipped. The new, fully equipped Betsamoya Guest House, nestling among the trees, offers two bedrooms (both *en suite*). Restaurant available.
Further information: Phophonyane Lodge, P O Box 199, Piggs Peak, tel 7-1319. For details about the casino, contact Protea Piggs Peak Hotel and Casino, P O Box 385, Piggs Peak, tel 7-1104/5.

TISHWESHWE CRAFTS
Malkerns

Ingenious crafts from all over the African continent are on display at Tishweshwe Crafts, which is housed in a series of quaint thatched cottages on the side of the Manzini/Malkerns Road. Prepare yourself for a fascinating collection that includes ebony carvings from Malawi, rugs and carpets, soapstone statues, grass baskets and tableware, jewellery, mohair jerseys, tapestries, leather goods, fabrics, Swazi candles and cards.

There's also a broad selection of books, travel guides and works outlining the history and politics of Africa.

After your visit you can indulge your taste buds at the restaurant attached to the shop.

Sister shops of Tishweshwe Crafts are found at the Swazi Plaza in Mbabane, at the New Mall in Mbabane, at the Royal Swazi Sun Hotel, and at the Lugogo Sun Hotel in the Ezulwini Valley. The shops

all belong to a holding company called INALA (meaning 'Prosperity for all'), which specializes in top-quality African products, so you can be sure you're not buying a dud!

A curio vendor in the Ezulwini Valley. This part of Swaziland bristles with craft centres and colourful roadside stalls.

Map: page 363, 4C
Tishweshwe Crafts are in the Malkerns Valley. From Mbabane take the road to Manzini. Turn right to Malkerns. Tishweshwe lies 1km further along, on the right. The centre is well signposted.
Details: Open every day 08h00-17h00.
Accommodation: There are a number of hotels, varying in luxury, near Tishweshwe. The Royal Swazi Sun Hotel and Casino (Private Bag, Ezulwini, tel 6-1001) offers everything your heart desires, including an 18-hole golf course. The Lugogo Sun (Private Bag, Ezulwini, tel 6-1101/6-1550) is in the same grounds as the Royal Swazi Sun, and is Swaziland's largest hotel. Nearby, the Ezulwini Sun has a wide variety of entertainments (P O Box 123, Ezulwini, tel 6-1201). The Smokey Mountain Lodge offers 16 self-contained chalets (P O Box 21, Ezulwini, tel 6-1291).
Further information: Tishweshwe Crafts, P O Box 376, Malkerns, tel 8-3336.

SWAZILAND

WHITE-WATER RAFTING ON THE GREAT USUTU RIVER
Mkhaya Game Reserve

Map: page 363, 5D/E
From Mbabane take the main road to the southeast, past Siphofaneni, to Phuzumoya on the Big Bend road. Immediately after crossing over the bridge at Phuzumoya, turn left off the tar. A guide will meet you at the Mkhaya signpost. He will direct you to the ranger's base, where you leave your car (a 24-hour guard will ensure its safety). A ranger-driven Land Rover will then ferry you the rest of the way – and throughout your stay at Mkhaya.

Details: Book ahead. Overnight visitors are met at the gate at 10h00 or 16h00. Alternative times available on request. One-day river-rafting trips are available all year round.

Accommodation: There's an attractive two-bedroomed, stone-and-thatch cottage, as well as luxury safari tents at Stone Camp, within the riverine forest in the southeastern corner of the reserve. Each tent has hot and cold water on tap, and a toilet. Shower facilities are communal. All meals, many with an authentic African flavour, are cooked and served at the camp fire. Take precautions against malaria.

Further information: Mkhaya Game Reserve, P O Box 234, Mbabane, tel 4-4541 (after hours tel 6-1591/2/3).

One of the greatest attractions of this unique reserve, in the secluded southwestern corner of Swaziland, must surely be its rhinos. Who could resist the opportunity to drive in an open Land Rover, or even to walk (with a guide, of course) through bushveld peppered with wildlife, and the chance of a sudden, face-to-face encounter with a rhino.

The rhinos really owe their survival to the dedicated efforts of one of Swaziland's pioneering conservationists, Ted Reilly, who owns Mkhaya Game Reserve, and who is the founder of Mlilwane Wildlife Sanctuary to the west.

Mkhaya was established originally as a refuge for the indigenous Swazi Nguni breed of cattle which, in the 1970s, showed signs of becoming another name on the world's list of extinct species. Reilly purchased the Mkhaya area – a 6 200-ha stretch of Lowveld savannah – as a sanctuary for the Nguni, then decided to diversify by introducing game to the area.

In 1981 Mkhaya was declared a nature reserve, and is now a refuge, not only for black and white rhinos, but also for a variety of other game, including such species as elephants, giraffes, warthogs, roan and sable antelope, kudu, nyala, tsessebe and hippos. Endangered bird species at Mkhaya include bateleur and martial eagles.

Ranger-led walks and Land Rover drives through the undergrowth of this veritable Noah's Ark are not the only enticements to visiting the reserve. You can also try some white-water rafting on the Great Usutu River, which forces its way through the Bulungu Gorge in a series of explosive rapids and waterfalls that challenge the most adventurous of river-runners.

Eight-man inflatable dinghies or two-man rafts, skippered by professionals, carry visitors 10 to 20 km down this mighty river, taking in some tranquil stretches of water where you do a bit of bird-watching. You stop at a plunging waterfall for lunch, and are given the opportunity to try your hand at abseiling.

Book well in advance: the thrill of white-water rafting at Mkhaya has become increasingly popular with both day-visitors and overnight guests.

With an air of resolute determination, a band of river-rafters faces the rapids on Mkhaya's Great Usutu River.

African fish eagle – monarch of the thermals

Like a jet-fighter on a bombing run, the African fish eagle hurtles towards the river, eyes locked onto a murky shadow below. Then, with surprising grace and speed, outstretched talons slice through the surface, latching instantly on a large and wriggling fish.

With its prey secure, the fish eagle half pauses in flight to adjust to its heavy load, then, with a surge of power, bears it off to dine at leisure.

The African fish eagle *(Haliaeetus vocifer)* is one of the most magnificent and, fortunately, the most plentiful of the African birds of prey. With its distinctive white head, neck, breast and tail feathers, and its long, black wings which span about two metres, the fish eagle in flight is nothing short of an aerodynamic wonder. It glides effortlessly on the thermals, wing tips angled for optimum efficiency in the air.

Usually found in swamplands and along the shores of large, tree-lined bodies of inland water, it is strictly territorial, and a mating pair will often spend their entire lives in the same small corner of marshland.

The eagles spend most of their days in the treetops, scanning the water for the telltale flicker of a fish. Although they prefer aquatic life, these eagles also prey on the eggs and nestlings of other birds. Frogs and, in rare cases, aquatic birds and small mammals, also constitute part of their diet.

Fish eagles lay their eggs in midwinter, in large, grass-lined stick nests. Two eggs are laid at a time and these are incubated by both parents. The young stay with their parents for about four and a half months before they decide to leave the nest, which may be used for years by the same parent couple.

The fish eagle's haunting cry, made both on the wing and from its perch, is instantly identifiable.

An African fish eagle swoops down with elegant, deadly precision to snatch its victim from the water.

NAMIBIA

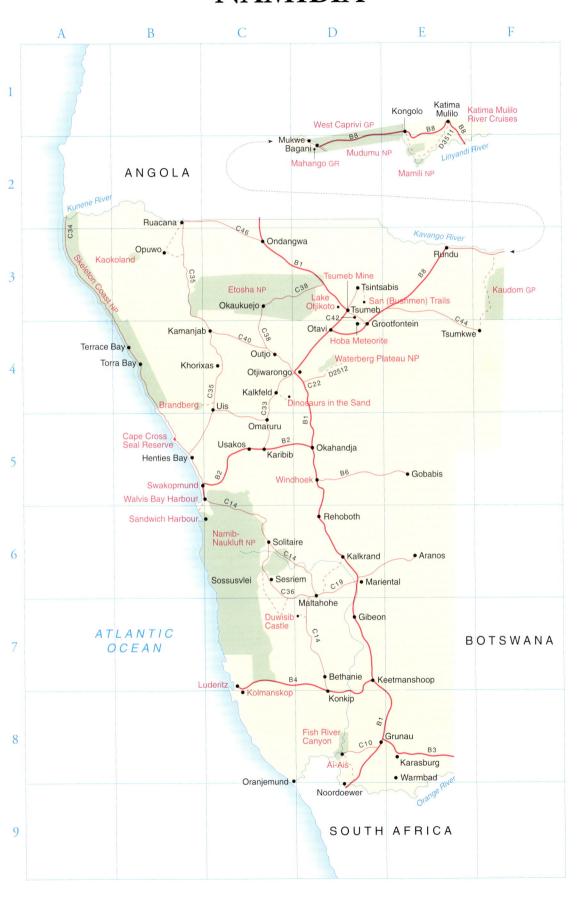

AI-AIS
North of Orange River

Map: page 371, 8D
Turn west off the B1 main road, 37 km north of the Noordoewer border post on the Orange River. The D316, a good gravel road, bisects a 72-km plain to the C10. Turn left, and drive carefully for 10 km through the pass to Ai-Ais.
Details: Open daily sunrise to sunset, from the second Friday in March to 31 October. Admission fee charged.
Accommodation: Luxury flats, huts with communal ablution facilities, swimming pool and hot tubs, camping and caravan sites.
Further information: Directorate of Tourism and Resorts, Ministry of Wildlife, Conservation and Tourism, Private Bag 13267, Windhoek, tel (061) 23-6975/6/7/8.

Ai-Ais is an oasis of green palms and riverbed reeds in a lunar crater at the bottom of the Fish River Canyon.

Here a hot spring, known to the Khoikhoi as the 'waters of fire', has been tamed into a sinuous pool where you can soak in the mineral waters and soothe your soul.

From the riverbed in front of the holiday complex, with its air-conditioned flats, lawns and shady camp sites, you look straight up at black-brown pyramids of blasted rock.

Were it not for the Fish River, which flows quietly beneath the sands for much of the year, and the green reed banks where you can hear the soft *kwit-kwit* of bee-eaters, this would be death valley.

Known to the San (Bushmen) for thousands of years, it was rediscovered by a Nama shepherd in 1850. German soldiers, harried by General Louis Botha's South African forces in 1915, used it as a hideaway to recover from their wounds.

Even today, the approach road through the jagged sandstone and lava is an awesome, hairpin descent.

The healing waters of the spring bubble to the surface at 60°C. The water is piped into indoor pools, Jacuzzis and an open swimming pool, where all aches and pains are eased away.

The resort is closed from November to mid-March, for this is the time when the Fish River can rage through the 161-km canyon in turbulent flood. In 1972, a year after the resort was opened, the luxury complex was nearly washed away.

Bouldered dykes now protect this luxuriant haven where the waters are hot, but where the winds of the canyon are surprisingly cool.

The spa at Ai-Ais, where hot springs have been channelled into a pretty pool to provide relief for any number of muscular aches and pains.

BRANDBERG
West of Omaruru

Map: page 371, 4B
From Uis Mine, 129 km west of Omaruru, drive north on the C35 for 14 kilometres. Turn west at the Witvrou ('White Lady') sign for 28 kilometres.
Details: Open sunrise to sunset throughout the year. No admission fee.
Accommodation: The nearest accommodation is at Brandberg Rest Camp, Khorixas, P O Box 35, Khorixas, tel (062262) 235. There is a small rest camp at Uis Mine with 4-bed bungalows, each with a kitchen and bathroom.
Further information: Directorate of Tourism and Resorts, Ministry of Wildlife, Conservation and Tourism, Private Bag 13267, Windhoek, tel (061) 23-6975/6/7/8.

Seared in petrified seams of lava, the ancient whaleback of the Brandberg, Namibia's highest massif, rises 2 573 m above the surrounding plains north of the coastal town of Swakopmund.

At times totally blanketed in mist, this 500-million-year-old island of granite seems to catch fire at sunset.

Its 30-km-wide bulk, with overlapping horseshoe folds fringing the slopes, is quite foreboding to all but mountaineers and scramblers. But perennial springs in the lower valleys enable such animals as klipspringer, Hartmann's mountain zebras and some leopards to survive. The mountain's starkness is muted to some extent by the camelthorn, fig trees and grass that cover its ravines. One of them, the Tsisab Ravine, leads to the White Lady rock painting which depicts a 40-cm-tall figure with a hunting bow.

The painting was discovered in 1918, and although some have surmised that the work depicts a lady, it is now believed that the figure actually is that of a clay-bedecked boy undergoing a ritual initiation ceremony.

The rock engravings at Twyfelfontein, and the conspicuous 35-m finger of limestone known as Vingerklip, are well worth stopping for on the drive from Brandberg to Khorixas.

BUSHMAN ROCK ART
See page 374

CAPE CROSS SEAL RESERVE
North of Henties Bay

Eyes closed, noses in the air as if catching the scent of the sea, thousands of Cape fur seals bask on the sunny, wave-lashed promontory of Cape Cross, 115 km north of Swakopmund.

It is much the same today as it was when Portuguese navigator Diego Cao landed here in 1485 to erect a stone cross, Western man's first real foothold in southern Africa.

An exact replica of this four-metre *padrao* (the original stands in a Berlin museum) today overlooks a circular wall from which you can view the seal colony from close quarters.

The seals flap, grunt, fight and flaunt all over the glistening black rocks, while others cavort with aplomb in the thundering rollers. On sandy patches they flop asleep against any convenient rock or neighbour's tummy.

A huge 300-kg, teeth-snapping male lunges at a trespassing Romeo, then turns to gently touch noses with one of his small, doe-like spouses (numbering up to 25 in one harem).

The roly-poly pups, brown and honey-coloured, bleat like lambs for their mothers, their cries instantly recognized.

A quarter of the pups at Cape Cross are lost to brown hyaenas and jackals. Because seals are fish-eaters, the aroma at the colony is pungent.

The seal population at Cape Cross, with its adjoining bay of pastel desert colours, numbers up to one hundred thousand. These animals have been exploited for centuries, but today the area is a reserve where the seals are free to breed and relax in the sun.

At the Ebbtide Curio Shop you can see the proprietor's collection of rusted anchors, shipwreck flotsam and an old pigeon roost from the days when these reliable birds were the only link with Swakopmund.

Map: page 371, 5B
Drive 76 km north from Swakopmund along the coastal road.
Details: Open daily 10h00-17h00 (closed Fridays). Admission fee at the gate. No pets or motorcycles.
Accommodation: None in the reserve, but there is a rest camp with bungalows at Henties Bay – Desert Rose Holiday Resort, P O Box 124, Henties Bay, tel (06442) 181. Also at Henties Bay is the Hotel De Duine (P O Box 1, Henties Bay, tel (06442) 1), with 10 rooms and a restaurant. Swakopmund offers a variety of accommodation.
Further information: As for 'Dinosaurs in the sand' *(see next entry)*.

The padrao at Cape Cross pays tribute to Diego Cao, the mariner who landed at this spot in 1485.

A rumble-tumble of seals bob and cavort in the shallows before sunning themselves on the shores of the icy Atlantic at Cape Cross.

PLACES TO VISIT

BUSHMAN ROCK ART

Bushman rock art is believed to be essentially of religious or spiritual significance, although various researchers have taken many years and much controversy to reach this conclusion.

The frugal, and often Spartan, hunter-gatherer lifestyle of the San-speaking people, involving communal sharing of meagre resources, an absence of political elites, an ecological sensitivity to nature's gifts, and full participation by women, has often been romanticized. But these Stone-Age people, who have been in southern Africa for at least 27 000 years, have had a tough life.

They were not untouched by jealousy, anger, disease and deprivation. Their creator seemed distant to them, while their other trickster god was always around to stir up mischief. So they sought to cure their difficulties by mutual participation in a healing dance, in which one or more of their band, including women, would go into a trance, the others dancing or clapping rhythmically. This ritual would release *n/um* (potency or soul force), which supposedly captured the spiritual power of certain animals, encouraged springs to maintain their flow, and balmed all ills.

The mountains at Twyfelfontein reveal a legacy of rock engravings illustrating the richness of game that once roamed these thirstlands.

The Bushman's daily experience was filtered through his trance dance and cosmology, to emerge as a living art form on numerous rock overhangs, caves and in some cases exposed rock. There are about 43 000 figures in the Brandberg alone, and another 2 000 paintings in the nearby Twyfelfontein Mountains.

The Brandberg massif was first seen by Portuguese navigator Diego Cao in 1485, from a coastal distance of 80 kilometres. Its black lava hills, with pink granite domes and jumbled boulders, rise 2 585 m above the surrounding plain, a massive and forbidding outcrop, 50 km long and 30 km wide. Here you will see the 'White Lady', originally believed to have been of Mediterranean origin.

His eyes permanently puckered against the scorching Namibian sun, a San hunter scans the desert for prey.

In the Tsisab Ravine there are elegant white-chested antelope, the seven figures of the 'Girls' School', and impressionistic white ostriches.

The delicately etched Twyfelfontein engravings, often more beautiful than the paintings, show lions, giraffes and an intriguing series of patterns, circles and dots, which some scientists now believe represent the hallucinations experienced in the early stages of a trance dance.

European settlers often denigrated Bushman rock art, and certainly underestimated its significance and artistic value. Englishman Sir John Barrow, who journeyed through the Cape Colony in 1797-98, was an early exception.

most studied mountain in the world. Giraffes are often portrayed in Hungorob Gorge, with its 137 rock-art sites, while springbok feature in the equally awesome Amis Gorge.

In other parts of Africa the eland plays a major role. The animals are often so sensitively and accurately drawn in characteristic poses, they seem to leap off the rock at you.

Groups of animals are symbolic of an intact environment, whose harmonious, gregarious behaviour probably indicates the Bushman's communal wellbeing in this area at that moment in time.

Animals painted in other parts of Namibia, a hippo or fish, are imaginary,

An antelope immortalized in rock at Twyfelfontein. The hills here contain over 3 000 engravings, the richest collection of its kind on the continent.

Rock engravings at Twyfelfontein. Animals depicted include giraffes, lions, rhinos, antelope and elephants.

He marvelled at the 'force and spirit' of the paintings and engravings, and wondered why colonists regarded the artists as 'troops of abandoned wretches'.

To other dedicated researchers such as David Lewis-Williams and Harold Pager, Bushman artistry did not merely portray hunting techniques, certain dress rituals, customs and animals, but rather the major role played in San society by their spiritual beliefs. Paintings depicting strange figures, with streams pouring from their heads, creatures that were part man, part animal, and depictions of unnaturally elongated people, were all attempts to reflect potency, as it manifested itself to a person in trance.

In many ways Bushman bands were the first spiritual care groups. And their rock shelters were the cathedral repositories of their beliefs.

The Brandberg, first surveyed by Reinard Maack in 1918, is possibly the

and may be an attempt to spiritually 'capture' rain, for water was seen as a soul force, not merely food or drink.

Bushman art originally incorporated a greater use of the colour white, made from silica, china clay and gypsum. But not being earth pigments like the ochre ores and oxides of iron minerals, the traditional reds and browns we associate with Bushman paintings, they tended to fade. Animal fats were used to bind the crushed ore; fine brushes were used, even spatulas of wood or bone, and the painter's fingers. Today rain, and the very water seeping behind the rock canvas, are the greatest threat to Bushman art. Just as we are beginning to really appreciate their beauty and significance, we are on the point, it seems, of losing them for ever.

NAMIBIA

DINOSAURS IN THE SAND
South of Otjiwarongo

Map: page 371, 4C
Access to the *Otjihaenamaparero Farm* dinosaur-footprint site on D2414 is signposted 29 km southeast of Kalkfeld. Other fossilized footprints may be seen at the Waterberg Plateau National Park further to the north *(see separate entry)*.
Details: Open sunrise to sunset. Admission fee payable at farm. Please close the gates.
Accommodation: There is a rustic camp site on the farm. Nearby is the Mount Etjo Safari Lodge, P O Box 81, Kalkfeld, tel (06532) 44 or 1602; camping sites at the municipal rest camp in Otjiwarongo, Private Bag 2209, tel (0651) 2231. Otjiwarongo has 2 hotels.
Further information: Directorate of Tourism and Resorts, Ministry of Wildlife, Conservation and Tourism, Private Bag 13267, Windhoek, tel (061) 23-6975/6/7/8.

In the shadow of the brooding Mount Etjo massif, 29 km south of Kalkfeld, there is a pleasant, grassed valley graced by yellow-flowered camelthorn trees, and surrounded by hills. Today it is just a small farm, *Otjihaenamaparero*, but 200 million years ago it was a lake where dinosaurs walked.

Three-toed prints a metre long have been left in the overlapping plates of shiny sandstone, over a distance of 25 metres. The tracks were imprinted in wet sand, which petrified into stone.

Although there is no specific sign of its dragging tail, this dinosaur probably resembled a huge kangaroo, with the gait of an ostrich.

At the farm you open a few farm gates, arrive at a rustic braai site, then follow white-painted stones 300 m to an ancient lakeshore. The site has been declared a national monument.

Alone on this hillside, with a light wind blowing off Etjo Mountain, you stand in awe before these primeval footprints, conscious of the brevity of mankind's existence in the vastness of time.

Preserved in sandstone for about 200 million years, the imprint of a dinosaur's foot gives some idea of prehistoric life in this enigmatic land.

DUWISIB CASTLE
Near Namib-Naukluft National Park

Map: page 371, 7D
The castle lies 81 km southwest of Maltahohe. From Maltahohe travel south on the C14 for 38 km, then turn west onto the D824. After a further 12 km turn west onto the D831. Follow the signs for another 40 kilometres.
Details: Open 08h00-17h00. Entrance fee.
Accommodation: There are chalets and camp sites in the castle grounds. There are 3 bungalows on *Farm Duwisib* next to the castle. Contact P O Box 11659, Windhoek, tel (06632) 5-3004; or stay at the Maltahohe Hotel, P O Box 20, Maltahohe, tel (06632) 13.
Further information: Directorate of Tourism and Resorts, Ministry of Wildlife, Conservation and Tourism, Private Bag 13267, Windhoek, tel (061) 23-6975/6/7/8.

Wagner's wild music seems to echo in the wind from the tawny sandstone battlements of Duwisib Castle, a four-square, crusader fortress on the edge of the Namib Desert. None of Namibia's many castles matches Schloss Duwisib in size, grandeur and interior décor.

Carpets, ornate fireplaces, paintings and furniture in the 22 rooms speak eloquently of its gracious past.

Italian stonemasons, Scandinavian carpenters and Irish builders were imported by the eccentric Prussian cavalry officer Baron Hansheinrich Von Wolff, and his American wife Jayta, to build this castle on their beautiful farm *Duwisib*, 'place of the rainbow'.

Completed in 1909, it took some 20 oxwagons two years to ferry the materials 650 km across the desert from Luderitz Harbour. Von Wolff, a horse-breeder, died in the Battle of the Somme in 1916.

His horses were freed and are now part of the wild herd of the Namib Desert.

The gnarled branches of an old tree frame the battlements of Duwisib Castle, which is now preserved as a museum with some fine examples of German furniture and antiques.

ETOSHA NATIONAL PARK
Northern Namibia

'Land of dry water' sounds like an impossible contradiction, but then Etosha isn't straightforward. Others say the name means 'Place of mirages' or 'Great white place' and, once you're there, the derivations are obvious. It's the water, and not dry water, that brings the profusion of life.

The heat that takes away the water creates the mirages and, where the water has dried, it leaves a thin, salty crust, white in the silence of great open places.

In the far north of Namibia, the focus of the Etosha National Park is Etosha Pan, the remains of a prehistoric inland sea. The pan stretches 130 km from east to west, and it runs 72 km from north to south – over 6 000 sq km of flat, shining sand or, for just a few months every summer if the rains have been good, of shallow, shining water.

Then the white plains turn green, almost overnight, as the sleeping seeds of grasses wake and grow.

Grass seems almost the only ground cover in many parts of Etosha, but there is a large variety of trees too, and shrubs. West of Okaukuejo there's even an area known as the Haunted Forest, named not for ghosts, but for the dense growth of squat, swollen-stemmed moringa trees that usually thrive on rocky hillsides, but which here, in Etosha, have successfully taken to the sands.

The San believe that these trees were thrown from Paradise and, landing upside down, grew that way. In other parts of the subcontinent, it's a tale you might hear of the baobab.

On the eastern side of Etosha grow wild figs and tamboti, marula, makalani palms and thorn trees, all forming a mixed woodland with lower-growing and mostly deciduous shrubs.

Dotted around the southern rim of the great pan are water holes, their water levels mostly regulated by the complex nature of the geological structures that underlie the sands of Etosha.

Along this line, too, are the camps – Okaukuejo, Halali and Namutoni. Namutoni means 'high place that can be seen from afar', and the view from the ramparts of the old fort here is also wide.

Here, you feel, are tales of people and passions of long ago, to be discussed in

Map: page 371, 3B/C/D
From Tsumeb drive 82 km along the B1. Turn left onto the C38. From here it is 35 km to the Namutoni entrance. The western Okaukuejo gate is approached along the C38 from Otjiwarongo, a distance of 180 kilometres. The game-viewing dirt road between the 3 camps is fine for ordinary cars.

Details: Open sunrise to sunset all year round. Each person and vehicle is charged an entrance fee. Take malaria precautions. The 3 rest camps all have a shop, restaurant, swimming pool and filling station.

Accommodation: Air-conditioned bungalows, flats, camping facilities. Prebooking advisable. There are also three private luxury camps adjoining the park: Mokuti Lodge just outside Namutoni, P O Box 403, Tsumeb, tel (0671) 2-1084; Ongava Lodge to the south, P O Box 186, Outjo, tel (06542) 3413; and Hobatere Lodge to the west, P O Box 110, Kamanjab, tel (06552) 2022.

Further information: Directorate of Tourism and Resorts, Ministry of Wildlife, Conservation and Tourism, Private Bag 13267, Windhoek, tel (061) 23-6975/6/7/8.

Rapier-horned gemsbok slake their thirst at a water hole near Okaukuejo Camp, the site of Etosha National Park's headquarters.

A lone giraffe is finely etched against the scarlet skies of Etosha. Giraffes usually keep their long necks upright when sleeping.

the firelight. Overall, though, what possesses and absorbs visitors is the cycle of the wild, the response from afar to that far-reaching and wonderful scent of rain on the dry earth.

This is what makes Etosha, what summons up its life and, in response, attracts its visitors. Some of them choose to stay in one of the private lodges, each of which has access to the park and arranges game-viewing in its own transport, and provides guides.

Almost everyone spends some time at Okaukuejo, which is also the park's headquarters, and which lies at the western end of the pan. Here a permanent water hole is floodlit at night, and those who enjoy game-watching at their ease can look on, drink in hand as, just a few metres away, beyond a low stone wall, the animals detach from the darkness, drink, and make their leisurely departure. Elephants are regulars, while the dry season almost always brings black rhinos and lions. Somewhere out in the darkness gemsbok and zebras, kudu, springbok and wildebeest all wait their turn. Of the smaller mammals, only the black-backed jackals, much-fabled cowards of the animal kingdom, dare to drink in company with the king himself.

The main building at Namutoni, in the east, looks like an old-fashioned colonial fort, because that's how it was built in 1907, as a remote outpost of Germany's short-lived African empire. It marks the site of an earlier, and much smaller, fort that was destroyed in an attack. Among the larger antelope that favour this area are eland, kudu and gemsbok, springbok and black-faced impala. Giraffes and zebras are seen here too, as they are almost anywhere in Etosha. Cheetahs and leopards, those free and secretive spirits, may also simply appear and disappear. At the Klein Namutoni water hole the shy Damara dik-dik, Namibia's smallest antelope, is often seen in the long light of mornings and evenings.

A black rhino strides purposefully past the water hole at Okaukuejo, completely ignoring a flock of timid guineafowl. Unsociable at the best of times, rhinos are unpredictable and may charge if provoked.

Keenly tuned to the possibility of sudden attack, a group of giraffes and zebras refresh themselves at one of Etosha's water holes.

Almost midway along the 145 km between Namutoni and Okaukuejo is the third camp, Halali. The name is not local, but is an attempt to put into syllables the traditional German bugle call that once signalled the end of the hunt. And in Etosha the hunt has indeed ended.

Quite close to Halali are two rugged dolomite outcrops. The nearer one is called Tsumasa, and it harbours a cave, home to at least four species of bat.

A trail has been laid out on Tsumasa and offers good views from the summit, as well as the chance to identify trees and shrubs, all numbered and described in a brochure obtainable at Halali.

Abundant though they are throughout the park, birds are less easily identified, although there can be no mistaking the pink sheen of flamingoes massing at the water's edge in the rainy season. In all, some 325 species of bird have been recorded, from ostriches and eagles to water birds such as Egyptian geese, avocets, spoonbills, storks and ducks.

Elephants are mild-mannered monoliths, and may charge only when threatened or thwarted in their search for water in times of drought.

The Etosha landscape is at its most characteristic towards the end of the dry season (July to October), when the green cover has dried and gone, the smaller pools have dried up, and the animals move close to the water holes on the pan's southern edge. This is the best time for game-viewing.

An enchanted visitor to the area in 1876 wrote that 'all the menageries in the world would not compare to the sight' he had seen on a particular day. The wonder of it is still there.

The secret tricks of mirages

The deserts, heat and vast distances of Namibia convince you, at times, that you are seeing things. Water seems to shimmer across a bone-dry salt pan, mountains loom where there is no elevated land, and faraway animals seem to double in numbers. These are mirages.

The word mirage comes from the French '*semirer*', to be reflected. But reflection, strangely, has nothing to do with it, even though what you are seeing may look like someone is juggling a series of cracked mirrors in front of you. A mirage is an illusory image of reality, an object, for example, in the distance, that floats above or hovers below its normal position, and is very often twisted into strange shapes.

What takes place, in effect, is that our atmosphere, a fluid medium, becomes a huge lens bending the rays of light as they shine through it. This refraction, as it is called, depends on the varying layers of atmosphere, the temperature, pressure and the amount of moisture in the air. And what we actually see depends on the height from which we are viewing the scene, how the particular temperature is changing in the atmosphere, and the temperature itself.

We tend to think of mirages as desert phenomena, the visions a man dying of thirst might see as he stumbles, lost on the Skeleton Coast.

But the earliest recordings of mirages were made in the freezing ice plains of the North Pole by explorer Robert Peary in 1906. He saw snowy mountains floating above the endless ice horizon.

Mirages most commonly associated with the Namib Desert and the super-heated salt pans and gravel plains of Namibia are called inferior mirages, in which the mercilessly flat surfaces are seen as sheets of water.

They are, in fact, an inverted image of the sky, seen from a slight elevation above the layer of hot air.

FISH RIVER CANYON
Southern Namibia

Map: page 371, 8D
From the Noordoewer border, drive north for 41 km, and turn left onto the D316 turn-off for Ai-Ais and the Fish River Canyon. You may proceed a further 64 km, and turn left onto the C10, which also leads to Ai-Ais. Some 13 km before Ai-Ais, take the road leading north, and then west, to get to the Fish River Canyon (about 50 km from the turn-off).

Details: Open 06h00-22h00. Admission fee charged. Hiking trails can be booked May to September.

Accommodation: The Hobas Rest Camp, about 10 km from the main viewing point, has shaded camp sites, communal ablution facilities, a shop and swimming pool, but no fuel or chalets. For more luxurious accommodation you may choose to stay at Ai-Ais *(see separate entry)*.

Further information: Directorate of Tourism and Resorts, Ministry of Wildlife, Conservation and Tourism, Private Bag 13267, Windhoek, tel (061) 23-6975/6/7/8.

The stony, dune-coloured plain appears to have cracked open in cataclysmic fracture as you stand on the precipice of the Fish River Canyon.

Beneath you tortured ridges and cliffs, eroded over millions of years, fall 550 m to the riverbed, as the jagged scar of the canyon zigzags to left and right, to disappear in a blue haze of mountains.

Halfway down, a massive plateau extends to the rim of the ravine, as a lone mountain chat dives deep to some hidden perch. The chasm is 27 km across at its widest point, and 161 km long – second in size only to Arizona's Grand Canyon. The entire area around the canyon has been proclaimed a natural conservation area.

Reed banks far below frame the twisting contours of riverbed pools, providing the only touch of colour in this oven-fired abyss.

A number of tracks lead to various viewpoints along the rim of the canyon. One leads three kilometres down, past gravel flats littered with brown coal rocks to the second viewpoint. From this point, a sequence of plateaus lie in front of you like flattened mushrooms, tempting you to step onto them.

The main observation point, which overlooks the dramatic Hell Bend, marks the start of the 86-km-long Fish River Canyon Hiking Trail, which follows the course of the riverbed to Ai-Ais in the south. A chained descent, with steps cut into the rock, leads to the canyon floor. You need to be physically fit to undertake this four- to five-day trail, which passes hot springs, skirts jumbles of boulders, and exposes striking wind-sculpted rock formations. Take all your own provisions (fishing is allowed).

Be sure to book well in advance at the Directorate of Tourism and Resorts *(see address opposite)* as this trail is popular with those who have fallen in love with the canyon and its awe-inspiring scenery.

Camelthorn, wild tamarisk and quiver tree aloes host a prolific bird life along the reed pools of the deep canyon, home to both leopards and such game as Hartmann's mountain zebras and kudu.

The canyon is a geological panorama of the earth's convulsions over the last 1 800 years, as the lava, sandstone and shales heated, cooled and changed their shape. The dark streaks in the rock are lava-filled fissures known as dolerite.

Continual erosion and southward-moving glaciers scythed into the crust, followed by the erosive waters of the Fish River, which, at 800 km, is the longest in Namibia. Giant green powder puffs of melkbos dot the rock plains around the canyon as you drive 19 km to the Hot Springs viewpoint, a lovely, restful spot with its pool and palms.

Multihued rock strata, split, seamed and sculpted by aeons of erosion, form the steep-sided Fish River Canyon.

HOBA METEORITE
West of Grootfontein

'Beware of the falling meteorite!' reads the sign at the futuristic meteorite centre in the valley of the Otavi Mountains, about 20 km west of Grootfontein.

One hasn't plummeted down from the heavens in the last 80 000 years, since this 50-ton monster, the world's heaviest metallic meteorite, fell like a shooting star from deep space, but you can't be too careful. Little paths from the demonstration wall lead through rockeries, aloes and wild olive trees to the awesome black slab, the 400-million-year-old centre of attraction, in its tree-tiered arena.

The meteorite consists of 80 percent iron, with a mix of nickel, including a rare nickel isotope that enabled scientists to put an approximate date on its fall. There is also a sprinkling of such exotic minerals as cobalt and iridium.

Standing three metres square and as high as a man's thigh, the meteorite was first recorded in 1920 by local farmer Johannes Brits.

It was declared a national monument in 1955, and now its surrounding green lawns and birds make it a restful braai venue. But do keep an eye on the sky.

Map: page 371, 4D
Take the D8 Otavi road west from Grootfontein. A signpost leads to the meteorite, a 20-minute drive away.
Details: Open daily 08h00-17h00. There is an entrance fee, a refreshment kiosk, interpretive wall, picnic sites and toilets.
Accommodation: Bungalows and camp sites are available at the Grootfontein Municipality, P O Box 23, Grootfontein, tel (06731) 3100. Hotels include the Meteor Hotel, P O Box 346, Grootfontein, tel (06731) 2078/9; and the Nord Hotel, P O Box 168, Grootfontein, tel (06731) 2049. There is a guest farm, Dornhugel, P O Box 173, Grootfontein, tel (06731) 8-1611.
Further information: Grootfontein Municipality, P O Box 23, Grootfontein, tel (06731) 3100.

The massive Hoba meteorite has a mass of some 54 000 kilograms.

A small, hutted village crouches beneath a mist-shrouded Kaokoland mountain.

KAOKOLAND
Northern Namibia

Kaokoland is a brooding wilderness of jagged mountains hiding long, stony plains and dry, palm-tufted riverbeds. At least two 4x4 vehicles are essential to venture into its wastes, where there are no shops or fuel for 500 kilometres.

Isolated by the sea and dunes of the Skeleton Coast in the west, this vast tract of land rises through gravel flats, grassveld and dusty mopane scrub to the equally stark Ehomba, Otjiveze and Joubert mountains in the east.

Only in the far north, where the Kunene flows over the Ruacana and the Epupa falls, does nature relent of its harshness in a wash of tropical greenery. It was through this seemingly barren badland that the *Dorslanders*, a group of families who trekked from the Transvaal in search of religious and political freedom from the government of the time, and the threat of British colonial expansion, managed to trek to Angola in the late 1870s. On their journey they encountered the indigenous 17 000-strong population of traditional Herero and Himba, the latter in their leather skirts and powdered body make-up.

Their success in dwelling in the desert is due in part to their ability to coexist with the creatures of the arid wild.

Not far from Kaokoland's only town, Opuwo, the Hoarusib River begins its annual watery rampage.

Where it twists through a narrow canyon, the lower Hoarusib has created silt cliffs known as the 'White Temples', which look amazingly similar to Egypt's Valley of the Kings.

The mighty Kunene, nurtured by six northern rivers each year, sports lush river banks of giant sycamore figs, leadwoods, papyrus, lianas and thousands of palms – a glaring contrast to the arid hinterland.

At Epupa Falls you will see some of the rarest of Kaokoland's 400 bird species, including the grey and red Cinderella waxbill and the lovely rufous-tailed palm thrush. Be sure to keep a wary eye out for crocodiles here.

Map: page 371, 3 A/B
Kaokoland lies some 414 km northwest of Etosha, first along the B1, then along the C46. There is a good road to Opuwo, the local capital, with the only available petrol. Opuwo has shops, a good bakery, a post office and a large school.
Details: Avoid camping in riverbeds, as this disturbs the animals. Use only dead wood for fires. Remember that this fragile environment is easily ruined by tyre tracks which will not be erased for about 80 years.
Accommodation: There is a permanent tented camp at Epupa, about 145 km west of Ruacana, near the Epupa Falls. The camp takes a maximum of 8 guests in 2-bed tents. Bucket showers, toilets, meals provided, fishing and rafting on the Kunene. Flying is the only practical way to reach Epupa. Contact Top Travel, P O Box 80205, Windhoek, tel (061) 5-1975.
Further information: Directorate of Tourism and Resorts, Ministry of Wildlife, Conservation and Tourism, Private Bag 13267, Windhoek, tel (061) 23-6975/6/7/8.

KATIMA MULILO RIVER CRUISES
Northeastern Namibia

Map: page 371, 1E
Fly into Katima Mulilo, or drive 200 km west from the Victoria Falls (four border posts) on reasonable gravel roads, or 1 300 km northeast from Windhoek. It is 3 332 km from Johannesburg on tarred roads, except for 200 km through the Caprivi Strip.

Details: Minimum party of 15. Cruises operate mid-February to the end of May only. Prices include everything. Pick-ups can be at Katima Mulilo or Victoria Falls. Malaria precautions necessary. Passports and appropriate visas needed to enter Namibian, Botswanan and Zimbabwean waters.

Accommodation: The first night is at the Zambezi Lodge, P O Box 98, Katima Mulilo, tel (067352) 203. Subsequent accommodation is provided on board.

Further information: Zambezi Queen, P O Box 98, Katima Mulilo, tel (067352) 203.

As the dawn wind ripples gently across the rose-coloured waters, the *Zambezi Queen* weighs anchor, pulls out into midstream, and begins another day of elegant cruising on the great Zambezi.

In the lush, carpeted dining salon, with its zebras etched on mirror panels, guests arrive for a scrumptious breakfast that includes hot, home-made bread and steaming cona coffee. The Zambezi River is only a metre deep in September, with crocodiles lying open-mouthed on the sandbanks. But by February, rainfall in the mountains of Zambia and Angola increases this depth to seven metres.

For those with discretionary dollars, this is the time to fly into Katima Mulilo, the sandblasted little village in Eastern Caprivi where the elephants come down to drink. Below the golf course, chalets and green lawns of Zambezi Lodge, the *Zambezi Queen* lies waiting in the shade of fig trees, a white, treble-decked mirage from the Mississippi.

Here you choose your berth on this luxurious 45-m river boat for a four-day cruise downstream that will include game-viewing in the Chobe, and a visit to the Victoria Falls. The *Zambezi Queen* is powered by four diesel engines which generate a total of 600 horsepower. The boat has 13 air-conditioned staterooms and mirrored lounges that reflect exotic Indian brasserie, Chinese figurines and Egyptian papyrus prints.

It is the largest private vessel on the Zambezi River, and the only holiday river boat to navigate any of the rivers of the subcontinent. Each handmade cabin has its own bathroom and viewing deck.

Lie back in bed and view elephants, sitatunga, pink-eared hippos and the constant darting of swifts and weavers above the sparkling waters.

If you have a taste for luxury, try a river cruise aboard the exquisitely appointed Zambezi Queen.

Locals in traditional craft paddle down the mighty Zambezi, passing a thatched jetty on the way.

KAUDOM GAME PARK
Northeastern Namibia

Omurambas, or dry fossil riverbeds, streak the dusty savannahs of the seldom-visited Kaudom Game Park in northeastern Namibia.

Kaudom (*Xau* means buffalo, and *dum* means depression) covers 385 000 ha, and lies along Namibia's border with Botswana in the east.

It is without a doubt the country's most remote wilderness reserve, and only two four-wheel-drive vehicles are allowed per party along its deep sand tracks. There are no game fences to hamper the movement of the wild dogs, the large herds of gemsbok, roan antelope, kudu, elephants, lions and blue wildebeest in this untouched wilderness.

Nights at the rustic Sikereti Camp (in the south) and Kaudom Camp (in the north) are enchanting, with the stars forming a vast, diamond-studded canopy above you as you sit around the crackling flames of your camp fire listening to the sounds of the night.

In the rainy season the grass and reedbeds spring to life, making game-viewing difficult, and driving all but impossible. But in the dry months there is always game to see at the water holes and amongst the acacia, leadwood and false or bastard mopane trees of this pristine sanctuary.

Elephants are known to dig down under the sandveld, memory and smell telling them of the presence of streams that flow underground, west from the great Okavango waterway.

There is a good population of giraffes in the park and always a chance of spotting red hartebeest, eland, bat-eared foxes, spotted hyaenas and, with luck, a leopard high in a manketli tree.

Map: page 371, 3F
From the south turn east 57 km north of Grootfontein, onto the C44. Follow this for 222 km to Tsumkwe. From here it is 74 km to the entrance gate via Klein Dobe. From the north the park is signposted on the main B8 road for Katere, from where it is about 58 kilometres.
Details: Open year-round sunrise to sunset. Admission fee charged. Booking essential. No caravans or trailers. Bring food and water for a minimum of 3 days. Petrol available at Tsumkwe, Bagani, Mukwe and Rundu. Check road conditions before departing.
Accommodation: Both Sikereti and Kaudom camp sites have 4-bed huts (bring your own bedding), a picnic area and communal ablution facilities with flush toilets. Both camps are unfenced.
Further information and reservations: Directorate of Tourism and Resorts, Ministry of Wildlife, Conservation and Tourism, Private Bag 13267, Windhoek, tel (061) 23-6975/6/7/8; Charley's Desert Tours, P O Box 1400, Swakopmund, tel (0641) 4341; or Namib Wilderness Safaris, P O Box 6850, Windhoek, tel (061) 22-0947 or 22-1281.

A bat-eared fox stands sentinel as her brood take an afternoon rest in the scorching heat of the Kaudom Game Park.

The roads in Kaudom are long, dusty and lonely – visitors should remember to take adequate supplies of water, food and fuel.

NAMIBIA

KOLMANSKOP
East of Luderitz

Map: page 371, 8C
Kolmanskop lies 10 km east of Luderitz.
Details: The only way to visit the ghost town is to obtain a permit from the Luderitz Foundation and Tourist Information office, upper Bismarck Street, and then join one of the daily tours that are run every morning from Monday to Saturday.
Accommodation: There are 3 hotels in Luderitz: Bay View Hotel, P O Box 100, Luderitz, tel (06331) 288; Kapps Hotel, P O Box 387, Luderitz, tel (06331) 2701; and Zum Sperrgebiet, P O Box 373, Luderitz, tel (06331) 2976. You may also try the Luderitz Bay Guest House, P O Box 97, Luderitz, tel (06331) 3347.
Further information: Luderitz Foundation and Tourist Information, P O Box 233, Luderitz, tel (06331) 2532; Kolmanskop Tour Company, P O Box 45, Luderitz, tel (06331) 2445.

Kolmanskop is a ghost town on a desert dune near Luderitz Bay. The Atlantic winds whistle through the bare ribs of the rafters, and the open, sagging doors are piled two metres high with sand.

Long gone are the diamond days when men rushed to pluck the sparkling icestones from the desert sands, and built a town that could boast four skittle alleys, a hospital, a casino and even an orchestra for elegant soirees. Today, strolling its sand-heaped heights, you can still read the Gothic lettering above the bakery, and see the butchery, the soda-water plant that supplied free ice to every household, and the grand, double-storey mansion of the mine manager, with its Romeo-and-Juliet balcony and arched windows.

The plaster is peeling away, the corrugated iron roofing rattles mournfully in the windblasts, and sand eddies around debris in once lush gardens. Kolmanskop took its name from Johnny Coleman, a transport driver who had to be rescued there during a terrible sandstorm.

But it was railway maintenance foreman August Stauch who spurred the general interest in the area. In 1908 one of his workers handed him what they thought was a pretty, shining stone. Being a shrewd man, he recognized it as a diamond and rushed off to procure a

Old buildings at Kolmanskop stand fast, proudly resisting the advances of the ever-encroaching sand dunes.

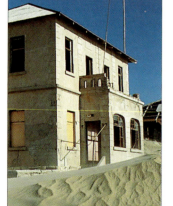

The desert wind moans in the cracks of the old homes at Kolmanskop, once a boom town.

Diamonds of the desert

Not far beneath the harsh sands of Namibia's desert coast north of Oranjemund lies a fortune in diamonds.

Concrete dykes keep the thunderous sea at bay as monster tracked excavators, the world's largest, and growling bulldozers, plough into the beach creating dunes behind them until the bedrock is laid bare.

Carefully screened workers, balaclavad against the chill Atlantic mist, then begin to pick, scrape and brush the rock which looks like petrified coral, rough and pock-marked.

But it is in these hidden crevices that the little white diamonds are found, nearly 100 percent of which are of gem quality. At Oranjemund 6 000 carats are mined each day. To do this, the world's largest opencast mine, the Consolidated Diamond Mine, removes 30 million tons of sand and earth each year.

The ancient Greeks looked with wonder at these beautiful flashing stones and considered them to be splinters from the stars. They were being mined in India 2 500 years ago, but only discovered in southern Africa in 1866 along the Orange River. And it was north of this river mouth in 1908 that the first Namibian gem came to light.

August Stauch, the railway maintenance foreman at Grasplatz near Kolmanskop, was an amateur geologist.

He suspected that there were hoards of diamonds lying on this wild coast, although it was many years before anyone realized it was the muddy waters of the Orange River that had brought them from the interior. Stauch instructed his labourers to keep an eye out for diamonds while clearing the railway track of drifting sand.

Before the day was out, young Zacharias Lewala returned with one and within 12 years Namibia was producing 20 percent of Africa's diamonds.

Stauch himself made a fortune, but died a pauper, and by 1950 Kolmanskop was a ghost town abandoned to the desert sands.

Diamonds are pure, colourless crystals compressed by the volcanic fire-force of the earth into a hardness 90 times that of the next hardest mineral, corundum.

In Namibia they are found north of Oranjemund along a hostile thirstland, where the wind scorches the rocky plains, and jagged mountains and distant old volcanoes swelter in the uncompromising sun.

prospecting licence. Within a few weeks prospectors poured in from the nearby railhead, and men even jumped ship to join the rush.

For at Kolmanskop the diamonds lay on the desert floor, and on the valleys between the dunes 'like plums under plum trees'. Workmen were seen abandoning wheelbarrows to scoop up the gems feverishly with their bare hands.

About 700 families came to live at Kolmanskop. Their standard of living was far more lavish than it had ever been in Europe. A swimming pool and playground were created, elegant residential bakeries were built, daily milk deliveries were made, and even a theatre was constructed by the town fathers for the amusement of the prospectors.

The lack of water, however, was a problem that could not be ignored. At first it was shipped in barrels from Cape Town to Luderitz, then hauled the nine kilometres by mule across the scorching dunes. Sea water – for use in the mine – was laboriously pumped 35 km from Elizabeth Bay.

Some was turned into drinking water in one of the world's first primitive desalination plants.

But the seams ran dry, diamond prices slumped in the Great Depression, Stauch left to die a pauper in Germany, and, in 1950, all mining ceased.

Steep-sided Lake Otjikoto, fringed by bush, is sanctuary to a fascinating fish life, including dwarf bream and the mouth-breeding Otjikoto cichlid. The lake became a national monument in 1972.

LAKE OTJIKOTO
West of Tsumeb

The turquoise waters of the 150-m-wide Otjikoto sinkhole lie sleeping far below the aloes and the screen of fig trees that twist and cling to its rim as if fearful of falling into its depths.

This former limestone cavern, known to the Herero as the 'place too deep for cattle', lies alongside the main B1 road, 20 km west of the old mining town of Tsumeb. It was formed when the roof of a huge subterranean cave fell in, leaving this steep-sided sinkhole.

A colourful mural of ostriches lines the entrance pathway, with its emerald grass and woodcarvings, as you descend to the rocky viewing platform. The pool is the natural home of several endemic fish species, including the rare and colourful Otjikoto cichlid.

The waters, believed to be bottomless, but actually measured at 55 m, occasionally rise, fed by subterranean streams. In 1915 they concealed the cannon of a retreating German army. Divers have recovered a perfectly preserved Krupps ammunition wagon, and a Sandfontein cannon. The latter may be viewed in the delightful Tsumeb Museum.

Map: page 371, 3D
From Tsumeb travel northwest on the B1 towards Etosha. The lake is near the road, about 20 km from Tsumeb.
Details: There is an admission fee, and the lake is open 07h00-18h00. A refreshment and curio kiosk and toilet facilities are available.
Accommodation: Try the municipal camp site in Tsumeb, P O Box 275, Tsumeb, tel (0671) 2-1056; the La Rochelle Guest and Hunting Farm, P O Box 194, Tsumeb, tel (0671) 1-1013; or 1 of the 3 reasonably priced hotels: Minen Hotel, P O Box 244, Tsumeb, tel (0671) 3071/2; Hotel Eckleben, P O Box 27, Tsumeb, tel (0671) 3051; Mokuti Lodge, P O Box 749, Tsumeb, tel (0671) 3084.
Further information: Tsumeb Tourism Centre, P O Box 779, Tsumeb, tel (0671) 2-0728.

LUDERITZ
West of Keetmanshoop

Map: page 371, 7C

From Keetmanshoop drive 316km west on the B4 to reach Luderitz. Beware of drifting sand across the road as you approach. The mounds are higher than you think.

Accommodation: Luderitz offers 3 hotels: Bay View Hotel, P O Box 100, Luderitz, tel (06331) 288; Kapps Hotel, P O Box 387, Luderitz, tel (06331) 2701; and Zum Sperrgebiet, P O Box 373, Luderitz, tel (06331) 2976. Luderitz Bay Guest House offers comfortable accommodation. Contact them at P O Box 97, Luderitz, tel (06331) 3347.

Further information: Luderitz Foundation and Tourist Information, P O Box 233, Luderitz, tel (06331) 2532; Luderitz Safaris, P O Box 76, Luderitz, tel (06331) 2719.

Church spires soar above the surrounding desert sands as you approach Luderitz, with its lovely little fishing harbour, steep streets and colourful colonial German mansions.

Its hinterland is somewhat ravaged by the diamond diggings of the forbidden Sperrgebiet, but the town itself tumbles down to choppy aquamarine waters and a narrow fjord, perfect refuge for the crayfish boats that bob in the wind.

'Enter with God', the carved door on Goerke House reads. On a foundation of chiselled stone, this hilltop diamond palace, with its pale blue exterior, dragon gargoyles and red, multipeaked roof, testifies to the solid wealth of Luderitz 90 years ago, when fortunes were made in nearby Kolmanskop.

Goerke House was built in 1909 by a German lieutenant who lived there for years, before returning to Germany. It now serves as a museum, and doubles as accommodation for VIP guests visiting the area. Ever since Bartolomeu Dias planted a cross in 1487 on the long finger of land that holds back the Atlantic gales, whalers, guano collectors, seamen and adventurers have sheltered in the bay.

A monument on Shark Island, which is now linked to the mainland, tells the fascinating story of Adolf Luderitz who, in 1881, paid the Hottentot chief Joseph Frederichs 10 000 Reichsmark and 260 rifles for the harbour.

A yacht trip around the peninsula's many hideaway coves will have energetic dolphins racing ahead of you at the bow, and there is a jackass penguin colony on Halifax Island.

But the essence of Luderitz is discovered walking the narrow up-and-down streets of the old town where double-storey colonial houses huddle in their past glory.

The best way to see Luderitz is on foot. Tours to the local karakul carpet-weaving factory or the oyster farm (both available all year) can be arranged at any travel agency in the town.

Strange desert creatures

The desert is home to a myriad creatures and plants which have adapted to their hot, dry environment in unique and marvellous ways. Two hundred and four species of vertebrate, including 121 reptiles, five types of frog, 44 bird species and 34 different mammals, live in the deserts of southern Africa.

The scorpions of the desert date back 400 million years, the most ancient of jointed-feet creatures. When baby scorpions are born they are popped into a brood pouch, and later placed on their mother's back in two rows, heads and pincers pointing outwards, and tails interlaced. In this piggyback style the mother feeds her young.

There are some devilishly clever creatures in the hunt-and-be-hunted wilds of the desert. One, the trap-door, or 'dancing white lady', spider, discovered the wheel. Endemic to the Namib dune sea, the spider has one ferocious enemy, the wasp, with which it continually plays hide-and-seek. The trap-door spider lives in a burrow in the side of a dune, sealing the entrance with a sandsilk trap-door. This usually fools the wasp, so the wasp digs down into the burrow from above.

As soon as the burrow is exposed, the spider makes a wild dash for freedom, flies onto its side, curls into a ball and hurtles down the slope, doing 44 cartwheels per second, or 10 m in 10 seconds, too fast for the wasp. The trap-door spider earned its alternate name because of its habit of performing a warning dance when threatened by a predator on the dunes.

Another creature that astonishes nature-lovers is the darkling, or tenebrionid, beetles which tilt their backs upward to collect the fog in the Namib. The fog condenses on their backs and trickles into their mouths.

The trap-door or 'dancing white lady' spider flees across the Namib dunes by folding its legs inwards and rolling cartwheel-style down the slopes.

MAHANGO GAME RESERVE
Western Caprivi Strip

Golden papyrus, with its topknot looking like a clown's wig, and its stem as thick as a man's wrist, grows tangled and tall along the banks of the Kavango River in the new Mahango Game Reserve, tucked away at the extreme western edge of the Caprivi Strip.

The papyrus is so prevalent that, in places, it is difficult to access this swift-flowing river. Early in the morning, as you approach one of the river's oxbow bends on foot, beneath a canopy of bastard mopane, wild seringa and giant bloodwoods, you can hear the water coursing past the reedbeds and around the sand bars.

The 25 000 ha that make up this reserve's unusually mixed habitat are home to elephants, tsessebe, wildebeest, oribi, buffaloes, sable and roan antelope, as well as rare red lechwe and sitatungas.

But it is the variety and busy number of birds that are so astounding. Drawn to the wetland feeding grounds, date palms and dense riverine forest are coppery-tailed coucals with their ominous beaks, Pel's fishing owls and the white and black swamp boubous that challenge you in pairs from the tops of papyrus.

The 300 species found in the reserve include a myriad raptors – palmnut vultures, swooping African fish eagles, martial eagles and bateleurs. Mahango is reputed to be the single best area in Namibia for bird-watching.

There is something primeval about a riverine forest, trees that have matured for hundreds of years in a wilderness untouched by man.

At Mahango you are encouraged to explore on foot in order to preserve its dry riverbed *(omuramba)*. There are no camping facilities, so you feel you are the first human to wonder at the soaring umbrella of trees above you, and the constant chuckle of the river as it infiltrates the papyrus beds.

There are two attractive game drives, both of which start some 500 m south of the main gate in the north. The road leading left takes you past a flood plain and a picnic site, while the one on the right (suitable for four-wheel-drive vehicles only) follows a course away from the river, onto more sandy terrain, where you may see a variety of game.

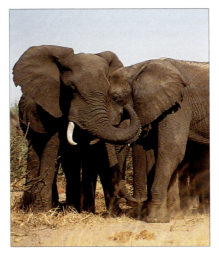

Elephants at the Mahango Game Reserve. Elephants consume as much as 200 litres of water and 250 kg of leaves, grass and bush every day.

Map: page 371, 2D
From Rundu travel 215 km east along the B8. Follow the sign at Bagani for 5 km to Popa Falls, and another 20 km to Mahango Game Reserve.
Details: Open sunrise to sunset year-round. Beware of elephants. An admission fee is payable at the gate. Best times to visit are August to October.
Accommodation: Mahango Game Reserve has no facilities for visitors, but to the north of the reserve is the Popa Falls Rest Camp, with 6 comfortable 4-bed huts, camp sites and a shop. Book at the Directorate of Tourism and Resorts *(see below)*. Alternatively, you can stay at Suclabo Lodge, northeast of Mahango (P O Box 894, Rundu, tel (067372) 6222). This private lodge has bungalows, restaurant, bar and swimming pool.
Further information: Directorate of Tourism and Resorts, Ministry of Wildlife, Conservation and Tourism, Private Bag 13267, Windhoek, tel (061) 23-6975/6/7/8.

MAMILI NATIONAL PARK
Central Caprivi Strip

Mamili is a maze of watery channels where the wild date palms hang over crystal streams.

The park's 40 000-ha wetland is really only a good rainy season and an obliging earth tremor away from joining the Okavango Delta of Botswana, with which it shares its Linyandi River border. This magnificent, unspoilt wilderness of flood plain and swampland was declared a national park in the early 1990s.

The Kwando River winds its way south for 100 km before breaking up into the narrow lily-covered waterways of the Mamili, lined with golden papyrus, lazy palms and shady marulas, ebonies and lovely *acacia albida*. These large trees, whose pods look something like rings of dried apple, can reach 30 m in height.

In times of flood it is not easy to get into Mamili, except by dugout canoe, but during the dry winter a four-wheel-drive vehicle will take you past the sylvan wetlands to such large islands as Lupala and Nkasa, both of which are home to a wide variety of bird and plant species.

Here crocodiles and hippos abound, and there are buffaloes, spotted hyaenas, a number of elephants, lions, wild dogs and shy sitatungas, which are specially adapted to walking across the reedbeds and lily lagoons.

Red lechwe, with their swept-back horns which they lay on their backs to negotiate a path through the reeds, love this secretive waterworld where man is not the only angler. Mamili's spectacular pageant of brightly plumed birds includes the little malachite kingfisher in its coat of many colours.

Long, red beak ready, it will sit on a dead branch, its bright, black eyes scanning the clear papyrus-fringed waters below for fish.

Map: page 371, 2E
Drive west from Katima Mulilo on the B8. At Matonga (47 km) turn left onto the D3501, which leads 40 km to Linyandi. Turn right onto the D3511 for about 48 km to Sangwali. Enquire here about the access track to Lupala Island and Mamili National Park.
Details: Check road conditions and camping possibilities with the Ministry of Wildlife, Conservation and Tourism at Katima Mulilo *(address below)*. Four-wheel-drive vehicles are essential.
Accommodation: Kalizo Fishing and Photographic Safaris operate a luxury lodge camp in Mamili. Contact them at P O Box 501, Ngwezi, Katima Mulilo, tel (067532) ask for 346.
Further information: Directorate of Tourism and Resorts, Ministry of Wildlife, Conservation and Tourism, Private Bag 13267, Windhoek, tel (061) 23-6975/6/7/8; Ministry of Wildlife, Conservation and Tourism, Private Bag 1020, Katima Mulilo, tel (067352) ask for 27.

NAMIBIA

MUDUMU NATIONAL PARK
Central Caprivi Strip

Map: page 371, 2D
From Katima Mulilo drive west on the main B8 road to Kongolo (125km). Follow the signs for Sangwali and Linyandi. There are scheduled flights by Air Namibia to Katima Mulilo, and an airstrip at Lianshulu.
Details: Open sunrise to sunset. Entrance fee. No public facilities. Contact the Ministry of Wildlife, Conservation and Tourism at Katima Mulilo *(see below)* before entering the park.
Accommodation: Southwest of the park lies the Nakatura camp site (no facilities). Contact Lianshulu Lodge at P O Box 142, Katima Mulilo, tel (067352) ask for 277, or book through Namib Safaris, P O Box 6850, Windhoek, tel (061) 22-0947.
Further information: Directorate of Tourism and Resorts, Ministry of Wildlife, Conservation and Tourism, Private Bag 1020, Katima Mulilo, tel (067352) ask for 27.

The double-decker, reedwall pontoon at Lianshulu Lodge, topped with a jaunty umbrella, provides a fish-eagle view of the surrounding golden mattress of reedbeds and massed riverine forest along the Kwando River in Mudumu National Park. This 85 000-ha conservation area comprises a wetland and swampland terrain filled with marvellous specimens of birds, mammals, amphibians and plants. Lilies float past like Hindu flame offerings – blue, yellow and white as you drift through the tranquil waterways.

At sunset the river, which divides Namibia from Botswana, provides a fiery canvas to the silhouetted trees, and an echo chamber for the grunting of lions in the mopane woodlands that roll back from the flood plains in a 30-km block of clay soil. In the dry Mudumu riverbed you may see a pack of wild dogs – Africa's most endangered carnivore.

Up to 500 migratory elephants visit Mudumu, and you often see them near the shallow Kwando River, which seldom exceeds 50 m in width, but which is host to ever-present crocodiles and pods of noisy hippos.

Early morning in the 800-sq-km park is a chorus of unsyncopated birdsong, as there are an incredible 400 species of bird, ranging from the painted snipe, hunching its way among the reeds at river's edge, to the startling African golden oriole in the mopane woodland, where giant baobabs and sausage trees also grow.

Lianshulu Lodge, west of Mudumu, is an enchanting complex of reed-and-thatch chalets overlooking the Kwando River. After a day in the wild you can cool off in its plunge pool before enjoying an excellent meal, or you may opt for a gentle sunset cruise on the pontoon.

NAMIB-NAUKLUFT NATIONAL PARK
Western Namibia

Map: page 371, 6C
Drive west from Mariental on the C19 to Maltahohe. Then take the C36. Turn left onto the D827 then right onto the D826 for NamibRand. Sossusvlei lies 167 km from Maltahohe.
Details: Entrance fees are payable at several gates which are open sunrise to sunset.
Accommodation: There is a government lodge at Sesriem, and camping sites at this and 12 other sites. Luxury tented dune camp at NamibRand, P O Box 5048, Windhoek, tel (061) 23-0616. *Die Duine Farm*, P O Box 131, Maltahohe, tel (06632) 6230, offers farm accommodation.
Further information: Directorate of Tourism and Resorts, Ministry of Wildlife, Conservation and Tourism, Private Bag 13267, Windhoek, tel (061) 23-6975/6/7/8.

There's something ironic about the cold ocean washing at the shores of a hot, dry desert, its dunes a frozen parody of the waves. The Namib-Naukluft National Park is such a desert, and it lies along the interminably bleak, fog-haunted coast of Namibia, stretching north from Luderitz to Walvis Bay. It's convenient to divide it into five sections, none of them at all the same as the others.

Sesriem and Sossusvlei
This is desert as the romantics picture it – seas of sand and soaring dunes. From the

A field of golden dunes, their ridges sharply edged by prevailing desert winds, reaches far into the Namib-Naukluft National Park.

camp at Sesriem, a hot but otherwise easy drive takes in Sesriem Canyon, where settlers found water, and modern tourists find welcome coolness. Mountainous dunes – among the world's highest – are the main attraction at Sossusvlei. Game-watching balloon trips are available.

Naukluft

Here are steep and spectacular cliffs in a reserve that was originally created to save Hartmann's mountain zebras. Streams flow far below the surface, sometimes rising to form cooling, crystal pools amid rocks sculpted by more abundant and more violent water that flowed untold millennia ago. Bird life is abundant, with a spillover of species from Namaqualand that lies just to the south.

The northern section

This lies between the Kuiseb and Swakop rivers, and features rocky plains bisected by the valley of the Swakop River. On these plains you'll see occasional columns of granite called inselbergs rising up like sentries above the thirsty land. In times of rain, the plains are covered by grass, and herds of springbok, zebras and gemsbok arrive to feast in the land of plenty.

Welwitschia Drive

This, the most northerly section of the park, is a short way from Swakopmund, along a route where numbered beacons mark points of special interest, ranging from lichen fields to rocky moonscapes, and from a dyke of intrusive dolerite to the place where South African soldiers camped during the First World War, in the conquest of what was then a German colony. There are ancient mine-workings and, of course, the welwitschia itself.

Sandwich Harbour

Bird migrants know Sandwich as a hospitable and refreshing stopover on their long journey between hemispheres. Here is water – much of it salty in the large lagoon, but there are also the mud flats, and springs of fresh water that form a chain of pools lined by sheltering reeds. The birds in countless numbers, and of many species, add splashes of colour and swirls of movement to some of Namibia's finest scenery *(see separate entry)*.

Rivers of sand at Sossusvlei

The magnificent red dunes of Sossusvlei twist upwards like a series of petrified rivers, dark on one side, sunlit on the other, reaching a height of 385 metres. Among the highest in the world, these dunes strongly resemble those of the Sahara Desert.

They are known as parabolic or cyclic dunes, and are caused by wind blowing from several directions simultaneously. They occur at the point where the Tsauchab River finally dies in a series of pans in the desert.

Composed largely of quartz sands, these dunes that look rather like cream-cake stars from the air, twist in five or six directions, and are all arrayed in a fiery palette of gold, ivory and maroon colours that have you reaching for your camera.

The clayey vlei itself is a shady spot, occasionally with water, where 500-year-old camelthorn trees provide welcome shade picnic sites. Strong winds buffet the vlei at from time to time, causing the sand-dune crests to burst into smoke as writhing blasts curl up the windward side, then break over the crest in an eerie explosion of gusting sand.

In 1986 the Tsauchab came down in flood, the first time in 10 years, attracting flamingoes, springbok, gemsbok and aquatic birds.

Sesriem Canyon, 55 km northeast or 'upstream' of Sossusvlei, is where the Tsauchab River disappears into a narrow gorge eroded into the rock and sand over centuries. This gorge – up to 30 m deep – is as narrow as 1,75 m in parts, and stretches for 1,5 kilometres.

The name Sesriem comes from the six ox-thongs which the thirsty trekkers tied together to raise a bucket of water from this deep canyon.

Massive dunes at Sossusvlei dwarf this solitary gemsbok.

NAMIBIA

SAN (BUSHMAN) TRAILS
Near Tsumeb

Map: page 371, 3D
Take the Tsintsabis road north from Tsumeb for 62 kilometres. Turn right onto the D3016 for 18 km, then first right onto the D3017, and follow the signs.
Details: The trails are intensive, and usually guided. They cover 2,5-4,5 km of fairly thick bush.
Accommodation: This is provided in Bushman huts, each separated by traditional fence bomas, or in more luxurious, thatched chalets. Both huts and chalets have modern ablution and cooking facilities.
Further information: San (Bushman) Trails, P O Box 689, Tsumeb, tel (06738) ask for 6222.

It is called *Xores*, the diminutive Heiqum Bushman, Theodore Xadeb, explains quietly, kneeling next to the low *Adenium bochemium* shrub.

Trail leader and local farmer Reinhard Friederich translates: 'Mixed with acacia gum, the sap of the shrub is used for arrowhead poison.'

This is only one of the many unusual – and educational – anecdotes you will learn if you venture onto a Bushman Trail organized on *Choant Sas* farm, 90 km from Tsumeb.

The trail is no ordinary excursion. You can elect to stay overnight in a beehive San hut made of poles tied with makalani palm thongs, and braai fresh kudu steaks beneath thick-trunked tamboti trees. Loeries *tok-tok* in the overhead purple-pod terminalia trees as you crouch on your haunches and your Bushman guide baits a bird trap or *!Uixuis*.

Further on, aardvark scrapings reveal the presence of a Tsoub sand well.

On the three-kilometre trail you will learn to make string from Sanseveria or Xui bark, coffee from white bauhinia beans, track a bat-eared fox, and grow to appreciate the tough, unromantic life of a hunter-gatherer.

SANDWICH HARBOUR
South of Walvis Bay

Map: page 371, 6B/C
Drive south from Walvis Bay along the coast road. After 4 km turn left at the fork. From here it's about 36 km to Sandwich Harbour. If you drive along the beach, take note of the tides. Alternatively, take the tracks that run parallel to the beach. Suitable for 4-wheel-drive vehicles only.
Details: Open year-round 06h00-20h00. Permits available from the Ministry of Wildlife, Conservation and Tourism, and from tour operators in Walvis Bay and Swakopmund.
Accommodation: Walvis Bay offers 4 hotels and 2 caravan/camping parks. Try Esplanade Park, a camping and caravan site with bungalows west of the harbour.
Further information: Namib Publicity and Tourism Association, 28 Kaiser Wilhelm Street, Swakopmund, tel (0641) 2224; Walvis Bay Municipality, P O Box 86, Walvis Bay, tel (0642) 5981 or 6145.

Sand dunes fold like whipped cream down to a crystal sea of birds at deserted Sandwich Harbour.

Thousands of birds migrate annually from as far as the Arctic to this shallow, 15-km wetland near Walvis Bay.

The subterranean watercourse of the Kuiseb River percolates silently into the lagoon beneath the awesome limbs of sand, to mix with the tidal sea that sweeps over the sand bar.

The resultant lagoon, with its reed pools and mud flats, provides a watery habitat for waders and water birds, sea birds and even land birds.

Modern man was originally attracted to Sandwich Harbour by the mountains of guano that covered the bay, but the venture to harvest guano for commercial purposes was unsuccessful.

Today Sandwich Harbour is strictly for the birds. The only way to explore this fragile and fascinating wonderland, and see its flamingoes, sandpipers and high, wheeling terns, is on foot.

And, for a lovely panorama of the lagoon, climb a dune. The sight of pink flamingoes flying gracefully above the pale apricot-coloured sands is a delight to any photographer.

White pelicans sun themselves at Sandwich Harbour's reed-fringed wetland area. In flight these birds form a V-shaped skein.

SKELETON COAST NATIONAL PARK
Far northwest coast

Howling winds whip the sand off the dunes in sheets and hurl them at the storm-lashed sea. Under this barrage of stinging grains you stoop for a bottle on the beach, and peer in, half expecting to see a scribbled message from a shipwrecked mariner.

Dozens of unwary travellers, their ships wrecked by mountainous waves, gale-force winds and treacherous reefs, have died on this desolate, 550-km strip of Namibia's northern desert coast.

Caught between an icy sea and a hinterland of baking dunes and barren, black-topped mountains, they have simply died of thirst and insufferable heat.

In spite of its ghastly associations with death, however, the Skeleton Coast is a place of rare beauty, changing moods and wonderful colours.

Divided into the southern park section and the northern tourism concession area, the Skeleton Coast has sprawling lichen-covered plains, secret riverbeds where elephants dig to drink, and colossal shifting dunes.

It offers perfect solitude, grandeur and constant surprises. Driving north of the Ugab River bed where stands of wild fig and tamarisk trees grow, and which demarcates the southern boundary, cormorants and gulls swoop over the turbulent surf.

At the two resorts of Terrace Bay and Torra Bay you can fish for kabeljou, galjoen and steenbras, while ghost crabs scurry past your tackle box.

Here black-backed jackals circle the lagoon, beachcombing for chicks and birds' eggs.

In years of very good rain, the coastal riverbeds serve as temporary home to populations of giraffes, gemsbok, brown hyaenas, caracals, zebras and even lions. North of Torra Bay creeping dunes loom over the beach.

Known as barchans, these crescent-shaped dunes, home to highly adapted spiders, termites, wasps and tenebrionid beetles, shift reluctantly before the relentless southwesterlies, and roar as their crests avalanche down the slipface.

Striped, dune-coloured Cessnas fly small parties of visitors into the far northern tourism concession area where, surrounded by the immensity of the desert, nature has created quicksand springs, clay castles that look like ancient Persian monuments, volcanic, metre-wide chunks of blue-white agate, and reed oases where springbok graze.

Map: page 371, 3/4 A/B
Drive north of Swakopmund for 194 km and you will cross the southern boundary of the park at Ugab River. Torra Bay camp site is another 104 km further on.
Details: Open year-round. Day-permits are available. Filling station at Torra Bay during December school holidays. Gates must be reached before 15h00. Only those with a reservation will be allowed into Torra Bay, which is only open 1 December to 15 January, or Terrace Bay. Normal vehicles may be used to enter and explore the southern section, but the northern section is best approached by air.
Accommodation: Camp sites at Torra Bay, and fully catered accommodation at Terrace Bay. Fuel, shop and bars at Terrace Bay (the resort caters mainly for fishermen).
Further information: Directorate of Tourism and Resorts, Ministry of Wildlife, Conservation and Tourism, Private Bag 13267, Windhoek, tel (061) 23-6975/6/7/8.

After good rains, the Uniab River rises to reach the sea near Terrace Bay in the Skeleton Coast National Park.

SWAKOPMUND
North of Walvis Bay

Swakopmund is a small seaside town on Namibia's Atlantic coast, that has uniquely retained all its turn-of-the-century German colonial charm and *gemutlichkeit* (wellbeing). The town, built at the mouth of the usually dry Swakop River, spreads out to the flat desert plains behind it. Immaculate, palm-lined streets, manicured gardens and gracious colonial buildings typify this pretty town.

On the approach from Windhoek the mountains seem to float on valleys of sand, while heat mirages shiver in rivulets that rise from the road.

The temperature stays relentlessly high as the desert becomes rolling dunes, dusted with graphite. Then, about 30 km from the coast, waves of fluffy, cooling, sea-freshened air envelop you. This is Swakopmund's secret elixir.

When the rest of the country reels in summer's heat and the winds dry a towel in 10 minutes, Swakopmund air-conditions its avenues of gorgeous palms and venerable burgher buildings with cool Atlantic air.

Practically every house, castle, cupola and bell-capped tower in Swakopmund has a date on it. Even new buildings maintain the elegant tradition.

From the old iron-girdered promenade pier, with its restaurant converted from a stricken tug, the little holiday town, with

Map: page 371, 5B
The drive west from Windhoek via Okahandja is 356 km on a good, tarred road, with many rest points.
Details: The boutiques, bakeries, cafes and old buildings are concentrated where Post Street forms an L-shape with the promenade. The museum is open daily 10h00-12h30, and 15h00-17h30. Entrance fee charged.
Accommodation: There are 15 hotels, and A-frame municipal chalets in Swakopmund.
Further information: Namib Publicity and Tourism Association, 28 Kaiser Wilhelm Street, Swakopmund, tel (0641) 2224; Swakopmund Municipality, P O Box 53, Swakopmund, tel (0641) 2411/2444.

NAMIBIA

Swakopmund has a distinctly Continental air, with its provincial German buildings set against the unlikely backdrop of the Namib Desert.

its red-and-white lighthouse, stretches back from the beachfront with gracious, old-world grandeur.

As you stroll along Kaiser Wilhelm, Moltke or Bismarck streets, only the wind-buffeted dunes that lead to the Namib-Naukluft National Park remind you that you are still in Africa.

The leaded windows, exterior wooden beams, and bonneted towers of the 44 historic buildings are pure Baltic seaside.

Worth visiting is the 'Mole', which was constructed originally as a harbour wall, but now serves as a protective sandbank for a fine, sandy beach.

Not far from Swakopmund are the Goanikontes lunar dunes, which are worth seeing, and a little further afield is the world's largest opencast mine, Rössing Uranium, where a million tons of rock are removed each week.

TSUMEB MINE
East of Etosha

Map: page 371, 3D
From Otjiwarongo drive north for 181 km on the B1 to reach Tsumeb.
Details: Tsumeb Museum open weekdays 09h00-12h00 and 15h00-18h00; and Saturdays 15h00-18h00.
Accommodation: There is a park for campers and a selection of reasonably priced hotels in Tsumeb. Try the Hotel Eckleben, P O Box 27, Tsumeb, tel (0671) 3051, or the cheaper Minen Hotel, P O Box 244, Tsumeb, tel (0671) 3071/2.
Further information: Tsumeb Tourism Centre, P O Box 779, Tsumeb, tel (0671) 2-0728.

Tsumeb is a rather tiny, and exceptionally pretty, mining town *en route* from Windhoek to Etosha Pan. Its village green, fed by the waters of the copper mine that tunnels beneath its streets, offers a lush canopy of flowering trees and soft dandelion grass. And the town's wide streets are lined with jacaranda trees and brilliant bougainvillea blossoms.

The green is bordered by homely colonial buildings, particularly in the main street. You will see the Church of St Barbara, with its pink tower bonnet, a handsome Lutheran church, and the conical bell tower of what appears to be another church, but is the old headquarters of Omeg Minenburo, an old mining company.

Iron-Age workers smelted copper at Tsumeb ('the place of frogs'), but only in the last 100 years has the world's greatest range of gemstones and minerals, 217 in all, been commercially exploited here. Mine tours have been discontinued, but you may see the stones in the Tsumeb Museum, which is located in an old German school building dating back to the early years of this century.

On display are samples of blue azurite, lichen-covered olivenite, aragonite, copper, lead and zinc.

Also in the museum you will see relics of an old German ammunition wagon and cannon, recovered from the bottom of Lake Otjikoto after being dumped there by retreating Germans in 1915.

Tsumeb has grown around its famous mine, the site of a fabulously rich treasure of mineral ore.

Namibia's rich harvest of salt

South Africa's salt supply for its plastics and chemical industries largely comes from Namibia and the area around Swakopmund and Walvis Bay. In a sense, it is man-made salt, as water is pumped from the sea into large, flat areas where it is left to evaporate, then pumped from one pan to the next until it eventually crystallizes.

The crystallized salt is washed in concentrated salt water to rid it of any sand, and it emerges far purer than the salt normally used at dinner tables.

These salt pans are best seen from the air. The bacteria in the pans differ according to the level of salt concentration and evaporation, and they colour the pans a kaleidoscope of lovely colours, ranging from green to deep red.

The largest of the natural salt pans lies in the salt-flats country between Meob Bay and Conception Bay in the Namib-Naukluft National Park.

Salt pans are flat depressions which were created by the sea before it retreated to new shores, leaving water residues that eventually evaporated to reveal such salts as chlorides of potassium, magnesium and sodium, as well as carbonates, calcium and sulphates.

The salt pans of Cape Frio in the far north, which has a seal colony, are 90 km long and several kilometres wide. These pans, which consist mainly of sand and concentrated brine, have a salt content of only about 25-30 percent. The salt pans at Angria Fria, which lie a little further north, contain high-quality salt up to 100 m deep.

Some four-wheel-drive visitors sometimes make the mistake of driving onto salt pans, a habit which is ecologically destructive and highly dangerous. The top salt crust is often only a few centimetres deep, and may conceal a soft slush of fine sand and water which can swallow a bulldozer.

Etosha is a vast saline lake and not a true salt pan. It certainly couldn't sustain its teeming game population if it were.

Framed by blue desert skies, these salt dunes near Swakopmund shimmer beneath the unblinking sun.

WALVIS BAY HARBOUR
Walvis Bay

The lagoon at Walvis Bay has a special significance – it is home to about half of southern Africa's flamingoes.

As the sun breaks through coastal mist over the sea, pontoons of these birds are illuminated in pink on the glistening water. The lagoon is flanked by an esplanade of palms, flowers and white benches.

At one end an information wigwam abuts onto the dune wetlands and the saltworks, all of which are part of the Namib-Naukluft National Park.

Here you will learn that the high nitrogen content of the Benguela Current and the warm, sunlit waters enable microorganisms to reproduce in sufficient abundance to support 25 000 birds.

Many of the birds migrate from inland pans such as Etosha, while others, such as Arctic terns and sandpipers, fly in from Russia and Siberia.

Discovered in 1487 by Bartolomeu Dias, Walvis Bay was used by whalers and guano collectors, and grew to become a major fishing port.

The town's harbour to the north of the reserve teems with trawlers, and the aroma of wet fish hangs heavy in the air.

The harbour at Walvis Bay bulges and bustles with fishing trawlers, fish-processing factories and the screech of scavenging gulls.

An estimated 500 000 tons of salt, practically all of southern Africa's annual requirement, is produced here, the pans doing double duty as an integral part of the bird sanctuary. The town is a vital link in a global bird network.

It supports at least half the world's chestnut-banded plovers, sandpipers *en route* to the Caspian Sea, thousands of terns, and the flamingoes.

Until 1994 the port of Walvis Bay and its hinterland belonged to South Africa, but in 1994 control was ceded to the Government of Namibia.

Map: page 371, 5B
Drive south from Swakopmund for 30 kilometres. At the roundabout take the second turn-off, into Union Street. Turn right into 5th Road, and left into Diaz Street. Continue for 1 km to the information display.
Details: No admission fee. Birds year-round, but more migrants in summer.
Accommodation: Large selection in Walvis Bay, but many visitors prefer Swakopmund.
Further information: Municipal Information Office, Civic Centre, P O Box 86, Walvis Bay, tel (0642) 5981.

NAMIBIA

WATERBERG PLATEAU NATIONAL PARK
East of Otjiwarongo

Map: page 371, 4D
Drive south on the B1 from Otjiwarongo for 27 kilometres. Turn left onto the C22 for a further 41 km, and left again onto the D2512 signposted gravel road.
Details: Open 08h00 until sunset, although closed 13h00-14h00 for payment of entrance fees. Jeep and bus tours of the plateau are available, and 3-day wilderness trails.
Accommodation: Comfortable bungalows in the Bernabe De La Bat Rest Camp on the wooded slopes of the escarpment. Caravan and camp sites also available. Restaurant, kiosk and swimming pool.
Further information: Directorate of Tourism and Resorts, Ministry of Wildlife, Conservation and Tourism, Private Bag 13267, Windhoek, tel (061) 23-6975/6/7/8.

As you pause to catch your breath on the Waterberg ('water mountain') Hiking Trail, the spine of the long mountain rises above you in a fusion of different colours: copper, gold and green.

The plateau – 48 km in length – sheers off sharply on all sides to slopes of lush woodland, coloured by the yellow pods of various species of acacia. In the distance, the ochre-coloured plains disappear into a blue haze.

The plateau, which is 250 m high, and, in parts, 16 km wide, supports one of the highest concentrations of indigenous plants in southern Africa. More than 479 species, including flowering aloes and fig trees, thrive here.

The Waterberg derives its name from the loose Kalahari sand on its table top, which acts as a sponge, absorbing the rain that sweeps across the arid plain.

The water percolates through the sand into the porous sandstone below, but is blocked by a layer of rock. It then flows sideways to appear as springs on the slopes of the mountain. The diversity of vegetation supports a large variety of game, some 90 mammal species in all, including giraffes, kudu, leopards, hyaenas, cheetahs, wild dogs and the endangered white rhinos.

Over 200 species of bird have been recorded – with pride of place being held by Namibia's only breeding colony of Cape vultures. A vulture restaurant has been opened to the public on Wednesday mornings. There are also 20 types of bat in the Waterberg.

The park is also home to at least 13 species of frog, including the rare black-and-orange-spotted *phrynomerus* frog.

During the dry season (from April to November) two hikes are available. The first is an accompanied three-day trail, in the west of the park; the second is a four-day unaccompanied trail along the south of the escarpment (starts on Wednesdays only). Take your own food and sleeping bag. For the less energetic, nine short, marked trails are available.

A monument at Waterberg honours soldiers who died here in battle between occupying German forces and local Hereroes.

Trailists overnight at a camp artfully concealed beneath the bizarre conical sandstone formations at Etjo, on the Waterberg Plateau.

WEST CAPRIVI GAME PARK
Caprivi Strip

Bastard mopane trees stand desolate in the hot winds that come gusting in from the dust-darkened horizons of West Caprivi Game Park.

Until the peace agreement of 1989, this entire area was out of bounds to casual visitors, but now its undisturbed beauty is destined to become a major attraction for wildlife-lovers.

Thorn scrub huddles beneath larger sausage, teak and ebony trees, cadging a little shade in the terrible heat of this endless woodland between the Kavango and Kwando rivers. The environment here is very similar to that at Mahango Game Reserve *(see separate entry)*, with a combination of flood plain, dune belts, acacia woodland and riverine forest.

The animal population here includes elephants, impala, kudu, roan antelope, waterbuck, reedbuck, buffaloes, lions, hippopotamuses and crocodiles. Their lives depend on the summer rains that water the sweltering veld.

The Caprivi, crossroads of rivers and rivalries, is a harsh, wooded wilderness where man has long traded in war.

Today the migrating elephants of the Caprivi, the giraffes, Burchell's zebras and impala can safely concentrate along the green forested banks of the Kwando, and jostle at the nearby pans of Ndwasa and Malombe.

Here they are joined by a chorus of birdsong (the birds are best seen on a boat ride past the islands and reed banks) and such water-loving creatures as sitatungas, shy lechwe and hippos.

A hard, three-hour journey to the western boundary brings you to the Kavango River as it rushes past the lovely rapids of Popa Falls, on its last journey into the desert.

Although you need a four-wheel-drive vehicle in the Caprivi Strip area, there is a good gravel road running east to west through the game reserve.

Map: page 371, 1/2D
East of Rundu the tarred road stretches for 190 km to Bagani (petrol available). Cross the Kavango River. The 191-km-long reserve is now on both sides of the gravel road.

Details: Travellers check in at the Susuwe office at the eastern end of the reserve. You may not leave the main road without permission. Kalizo Fishing and Photographic Safaris operate photographic tours. Contact them at P O Box 501, Ngwezi, Katima Mulilo, tel (067352) ask for 346.

Accommodation: There are two camp sites within the reserve: Nambwa in the southeast, and Chisu further north. Both lie on the banks of the Kwando River, but have no facilities. On the Kavango River in the west you may stay at the Popa Falls Rest Camp, with its comfortable four-bed huts and camp sites. You may also try Lianshulu Lodge (in the Mudumu National Park), P O Box 142, Katima Mulilo, tel (067352) ask for 277.

Further information: Directorate of Tourism and Resorts, Ministry of Wildlife, Conservation and Tourism, Private Bag 13267, Windhoek, tel (061) 23-6975/6/7/8.

The Kavango River drops in a series of gentle rapids at Popa Falls before continuing across the Kalahari towards its famous delta.

PLACES TO VISIT

WINDHOEK

ALTE FESTE

Map: page 397
From Independence Avenue drive east on Peter Muller Street, and turn right into Leutwein Street. Alte Feste is clearly visible on your left.
Details: Open 09h00-18h00 Monday to Friday; 10h30-12h30 and 15h00-18h00 Saturdays and Sundays. Closed on public holidays. No admission fee, but donations welcome.
Accommodation: There is a good restaurant and pub at the Alte Feste, tel (061) 22-6840, and a good selection of hotels in Windhoek.
Further information: The Curator, State Museum, P O Box 1203, Windhoek, tel (061) 293-4376.

German colonial troops or *schutztruppe* stormed the Nama Chief Jan Jonker Afrikaner's kraal overlooking Windhoek, where this 'old fort', with its white castle turrets, still stands in sombre elegance as today's State Museum.

War and genocide have characterized Germany's attempt to carve a colonial empire in this land of deserts and black mountains, leaving a legacy of handsome castles and forts throughout Namibia. Alte Feste, built by Congo explorer Captain Curt Von Francois, the founder of Windhoek, is the most famous.

One wing of the entrance verandah is a restaurant, the other the repository of ancient wagons and yellow field cannons. A plaque records that the stronghold was built originally 'to preserve peace and order between the rivalling Nama and Herero communities'.

The first of six halls you enter contains sepia pictures of the 100-year struggle of the Namibian people for independence.

A wind-up house organ, a cupboard made of paraffin tins, and a 1904 dining table and chairs, crafted by Siegfried Spaeder, one of seven soldiers who defended Namutoni Fort in Etosha against impossible odds, typify the museum's accent on colonial home life in a Victorian age.

One tower, which overlooks the fort's lovely grassed slopes and palms, affords panoramic views of old Windhoek.

These relics of the German occupation are on display on the verandah at Alte Feste.

DAAN VILJOEN GAME RESERVE

Map: page 397
The signposted turn-off to Daan Viljoen lies 20 km west of Windhoek, on the C28, a continuation of Sam Nujoma Drive.
Details: Open year-round sunrise to 13h00, and 14h00-17h00, although visitors may leave up to 23h30. Entrance fee.
Accommodation: Attractive 2-bed bungalows, fully equipped with kitchen utensils and bedding, and caravan sites near the lake. Restaurant, swimming pool, kiosk and picnic spots.
Further information: Directorate of Tourism and Resorts, Ministry of Wildlife, Conservation and Tourism, Private Bag 13267, Windhoek, tel (061) 23-6975/6/7/8.

The lake at Daan Viljoen Game Reserve, 24 km west of Windhoek, with its island of green reeds, walkway of weeping willows and thatched picnic umbrellas, is the focal point of this 50-sq-km park, a favourite with Windhoek residents.

At one end of this lake are rondavels and camp sites, while at the other a restaurant overlooks the Khomas Hochland hills to distant Windhoek.

From a dozen vantage points on the built-up lawns overlooking the tranquil lake, you can watch flotillas of water birds such as dabchicks and blue-billed maccoa ducks cruise past.

More than 200 species of bird have been identified in the park, and you can easily see 50 varieties in a day.

You will see Egyptian geese, looking like highwaymen with dark rings around their eyes, red-billed teals, coots, shy African shelducks, and, in some of the drowned trees, cormorants displaying their white, downy fronts.

There is an interesting circular drive which starts near the handsome stone entrance-arch, but probably the best way to explore this park is to take one of the two bushveld trails.

These trails (one is a 9-km walk, the other a 3-km ramble) wander through ridged mountain foothills, home to cliff-nesting black eagles, and decorated by a spiky variety of Africa's thorn trees:

WINDHOEK

candle-pod acacias with hairy leaves, sweetthorn, and also dense stands of camelthorn typical of semidesert areas.

In the dry riverbeds, rocks shine in the sun, the trees draw sustenance from the underground streams, and here you will spot eland, gemsbok, springbok and hartebeest with their twisted horns.

When the rains arrive at the end of each year, family groups of wildebeest and Hartmann's mountain zebras will stop to stare at you as you walk by.

KEY TO THE MAP
1 Alte Feste
2 Daan Viljoen Game Reserve
3 Namibia Crafts Centre
4 Tintenpalast
5 TransNamib Railway Museum

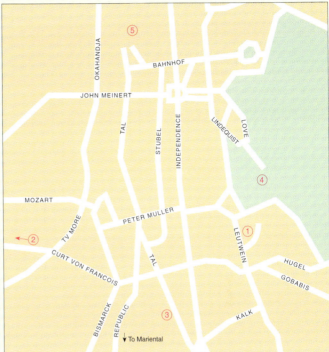

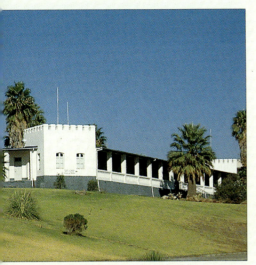

The romantic fort at Alte Feste was once the headquarters of the German administration of the territory known then as South West Africa.

NAMIBIA CRAFTS CENTRE

The colourful walls of the fascinating Namibia Crafts Centre are repainted annually in a school competition.

These walls enclose the courtyard of the ochre-coloured Windhoek Brewery, where the two-storey centre now displays 500 crafts from all over Namibia and Africa, as far north as Tanzania. In the blue and green centre in Tal Street you will see 50 stalls and a bewildering array of exciting buys.

At the entrance are huge woodcarvings which have been fashioned from roots dug up from central Namibia's dry sands and ancient riverbeds. Pitted and twisted, they reflect the agony of this thirstland's desert conditions.

Various other crafts on display include delicate items of San jewellery, such as beadwork and painted ostrich eggs, intricate carvings of animals, teak bowls, and masks of different shapes and sizes.

Animal footprints and a colourful mural lead upstairs where you can have a Herero woman's dress made for you, or buy an Angora jersey from Swakopmund.

From Okahandja there are quaint drinking glasses carefully etched with tiny animals, some semiprecious stones from Damaraland, marble tables from the Karibib Desert, Ovambo baskets, toys made of wood, and cotton duvets in bright colourful squares.

From Malawi are black, rough-faced masks, skeletal masks from Tanzania, Kenyan candleholders, green malachite bracelets from Zambia, and soapstone from Zimbabwe.

Circular rugs made from springbok hides are good value, as are the Kavango reed mats, carved tables, karakul carpets and Bushman powder bags.

Next door, in the Old Brewery, music and one-man shows are held in the converted Warehouse Theatre.

Map: Above
The Namibia Crafts Centre is at 40 Tal Street. It lies on the left of Tal Street, heading towards Garten Street.
Details: Open 09h00-17h30 Monday to Friday; and 09h00-13h00 Saturdays. From 1 May to 31 August 08h30-17h00; closed Sundays. No admission charge.
Accommodation: There are many good hotels in Windhoek.
Further information: Namibia Crafts Centre, P O Box 24204, Windhoek, tel (061) 22-2236.

The bright walls of the Namibia Crafts Centre conceal exuberant displays of handwork from across the continent.

WINDHOEK

Map: page 397
From Independence Avenue turn east into Peter Muller Street, and right into Leutwein Street. Tintenpalast lies on your left.
Details: Open 7 days a week 07h00-17h00. Walk freely around the lawns. Explain that you are a visitor to the policeman on duty, sign the book, and you will be shown around. No entrance fee.
Accommodation: There are numerous hotels in Windhoek.
Further information: The Tourist Rendezvous, P O Box 107, Windhoek, tel (061) 22-1225.

TINTENPALAST

This imposing, square-columned edifice, three storeys high and 150 m long, which once represented the hallowed ideals of German colonialism, today houses the Namibian Parliament.

Designed by government architect Gottlieb Redecker, who was responsible for many of Windhoek's lovely old monuments, it cost 450 000 marks, and was mainly constructed from imported German materials (although the wood came from Cameroun).

After the Desert War of 1915, the South African administration took over the building, and it remained in their hands for 75 years.

A policewoman will escort you inside, past long rows of offices where officials tend to the work of government, to cool, treed courtyards, twisted iron staircases and a parliamentary visitors' gallery. The palace overlooks Windhoek's loveliest gardens.

Large, formal lawns, shaded by old palms, flamboyants, ornamental pines and a profusion of flowers, feature a fountain and twin walkways arched with trailing bougainvillea.

The vista beyond stretches across the neo-Romanesque, Lutheran Church ('Christuskirche'), with its needle-thin tower, to the city and the Khomas Hills.

Its meticulous gardens studded with tall palms, Tintenpalast is the gracious and fitting home of the Namibian parliament.

Map: page 397
Drive west down Bahnhof Street off Independence Avenue. At the end turn right, and park facing the station. The museum is up the circular stairway to the left of the ticket entrance.
Details: Open 09h00-12h00 and 14h00-16h00 Monday to Friday; closed on public holidays. Entrance fee charged.
Accommodation: With a selection of good hotels, accommodation is easy to find in Windhoek.
Further information: The Curator, TransNamib Museum, Private Bag 13204, Windhoek, tel (061) 298-2186.

TRANSNAMIB RAILWAY MUSEUM

The chairs in the dining cars of old steam trains crossing Namibia had a special under-rack where gentlemen in transit could place their hats, while iron containers were filled with hot water and delivered to each compartment to keep m'lady's toes warm.

A thousand such fascinating objects covering the 100-year history of rail in Namibia can be found in the 10 halls of the TransNamib Museum in Windhoek.

One hundred years of Namibian rail history are recorded in Windhoek's elegant old railway-station building.

You will hear the whistle and shunting of trains as you explore this museum on the first floor of the elegant, gabled station which was built by the German administration.

The curator, Walter Rusch, personally and painstakingly collected every single item in the museum during his 40 years with the railways.

The numerous exhibits include lovely, resilient oak furniture made with dowels, train-ticket racks, Morse-code cabinets, washbasins, ancient typewriters, silver cutlery, leather pay-trollies, passenger-bedroll sealing machines, and a fascinating cast-iron telephone whose handle weighs a kilogram.

A much-prized item is a long-handled hammer, used to tap and test every wheel as the train chuffed into the station. The parking area outside the station features a tiny Puffing Billy, while today's ticketing concourse displays a wicker basket used to lower apprehensive passengers from liners in Luderitz Bay onto waiting boats.

BOTSWANA

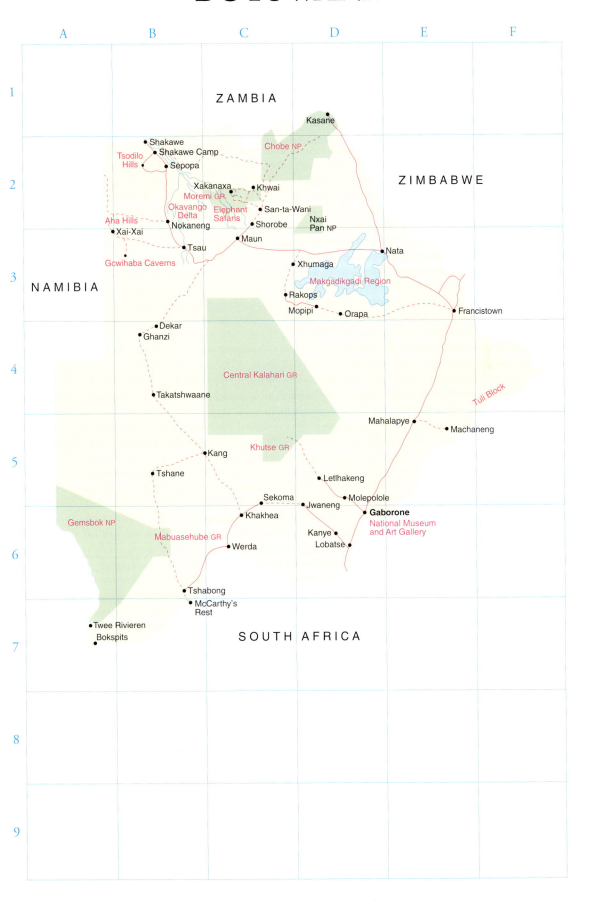

AHA HILLS
Northwestern Botswana

Map: page 399, 2A
From Maun drive 100 km south to Sehithwa. From Sehithwa travel north to Tsau, and follow the signpost just north of the town, to Drotsky's Caves. After about 40 km the track passes the small village of Xai-Xai and heads into the hills some 15 km further on. You can also take the road leading northwest for about 120 km to Nokaneng, then west for another 120 km to Gcangwa, and then south 30 km on the Xai-Xai road. As with most of the roads in the Kalahari, this latter road is for four-wheel-drive vehicles only.
Details: Open 06h00-18h00 April to September; 05h30-19h00 for the rest of the year. Nearest water at Gcangwa or Xai-Xai. Very little shade; no facilities. Travel in 2 fully equipped 4x4 vehicles, with water, food, tools, compass, map and fuel. Take malaria precautions.
Accommodation: Camping only, anywhere. Nearest accommodation at Drotsky's Cabins, 5 km from Shakawe; and Shakawe Fishing Lodge, 10 km from Shakawe. Book for both venues at Merlin Services, Airport Bag 13, Maun, tel 66-0351.
Further information: Gaborone National Museum and Art Gallery, P O Box 114, Gaborone, tel 37-4616.

The remote pink plateau of the Aha Hills (Aha means 'small rocks') emerges like a mirage, shimmering in the distance across the flat scrub-savannah of north-western Botswana.

The hills – a low, 245-km² plateau of dolerite, limestone and marble on the Namibian border – are not particularly dramatic in themselves, merely unexpected in this vast expanse of desolate bush, the western Kalahari home of the !Kung San (Bushmen).

A few of these hunter-gatherers still maintain their old traditional lifestyle, crossing the border fence now by means of stiles erected at strategic points. Most, however, gravitate towards the nearby villages of Gcangwa and Xai-Xai, where there are schools, water facilities and food-aid during drought months.

There are probably undiscovered caves lying deep in these limestone hills, part of the same formation as the Gcwihaba (Drotsky's) Caverns, some 85 km to the east *(see separate entry)*. The views from the top provide a panorama of vast plains interspersed with hills.

The skeleton of a tree rises hauntingly above the golden Kalahari bushveld, its branches withered by the uncompromising heat of the sun.

CENTRAL KALAHARI GAME RESERVE
Central Botswana

Map: page 399, 4C/D
Drive west from Francistown on the Orapa road for about 300 km to Rakops. From here, follow the sign for 55 km to Matswere Game Scouts Camp. If you're coming from Maun, ask for directions from the Duck Inn. The southern section can be reached from Gaborone via Molepolole.
Details: The gates are open 06h00-18h00 April to September; 05h30-19h00 October to March. Permit needed. Admission charged. No fuel or facilities in the reserve. Water is only available at the Matswere Game Scouts Camp.
Accommodation: Camping (no booking required) at Deception Valley, Piper's Pan and Sunday's Pan.
Further information: Department of Wildlife and National Parks, P O Box 131, Gaborone, tel 37-1405.

With an area of 51 800 km² the Central Kalahari Game Reserve is six times the size of Yellowstone National Park in North America. This savannah of endless grasslands, fossil riverbeds, pans and vast open spaces has an extraordinary beauty about it – a beauty that inspired explorers such as Moffat and Livingstone and, more recently, poet and writer Laurens van der Post.

Here, in the vast spaces, and in long silences broken only by the moan of distant lions, you can journey back to the days of the Bushman (San) hunters of old, and walk in their footsteps through the ceaseless seas of sand.

The word Kalahari comes from the local Tswana expression for 'the great thirst'. But it was known by other San names long before that. Before the reserve was opened to the public, it served as a refuge for the last remnants of the Kalahari's San. Today there are about 300 who have survived the depredations of man and his great enemy, drought.

There are four fossil rivers in the reserve, very few sand dunes, and a proliferation of pans in the north, which, when they are full, are a magnet for game. Deception Pan and its water holes are the best game-viewing areas.

Here you may see gemsbok, springbok, hartebeest, brown hyaenas, giraffes, wildebeest, bat-eared foxes and honey badgers – those tough little fighters that are usually found near water.

You will probably also see lilac-breasted rollers, in their pink-and-blue plumage, and such other species as guinea fowl, korhaans, snake eagles and ostriches.

Showman of the desert

The bat-eared fox is the prince of performers. Even the streetfighter ethics of a marching baboon troop cannot match the entertaining virtuosity of this pretty little animal with the round, all-hearing ears and coat of glossy grey.

He is tiny, weighing no more than a large book, and standing just 30 cm at the shoulder – about the height of a small dog. The species *(Otocyon megalotis)* belongs to a subfamily of its own, and is not closely related to either the foxes or dogs.

Bat-eared foxes love the open country, especially Nxai Pan and the Kalahari, where you'll see them darting from one termite mound to another in a frenzy of expectation, because the big ears can actually hear the movement of the termites deep in the mound.

A foraging fox will pause, dig away, look up, dig again, eat a tasty termite or two, do a swivel and scuffle, then scratch away again. When it's had its fill, it quite often sits atop the mound, as if safeguarding the mother lode, and savouring the next repast. But let a lizard or mouse move into view, and the fox is off again in a Charlie Chaplin chase. It is unbelievably nimble, and though the rodent may twist, duck and turn, the fox will duplicate its every move with lightning speed.

It's an up, down, double-back pantomime of jerk-start action that invariably corners the prey. Locusts are another delicacy the bat-eared fox fancies, and it will soon unearth them too, hide as they may in the desert sands.

Even the animal's face, with its dark muzzle, black eyes and white, furry sweatband across the forehead, is entertaining. It is, in fact, a lovely mixture of colours: brown, white, grey and black. Both the creature's bushy tail and legs are black.

The bat-eared fox is the symbol used by Botswana's Department of Wildlife and National Parks. It is usually seen in pairs, lives in holes in the ground and bears about six young each summer. It can chatter away like an old crone when it gets upset, but usually makes a rather appealing, soft 'who-who' call.

The bat-eared fox feeds mainly on insects, especially termites.

CHOBE NATIONAL PARK
Northern Botswana

More than 11 000 km² of magnificent wilderness terrain to the south of the Linyanti-Chobe river system, Botswana's common border with the Caprivi region of Namibia, have been set aside as the Chobe National Park, one of Africa's premier wildlife conservancies.

The rivers (they are in fact two sections of the same watercourse), the flood plains and seasonal swamps in the north, and the scrublands, grassy savannah and natural pans of the drier interior, are the main attraction for great herds of herbivores that trek in from the north-central wastelands of the country.

Especially notable are the elephants that congregate around the river reaches during the rainless winter months. At optimum times they number a remarkable 35 000 – the largest concentration in any of the continent's parks.

The other game populations are also impressive. Buffaloes are there in huge numbers, blue wildebeest in lesser. The diversity of antelope includes water-adapted red lechwe, Chobe bushbuck (brighter in colouring than their conventional cousins), kudu, impala, sable and roan antelope, tsessebe, and the increasingly rare puku, which is at the southern limit of its range on the Puku Flats. The wetlands here sustain a large number of hippos and crocodiles.

About 460 different kinds of bird have been recorded within the Chobe park, a superb array of avifauna, seen at its most varied and colourful in the northern wetlands. The waters and the lush vegetation support fish eagles and reed cormorants, egrets, knob-billed and white-faced ducks, Egyptian geese, marabou and saddle-billed storks, herons, ibises, kingfishers, colonies of busy little carmine bee-eaters and much else.

Running southwards from the forest- and papyrus-fringed Linyanti is the

Map: page 399, 2C/D
Northern Chobe is reached by road from Livingstone in Zambia, Victoria Falls in Zimbabwe, and over Ngoma Bridge from Namibia. There are scheduled flights to Kasane, and landing strips at Savuti and Linyanti. You will need a 4x4 vehicle to travel within the park.

Details: Open throughout the year. November to May are the best months, although Savuti has good game all year.

Accommodation: There are 3 venues in Kasane, 2 in Serondella, 4 in Linyanti and 3 in Savuti. Public camp sites are at Savuti, Linyanti, Kasane, Ngoma, Kazungula, Serondella and Ngwezumba. Try Chobe Game Lodge, P O Box 43, Kasane, tel 65-0340; Chobe Chilwero, P O Box 22, Kasane, tel 65-0234; Chobe Safari Lodge, P O Box 10, Kasane, tel 65-0336; Kubu Lodge, P O Box 43, Kasane, tel 65-0312; Cresta Mowana Safari Lodge, P O Box 266, Kasane, tel 65-0300.

Further information: Department of Wildlife and National Parks, P O Box 131, Gaborone, tel 37-1405.

A lioness shows her cubs the way into the long grass. Litters usually comprise two to three cubs, but up to six have been recorded.

Savuti Channel, a barely discernible 100-km-long conduit connecting the river with the now dry Savuti marshlands and, beyond, the Mababe Depression. No water has flowed along the channel for almost 20 years.

The Mababe was once a lake that covered most of northern Botswana, but today, for all but a few months during each decade, it unfolds before you as a vast, grassy, treeless flatland, apparently devoid of life.

With the rains, though, come the giraffes, the elephants and the buffaloes, the tsessebe and the zebras (up to 25 000 zebras migrate down from the north). And following them are the inevitable carnivores. The Savuti area is renowned for its leopards and cheetahs, hyaenas, wild dogs and, especially, for its lions.

For the comfort-conscious visitor, the most inviting part of the Chobe is its northeastern corner, the 35-km stretch of river frontage that extends westwards from Kasane, the park's administrative headquarters.

Kasane is a rapidly developing little centre, boasting hotels, shops, supermarket, banks and an international airport. Along and near the river banks to either side are some splendid private venues – the five-star Chobe Game Lodge, Chobe Chilwero, the old, established and charming Chobe Safari Lodge, the Swiss-style Kubu Lodge, and the luxurious Cresta Mowana Safari Lodge.

Collectively, they provide the visitor with just about everything he could need or want from a safari holiday. On offer are game- and bird-watching expeditions, nature-walks, facilities for fishing, boating and kayaking, light-aircraft and helicopter sightseeing flights, and trips to the Victoria Falls 70 km to the west.

Silhouetted against the warm sunset skies, two elephants confer at the water's edge. Elephants often travel at night, following well-worn game paths through the bush.

ELEPHANT SAFARIS
Okavango Delta

Map: page 399, 2C
Take a flight to Maun, then an all-inclusive charter by smaller aircraft to Nebeka airstrip near the midwestern edge of the Moremi Wildlife Reserve, where your safari operator will transport you on a 4x4 journey to the camp.
Accommodation: At Abu's Camp you will be splendidly accommodated in 1 of 5 'Out of Africa'-style safari tents, with an open-air bucket shower and the services of an expert chef.
Further information: Ker and Downey Safaris, P O Box 40, Maun, tel 66-0211/2/3 or 66-0375.

You will probably never get closer to the game of the Okavango Delta than from a howdah perched atop an African elephant – sitting even higher than an elephant's eye! You are seen as part of the natural world, virtually ignored even by the other elephants, and allowed to come right alongside.

Several years ago American conservationist Randall Jay Moore brought a group of trained elephants back to their ancestral habitat in Africa. Abu, a huge tusker, is the leader of six adults and a 'brat pack' of young apprentices.

The safari sets out from (naturally) Abu's Camp, not far from the Xhenega River in the southern delta, to rock along beneath huge ebony trees, ilala palms, and beside the lily-dappled waterways.

Each of the adults is guided by a mahout (elephant trainer), who sits with you atop the animal's head.

Abu is something of a film star, having featured in several Hollywood epics, including *Circles in a Forest* and, more recently, *The Power of One*.

In the latter, the script calls for Abu to mock-charge the film's six-year-old star several times, stopping only metres in front of the boy (and his mother, who was watching close by!).

The elephant safaris, the world's first non-Indian variety, do not actually involve overnight stops, but, rather, excursions from base camp lasting a few hours each. Abu's Camp is a rugged patch of Africa, with luxury safari tents and bucket showers.

GCWIHABA CAVERNS
Northwestern Botswana

Thousands of stalagmites rise from the floor, and giant stalactites, some of them more than six metres long, descend in stately splendour from the ceiling of the magnificent Gcwihaba ('hyaena's lair' in the local San dialect) chambers, located in the remote wasteland 250 km west of the Okavango Delta.

The labyrinth, on the parched flank of the ancient Gcwihaba River Valley, is more popularly known as Drotsky's Caves, after a farmer who visited them in the early 1930s – the first white man, apparently, to do so. Since then it has been a source of keen interest to geologists and climatologists for the light it sheds on the weather patterns of the region's distant past.

The complex is open to the public, but recommended only for the more intrepid explorer. Neither the site nor the long overland route westwards offers visitor facilities. To get there you'll need a four-wheel-drive, and provisions, water and fuel to last you at least two days, preferably three. The caves are unlit, so bring torches.

There are two known entrances. A track leads to the main one (with an information board outside it) and the second is about 200 m from the first.

Maps are available from the Botswana Society at the National Museum in Gaborone, but you won't find any marked trails other than the fragile lengths of cord strung out along the passageways (watch out for bats and barn owls). If you're happy with these conditions, you'll find the excursion both exciting and rewarding.

Map: page 399, 3B
The easiest route to the caverns is from Maun via Tsau on about 150 km of tarred road. About 1,5 km past the turn-off to Tsau, take the road to the left at the sign for Drotsky's Caves. After some 146 km of sandy road (a 4-wheel-drive vehicle is essential) you will reach a second sign pointing left. A bush track leads 26 km to the caves.
Details: Open 06h00-18h00 from April to September; 05h30-17h00 October to March. Admission charged. No water and little shade (nearest water at Xai-Xai, where there is a police station and rural stores).
Accommodation: Camping is allowed anywhere, but there is no formal accommodation. The nearest hotel accommodation is at Maun and Shakawe.
Further information: National Museum and Art Gallery, P O Box 114, Gaborone, tel 37-4616; Botswana Society, P O Box 71, Gaborone, tel 35-1500.

The dry Auob River weaves a sinuous path through the Kalahari, west of the Gemsbok National Park.

GEMSBOK NATIONAL PARK
Southwestern Botswana

A lone male gemsbok stands sentinel on the edge of a massive, rolling dune, the dying sun illuminating the red oxide of the sand, the animal's very distinctive victory horns, and its beautifully marked black-and-white face.

This is the ultimate Kalahari, the vast semidesert wilderness that covers two-thirds of Botswana. The national park lies in the remote southwest of the country, a wild and lonely region of shifting duneland. Here and there the terrain is scantily clad with grass, scatterings of thorn scrub and drought-resistant trees, and incised by ancient watercourses.

The park's southwestern boundary is the almost always dry Nossob River, which also forms part of the common

The black-breasted snake eagle has short toes adapted to grasping the cylindrical bodies of snakes.

Map: page 399, 6A
Entry is usually from the South African side, via the Bokspits border post and Twee Rivieren – the most southerly of the camps.
Details: Open 06h00-18h00 April to September; 05h30-17h00 October to March. Admission charged.
Accommodation: Camp sites (no pre-booking necessary) at the Twee Rivieren entrance in the south, with ablution facilities, and three others in the park, none with facilities. Go through the South African border post (08h00-16h00) for access to luxury chalets at Mata Mata (fuel), Nossob and Twee Rivieren.
Further information: Department of Wildlife and National Parks, P O Box 131, Gaborone, tel 37-1405; South African National Parks Board, P O Box 787, Pretoria 0001, tel (012) 343-1991.

border with South Africa's Kalahari Gemsbok National Park.

There are no fences, and the animals move freely between the two sanctuaries.

For many years the Gemsbok National Park was closed to visitors, but it is now being upgraded for tourism. Access is via either Tshabong, or from the rather more highly developed South African side.

The Gemsbok park is the oldest of Botswana's parks, and although it cannot match the Moremi or Chobe *(see separate entries)* for wildlife interest, the animals are there, and in abundance.

You won't see elephants or buffaloes – they belong to the northern areas – but there are plenty of gemsbok, wildebeest, eland, red hartebeest and, inevitably, attractive little bat-eared foxes to draw the eye. Herds of springbok wander among the camelthorns, blackthorns and other acacias of the fossil riverbeds.

Lions and leopards are well represented, and the night-time silence around your camp fire is often pierced by the eerie whoop of hyaenas.

You will need a four-wheel-drive to explore the great spaces. The best time to visit is after the rains (if indeed they come), from March to early May. The most rewarding game-viewing route is the Nossob's bed, though not, of course, during the infrequent periods of flow.

Some of the camping spots are lovely: the bare, arid countryside can, at certain times and in a certain light, become hauntingly beautiful.

The Kalahari's sands derive their ochre colour from iron oxide on the outer surface of each grain of sand.

Springbok congregate at a water hole. These beautiful animals once formed large herds which thundered across the country in great migratory waves, destroying fences and grazing lands in their path.

KHUTSE GAME RESERVE
South-central Botswana

Map: page 399, 5C
From Gaborone drive northwest for 240 km (about 5 hours) to the Khutse gate. The road is tarred to Letlhakeng. The remaining 100 km requires a 4x4 vehicle. Take fuel for the return trip of 700 km (Molepolole is the last stop for petrol).

Details: Open 06h00-18h00 April to September; 05h30-19h00 October to March. Entrance fee charged. Map on display at the gate. You can hire a San guide at Khutse Pan, just inside the reserve. Take all provisions.

Accommodation: Camping sites at the gate and at the attractive Moreswa (also called Moraye) Pan (41km from the main gate), with its 2 trees. No ablution facilities except at the gate camp.

Further information: Department of Wildlife and National Parks, P O Box 131, Gaborone, tel 37-1405.

Sparsely grassed plains, ancient riverbeds, fossil dunes, scatterings of hardy trees and, most distinctively, a series of 60 or so seasonal pans – these are the physical ingredients of this 2 500-km² sanctuary.

The pans, which are linked by a 130-km circular track that starts and ends at the Galalabodino Game Scout Camp north of the village of Salajwe, are bone dry for most of the time, bare and blindingly white in the hot sunshine. They once formed part of a long-gone river system and, for a brief period after the November rains, are covered by a colourful array of wildflowers.

The Khutse is the southern extension of the much larger Central Kalahari Game Reserve *(see separate entry)*, and its wildlife complement is similar. Desert-adapted gemsbok, wildebeest, red hartebeest and other migratory species are prominent among the larger animals. Bat-eared foxes, caracals, porcupines, pangolins and mongooses are among the smaller. The concentrations, however, are modest – the harsh droughts of the 1980s have kept their numbers down.

Game-viewing is nearly always good around the 60 or so pans in the reserve, including the Molose Pan in the west, which is fed by a borehole. Bird life is surprisingly prolific. Sit with a pair of binoculars, in as much shade as you can find, and you're quite likely to see a fair sprinkling of the 150 or so seasonal species, including the white-backed vulture and the kori bustard.

The latter has a 7,5-m wingspan, weighs up to 40 kg (it is the world's heaviest flying bird), and its white-throat display is entertainingly reminiscent of the can-can dance.

The gemsbok is able to survive the harshest droughts by unearthing and eating subsurface roots and bulbs.

MABUASEHUBE GAME RESERVE
Southwestern Botswana

You could easily wander for a whole week without encountering another human presence in the Mabuasehube, which must rank among the most arid and remote of Africa's conservancies.

The Mabuasehube, which borders on the Gemsbok National Park *(see separate entry)*, is known for its herds of migratory antelope, its carnivores and for six large, usually dry, pans flanked by the ochre-coloured sand dunes that give the reserve its name (a corruption of 'Mabuashegube', meaning 'red earth' in the local Segologa dialect).

The Bosobogolo Pan is especially well endowed with wildlife, notably its herds of leaping, prancing, brown-and-white springbok. Among the other game animals are red hartebeest and eland, wildebeest and the superbly adapted gemsbok. Close on the scent of these herbivores are lions, brown hyaenas and caracals. In the evenings, small nocturnal creatures such as Cape foxes, meerkats and black-footed cats may be seen hovering around the edge of the pans.

Some 170 species of bird have been identified in the Mabuasehube reserve. Best viewing spots are the dunes to the south of the pans which, after the occasional rains, become colourful and noisy with waterfowl.

This particular part of Botswana was the stamping ground of Robert and Mary Moffat, the missionary couple who based themselves at Kuruman 180 years ago, and where they translated the Bible into Tswana, printing it themselves in the desolate wilderness. Their daughter Mary married David Livingstone, the great explorer.

The manes of male lions tend to darken, from a light tawny gold in younger animals, to almost black in older individuals.

Map: page 399, 6B/C
There are 3 main routes to Mabuasehube. From South Africa travel north from McCarthy's Rest via Tshabong. From the north travel south via Kang and Tshane. The third, and best, route is that from Gaborone west to Khakhea (shop), via Lobatse, Kanye, Jwaneng (last petrol stop) and Sekoma. From Khakhea drive south to Werda for about 55 kilometres. Watch out for an unmarked turning to the west, some 1,5 km before crossing the dry Moselebe River bed. From here a straight 143-km track leads to Mabuasehube.

Details: Open 06h00-18h00 April to September; 05h30-19h00 October to March. Admission fee payable at gate.

Accommodation: No facilities within the reserve. Camping at the Game Rangers' Camp only, where water is normally available. But arrive fully equipped and with provisions (including water).

Further information: Department of Wildlife and National Parks, P O Box 131, Gaborone, tel 37-1405.

BOTSWANA

MAKGADIKGADI REGION
North-central Botswana

Map: page 399, 3D/E
Drive from Maun on the new Maun-Nata tar road. At the village of Motopi on the Boteti River, 70 km from Maun, take the old Nata road east for 18 km, then turn right and travel for nine kilometres. At the crossroads turn left and drive for 55 km to Xhumaga Village. Nxai Pan, halfway between Nata and Maun, is clearly signposted, with the gate 35 km from the road.

Details: Opening times 06h00-18h30 April to September; 05h30-19h00 October to March. Best game-viewing months in Makgadikgadi are April to July; at Nxai Pan December to April. Four-wheel-drive vehicles only. Petrol and provisions can be purchased at Maun, Nata, Gweta and Mopipi. Park fees payable at the Game Rangers' Camp on the old road.

Accommodation: Nata Safari Lodge (Private Bag 10, Francistown, tel 61-1210) has large, 3-bed chalets and offers breakfast and dinner. Swimming pool. Camping allowed. Gweta Rest Camp (P O Box 124, Gweta, tel 61-2220) offers self-service thatched rondavels. Camping within the park is allowed only at Xhumaga and Njuca Hills in the Makgadikgadi section, and South and North camps in Nxai Pan. No reservations needed.

Further information: Department of Wildlife and National Parks, P O Box 131, Gaborone, tel 37-1405.

Millions of years ago the great, shallow depressions of east-central Botswana were an inland sea, a flood plain 300 km wide and up to 30 m deep, fed by a triumvirate of rivers – the Okavango, the Chobe and the mighty Zambezi.

Then the climate changed, seismic disturbances shifted the earth, the rivers changed their courses, and gradually Makgadikgadi (pronounced 'muckhurryhurry') became what it is today: an austere 3 900-km² wilderness of salt, and pale, wafer-crusted clay, dazzling to the eye, animated by mirages that dance and shimmer in the air.

But when the first rains come, usually in November or December, the desolate landscape is transformed, delineated into a series of huge pans covered by sheets of water a few centimetres deep.

At the beginning of these wet spells, shrimps, algae and other tiny, highly nutritious organisms hatch from their long-dormant eggs to provide a feast for great multitudes of waterfowl (one sighting is reputed to have encompassed more than a million individuals).

Flamingoes arrive in their tens of thousands, an amazing extravaganza of reflected pink and white.

Other species keep them company: hordes of pelicans, black-and-white marabou storks, with their ungainly, balding pates, black-winged pratincoles, graceful wattled cranes and fish-eagle pairs flying in from the delta region.

Largest of the pans are the Ntwetwe and the Sowa (or Sua). Smaller and rather different in character are Nxai to the north, and Lake Xau to the south. Nxai in fact is no longer a typical salt pan but, rather, a grassy, game-rich, mopane- and acacia-studded plain.

Here and there the flat surfaces are broken by vegetated 'islands', pockets of richer soil that manage to sustain their own tiny wildlife habitats. Unusual among these is Kubu, a 10-m outcrop of boulders and baobabs that supports a complex of ancient stone-walled ruins.

The region is rich in animal and bird life. The plains game also migrates according to the dictates of the season and the availability of food and water. During the long, dry periods the herds of wildebeest and zebras, springbok and red hartebeest – together with their many predators – are to be found in the open country to the west, but when the rainy season comes the herds start migrating eastwards, especially onto the broad grasslands between Ntwetwe and Nxai.

The whole of Nxai Pan, and part of Ntwetwe, have been consolidated into the huge Makgadikgadi Game Reserve. Towards the east is the 310-km² Nata Reserve – which, in times of flood, serves as a magical wildfowl habitat.

Escaping the fierce midday heat at Moremi Game Reserve, a male lion rests on the outskirts of a thicket.

MOREMI GAME RESERVE
Okavango Delta region

For variety, wildlife interest and sheer beauty, few corners of Africa can compare with the Moremi. The 1 800-km² reserve extends across the northeastern segment of the Okavango Delta and beyond, into the drier country towards the Chobe National Park, to encompass a quite superb diversity of habitats.

Here, in the tropically lush wetland section, there are broad channels and lagoons, flood plains, forested islands, dense papyrus- and reedbeds, giant strangler figs and fan palms, and swathes of mopane woodland that give way to riverside acacia and grassland.

Most of the islands are tiny, many of them little more than giant termite mounds that nurture a tree or two. Some are large. Chief's Island is an enormous 100x15-km expanse of grassy plain and forest, girded by two slow-moving rivers, all of which sustain a wondrous array of birds and animals.

The Moremi is a prime conservation area. Human encroachment is kept to a minimum, and the wildlife remains relatively undisturbed – and unrestricted. There are no artificial barriers (apart from the veterinary cordon far to the south), and the larger herbivores are free to move along some of the ancient migratory paths that cut through the reserve.

Here you'll find splendid herds of elephants and buffaloes, zebras, kudu, impala, scimitar-horned sable antelope, tsessebe, Chobe bushbuck, water-loving lechwe, and the full complement of predators, from lions and leopards down to wild cats and other small nocturnal hunters, such as genets.

The dry months, the best for game-viewing, are those (April to October) during which the elephants converge on the Khwai River.

Well over 400 different kinds of bird make their home in the Moremi, some of the more striking of them on and around the limpid lagoons. Always a delight to the eye are the African and lesser jaçanas, as they make their delicate, strutting way across the dense mantles of water lilies.

In August, at Xakanaxa, Gcodikwe and other high-density housing areas known as heronries, breeding colonies of goliath herons are joined in the shallows, and among the low trees and swamp-fig thickets, by storks (marabou, yellow-billed and saddle-billed), sacred ibises and pelicans in great, flapping, noisy, colourful traffic jams.

The Moremi has a limited internal road network: it follows a triangular route from South Gate to the wetlands of the Third Bridge area in the east, and then back to North Gate.

There is no permanent public accommodation within the reserve. But camping sites have been established at the two gates, at Third Bridge and at nearby Xakanaxa. The amenities are basic, and the camps tend to be crowded during holiday periods.

Perhaps more inviting are the score or so private safari lodges that flourish around the perimeter of Moremi Game Reserve. The curiously, and in some ways aptly, named Oddballs Camp (eccentric characters do tend to feature among its clientele) caters for the younger and the more adventurous visitor, but, generally speaking, the venues are small and expensive. Each has its own very distinctive character.

Standard attractions include comfortable sleeping arrangements (in chalets or well-appointed East African-style tents), highly personalized service, good, sustaining food, trips by powerboat, pontoon and mokoro *(see box)*, game drives in the dryland parts, walks, birdwatching and photographic forays.

Camps Okavango and Moremi are among the most luxurious. Khwai River Lodge, overlooking the flood plain near North Gate, is the oldest.

Camp Okuti and the fairly small Delta Camp are charmingly intimate. Machaba is for the game-spotter. Tree-shaded Xugana has an especially beautiful lagoon setting. Xakanaxa and Pom Pom are famed for their bird life.

Map: page 399, 2B/C
From Maun drive northeast on the tarred road which changes to sand after Shorobe. Shortly after leaving Maun the road forks – take either turning, they both go to the same place. Beyond Shorobe continue for 29 km to a turn-off marked Moremi South Gate. The total distance from Maun to the gate is 95 kilometres. Only 4x4 vehicles can enter Moremi. Airstrips at Khwai, Xakanaxa and San-ta-Wani.

Details: Open 05h30-19h00 October to March; 06h00-18h30 April to September. Admission charged.

Accommodation: There are no lodges in the reserve, but numerous luxury camps dot its borders. Excursions into Moremi are made from these lodges. Try Camp Moremi or Camp Okavango, Private Bag 10, Maun, tel 66-0564/9; Oddballs or Delta Camp, c/o Okavango Tours and Safaris, P O Box 39, Maun, tel 66-0220; Camp Okuti, Private Bag 49, Maun, tel 66-0307; Machaba or Pom Pom, c/o Ker and Downey Safaris, P O Box 40, Maun, tel 66-0211/2/3; Xugana, c/o Okavango Expeditions, P O Box 69859, Bryanston 2021, tel (011) 708-1893/5; Xakanaxa, Private Bag 26, Maun, tel 66-0222. Public camps, administered by the Department of Wildlife and National Parks (P O Box 131, Gaborone, tel 37-1405), lie within the reserve.

Further information: Department of Wildlife and National Parks, P O Box 131, Gaborone, tel 37-1405.

Mokoro magic in the waterways of the Delta

Perhaps the most restful, and certainly the most environmentally friendly, way of exploring the waters of the Okavango and Moremi is by mokoro, the traditional dugout canoe. Guided by an expert African poler, it skims swiftly and silently over the placid surface through a timeless landscape of giant riverine trees, dense beds of papyrus and reeds and, everywhere, carpets of blue and white water lilies.

The mokoro (plural: mekoro) is a comparatively heavy craft, customarily fashioned with an adze axe from such hardwoods as mukwa and acacia. For every canoe made, though, a giant, long-lived tree is felled, which threatens serious ecological damage. The increasing number of visitors to the region compounds the threat, and some of the more conservation-conscious safari camps are switching over to fibreglass.

Most of these luxury venues offer organized mokoro excursions. But if you're adventurous, there's nothing to prevent you hiring one to take you into the watery wonderland on your own. Try to find a poler who knows his animals, birds and plants, as well as his way around the labyrinthine channels.

A good guide will teach you much of the ways of the wild, help you set up camp, cook your food, and provide amiable company around the evening fire. You won't need a tent in the dry season (but take blankets or a sleeping bag – the nights can be surprisingly cold). A mosquito net is essential.

Visitors glide through the lily-covered waterways of the Okavango Delta in a mokoro (dugout canoe).

NATIONAL MUSEUM AND ART GALLERY
Gaborone

Map: page 399, 6D

The National Museum and Art Gallery is in Independence Avenue, not far from the Library and Town Hall-end of the mall, the hub of Gaborone. From Queens Road turn left into Independence Avenue, and then turn first right.

Details: Open 09h00-18h00 Tuesdays to Fridays; 09h00-17h00 Saturdays, Sundays and public holidays. Closed Mondays, Christmas Day and Easter weekend. Admission free. Crafts shop.

Further information: National Museum and Art Gallery, P O Box 114, Gaborone, tel 37-4616.

Visitors to Gaborone, the country's young, fast-growing and attractive little capital city, should not leave without spending an hour or two in this delightful compound of museum and gallery.

The exhibits tell the story of man and animal in Botswana, exploring in visually striking terms the environment that enables them to coexist. The dioramas and displays are colourful, well lit and well conceived.

Especially impressive are the mounted animals – the bat-eared foxes whose large and ultrasensitive ears can easily pick up the sounds of larvae burrowing away in the ground; the graceful desert lynx; the secretive and nocturnal caracal, which can flush birds from their cover and leap for them in the air, and many others.

To the San desert-dwellers the caracal was known as the morning star, or the bird of dawn. But this lovely piece of imagery, like so much else, properly belongs to a time that has passed: the hunter-gatherer lifestyle has virtually come to an end in Botswana.

The traditional San communities *(see box)* lived in total harmony with their desert environment. The museum shows how they survived its harshness, even thrived within it, hunted with poisoned arrows, dug in the sandy earth for edible roots, and sought the tsamma melon – often their only source of water in the long, dry months.

Sculpture artefacts, crafts and fabrics from many parts of Africa south of the Sahara are also on view. Notable is the basketwork, for which the people of Botswana are famous.

In the art section you'll see, among other things, works by early explorer-artists such as Thomas Baines, who travelled with the great David Livingstone until the two quarrelled. His fearsomely colourful painting of 'The Gnoo' hangs in the gallery.

THE OKAVANGO
Northwestern Botswana

Map: page 399, 2B/C

Access to the delta is usually by all-inclusive safari boat or light aircraft from Maun or Kasane, to an island near one of the camps. The panhandle and Shakawe are 370 km by road from Maun. With the right guide, you can travel by boat from Maun all the way to Shakawe.

Details: The climate is most pleasant in April/May and August/September. Bird-lovers should visit between October and January, when migrants from the northern hemisphere flock to the delta. Much of the Okavango is not formally proclaimed as a reserve; access is unrestricted. There are organized horseback, elephant and houseboat safaris within the delta region.

Accommodation: There are 4 fishing lodges in the panhandle, lodges in the southern (sometimes called eastern) Okavango, and 7 in the central delta, plus privately run camp sites in the south and north. Maun, the usual access point, has hotels, lodges and camp sites.

Further information: Department of Tourism, Private Bag 0047, Gaborone, tel 35-3024.

The huge Okavango Delta is a natural fairyland of a thousand islands in a thousand streams, born of a great river's determination to reach the sea. Its efforts are in vain, for no matter how much it floods, its strength is trapped in, and sapped by, the desert sands.

Generous midsummer rains which fall in Angola's highlands fill the river (the Okavango is known as the Kubango in its upper reaches), which meanders southeastwards for a distance of 1 600 km, then crosses Namibia's dry Caprivi Strip to enter Botswana.

There the waters flow through the 100-km-long, comparatively narrow 'panhandle', before spreading out across the Kalahari to form one of the world's few great inland deltas.

The delta ranks among the finest of wetlands, an immense, fan-shaped, emerald wilderness of waterways large and small, oxbow lakelets, lagoons, fertile flood plains and lush riverine forests of wild date and ilala palms, sausage trees laden with their salami fruit, giant strangler figs, and many others. The Okavango region nurtures over 1 000 species of plant – more than any other similar-size region in Africa.

The gradient of the land is one in several thousand, almost imperceptible, and the annual surge is slow. It takes several months for the seeping waters to reach their southeastern extremity around the Maun area. But during this time some 16 000 km² of northern Botswana have been inundated.

There are many large stretches of open water, limpid expanses studded by wooded islands and islets. Most of the flood, though, makes its languid way along a myriad narrow, meandering,

maze-like channels, their outlines difficult to discern through the profusion of water lilies and hippo grass, the reeds and the dense and mysterious beds of papyrus. The flow is so gentle that the sediments remain undisturbed and the water marvellously translucent.

Much of the delta's permanent flood lies in the panhandle area. Here the river, fresh from its highland sources, is still rich in nutrients, and they sustain a splendid variety of fish, 80 different species in all.

These, in turn, attract the birds – and the sporting angler. The catches are excellent, especially of tigerfish but also of bream – a delicacy favoured by Pel's fishing owl. More of these rare raptors hunt in the Okavango than anywhere else in the world.

The panhandle is also the home of the Bayei and Hambukushu fishermen and wetland farmers. Their settlements are dotted all along the banks up to the busy little centre of Shakawe, departure point for the Tsodilo Hills, and their 3 000 San paintings *(see separate entry)*.

The northeastern part of the delta, and some of the drier country beyond, have been set aside as the Moremi Game Reserve *(see separate entry)*, a formally protected area which is rich in game. The remainder of the swamplands also has its animals, though the spectrum is relatively modest in size and diversity.

The migratory wildlife, which was once abundant, has suffered from human encroachment and the exploitation of the surrounding grazing lands. Moreover, the delta's soils are poor, and the vege-

Lilies of the delta

Waxy lilies thrive in the swamplands of the Okavango. They seem like manna thrown across the waters as they open, blue and pink, yellow and white, to the warming sun. There are probably more of them floating, in all their gorgeous varieties of colour, among the channels, lagoons and hidden creeks of these wetlands than anywhere else in the world.

At sunset they close their petals, but by midmorning they are opening up again, swishing at your side as your mokoro glides past. When the wind blows the lily's leaves turn, and you can see they are red underneath, with long, supple shoots drifting down through the crystal depths.

Most belong to the species *Nymphaea caerula*, the prefix derived from one of the four mythological spirits of nature (seen as a lovely young woman), the suffix a reference to the blues and mauves in which it predominantly displays itself.

Water lilies are generally widespread throughout Africa, from the southern subcontinent up to Egypt, where in ancient times they were a favourite of the Pharaohs. They also have their place, both decorative and functional, in the modern world. Horticulturists have developed ornamental hybrids that grace many water gardens. More prosaically, they serve as a dietary supplement in times of need, and as an astringent flavouring used in local stews. Near Shakawe, in the upper reaches of the delta's panhandle, the women swim out to harvest the plants.

Keep a lookout for two other pretty Okavango varieties. *Nymphaea lotus*, the cream-and-yellow-centred night lily, opens only in late afternoon, and closes around midnight. It is more common in the northern delta, where the water is deeper and the flow faster. Smaller and even prettier is the tiny snow lily.

Simple reed floats are used to support fishing nets used by local fishermen in the lily-covered waters of the Okavango.

An aerial view of the meandering, reed-fringed waterways and rich swamplands of the Okavango Delta.

BOTSWANA

Mekoro are the traditional vehicles of the Okavango, gliding easily through the shallow channels.

tation, despite its apparent lushness, is not especially sustaining.

Nevertheless, buffaloes are plentiful in the grassier parts; hippos and crocodiles ever present amongst the waterways. Elephants occasionally venture onto the flood plains, giraffes into the peripheral woodlands. The aquatic red lechwe, whose hooves have adapted to the slippery ground, can often be seen darting through the reeds.

The watery wilderness is also home to the spiral-horned sitatunga, an antelope adept at moving swiftly over the waterlogged terrain, and an excellent swimmer. Sometimes when threatened it submerges itself in the water. Among the smaller mammals, of which there are a great many, is the Cape clawless otter.

The delta's bird life is superb. Well over 400 species are represented. There is less avian variety in the middle reaches than towards the south, probably because the vegetation lacks dramatic diversity. But the ungainly marabou storks in their jostling, untidy colonies, wattled cranes, geese, ducks, lily-trotting jaçanas, herons, cormorants, darters, and kingfishers atop bare sticks – all the birds which love water more than land – are there. And always the haunting cry of the fish eagle as it sits high in a tree, eyeing the waters for the silvery flash of bream or tigerfish.

Maun, in the south, is the traditional Batawana capital, and gateway to the delta. It used to be a romantically rugged, Out-of-Africa staging settlement, but much of the old glamour has gone. It now boasts tarred road links with Gaborone, Francistown and other centres, an international airport, shopping malls, stores, banks and service stations. Its streets are busy with gleaming new saloons and pristine four-wheel-drive vehicles. Many safari firms have offices, or are represented, in town.

You cannot drive into the delta, but many of its lodges and camps have their own airstrips. Getting to some involves a boat trip, as well as a light-aircraft flight.

There are some 40 of these venues in the wetland region, and more are making their appearance annually. They are privately owned and managed (the only public facilities are in the Moremi Game Reserve). Each has its own individual character and attractions. All are inviting; some are lovely.

Independent travel is difficult in the delta region, and the great majority of visitors get to know the swamplands as guests of one or other of the operators.

The inclusive tour packages on offer are varied and flexible, and are mostly tailored to meet the needs of the client. A typical one will take in – among other things – transport, a comfortable bed (either in a luxurious tent or a more permanent structure of reeds and poles, or brick, under thatch), companionable eating and drinking. Packages also tend to include professional guides who take you on game-viewing, bird-watching, fishing and photographic forays. There are also expeditions by mokoro, the traditional dugout canoe *(see box, page 407)*.

Palm trees and other giants of the waterways are boldly silhouetted by the tints of the setting sun.

TSODILO HILLS
Northwestern Botswana

The god of the *!Kung* Bushmen named two of the four hills of Tsodilo, calling them Male and Female. The third is known as the Child; the fourth is an orphan with no name.

Rising 420 m sheer above flat, lush bushland in the far northwest of Botswana, a mere 50 km from the long panhandle of the Okavango Delta, it is easy to understand why this rugged moonscape of tumbled stones, many covered in lichens of green and gold, came to mean so much to the ancients.

They have been home to the San (and more recently to a Bantu-speaking Hambukushu community) for the past 30 000 years, and in the later millennia the rock faces and caves have been decorated with more than 3 000 delicate paintings. Many of the subjects are of outstanding quality. The oldest dates back about 4 000 years.

Especially notable among the rock-art classics are the various stylized depictions of penguins and whales (improbable though it may seem, the artist must have visited the sea), and the painted outcrop known as Van der Post's Panel. The sites are easily accessible.

The views from the top of the Male – it's a tough scramble to get there – are memorable, especially at dawn and sunset. There are challenging ascents, too, for the experienced climber.

Map: page 399, 2B
Turn left at the Botswana National Museum and Art Gallery sign (zebra stripes) about 10 km south of Sepopa, for a difficult 53-km, 3-hour run. Travel in 2 vehicles and be prepared to dig and winch in heavy sand. The 41-km route from Shakawe Fishing Camp is also a difficult sandy road.

Details: Open 05h30-19h00 October to March. Thereafter 06h00-18h00. Admission charged. Fuel only at Maun, Shakawe Fishing Camp and Shakawe, where there is also a trading store for basics. Airstrip. See Monuments Officer for a San guide.

Accommodation: Camping allowed anywhere. Try the large cave between the Male and Female hills. Near the airstrip there is a well for water. Otherwise the nearest accommodation is at Shakawe, Drotsky's Cabins and Shakawe Fishing Lodge. For reservations contact Merlin Services, Airport Bag 13, Maun, tel 66-0351.

Further information: National Museum and Art Gallery, P O Box 114, Gaborone, tel 37-4616.

The San's battle for survival

The dice have been loaded against the San, or Bushman, people – the hunter-gatherers of the hot Kalahari, and perhaps the finest of all pre-historic artists. Like the Aboriginals of Australia and the Amerindians of the North American plains, their lifestyle has disintegrated under the hammer blows of modern supermarket culture.

Until fairly recently Botswana's Bushmen – or Remote Area Dwellers, as politically correct officialdom prefers to call the desert communities – were able to continue in their time-honoured ways in the great thirstlands, where the heat and the distances and a benevolent government kept the corrosion of civilization at bay. That has all gone now.

During the past two decades or so nearly all the country's San have drifted to farms and villages, where, despite the goodwill of an open-handed administration, most live a life of unemployment and dependency.

The soul force of these gentle folk evolved in the great spaces washed with sun – the Kalahari of Namibia and Botswana. Long ago, before the coming of more territorial and aggressive Bantu-speaking migrants from the north, their range was much wider. They were dominant in an immense area, stretching from East Africa to the southern Cape shores, and across the subcontinent, from the Atlantic to the Indian oceans.

Left alone, and with limitless room in which to roam, they developed a free-spirited and harmonious relationship with the world around them. Theirs was a sharing society, where urban neuroses, competition and greed were unknown, and in which the oneness of all things, animate and inanimate, was sacred.

The San had no chiefs. All their decisions were made communally, within groups that varied in size (according to season and the availability of resources) from small family units to bands of up to 80 members. Each group had its own, clearly defined territory; men and women enjoyed equal status.

The women gathered the fruits of the desert, such as tsamma melons (a source of both food and water), wild cucumbers and other edible drought-hardy plants. The men hunted with bow and poison-tipped arrow. They were superb trackers of game.

The hunt was a crucial part of overall San culture, an event that held profound mystical (as well as dietary) significance. But it was conducted sparingly, and always on the assumption that the prey had as much right to life as the hunters.

When the kill had been made, the entire group joined in the night-long feast, singing and dancing in trance-like ritual around the fire. During these hours the great healing force called *n/um* would flow over the celebrants, keeping the wily evil god away. The good creator-god stood rather more remote from the affairs of man.

Today in settlements where poverty and alcohol are rampant, and the ancient ways are a mere memory, the healing dance must be performed regularly and frequently. For the San's world has crumbled, and he can see no guiding star before him.

Two members of a San family near the Aha Hills. Although the San once occupied large parts of southern Africa, their numbers have dwindled to precarious proportions in recent decades.

BOTSWANA

TULI BLOCK
Eastern Botswana

The ruggedly beautiful, wedge-shaped region that lies between the Limpopo and Shashe rivers in the east is comparatively fertile and quite heavily populated, by Botswana standards.

But most of the people live in the urban centres of the western sector, along the line of road and rail leading north into Zimbabwe, leaving the land – the open plains and mopane woodlands, the jagged sandstone hills and the still-prolific wildlife of the area – to farmers and ranchers, and to the fortunate owners of some of Africa's most inviting private game reserves.

The most exclusive of these last is probably Mashatu, whose 30 000 or so hectares are home to the world's largest privately conserved elephant population. The animals are descendants of the once-great herds of the Limpopo Valley, slaughtered to the brink of extinction by 19th-century ivory hunters.

Here, from a radio-controlled safari vehicle, you'll also see giraffes and zebras, a variety of antelope, lions, leopards (if you're lucky), hyaenas and cheetahs, as well as plentiful bird life.

'Base camp' is either the luxurious Majale Lodge (swimming pool, cocktail bar overlooking the illuminated water hole, 'his' and 'hers' shower rooms *en suite*), or the Thakatu tented camp with well-appointed, twin-bed units.

As attractive in its own, highly distinctive, way is Tuli Safari Lodge, focus of a 7 500-ha reserve on the banks of the Limpopo River. The lodge itself, comprising thatched chalets, is set in six hectares of park-like gardens. The pool area is surrounded by magnificent sandstone rocks, and the bar is built around a 600-year-old Mashatu tree. The patio looks down on a waterfall and its pool (also illuminated), magnet for a splendid parade of animals.

Nkolodi, a self-catering tented camp, is situated some three kilometres from the main lodge.

Map: page 399, 4E/F
The traffic-free (wide tar) scenic route is along the Botswana border, passing through Ellisras and Alldays. Otherwise via Pietersburg from Johannesburg, or from Gaborone via Mahalapye and Machaneng (2-wheel-drive), both 5-hour drives. From Zimbabwe and Beitbridge turn right just before Messina. There is an airstrip at Tuli Lodge, where customs and immigration formalities, landing fees and airport tax can be handled. Prior clearance from Civil Aviation, P O Box 250, Gaborone, tel 37-1397. Air Botswana has flights to Tuli from Gaborone, Maun and Victoria Falls.
Accommodation: Mashatu Game Reserve offers luxury safari accommodation at Majale Lodge, as well as the tented Thakatu Camp; book through Rattray Reserves, P O Box 2575, Randburg 2125, tel (011) 789-2677. For reservations at Tuli Safari Lodge and Nkolodi Camp, contact Tuli Safari Lodge, P O Box 32533, Braamfontein 2017, tel (011) 482-2634/482-2620.
Further information: Tuli Safari Lodge, P O Box 32533, Braamfontein 2017, tel (011) 482-2634/482-2620.

A herd of zebras, their magnificent coats glinting in the sun, streaks across the veld. These timid creatures often bolt at the slightest hint of danger.

A pioneer graveyard at Fort Tuli, on the banks of the Shashe River, marks the point at which Cecil Rhodes's pioneer column entered Zimbabwe.

ZIMBABWE

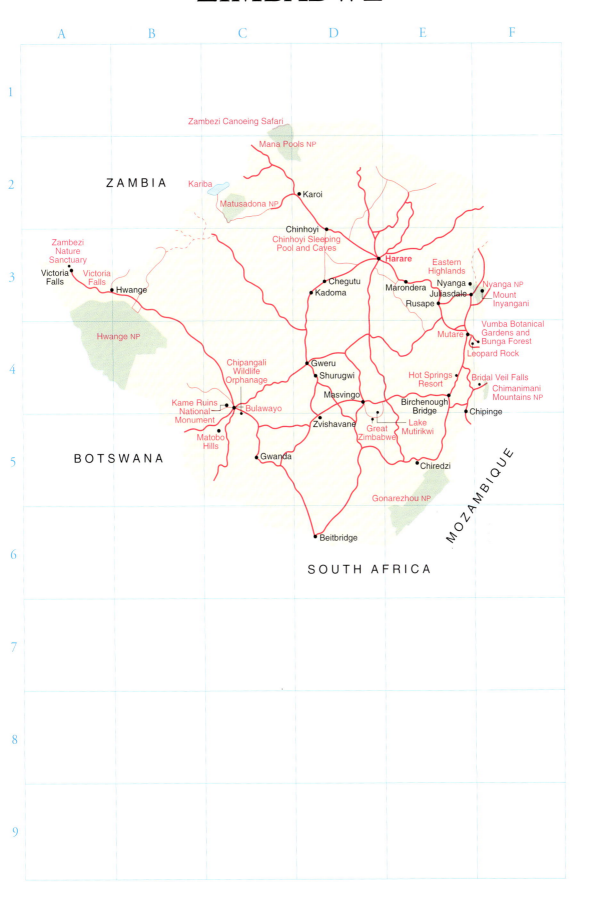

BRIDAL VEIL FALLS
Chimanimani Mountains

Map: page 413, 4F
Follow the sign near the Chimanimani Arms Hotel to the falls, 5 km from the village. Keep right at all forks. Check on road conditions at the hotel.
Details: National Parks site open 06h00-18h00. No entrance fee, tours or public transport. Ablutions, braai and picnic sites. No swimming, camping or fishing.
Accommodation: Chimanimani Hotel, P O Box 5, Chimanimani, tel (26) 511, offers comfortable accommodation; for backpackers, Heaven Lodge, P O Box 18, Chimanimani, tel (26) 450, is recommended.
Further information: Manicaland Publicity Association, P O Box 69, Mutare, tel (20) 6-4711; The Chief Executive Officer, Chipinge Rural Council, P O Box 19, Chipinge, tel (27) 2733 or 2350.

Morning light sparkles like reflections off a stained-glass window at Bridal Veil Falls, where delicate folds of white spray tumble 50 m between forest- and fern-clad cliffs.

Hidden, seemingly a thousand kilometres from anywhere, these falls lie near the source of the Nyahodi River, in the foothills of the Chimanimani Mountains.

Two conspicuous trees in the parkland at the falls – one dark and one light – twist and grow together, symbolizing perhaps the symphony and dream-like quality of this sylvan glade, rich in birds, mist and mountain windsong.

A narrow path leads through pristine picnic lawns and acacia trees to a small, quiet pool into which the river cascades. Smooth boulders provide perfect seats at the edge of the clear water.

You feel you should be making a wish as you look straight up at the falls, strelitzia fronds waving in the breeze, and spray falling gently on your face.

To reach this romantic bower you will have to put up with a 15-minute rough ride on a gravel road. A two-wheel-drive car will get you there, but drive slowly. Nearby Chimanimani Village, originally called Melsetter, after trekker Thomas Moodie's home in the Scottish Orkney Islands, has a recreational club, an English village church and a lovely old-style country hotel.

Bridal Veil Falls cascade in a delicate tracery of white over velvety moss-covered rocks.

BULAWAYO
See page 415

CHIMANIMANI MOUNTAINS NATIONAL PARK
Eastern Highlands

Map: page 413, 4F
From Birchenough Bridge take the main road east, twisting through forest plantations for some 108 km to reach Chimanimani. If coming from Mutare, follow the main road south for about 68 km, and turn east to Cashel. Continue past Cashel (26 km) for a further 68 km to Chimanimani.
Details: Open sunrise to sunset. Entry fee and camping fee payable at base camp. Otherwise free camping anywhere in the park. The mountain climbers' hut is a refuge, and neither exclusive nor furnished. Use caves as overnight shelters.
Accommodation: Chimanimani Hotel, P O Box 5, Chimanimani, tel (26) 511; or, for backpackers, Heaven Lodge, P O Box 18, Chimanimani, tel (26) 450; and the Frog and Fern Bed and Breakfast, P O Box 75, Chimanimani, tel (26) 294.
Further information: The Chief Executive Officer, Chipinge Rural Council, P O Box 19, Chipinge, tel (27) 2733 or 2350; Manicaland Publicity Association, P O Box 69, Mutare, tel (20) 6-4711.

Your first view of the Chimanimani Mountains from a hiking trail is often that of jagged granite, emerging out of the mist like a Japanese woodcut in stark silhouette. Before you, a flash of sunlight reveals dwarf msasa trees and wild russet proteas, while at your climbing boots you'll probably see a filigree spider's web and waves of themeda tiandra grass bowed low under droplets of dew.

The Chimanimani Mountains, which are accessible only on foot from the National Parks Base Camp some 16 km from Chimanimani Village, are probably the loveliest mountains in Zimbabwe.

For hikers, the park is a paradise. There are rivers and lakes, fringed with proteas and wild fig trees, as well as mountains, gorges and caves. There is a profusion, too, of waterfalls, one of the loveliest being near the old Outward Bound Adventure School. The mountain peaks are all over 2 000 m high; from one of them, some say, you can see the lights of Beira at night.

Probably the best way to get to this, the most southerly of the country's eastern mountains, from Mutare is to drive south via the Birchenough Bridge. Chimanimani lies about 150 km south of Mutare.

Stop near the Chipinge turn-off, about 50 km east of Birchenough Bridge, to see the well-maintained grave-site of Scots Afrikaner-trekker, Thomas Moodie. Five kilometres further on is the Ponte Italia, where a bullet-scarred plaque commemorates the construction of this stone culvert by Italian prisoners of war in September 1944.

From the base camp there are two more popular routes over this storm-lashed barrier of mountains. One is a two-hour climb via Bailey's Folly to the mountain hut. The second penetrates the scenic Banana Grove.

Turret Towers, one of several high points in the Chimanimani, is known to local folk as Mwenje (to be squeezed), referring to the narrow gap in the range through which the Musape River flows into Mozambique.

The Chimanimani Mountains are the focal point of a coffee-growing area that includes the 65-km scenic gravel route to Cashel, an eland reserve on Nyamazure Hill, and Bridal Veil Falls. There's also the mysterious Haroni-Rusitu lowland rainforest, and the 1 000-year-old, 66-m-high big tree in Chirinda, which has been declared a national monument.

PLACES TO VISIT

BULAWAYO

CHIPANGALI WILDLIFE ORPHANAGE

Set in the lee of the distant Matobo Hills, Chipangali is a vital sanctuary for wild animals which have been orphaned or injured. The many species of animal kept there include, amongst others, black-maned lions, leopard tortoises and black-backed jackals. Among the wide variety of birds are lesser flamingoes and crested cranes. The animals are kept in spacious, tree-shaded enclosures closely resembling their habitats in the wild.

Paved walkways take you past such delightful enclosures as the aloe-adorned Antelope Alley, where you can meet such guests as klipspringer and duiker, which have been particularly vulnerable to urban sprawl and indifference in the past.

Grunting lions, hungry perhaps for their evening meal, draw visitors to the carnivore area, where you'll encounter such mammals as hunch-shouldered hyaenas, cheetahs, wild dogs, leopards and caracals. Flamingoes dominate the soaring Flight Aviary, a special water-wonderland of birds a stone's throw from reed-lined pools inhabited by crocodiles. You'll even find exotic species such as the Mona monkey from Nigeria.

For those with an interest in things slithery, the Python House near the sanctuary's restaurants offers a four-metre-long African rock python, which is protected by Zimbabwean law. Known as *Shato* in Shona, the python coils itself around its prey, suffocating it to death.

If you want to stay overnight, there's a bush camp at Chipangali, with four comfortable two-bed chalets. There's also an interpretive centre, an attractive tea garden and an information gallery, which houses an interesting, if macabre, collection of animal skulls and strange things in bottles.

Map: page 417
From Bulawayo City Hall 'under the clock', take Leopold Takawira Avenue (the road to Beitbridge and Johannesburg) southeast for 24 kilometres. Chipangali's stone entrance-arch is on the right.
Details: Open 10h00-16h30 year-round. Closed on Mondays (but not if Monday is a public holiday) and Christmas Day only. Admission charge.
Accommodation: There are four 2-bed huts in a comfortable bush camp.
Further information: Chipangali Wildlife Orphanage, P O Box 1057, Bulawayo, tel (9) 7-0764; Bulawayo Publicity Association, P O Box 861, Bulawayo, tel (9) 6-0867.

An African rock python – one of the fascinating inhabitants of the wildlife orphanage.

KAME RUINS NATIONAL MONUMENT

Zimbabwe means 'house of stone', and it is justly famous for its stone-wall or *mazimbabwe* ruins. Like balancing rocks they are all over the country, some 150 major sites in all. One of the best places to see them is in the lovely valley of the Kame ('slow-flowing') River, only 20 km from Bulawayo, along a quiet country road.

The undulating, 1,5-km area beneath towering monkeythorn and purple-pod acacia trees is filled with relics from the country's fascinating past. The pristine riverside beauty, the gentle trees and the wild hills of this little valley have attracted man for thousands of years.

There is evidence that hunter-gatherers lived in the area 200 000 years ago; while more recently (1 000 years ago) Iron-Age dwellers built their village here.

The stone structures here are similar to, but more decorative than, those at Great Zimbabwe.

First stop for visitors is the interesting site museum, where you can learn a lot about the history of the ruins, and the Torwa and Rozvi people who built them 500 years ago.

There are attractive displays of Kame pottery, colourfully decorated with red haematite and black graphite; carved felines, soapstone pipe bowls and whorls for spinning cotton.

Among the other items which have been excavated are a draughts-like game called *isafuba*, some glass jewellery beads, pieces of Ming porcelain, and even an old 17th-century European spoon, such as the type Jan van Riebeeck may have used.

The rather rocky path to the hill ruins, the most sophisticated of Kame's five complexes, is lined with euphorbias and marula trees, as it twists up past platforms to what was probably the king's domain.

Kame was not built for fortification but mainly for prestige, and, like Great Zimbabwe, the ordinary folk lived in ordinary huts in the lower-lying areas between the palaces of the mighty.

Map: page 413, 4C and 417
From Bulawayo City Hall go west up Leopold Takawira Avenue. Turn left into Main Street, right into 11th Avenue, and continue for 4 kilometres. Turn left and immediately right into Khami (the old spelling) Road for another 14 kilometres. Turn right at the 'Kame Ruins' sign, and drive for 2 km on a gravel road that runs past an old farmhouse, 'Green Gables'.
Details: Open daily year-round 07h30-16h30. Admission fee charged. Toilets, drinking water, braai and picnic areas. Curio seller.
Accommodation: Bulawayo offers a wide variety of accommodation both in the city and in the outlying areas.
Further information: The Director, Natural History Museum, P O Box 240, Bulawayo, tel (9) 6-0045; Bulawayo Publicity Association, Fife Street, Bulawayo, tel (9) 6-0867.

BULAWAYO

MZILIKAZI ART AND CRAFT CENTRE

Map: page 417
The centre is in the northwestern corner of the city. Go north along Lobengula Street, and turn left at Masotsha Ndlovu Way, which becomes the Old Falls Road. Mpilo Hospital and Mzilikazi Art and Craft Centre are 3,5 km along this road.
Details: Open Monday to Friday 08h30-12h30. Closed weekends and public holidays. No entrance fee. Free guided tours. Most tour companies in Bulawayo conduct city tours that include Mzilikazi. Public transport on the Mpilo bus from Lobengula Street terminus will get you to Mzilikazi.
Further information: The Manager, Mzilikazi Art and Craft Centre, P O Box 7008, Mzilikazi, Bulawayo, tel (9) 6-7245; Bulawayo Publicity Association, P O Box 861, Bulawayo, tel (9) 6-0867/7-2969.

Seeing the various artists at work moulding clay, working with iron, and screen-printing at Mzilikazi Art and Craft Centre, makes a visit to this large complex a rewarding experience.

The art and craft centre is named after the 'great bull elephant', Mzilikazi, the warrior-chief who fled from Zululand with 300 of his Khumalo followers in the late 1830s to found a nation in the west of Zimbabwe.

Because the centre lies in the vibrant, high-density suburb of Mzilikazi in Bulawayo, you will be able to hear a good cross section of Zimbabwe pop music, quite the rage among young people, as you walk around and watch various crafts being practised.

The centre was started in 1963 to help township women earn a living. The growth of crafts in Zimbabwe has been meteoric: you will find wooden hippos, soapstone figurines, crocheted bedspreads, pots, baskets and bangles on every main road in the country. At Mzilikazi up to 150 people at a time are enrolled in the learning and making of an enormous range of earthenware and ceramic pottery.

Skills include fine art, drawing, iron-sculpting, stonework, commercial art, carpentry and advertisement designs.

Mzilikazi exports regularly to various countries, and profits are ploughed back into the school.

At Bulawayo Home Industries, also in Mzilikazi Square, ilala-palm baskets, batik wall-hangings and banana-stem bread-holders are among the many items which are manufactured.

NATURAL HISTORY MUSEUM

Map: page 417
Turn north just past the fountain, off Leopold Takawira Avenue (the Beitbridge road), 1 km from the Publicity Association. Security parking available.
Details: Open daily 09h00-17h00, except Good Friday and Christmas Day. Entrance fee and explanatory map at the entrance. No photography. Small shop, tearoom.
Further information: The Director, Natural History Museum, P O Box 240, Bulawayo, tel (9) 6-0045; Bulawayo Publicity Association, P O Box 861, Bulawayo, tel (9) 6-0867/7-2969.

A staggering 75 000 animal species are housed in Bulawayo's Natural History Museum, the largest collection in the southern hemisphere, and the city's premier attraction.

The museum, a smart, Colosseum-like building situated amidst the trees, lawns, fountains and aviary of Centenary Park, is a mecca for conservationists, zoologists and nature-lovers.

This museum does not believe in row after row of dusty displays. The exhibits are presented in an uncannily realistic manner, in original wildlife settings. A sign at the entrance to the Lowveld Hall reads: 'Please keep to the game path'.

In the hall, beneath a man-made fig tree (the veins on the leaves were hand-painted), is a reconstructed wilderness scene, dominated by a huge elephant – the second-largest ever mounted.

Other species here include buffaloes, zebras, giraffes, eland and four lions. To complete the fantasy of the wild, animal sounds emanate from some loudspeakers. There is even a tiny stream at your feet, and the fresh spoor of passing game.

Among other major attractions at the museum are the colourful bird collection, the most comprehensive in Africa, and the fascinating insect displays.

The Hall of Chiefs features important highlights of the history of Zimbabwe, including the culture of the builders of Great Zimbabwe 700 years ago, and fascinating mementos of the life and times of Cecil John Rhodes, the founder of Rhodesia. These include photographs of his crowd-lined funeral journey from Cape Town to the Matobo Hills, where he was laid to rest.

The Geology Hall contains a reconstructed Bulawayo gold mine, complete with low, rocky tunnel, rail line and skip, while in the Hall of Man life-size figures pursue their daily tasks in a variety of exceptionally realistic and sympathetic settings, showing man as a primitive hunter, artist, farmer, warrior, trader, miner and, finally, healer.

BULAWAYO

STEAM TRAIN

Puffing through Hwange, one of the world's great game parks, in an old-fashioned steam train *en route* to the Victoria Falls is an experience few are ever likely to forget.

Yet this opportunity is available once a month on the *Zambezi Express* to anyone who's interested, courtesy of a Zimbabwe rail company.

The coaches are pulled by a 15th-class, Garratt articulated steam locomotive, a 28-wheeled, chuffing, coal-fired monster that is every train-enthusiast's dream. And the interior shows an elegance quite unequalled perhaps by modern trains. For the class-conscious, there's emerald class and ivory class, as well as a luxury dining car, private lounge and a library.

Nostalgic train journeys such as the Trans-Siberia, the Orient Express and the Pacific Coast-to-Coast have long been popular, but a journey that affords you views of elephants, lions or herds of thundering buffaloes is unique, particularly if you're sipping a glass of chilled wine and enjoying a good meal at the same time.

Cape to Cairo was Cecil Rhodes's imperial dream for his railway. The first train, *Pride of the Road,* arrived in Bulawayo on November 4, 1897, from Mafikeng, of siege and Baden-Powell fame. By 1902, Bulawayo was connected by rail to Salisbury (Harare) and Beira, thus completing the Atlantic and Indian oceans link-up. In 1904 the railway reached Victoria Falls, and, in 1909, the Congo border.

The expansion and development of railroads through Zimbabwe at the turn of the century are highlighted at the Railway Museum in Bulawayo, where you can see some of the original trains and equipment used at the time.

The trains include nine giant locomotives dating from 1896. There is a 20-ton locomotive of 1897 vintage, a 60-ton 1906 6th class, and a 111-ton American 9A-class locomotive, built in 1917.

You can climb in and see the ancient brass, and visualize the stoker at his blazing fires. Rhodes's private Pullman Saloon (which carried his body in state from Cape Town to near his grave-site high up in the Matobos) is also there, as is a museum coach.

And standing there, as if waiting for the train to pull in, is a fascinating 70-year-old, tin-roofed station building, complete with notice board, rain gauge, lamps and fire buckets.

Map: below
To get to the Bulawayo Railway Museum (in Prospect Avenue) from the City Hall in central Bulawayo, take Leopold Takawira Avenue west to Fort Street. Turn left, passing 8th-15th avenues. At the difficult industrial-area intersection, turn right into Preston Avenue, right into Josiah Chinamano Avenue, and left into Prospect Avenue.
Details: Open Tuesdays, Wednesdays and Fridays 09h30-12h00 and 14h00-16h00. Open Saturday and Sunday afternoons 14h00-17h00. Admission fee charged. No restaurant.
Further information: Railway Historical Committee, P O Box 603, Bulawayo, tel (9) 36-3318; Rail Safaris, 23 Prospect Avenue, Raylton, tel (9) 7-5575; Bulawayo Publicity Association, P O Box 861, Bulawayo, tel (9) 6-0867 or 7-2969.

KEY TO THE MAP
1 Chipangali Wildlife Orphanage
2 Kame Ruins National Monument
3 Mzilikazi Art and Craft Centre
4 Natural History Museum
5 Steam Train

A steam train, resplendent in shiny green and red livery, thunders through the veld near Bulawayo. Many of these locomotives can be seen in full retirement at the Railway Museum.

ZIMBABWE

CHINHOYI SLEEPING POOL AND CAVES
Great North Road

Map: page 413, 3D
Drive west from Chinhoyi on the main (Kariba) road for 8 kilometres. The signposted caves are on the left.
Details: Open sunrise to sunset. Chinhoyi Caves Recreational Park is administered by the National Parks and Wildlife Management Board. An admission fee is charged.
Accommodation: You can stay at the Caves Motel, P O Box 230, Chinhoyi, tel (67) 2340/2-3751 (there is a petrol station here); or at the more up-market Orange Grove Motel and Caravan Park, P O Box 436, Chinhoyi, tel (67) 2785/6.
Further information: Chinhoyi Caves Recreational Park, Private Bag 7713, Chinhoyi, tel (67) 2-2723. Reservations: Central Booking Office, National Parks and Wildlife Management, P O Box 826, Causeway, Harare, tel (4) 70-6077/8 or 72-6089.

The delightful sleeping pool at Chinhoyi Caves, near the northern Zimbabwe farming town of the same name, reflects the blue of the open veld sky. At noon, with maximum light overhead, the pool's translucent depths seem to conceal a fairy-tale world of myth and mystery.

Ninety-one metres deep, the pool forms part of a labyrinth of ghostly underground passages and tunnels, with names such as Wonder Hole, Dark Cave (although it has lights), and the 'Sink of Bats'. Scuba divers have gone down to the bottom of the pool, and believe it may be part of a far larger body of water. Excavations have shown that people lived here 1 500 years ago.

The Shona knew the caves as *Chirorodziva* or 'pool of the fall', because victims of Zululand's rampaging Nguni warriors were thrown into the water from the top of the caves in the 1830s.

There's a really lovely park outside the caves, which offers camping/caravan sites sheltered by mukwa, Cape fig, msasa and combretum trees. It is a quiet, relaxing spot to stop over *en route* to Kariba or Mana Pools on the Zambezi.

Chinhoyi's fathomless pool of deep blue, shot through with flashes of turquoise, is wreathed in local myths and legends.

EASTERN HIGHLANDS
Eastern Zimbabwe

Map: page 413, 3E
From Harare travel east towards Mutare. After 170 km turn left at Rusape town for another 100 km, to the clearly marked entrance to the Nyanga National Park.
Details: There's an endless variety of scenic walks. One of the best walks leads from the Troutbeck Inn south to the foot of Mount Inyangani.
Accommodation: There are 6 hotels in the area, including the popular Troutbeck Inn, Private Bag 2000, Nyanga, tel (298) 305/6.
Further information: Manicaland Publicity Association, P O Box 69, Mutare, tel (20) 6-4711.

There's no mistaking the African sunrise, but the growing light reveals a landscape that, though African in its sheer extent, is gentler and more softly rounded than almost any other corner of this vast continent. It is this scenery of Nyanga National Park, cool and restful, that makes a wonderland of the Eastern Highlands.

The highest mountain in Zimbabwe, Inyangani rises to 2 592 m from a great, granite plateau that, in the east, drops sheer and sudden to the lowlands of Mozambique and the tropical Honde Valley. Streams, gathering momentum to become mighty rivers, flash down gorges of dense, indigenous forest and misty slopes planted with sighing plantations of pine and eucalyptus.

Apart from a range of accommodation in the park itself, there are several hotels in the area – including a home built for Cecil Rhodes. A hard-headed businessman and politician, he was little noted for his appreciation of natural scenery, but the Highlands captivated him. It's easy to understand why.

Some favourite pastimes in the Highlands – apart from lazy nature-watching or just enjoying the scenery –

are walking, boating and year-round fishing in some of the best-stocked trout waters to be found anywhere.

The slopes of Inyangani demand special care in the rain or mist, and can be reached only on foot, but a short drive along a good gravel road leads to the high place called World's View.

Of all places so named, this must be the original. There are ancient stone walls and enclosures to explore and ponder over, tea and coffee plantations to be visited, and farms where you can sample an impressive range of local cheeses. It's all very different – and delightful.

A patchwork of multicoloured foliage covers the steep granite cliffs overlooking Burma Valley, a fertile, cultivated area in the Eastern Highlands.

GONAREZHOU NATIONAL PARK
East of Chiredzi

This 5 000-sq-km expanse of wild, hot, dry, low-lying baobab and mopane bush country nudging the verdant borders of Mozambique and South Africa is potentially one of Africa's finest wilderness areas.

The name means 'the place of the elephant', and, indeed, the lumbering pachyderms are there in impressive numbers. More than 6 000 of them roam the great open spaces, migrating freely between Gonarezhou and neighbouring countries.

Poaching, civil strife in Mozambique, and the proliferation of firearms, though, have exacted a tragic toll. Consequently, the animals, considered gentle enough elsewhere, tend to be temperamental in Gonarezhou. The official pamphlet warns that 'they bear a grudge against man, due to persecution and harassment over the years' – and visitors are urged to keep their distance.

The park's wildlife complement also embraces buffaloes, giraffes, zebras, kudu, the timid suni, the rare Lichtenstein's hartebeest and many other antelope. Large herds of eland commute seasonally between Gonarezhou and South Africa's Kruger National Park. Handsome, shaggy-coated nyala, scarce at one time, are now commonly seen. Lions and leopards are among the carnivores; hippos and crocodiles haunt the riverine parts.

The park is divided into two distinct sections, each with its own road network (there are no internal connections: the land between them remains an untouched wilderness).

To the north is Chipinda Pools, a rugged area suitable only for four-wheel-drives, and bisected by the Runde River on its way to join the Save River in the east. The Runde, Gonarezhou's major watercourse, is flanked for 32 km of its length by the dramatic red sandstone ramparts of Tjolotjo Cliffs (seen at their most striking when bathed in the light of the setting sun), and at one point tumbles

Map: page 413, 5/6E
From Beitbridge, drive 187 km north to Ngundu on the road to Harare. Turn right for the 105-km drive to Chiredzi. Continue to Chipinda Pools and the National Parks turn-off (122 km from Ngundu). There are 2 turn-offs leading to the park – 1, after a further 30 km from Chiredzi, to Induna, and the second (55 km from Chiredzi), to Mahenye.

Details: Open 06h00-18h00 year-round. Admission fee charged. Travel on game-viewing roads restricted November to April.

Accommodation: There are lodges at Mahenye and Induna, and camping/caravan sites at Chipinda Pools. At Chinguli, in the centre of the park, there is a comfortable rest camp. In the south, at Swimuwini, there are 5 National Parks chalets (no cutlery or crockery), and various caravan and camping sites.

Further information: The Director, National Parks, P O Box CY140, Causeway, Harare, tel (4) 70-6077; The Warden, Chipinda Pools, Private Bag 7003, Chiredzi, tel (31) 2980.

Goliath herons swopping incubation posts. Their pale greenish eggs take about 30 days to hatch.

down a steep, rocky gorge in a spectacular sequence of 10-m waterfalls.

These are the Chivilila Rapids, venue of one of Chipinda's two pleasant rest camps. Much further downstream, at the confluence of the two rivers near the Mozambique frontier, is the Tambohanta Pan, an extensive wetland area during the rainy season, and a magnet for the animals, including some 230 bird species of the region – egrets, storks, wild ducks and many others.

Mabalauta, the park's 2 000-sq-km southern section, is the area in which you will find the densest concentration of elephants and other big game.

Part of the boundary is formed by the substantial Mwenezi River, along whose banks five caravan/camping sites, and the thatched chalets of the attractive Swimuwini Rest Camp, have been established. Elsewhere there are some beautiful picnic sites and observation points, one of which is sited atop a cliff overlooking crocodile pools. Four circular, four- to five-day wilderness trails have been charted, three in the north and one in the Mabalauta area.

GREAT ZIMBABWE
Masvingo

Map: page 413, 5D
The monument lies 28 km south of Masvingo. From Beitbridge travel north for some 200 km until you reach Riley's Garage. Turn right here, and continue for 21 km to reach Great Zimbabwe. United Air operates a weekly 12-seater flight from Harare to Masvingo on behalf of Air Zimbabwe.
Details: Open 06h00-18h00. Entrance fee charged. Several guided tours daily starting at 08h00. Restaurant, curio- and bookshops.
Accommodation: The luxurious Great Zimbabwe Hotel, with its own access to the ruins, is part of the Zimbabwe Sun Group (Private Bag 9082, Masvingo,
tel (39) 6-2274/6-2449). The pretty camping facilities at the ruins, 800 m from the hotel, include ablution and cooking facilities.
Further information: Masvingo Publicity Association, P O Box 340, Masvingo, tel (39) 6-2643. To book camp sites, contact Great Zimbabwe National Monument, P O Box 1060, Masvingo, tel (39) 6-2080.

The huge enclosure at Zimbabwe Ruins is one of the great sights of Africa – an ageing monument to what was once a booming city of 40 000 people.

The country of Zimbabwe is named after these brooding, 11-m-high walls or 'houses of stone' that cover 720 ha of the Mutirikwi Valley, halfway between Harare and Beitbridge.

Great Zimbabwe, as these ruins are known, is the largest complex of its kind in sub-Saharan Africa, and was built 700 years ago by the ancestors of the Shona.

This former city was such an awesome masterpiece of architecture and construction that early European explorers were convinced it was built by King Solomon or the Queen of Sheba.

Carbon-dating and anthropological and archaeological investigations have shown its ancestral African origins.

The Zimbabwe complex is divided into three areas: the Great Enclosure – an elliptical, 243-m-long and 10-m-high wall surrounding the living quarters of the king (this is the largest single structure in Zimbabwe); Hill Complex, a complex of enclosures and giant boulders overlooking Lake Mutirikwi; and, finally, the aloe-decked Valley Ruins where the ordinary people lived, and where today there is a quite fascinating reconstructed Shona-Karanga village.

The Great Enclosure, with its boma, wall-enclosed huts and its soapstone birds perched on poles, was actually an up-market version of a normal Shona village. It was built, not so much for defence, but more as a display of wealth and power. Similar, but smaller, Zimbabwe ruins are scattered throughout the country.

A feature of the ruins is the many chacma baboons which climb all over the tumbled stones and great chiselled walls, shaking and disturbing the centuries-old work of the masons who carefully dry-placed the grey, and now lichen-covered, granite bricks.

Not far from Great Zimbabwe is the beautiful Lake Mutirikwi (well known amongst the Zimbabwean angling fraternity for its great bass-fishing), and historic Masvingo, the first laager site of Cecil Rhodes's 1890 pioneer column.

The Great Enclosure at Great Zimbabwe stands sentinel over the grassy slopes that once were the home of a thriving Shona state.

PLACES TO VISIT

HARARE

CHAPUNGU SCULPTURE PARK

Huge bateleurs carved in stone loom over the imposing thatched entrance gate to the Chapungu Sculpture Park, site of what is believed to be the largest collection of Zimbabwe stone sculpture in the world, on the outskirts of Harare.

Here, surrounded by seven hectares of rolling lawns, you can cross the footbridge of a lovely lake, and watch flotillas of ducks, and Tapfuma Gutsa's beautiful sculpture of a swallow skimming the water lilies.

Exhibition lawns, attractive rockeries, woodlands and indoor galleries offer fascinating insights into the world of contemporary Zimbabwe sculpture, which began during the 1960s, and is highly regarded internationally.

More than 200 works by about 100 artists are on display, some twice the height of a man and weighing several thousand kilograms.

Twelve artists work in residence at Chapungu, and it is a common sight to see the sculptors chiselling away at the gigantic blocks of opal stone, limestone, springstone or the favourite, serpentine, transforming them into exquisite life. The artists' subject matter covers the full range of traditional Shona themes, as well as more contemporary issues.

Mbira thumb-piano music – a quintessential sound of Africa – is one of the attractions at Chapungu, and you can listen to it as you relax in the thatched garden restaurant, a replica of a 19th-century Shona village.

Other attractions are a craft shop, a traditional healer and traditional dancing by the very lively Boterekwa Traditional Dance Group, who perform twice daily at weekends.

Map: below
Take Samora Machel Avenue from town east towards Mutare for 8 kilometres. Turn right into Harrow Road, opposite the Caltex Service Station and high palm trees. Sign and entrance gate clearly visible.

Details: Open 08h00-18h00 Monday to Friday; 09h00-18h00 Saturdays and Sundays. Traditional dancing Saturdays and Sundays 11h00 and 15h00. Admission fee charged. Parking in security area. Chapungu guides within complex. Light meals and refreshments in the garden restaurant. Detailed catalogues of the sculptures available.

Further information: The Exhibitions Curator, P O Box 2863, Harare, tel (4) 48-7113.

EWANRIGG BOTANICAL GARDEN

There are 15 species of brightly coloured sunbird in Zimbabwe, and many of them come and poke their long beaks into the 57 varieties of flaming aloe that flower through most of the Zimbabwe winter at Ewanrigg Botanical Garden, 35 km from downtown Harare.

In a hilly msasa woodland, surrounded by some of the country's richest cattle farms, vineyards and maize lands, the 85 ha of garden proudly flaunt bank after bank of flowers, amongst them fuchsias, Barberton daisies, bougainvillea and gorgeous aloes.

Neat, narrow paths weave in and around the flowerbeds, rising in a series of gentle levels through bamboo groves, a water garden, rockeries, herbarium, huge cacti and trees alive with birdsong. On one side of the gardens a vast green valley of rolling lawns separates picnickers from the forest trails in the hills, where the msasa trees blaze in autumn colours.

The aloe, often seen growing wild at Great Zimbabwe and in the ancient ruins of the towering Nyanga Mountains, is actually part of the lily family. Its name comes from the Arabic word for these prickly, primeval plants, whose leaves bear some resemblance to the upward-reaching tentacles of an octopus.

Farmer Harold Christian began the Ewanrigg Garden collection in the 1920s, naming the park after his brother, Ewan, who was killed in World War II. Rigg means ridge in Welsh.

Another special feature of the gardens is the cycads. Looking like giant feather dusters or Aztec topknots, these strange plants flourished throughout southern Africa 300 million years ago. Today they are a dying species, with only tiny pockets left in the Karoo, KwaZulu-Natal, the Eastern Cape, and in Zimbabwe, along the slopes and river banks of the eastern mountains.

The best months for travellers to visit the park are June, July and August, when the aloes flower in a fiery display of reds, orange and gold. Ewanrigg is known to have one of the world's finest collections of these lovely, hardy succulents. The most recent feature at Ewanrigg is a beautifully laid-out, lovingly tended and labelled herb garden.

KEY TO THE MAP
1. Chapungu Sculpture Park
2. Ewanrigg Botanical Garden
3. Heroes' Acre
4. Lake Chivero
5. Larvon Bird Gardens
6. Mbare Musika Market
7. National Archives

Map: above
Take Samora Machel Avenue east towards Mutare. At the traffic lights, turn left into Enterprise Road, and drive for 21 km to the Mutoko and Shamva fork. Take the Shamva road for another 21 km, then turn right at the signpost, for the final 5-km drive to the park entrance.

Details: Open 08h00-18h00 (earlier by prior arrangement with the curator). Admission fee charged. Picnic and braai sites (wood available) near the entrance. Ablution facilities but no camping. Woodland trails with tree species tagged. Dogs permitted. Petrol available 6 km from Ewanrigg, at the Mermaid's Pool turn-off. Plants for sale.

Further information: The Curator, Ewanrigg Botanical Garden, P O Box 8119, Causeway, Harare, tel (74) 2-3720.

HARARE

Map: page 421
Take Second Street, north of Africa Unity Square, and turn immediately left into Samora Machel Avenue (Bulawayo Road). The eternal-flame tower 7 km along this road is clearly visible.
Details: Permits are available from the Public Relations Office, Ministry of Information, Fifth Floor, Linquenda House, Baker Avenue. Admission free with a permit. Pink guidebook free. Ample parking.
Further information: The Public Relations Officer, Ministry of Information, P O Box 8150, Causeway, Harare, tel (4) 70-6891.

Map: page 421
From Harare drive along Samora Machel Avenue, west towards Bulawayo for 30 km, passing the Snake Park (14 km), Larvon Bird Gardens (15 km) and the Lion Park (21 kilometres). Turn left at the National Parks sign, onto Spillway Road. Proceed for 7 kilometres. The Lake Chivero road turn-off for the National Parks Caravan Park and Hunyani Hills Hotel is some 30 km from Harare.
Details: Open daily 06h00-18h00. Admission charge.
Accommodation: Harare and its environs offer varied accommodation.
Further information: The Public Relations Officer, National Parks and Wildlife Management, P O Box CY140, Causeway, Harare, tel (4) 79-2782/4/6-9; Central Booking Office, National Parks and Wildlife Management, P O Box 826, Causeway, Harare, tel (4) 70-6077/8 or 72-6089; Hunyani Hills Hotel, P O Box 2852, Harare, tel (4) 70-5913; Harare Publicity Bureau, P O Box 1483, Harare, tel (4) 70-5085/6/7.

HEROES' ACRE

Mutoko gold is the name of the velvet black granite used at Heroes' Acre. It forms the polished base for the giant Unknown Soldier statue of two men and a woman, guerrilla warriors in the long and bloody struggle that changed Rhodesia into Zimbabwe.

Twenty-five thousand people died in this 16-year war. Some of the military leaders, including Josiah Tongogara, who led Mugabe's army, are buried here, on a hilltop msasa woodland site affording the best views of Harare.

Others who have found their final resting place in Heroes' Acre are Robert Mugabe's wife, Sally, various chiefs, journalists, trade unionists, teachers, the writers of the revolutionary rhetoric, and a number of political prisoners such as Maurice Nyagumbo, who was incarcerated for some decades, and Leopold Takawira, who died in prison.

More than 250 people, including seven artists from North Korea, and various local craftsmen, were involved in the Heroes' Acre project. And the end result is impressive – a 40-m eternal flame rises gracefully into the air, and there are two stately mural shrines which depict scenes from the war and the long liberation struggle.

Yet the stillness of those long gone is not total here. The sounds of children playing down below drift across the bronze statues, and the graves where flowers are still tended by relatives.

LAKE CHIVERO

Chivero, a lovely lakeshore game park half an hour from Harare, is the city's popular weekend water playground.

You can see white rhinos, giraffes, sable, zebras and wildebeest along the gravel roads that wind through Lake Chivero's pretty msasa woodlands and savannah plains. There are, however, no elephants, buffaloes or big cats, such as lions. Lake Chivero is situated on the Manyame

The wooded shores of Lake Chivero are sanctuary to a wide variety of game, ranging from white rhinos and buffaloes to vervet monkeys.

River, which starts its journey on the central Zimbabwe watershed near the wine-producing town of Marondera, and which flows eventually into the Zambezi and Cahora Bassa Dam in Mozambique.

It was first dammed in 1952, creating the 16-km-long Lake McIlwaine, now Chivero. Its sister lake, Manyame, is 25 km distant. These two lakes provide Harare with most of its water. Chivero's game reserve on the south bank, and its holiday facilities on the north, make it the favourite choice.

On the south bank a variety of walking trails bypasses rock paintings, and leads to an attractive picnic site at Bushman's Point. Other drawcards here are pony trails led by National Parks staff, angling and boating.

The lake's north bank, with its tall trees and circling wooded hills, is the site of the Lake Tea Garden and the thatched Hunyani Hills Hotel, in a lakeshore safari setting of cassias and bougainvillea. The Mazowe and Jaçana yacht clubs host regular sailing camps for children.

The north shore also boasts at least 10 watersport clubs. Swimmers should be aware that Chivero has both bilharzia and crocodiles.

LARVON BIRD GARDENS

The distinctive call of the fish eagle invariably greets you as you cross the ornamental bridge over the lake into Larvon Bird Gardens, a lovely wild-bird orphanage just beyond the western outskirts of Harare.

The orphanage, similar in many ways to Bulawayo's animal orphanage, serves as a sanctuary for 240 species. Some of the birds have been hand-reared from eggs; others brought to the aviary because they have been wounded or abandoned.

Signs direct you to the Soaring Raptor Aviary, home to eight species of eagle and five species of vulture, including Cape vultures. The tiny pearl-spotted owl is one of 11 which stare at passing visitors from across the way.

A pleasing aspect of the orphanage is the fact that most of the species, including such birds as goliath herons, crowned cranes, marabou storks, Indian mynahs and ostriches, have their own spacious gardens.

Other attractions include a flamingo pool, parrot house, and a walk-through aviary with a delightful assortment of trees, shrubs and tiny pools.

There are 640 species of bird in Zimbabwe, and the Larvon Bird Gardens is the ideal spot to begin learning about their habits and habitats.

Map: page 421
Take Samora Machel Avenue west towards Bulawayo for 15 km from the centre of town. At the Lake Service Station turn left into Oatlands Road, following the sign. The road leads 1km to the entrance.

Details: Open 10h00-17h00 weekdays; 09h00-17h00 weekends and public holidays. Admission fee charged. Waterfowl fed at 16h00. Tea garden. Curio shop. There are potteries, craft shops and a snake park 500 m before the Larvon turn-off.

Further information: The Proprietors, Larvon Bird Gardens, P O Box 6708, Harare, tel (4) 2-9816.

A crowned crane displays its vivid plumage. These striking birds usually inhabit vleis or marshy grasslands.

HARARE

Map: page 421

Mbare Musika Market lies 5 km south of the city centre. Travel towards Bulawayo along Samora Machel Avenue. Turn left at the traffic lights into Rotten Row. At the fifth set of traffic lights along this road (2 km), turn right into Remembrance Drive. Proceed for 500 m, then turn left into Chaminuka Street, and drive 1 km past Rufaro Football Stadium and Canon Paterson Craft Centre.

Details: Open daily 07h00-17h00 year-round. No entrance charge. Park outside produce market. United Touring Company offers Mbare as part of a twice-daily city tour.

Further information: Harare Publicity Bureau, P O Box 1483, Harare, tel (4) 70-6681/8.

MBARE MUSIKA MARKET

Here's a crowded, noisy crossroads for city slickers, farmers, saints, crooks and craftsmen – a place where all kinds of businesspeople mix with beggars. This is Mbare Musika, one of Zimbabwe's busiest country bus terminuses, and its most colourful marketplace.

More than 100 vendors display an extraordinary assortment of wares in the neat rows of curio and craft stalls in the main hall. Masks, drums, soapstone carvings, painted bangles, piles of snuff, wire bicycles, gourds of stolen telephone wire, cowhorn snuffboxes and walking sticks are just a fraction of the multitude of items on sale.

Prices of all goods here are marked, and all are instantly negotiable. Everybody speaks English, and most are masters in the art of wheeling and dealing in different currencies.

There's an easy-going atmosphere at Mbare: joke, chat, pay a fair price, and you will make instant friends. And if by unlikely chance an artful dodger eyes your camera, there will be half a dozen hearties ready to pounce on him.

The main produce market has broom-sized bundles of leaf tobacco, bath sponges (or heel rubbers for barefoot walkers) made from tractor tyres, second-hand Chinese spanners, Zambian wrap-arounds, stringless guitars, and, in one corner, an exotic coterie of one-eyed gentlemen offering *muti* (medicines).

If you're after travel goods, look for a little camp of vendors beneath towering pylons. Here you'll find various travelling bags, including a canvas-lined carryall known to the streetwise as a comrade bag.

The bus terminus itself is Dodgem city. The travel-worn, diesel-belching buses carry an incredible mix of ploughs, chickens, beds and 44-gallon drums in a wide variety of colours.

For an experience with a difference, why not buy a roasted chibage mealie to sustain you, and take a country ride? This is the ideal way to see Zimbabwe.

Mbare Musika Market bulges with a continuous pageant of vociferous traders, haggling with customers over vibrantly coloured wares.

NATIONAL ARCHIVES

If you want a copy of a Portuguese map of Africa drawn in 1573, written in Latin, and not very accurate, the National Archives is the place to get it.

In addition you will have access to 30 000 photos recording aspects of Zimbabwe's history, and featuring such subjects as kings, explorers, hunters, dancers, soldiers and farmers. There are also classic snaps of grandpa's Model-T Ford crossing rivers, and long-gone, grand hotels, with gables and porches, and hitching posts for horses.

The Archives also house the world's finest collection of paintings by Thomas Baines, the well-known explorer who

HARARE

travelled up the Zambezi 130 years ago with David Livingstone.

Other attractions of the National Archives are the library, with more than 40 000 books about Zimbabwe, and an extraordinary audiovisual department that offers, amongst other things, 1951 Government training films and renditions from the penny whistle of jazz artist Spokes Mashiyane.

Map: page 421

From Africa Unity Square take Baker Avenue East, and turn left into 7th Street. After about 2 km this road becomes Chancellor Avenue, runs past State House, and is commonly known as the Borrowdale Road. Turn right into Churchill Avenue East at the traffic lights, right again into Hiller, right into Ruth Taylor, and left into Archives. Total distance 3,5 kilometres.

Details: Open 08h30-16h00 Monday to Friday; 08h00-12h00 Saturdays. Closed Sundays and public holidays. Free parking available. No admission fee.

Further information: The Director, National Archives, Private Bag 7729, Causeway, Harare, tel (4) 79-2741.

Ferocious might of the buffalo

The most dangerous animal in the bush is a charging buffalo *(Syncerus caffer),* as some unfortunate travellers in southern Africa have found to their cost. And even when it is not charging, this noble creature is respected and feared by the most experienced game rangers in the subcontinent.

Weighing in at 700 kg, and standing 1,4 m at the shoulder, the male buffalo, with its wicked horns and sturdy hooves, is capable of flattening just about anything that stands in its way. There are few wilderness-lovers in Zimbabwe who have not heard of at least one person having been charged, if not killed, by one of these beasts.

They emerge from nowhere and simply charge. And while a lion or elephant can be sidetracked by a shout or handclap, not so a buffalo. It will just keep coming. That is when a fair degree of common sense, a fast pair of legs and a sturdy tree nearby come in handy. Nature normally provides the adrenalin.

The males are mainly black, while the females have just a tinge of reddish-brown.

Both sexes have horns, distinctive for their upturned swing.

Buffaloes once inhabited great parts of southern Africa, but today they are located mainly in a northern belt stretching from Namibia to Mozambique. Sizable herds are found in the Kruger National Park and parts of Zimbabwe. In Hwange, for instance, herds number several thousand.

Buffaloes like to drink mornings and evenings, and prefer to keep to the shade of large trees and bush during the heat of the day.

The name buffalo comes from the Greek word for ox. The animal is related to the far more gentle American bison and the water buffalo of Asia.

A buffalo herd at a drinking hole. Males on the perimeter keep a lookout for predators.

When angered, male buffaloes will charge, lowering their horns at the last minute to toss their tormentor into the air.

425

ZIMBABWE

HOT SPRINGS RESORT
Chimanimani

Map: page 413, 4E
Travel 85 km south from Mutare on the Birchenough Bridge Road. The resort lies 19 km south of the Cashel turn-off, and 53 km north of the bridge. There is an airstrip 9 km from Hot Springs.
Details: Open year-round. Entrance fee charged. Facilities include equipped conference room, aromatherapy, Chimanimani hiking trails, tennis, squash, bowls.
Accommodation: There are 12 thatched, fully furnished double lodges, with *en suite* facilities.
Further information: Hot Springs Resort, P O Box 190, Nyanyadzi, tel (26) 361/7/8.

Rainbow-coloured bee-eaters hover and hunt insects as you sit in the shade of ilala palms and acacia trees at the lake of Hot Springs Resort.

This lovely bushveld spa overlooking the Karoo-like Maranke Hills in the west, lies in the lee of the mighty Chimanimani Mountains, in an area quite famous for its delicious honey and its hard-working peasant bee farmers.

Hot Springs is justly proud of its dazzling variety of bird species, attracted by the continuous flow of warm water, and of its profusion of tall exotic and indigenous trees.

The medicinal alkaline waters of Hot Springs take 40 years to percolate down through the rock from their source high on the Chimanimani plateau. They descend for about five kilometres before the earth's hidden pressure brings them bubbling to the surface again.

Hot Springs, with its inviting lakeside restaurant and its attractive thatched chalets, is one of only two developed hot-spring sites in the country.

The piping-hot waters, which have a mineral-mix second only to Rotorua in New Zealand, fill a 30-m open pool surrounded by lawns, gracious trees and unique forest root carvings. A cold splash pool flanks the main baths.

Since the days of the ancient Romans, man has always 'taken the waters' at hot spas worldwide, usually to thaw out rheumatism, arthritis and the many ills of the blood, real and imaginary, to which flesh and indulgence make us heir.

Hot Springs can go further back: Stone-Age tools found in mint condition near the resort indicate that its balming waters were used by hunter-gatherers thousands of years before today's bathers came to refresh body and soul among the avenues of bougainvillea, sedge, pawpaw, flame trees and butterflies that divide the chalets from the magical springs.

Local folk in this remote resort recall a more recent legend in which mythical woodcutter spirits would sometimes be heard chopping the wood that stokes the spring's cauldron fires.

Rustic but charming A-frame chalets provide comfortable accommodation for visitors to the Hot Springs Resort.

HWANGE NATIONAL PARK
Western Zimbabwe

Hwange is Zimbabwe's big one – about 15 000 sq km of savannah parkland along the Botswana border – and home to just about every African animal you ever wanted to see. The chances of seeing them are good, and it's all conveniently close to Victoria Falls.

Sunset at Nyamandhlovu Pan, for instance, generally sees at least a dozen game species at the water, with the highlight of the evening's viewing still to come. This is the arrival of the elephants – perhaps 50 or more of these giants, grey and ghostly, scattering the lesser creatures as they make their own stately way towards the water.

A little of the stateliness disappears once they actually get to the water, splashing and wading, gurgling and spraying and drinking – with an adult swallowing anything up to 250 litres in 20 minutes. All of Africa's animals once lived like this, and the sight is a memorable one.

The area around Hwange was once the royal hunting preserve of the Ndebele kings, and although white hunters and settlers later took a heavy toll, the variety and the numbers of game are once again impressive. Here, in fact, are some of the densest wildlife concentrations on the entire continent. And Hwange became a reserve almost by accident, because the soils were too poor for farming, and because water was scarce.

To maintain a state of equilibrium, the elephant population is kept at around 22 000, while the park also supports 15 000 buffaloes, 3 000 giraffes and many thousands of other animals, including roan and sable antelope, black and white rhinos, wildebeest, tsessebe, impala, gemsbok and kudu. There are predators in abundance, too, with leopards and

---

Soul of the white termite

In Hwange National Park, as in many other parts of Zimbabwe, hundreds of ochre mounds punctuate the countryside. These so-called 'ant hills' or, more correctly, termitaria, are living monuments of a highly industrious community of insects – the termites (also known as white ants).

Each is a totally self-sufficient unit, closed and air-conditioned, comprising a series of dark, damp nest chambers, all interconnected by an elaborate system of tunnels.

Temperature and humidity are maintained at constant optimal levels, producing an ideal microclimate which is essential to the survival of the species.

Termite mounds are made from a mixture of soil, saliva and faeces, and can be very hard – so hard, in fact, that they can support the weight of a sleeping elephant. The mounds are veritable fortresses, difficult to penetrate. But antbears and pangolins quite often succeed. Spiders, beetles and bugs get into the mounds that have open chimneys, while marauding bands of soldier ants come into the attack once the mound is breached or when the termites are busy constructing.

In a termite colony there is a distinct division of labour. First comes the King and Queen with their own bedchamber. They do not swop spouses, remain loyal to one another for life and produce up to 30 000 eggs a day. Then there is a group of potentially amorous activists waiting in the wings, ready to take on reproductive duties should one of the royal pair collapse under the strain of his or her respective responsibilities.

Sterile big-headed soldiers, male and female, defend the colony with nasty, biting jaws, squirting chemical warfare, and bluff.

By far the greatest proportion of termites in any colony are the working masses: the nannies, the food gatherers, construction and domestic help.

Termites play an extremely valuable role in nature: by breaking down dead vegetation they assist the recycling process, and at the same time aerate and fertilize the soil.

A lookout point at Hwange National Park, once the royal hunting preserve of Mzilikazi, founder of the Ndebele nation. The area was first declared a game reserve in 1928, and achieved national-park status in 1949.

Map: page 413, 3/4A/B
From Bulawayo travel west on the main road to Victoria Falls. To reach Main Camp, turn left 17 km after Gwai River (265 km from Bulawayo), and continue for 24 km to the camp. To reach Sinamatella Camp, follow the main road for 330 kilometres. Just before you reach the town of Hwange, turn left – Sinamatella lies 40 km further on. For Robins Camp, follow the main road for 390 km, turn left, and follow the clearly signposted road for about 70 km to reach the camp. Air Zimbabwe operates daily flights into Hwange National Park. The nearest rail station is at Dete, 24 km from Main Camp.

Details: Main, Nantwich, Bumbusi, Lukosi and Sinamatella camps are open all year from sunrise to sunset, but Robins is closed during the wet season (1 November to 30 April). Admission fee charged. Licensed restaurant, shop and petrol. Bring binoculars, bird book, sunscreen, jacket and hat. Take precautions against malaria.

Accommodation: Fully equipped, rustic National Parks chalets at Main Camp, Robins Camp and Sinamatella offer a combination of two- and four-bed accommodation. Some share cooking and dining facilities. Bookings through Central Booking Office, National Parks and Wildlife Management, P O Box 826, Causeway, Harare, tel (4) 70-6077/8 or 72-6089. There is one large hotel and many luxury safari lodges. Try Sikume Tree Lodge, Private Bag 5779, Dete, tel (18) 2105.

Further information: The Public Relations Officer, National Parks and Wildlife Management, P O Box CY140, Causeway, Harare, tel (4) 79-2782/4/6-9.

At the Hwange National Park, two male giraffes spar for their position in the hierarchy within the herd. Serious injury is rare.

lions making up the famous Big Five, together with the elephants, buffaloes and rhinos.

More than 400 bird species go about their daily chores among vegetation that ranges from stunted mopane scrub and sparse grasses in the central and southern regions, to some of Zimbabwe's finest teak forests in the northeast.

On the fringes of the Kalahari, Hwange itself was probably also a desert at some distant time, followed by a wetter period that has left traces in the form of 'fossil rivers' to be seen at Kennedy Pans and Linkwasha Vlei, east of Main Camp.

Main Camp is closest to the Victoria Falls-Bulawayo road and close to an airport served by the national airline. It lies on a tarred road which continues for a further 76 km to reach the Shumba picnic site. The hides that overlook the pans at Nyamandhlovu and Guvalala are also situated just off this road.

Main Camp has all the comforts of home, and more, with bar and restaurant, lodges, cottages, chalets and – a little closer to nature – camping/caravan sites. Main Camp is up at the northwestern corner of the park and is the base for no fewer than nine game-viewing drives that range in length from 16 to 120 kilometres. If you want to experience the thrill of the wild on the ground, guided foot safaris are available.

Robins Camp, more than any other part of the park, is the heart of lion country, and also attracts more tsessebe and reedbuck. It's also the start of a fairly demanding game-viewing drive to the crocodile pools on the Deka River. Accommodation at Robins includes chalets, with outdoor cooking facilities, camp sites and caravan parking.

The camp is named after a former owner who, in the midst of game country, was totally absorbed in his hobby – astronomy. He built the concrete tower that is now part of the administrative centre and, up here, spent his nights studying the stars. Daytime was for sleeping, and when reclusive Herbert Robins died in 1939, he bequeathed his property to the nation.

Robins lacks a bar and restaurant, and if these are deficiencies, they are compensated for at Sinamatella Camp, set on a high, rocky ridge overlooking the Sinamatella Valley.

The bush here is noticeably thicker than at Main Camp, and there are dams and vleis – notably Detema and Mandavu, both of which have picnic sites – where game-viewing is excellent.

Observant viewers notice that, just as the Robins Camp has something of a monopoly on lions, so Sinamatella seems to attract far more leopards than the other areas. Sinamatella is well provided, and has the full range of comfortable accommodation, from lodges, cottages and chalets to camping/caravan sites. There are also the shop, bar and restaurant, of course, but among the chief attractions are the game-viewing drives, specially the Lukosi River loop.

Although there's plenty to see and do in Hwange National Park, its developers have never lost sight of the fact that the aim of conservation is to conserve. Development around the main centres in the park has been relatively intense, but by far the greater part of Hwange is inaccessible to the casual tourist, and is kept as a true wilderness area and a living relic of what Africa really was like in the time before exploitation. One day it may cautiously be opened.

In the meantime, though, Hwange offers more than enough for most people.

PLACES TO VISIT

KARIBA

ANDORA HARBOUR

Andora harbour nestles at the foot of rugged baobab hills, banana groves and colourful African suburbia, just around the corner from Kariba Dam. It is a young, rough-and-ready fishing harbour that carries the heavy smell of diesel or racked kapenta fish, and constantly echoes the sound of the shipwright's hammer. Here you are quite likely to see an elephant come walking down to the water, ignoring man's presence with impunity.

Apart from the elephants, leopards regularly cross the main airport road into town, and there's no shortage of other wild animals that appear in Kariba Harbour and village at any time. So take care.

Andora, like its namesake in Spain's high Pyrenees, is tucked away in folds of hills, protected against the fury of the lake's sudden storms.

The little town is the starting point of the increasingly popular 22-hour Kariba ferry journeys, and numerous other boating expeditions across the lake.

Coxswains have to manoeuvre around hippos in the harbour as they tie up alongside the floating fuel station. Ice, bait, taxidermy, and houseboat-hire are all arranged at Andora Harbour.

Overlooking Andora is the little hilltop village of Kariba Heights, noted for its circular Santa Barbara Church, built by Italian construction workers in memory of their colleagues who died during the construction of the Kariba Dam in the late 1950s. Not far away is a memorial plaque to Operation Noah, a rescue operation mounted by ranger Rupert Fothergill, that saved 5 000 animals from drowning when the waters of the Zambezi rose behind the dam wall.

KEY TO THE MAP
1 Andora Harbour
2 Kariba Dam
3 Kariba Ferry Cruise
4 Lake Kariba
5 Safari Islands
6 Tigerfishing

Map: below
From Harare take the Lomagundi or Chirundu road northwest for 300 km, passing through Banket, Chinhoyi and Karoi. Turn left at Makuti before Cloud's End Motel and drive for 77 kilometres.
Details: Open to visitors at all times.
Accommodation: Wide variety of good hotels, cottages and camp sites. Try the Caribbea Bay Resort and Casino, P O Box 120, Kariba, tel (61) 2453/4; Cutty Sark Hotel, P O Box 80, Kariba, tel (61) 2321/2; Lake View Inn, P O Box 100, Kariba, tel (61) 2411/2; Kariba Breezes, P O Box 3, Kariba, tel (61) 2433/4.
Further information: The Director, Kariba Publicity Association, P O Box 86, Kariba, tel (61) 2328.

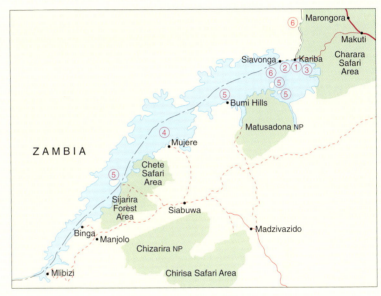

KARIBA DAM
Lake Kariba

In the ChiShona dialect it is *kariwa* – a flat, stone structure, and the structure holds back and harnesses the great Zambezi River where it forms the boundary between Zimbabwe and Zambia. Some 600 km downstream from where it provides the mighty spectacle of Victoria Falls, the Zambezi enters a gorge no more than a few hundred metres wide. Here is the wall, a curving, concrete construction, 128m high, carrying an international highway across its entire length of 633 metres.

The inland sea stretches back for 285 kilometres. But the building of the wall, completed in 1959 to contain what was then the world's largest man-made lake, created more than a dam and a source of hydroelectricity. Kariba – lake, dam, village and recreational area – is one of Zimbabwe's major attractions.

From the air you can see the double-curved wall stoutly straddling the gorge, and the main resort area along the sweep of coast from Camp Hill to Mopani Bay. Water-skiers leave spreading, chevron-

Map: above
From Harare drive northwest along the main road, through Chinhoyi and Karoi to Makuti. Take the turn-off to the southwest, to Kariba (77 km further on). Kariba lies about 365 km from Harare.
Details: No entrance fee. Dam can be viewed at any time. Refreshments and curio shop at viewpoint. Take your passport if you wish to walk on the dam wall.
Accommodation: See under Lake Kariba.
Further information: Kariba Publicity Association, P O Box 86, Kariba, tel (61) 2328. United Touring Company, c/o Caribbea Bay Resort and Casino, P O Box 120, Kariba, tel (61) 2453/4, offers ground tours and aircraft flips over the dam.

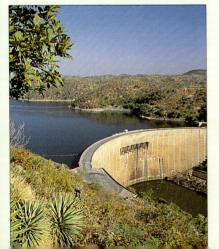

Nyaminyami, the 'river god', keeps a benevolent eye over the retaining wall of the Kariba Dam, which covers over 5 000 square kilometres.

429

like trails on the water, crisscrossed by the bright wings of boardsails.

Leisurely ferries laden with sightseers are among the many classes of boats which are moored or under way at this relatively busy end of Kariba.

Anglers go in search of bream and the fighting tigerfish. Along the shoreline are several hotels and casinos, yacht clubs and marinas, and there's even a harbour for commercial fishing boats.

The road that winds in from the airport (and all the way from Harare), becomes Lake Drive, and swings past the Batonka village and museum. The Batonka people formerly lived in the Zambezi Valley upstream of the dam wall and, in a major resettlement exercise, some were placed here.

Just past the road that turns down to the camping/caravan area, there's a distinctly modern little building up on Kariba Heights. This is the church of Santa Barbara, built by the Italian dam builders as a memorial to comrades lost during the years of construction.

After skirting the Sugar Loaf, Lake Drive reaches the Information Bureau, housed in the Observation Building that overlooks the gorge and the wall. On the rare occasions when all six floodgates are open, water is released in a thunderous cascade that sends plumes of spray drifting high into the hot air.

KARIBA FERRY CRUISE
Lake Kariba

Map: page 429
Drive from Harare to Kariba (365 km), turning left at Makuti. From Bulawayo drive 375 km to Mlibizi, turning right at the Kamativi turn-off.
Details: Departures from Andora Harbour usually Mondays, Tuesdays; Thursdays and Fridays from Kariba. Board ferry at 08h00 for 09h00 departure, arriving next day at 07h00. Fifty percent deposit on booking. No animals.
Accommodation: Caribbea Bay Resort and Casino, P O Box 120, Kariba, tel (61) 2453/4; Cutty Sark Hotel, P O Box 80, Kariba, tel (61) 2321/2; Lake View Inn, P O Box 100, Kariba, tel (61) 2411/2; Kariba Breezes, P O Box 3, Kariba, tel (61) 2433/4.
Further information: Kariba Ferries, P O Box 578, Harare, tel (4) 6-7661; Kariba Publicity Association, P O Box 86, Kariba, tel (61) 2328.

The Kariba ferry leaves Andora Harbour, carrying both passengers and cars along the length of the lake.

The iron ramp crashes down on the concrete slipway at Andora Harbour, and the queue of waiting cars begins to nudge forward into the dark, cavernous belly of the *Sealions* car ferry that will take you on the 22-hour, 282-km journey down the length of Lake Kariba.

The *Sealions*, which carries 15 vehicles and 70 passengers, and the *Seahorse* ferry (eight vehicles and 40 passengers) are diesel-chugging workhorses. And although these ferries don't have such luxuries as cabins, slot machines and air-conditioned boutiques, they do have a comfortable glass-enclosed passenger lounge and a sundeck. The meals are huge, galley-fresh and communal, the beers cold. At night you sleep on reclining chairs or paliasses – no great inconvenience when you can watch elephants basking on the shore, or see the sun go down in a searing runway of fire across the vastness of the lake.

The first leg of the journey passes between Rhino Island and Sampakaruma Island, both of which were hills on the Zambezi Valley floor before the waters of Lake Kariba rose. A cold buffet lunch is served as the ferry enters the Sibilobilo Lagoon, which is surrounded by a series of game- and bird-rich islands.

Tiger Fish Gap, between two of these islands, is the approach route into Kota Kota Narrows, named after the mountain on the Zambian shore.

When the ferry reaches the Sengwa Basin in the afternoon, it pauses to allow those who have the nerve, to take a dip.

Sunset usually means a scramble for cameras and a drink. Supper is at 20h00. Most passengers then choose their chair for the night.

One or two, however, will chat to the skipper, behind his glow of navigation lights and radar. During the night the ferry passes through the Chete Gorge.

Later, Binga Village emerges as a row of lights on the shore. The next morning the ferry docks at Mlibizi, a small fishing village with comfortable lodges, and a two-hour access to Chizarira or Hwange national parks.

LAKE KARIBA
Zambezi River

The roaring waters of the Zambezi River surrender their might into the expanse of Lake Kariba – an inland sea, some 282 km long and 30 km wide.

Fringed by lush, green grass and the skeletons of trees long dead, Lake Kariba has a haunting beauty about it, enhanced by the variety of animal life on its shores.

Elephants, impala, hippos, crocodiles, buffaloes, waterbuck, and a variety of other, smaller animals, are drawn to these shores for sustenance and ablutions. And this is what makes Kariba so special. You can hire a houseboat, a simple outboard or a canoe, and cruise the quiet waters of this giant African lake, as the animals graze or drink along the shoreline.

The 35-m triple-decker houseboat, *Catalina*, is a large motor cruiser with staterooms, television and video. The 18-passenger, open-plan *Karibezi* has a refreshing swimming cage alongside to protect you against crocodiles.

Other vessels are the *Marimba*, which has *en suite* double cabins, and three decks for lazing the cruise away, and the *Sanjika* motor vessel, a typical, canopied Kariba launch. Or you may care to try the luxurious *Belinda*.

The MV *Southern Belle* is a cosy, 50-m multideck Mississippi paddle steamer, complete with conference room, plunge pool, boutique, 21 cabins and a crew of 32 to pamper the occupants. A double staircase is situated amidships, and leads to the Schooner Bar.

The key to cruising Kariba is to find a good fishing creek, off Bumi or the Sanyati Gorge, perhaps, and a hideaway nook on the shore to anchor at night.

The lake is home to many privately owned yachts, which often set sail when the wind forces the powerboats to run for cover. Probably the largest sailboats on the lake are a flotilla of Wharram Tiki 30 catamarans that sail together as a group with a mother ship.

Another cruising option is a wooden safari floatboat up the Ume River, that comes with solar heating and a professional game guide. Finally, if all else fails, there's always a windsurfer, or, for old salts, a diesel-driven, blustery kapenta rig. And a tot of grog.

Map: page 429
Kariba lies about 365 km from Harare.
Details: Sudden storms can be violent, with substantial waves, strong winds, and even hail. Find an island, and hide in its lee or tuck your craft behind the burly Kariba ferry. The temperature on the lake can go as high as 40°C.
Accommodation: Kariba offers a wide variety of accommodation. Try Caribbea Bay Resort and Casino, P O Box 120, Kariba, tel (61) 2453/4; Cutty Sark Hotel, P O Box 80, Kariba, tel (61) 2321/2; Lake View Inn, P O Box 100, Kariba, tel (61) 2411/2; Kariba Breezes, P O Box 3, Kariba, tel (61) 2433/4.
Further information: The Lake Captain, P O Box 10, Kariba, tel (61) 2389; Kariba Publicity Association, P O Box 86, Kariba, tel (61) 2328.

The setting sun burnishes the still waters of Lake Kariba's eastern basin, home of the popular Matusadona National Park.

SAFARI ISLANDS
Lake Kariba

Spread out along the rugged southern shore of Lake Kariba, with its eerie, drowned forests, fish eagles and flaming sunsets, is a series of tantalizing safari resorts, many situated on small islands, some tucked quite unobtrusively into the mountainous and serenely beautiful Matusadona National Park shoreline.

These thatched wilderness hideaways, usually with 10 to 20 chalets, swimming pools and cosy reed-lined restaurants, specialize in boat and walking safaris. It is here that you will find some of the most informed and experienced guides in the safari business.

Elephants, buffaloes and lions are plentiful in these areas and the bird life is particularly rewarding.

One of the most attractive of the safari resorts is Bumi Hills Safari Lodge on the southern shore, with its luxurious cliff-perched chalets overlooking browsing elephants. Another popular retreat is Fothergill Island, east of Bumi Hills, named after the ranger who rescued 5 000 animals threatened by the rising waters of Lake Kariba in the late 1950s. Fothergill is the largest of the island resorts, and certainly one of the most beautiful. The island has a striking safari camp with thatched chalets and a swimming pool. Various game-viewing, photographic and fishing excursions are offered daily.

Spurwing Island, which lies just to the west of Fothergill Island, and faces the

Map: page 429
The safari resorts usually do powerboat pick-ups from Kariba town marinas, or light-aircraft transfers from Kariba Airport, which services flights from Harare and Victoria Falls.
Details: The journey across the lake takes 30-60 minutes, and is usually avoided when the weather is bad.
Further information: Any travel agent or the Zimbabwe Tourist Office, P O Box 2398, Johannesburg 2000, tel (011) 331-3137; Bumi Hills Safari Lodge, P O Box 41, Kariba, tel (61) 2353; Fothergill Island Safaris, Private Bag 2081, Kariba, tel (61) 2253, 2378/9; Spurwing Island, P O Box 101, Kariba, tel (61) 2466/2265; Kariba Publicity Association, P O Box 86, Kariba, tel (61) 2328.

Matusadona Mountains, has a magnificent double-storey, thatched pub, and viewing platform.

Sanyati Lodge is particularly remote, resting on a craggy precipice overlooking Lake Kariba, where it joins the Sanyati Gorge, haunt of bream and fanatical fishermen. Charara, Water Wilderness, Chizarira and a dozen others also offer seclusion, game-viewing, fishing and impossibly beautiful Kashmiri sunsets.

There are numerous fishing resorts along the shores of Lake Kariba, at Binga, Mlibizi and Deka. You can reach them from Bulawayo or the Victoria Falls.

For the man of adventure, modest means and local knowledge, the National Parks chalets near Tashinga are particularly exclusive, wild and wonderful. But it is still the safari islands and their lodges across the lake from Kariba Village that are the most popular.

Kariba's warm waters teem with fish, enticing anglers from all over the world to try their luck.

TIGERFISHING
Lake Kariba and Zambezi River

Map: page 429
Lake Kariba's eastern basin is 365 km from Harare. The western basin is 375 km from Bulawayo. Chirundu (for Zambezi River fishing) is 351 km from Harare. Victoria Falls is 437 km from Bulawayo.

Further information: The 'Master Angler', P O Box BW550, Borrowdale, Harare, tel (4) 88-5660; Kariba Publicity Association, P O Box 86, Kariba, tel (61) 2328.

Razor-sharp teeth, fearsome tenacity and a fighting spirit second to none combine to make the tigerfish one of the most sought-after angling quarries in southern Africa's rivers and lakes.

Described as the roughest and toughest game fish in Africa, the 'tiger' *(Hydrocynus forskahlii)* can snap steel traces, swallow swivels, and throw practically any hook with impunity.

To give anglers excellent opportunities to pit their skills against this voracious striped predator, several fishing camps have been established along the Zambezi. Tigerfish are also caught in abundance along the Limpopo and Hunyani rivers, and along the lower reaches of the Save/Runde and Pungwe rivers.

An international tigerfishing tournament held annually at Lake Kariba is recognized in the Guinness Book of Records as the biggest freshwater angling competition in the world. It has been held annually since 1962, and attracts some 300 teams and 500 boats.

To ensure that Zimbabwe's tigerfish populations are not threatened in any way, local sportsmen favour a 'catch and release' policy, returning their victims to the water after reeling them in.

The largest tigerfish are usually caught on the troll at low speed, using a spinner and ball-bearing swivel. Bright-bladed lures are best.

If you're fishing for tigerfish in the Zambezi River in summer, use live bream as bait on a 5-10 kg breaking-strain line.

Be prepared to lose lots of hooks and traces in the submerged forests when a tigerfish shoal eventually cruises by and switches on to your presence.

Tigerfish quite like noise, a characteristic not common in other fish species. So you can chat, open a beer, swop jokes, but be ready: to catch a tigerfish in that lake, let alone get him into the boat, takes skill, sweat and endurance. The record stands at 15,5 kilograms.

Many keen Zimbabwean fishermen have their tigerfish mounted, and there are taxidermists at Kariba, Victoria Falls and Harare.

Be sure to ask the locals or your boat skipper where the best fishing spots are, and take a cooler box along for your bait and refreshments.

LAKE MUTIRIKWI
Great Zimbabwe

The Beza mountain range is the outstanding sight as the visitor drives towards Great Zimbabwe and the lovely lake which began to spread out along the valley to the north of the ruins when the Mutirikwi River was dammed. These sombre, sculpted hills jut out of the flat woodland like a phalanx of pyramids.

Lake Mutirikwi is, in fact, enveloped by hills, a good reason why this spot was chosen for the construction in 1961 of a dam to feed the Lowveld sugar-cane fields. The area was originally called Kyle, perhaps because it reminded homesick settlers of distant Scotland.

A game park and National Parks recreational facilities now occupy the north bank (access is via the Birchenough Bridge road).

You can take a game-viewing pony trail through the park, and see Lichtenstein's hartebeest, giraffes, hippos, oribi, sable, leopards, and any one of the 34 other mammal species. There's also a variety of birds. One of the best drives through the game park is that from the southern shore, which crosses over the 309-m-long dam wall.

This scenic drive takes visitors through communal lands, and right around Glen Livet Circular, a panoramic mountain drive that ends back at the National Parks chalets overlooking the lake. The 15-km lake itself is home to a thriving population of large-mouth bass, some of which can reach a total weight of four kilograms at Mutirikwi.

There is an arboretum in the park and a good interpretive centre that features the 140-million-year history of the Nile crocodile, a reptile with which Mutirikwi is well endowed.

Map: page 413, 5D
Take the A9 east out of Masvingo towards Birchenough Bridge. Turn right 13 km from town. Follow the signs to the National Park entrance.
Details: Open 06h00–18h00. Admission fee charged (includes fishing licence). No fee for southern shore or dam-wall drive. Bilharzia and crocodile warning.
Accommodation: Southern shore: Mutirikwi Lake Shore Lodges, P O Box 518, Masvingo, tel (39) 7151, offers fully furnished lodges with modern facilities; Masvingo also offers a wide variety of accommodation, ranging from camping/caravan sites to bed-and-breakfast facilities; and the luxurious Great Zimbabwe Hotel, Private Bag 9082, Masvingo, tel (39) 6-2274. On the northern shore, within the Lake Kyle Recreational Park, are fully equipped lodges with one or two bedrooms.
Further information: The Director, Masvingo Publicity Association, P O Box 340, Masvingo, tel (39) 6-2643; Central Booking Office, National Parks and Wildlife Management, P O Box 826, Causeway, Harare, tel (4) 70-6077/8 or 72-6089.

Seeking respite from the relentless Zimbabwean sun, elephants cool their toes in the waters of Lake Mutirikwi.

LEOPARD ROCK
Mutare

This sumptuous mountain resort, which lies about 38 km from the town of Mutare, was described by England's Queen Mother as the most beautiful place in Africa, when she stayed in Zimbabwe's Eastern Highlands in 1953.

At the time it was a rambling Scottish, castle-like inn – a gracious Norman-towered hotel in the pristine country setting of the Vumba 'mountains of mist'.

Twenty years later, when the liberation war engulfed Rhodesia, Leopard Rock became the unfortunate target of a number of guerrilla rockets, and was subsequently virtually abandoned.

Just one guardian remained, the white-haired head waiter known as Damson, who showed occasional visitors around the empty halls and children's playroom, with its echoes of the past and distant memories of the Seymour-Smith and Milton families who built it.

Then in 1993, tobacco baron Tony Taberer poured millions into the hotel, transforming it once again into a rather beautiful mountain resort, with casino, conference rooms, croquet lawn, conservatory and an 18-hole championship golf course, possibly the finest in Africa.

The hotel's locality on the coffee- and protea-growing slopes of the Vumba Mountains is ideal for such outdoor activities as horse-riding, bird-watching and exploring the vast complex of trails that crisscross these mountains overlooking Mozambique.

Map: page 413, 4E
Take the Birchenough Bridge Road from Mutare, driving south down Herbert Chitepo Street. Go under the railway bridge, past the service station, and take the next turning left into the Vumba road. Keep to this twisting, tarred road (avoid the Burma and Essex Valley turn-offs) for 38 kilometres. Then turn right and drive 1 kilometre.
Accommodation: The luxurious Leopard Rock Hotel has 58 double rooms and 1 single room, as well as a golf course and casino. There are 4 other hotels and a dozen different holiday cottages available in the Vumba.
Further information: Leopard Rock Hotel, P O Box 1322, Mutare, tel (20) 6-0170/1/7.

MANA POOLS NATIONAL PARK
Zambezi River

Map: page 413, 1/2C
Mana Pools is situated some 400 km northwest of Harare, on the road to Chirundu. Turn right onto a gravel road 6 km north of Marongora (where permits must be obtained), drive 30 km to Nyakasikana Gate, and then 42 km to Nyamepi Camp.
Details: Open in the dry season (15 April to 15 November) only. Nearest shop and petrol are at Makuti 100 km distant. Fishing and swimming permitted in the Zambezi. Walking is permitted unaccompanied.
Accommodation: Camping/caravan sites; Rukomechi and Chikwenya luxury lodges.
Further information: For reservations, contact the Central Booking Office, National Parks and Wildlife Management, P O Box 826, Causeway, Harare, tel (4) 70-6077/8 or 72-6089.

This national park on the Zambezi River is probably the wildest and most beautiful of all Zimbabwe's parks. Named after several pools along the alluvial flood plains of the Zambezi, it occupies 65 km of river frontage and covers a total area of 2 200 square kilometres.

It is so rich in game that guests at the park's two main safari lodges often have to pick their way around elephants, buffaloes, lions and hyaenas to reach the riverside thatched pub or alfresco tub.

Hundreds of hippos flaunt themselves in the river, yawning by day, honking by night. On the sandbanks crocodiles laze in the sun, their motionless forms contrasting with the background ballet of impala prancing through the long grass.

Regiments of baboons, highly intelligent creatures that are a joy to watch, trek up the sand rivers in the dry season, while hornbills, kingfishers, jaçanas, vultures, eagles and bee-eaters, as well as 350 other species, decorate the river banks, the acacia, albida and sausage trees, the jesse bushes and mopanes.

The best time to visit Mana Pools is during the dry season (from August to October), when herds of animals are attracted by the flood plain's abundant water and lush grasslands.

Mana Pools is a focal point for canoe-safari enthusiasts, and it was here that Zimbabwe's Zambezi Society was established to safeguard this wilderness from dam builders, mineral and oil exploration, and rhino poachers.

Its tree-lined banks thrown into stark outline by the setting sun, the Zambezi flows its sluggish way through Mana Pools National Park.

MATOBO HILLS
South of Bulawayo

Map: page 413, 5C
Head southwest from Bulawayo along the A47 for 32 kilometres.
Details: Open daily 06h00-18h00. Admission fee charged. There is also a charge for picnicking in the park. No petrol. Beware bilharzia.
Accommodation: National Parks chalets, camping/caravanning facilities at five sites; Matobo Ingwe Motel, P O Box 8279, Belmont, tel (838) 322; and several safari lodges on the park's periphery.
Further information: Central Booking Office, National Parks and Wildlife Management, P O Box 826, Causeway, Harare, tel (4) 70-6077/8 or 72-6089.

The locals call it 'Malindidzimu', the place of benevolent spirits. And no wonder, for there is a mysterious, almost eerie, feel to the jagged beauty of the Matobo Hills, described by Rhodesia's founder, Cecil John Rhodes, as 'one of the views of the world'.

Black eagles soar in the restless winds, swooping and diving high above the grandeur of tumbled red hills. The hills got their name from Mzilikazi, founder of the Ndebele nation, who likened the great granite outcrops to the bald heads (amaTobo) of his indunas.

Rhodes often rode these hills alone on horseback and, appropriately, his remains are buried here in a really breathtaking amphitheatre of giant boulders atop a hunched whaleback called 'World's View'. Nearby lie the remains of Leander Starr Jameson, leader of the Jameson Raid that helped precipitate the Anglo-Boer War. To complete the pantheon there is a monumental frieze of Major Alan Wilson's last stand and annihilation by Ndebele impis on the Shangani River during the first Chimurenga War.

The Matobo Hills form a vital part of the Matobo National Park, haunt of leopards, baboons, rhinos, hyaenas, sable, tsessebe, caracals, giraffes, klipspringer and other smaller mammals.

The park's attractive wooded valleys, grassy marshlands and streams support about 175 species of bird, many of which you can see along the park's scenic roads.

Among the park's attractions are its various San (Bushman) rock art, fishing in the Mpopoma and Maleme dams, exploring the wilderness and pony trails.

The Matobo Hills – a tumble of granite masses sculpted and scored by the elements.

Spiritual galleries of the San

The caves in the rugged Matobo Hills are exquisite galleries of precious art, fashioned by the San hunter-gatherers over thousands of years.

Using blood-coloured oxides of iron, and often very fine brushes, the San's extraordinary tapestry on the rock faces records their nomadic lifestyles, the animals they hunted, and their deep sense of spirituality.

The central religious experience of the artists, who were probably related to the !*Kung* San of modern-day Botswana, was *n/um*. This was a spiritual force, to deflect or cure evil, usually released communally through a trance dance.

San art followed very strict conventions – stylized, abstract, often with symbolic overtones – but always with a marvellous vibrancy, especially in their portraits of animals that seem almost to move on the walls of the many high overhanging caves of the Matobos.

Five large rhinos are painted in the small White Rhino shelter, plus a lion, birds, hippos, wildebeest and hunters.

The Gulubahwe Cave features a snake on the wall, together with the rather hunch-shouldered human figures typical of the Matobos.

Pomongwe Cave has been excavated, but its paintings have been all but obliterated by the application of an oil-and-glycerine mix to them in the 1920s, in an ill-considered attempt to preserve what had been there for many thousands of years anyway.

Nswatungi Cave, on the other hand, is fascinating, with its main panel featuring two large polychrome or multicoloured giraffes, an artistic rarity.

Inanke Cave is considered by many to be the high point of prehistoric art in the Matobos. The long column of animals – giraffes, zebras, eland, and even fish – is painted in various shades of ochre and white. There are also huge, unforgettable human figures in Inanke, a special feature of the Matobos.

But the masterpiece that distinguishes Inanke is a large, abstract design of 16 dark rectangles in white and rusty yellow, capped with what looks like a series of eggs, or clouds, probably representing the spiritual energy and extraordinary trance power of *n/um*.

MATUSADONA NATIONAL PARK
Northwest Zimbabwe

In a way, it's not untrue to say that Matusadona National Park was created by steel and concrete. The dam wall of Kariba caused the waters of the Zambezi to back up, gradually flooding the river's long valley. As the waters rose, Operation Noah swung into action and, in about the space of two years, dedicated men in an assortment of little boats saved at least 5 000 animals.

The achievement of the greatest animal-rescue operation ever undertaken is recorded on a plaque on the face of the Zambezi escarpment overlooking Matusadona. It was at Matusadona that most of the animals were restored to safety – and freedom.

Lake Kariba today forms the northern boundary of Matusadona, and provides the usual route of entry, a 20-km voyage from the town of Kariba. The reserve is bounded by the verdant valleys of the Ume and Sanyati rivers, both partly flooded, leaving 12 km of the narrow Sanyati Gorge like some strangely located Norwegian fjord, where African trees cling to the cliffs, and African birds wheel and call above your boat.

The bird life of Matusadona is one of its outstanding features and, for the fish eagle in particular, the remnants of the drowned forests of Kariba provide an abundant bonus of nesting sites.

More than 240 bird species have been recorded, including many waterfowl, and, for birds as well as for many human visitors, it is Lake Kariba that is the focus of Matusadona. These warm waters are home to at least 20 angling species, from the internationally renowned tigerfish to bream, eels, catfish and Cornish Jack. On a larger scale, hippos and crocodiles are rarely far away.

Apart from privately run safari lodges, there are various lodges and camp sites at Tashinga, which is also the park head-

Map: page 413, 2C
Powerboats leave from Andora Harbour. Overland it is 150 km west of Karoi, off the Harare-Lusaka road. Saloon cars can drive from Karoi to Mlibizi (and on to Victoria Falls), but the 82-km turn-off to Matusadona is strictly for 4-wheel-drive vehicles only.

Details: Open year-round. Admission fee charged (but not for fishing parties in powerboats or houseboats).

Accommodation: Camping at Tashinga, and at other less-developed camp sites. Exclusive (1-party only), fully equipped, rustic chalets at Ume, Mbalabala and Muuyu. Maximum 12 people; minimum 1-week stay.

Further information: Central Booking Office, National Parks and Wildlife Management, P O Box 826, Causeway, Harare, tel (4) 70-6077/8, or 72-6089.

quarters, and there is a camp site at Sanyati West, near the Sanyati Gorge.

Guided trails head for the hills that, with a plateau covered with mopane scrub and woodland, make up much of the Matusadona landscape in the hinterland of the lakeshore.

Africa's Big Five – elephants, buffaloes, rhinos, lions and leopards – are present in good numbers, and you may also be lucky enough to see cheetahs.

At Matusadona you will hear many stories about the determination that goes with instinct. The lake reached its capacity level in the 1960s, cutting a new line along the Zambezi, and also erecting a barrier across the migration routes of buffaloes and elephants.

More than 20 years later, herds and individuals were observed still trying to follow the ancestral pathways, none with a greater determination than a pair of elephants in 1982.

They swam clean across the lake from south to north, covering no fewer than 40 km, and spending, park officials calculated, some 30 hours in the water. Exhausted, the elephants staggered ashore near Kariba Village, rested awhile, and went their way.

Several thousand buffaloes graze on Matusadona's grasslands. Don't be fooled by their placid gaze – these animals can attack fearlessly.

MOUNT INYANGANI
Eastern Highlands

Map: page 413, 3F
From Mutare drive north for about 75 km to Juliasdale. Continue north for another 9 km, and turn east at the Rhodes Nyanga Hotel and National Parks Headquarters turn-off. Keep to the right, then swing left, avoiding the scenic road to Pungwe View. Drive past the Ministry of Agriculture and Water Development Fruit Experimental Station on the left, and the pony stables on the right. You will see the mountain ahead of you (14 km from the turn-off).
Details: No entrance fee, but inform the National Parks office that you are climbing. Do not begin climbing before sunrise or after 14h00. Entrance fee for Nyazengu Trail. Do not walk or climb alone.
Accommodation: The nearby Rhodes Nyanga Hotel, Private Bag N8024, Rusape, tel (298) 377, offers comfortable accommodation. There are camping/caravan sites near the park entrance, as well as a self-catering cottage on the property of a trout hatchery.
Further information: Central Booking Office, National Parks and Wildlife Management, P O Box 826, Causeway, Harare, tel (4) 70-6077/8 or 72-6089.

Anyone with four hours to spare, and who is reasonably fit, can climb this mountain, Zimbabwe's highest (2 592 m).

Overlooking the Mozambique plains and the tropical Honde Valley, with its banana and tea plantations, Mount Inyangani rises in a series of rolling, treeless downs to a point where you climb through a fairyland of proteas, wildflowers and mountain streams to the saddle. From here a level path winds through the marshy upland plains and lichen-covered rocklands to the summit.

Be sure to bring along an anorak, penknife, matches and binoculars. The mist descends suddenly, so keep to the Zimbabwe Mountain Club's track, which is well marked with yellow arrows.

The summit is marked by a tower and a height beacon, and affords exceptional views of the countryside below. All of Africa seems to unfold below you, with the wind blowing up strongly from the vastness of Mozambique.

If you're lucky, you'll see eagles floating on the thermals, or a dainty-footed klipspringer stepping across the rocks.

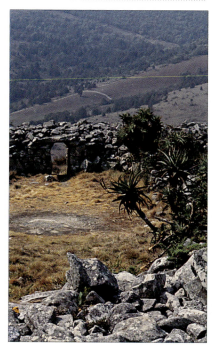

The ancient remains of a stone-walled village lie silently tucked into the mountains near Nyanga in the Eastern Highlands.

MUTARE
Eastern Highlands

The most dramatic view of Mutare, the prettiest of Zimbabwe's towns, is from the top of Mutare Heights at sunset. From here the heavens reveal a panorama of changing colours, while below, the lights of this holiday town begin to twinkle in tandem with the fading light. (To get there, take the three-kilometre winding gravel road off Christmas Pass, which is just to the west of the town.)

Mutare lies 298 km from the Indian Ocean, on the railway route between Beira and Harare. It started life as a gold-mining camp near Penhalonga, changed sites, then, with the coming of the railway in 1896, moved to its present spot.

Mutare consists essentially of two elegant main streets, palm-lined with old colonial buildings. The excellent museum is strong on cultural history, vintage cars and firearms. Other attractions in the vicinity are a game reserve, Cecil Kop, Murahwa's Hill where you'll find Iron-Age ruins, and an 1897 house named Utopia, which is furnished as it was 100 years ago, when it was occupied by the parents of the poet and philanthropist Kingsley Fairbridge.

If you like old houses, take a look at the elegant police station in Herbert Chitepo Street (Old Main Street) or visit Jenny's Cottage in 8th Avenue.

Map: page 413, 4E
Take Samora Machel Avenue east out of Harare, and drive for 263 kilometres. Pause for lunch at Malwatte Farmhouse Restaurant, east of Marondera, or Halfway House, near Headlands.
Details: There are daily train services, and Express Motorways operates a daily bus service from Harare.
Accommodation: Mutare offers hotel, holiday-cottage and bed-and-breakfast facilities, ranging from the luxurious Leopard Rock Hotel – P O Box 1322, Mutare, tel (20) 6-0170/1/7 – to the small, but very comfortable, Castle Private Guest House, P O Box Mutare, tel (20) 21-0320; Malwatte Farmhouse Restaurant, P O Box 23, Mutare, tel (79) 34-4121, 1/34-4112.
Further information: Manicaland Publicity Association, P O Box 69, Mutare, tel (20) 6-4711.

In the Nyanga Mountains, a centuries-old stone village and cattle pit are preserved as a museum.

NYANGA NATIONAL PARK
Eastern Highlands

Most of this lovely highland park, with its scented mountain air, trout streams, open vistas, lakes, wildflowers, forests and holiday cottages, was a gift to the nation by the Victorian imperialist Cecil John Rhodes. His original stables and homestead are now a small country hotel and adjacent exhibition centre, amongst ancient oak and gum trees. Nyanga National Park has always been a premier holiday attraction for settlers, farmers and now expatriate aid-workers. One visitor commented how much it reminded her of her native Scotland. The area is, in fact, part of the Great Rift Valley that runs the length of Africa's eastern flank.

The park is a combination of grassland, lakes, valleys and hillside montane forest of dwarf brachystegia trees trailing wisps of 'old man's beard' in the icy winds.

But this was not always the case – the woodlands once supported a substantial Iron-Age farming population who built stone terracing walls, sunken cattle enclosures and hilltop forts here. Today remnants of these structures serve as idyllic picnic spots or viewsites for visitors.

Good tar/gravel roads link the park's three villages, Nyanga, Troutbeck and Juliasdale. Each of the villages offers hotels (one with a casino), trout-fishing and horse-riding, and a tiny village church overlooking the mountains. Magnificent scenic spots as Pungwe Gorge, Mutarazi Falls (second-highest in Africa), Udu Dam and Nyamgombe River are all within easy access.

Game in the park, particularly in the more remote valleys, includes wildebeest, kudu, waterbuck and leopards.

Cream teas are the order of the day at the small cottage hotels, and if you do not enjoy walking, Nyanga National Park will soon change that. Artists are drawn to its misty landscape of mountains, lakes, eagles, flowers and butterflies.

Map: page 413, 3E/F
From Harare, take the Mutare road. Turn left at Rusape, 170 km from Harare, and continue for another 100 km to the clearly signposted National Park entrance. From Mutare, the Nyanga road turn-off is on the western side of Christmas Pass, 10 km from the town. There is an airstrip at the Brondesbury Park Hotel.
Details: Park open permanently. No entrance fee. Petrol at Nyanga Village, Juliasdale and Troutbeck.
Accommodation: National Parks camp sites at Nyangome and Mutarazi – contact Central Booking Office, National Parks and Wildlife Management, P O Box 826, Causeway, Harare, tel (4) 70-6077/8 or 72-6089. For hotels, try Troutbeck Inn, Private Bag 2000, Nyanga, tel (298) 305/6.
Further information: The Director, Manicaland Publicity Association, P O Box 69, Mutare, tel (20) 6-4711; The Public Relations Officer, National Parks and Wildlife Management, P O Box CY140, Causeway, Harare, tel (4) 79-2782/4/6-9.

PLACES TO VISIT

VICTORIA FALLS

FALLS CRAFT VILLAGE

Map: below
The Falls Craft Village is situated just behind the post office, in a crescent of curio shops and open-air sculpture markets. Follow Adam Standers Road off Livingstone Way for 100 metres.
Details: Open daily 08h30-17h00 (Sundays 09h00-13h00) all year round, except Christmas Day. Admission fee charged. Craftsmen, particularly wood sculptors, at work.
Further information: Falls Craft Village, P O Box 49, Victoria Falls, tel (13) 4309; Victoria Falls Publicity Association, corner Park Way and Livingstone Avenue, Victoria Falls, tel (13) 4202.

Ferocious Shangani warriors dance and sing outside this colourful, walled village to entice visitors into its exotic boma. Do not be daunted. It is well worthwhile, and probably the best of its kind in the whole of Zimbabwe.

Inside the large enclosure, while young Shona women dance their high-speed shake-shake routine, a guide will show you around the 30-or-so huts of all shapes and sizes, depicting every aspect of Zimbabwe's multicultural rural life.

From the Limpopo in the south, there is a Venda chief's hut; from the Nyanga Mountains, an iron-smelting furnace; from the Zambezi River, a Tonga hut, built on stilts to protect the children from predators.

There are also a number of genuine traditional artefacts, which have been collected throughout the country, and a rather Spartan Bushman shelter from the middle of the Kalahari.

The huts in the Falls Craft Village are amazingly varied in design. Walking around them conjures up what life must have been like in Great Zimbabwe 700 years ago, when 40 000 people lived in the valley separating the great walled enclosures of the ruling families.

The tour exits through a large and fast-cash curio shop, but before buying, pop in to see the Ndebele *n'anga* (witchdoctor) in his low-slung, creeper-covered hut. He will throw the bones for you, consult the spirits, and make a quick demand for payment if you photograph him.

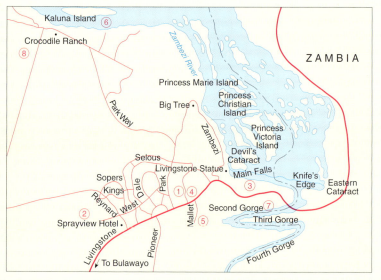

KEY TO THE MAP
1 Falls Craft Village
2 Flight of Angels
3 Rainforest
4 Traditional Dancing
5 Victoria Falls Hotel
6 Victoria Falls River Cruise
7 White-Water Rafting
8 Zambezi National Park

FLIGHT OF ANGELS

Map: above
There are pick-ups for fixed-wing and helicopter flights from all Victoria Falls hotels and selected travel agents. Sprayview Airfield is off Reynard Road. Turn off Livingstone Way, in front of Sprayview Hotel – the airfield is 500 m further on.
Details: Flights usually operate every 15 to 20 minutes during daylight hours from Sprayview Airfield. Contact United Air, P O Box 50, Victoria Falls, tel (13) 4530; Southern Cross Aviation (at the Elephant Hills Hotel), P O Box 210, Victoria Falls, tel (13) 4618; Batoka Sky, Safari Par Excellence, P O Box 44, Victoria Falls, tel (13) 4424.
Further information: Zimbabwe Tourist Development Corporation, P O Box 8052, Causeway, Harare, tel (4) 79-3666; Victoria Falls Publicity Association, corner Park Way and Livingstone Avenue, Victoria Falls, tel (13) 4202.

'But no-one can imagine the beauty of the view from anything witnessed in England,' missionary explorer David Livingstone wrote about his first sight of the Victoria Falls on 16 November 1855. 'Scenes so lovely must have been gazed upon by angels in their flight.'

David Livingstone did not really discover the Victoria Falls. San, Kololo, Lozvi, Tonga, Ndebele, and possibly even Arab trader, Portuguese explorer and Boer voorloper gazed on these beautiful falls before him. But by his intrepid adventures and courage he made them known to Europe and America.

One way of seeing them is by aircraft. It was Ted Spencer, a man long associated with the falls, who pioneered the 'flight of angels' in the 1940s. His fame was based on his feat of flying under the Victoria Falls Bridge. In the old days, pilots of Air Zimbabwe's predecessor, Central African Airways, used to circle low over the falls to give visitors their first breathless view of this princess of waterfalls.

Angel flights now include two Bell Jetranger helicopters that buzz daily like dragonflies before a typhoon, over the falls and up the river. Two microlites from Zambia's Batoka Sky Company (named after the Zambezi River Gorge) offer four trips a day.

Both United Air and Southern Cross Aviation offer 30-minute air safaris encompassing the Victoria Falls National Park and environs, giving you a superb view of the game, especially along the banks of the Zambezi River.

All of these excursions provide unparalleled views of the falls, the gorges and the meandering Zambezi, with its rich riverine forest, elephant populations and pods of hippos near the rocky rapids. Conservationists are concerned, however, that the aircraft tend to frighten the game, and threaten the fragile tranquillity of this World-Heritage Site.

Soon Livingstone's angels may need to pause a little longer in their flight, if this vision of loveliness is to be protected.

Neither clouds of spray nor the failing evening light can dim the magnificence of 'the smoke that thunders'.

The luxuriant rainforest at Victoria Falls is sustained by the clouds of spray spun upwards by the force of the falling water.

RAINFOREST

The rainforest, drenched in repeated updraughts of billowing rainbow-tinged spray, was probably explorer David Livingstone's first view of the Victoria Falls, known in the local dialect as *mosi-oa-tunya* – the smoke that thunders.

Livingstone must have been truly awed as he crawled forward to the basalt lip of Kazeruka (now Livingstone) Island, watching the river swirling in the angry gorge below, and the falls thundering to the left and right.

If you want an unusual view of the falls and the adjacent rainforest, follow the path to the right from the National Parks entrance gate, to Danger Point (which faces Zambia and the palm-lined Eastern Cataract) and the Boiling Pot.

Below, you will probably see guests of the 'float of angels' safaris admiring the view from rafts.

The paved pathway from here leads back along the edge of the falls, and affords spectacular views of Rainbow Falls, Horseshoe Falls and Livingstone Island. Thornbrush has been carefully placed to prevent anyone from falling over the edge.

As you leave the ilala palms behind you, the rainforest begins. Opposite Main Falls, mahogany, ebony and fig-tree giants, together with ferns, flowers, butterflies and birds, compete with the scenic splendour of the Zambezi plunging over the brink of the falls at a rate of 500 million litres a minute.

The Victoria Falls hold no records for size, height or volume of water when compared to other great waterfalls of the world, such as Venezuela's 979-m-high Angel Falls, or the 11-km-wide Khone Falls in Laos. But the falls do comprise the largest and most visible single curtain of falling water in the world.

As you emerge from the rainforest, probably soaked, you approach the Devil's Cataract, the highlight of your visit to the falls. Here, from several viewpoints, you will see the green-white water roaring two metres from your feet in a maelstrom of fury and majesty into the chasm below.

Map: page 438
The entrance to the rainforest and the Victoria Falls National Park is off Livingstone Way, 300 m from the bridge border post, at the car park. Go through the interpretive display and turn right. Allow 2 to 3 hours for the excursion.

Details: Open sunrise to sunset. To visit at other times contact the National Parks and Wildlife Management. Admission fee charged. Game includes small antelope and many birds. A raincoat and rainhat are essential. Toilet facilities, paths and rustic forest benches. Sunlight on spray can be dazzling for photography.

Accommodation: No restaurant or accommodation in the rainforest. But there is a wide range of hotels, National Parks chalets and camping facilities in Victoria Falls Village.

Further information: The Public Relations Officer, National Parks and Wildlife Management, Matabeleland North, Private Bag 5925, Victoria Falls, tel (13) 4558; Victoria Falls Publicity Association, corner Park Way and Livingstone Avenue, Victoria Falls, tel (13) 4202.

VICTORIA FALLS

Map: page 438

The boma-encircled Craft Village is behind the Victoria Falls Post Office, off Livingstone Avenue. You can walk there from most hotels. The Victoria Falls Hotel is on Mallet Drive, near the railway station.

Details: Shows nightly at 19h00 (except Christmas night). Admission fee charged. The dancing at the Craft Village is part of its normal daily tours. You can buy masks, costumes, musical instruments and drums at the Victoria Falls curio quarter.

Accommodation: Victoria Falls Hotel offers luxurious colonial-style accommodation. Write to: P O Box 10, Victoria Falls, tel (13) 4764.

Further information: Victoria Falls Publicity Association, corner Park Way and Livingstone Avenue, Victoria Falls, tel (13) 4202; Falls Craft Village, P O Box 49, Victoria Falls, tel (13) 4309.

TRADITIONAL DANCING

The solid beat of drums, rattling gourds and the deep, harmonizing chant of Africa merge against the background roar of the Victoria Falls as the multistriped Makishi dancers take centre stage for a breathtaking performance of traditional dancing.

Tufted leggings rise from the African dust, animal-skin kilts shake in the frenzy of moving bodies, and assegais rise up then come crashing down on great oxhide shields as the dancers perform ritual war dances that go back to the days of the Zulu king, Shaka.

You just have to close your eyes to imagine 5 000 Zulu warriors cresting the horizon in the early dawn, battlelines drawn, and assegais poised for battle.

There are two evening dance troupes at the Victoria Falls, one at the Victoria Falls Hotel, and the other at the Falls Craft Village. Both groups are spectacular and, in the process of trying to outdance each other, will provide you with an unforgettable evening.

Seventy-five dancers and drummers perform 13 different traditional or African folk dances nightly at the Falls Craft Village. The musical accompaniment – trumpeting kudu horns and rumbling drums – have become almost as familiar as the crash of the falls.

Traditional dancers step to the hypnotic beat of rhythmic drums under a star-studded canvas.

Map: page 438

Going towards the falls along Livingstone Way, turn right at the Makasa Sun Casino Hotel into Mallet Drive. The Victoria Falls Hotel is 300 m further along. If you are arriving by train, the hotel is just visible behind trees, 100 m to the right of the station.

Details: The hotel welcomes residential guests day and night. Casual guests may attend lunch on the terrace or the braai at night. There are 140 suites and rooms, a swimming pool, billiard room, boutiques, tennis courts, chapel, children's playground and library. Footpaths lead from the front of the hotel down to the Zambezi's Third Gorge, and another to the rainforest.

Further information: The Guest Relations Officer, Victoria Falls Hotel, P O Box 10, Victoria Falls, tel (13) 4751 up to 4764.

VICTORIA FALLS HOTEL

Stand in the gardens of the Victoria Falls Hotel for the perfect view of the spray of the thundering falls, its mist-smoke throwing a halo around the spidery bridge and chasm in the morning sun.

The Victoria Falls Hotel sits regally above the Zambezi gorges, in a clifftop setting of ancient teak and mango trees, palms, and courtyard lily ponds.

You almost expect to see ladies with lace parasols playing croquet on the rolling lawns, waiting to eat cucumber sandwiches for tea. Which, of course, is precisely what did happen when the hotel originated in an era of devil-may-care elegance 90 years ago.

The British Empire was at its height, and the falls attracted adventurers from around the world (a thousand visitors arrived for the first river regatta in 1909). And it still does – Zimbabwean helicopters fly angel flips in the sunlit skies overhead. And in the river below the hotel's lush gardens, American rafters ride the white-water rapids.

For those with a touch of Indiana Jones in their soul, there is the option of a splatgun safari, using washable paint to bag an elephant, an exercise which has been described by its promoters as ecohunting. But the old-world aristocrat, the Victoria Falls Hotel, smiles benignly.

For her there is nothing much that is really new under the midday sun. The First Victoria Falls Hotel of 1904 was

The elegant façade of Victoria Falls Hotel, where diners on the terrace overlook the Zambezi River as it churns through Second Gorge.

made of wood and corrugated iron and raised off the ground to keep the white ants at bay and provide ventilation.

Air-conditioned luxury and Rangoon fans have long taken over in the gracious green-and-white lounge of the hotel, where you are quite likely to bump into the royal, rich and famous.

Another quiet corner as you snoop around this lovely, and always surprising, hotel is the little chapel of Saint Mary Magdalene, consecrated over 60 years ago. On one of the antique wicker chairs, a prayer book lies open for the pilgrim traveller.

The hotel was originally built, and to this day is owned, by Zimbabwe Railways. Old steam trains, some from as far away as Cape Town, pull up at the delightful wood-and-stone station that lies behind a phalanx of giant trees (and a host of vervet monkeys) only 100 m from the hotel.

As night falls, the drums of the hotel's Africa Spectacular dance extravaganza are heard in the distance, as guests sit down to feast on a tender piece of crocodile tail in the Livingstone dining room, with its pale gold walls and Grecian columns.

A cruise on the Zambezi in the warm blush of the evening sun is an unforgettable experience.

VICTORIA FALLS RIVER CRUISE

You can cruise the wide, green expanse of the Zambezi above the Victoria Falls, with its brooding shoreline forests and noisy hippos, in a klepper Canadian canoe, a double-deck booze boat, an outboard chugging pontoon, a powerboat, or a craft called a crocodil, which has to be inflated.

There are dawn cruises, sundowner cruises, lunchtime cruises, and, in fact, everything but submarine dives. The best of them all are the canoe excursions, which range from three kilometres to three days, and start as far away as the Kazangula Forests, 80 km upstream.

In its journey through Zimbabwe the Zambezi can be as wide as two kilometres, or as narrow and rock-strewn as the beautiful Katambora, Sansimba or Kandahar rapids, which are the main attraction for white-water rafters.

Here the adventurous will pass palm islands such as Tsowa and Chundu, see elephants fording the river, and carefully navigate past lazy hippos in midstream. And there's an endless variety of game and birds along the river banks as you cruise through the Zambezi National Park.

If sleeping under the stars to the snorts of hippos and the whoops of hyaenas is not for you, try a sundowner cruise nearer the falls. The game here is not as plentiful, but there are plenty of birds in the forests of the huge royal islands: Princess Victoria, Princess Christian and Princess Elizabeth. And you will usually see antelope and warthogs below the ilala palms of the rustic and cosy National Parks cottages, opposite Lwanda Island.

The Zambezi always appears so open and pristine, particularly after a squall comes tumbling up the river, that it is easy to believe you are the first to experience its quiet beauty. But, in fact, San hunter-gatherers lived in the Zambezi area for thousands of years before Iron-Age farmers arrived at about the time of Christ. And all cruised the Zambezi not far from the thundering smoke in some form of precarious tree dugout or skin-stretched canoe.

Local Victoria Falls residents actually water-ski on the Zambezi, fishermen dart across its rapids, and a national airline used to land flying boats near the falls. But all the water inevitably finishes up going over the brink, so whether you're cruising, fishing or white-water rafting, you should always be sure to exercise some measure of care.

Map: page 438

Flights into Victoria Falls daily from practically any southern African capital. There's also a daily train from Bulawayo, with comfortable berths and dining. By road, Victoria Falls is 439 km from Bulawayo, 1 491 km from Johannesburg.

Details: There is no fee for cruising or fishing in the Zambezi, as it is in international waters. There are dawn, lunch and sunset cruises with pick-ups from hotels.

Accommodation: Choice of large hotels, including the Victoria Falls Hotel *(see separate entry)*; Elephant Hills Hotel, P O Box 300, Victoria Falls, tel (13) 4793; Makasa Sun Hotel, P O Box 90, Victoria Falls, tel (13) 4275; A'Zambezi River Lodge, P O Box 130, Victoria Falls, tel (13) 4561; and the Sprayview Hotel, P O Box 70, Victoria Falls, tel (13) 4344. There are also a number of luxury safari lodges, National Parks chalets and town-council caravan and camp sites.

Further information: Victoria Falls Publicity Association, corner Park Way and Livingstone Avenue, Victoria Falls, tel (13) 4202.

VICTORIA FALLS

Map: page 438
To book, contact any Victoria Falls safari company, travel agent, tour operator or hotel. There is a strenuous climb in and out of the river gorge, the worst part of the full-day expedition.

Details: Age doesn't really matter, mental approach does. There are numerous options, depending on the time of year (low and high water), ranging from one to seven days. August through December is best, as there is very little action in the high-water months (February to May).

Further information: Safari Par Excellence, P O Box 108, Victoria Falls, tel (13) 4510; Shearwater Adventures, P O Box 125, Victoria Falls, tel (13) 4471 or 4648; Victoria Falls Publicity Association, corner Park Way and Livingstone Avenue, Victoria Falls, tel (13) 4202.

WHITE-WATER RAFTING

The grade-five, low-water run through the Zambezi's turbulent gorges below the Victoria Falls is probably the wildest one-day run in the world. You have to be slightly mad (and 16-60 years old) to do it. But it is exhilarating beyond compare. Yes, there is an element of danger, but there have been very few accidents.

High-water runs are usually in July and August, while the low-water runs (when the rapids are real bone-shakers) go through from August until December.

David Livingstone, who tried everything at least once, rode several Zambezi rapids (near Kariba Gorge) in a canoe in 1860. Jack Soper, founder of today's Victoria Falls curio shop, did the same earlier this century.

But the sport of white-water rafting on the Zambezi, as we know it, started with the North American adventure company, Sobek, in 1981. Their name comes from the ancient Egyptian river god, which they adopted in 1973 when they first braved the Omo and the Awash rivers of Ethiopia. Sobek have pioneered 200 rivers in 60 countries.

Next to test their courage was an expedition of Harare schoolboys led by a Jesuit priest, using a home-made rubber tyre and bamboo Kontiki craft.

Today white-water rafting is a major industry, the focal point of the annual Zambezi River Festival, and the main reason why many, especially young, people visit the falls.

River-runners, in groups of five to seven people, meet in the early morning, listen to a safety pep talk, don life jackets and helmets, and tackle the water with one trained oarsperson at the helm.

Each run usually covers 10 rapids, and up to 22 km of bucking, twisting, screaming adventure. The oarsperson calls out when to shift your weight and how to pop out of the maelstrom if you are thrown overboard.

The ferocity of the Zambezi as you are blasted through the gorges (some just 12 m wide) is combated by the flexibility of the big rubber rafts, growing confidence in your raftmates, and the sheer adrenalin rush of riding the roughest rapids in the world.

The quiet stretches of water between the rapids, and the high cliffs on either side, bring welcome contrast and relief. But soon the current builds up again, the river rumbles and churns, and once again you are hurled over the precipice or slammed into surging walls of green, white water.

Then suddenly it is all over. You look at the oarswoman. She shakes her head. That was the last one. Now as you drift across the calm, 100-m-deep water of the Batoka Gorge, you realize, finally, that you've done it. You've joined that elite band of river-runners that have challenged – and beaten – the Zambezi.

Now you can buy the T-shirt, wear the rafter sandals and, at the Explorer's Pub that night, you can proffer sage advice to tomorrow's hesitant greenhorns.

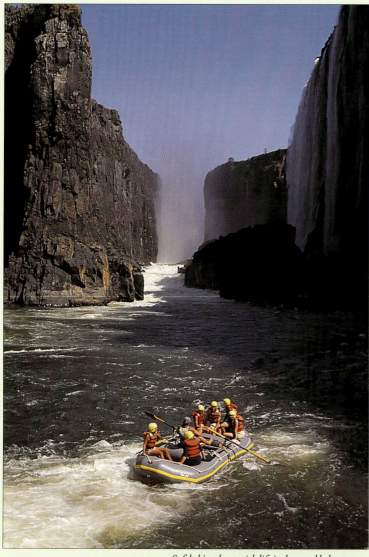

Safely kitted out with life jackets and helmets, intrepid adventurers brave the foaming white waters beneath the falls.

VICTORIA FALLS

ZAMBEZI NATIONAL PARK

The royal sable antelope, with its dark, glistening coat and needle-sharp horns, is a common and beautiful sight in the Zambezi National Park that fringes the river upstream from the Victoria Falls.

There are 25 attractive fishing and picnic sites in this smallish, quiet park alongside the Zambezi. All are gently shaded by giant trees, and overlook the sparkling rapids and ilala-palm islands of the wide Zambezi.

The park, which stretches 40 km to the west, and 24 km to the dry wilderness of the Matetsi Safari Area in the south, is the natural sister of the Victoria Falls rain-forest National Park.

Ebony, fig and acacia albida trees, all big, towering giants, guard the river bank, with its circular 90-km Zambezi drive, which crosses such tributaries (often dry) as Mpala Jena, Siamunungu, Sansimba and Chomunzi.

The park covers an area of 56 000 ha, and its rustic riverside chalets, just five kilometres from the Victoria Falls, are very popular amongst locals. There's game literally in your back yard and personal 'garden', a strip of cleared bush running down to the river.

An excellent game-viewing spot is the open Njako Pan platform (take the Chamabonda Drive), where you may see sable, lions, elephants, bat-eared foxes and a large variety of birds. If you wish to overnight in a safari lodge, consider Westwood, just outside the park, and Imbabala at Kazangula. Both are on the Zambezi, and both specialize in guided river and game trails.

Map: page 438
Regular air connections to the Victoria Falls from Zimbabwean and South African cities.
Details: Open 06h00-18h30 or 24 hours for chalet residents. Admission fee charged. No public transport, restaurant or store. Victoria Falls Village is 5 km away.
Accommodation: Central Booking Office, National Parks and Wildlife Management, P O Box 826, Causeway, Harare, tel (4) 70-6077/8 or 72-6089; Westwood Game Lodge, P O Box 132, Victoria Falls, tel (13) 4614; Imbabala Safari Lodge, P O Box 159, Victoria Falls, tel (13) 43-1521. The crocodile ranch is at the park entrance.
Further information: The Warden, Zambezi National Park, Private Bag 5920, Victoria Falls, tel (13) 4222.

An aerial view of the falls. The best time to visit is between February and May, when the river is in full spate.

The moon shines silver in the purple night sky, casting a metallic sheen over the waters of the Zambezi.

443

VUMBA BOTANICAL GARDENS AND BUNGA FOREST
Eastern Highlands

Map: page 413, 4F
The signposted access road turns left off the main Vumba road, 32 km south of Mutare.
Details: Open 07h00-17h00 daily. Admission fee charged. Camping/caravan sites. Swimming pool, golf course at Leopard Rock, nearby tennis court. Tea garden. Basic provisions and petrol nearby.
Accommodation: No accommodation in the gardens, but plenty in the vicinity to suit every pocket. No pets.
Further information: The Curator, Vumba Botanical Gardens, Private Bag V7472, Mutare, tel (20) 8-1293 or 21-2722; The Director, Manicaland Publicity Association, P O Box 69, Mutare, tel (20) 6-4711.

There is a lovely garden in the Vumba Mountains in eastern Zimbabwe – a Garden of Eden that bares its soul in an exquisite tapestry of lakes, flowers and verdant forests.

Perched near the edge of a 1 000-m drop overlooking Mozambique and Lake Chicamba Real, the Vumba Botanical Gardens are a sanctuary for thousands of flowering plants, including such species as azaleas, fuchsias, hydrangeas, cycads, orchids and countless other exotic and indigenous flowers, trees and plants.

It is surrounded by evergreen and seemingly endless rainforest (the Vumba Botanical Reserve).

Green-fingered English exile Fred Taylor from Manchester lovingly created the park between 1920 and 1950.

National Parks are now in charge of these gardens, where the bird life is one of the most prolific in Zimbabwe. The Bunga Forest, on either side of the road leading down to the Botanical Gardens, is particularly attractive, with its huge, mossy trees.

The sun's rays filter through the thick forest canopy in the attractive Vumba Botanical Gardens.

ZAMBEZI CANOEING SAFARI
Zambezi River/Mana Pools

Map: page 413, 1C
Pick-ups take place at Harare or Kariba airports or at the Marongora entrance to Mana Pools National Park.
Details: May to October only. Cost includes accommodation, meals, drinks.
Further information: Tour operators include Bushlife Zimbabwe, P O Box GD305, Greendale, Harare, tel (4) 49-6628 or 49-6113; Shearwater Adventures, P O Box 3961, Harare, tel (4) 73-5712.

Early morning on the Zambezi. The river mists float above the water and the reeds, giving everything a fragile beauty. In the shallows a goliath heron stabs at a fish; in midriver a pod of hippos snorts uncomfortably after a noisy night.

Nearby, six canoeists, refreshed after a comfortable night's sleep in walk-in tents, push off the sandbank in their two-man canoes, ready to face another magical day on the river.

The party is on the second day of a canoeing safari that is taking them from the sandy Ruchomechi River past the Mana Pools National Park to Chikwenya Island, possibly the most beautiful stretch of river and wilderness in the whole of southern Africa. Leading them is a highly experienced river and bush guide.

Those who have done it, who have witnessed the river in all its moods, and seen the elephants, the impala, the lions, the birds, the wondrous forests, the mountains tinged with fire, and, above all, who have experienced the lovely silences of the wild, return with a new and invigorating vision on life.

The canoes are ideal for drifting close to an island in midstream to watch a sleepy crocodile or delicate jaçana wader. And you don't have to be an expert to handle one.

The paddles are lightweight, and the canoes are exceptionally stable. As you proceed downstream in a light current with no rapids, there's really very little work to do.

Along the way the guide will stop at selected spots for game walks.

The Mana Pools flood plain looks anything but a flood plain before the rains. Huge acacias, albida trees covered by flaming combretum creeper, baobabs and sausage trees dominate the dusty parkland. With the onset of the rains in November, an incredible natural garden of lush green lawns and scattered pools forms beneath the canopy of flower-garlanded trees.

There are several canoeing options, ranging from three- to nine-day trips which start as far upstream as Kariba Dam, and end at Kanyemba on the Mozambique border.

Your guide will steer you around some of the 3 000 hippos in the river – these huge 'water horses', as the Greeks called them, don't like to be interfered with. Crocodiles, on the other hand, tend to show a lot of interest in you, if you decide to go swimming.

For the rest, the delicate tapestry of wildlife is there to be enjoyed: the lions, zebras and kudu; the carmine bee-eaters and the malachite kingfishers flashing past; the butterflies and spurwing geese; the nightly whoops of hyaenas – all these will awaken the spirit of Africa, and bring you back for more.

Canoeing down the Zambezi enables adventurers to experience face-to-face encounters with a variety of animals, including elephants.

The bountiful harvest of the sausage tree

You will never fail to identify a sausage tree – its fruit looks like giant salami. These great, rough-skinned pods hang from the tree's branches by the hundred, as if deliberately tied there to catch your attention.

Never study your route map under a sausage tree (scientific name *Kigelia africana*) – the pods come down like boulders, especially between December and June.

Usually 50 cm in length, these greyish pods can grow up to a metre in length, weigh as much as 10 kg, and be up to 18 cm thick.

Close up they tend to appear as overgrown bathroom sponges, but hard. The thick-trunked and handsome tree itself grows up to 18 m high. Its circular crown gives it an oak-like appearance.

The bark is greyish in colour, and, when the trees are particularly big, the trunk flakes in round patches.

The celebrated missionary and explorer David Livingstone once camped under a sausage tree in northeastern Zimbabwe, and to his later embarrassment he carved his initials in it. These have long since been obliterated.

The kigelia is part of what botanists call the Bignoniaceae or jacaranda family, and its fruit, leaves and flowers attract a variety of animals, including such mammal species as giraffes, baboons and elephants.

You may even see bats high up in a tree, pecking away at the flowers.

The sausage tree is said to have several medicinal uses. Children with stomach upsets are given a mixture of the fruit and bark ground down and boiled in water, and some herbalists use it to treat rheumatism and syphilis. An extract from the fruit is used in a cream for treating skin lesions, the sort you get from suntanning.

Research continues, to see if the kigelia cream is effective against melanoma cells. Should this prove to be the case, then the harvest of the benign sausage tree will become very valuable indeed.

The aptly named sausage tree has seed pods whose contents are said to help in the treatment of skin cancer.

ZAMBEZI NATURE SANCTUARY
Victoria Falls

Map: page 413, 3A
From Livingstone Way, turn north towards the river, onto Park Way. Continue for 5 km (the Zambezi River is on your right). The crocodile ranch is on the left, just before the Victoria Falls Boat Club and the entrance to the Zambezi National Park.
Details: Open year-round 08h00-17h00, except Christmas Day. Admission fee charged. Tea garden beneath shady sycamore fig and waterberry trees. Children's farmyard. 'Old Crocarosity' shop.
Further information: The Manager, Zambezi Nature Sanctuary, P O Box 18, Victoria Falls, tel (13) 4604.

Crocodiles are awesomely ugly, especially when you see them only a metre away, basking with mouths open on the sun-dappled banks of the Zambezi Nature Sanctuary, near the Victoria Falls.

Set in a pretty butterfly forest near the entrance to the Zambezi National Park, the sanctuary is within sight of the mighty river itself.

A woodland path leads from the entrance to the nursery, where crocodiles are hatched from eggs collected along the banks of the Zambezi. Some of these hatchlings are returned to their ancestral river once they are old enough to survive on their own.

There are 10 000 crocodiles in the sanctuary, all carefully divided into age-group pools and gardens. There's also a wild-cat sanctuary, where creatures such as caracals, leopards and servals are taken care of on behalf of the Chipangali Orphanage in Bulawayo.

Other attractions are a leather workshop, where you can buy belts and bags, and a 50-seat auditorium museum, which offers video shows daily.

Where the sanctuary fence abuts onto the bush there is an open-air 'vulture restaurant', where these scavengers feast on surplus meat and bones left them by the sanctuary's management.

Leopards are generally nocturnal, and are equipped with extra-long whiskers to detect obstacles in the dark.

Easily identified by its tufted ears, the caracal is a solitary creature, preferring to hunt alone at night.

INDEX

A

Abe Bailey Education Project 42
Abel Erasmus Pass 86, 87
Addo Elephant National Park 186, 198
Adler Museum of History of Medicine 10
African Art Centre 112-13
Afrikaans language 251
Agter-Paarl 228
Agulhas lighthouse 216, 217
Aha Hills 400
Ai-Ais 372, 380
Air Force Museum 62-3
Akkerendam Nature Reserve 327
Alanglade 100
Albany Museum 188, 215
Albert Falls Nature Reserve 128
Alexander Bay 316
Alexander McGregor Memorial Museum 333
Alexandra Park 136
Aliwal North 197
Allemanskraal Dam 352
Aloe Fjord 69
Alte Feste 396, 397
Amatola Hiking Trail 172-3
Ambagswerf (Crafts Green) 224
Amis Gorge 375
Amphitheatre
    Cape Town 280
    Drakensberg 151, 350
Amphitheatre Gardens (Durban) 113
Andora Harbour 429, 430
Andrieskraal 187
Andries Pretorius Monument 306
Andries Vosloo Kudu Reserve 190
Anglo-Boer War 10, 29, 31, 89, 95, 107, 340, 345, 346
Anglo-Boer War Memorial 306
Anglo-Zulu War 162, 163
Angria Fria 393
Anreith, Anton 265, 267, 269, 272, 275, 287
Apies River 30, 34
Apple Express 186-7, 210
apple orchards 230
Arbeidsgenot Museum 300
Arboretum 178
Arcadia 36, 38
Arcadia Park 30
Arniston 214
Arts and Crafts Market (Cape Town) 279, 280
Ashton 217
Assagay Safari Park 144
Assegaaibosch Nature Reserve 236
Auckland Park 24
Aukland Nature Reserve 178, 179
Auob River 403
Austin Roberts Bird Sanctuary 28, 31
Avalon Springs 221, 222
Aventura Vaal Spa 330

B

baboons, chacma 284
Backsberg 258
Badkloof 221
Badplaas 42-3
Bain, Andrew Geddes 188, 226, 309
Bain's Kloof Pass 226-7, 228
Bain, Thomas 217, 226, 302, 311, 321
Bakenskop 304
Baker, Sir Herbert 10, 11, 22, 30, 38, 100, 247, 274, 292, 293
Bakoni Malapa Museum 72
Ballotina 252
Banzi Pan 161
baobab trees 78
Barnard, Chris 301
Barnato, Barney 31, 335
Baroa ba Bararo 361
Bartolomeu Dias Museum 200
Basotho Pony Project 355, 357
Bathurst 191
Batonka village and museum 430
Battle of Blood River 140, 154-5
Baviaanskloof 187
Baviaanskloof Forest Reserve 187
Baynesfield Estate 128
Bay of Plenty 114
beaches,
    Cape Town 282-3
    Durban 116
    East London 175
    Port Elizabeth 194
Beacon's Nek 187
Beaufort West 301, 305, 311
Beaufort West Museum Complex 301
Belfast 47
Bellingham 256
Bells Rock 227
Belvidere Church 25, 204-5
Belvidere Estate 204, 205, 210
Ben Alberts Nature Reserve 73

Bendigo Mine 206
Ben Lavin Nature Reserve 73
Ben MacDhui 197
Benoni 60
Bensusan Museum of Photography 10
Berea 121
Bergh House 249
Bergkelder 243
Bergplaas State Forest 211
Berg River Valley 227, 240
Bergville 151
Berlin Falls 98, 108
Bethlehem 348
Betty's Bay 232
Bhabhathane Community Project 227
Bhanga Nek 159
Biedouw Valley 321, 327
Big Hole 334
Blaauwklippen 260, 261
Black Hills 75
Blanco 309
blesbok 352
Blettermanhuis 248, 249
Bloemfontein 344-6
Bloemfontein Zoo 345
Bloemhof Dam 347
Bloemhof Dam Nature Reserve 347
Blood River Monument 154-5
Bloubergstrand 282
Blou Pont 217
bluebuck 215
Blue Mountain Pass 355
Blue Waters Beach 250
Blyde Forest Reserve 98
Blydepoort Dam 86
Blyde River 87, 104
Blyde River Canyon 86-7, 109
Blyderivierspoort Nature Reserve 86, 87
BMW Pavilion 280
Bobs Glyvalle waterfall 80
Boiling Pot 180
Bo-Kaap 273
Bo-Kaap Museum 273
Bonnet Pass 98
bontebok 214
Bontebok National Park 214-15
Boosmansbos Wilderness Area 215
Borakalalo 74
Boschendal 230, 256, 257
Bosobogolo Pan 405
Botanic Garden, Johannesburg 11, 17
Botanical Garden(s)
    Durban 114
    Harold Porter (National) 232
    Karoo (National) 237
    Kirstenbosch 288-9

Lowveld (National) 96
Natal (National) 136-7
Pretoria (National) 36-7
Botha's Hill 143
Botsoela Falls 357
Bottelary Co-operative Winery 261
Bottelary road 230
Boulders 283
Bourke's Luck Potholes 86, 87, 98, 104
Braamfontein 12, 23
Braamfontein Spruit Trail 11, 13
Brandberg 372, 374, 375
Brandvlei 301
Brandwacht Mountains 237
Bratina (fraternity cup) 31
Breakfast Rocks 240
Bredasdorp 216, 218, 219, 221
Breede River Valley 226, 228
Bretagne Rock 240
Bridal Veil Cataract 179
Bridal Veil Falls
    Sabie 89, 109
    Zimbabwe 414
Brits 44, 74
Brixton Tower 24
Broederstroom 43, 49
Brozel, Gunter 239
Bruma 13
Brummeria 36
Bryanston 22
buffalo 425, 436
Buffels Bay 202, 284
Buffelskloof 302
Buffelsnek woodlands 212
Buitenverwachting 287
Bulawayo 415-17, 434
Bunga Forest 444
'Bunny Park' 60
Burgerhuis 244, 245
Burgers Park 31
Burma Valley 419
Bushman paintings, see San rock art
Bushman's Nek 361
Bushmen's Pass 354
Butha Buthe 359

C

Caledon 216, 217
Caledon Wildflower Garden 216
Calitzdorp Spa 302
Calvinia 327
Campanile 193
Campbell, Killie 121
camphor tree 254
Camps Bay 282, 283
Cango Caves 300, 302, 303
Cango Crocodile Ranch and Cheetahland 303

447

INDEX

Cango Ostrich Farm 312
Cango Valley 302
Cao, Diego 373, 374
Cape Agulhas 214, 216-17
Cape Cross Seal Reserve 373
Cape Dutch architecture 235
Cape Flats 250, 292
Cape Frio 393
Cape of Good Hope Nature Reserve 284-5
Cape Point 284-5, 296
Cape St Francis 190
Cape Town Castle, *see* Castle of Good Hope
Cape Town Harbour 269-70
Cape Vidal 167, 168
Caprivi Strip 387-8, 395
caracal 446
Carletonville 42
Carlton Centre Panorama 12
Carolina 42
Castle of Good Hope 25, 264
Cathedral of St Michael and St George 189
Cathedral Peak 146-7
Cathkin Peak 148
Cecil Kop Game Reserve 437
Cederberg Wilderness Area 316-17, 327
Centenary Nature Reserve 221
Central Highlands Scenic Drive 354-5
Central Kalahari Game Reserve 400, 404
Ceres 228
Ceres Fruit Route 228
Cetshwayo 162, 163
Ceylon State Forest 88, 89
Champagne Castle 148
Chapman's Peak 285
Chapungu Sculpture Park 421
Charter's Creek 169
Chatsworth 120
Cheche's Pass 355
cheetahs 44, 45
Chelmsford, Lord 162, 163
cherry festival 350
Chimanimani Mountains 414, 426
Chimanimani Mountains National Park 414
Chinhoyi Sleeping Pool and Caves 418
Chipangali Wildlife Orphanage 415
Chipinda Pools 419
Chiredzi 419
Chivilila Rapids 420
Chobe National Park 401-2, 404, 406
Chobe River 401, 406
Christiana 330
Christuskirche 398
Church of the Good Sheperd 293
Church of the Holy Trinity 204, 205
Church of the Vow 140, 155

Church Square 29
Church Street 252
Citrusdal 316, 318
citrus estates 318
City Deep 20
Civic Theatre 12
Clan Lindsay Rocks 180
Clanwilliam 316, 318, 321, 323, 327
Clanwilliam Dam and Nature Reserve 318
Clanwilliam Wildflower Garden 318
Clarens 348
Clifton 282, 283
Cockscomb Forest Station 187
Coffee Bay 173, 176, 205
Cogman's Kloof 217, 226
Coleskeplaas 187
Company Gardens 266-7
Compasberg 314
Conception Bay 393
Confidence Reef Mine 51
Constantia 285, 286
Constantia Manor House 235
Constantia Market 285
Contreberg Reserve 327
Cook, Captain 293
Cosmos 49
C P Nel Museum 304, 313
Cradock 192
crane
 crowned 125, 423
 wattled 48
Crocodile Centre (St Lucia) 168
Crocodile River 43, 73, 91, 96, 110
Crocodile River Arts and Crafts Ramble 43-4
crocodiles 129
Crocworld (Scottburgh) 129-30
Crown Mines 14
Cullinan 58
Cultural History Museum 68, *see also* South African Museum
Cwebe Nature Reserve 174, 183
cycads 79, 96, 191, 288

D

Daan Viljoen Game Reserve 396-7
Dacres Pulpit 227
da Gama, Vasco 297
Danger Point 229, 285
Darling 324, 327
dassies 157
Debengeni Falls 74, 77
Deception Pan 400
deer, sambar 339
De Gang 310
De Havilland Hornet Moth 62

De Hoek State Forest 74, 77
De Hoop Marine Reserve 219
De Hoop Nature Reserve 218-19
De Kaap Valley 42
Delaire 261
Delheim 260, 261
Delta Municipal Park 13
De Mond 217
Deneysville 69
Dennebos 210
De Oude Kerk Volksmuseum 252-3
De Rust 300, 302, 309
desert creatures 386
De Vasselot 208, 212
Devil's Knuckles 95
Devil's Peak 292, 296
Devil's Pulpit 86
de Wet, Christiaan 344
De Wet House 253
De Wildt Cheetah Research Centre 44-5
De Wildt Herbal Centre 46
Diagonal Street 18
diamond-mining
 Namibia 384
 West Coast 316
Dias, Bartolomeu 200, 393
Dias Monument 200
Dias's caravel (replica) 200
Die Akkers 80
Die Berg 47
Die Braak 242, 244-5
Die Hel 300, 302, 311
Die Kelders 229
Die Noute 309
Diepkloof Visitors' Centre 64
Diepwalle State Forest 201, 211, 212
Dieu Donne 256
Diggers Museum 330
Dingane 154, 155
dinosaur footprints 376
Dinosaur Park 88
Dlinza State Forest 155
Dock Road Complex 278-9
Dombeya Farm 262
Dorphuis 313
Dorp Street 242
Dorslanders 381
Double Drift Reserve 190
D'Ouwe Werf 245
Drakenstein Valley 230
Driekop Gorge 98
Dromedaris (replica) 25
Drostdy
 Graaff-Reinet 306
 Swellendam 223
Drostdy Museum 223
Drotsky's Caves 400, 403
Duggan-Cronin Gallery 333
Duiker Island 286, 289
Duiwelskloof 79
Duiwe River Valley 208
Dullstroom Dam Nature Reserve 47
Dundee 154, 162
Dunn, John 155

Durban
 beachfront 113, 114, 116-19
 central 112, 115, 121, 122, 124, 126
Durban Art Gallery 115
Durban City Hall 115
Durban North 120, 125, 126
Dutch Reformed Church
 Graaff-Reinet 307
 Nieu-Bethesda 310
Du Toit's Kloof Pass 227, 228
Duwisib Castle 376
Dwaalheuwel Spruit Bridge 97
Dwesa Nature Reserve 174, 183

E

eagle
 African fish 370
 black 157
 black-breasted snake
Eastern Caprivi 382
Eastern Highlands 418-19, 436-7, 444
Eastern Shores Nature Reserve 168
East London 174-5
East London Museum 175
Ebenezer Dam 75, 77
Echo Caves 86, 87
Eerste Tol 226, 227
Egyptian goose 241
1820 Settlers 189
Eikendal 261
Eilandvlei 207
Elandsberg 97, 109, 179
Elands River Falls 97, 109
elephants 93, 170, 186, 379, 387, 402, 433
Elephant Safaris 402
Elgin 230, 231
Elim 219
Elizabeth Bay 385
Emakhosini 162
Emmarentia Dam 11, 17
Entabeni State Forest 82
Epupa Falls 381
Erfurthuis 248
Eshowe 155, 164
Estcourt 149
Etosha National Park 377-9, 392
Etosha Pan 377, 393
Evelyn Valley 172
Ewanrigg Botanical Garden 421
Eye of Kuruman 330, 341
Ezulwini Valley 364, 367, 368, 369

F

Faerie Glen Nature Reserve 55
Fairview 258

448

INDEX

Fairy Knowe 210
Falls Craft Village 438
   traditional dancing 440
False Bay 250, 285, 295
False Bay Park 166
Fanie Botha Hiking Trail 88-9, 104
Fanie's Island 169
Featherbed Bay Beach 205
Featherbed Nature Reserve 205, 206
Feather Market Hall 193
Ferncliffe Trail system 138-9
Ficksburg 350
Fika Patso Dam 350, 351
First National Bank Museum 15
First Raadsaal 344
Fish Hoek 283
Fish Hoek Valley 295
Fish River Canyon 372, 380
Fitzsimons, F W 195, 196
Fitzsimons Snake Park 117
flamingoes 34
Fleamarket World 13
Flight of Angels 438
Florence Bloom Bird Sanctuary 11, 13
Florida Lake 48
Flower Market (Johannesburg) 20
Forbe's Reef 366
Fordsburg 23
Foreshore 270
Forest Falls 110
Fort Frederick 194
Fort Klapperkop 31
Fort Nongqayi 155
Fort Tuli 412
Fort Wynyard Museum 290
Fossil Trail 305
Foster's Folly 312
Fothergill Island 431
Fountains Valley Recreation Resort and Nature Reserve 30
Four Passes Drive 228, 230-1
Fourth Raadsaal 344
Four Ways 55
fox, bat-eared 383, 401
Franklin Nature Reserve 345
Franschhoek 230, 231, 235
Franschhoek Pass 230, 231
Franschhoek Vineyards Co-operative 256-7
Franschhoek Wine Route 256-7
Fransie Pienaar Museum 310
fynbos 218, 229, 288

G

Gaborone 408
Gaika's Kop 179
Gamka Mountain Nature Reserve 302, 304
Gamka River Valley 302
Gamkas Kloof 300, 302, 311
Gamtoos River Bridge 187
Gamtoos River Mouth 190
Gansbaai 229
Garcia's Pass 226
Gardiner Street Jetty 115
Gariep Dam 347
Gariep Dam Nature Reserve 347
Garsfontein 55
Gately House 175
Gcangwa 400
Gcwihaba Caverns 400, 403
Geju plateau 172
gemsbok 377, 389, 405
Gemsbok National Park 331, 403-4, 405
Genadendal 220
General J I J Fick Museum 350
Geological Museum 13
George 202, 203, 210, 302, 309
George Museum 202
George's Valley 75
Giant's Castle Game Reserve 149-50
Gideon Malherbe House 251
Gideon Scheepers Memorial 306
giraffes 377, 428
Goanikontes lunar dunes 392
God's Window 87, 88, 98, 108
Goede Hoop Church settlement 187
Goegap Nature Reserve 319, 327
Goerke House 386
Goetz/Fleischack Museum 57
Golden Acre 265
Golden Gate Highlands National Park 348-9, 351
Golden Mile 114, 116-19
Gold Reef City 14-15
Gonarezhou National Park 419-20
Gonubie 174, 176
Gordon's Bay 230, 231, 241
Gordon's Rock 240
Gottland House 312
Gouda 228
Goudveld State Forest 211
Goukamma Nature Reserve 202
Goukamma River 202
Goukamma Valley 210
Government Avenue 267, 274
Gqunube River 176
Graaff-Reinet 306-8, 310, 314
Graaff-Reinet War Memorial 306
Grabouw 230, 231, 237
Grahamstown 188-9, 190
Graskop 86, 87, 88, 98, 108, 109
Gravelotte 76
Gray, Sophy 205
Greater St Lucia Wetland Park, *see* St Lucia
Great Fish River Reserve 190
Great Synagogue 271
Great Usutu River 370
Great Zimbabwe 415, 416, 420, 421, 433
Green Belt Trails 138-9
Greenmarket Square 268
Green Point 293
Green Point Fleamarket 286
Grey, Sir George 267
Greyton 220
Greyton Nature Reserve 220
Groenland Mountains 231
Groenvlei 202, 207
Groot Constantia 25, 285, 286-7
Groote Kerk 269
Groote Schuur 247, 292
Grootfontein 381
Groot Marico 340
Groot River estuary 209
Groot River Pass 208
Grootvadersbos Nature Reserve 215
Grosvenor House 248, 249
Gydo Pass 226

H

Ha Baroana 354, 356, 360
Haelkop 236
Haenertsburg 75, 77
Ha Khotso 356
Ha Letuka 355
Halifax Island 386
Ha Marakabei 359
Hangklip State Forest 82
Hans Merensky Nature Reserve 75
Ha Ntsi 354
Happy Valley 194
Harare 421-5
Hardeveld 326
Hare Krishna Temple of Understanding 120
Harkerville State Forest 211
Harold Porter National Botanical Garden 232
Harrismith 350, 351
Hartbeespoort Dam 43, 49, 50
Hartbeespoort Dam Nature Reserve 49
Hartbeespoort Dam Snake and Animal Park 49, 50
Hartenberg Estate 261
Haunted Forest 377
Hazelmere Nature Reserve 130
Heidelberg 50, 64
Heidelberg Motor Museum 50-1
Helderberg Nature Reserve 233
Helderberg Peak 233
helicopter trips 270, 279
Helshoogte Pass 230
Henties Bay 373
Herbert Baker Street 31
Hermann Eckstein Park 26
Hermanus 234
Hermanus Harbour Museum 234
Heroes' Acre 422
Heroncliff 187
heron, goliath 420
Herrie the Elephant 300, 309
Hester Malan Nature Reserve 319
Hester Rupert Art Gallery 307
Hex River range 228
Heys, George 32
Highgate Ostrich Farm 313
hiking precautions 147
Hillbrow 10, 11
Himeville 150
History Museum
   Grahamstown 188
   Mossel Bay 200
Hlane Royal National Park 364
Hluhluwe-Umfolozi Park 156-7, 162
Hlumuhlumu Mountains 43
Hoarusib River 381
Hoba Meteorite 381
Hoedspruit 87
Hogsback 172, 178-89
Hogsback State Forest 178
Hole in the Wall 173, 176, 177, 183
Hololo Valley 359
Honde Valley 436
Honeydew 43
Honnet Nature Reserve 82
Horse Memorial 194
Horseshoe Falls
   Sabie 109
   Wild Coast 180
hot-air ballooning 56, 132
Hot Springs Resort 426
Hottentot-Hollands Nature Reserve 237
Hottentot-Hollands range 230, 231, 233, 241, 254, 285, 292
Hout Bay 283, 285, 286, 289, 295, 298
Howick 131, 132, 142
Howick Falls 131, 142
Huberta 177
Huguenot Memorial and Museum 235
Huguenot Tunnel 228
Humansdorp 187
Humewood Beach 194
Hungorob Gorge 375
Hwange National Park 417, 427-8

I

Ifafi 49
impala 60, 168

INDEX

Indian Market (old)
  Durban 126
  Johannesburg 19
Ingomana River Mouth 174
Injasuti 149
iPithi Falls 131
Irene 62
Irma Stern Museum 287
Isaac Stegmann Nature
  Reserve 63
Isandhlwana 162, 163
Island Lake 207
Itala Game Reserve 157-8

J

Jacaranda Route 30-1
jackal, black-backed 331
James Hall Museum of
  Transport 16, 25
Jan Felix Lategan Memorial
  gun collection 307
Japanese Gardens 120
Jean Craig Pottery 262
Jeffreys Bay 190
Jewish Museum 271
J G Strijdom Tunnel 86
Johannesburg Art Gallery 16,
  22
Johannesburg city 12, 18, 25
Johannesburg Stock
  Exchange 18
Jonkershoek State Fisheries
  Station 235-6
Jonkershoek State Forest 235,
  237
Jonkershoek Valley 236-7,
  262
Joostenberg 235
Joubert House 221
Joubert Park 16
Jubilee Creek 206
Jubilee Square 291
Jukskei River 11, 55
Juma Mosque 121
Just Nuisance 291

K

Kaaimans River and Falls 203
Kaaimans River Bridge 203,
  210
Kaffrarian Museum 177
Kalahari Gemsbok National
  Park 331-2, 404
Kalk Bay 295
Kalkfeld 376
Kame Ruins National
  Monument 415
Kanoneiland 332
Kaokoland 381
Kariba 429-32
Kariba Dam 429-30
Kariba Ferry Cruise 430, 431
Kariba Heights 429, 430
Karkloof Falls 142
Karoo National Botanical
  Garden 237

Karoo National Park 305,
  314
Karoopoort 226
Karoo scenic drives 302
Kasane 402
Katberg Pass 226
Katima Mulilo 78, 382
Kaudom Game Park 383
Kavango River 395
Keetmanshoop 386
Kerzner, Sol 65
Ketane Falls 357
Kettlespout Falls 179
Keur River Bridge 309
Khatibe Peak 359
Khomas Hochland 396, 398
Khorixas 372
Khutse Game Reserve 404
Killie Campbell Africana
  Library 121
Killie Campbell Museum
  121
Kimberley 333-8
Kimberley Mine Museum
  334-5
Kimberley Tram 336
King Edward VII Tree 201
King's Beach 194
King William's Town 172
Kirstenbosch Botanical
  Garden 201, 288-9
Klapmuts 228
Klein Constantia 287
Klein Drakenstein 239
Kleinplasie 238
Kleinpoort 187
Klipvoor Dam 74
Kloof 131
Kloofendal Nature Reserve
  51
Kloof Falls 131
Knysna 201, 202, 204-6,
  207, 210, 212
Knysna Heads 206
Knysna Lagoon 206
Kogelberg 241
kokerboom 322
Kolmanskop 384-5
Kommandosnek 49
Kommetjie 285
Koopmans-De Wet House
  272
Koos Raubenheimer Dam
  302
Koppie Alleen 219
Kosi Bay Nature Reserve
  158-9
Koue Bokkeveld 228
Kowie Canoe Trail 191
Kraalbaai 324
Kransberg 73
Krantzkloof Nature Reserve
  131
Kromdraai 43, 59, 63, 70
Krugerhof 89
Kruger House Museum 31
'Kruger Millions' 107, 177
Kruger National Park 75,
  90-4, 96, 101, 419
  rest camps 91, 93, 94

  touring in the 91
  when to visit the 91
Kruger, President Paul 15,
  31, 89, 97
  statue of 29
Krugersdorp 43, 52
Krugersdorp Game Reserve
  52
Kruisrivier 302
Kruithuis 244
kudu 160
Kuiseb River 389, 390
Kunene River 381
Kuruman 330, 341, 405
KwaGqokli Hill 162
Kwa Maritane 56
KwaMuhle Museum 122
Kwando River 387, 388,
  395
KwaZulu Cultural Museum
  162
KWV 258, 259
Kyalami 53

L

Laborie 258
Ladismith 311
Lady Eleanor 291
L'Agulhas, *see* Cape Agulhas
Laingsburg 305
Lake Bhangazi 168
Lake Chivero 422-3
Lake Kariba 431, 432, 435
Lake Mutirikwi 420, 433
Lake Otjikoto 385, 392
Lake Pleasant 210
Lakes District 207-8
Lake Sibaya 159
Lake Xau 406
Lambert's Bay 320, 327
Lamont Hussey Observatory
  345
Landskroon 258
Langebaan 324, 325
Langeberg 215, 217, 221,
  222
Langeberg Dunes 342
Langenhoven, C J 300, 309
Langkloof 186, 230
Langvlei 207
Lanseria 43
Lanzerac 236
Lapalala Wilderness 76
Lapalala Wilderness School
  76
La Provence 257
La Rochelle 16, 25
Larvon Bird Gardens 423
Latimer's Landing 175
Le Bihan Falls 356, 357
Leboela Falls 357
Lebombo Mountains 368
Leeu-Gamka 310
Leipoldt, Louis 321
Leopard Rock 433
leopards 103, 446
Leopard's Kloof 232
Le Roux Town House 313

Lesotho crafts 358
Lesotho Horse Trails 357
Letaba River 75, 81
Letsitele 75
Leydsdorp 76, 78
Libertas Parva 246
Lichtenburg 80, 339
Lichtenburg Game Breeding
  Centre 339
Likalaneng 355
Likalaneng Pass 355
Limietberge 226, 227
Limpopo River 11, 78, 412
Linyandi River 387, 401
Lion and Game Park (Natal)
  133
Lion Cavern 366
Lion Park (Muldersdrift) 53
lions 26, 52, 92, 331, 402,
  405, 406
Lion's Head 295, 296
Lippizaner Centre 53
Lisbon Falls 98, 108, 109
Little Top 117
llama 80, 339
Llandudno 282
Lobamba 364-5
Local History Museum 122
loerie, Knysna 198
Londolozi Game Reserve 103
London Nature Reserve 98
Lone Creek Waterfall 88, 109
Long Street 272
Long Tom Pass 95
Lord Milner Hotel 305
L'Ormarins 257
Loskop Dam 54
Lost City 56, 65-7
Loteni Nature Reserve 150
Louis Trichardt 73, 82
Louwsburg 157
Luderitz 384, 386, 388
Lutyens, Sir Edwin 16, 22
Lydenburg 95
Lynwood Glen 55

M

Mababe Depression 402
Mabalauta 420
Mabibi 167
Mabuasehube Game Reserve
  405
macaw 125
Machache Peak 354
Maclear's Beacon 288
Mac-Mac Falls 88, 89, 110
Mac-Mac Pools 88, 89, 110
Mac-Mac State Forest 88,
  104
Macrorie House 137
Maden Dam 172
Madonna and Child
  Waterfall 179
Mafadi Peak 149
Mafeteng 354
Magaliesberg 12, 25, 40, 44,
  45, 49, 60
Magersfontein 340

INDEX

Magersfontein Battlefield and Museum 340
Magnolia Dell 31
Magoebaskloof 74, 77, 80, 81, 84
Magoebaskloof Pass 75, 77
Mahango Game Reserve 387, 395
Mahlasela Pass 359, 360
Mahulungwane Falls 366
Makgadikgadi Game Reserve 406
Makhaleng River Valley 355
Mala Mala Game Reserve 102
malaria 94
Malay Quarter 273-4
Malealea Lodge 357
Maletsunyane Falls 356, 357
Malgas Ferry 220
Malkerns 369
Malolotja Falls 366
Malolotja Nature Reserve 366
Maltese Cross 317
Maluti Mountains 348, 354, 357, 359, 362
Mamili National Park 387
Mampoer Tour 340
Mamre Mission 238-9
Mana Pools National Park 434, 444
Mandela, Nelson 20, 293
Mankelekele Mountains 88, 106, 107
Mankwe Lake 56
Mantenga Falls 367
Mantenga Handicrafts Centre 367
Mantsonyane 355
Mapelane 167
Maputaland 158, 159
Maputaland Marine Reserve 167
Marais, Newald 239
Marakabei 355
Maranke Hills 426
Marcus Bay 214
Margate 132
Maria Moroka National Park 349
Mariannhill Monastery 122
Mariepskop 86, 87
Marie Rawdon Museum 305
Marine Hall 196
Mariner's Wharf 289
Maritime Museum 200
Maritzbos Indigenous Forest 89
Market Theatre 19
Marks, Sammy 29, 61
Marloth Nature Reserve 221
Marriamen Temple 140
Martello Tower 290
Martins, Helen 310
Mary Fitzgerald Square 21
Maseru 354, 356, 357, 362
Mashu Museum of Ethnology 121
Masvingo 420

Matelile Pony Owners' Association Centre 357
Matetsi Safari Area 443
Matjiesfontein 25, 302, 305
Matobo Hills 415, 416, 434-5
Matobo National Park 434
Matusadona National Park 431, 435-6
Mauchsberg Peak 88
Maun 410
Mayville 224
Mazeppa Bay 180
Mbabane 364
Mbare Musika Market 424
McGregor Museum 337, 340
Mdedelelo Wilderness Area 146, 148
Meerhof 49
Meiringspoort 302, 309
Melrose Bird Sanctuary 11
Melrose House 31, 32-3
Melville 11, 17
Melville Koppies Nature Reserve 11
Memorial Church 140
Meob Bay 393
Messina Nature Reserve 78
Metropolitan Methodist Museum 268
Meyerspark Bird Sanctuary 55
Mfihlelo Falls 183
Mhlangamphepha Valley 366
Middelburg 54
Middelkop Tea Estate 81
Midmar Dam 132-3
Midmar Dam Nature Reserve 132-3
migrant birds 325
Millwood House and Mine 206, 211
Milnerton 282, 293
Mimosa Lodge 312
mine tours 14, 15, 100, 316
Miniland (Santarama) 25
Minitown (Durban) 118
Mint (old)
    Gold Reef City 15
    Pretoria 29
mirages 379
Missionary Museum 177
Mitchell's Pass 226
Mkambati Nature Reserve 180, 183
Mkhaya Game Reserve 370
Mkhomazi Wilderness Area 150
Mkuze 160
Mkuzi Game Reserve 160-1
Mlambonja Wilderness Area 147
Mlawula Nature Reserve 368
Mlibizi 430, 432
Mlilwane Wildlife Sanctuary 364, 368-9, 370
Mnandi Beach 250
Modjadji Nature Reserve 79
Moeketsi, Kippie 19

Moerdijk, Gerard 39
Moertjiesklip 309
Moffat Mission 341
Mogwase 56
Mokhoabong Pass 355
Mokhotlong 358, 359, 361
mokoro trips 407, 410
Molimo Nthuse Mountain Lodge 355
Molimo Nthuse Pass 355, 357
Molose Pan 404
Monk's Cowl 148
Montagu 217, 221
Montagu Mountain Nature Reserve 217
Montagu Pass 302, 309
Montagu Rock 227
Montagu Spa 221-2
Montrose Falls 110
Moreleta Spruit Hiking Trail 55
Moremi Game Reserve 404, 406-7, 409
Morgenhof 261
Morgenzon State Forest 104
Moshoeshoe 362
Mossel Bay 200, 302, 313
Mostert's Mill 289
Moteng Pass 359
Motete Valley 360
Motswari Private Game Reserve 101-2
Mountain Zebra National Park 192
Mount Etjo 376
Mount Inyangani 418, 419, 436
Mount Sheba Nature Reserve 97
Mouton-Excelsior 257
Mowbray 287, 289
Mpande 112, 155, 162
Mpushini Falls 155
'Mrs Ples' skull 63
Mswati III 364
Mtfombotsi Forest 364
Mtubatuba 156
Muckleneuk 121
Mudumu National Park 388
Muizenberg 250, 283, 290, 291, 295
Muldersdrift 43, 53
Multiflora 20
Munroeshoek Cottages 200
Murahwa's Hill 437
Murray Bay 293
Murrayfield 55
Murray, Rev Charles and Andrew 307, 308
MuseumAfrica 10, 13, 19, 20-1
Museum of Science and Technology 33
Musical Fountains 25
Mutarazi Falls 437
Mutare 414, 433, 437
Mutirikwi Valley 420
Mzilikazi 427, 434

Mzilikazi Art and Craft Centre 416
Mzimvubu River 182

N

Namaqualand 326, 327
Namibia Craft Centre 397
Namib-Naukluft National Park 376, 388-9, 392, 393
Nasrec 21
Natale Labia Museum 290
Natal Maritime Museum 123
Natal Museum 137-8
Natal Sharks Board 134-5
Nata Reserve 406
National Archives (Zimbabwe) 424-5
National Arts Festival 189
National Cultural History Museum 68, *see also* South African Museum
National Exhibition Centre 21
National Museum and Art Gallery (Gaborone) 408
National Museum of Military History 22
National Women's Memorial 346
Natural History Museum
    Bulawayo 416
    Cape Town 266
Natural Science Museum 115
Nature's Arch 205
Nature's Valley 201, 208, 209, 212
Naukluft 389
Naval Hill 345
Naval Museum 290
Ncwala Festival 364, 365
Ndedema Gorge 147, 148
Ndumo Game Reserve 161, 170
Nederburg 239-40, 258
Neethlingshof 261-2
Neil Ellis Wines 236, 262
Nelson's Caves 211
Nelspruit 88, 96, 106, 110
New Agatha Forest Station 80
Newlands 288, 294
Newlands Stadium 294
New Muckleneuk 28
New Small Craft Harbour 123
Newtown 10, 13, 19, 20
Ngwenya iron-ore mine 366
Ngwenya Peak 366
Nhlohlela Pan 160
Nico Malan Theatre Centre 274
Nieu-Bethesda 310
Nieuwekloof Pass 226, 228
Nodwengu 162
Noordhoek 283, 285, 295

451

INDEX

Noordhoek Peak 295
Norvalspont 347
Nossob River 403
Nsumo Pan 160, 161
Ntwetwe Pan 406
Nutcracker Valley 104
Nuweberg 237
Nuwekloof 187
Nuweveld Mountains 305
Nxai Pan 406
Nyamgombe River 437
Nyamithi Pan 161
Nyanga Mountains 421
Nyanga National Park 418, 437
NZASM Tunnel 97, 109

O

Oberon 49
Observatory Museum 188
Oceanarium 195, 196
Ohrigstad 86
Okavango Delta 387, 402, 403, 406, 408-10
Okiep 327
Old Church Museum 252-3
Old Courthouse 122
Old Drostdy 253
Old House Museum 122
Old Presidency 345
Old Residency
 Graaff-Reinet 307
 Simon's Town 291
Old Smithy 309
Old Synagogue 271
Old Toll House 354
Old Town House 268
Olifants River 86, 90, 91
Olive Schreiner House 305
Olivier Towers 312
Olthaver House 15
Omaruru 372
Ondini Historic Reserve 162
Oom Samie se Winkel 246-7
Operation Genesis 56
Operation Noah 429, 435
Opuwo 381
Orange River 322, 323, 332, 372
Orange River Canoe Trails 320
Orange River Mouth 316
Oranjemund 384
Oranjeville 69
Organic Market 22
Oribi Gorge Nature Reserve 135
Oriental Plaza 23
ostrich palaces 312-13
Otavi Mountains 381
Otjihaenamaparero Farm 376
Otjikoto cichlid 385
Otjiwarongo 394
otter, Cape clawless 183
Otter Trail 208, 209, 212
Oude Libertas Centre 247
Oude Meester Brandy Museum 247
Oudepost Reserve 327
Oudtshoorn 300, 302, 303, 304, 309, 311, 312-13
Ou Kaapseweg 295
Ouma Plaas Doll's House 330
Outeniqua Choo-Choo 203, 210
Outeniqua Hiking Trail 211
Outeniqua Mountains 207, 211, 212, 302
Outeniqua Pass 309
Overberg 230
Oviston Nature Reserve 347
Owl House 310

P

Paardeberg 227
Paarl 227, 239, 240, 250
Paarl Mountain 227
Paarl Mountain Nature Reserve 240
Paarl Rock 240
Paarl Rock Brandy Cellar 258-9
Paarl Wine Route 258-9
Paddagang 253
Padkloof Pass 342
padrao
 Cape Cross 373
 Mossel Bay 200
Pakhuis Pass 321, 327
Palace of Justice 29
Panorama Route 87, 98, 108
Papegaaiberg 243, 247
Parke's Cottage and Shop 206
Parktown/Westcliff Urban Walk 11
Parkview 26
Parliament 274
Parliamentary Museum 274
Parsonage 253
Pass of Guns 360
Peatties Lake 128
pelicans 161, 390
Pelindaba 43
Pella Mission Church 341-2
Penny Ferry 279, 280
Petticoat Lane 55
PheZulu 143-4
Phophonyane Falls 369
Phophonyane Nature Reserve 369
Phuthaditjhaba 350
Pickering Memorial Garden 333
Pickhandle Mary 21
Pierneef, J H 34-5, 246
Pierneef Museum 34-5
Pietermaritzburg 128, 133, 136-41
Pietermaritzburg Station 25
Pietersburg 72, 79
Pietersburg Game Reserve 79
Piggs Peak 369
Pilanesberg National Park 56, 66
Pilgrim's Rest 89, 97, 98, 99-100, 104
Pinehurst 313
Pinetown 122
Pinnacle, the 88
Pinnacle Nature Reserve 98
Pioneer Open-Air Museum 55, 57
Pioneers of Aviation Memorial 338
Pioneers' Park 16, 25
Pirie Forest 172
Plains of Camdeboo 314
Planetarium
 Cape Town 266, 275
 Johannesburg 23
Platberg Peak 232
Player, Ian 156
Plettenberg Bay 208, 211
Police Museum 35
Popa Falls 395
Port Alfred 191
Port Edward 143, 184
Port Elizabeth 186, 187, 190, 193-6, 197, 198
Port Elizabeth Museum Complex 195-6
Port Grosvenor 181
Port Shepstone 135
Port St Johns 182
Postberg 324
Postmasburg 342
Post Office Tree 200
Potberg Mountain 218, 219
Potchefstroom Museums 57
Potgieter, Hendrik 40
Potgietersrus Game Reserve and Breeding Centre 80
Premier Diamond Mine 58
President Pretorius Museum 57
Pretoria
 central 28, 29, 31-5, 37
 east 55
 north 40
 south 39
Pretoria Aquarium and Reptile Park 28, 34
Pretoria Art Museum 30, 36
Pretorius, Andries 57, 154, 155
 house of 141
Pretorius, President M W 57
Prince Albert 310, 311
Prince Alfred's Pass 226
Prince's Park 29
Prospector's Trail 89, 104
Protea Park 31
puff adder 195
Pungwe Gorge 437
python, African rock 415

Q

Qiloane 362
Qiloane Falls 357
Qora Mouth 180
Queen Elizabeth Park 138, 139
quivertree 322
QwaQwa Conservation Area 350-1

R

Raadsaal 29
Railway Museum
 Bulawayo 417
 Matjiesfontien 305
railways 210
Rain Queen 79
Ramskop Municipal Nature Reserve 318, 327
Rand Easter Show 21
Rand Regiments Memorial 22
Ratombo Nature Reserve 82
Reilly, Ted 368, 370
Reinet House 307, 308
Rembrandt van Rijn Art Gallery 246
Reptile and Snake Park (Margate) 132
Reptile Park (Pretoria) 28, 34
Rex, George 204
Rhebokskloof 259
Rhenish Mission complex 245
rhinoceros
 black 378
 white 59, 156, 190, 352
rhinoceros iguana 28
Rhino Nature Reserve 59, 70
Rhodes 197
Rhodes, C J 230, 240, 267, 292, 335, 337, 412, 416, 418, 434, 437
Rhodes Cottage 291
Rhodes Memorial 292
Ribaneng Falls 357
Richtersveld National Park 322
Rietvlei Recreational Area 293
river cruises
 Katima Mulilo 382
 Victoria Falls 441
Riviersonderend Valley 231
Roaring Sands 342
Robben Island 293, 295
Robberg Nature Reserve 211
Roberts, Margaret 46
Robinson Pass 226, 302, 313
Rocher Pan Nature Reserve 327
Rodin, Auguste 22
Roma 354
Rondebosch 292
Rondevlei 207, 208, 210
Rondevlei Nature Reserve 294
Roodepoort 48, 51
Roof of Africa Drive 359-61
Rooibos Tea Estates 323
Rooikat Trail 80
Rorke's Drift 162-3

Rorke's Drift Arts and Crafts Centre 163
Rorke's Drift tapestries 112-13, 162, 163
Rosebank 287
Rössing Uranium Mine 392
Rottcher Wineries 104
Rovos Rail 105
Royal Natal National Park 151-2, 350
Ruacana Falls 381
Rugby Museum 294
Rugged Glen 152
Ruiterbos 302
Runde River 419
Rus in Urbe 312
Rustenburg Nature Reserve 60
Rust-en-Vrede Waterfall 302
Rust-en-Vreugd 275
Rynfield Children's Park 60

S

SABC Broadcasting Centre 24
Sabie 88, 95, 105, 109, 110
Sabie Forestry Museum 105
Sabi Sabi Private Game Reserve 103
Sabi Sand Game Reserve 103
sable antelope 52
Safari Island 431-2
Safari Ostrich Farm 313
Saldanha Bay 324
salt-mining 393
SA Maritime Museum 278
Sam Knott Nature Reserve 190
Sammy Marks Museum 61
San (Bushman) Trails 390
sand dunes 388, 389
Sandton 12, 24, 53, 55
Sandton City 24
Sandveld Museum 320
Sandveld Nature Reserve 347
Sandwich Harbour 389, 390
Sandy Bay 282
Sani Pass 358, 359, 361
San people 411
San rock art 20, 21, 147, 150, 360, 374-5, 435
Santa Barbara Church 429, 430
Santarama Miniland 25
Sanyati Gorge 432, 435
Sapekoe Tea Estate 77, 81
sardine run 116, 119
SAS Somerset 280
sausage tree 445
Save River 419
Savuti Channel 402
Saxonhof 242
Saxonwold 22
Schaapen 324
Schoemanskloof 110
Schoemansville 49
Schreuderhuis 249
Scottburgh 129
Scottzkloof 310

seal, Cape fur 286, 373
Sea Point 282, 293
Sea World 118
Sehlabathebe National Park 360, 361
Semonkong 356, 357
Sendinggestig 272
Sendingkerk 301
Sendingpastorie 301
Senqunyane Lodge 355
Senqunyane River 354, 355
Senqunyane Valley 355
Senqu River 359
Seodin 341
Serala Forest Station 84
Serpentine, the 207, 208, 210
Sesriem Canyon 389
Seweweekspoort Mountain 300, 311
Seweweekspoort Pass 302, 311
Shakaland 164
Shamwari Game Reserve 197
Shark Island 386
Shark Point 180
sharks 134
Shashe River 412
Sheik Yusuf 273
Shelley Beach 180
Shell Museum 200
Shipwreck Museum 216, 221
shipwrecks 181
Sibaya 159
Signal Hill 295
Silaka Nature Reserve 182
Silotwane Peak 366
Silverglen Nature Reserve 142
Silvermine Nature Reserve 295
Silverton 55, 57
Silverton Ridge 36, 37
Simonsberg 230
Simon's Town 290, 296
Simon's Town Museum 291
Sir Lowry's Pass 230, 231, 241
Sister Henrietta Stockdale Chapel 338
Skeleton Coast National Park 381, 391
Skeleton Gorge 288
Skilpad Wildflower Reserve 327
Skurweberg range 228
Slanghoekberge 226
Slangkop Lighthouse 285
Smuts, Gen J C 62
 statue of 277
Smuts House Museum 62
Snake Park
 Durban 117
 Hartbeespoort 49, 50
 Port Elizabeth 195
Sneeuberg range 314, 316
Snoek Festival 289
Sobhuza II 364, 368
Sodwana Bay National Park 159, 167

Somcuba 107, 177
Somerset West 230, 231, 233, 254
Sossusvlei 389
South African Air Force Museum 62-3
South African Library 267
South African Museum 265, 266, 275, 276, 288
South African National Gallery 277, 290
South African War 22, 272
Soutpansberg Hiking Trail 82
Soutpansberg Mountains 73, 82
Sowa Pan 406
Soweto Tours 25
Spandau Kop 314
Spier 262
spider, 'dancing white lady' 386
Spier 262
springbok 332, 404
Springbok 319, 327
Spurwing Island 431
Sri Siva Soobramoniar Temple 140
Stadshuis 301
State Bank (old) 29
State Theatre 37
steam-train trips 14, 25, 105, 210, 417
Steenberg mountain wilderness 295
Steenbras Dam 241
Steenkampsberg range 47
Stellenbosch 230, 236, 242-9, 255
Stellenboschberg 236
Stellenbosch Village Museum 148-9
Stellenbosch Wine Route 260-2
Stellenryk Wine Museum 246
Stempastorie 296
Sterkfontein Caves 63
Sterkfontein Dam 351
Sterkfontein Dam Nature Reserve 351
St George's Mall 277
Stinkhoutdraai 309
St James 291
St James Anglican Church 308
St Lucia 159, 160, 165-9
St Lucia Estuary 168
St Lucia Game Reserve 169
St Lucia Marine Reserve 167
St Lucia Nature Reserve 168
St Lucia Park 169
St Mary's-on-the-Braak 245
stork, marabou 364
Storms River Mouth 209, 212
St Patrick's-on-the-Hill 178
Strand 230, 231
Strandfontein Pavilion 250
Strijdom Square craft market 37

Struben Dam 55
Struisbaai 217
Studtis 187
Sudwala Caves 88, 106-7, 110
Suikerbosrand 50, 64
Suikerbosrand Nature Reserve 64
Sun City 56, 65-7
Sundays River Valley 186
Sundial Peak 86
Swakopmund 372, 373, 389, 391-2, 393
Swakop River 389
Swartberg 216, 300, 309, 310
Swartberg Pass 226, 302, 311
Swartland 227
Swartvlei 207, 211
Swartwater Dam 350
Swazi crafts 367
Swaziland National Museum 365
Swellendam 214, 220, 221, 223-4
Sydenham Road 114

T

Taal (Language) Monument 250-1
Table Bay 293
Table Mountain 227, 231, 240, 288, 289, 296-7
 myths about 297
Table Mountain Cable Car 296
Table Mountain Reserve 297
Table Top 210
Tambohanta Pan 420
Taung 63
tea cultivation 77, 81
Telkom Exploratorium 278
Tembe Elephant Park 170
termites 427
Terrace Bay 391
Tewate Wilderness Area 168
Thaba Bosiu Highlands 362
Thaba Nchu 349
Thaba Ntlenyana 358
Thaba Putsoa Mountains 357
Thaba Tseka 354, 355
Thabazimbi 73
Theewaterskloof Dam 231
The Island 180
The Old Gaol 224
The Playhouse 124
The Posthouse 220
The Sentinel 285, 286, 350, 351
The Window 216
The Workshop 124-5
Thibault, Louis 235, 252, 253, 265, 272, 275, 287, 306
39 Steps Waterfall 179
Thornhill 187
Three Bushmen 361

INDEX

Three Rondavels 86
Tienie Versveld Wildflower Reserve 324, 327
tigerfishing 432
Timbavati Private Game Reserve 101-2
Tintenpalast 398
Tishweshwe Crafts 369
Tjolotjo Cliffs 419
Tlaeeng Pass 360
Tobacco Tour 340
Tollhouse 309
Toorwaterpoort 300
Tor Doone 179
Torra Bay 391
Totius House Museum 57
Touws River Estuary 207
TransNamib Railway Museum 398
Transnet Museum 25
Treaty of Vereeniging 32
Tsehlanyane Valley 359
Tshipise Spa 82
Tsisab Ravine 372, 375
Tsitsikamma Hiking Trail 208
Tsitsikamma National Park 208, 209, 212
Tsodilo Hills 409, 410-11
Tsumeb 385, 390, 393
Tsumeb Mine 392
Tsumeb Museum 385, 392
Tswaing Crater Museum 68-9
Tugela River 151
Tulbagh 228, 252-3
Tuli Block 412
turtles, sea 167
Tuynhuys 266
Tweede Tol 227
Tweefontein State Forest 88
Two Oceans Oceanarium 280
Twyfelfontein 372, 374, 375
Tyumie River Valley 178
Tzaneen 74, 75, 77, 80, 81

U

Udu Dam 437
Ugab River 391
Uiterwyk 262
Ulundi 162
Ulundi Battle Monument 162
Ulundi Memorial 162
Umfolozi 156, 157
Umgeni River Bird Park 125
Umgeni River Mouth 116
Umgeni Valley Project 142
Umhlanga 134
Umhlanga (Reed Dance) 364
Umtamvuna Nature Reserve 143
Umtata River Mouth 173
Umzimkulwana River 135
Umzinto 144
Uniab River 391

Union Buildings 22, 30, 38, 248
Union Monument 306
Unisa 31
University of Pretoria 31
University of Stellenbosch 243
Upington 332
Urquhart House 308
Utopia House 437
Uvongo Bird Park 132

V

Vaal Dam 69
Vaal Dam Nature Reserve 69
Vaalhoek 98
Vaalwater 76
Vale, W T 33
Valhalla 62
Valley of a Thousand Hills 133, 143-4
Valley of Desolation 314
Valley of Ferns 212
van der Stel, Simon 242, 243, 254, 266, 286
van der Stel, Willem 254, 267
Vanrhynsdorp 327
van Riebeeck, Jan 265, 266, 270, 289, 293
Van Ryn Brandy Cellar 251
Van Ryneveld's Pass 226
Van Staden's River Bridge 187, 197
Van Staden's River Mouth 198
Van Staden's Wildflower Reserve 197, 198
van Wouw, Anton 29, 39, 246, 346
Velddrif 327
Venning Park 30
Vergelegen 254-5
Verloren River Valley 187
Verneukpan 301
Vernon Crookes Nature Reserve 144
Verulam 130
Verwoerdburg 30
Victoria and Alfred Waterfront 278-80, 286
Victoria Bay 210
Victoria Embankment 115, 123
Victoria Falls 402, 417, 427, 429, 438-43, 446
 rainforest 439
 river cruises 441
 traditional dancing 440
Victoria Falls Hotel 440-1
Victorian House, the 253
Victoria Park 216
Victoria Street Market 126
Victory Park 13
Viljoen's Pass 230, 231
Villiera 259
Vineyard Trail 255
Vingerklip 372

Virginia Airport 126
Vlottenburg 251
Voortrekker Monument and Museum (Pretoria) 39
Voortrekker Museum (Pietermaritzburg) 140-1
Vumba Botanical Gardens 444
Vumba Mountains 433

W

Waenhuiskrans 214
Walker Bay 229
Walker, Clive 76
Walker Point 202
Walvis Bay 388, 390, 391, 393
Warmbaths Spa 83
Warm Bokkeveld 228
War Museum of the Boer Republics 346
Waterberg Mountains 73, 76
Waterberg Plateau National Park 394
Waterfall Bluff 183
water lilies 409
Waters Meeting Nature Reserve 191
Waterval-Boven 97, 109
Waterval-Onder 89, 109
Watervalspruit 98, 108
Water Wonderland 119
Welgeluk 313
Wellington 226, 228
Weltevrede 310
Welwitschia Drive 389
Wemmer Pan 25
West Caprivi Game Park 395
West Coast National Park 324-5, 327
Westlake 295
whales 276
Whale Well 276
White Lady rock painting 372, 374
White River 104
white-water rafting
 Great Usutu River 370
 Victoria Falls 442
Wiesenhof Wild Park 262
Wild Coast 173, 174, 176, 180, 181, 182
Wild Coast Hiking Trail 183
Wild Coast Sun 184
Wilderness 203, 207
Wilderness Lagoon 207
wildflowers 326-7
Willem Pretorius Game Reserve 352
William Campbell Furniture Museum 121
William Fehr Collection Museum 264
Willowmore 187
Winburg 352
Windhoek 396-8
wine-making 257

wine routes 256-62
Winterberg 252
Winterhoek Mountains 198
Winterton 146, 148
Witsieshoek Mountain Resort 350
Witte River Gorge 226
Witte River Valley 227
Witzenberg 228, 252
Wolfberg Arch 317
Wolkberg Mountains 75, 84
Wolkberg Wilderness Area 84
Wolseley 228
Wolwekloof 227
Wonderboom Fort 40
Wonderboom Nature Reserve 40
Wonder Cave 59, 70
Woodbush Forest Plantation 77
Woollan, Benjamin 18
Worcester 237, 238
Worcester Wine Route 238
World of Birds 289, 298
World's View
 Pietermaritzburg 138, 139
 Zimbabwe 419, 434
Wupperthal 321, 327, 328
Wylie Park 141

XYZ

Xai-Xai 400
yellowwood trees 201
Ysternek Mountain Fynbos and Forest Nature Reserve 212
Yzerfontein 324
Zambezi National Park 443
Zambezi Nature Sanctuary 446
Zambezi Queen 382
Zambezi River 382, 406, 429, 431, 432, 434
 canoeing safari 444-5
Zambezi River Festival 442
Zanddrift 224
Zandwijk 259
zebras 59, 378, 412
 Burchell's 90, 166
 Cape mountain 192, 304
Zeekoevlei 294
Zimbabwe Ruins, *see* Great Zimbabwe
Zoo Lake Park 26
Zoological Gardens
 Johannesburg 22, 26
 Natal 133
 Pretoria (National) 28, 29, 34, 80, 339
Zulu beadwork 112
Zululand Historical Museum 155
Zulu traditions 144, 164
Zuurberg National Park 198
Zwartkop Mountain 59
Zwartkoppies Hall 61

PICTURE CREDITS

Picture credits for each page read from top to bottom, using the top as the reference point. Where the tops of two or more pictures are on the same level, credits read from left to right.

Abbreviations:
AAI – Anka Agency International
ABPL – Anthony Bannister Photo Library
AI – African Images
PA – Photo Access
NPB – Natal Parks Board

PRELIMS: 3 Herman Potgieter/ABPL. 8 Mark van Aardt.

JOHANNESBURG: 10 Walter Knirr, Jeannie MacKinnon. 11 Jeannie MacKinnon. 12 Walter Knirr/PA, Jackie Murray. 13 Walter Knirr. 14 Walter Knirr. 15 Both Walter Knirr. 16 Johannesburg Art Gallery. 17 Both Jeannie MacKinnon. 18 Walter Knirr. 19 Jackie Murray. 20 Both Jackie Murray. 21 Both Jackie Murray. 22 Lorna Stanton/ABPL. 24 Walter Knirr, Jackie Murray. 25 Walter Knirr. 26 Walter Knirr, Mark Tennant/AI.

PRETORIA: 28 Rick Matthews. 29 Duncan Butchart/AI, Zelda Wahl. 30 Walter Knirr. 31 Jackie Murray, Frik Dreyer/National Cultural History Museum. 32 Mike Ettershank/AAI. 33 Walter Knirr, Museum of Science & Technology. 34 Duncan Butchart/AI. 35 Both Frik Dreyer/National Cultural History Museum. 36 R Viljoen. 37 Koos Delport/PA. 38 Walter Knirr. 39 Mark van Aardt, Keith Young. 40 Chris van der Merwe/AAI.

HIGHVELD: 42 Walter Knirr. 44 Z Botha, Anup Shah/ABPL. 45 Roger de la Harpe. 46 Jackie Murray. 47 Peter Pickford. 48 Peter & Beverly Pickford/Focal Point, Walter Knirr. 49 C L Gittens/PA. 50 J Marais/AAI, R Viljoen. 51 Sarah/Cos Coronaios/ABPL. 52 Walter Knirr, Anthony Bannister/ABPL. 53 Walter Knirr. 54 Lorna Stanton/ABPL. 55 Jackie Murray. 56 Rick Matthews, J Marais/AAI. 57 Frik Dreyer/National Cultural History Museum. 58 Jeannie MacKinnon, Jane-Anne Hobbs. 59 Anthony Bannister/ABPL, Roger de la Harpe. 60 Shawn Benjamin, Lisa Trocchi/ABPL. 61 Both R Viljoen. 62 SA Air Force Museum. 63 Gerald Cubitt. 64 Lorna Stanton/ABPL. 65 Walter Knirr. 66 Walter Knirr, Herman Potgieter/ABPL, Anthony Bannister/ABPL. 67 Peter Pickford. 68 Frik Dreyer/National Cultural History Museum. 69 Walter Knirr. 70 Sarah/Cos Coronaios/ABPL, Walter Knirr.

NORTH TRANSVAAL: 72 Both Jacques Jordaan. 73 Anthony Bannister/ABPL. 74 Walter Knirr. 75 Walter Knirr. 77 Keith Young, Walter Knirr. 78 Both Lanz von Hörsten. 79 Mark van Aardt. 80 Walter Knirr, Gerald Cubitt. 81 Tea Council of SA. 82 Friedrich von Hörsten. 83 Walter Knirr. 84 Gerald Cubitt.

LOWVELD AND ESCARPMENT: 86 Keith Young. 87 Mark van Aardt. 88 Walter Knirr. 89 Mark van Aardt. 90 Mark van Aardt, Lanz von Hörsten. 91 Keith Young. 92 Pat Donaldson/ABPL. 93 Lanz von Hörsten. 94 Lanz von Hörsten, David Steele/PA. 95 Mark van Aardt. 96 Mark van Aardt. 97 Walter Knirr. 98 Walter Knirr. 99 Herman Potgieter/ABPL. 100 David Steele/PA, Walter Knirr. 101 David Steele/Getaway/PA. 102 David Steele/PA. 103 David Steele/Getaway/PA, Robert C Nunnington/ABPL. 104 Walter Knirr/PA, C Friend/PA. 105 Mark van Aardt. 106 Both Mark van Aardt. 107 Mark van Aardt. 108 Walter Knirr. 109 Both Walter Knirr. 110 Walter Knirr.

DURBAN: 112 N Sutherland/PA. 113 Ted Brien/PA, Walter Knirr/PA. 114 Both Walter Knirr. 115 Walter Knirr. 116 Walter Knirr. 117 Roger de la Harpe/ABPL, Walter Knirr/PA. 118 Ivor Migdoll, Walter Knirr. 119 Ivor Migdoll, Walter Knirr. 120 Both Mark van Aardt. 121 Ivor Migdoll. 122 Ivor Migdoll, L A Mettler. 123 Ivor Migdoll. 124 R Viljoen, Mark van Aardt. 125 R Viljoen, Jeannie MacKinnon. 126 Ivor Migdoll.

CENTRAL KWAZULU-NATAL: 128 Shaen Adey, Roger de la Harpe. 129 Shaen Adey. 130 David Steele/PA, Nigel Dennis/ABPL. 131 Roger de la Harpe. 132 Walter Knirr, Shaen Adey. 133 Roger de la Harpe/NPB. 134 Planet Earth/J D Watt/PA, Planet Earth/Doug Perrine/PA. 135 Mark van Aardt. 136 Roger de la Harpe. 137 Roger de la Harpe. 138 Cindy Mothilal/NPB, Roger de la Harpe. 139 Roger de la Harpe. 140 Both Cindy Mothilal/NPB. 141 Dr F le Roux/PA. 142 Roger de la Harpe. 143 Roger de la Harpe/NPB, Mark van Aardt. 144 Walter Knirr.

DRAKENSBERG: 146 Walter Knirr. 147 Walter Knirr. 148 NPB. 149 Roger de la Harpe. 150 HPH Photography/PA, Roger de la Harpe. 151 Shaen Adey. 152 Roger de la Harpe/NPB.

NORTHERN KWAZULU-NATAL: 154 Walter Knirr. 155 Local History Museums' Collection, Durban. 156 Roger de la Harpe, Roger de la Harpe/NPB. 157 Roger de la Harpe/ABPL. 158 Roger de la Harpe/NPB, Robert C Nunnington/ABPL. 159 Duncan Butchart/AI, David Steele/PA. 160 Shaen Adey/ABPL, Pat de la Harpe. 161 Nigel Dennis/ABPL. 162 David Steele/PA. 163 David Steele/PA. 164 All Roger de la Harpe. 165 Roger de la Harpe/ABPL. 166 Ivor Migdoll. 167 Roger de la Harpe/ABPL. 168 Shaen Adey, Peter Pickford. 169 Roger de la Harpe/ABPL, Roger de la Harpe. 170 Both Shaen Adey.

TRANSKEI: 172 David Bristow. 173 Jackie Murray. 174 David Bristow. 175 Mark van Aardt. 176 Zelda Wahl, Jackie Murray. 177 Zelda Wahl. 178 Gwynneth Glass, Zelda Wahl. 179 Both Zelda Wahl. 180 Peter Pickford. 181 Local History Museums' Collection, Durban. 182 Both Peter Pickford. 183 Owen Coetzer/Getaway/PA, Peter Steyn/PA. 184 Mark van Aardt.

SOUTHEAST CAPE: 186 Friedrich von Hörsten. 187 Landmarks/Larsson. 188 Zelda Wahl. 189 Zelda Wahl. 190 Paul Funston/ABPL, Landmarks/Hosten. 191 Gwynneth Glass. 192 Gwynneth Glass, Lanz von Hörsten. 193 Landmarks/Hosten. 194 Landmarks/Matthews. 195 Zelda Wahl, Gwynneth Glass. 196 Friedrich von Hörsten, A de Gouveia/PA. 197 Gwynneth Glass. 198 CNC Photography/Cape Nature Conservation.

GARDEN ROUTE: 200 Lanz von Hörsten, Mark van Aardt. 201 Shaen Adey. 202 Zelda Wahl. 203 Lanz von Hörsten, Mark van Aardt. 204 Anthony Bannister/ABPL, Zelda Wahl. 205 Mark van Aardt. 206 Peter Pickford. 207 Walter Knirr. 208 Both Mark van Aardt. 209 Lanz von Hörsten. 210 Gwynneth Glass, Fred Roth/PA. 211 Marianne Alexander. 212 Lorna Stanton/ABPL.

SOUTHERN CAPE: 216 Richard du Toit/ABPL, Gwynneth Glass. 217 Cape Nature Conservation. 218 Walter Knirr. 219 Richard du Toit/ABPL, Mark van Aardt. 220 Both Shaen Adey. 221 Richard du Toit/ABPL. 222 Mark van Aardt, Friedrich von Hörsten. 223 Walter Knirr. 224 Mark van Aardt, Keith Young.

SOUTHWEST CAPE: 226 Keith Young. 227 David Steele/PA. 228 Hein von Hörsten/ABPL. 229 Peter Blake, Colin Paterson-Jones. 230 Zelda Wahl. 231 Peter Blake. 232 Both Friedrich von Hörsten. 233 Friedrich von Hörsten.

PICTURE CREDITS

234 Mark van Aardt. 235 Peter Blake, Shaen Adey, Hein von Hörsten. 236 Shaen Adey/ABPL, Alain Proust. 237 Peter Pickford, Gwynneth Glass. 238 Both Zelda Wahl. 239 Walter Knirr. 240 Friedrich von Hörsten. 241 Walter Knirr, HPH Photography/PA. 242 Keith Young, Walter Knirr. 243 Keith Young. 244 Both Mark van Aardt. 245 Mark van Aardt, Gwynneth Glass, Peter Blake. 246 Keith Young, Mark van Aardt. 247 Mark van Aardt. 248 Both Zelda Wahl. 249 Both Zelda Wahl. 250 Keith Young, Mark van Aardt. 251 Peter Blake. 252 Hein von Hörsten. 253 Zelda Wahl, both Keith Young. 254 Lanz von Hörsten. 255 Kate Zari Roberts, Peter Blake. 256 Peter Pickford. 257 Mark van Aardt, Jeannie MacKinnon. 258 Alain Proust, Mark van Aardt, Peter Blake. 259 Walter Knirr, Alain Proust. 260 Peter Blake, Alain Proust. 261 Peter Blake, Jeannie MacKinnon. 262 Peter Blake.

CAPE TOWN: 264 Both Zelda Wahl. 265 Shawn Benjamin, Pat de la Harpe. 266 Shawn Benjamin, Zelda Wahl. 267 All Shawn Benjamin. 268 Hein von Hörsten, Zelda Wahl. 269 Shawn Benjamin, Walter Knirr. 270 Private Collection/SA National Gallery. 271 Zelda Wahl. 272 Both Shawn Benjamin. 273 Zelda Wahl. 274 R Viljoen. 275 Both Zelda Wahl. 276 Shawn Benjamin, R Viljoen. 277 SA National Gallery, Zelda Wahl. 278 Zelda Wahl. 279 Zelda Wahl, both Gwynneth Glass. 280 Zelda Wahl, AI, Mark van Aardt.

CAPE PENINSULA: 282 Zelda Wahl. 283 Peter Pickford, Peter Pickford, Roger de la Harpe, Peter Pickford. 284 Mark van Aardt, Friedrich von Hörsten. 285 Mark van Aardt, Walter Knirr. 286 Friedrich von Hörsten. 287 Both Zelda Wahl. 288 Zelda Wahl, Gwynneth Glass. 289 Walter Knirr. 290 Keith Young. 291 Jeannie MacKinnon, Lanz von Hörsten. 292 Peter Pickford, Mark van Aardt. 293 Gerald Cubitt. 294 Mark van Aardt. 295 Gwynneth Glass. 296 Walter Knirr. 297 Mark van Aardt. 298 Peter Chadwick/ABPL.

KAROO: 300 Shaen Adey. 301 Zelda Wahl. 302 Friedrich von Hörsten. 303 Jeannie MacKinnon. 304 HPH Photography/PA. 305 Shawn Benjamin. 306 Keith Young, E S Whitlock. 307 Walter Knirr. 308 E S Whitlock. 309 Both Zelda Wahl. 310 Keith Young, Shaen Adey. 311 Walter Knirr. 312 Jeannie MacKinnon, Jeannie MacKinnon, Lanz von Hörsten. 313 Lanz von Hörsten. 314 H W Rayner.

WEST COAST: 316 Anthony Bannister/ABPL. 317 Hein von Hörsten/ABPL. 318 Shaen Adey. 319 Lanz von Hörsten. 320 Charles Didcott/Felix Unite River Adventures. 321 David Steele/Getaway/PA. 322 Walter Knirr. 323 Walter Knirr. 325 Walter Knirr/PA, Anthony Bannister/ABPL. 326 Walter Knirr. 327 Walter Knirr. 328 Zelda Wahl, David Steele/PA.

THE INTERIOR: 330 Walter Knirr. 331 Roger de la Harpe, Friedrich von Hörsten. 332 Friedrich von Hörsten. 333 Both McGregor Museum. 334 Zelda Wahl, Mark van Aardt. 335 Walter Knirr, Zelda Wahl. 336 Mark van Aardt. 337 Both McGregor Museum. 338 Brian Johnson Barker. 339 Anup Shah/ABPL, Lisa Trocchi/ABPL. 340 Peter Lawson/PA, Colla Swart/ABPL. 341 Zelda Wahl.

FREE STATE: 344 Walter Knirr. 345 Walter Knirr. 346 All Walter Knirr. 347 Walter Knirr. 348 Walter Knirr. 349 Lanz von Hörsten, Rick Matthews. 350 Keith Young. 351 Keith Young. 352 Both Friedrich von Hörsten.

LESOTHO: 354 Dirk Schwager. 355 Dirk Schwager. 356 Dirk Schwager. 357 Dirk Schwager. 358 Peter Pickford. 360 Gerald Cubitt. 361 Both Gerald Cubitt. 362 Dirk Schwager.

SWAZILAND: 364 Big Game Parks. 365 Dirk Schwager. 366 Dirk Schwager. 367 Dirk Schwager. 368 Big Game Parks. 369 Jackie Murray, Rick Matthews. 370 Big Game Parks, Peter Pickford.

NAMIBIA: 372 Mark van Aardt. 373 Paul Tingay. 374 Zelda Wahl, Peter Pickford. 375 Roger de la Harpe, Peter Pickford. 376 Both Mark van Aardt. 377 Roger de la Harpe, Friedrich von Hörsten. 378 Friedrich von Hörsten, Clem Haagner. 379 Roger de la Harpe. 380 Mark van Aardt. 381 Both Mark van Aardt. 382 Both Paul Tingay. 383 Lorna Stanton/ABPL, Mark van Aardt. 384 Both Walter Knirr. 385 Gerald Cubitt. 386 Anthony Bannister/ABPL. 387 Mark van Aardt. 388 Mark van Aardt. 389 Mark van Aardt. 390 Gerald Cubitt. 391 Roger de la Harpe. 392 Mark van Aardt. 393 Zelda Wahl. 394 Anthony Bannister/ABPL. 395 Zelda Wahl. 396 Both Gerald Cubitt. 397 Zelda Wahl. 398 Marianne Alexander, Gerald Cubitt.

BOTSWANA: 400 Hein von Hörsten. 401 Richard du Toit/ABPL. 402 David Steele/Getaway/PA, Roger de la Harpe. 403 Both David Steele/Getaway/PA. 404 Both David Steele/Getaway/PA. 405 Both David Steele/Getaway/PA. 406 Gerald Cubitt. 407 Walter Knirr. 408 Mark van Aardt. 409 Roger de la Harpe. 410 Roger de la Harpe, Patrick Wagner/Getaway/PA. 411 Rick Matthews. 412 David Steele/Getaway/PA, Brendan Ryan/ABPL.

ZIMBABWE: 414 Paul Tingay. 415 Anthony Bannister/ABPL. 416 B & L Worsley/PA. 418 Mark van Aardt. 419 Gerald Cubitt. 420 Jan Teede/ABPL, Mark van Aardt. 422 Mark van Aardt. 423 Lorna Stanton/ABPL. 424 Paul Tingay. 425 Lex Hes/PA, J & B Photography/PA. 426 Paul Tingay. 427 Marianne Alexander. 428 M Philip Kahl/ABPL. 429 Roger de la Harpe/ABPL. 430 Marianne Alexander. 431 Peter Pickford. 432 Peter Steyn/PA. 433 Friedrich von Hörsten. 434 Gwynneth Glass. 435 David Bristow/Getaway/PA. 436 Gerald Cubitt, Brendan Ryan/ABPL. 437 Mark van Aardt. 439 Mark van Aardt, Jeannie MacKinnon. 440 Mark van Aardt, Roger de la Harpe. 441 Mark van Aardt. 442 Patrick Wagner/Getaway/PA. 443 Mark van Aardt, Peter Pickford. 444 Gavin Thomson/ABPL. 445 Phillip Richardson/ABPL, Clem Haagner/ABPL. 446 P J Wagner/PA, Peter Steyn/PA.

Front cover: Walter Knirr
Back cover: Zelda Wahl

Reproduction by Hirt & Carter (Pty) Ltd, Cape Town
Printed by SNP Printing (Pte) Ltd, Singapore